The DREAM Interpretation Dictionary

Symbols, Signs, and Meanings

J.M. DeBord

VISIBLE INK PRESS

Detroit

ABOUT THE AUTHOR

 **J.M. DeBord**, who is known as *RadOwl the reddit dream expert* on the popular website reddit.com, is the author of *Dreams 1-2-3: Remember, Interpret, and Live Your Dreams*. He has appeared as a featured dream expert and dream interpreter on numerous media programs, including *Coast to Coast AM, Darkness Radio*, and *The Moore Show*. He has touched millions of lives with his insights and answers, gaining him international acclaim for his ability to demystify dreams and their interpretation. He has a bachelor of arts from the University of Cincinnati and lives in Tucson, Arizona.

ALSO BY VISIBLE INK PRESS

Ancient Gods: Lost Histories, Hidden Truths,
and the Conspiracy of Silence
By Jim Willis
ISBN 978-1-57859-614-0

Angels A to Z, 2nd edition
by Evelyn Dorothy Oliver, Ph.D.,
and James R Lewis, Ph.D.
ISBN: 978-1-57859-212-8

Armageddon Now: The End of the World A to Z
by Jim Willis and Barbara Willis
ISBN: 978-1-57859-168-8

The Astrology Book: The Encyclopedia of
Heavenly Influences, 2nd edition
by James R. Lewis
ISBN: 978-1-57859-144-2

The Dream Encyclopedia, 2nd edition
by James R Lewis, Ph.D.,
and Evelyn Dorothy Oliver, Ph.D.
ISBN: 978-1-57859-216-6

The Encyclopedia of Religious Phenomena
by J. Gordon Melton, Ph.D.
ISBN: 978-1-57859-209-8

The Fortune-Telling Book:
The Encyclopedia of Divination and Soothsaying
by Raymond Buckland
ISBN: 978-1-57859-147-3

The Handy Bible Answer Book
By Jennifer R. Prince
ISBN 978-1-57859-478-8

The Handy Islam Answer Book
By John Renard, Ph.D.
ISBN 978-1-57859-510-5

The Handy Mythology Answer Book
By David Leeming, Ph.D.
ISBN 978-1-57859-475-7

The Handy Religion Answer Book, 2nd edition
By John Renard, Ph.D.
ISBN 978-1-57859-379-8

Real Miracles, Divine Intervention,
and Feats of Incredible Survival
by Brad Steiger and Sherry Hansen Steiger
ISBN: 978-1-57859-214-2

Real Monsters, Gruesome Critters,
and Beasts from the Darkside
by Brad Steiger and Sherry Hansen Steiger
ISBN: 978-1-57859-220-3

Real Visitors, Voices from Beyond,
and Parallel Dimensions
by Brad Steiger and Sherry Hansen Steiger
ISBN: 978-1-57859-541-9

The Religion Book: Places,
Prophets, Saints, and Seers
by Jim Willis
ISBN: 978-1-57859-151-0

The Spirit Book: The Encyclopedia of Clairvoy-
ance, Channeling, and Spirit Communication
by Raymond Buckland
ISBN: 978-1-57859-172-5

The Witch Book: The Encyclopedia of Witchcraft,
Wicca, and Neo-paganism
by Raymond Buckland
ISBN: 978-1-57859-114-5

Please visit us at visibleinkpress.com

The
Dream
Interpretation
Dictionary:
Symbols, Signs,
and Meanings

Copyright © 2017 by Visible Ink Press®

Visible Ink Press®
43311 Joy Rd., #414
Canton, MI 48187-2075

Visible Ink Press is a registered trademark of Visible Ink Press LLC.

Most Visible Ink Press books are available at special quantity discounts when purchased in bulk by corporations, organizations, or groups. Customized printings, special imprints, messages, and excerpts can be produced to meet your needs. For more information, contact Special Markets Director, Visible Ink Press, www.visibleink.com, or 734-667-3211.

Managing Editor: Kevin S. Hile
Art Director: Mary Claire Krzewinski
Typesetting: Marco DiVita
Proofreaders: Brian Buchanan and Barbara Lyon
Indexer: Larry Baker

Cover images: Shutterstock

Library of Congress Cataloging-in-Publication Data
Names: DeBord, J. M., author.
Title: The dream interpretation dictionary : symbols, signs, and meanings / by Jason M. DeBord.
Description: 1st [edition]. | Detroit, MI : Visible Ink Press, 2017.
Identifiers: LCCN 2017001712| ISBN 9781578596379 (pbk. : alk. paper) | ISBN9781578596584 (epub) | ISBN 9781578596577 (pdf)
Subjects: LCSH: Dream interpretation—Dictionaries. | Dreams—Dictionaries.
Classification: LCC BF1091 .D43 2017 | DDC 154.6/303—dc23
LC record available at https://lccn.loc.gov/2017001712

Printed in the United States of America
10 9 8 7 6 5 4 3 2 1

TABLE OF CONTENTS

Introduction   [ix]

INTRODUCTION

The woman in the audience at a workshop I hosted raised her hand and asked me what it means to dream about losing a tooth. I told her to focus on the idea of losing something important, and her facial expression grew more serious. She said, "I heard that it means someone close to you is going to die."

"That's wrong in most cases," I assured her. "I know someone who dreamed about losing a molar soon after having a miscarriage. The symbolism fit the circumstance because a molar is deeply embedded in the mouth, and a fetus is embedded in the womb. Loved ones are deeply embedded in your life, so losing a loved one is comparable symbolically to losing a molar. But out of hundreds of dreams featuring teeth I've helped interpret, only a few have connected with a loss like that. Losing a tooth is much more likely to mean the loss of something like reputation or status or loss of opportunity or a relationship. Or it can be an expression of anxiety."

I told her about the young man I chatted with at reddit.com, one of the world's largest social media sites, where I'm known as *RadOwl the dream expert*. He dreamed about dining with his father and his teeth falling out when he opened his mouth to speak. He'd just come out as transgender to his father and conversations between them had become awkward to say the least. The meaning is clearly shown in the action of losing teeth while talking with his father. Plus, as soon as I suggested to the young man that the dream could reflect difficulty talking with his father, the idea rang a bell with him.

The woman at my workshop was relieved to understand her dream that way—she probably wasn't about to lose a loved one—and her question provided a great opportunity to make a point that's repeated throughout this book.

A symbol is understood in the context of the dream-story, the actions involving it, and how it fits together with other details. Symbols by themselves can mean all sorts of things. Never jump to conclusions. Even dreams about murder or winning the lottery are usually symbolic, and the imagery shouldn't be taken literally. It's figurative.

In a roundabout way, now you know why I wrote this book. Too much bad information about dreams masquerades as expert opinion. A book needed to be written by someone who knows better, so that fewer people are worried or fooled by something they read from questionable sources. However, I prefer to look on the bright side and say this book is for everyone looking for high-quality sources, like me during my early days of dreamwork.

Back then (in the mid-1990s), all I had to refer to were books written by psychiatrists such as Carl Jung and Sigmund Freud. I'd wake up with a head full of dream memories and hunt around for anything to help me understand them. Usually, the books weren't very helpful. They provided interesting insights into dream psychology, but not so much about my dreams.

You could say that this book is my answer to dream books that are too academic, too disconnected from everyday reality, or too misinformed to be much good to anyone. It provides you with a *step-by-step system* for dream interpretation, DREAMS 1-2-3, that I have developed over the course of two decades and used to help thousands of people understand their dreams and benefit from them.

A COMPLETE SOURCE: DREAM DICTIONARY, GUIDE, AND ENCYCLOPEDIA ALL IN ONE

My answer is to give you a book that's a dream dictionary with a built-in interpretation guide and encyclopedia of concepts important for understanding dreams—a complete source. It is a book you can flip through when you wake up from a dream and want answers, a book that provides examples from the dreams of people from all walks of life and all around the world, and a book that is written by someone who knows a lot about dream theory and psychology, but it doesn't get lost in any academic minutiae. This is a book that's easy to follow and explains the subject simply yet thoroughly, and always keeps sight of the goal of making dreams understandable for everyone.

The biggest shortcoming of most dream dictionaries is they give the impression that a symbol can be explained in a few sentences. That answers are definitive when at best they're speculative. Some dream dictionaries are ridiculously inaccurate, vague, or broad. Some are just ridiculous and take advantage of the fact that any meaning can be ascribed to any dream symbol and most people don't know better. I can't tell you how many dream dictionaries I've flipped through thinking to myself *where the hell do they come up with this stuff?*

No book can cover every way dreams create meaning. Symbols defy being boiled down to neat definitions because they're based mostly on your personal associations and are as complex and varied as the people who dream about them. And besides that, *only you know what your dreams really mean.*

What you want is a book that tells you *why* a dream means what it does. That *shows* the process of dream interpretation and *explains* it in clear, concise language. That gives *answers* and the information needed to reach them on your own. A book that *teaches*.

Why Bother—Aren't Dreams Meaningless?

At this point, you might not know much about how dreams work. You might not even know that dreams are meaningful—deeply meaningful and important—but soon you will understand— and not only understand, you will know how to use your dreams to benefit and enhance your life.

The first question I am often confronted with at my workshops and lectures is *aren't dreams just brain farts?* To which I reply, some dreams are meaningful and some aren't, and it's easy to tell the difference. I'll show you later.

Most people I talk to about this subject don't know how to delve into the meaning of their dreams, so they don't bother with it. They wake up, and … poof! the memories of their dreams are gone. Why bother trying if you think it's pointless?

Because of a theory popularized in the 1980s known as *activation-synthesis*, the idea leached into popular culture that dreams are brain farts. But if the truth was widely known that dreams are meaningful and can be enormously significant, the popularity of dreamwork would explode overnight. You don't have to be a guru or psychologist to benefit from your dreams. Just work at it.

Dreams tell you about your physical health, your mental and emotional health, your relationships, your work, your mind, your heart, your ambitions, wishes, and desires. They bring you closer to who and what you truly are in the deepest inner reaches of your being. And working with them can be the best thing you ever do for yourself. You can make your dreams come true and live them in the fullest sense.

Many great and notable people pay close attention to their dreams. Albert Einstein, Larry Page, Paul McCartney, Stephen King, Otto Loewi, Elias Howe, Christopher Nolan, and Thomas Edison are some of the most notable examples, but the list of smart, successful people who follow their dreams is miles long.

Are you ready to add your name to the list?

My Approach

Some dream analysts call themselves Freudians. Some are Jungians. Some are students of Gestalt. Some are students of neuroscience, others of behavioral science. I am none of them, and all of them.

Every scientific theory of dreaming has at least some merit, even the ones that claim that dreams are meaningless. It's true. *Some* dreams are meaningless, just imagery behind your eyes, but most are meaningful, even just for the small bit of self-knowledge you can gain about how your mind works.

However, why adhere to one school of thought or tradition over others when they all have something good to offer? Why limit yourself like that?

My approach is that dreams are stories told through symbolism and can be analyzed the same basic way you would analyze a novel or movie. And your feelings can tell you more than anything else about your dreams. Some dreams skim the surface of who and what you are, and some plumb the deepest reaches. You are the best interpreter of your dreams; you just need to know how. Anyone can do it—it's not as difficult as it can appear.

Far and away, though, one great teacher has influenced my approach more than others. Dr. Carl Jung, the Swiss psychiatrist. Most people have at least heard of him, but few folks these days know the huge influence he is on twentieth- and twenty-first-century thought. His work has influenced everything from quantum physics to personality theory. The mainstream scientific community turned its back on Dr. Jung because he dared to delve into subjects such as mysticism and alchemy in pursuit of better understanding consciousness and its development. Every great, original thinker has faced the same blowback from the mainstream, and only time can prove whether they were correct. Have you ever heard of the book *One Hundred Authors Against Einstein*? Guess who won that debate?

Within everyone is a much greater person, Jung taught, and dreams are its spokesperson. I'm here to spread that good news while building on the contributions of other teachers and thinkers such as Edgar Cayce, Robert A. Johnson, Robert Moss, Ann Faraday, and Larry Pesavento.

How to Use This Book

This is a big, big book, but it's not complicated. It's designed to be taken a little at a time like a dictionary or encyclopedia, or read cover to cover. Breathe a sigh of relief if the thickness of this book is daunting. You have the rest of your life to read it.

The entries in the *Dream Interpretation Dictionary* interconnect, so delving into the meaning of a dream is like following a breadcrumb trail. Read the entry for *Family* to see what I mean. Not only does it thoroughly cover the subject, it lists related entries under "see also." Think of them as clues, and you are the detective piecing them together.

For example, ideas about what it means to dream about your mom can be found in the entries for *Mother* and *Family*. You have a dream about your mom, and it refers also to your father, so you look up *Father*. Under "see also" you notice the entry for *Parents* and look up that entry. In a general sense, traditional parents are a woman and man, so you look up *Woman* and *Man*. The setting of the dream is your family home, so you look up the entry for *Family Home*. A family home is, in a general sense, a home, so you look up *Home*.

That's how you follow the clues. They circle right back to *Mother*.

Or you dream about crashing a car into a wall at a fork in the road, and the passengers are some of your friends. Begin with the entry for *Car*, then look up *Crash*, the main symbol, and action. Look up *Road* and *Wall*, since they're part of the story. Finally, look up *Friend* and *Passenger* and connect the dots. It might also help to look up *Group* since multiple passengers are technically a group. *Fork in the road* is a metaphor, and "Figuring Out Your Dreams" shows you how metaphors are used in dreams.

The meaning of a dream is often found by starting with the main symbol, looking up related symbols in the dictionary, and seeing the connections between them. They all fit together somehow, usually around a subject or theme.

The *Dream Interpretation Dictionary* can't cover every possible meaning for every dream symbol, so you will refer often to the "Figuring Out Your Dreams" appendix at the back of this book, which gives an overview of how to understand dreams and specific advice and techniques for their interpretation. It's your foundation. Even though it's at the back of this book, read it first.

The Dream Theatre

Your other foundation is your understanding of the environment in which a dream-story is told: your head! More specifically, your psyche or mind. When you understand that most details of most dreams are based on what's happening between your ears and that what you experience in a dream is a story based on your life—especially your inner life—you have an approach to understanding your dreams that works in most cases. What you're trying to understand is yourself as seen from the broader perspective of your unconscious mind.

See the entry for *Psyche* to really get the picture, and follow the breadcrumb trail given in the "see also" list.

More importantly, you want to understand the reasons and purposes for dreams. In the short term, dreams help you process your daily life and learn from it. Most dreams connect with what happened the previous day in your life or look ahead in anticipation of what's soon coming. Long term, dreams help to unite the conscious mind with the unconscious mind to make you a complete person. This subject is addressed in-depth in "Figuring Out Your Dreams."

Even a book this big can't cover every possibility for symbolism, but you can read between the lines and do your own detective work. For example, you dream about running backward and it's not specifically mentioned in this book. However, you can look up the entries for *Run* and *Backward* and tie the ideas together. Running can symbolize a rapid pace, and backward can mean going backward in your life. Tie the two ideas together and it can mean rapidly moving backward in life.

Hub Entries

Some entries act as hubs for all related entries. Take *Family*, for example. Every type of family member and family-related subject in *The Dream Interpretation Dictionary* is found under the "see also" list at the bottom of that entry. Use the hub entries to thoroughly explore a topic. When read together, they provide a complete overview, along with loads of specifics and examples.

Here's a handy list of hub entries: Actor, Airplane, Animals, Archetypes, Arena, Army, Baby, Beauty, Birds, Body, Building, Bully, Car, Child, Clothing, Colors, Crime, Death, Disaster, Doctor, Drugs, Earth, Emotions, Enemy, Escape, Evil, Face, Fall, Family, Famous, Fight, Fire, Fly, Food, Games, God, Group, Home, Hospital, Insects, Job, Man, Marriage, Money, Monster, Penis, Police Officer, Pregnant, Psyche, School, Sex, Shapes, Shop, Space, Thief, Time, Unconscious Mind, Vagina, War, Water, Weather, Woman.

Some Favorite Entries

Armageddon
Bear
Cancer
Death
Deceased Loved Ones
Devil
Facebook
Fellatio
Fisting
Grim Reaper
Hooker
Jesus
Kanye West
Nightmare

Nuclear War
Numbers
Penis
Phallic Symbol
Sex
UFO
Vagina
Zombie

Remembering Dreams

A research study about dream recall found that more than half of participants had little or no recall of their dreams. That means most people wake up and draw a blank. No dream memories. They might even assume they don't dream, but everyone dreams and everyone can remember their dreams.

Think of it like doing an exercise. If you are out of shape, the first time you try to do a pull-up or jog a mile might be laughable, but with practice, it gets easier. If you have never tried to remember your dreams, that muscle is going to need a lot of strengthening before it performs optimally.

Remembering dreams boils down to two main factors:

1. Time

2. Desire.

Make time and want to do it. Simple as that. Search the Internet for "help remembering dreams" to go into depth about this subject. Here I will cover it briefly in a handy "Top-10 List."

Ten Tips for Remembering Dreams

1. Before falling asleep, remind yourself that you will dream and want to remember.
2. Get enough restful sleep. The more you sleep, the more you dream.
3. When you wake up, *keep your mind clear* and *think only about what you were dreaming.*
4. Stay in the same position you are in when you wake up.
5. Keep a dream journal near your bedside and use it.
6. Wake up a few minutes early.
7. Go to bed sober and avoid sleep aids. Certain sleep aids don't actually help you sleep; instead, they create amnesia.
8. Take B vitamins. They aid memory and stimulate dream recall.
9. Practice. Practice. Practice.
10. Wake up in the middle of the night. It's a habit of people with high dream recall.

Recurring Dreams—Oh, You Again

Recurring dreams deserve special mention. They tend to be the dreams people remember best and are a popular subject for questions from my audiences at workshops and lectures.

Recurring dreams are the fruit hanging lowest on the tree, the easiest to grasp and bite into. They offer tremendous opportunity for understanding the themes and motifs of your life. Once you grasp the meaning of a recurring dream, it acts as an answer key for other dreams of the same type, and for recurring subjects, themes, and symbols.

Recurring dreams come in three flavors:

1. "Just another day" dreams: you go to work, go to school. You see your friends, see your family. Anything that's a regular part of your life is likely to recur in the subjects and imagery of your dreams.

2. Serial dreams: characters, settings, symbols, themes and actions recur. The dream-stories vary, but the details are familiar.

3. Identical dreams: you find yourself back in the same scenario and know how it's going to play out, like the movie *Groundhog Day*.

The first type of recurring dream is no mystery. Dreams reflect your daily life, and whatever is a regular part of it is going to be reviewed nightly. Just another day.

Serial dreams, the second type, are common. Your dreaming mind rummages through your memories looking for ways to tell you stories and takes note of what works best for you. These dreams can be like sequels to a movie or episodes of a television show that continue a story. Serial dreams are sometimes called "dream series."

I dream a lot about working as a waiter. Many tables of people all need something from me, making me anxious about getting it all done. The stories vary, but the basic idea is the same. This theme arises when I'm anxious about getting everything done on my to-do list, or when I feel pulled in many directions at once. It's a feeling I know well from my past experience as a waiter and these days as a busy author and public figure.

Whenever this type of dream recurs, I know it connects somehow with the above ideas, or with the type of work and what it involves: waiting on people and caring for their needs, cleaning up, using my personality to charm and impress.

The third type of dream—the *Groundhog Day* dream—is a different animal. The story doesn't continue, it loops back and starts over. It can start over within the same dream, on the same night of dreaming, or over several nights of dreaming. This type of recurring dreams tends to vex the dreamers who have them. They sense that a message is trying to get through something important.

Once you get the message and act accordingly, these recurring dreams either stop or progress to the next scene. Otherwise, in my experience, the story is repeated the same way. Something needs to change.

Abduct—See: *Kidnap*

Abortion—In simplest terms, to abort means to stop. In a dream it can indicate that something has been, or needs to be, aborted: a plan, relationship, idea, thought process.

The word is used in the sense of "abort the mission" and "abort the plan." Dreams like to make comparisons and visual wordplays, so abortion in a dream can symbolize something like canceling a date or backing out of a commitment. It's aborted.

Abortion can mean something is blocking progress or causing harm and needs to stop. Danger lurks. Stop now before things get worse.

When a sense of relief accompanies an abortion, it can mean something ended that was causing concern or anxiety.

An accidental pregnancy is sometimes a problem, so an abortion can symbolize a solution. Whatever is aborted needs to go. Time to let go or change direction.

Abortion can symbolize rejecting something trying to psychologically or emotionally burrow into you, as a fertilized egg burrows into the uterine wall. See: *Worm*.

Dreams can create symbolism based on the perception of what it's like to have one—it's invasive and difficult—and the emotions experienced: anxiety, separation, relief, regret. In which case, abortion is more about the feelings it invokes than the specifics of the symbolism.

Abortion implies not getting the result you want. Maybe you took a risk or tried something new, and it didn't work out.

It implies starting over, trying again.

Dreams can create symbolism related to the controversy of abortion and how it sharply divides people. For example, a woman dreams that her niece is pregnant and wants to have an abortion, creating a huge controversy in the family. In reality, her niece wants to drop out of college, and that's what's causing the controversy. Abortion connects with the overall circumstances because getting pregnant is a reason that some women drop out of school.

Abortion protesters might symbolize feeling like you are on the other side of an important issue, or feel divided from a group.

If you have had an abortion and dream about it, you could be working through unresolved feelings or issues related to it. It can mean you fear getting pregnant, or making a big mistake. Dreaming about an abortion when you're actually pregnant can express fear of miscarriage. See: *Miscarriage*.

Being forced to have an abortion in a dream can symbolize doing something against your will, such as end a relationship or give up on an idea, or being prevented from doing something that you want to do. It can symbolize fear that you won't be able to follow through on something important to you.

Dreaming that a friend or relative has an abortion can indicate that something unhealthy about the relationship needs to end, or you have a low opinion of the person.

Dreaming about a pregnant female you know having an abortion can symbolize fear that the person will miscarry, or is not ready to be a parent.

Abortion is the termination of a pregnancy. See: *Pregnant.*

For some people, it's murder. See: *Murder.*

For a married, monogamous woman, an abortion can reflect concerns for her husband. If she was supposedly pregnant, the child would be expected to be his, so an abortion can indicate concerns about his well-being or the state of their marriage. The symbolism is built around the idea that her husband is not ready to be a father. The idea extends to significant others and boyfriends.

Someone married and having an affair can dream about an abortion as a way of expressing fear about getting caught. Getting pregnant, or getting someone pregnant, is hard to hide.

See also: *Baby, Caesarean Section, Death, Fetus, Guilt, Miscarriage, Murder, Pregnant*

Above—A primary way dreams create symbolism is through the use of physical representations. So what does it mean that something is above you, or above something else?

It's a way of saying it's admired. It has higher authority, status, or importance. It comes first.

Above can mean perspective: See: *Balloon.*

It can mean thoughts and thought processes: See: *Attic.*

Take note especially of discrepancies represented in imagery of above and below. For example, wearing underwear on your head can symbolize putting priority on sexuality, or that it fills your thoughts.

See also: *Ascend, Attic, Balloon, Below, Birds, Building, Skyscraper*

Abscess—Dreaming about an abscess suggests a loss, something you will miss like a tooth. See: *Teeth.*

It can symbolize something that's been held on to for too long. It's festering.

It can symbolize defect of character, or negativity. Negativity festers and causes pain.

An abscess is a wound, and dreams can use a wound to the body to symbolize a wound to the psyche. The characteristics of the dream wound define the symbolism. An abscess is an infection. So then the question is, what's infecting you? What's brewing beneath the surface? See: *Infect, Wound.*

An abscess in the mouth can symbolize an inarticulate pain—the mouth is used to communicate, and an abscess is painful, so the ideas connect to create symbolism. It can symbolize using words to wound. See: *Mouth.*

It can symbolize the sort of pain that comes from the deepest depths of a person; for example, from the loss of a cherished loved one, or existential angst. See: *Pain.*

It can mean that an illness of the mind or body is passing, or a time of pain or suffering soon will be over. It's come to the surface, and now you can be rid of it. See: *Illness.*

An abscess can symbolize disgust with the body and its functions, such as defecation and urination. See: *Excrement.*

A body covered in abscesses can symbolize fear of loss of material wealth or possessions. Or think of it as the many self-wounds that develop from excessive self-criticism, or self-hatred. It's a picture of how you feel.

See also: *Excrement, Illness, Infect, Maggots, Mouth, Pain, Roach, Wound*

Absorb—See: *Digest*

Abuse—Think of abuse as a physical representation of a personal situation, an exaggeration that in its way sums up a situation or how you feel.

It could reflect a physically abusive situation, but more often it's figurative. For instance, your spouse doesn't really hit you as in the dream, but it feels like abuse when he or she insults you, starts an argument or acts oblivious.

Go further with the idea, and abuse can apply to a wide range of situations. Substances can be abused. A friendship can be abused. Trust can be abused. In this sense, abuse means "to take advantage" or "misuse." Authority can be misused and shown in scenes of someone's being slapped around or otherwise abused by an authority figure.

Characters that abuse you in a dream can symbolize ways you abuse yourself, especially by being too hard on yourself. Most dream-characters are projections from your inner world, so a character that is abusive is likely to connect somehow back to you. Throwing rocks is known to symbolize abusive ways you talk to yourself. It can symbolize hurled insults, whether you insult yourself or someone else. The feeling of being hit by a rock is a representation of emotional and personal impact. Words can hurt.

Dreaming about dishing out abuse can reflect coarseness in your character. You come on strong and affect the people around you. Perhaps the exaggeration into physical abuse is to help you see the impact you have, in which case there might be an underlying message that it would be wise to tone it down.

Being abusive in a dream can express a wish to lash out or pay back for perceived wrongs, as when a victim turns the tables. Meek and mild people are known to dream about scenes of abuse and violence, and they have the hardest time recognizing that it's an exaggerated way of acting out their deepest feelings. In which case, dreaming about abuse is compensation. It's the flip side of the conscious personality, and it's a sign that under the right circumstances the Hulk hidden inside can pop out. See: *Compensation.*

Dreaming about a child being abused can indicate that someone is taking advantage of your innocence or naiveté, or that a young part of yourself feels left out of your life. It can mean you miss the simplicity and fun of childhood. See: *Child, Innocent.*

See also: *Beat, Child, Compensation, Conflict, Doll, Fight, Fist, Handicap, Rape, Toy, Wound*

Abyss—When you "face the abyss," it means you are at a point where the next step is personal darkness or tragedy. You are at a momentous point in your life.

An abyss can symbolize hopelessness, fear, or despair. It's a dark place where lives are lost, and in a figurative way it can express your feeling of being lost or hopeless. It can symbolize a hopeless situation you can't escape.

On the other hand, an abyss can describe something that seems insurmountable. Leaping over an abyss can symbolize overcoming a seemingly insurmountable obstacle or difficulty.

To look into an abyss can be to glimpse the unknown aspects of yourself. The abyss can symbolize your unconscious mind, which has depths that most people do not know about and can be frightening when it isn't understood. In the abyss are your unknown depths. See: *Cave.*

An abyss can symbolize something dark about a person, a void within him or her, especially if the scene is accompanied by howling or scratching, or reference is made to hell or damnation.

See also: *Cave, Cliff, Climb, Cry, Dark, Dead End, Demon, Depression, Fear, Hell, Unconscious Mind*

Accelerate—See: *Car*

Accent—To dream about speaking with an accent can symbolize difficulty expressing yourself. Do you feel misunderstood? Are your words just not coming out right?

Take the idea further. Perhaps you are not expressing your feelings or articulating your thoughts the way you want to.

Using an accent that draws positive attention to you might mean you give off the impression of confidence or sophistication. Sometimes people with accents are considered interesting or intriguing. If an accent draws negative attention, it might mean you feel insecure or persecuted. The symbolism is based on the fact that the wrong accent used around the wrong people can spell trouble.

Accents are sometimes viewed as exotic and foreign. Those associations can be stretched by dreams to include anything that falls outside your scope of experience, or is foreign to you. For example, computer languages are foreign to most people who don't study computer programming. Engineering, medicine, and science have specialized languages and lexicons that to outsiders sound foreign and confusing. You might recognize the words used, but not the meaning or subtext. See: *Foreign.*

A dream-character that speaks with an accent might symbolize something about yourself or another person you don't fully understand. It can mean you have part of the picture but not the whole thing. Something is puzzling or quirky.

Because understanding someone speaking with an accent requires more attention than usual, it can mean you really need to listen. You aren't giving something the attention it needs. Or something is "lost in translation." Listening closely to understand an accent can be a way of drawing attention toward something about yourself you need to understand.

An accent that's difficult to understand can symbolize something that's misunderstood, or a situation is looked at from different perspectives.

Accent in another sense means "to emphasize." It's important, worthy of attention, and can be symbolized as a dream-character who speaks with an accent.

See also: *Foreign, Mouth, Talk, Teeth*

Accident—See: *Crash*

Accomplice—When you act as an accomplice in a dream, it can mean you participate in sabotaging or harming yourself. You follow along with a thought process or impulse that leads to trouble.

Your shadow side can recruit your ego as an accomplice. It's a good representation because your shadow talks you into doing things you wouldn't otherwise do. See: *Shadow.*

Being an accomplice can symbolize that you follow along with someone or something that's a bad influence on you. For example, a young man dreams about being an accomplice to an arsonist who burns down the house of a famous actress. The actress is the sort of woman the young man

wants as a mate, and burning down her house symbolizes the ways he sabotages himself when it comes to finding a woman to love.

The presence of an accomplice, or acting as an accomplice, suggests bad intentions or a guilty conscience. See: *Guilt.*

See also: *Burglary, Guilt, Shadow, Thief*

Accountant—An accountant in a dream can symbolize "keeping the books." The dream might be about your finances, but dreams are usually not so obvious. Instead, an accountant can symbolize other ideas based on the root word "account," such as when it means keeping track of something, or a summary of an event or situation. For example, a witness to a crime gives an account of what happened, but it's still a perspective, not necessarily objective truth.

An accountant in a dream can represent strategizing to save money, and the part of yourself that plans and strategizes.

It can symbolize careful planning, a deliberate approach, or taking things a step at a time.

Expand the idea and "keeping the books" can mean keeping track of something like how often your roommate does the dishes or your significant other says, "I love you." In which case the accountant is the side of you that keeps score.

Expand further and an accountant can symbolize avoiding social contact. It can symbolize isolation, tedium, or repetition.

Another association with accounting is that it's a specialized field that requires training and a certain temperament. Accountants are focused, sometimes single-minded. They're good with numbers.

Accounting is inflexible, generally. The numbers add up or they don't. People say that something doesn't add up when they spot an incongruity or have a hunch that something isn't right.

An account can be an opposite image of the way you are, and if so, it implies the need to meet somewhere in the middle. You don't have to be as focused as an accountant, for example, but if you are unfocused or easily distracted, then your dreams can use an accountant to compensate and even help you find the ability to concentrate. The contrast can be a way of highlighting certain behaviors or thought patterns.

See also: *Bank, Compensation, Math, Money, Purse, Wallet*

Accuse—See: *Court, Criminal, Guilt, Police Officer*

Acid—Acid is a corrosive something that's eating at you, such as stress, guilt, or tension. Character flaws such as cynicism and corruption can be corrosive. The possibilities for symbolism are plenty because many things in life can be described as corrosive.

On the other hand, acid can be cleansing. The symbolism derives from acid's use as a cleanser, something that eats away the muck. Dreams can use it to describe dissolving resistance, letting go, or eating through the outer layers to reveal the true person underneath.

The face is the seat of personal identity, so acid thrown into the face can symbolize insults or attacks on your character.

Dreams love to use wordplays, so acid might mean LSD or another psychedelic drug. Taking acid in a dream can refer to a psychedelic experience you have had. But people who have never done the drug can dream about it, too, on the basis of perceptions of what it is like and what it is supposed to do for them. For example, acid can be symbolism for surreal experience, outside-the-box thinking, inner exploration, acting out of character, making poor decisions, or seeking insight about life and the nature of reality.

See also: *Drugs, Face*

Actor—An actor can symbolize the roles in life you play: spouse, son, daughter, parent, employee, sibling, friend. In those roles you are expected to act and be a certain way. The role can be formal—like priest or doctor—or informal—such as playing the role of friend who gives advice, or a person who fixes problems.

When the roles you play conflict with your inner desires and true character, that tension will generate conflict likely to be exposed in dreams. For example, some parents want their children always

to play the role of a child in the relationship, but that role might not fit a teenager or adult child who has outgrown it. In which case, you could dream about an actor who refuses to work or step onstage.

Being an actor can mean unconsciously following patterns, the scripts for what you believe about yourself and your life that are deeply embedded in your being and largely outside your awareness.

Being an actor can refer to the persona you project, or the ideal version of yourself you want the world to see. It's not a facade but a product of your wishes and imagination. See: *Persona*.

Then again, maybe you are faking it. See: *Imposter*.

Being an actor can be a metaphor for feeling like you are onstage, expected to perform a certain way. Or you are the center of attention. You enjoy the spotlight. Or you desire fame, recognition, wealth, or attention. See: *Stage*.

Because actors are directed, the symbolism can relate to directing your life or sense of personal direction. It can symbolize being manipulated to do someone's bidding. Reverse the idea, and in an actor being directed you could see a projection of how you manipulate people and situations. See: *Director*.

A famous actor can be a projection of something about yourself, especially the roles you play or your personality. For example, actor Jim Carrey is known for playing buffoonish roles, so in a dream he could symbolize a buffoonish side of your personality, or a ridiculous situation. But he is also known for being a deep guy offstage, and that association can be used in your dreams, too. It depends on what you know about him and how the dream-character behaves.

See also: *Camera, Director, Documentary, Famous, Hollywood, Imposter, Mask, Movie, Ovation, Persona, Spotlight, Stage*

Addict —An addict is someone who can't control a habit or vice. Described in simplest terms, it means out of control, powerless over an obsession or compulsion, or a situation is out of hand.

A dream about being an addict can connect with an actual addiction, but many things in life beyond drugs can be addictive: food, attention, sex, excitement, love, games, work. Dreams create physical representations of personal situations, and drug addiction is a ready-made comparison to other sorts of addictions.

Another common perception is that people abuse substances to cope with the stresses of everyday life, or to fill a void. It can mean something or someone is missing from your life. It's exaggerated, but fits how you feel. Drug abuse could symbolically connect with other types of abuse. See: *Abuse*.

Addicts make other people responsible for them, avoiding responsibility for themselves, so it's possible that an addict in your dream can symbolize avoiding responsibility.

Addicts are commonly looked down on, so there are possibilities for symbolism related to arrogance or feelings of superiority, or for seeing yourself as above something or someone. For example, maybe you think you're too good to do chores, or to date someone from a lower class.

A drug addict can symbolize low opinion. An addict in a dream can represent low self-esteem because addicts are commonly viewed as lacking it.

It can symbolize desperation.

To dream about being in a group of addicts can connect with feeling that you don't fit in, or don't understand your behavior when among groups of people. The symbolism is created from the association that drug use makes people act differently.

The entry for *Drugs* goes into more detail and provides examples.

See also: *Abuse, Anxiety, Cocaine, Crash, Drugs, Food, Sex, Zombie*

Adopt—To dream about adopting a child can symbolize taking on something new, such as adopting a new character or personality trait, lifestyle or hobby. Parts of yourself can take form as dream-characters, so to adopt a character in a dream can mean accepting and integrating a part of yourself. You adopt it into your personality or thought processes.

Adoption can connect with being a parent or provider, and that association can branch out far and wide. For example, you have a friend who

needs a lot of guidance and encouragement. It's like adopting a child.

Adoption can reflect a wish to be a provider or play the role of parent, to provide care and love. It can symbolize a protective parental instinct. Teachers and other professionals who work with children use the word "adopt" to describe their relationships with some of the children under their care. It suggests a special bond between them. A sibling can, in a sense, play the role of parent when he or she takes care of other siblings.

Adopted can mean accepted, such as being accepted into a social group, or accepting something as fact.

Dreams can play with words, so adopting can mean "take on" in the sense of adopting an idea, belief, or responsibility symbolized as a person or pet.

If you want to have a child and haven't been able to, adoption in a dream can be a suggestion to look into the possibility. Alternately, adoption can mean "substitute." For example, some couples treat their pets like children and "adopt" them. See: *Pet*.

The symbolism gets deeper for people who were adopted. Their dreams can explore related subjects such as the desire to know more about their biological parents.

Dreaming about giving up something for adoption suggests that you need help handling something—it's too much work or responsibility. If your thoughts during the dream are along the lines of "I don't want it," adoption is more likely to mean you want to give up something completely. If your thoughts are "I need help with it," adoption is more likely to mean "help!"

People say that something like a project or idea is their "baby." Or their baby is their car or home. They're saying, "This is mine; it's important to me."

A young woman dreams about being pregnant with five babies—an overwhelming proposition—and thinking through her options. Adoption seems like the best route. The dream flips from a scene of making a doctor's appointment to being in a classroom at her college, with classmates, discussing their ongoing job training. Suddenly she feels like she's ready to give birth and heads toward the hospital. The teacher comes along for part of the trip but is unable to keep up.

The dream is about five projects given to her as part of her job training. The amount of work and learning involved to complete them is overwhelming, like having five babies at the same time. What she has learned in school is going to carry her only so far, as symbolized by the teacher going along for part of the trip but being unable to keep up. The solution for the dreamer is to "adopt" the projects, which she calls "my babies." It's a way of tapping into a deeper level of commitment and personal resources. If she treats the projects like babies she's adopted, she's more likely to succeed. Problem solved.

See also: *Abortion, Baby, Child, Family, Miscarriage, Orphan, Pet*

Adultery—See: *Affair, Cheat*

Adversary—See: *Opponent*

Affair—To dream about having an affair can indicate a sexual desire that needs to find expression in your life. See: *Sex*.

However, while that assumption tends to be the first that comes to mind after one dreams about having an affair, dreams are more likely to create symbolism based on other associations, such as the excitement or adventure of an affair.

For example, maybe the thought of quitting your job and living on an island crossed your mind, and the desire is growing in you to actually do it. Your relationship with the thoughts has become like an affair, something that secretly stimulates you or captures your imagination. The idea extends to artistic projects, spiritual pursuits, and intellectual fascinations. See: *Embark*.

An affair can relate to adultery. Rarely, though, is an affair represented directly in a dream as the stereotypical "meet at a motel" scenario.

An affair can symbolize cheating on someone who is not a spouse, such as a boyfriend or girlfriend. See: *Cheat*.

Some affairs are nonsexual. They are "affairs of the heart," strong emotional connections to someone who is not your spouse or mate. The idea extends beyond relationships to include situations such as putting your heart into your work, or having zest for a subject, intellectual pursuit, attending a particular church, or associating with a group of people.

Spiritually oriented people are known to dream about affairs as symbols of their relationship with a higher power. It captures related feelings and thoughts and sums them up in one image. See: *Spirit*.

See also: *Adultery, Cheat, Embark, Heart, Hotel, Journey, Panic, Sex, Spirit*

Afterlife—To dream about the afterlife can connect with trying to escape a hardship in this life. You want it to be over.

It can represent something you have been putting off. For example, people say they will do this or that when they get time or reach the next phase of life—"I'll start painting once my kids are grown," or, "There will be plenty of time to travel later in life." Perhaps it's something that shouldn't be put off.

Some dreams about afterlife address spiritual beliefs. People who strongly believe in an afterlife can dream about it as a way of processing information they receive, such as scriptures they read or sermons they hear.

People who don't believe in an afterlife can be challenged by powerful and vivid dreams about it. Atheists have been known to become spiritual after having dreams that rearranged their notions and beliefs. It's one thing to conceptualize something you have not experienced and quite another to experience it fully and realistically in a dream.

It's also possible to dream about deceased loved ones in the afterlife. It can symbolize something such as the hope that the person is "in a better place." But you can also dream about deceased loved ones as a way of actually connecting with him or her in the afterlife. It's an idea that will severely challenge people who think that death is the final end. It's something that you have to experience for yourself—don't take my word for it. It's a fact in the dream world, and dreams have to be treated as a reality unto themselves. See: *Deceased Loved One*.

However, usually the afterlife is used as symbolism. For example, a man dreams about being in the afterlife and going to a sterile white office building. He waits to be told what his job assignment will be. Everything is very orderly and subdued. A supervisor tells him that his job will be janitor. It's upsetting, but he figures he can work his way up.

The dream reflects a situation at his work; the company he works for is being sold. The owner tells him he will be hired by another company owned by the same person, but his position will be entry-level. The dream sums up the situation and his feelings about it. Being a janitor in the afterlife means he's starting over and working his way up from the bottom.

See also: *Angel, Deceased Loved One, God, Heaven, Hell, Soul, Spirit*

Age—See: *Child, Elderly, Teenager, Young*

AIDS—To dream about AIDS can express fear of sexual disease. While attitudes toward AIDS are changing and the disease is no longer a death sentence, fear of it is still pervasive. It can be an irrational fear that is largely subconscious, stemming from taking risks that can expose you to the virus that can cause AIDS. See: *Disease.*

Another possibility is that a dream about contracting AIDS symbolizes loneliness or ostracism. You might wonder why people will not get close to you—what's so wrong about you? Or you feel like a pariah, untouchable. This association with AIDS is less prevalent in modern times, but during the early years of the disease it was perceived as a sort of plague, and the people who had the disease were treated like lepers. Keep in mind that dreams can project these thoughts and feelings onto a character, so in the dream it's not you who has AIDS.

Dreams can use this theme to sum up your feelings and perceptions about someone you know. For example, the kid at school or co-worker whom no one talks to or who is shunned.

Consider the possibility of wordplay in a dream that refers to AIDS. Perhaps it really means "aid," as in give help.

Rarely does a dream about AIDS mean you have it, but if it recurs, or the dream is that powerful, it might mean you have it or are in danger of getting it. The actor Charlie Sheen dreamed about catching HIV years before it actually happened. That's not to say the dream was prophetic, but that he recognized that his lifestyle made it likely.

See also: *Disease, Fear, Illness, Parasite, Subconscious*

Air—Air is ubiquitous and essential for life. These facts about air and many others can be used by dreams to create symbolism. The symbolism is especially noticeable in figures of speech such as *light as air, up in the air, clear the air, walking on air.*

If you dream about air, ask yourself whether a figure of speech is acted out. The symbolism will show in the actions and other details and will be used to describe something about you and your life. And remember, dreams don't draw attention to something unless it's necessary. If air is part of the story, then it means something.

Air is intangible, just as thoughts are intangible, so air can symbolize thoughts and the direction of thought processes. Air creates lift and makes objects rise, and your thoughts can lift you up or rise in the senses of gaining in insight and clarity or improving in quality. Many air-related analogies and comparisons are used to describe thoughts, the most obvious being air quality.

Cloudy or smoggy air can symbolize cloudy thinking, confusion, or disagreement. If you "clear the air," it means you take steps to see a situation clearly.

Air can be used to describe feelings and emotions. Feelings and emotions move and move you, and air moves, too. They can seem to come from nowhere, like a sudden gust of wind. You can feel "light as air," "tempestuous," or "stormy." Water is a more common way of symbolizing feelings and emotions, but dreams will pick whatever symbolism best fits the situation.

Air is associated with wind, and wind can indicate direction in your life, or lack of direction, "going wherever the wind blows." Wind can indicate the direction thoughts are going in about a subject. Strong wind can symbolize something slowing you down or trying to push you in another direction. Lack of wind can symbolize lack of motivation or energy—no "wind in your sails." A wind at your back has the opposite symbolism.

Air in a dream can refer to the air you breathe. An obstructed airway can spark powerful dreams in response. See: *Chimney.*

See also: *Balloon, Chimney, Collective Unconscious, Float, Fly, Hang, Nose, Panic, Storm, Strangle, Tornado*

Airplane—Airplanes take us to destinations. In our lives we go to destinations when we reach for goals, achieve ambitions, or arrive at new phases of life. This use of the symbolism of airplanes is the most common, though the possibilities are far and wide.

Planes in dreams are commonly used to symbolize "going places" in life, because planes take us to destinations, and dreams use analogies and comparisons to create symbolism. Ambitions and goals are destinations in your life you want to reach, and a plane is the fastest vehicle for reaching a destination. Slower-moving vehicles are used to symbolize goals and personal destinations that take longer to reach.

However, all symbols have variations, and a plane flying away from you can symbolize a situation or ambition that's quickly getting away from you.

Planes are associated with freedom. See: *Fly.*

They're associated with far-reaching thoughts. See: *Air.*

In dreams about airplanes, the meaning of the symbolism can be defined by your role in the situation and the nature and circumstances of the flight. Are you a passenger or a pilot? Being the pilot of the plane implies that you make the decisions or are the one responsible, especially in a group situation. If you are the passenger, then it can mean you are along for the ride and don't control the direction or make the decisions. See: *Passenger, Pilot.*

Is the plane a commercial jet, a jet fighter, a crop-duster? A jet fighter is the image of adrenaline

rush and excitement, while a crop-duster can symbolize taking things slow and easy.

Flying an airplane can symbolize the control you have in reaching a destination. Flying with confidence can represent feelings of control—you know where you're going in life and how to get there. Hesitance or inability to fly can symbolize lack of control or uncertainty. You don't know where you're going or how to get there, or you're learning as you go.

Flying in an airplane can symbolize high ideals or lofty goals, symbolism created by the fact that planes fly high in the sky. If the plane flies too high, or is limited in how high it can go, you might be overreaching and need to be more grounded. If the plane flies too low, you might be aiming too low. You can set your sights higher. See: *Fly.*

Arriving in an airplane can symbolize that you have arrived at a destination in life. For example, you have found the success you seek, a risk pays off, or a new phase of life begins. See: *Airport.*

Departing in an airplane can symbolize "taking off." For example, an airplane taking off can symbolize a new and exciting romantic relationship, or a project that gets off the ground. It can symbolize desire to escape. See: *Embark, Journey.*

A business owner dreams that he boards an airplane and it taxis down the runway. He stands at the doorway and beckons his employees to catch up and jump aboard. The imagery symbolizes his efforts to get his employees to catch up with him. The business is taking off, and he is way ahead of them. He wants them to catch up.

A plane disappearing into the clouds suggests the idea of wanting to get away or disappear.

A plane crash can symbolize an ambition or goal that isn't reached. It can symbolize a disaster or calamity—a job or relationship that ends, a plan that falls through, illness or death. See: *Crash.*

Turbulence while flying in a plane can indicate difficulties in life. They could come from an external source, such as arguments with a spouse, ill health, or trouble handling schoolwork. Or the source can be in your emotions or psyche. Something is rocking your boat.

Because planes are a fast way of traveling long distances, they can symbolize being in a hurry, or sudden changes. See: *Jet*.

For people who travel a lot on airplanes, the symbolism can relate to the reasons they travel, like business or leisure. For example, some business travelers who are constantly bombarded by phone calls and emails catch a break only while on a plane (though in-flight Wi-Fi means there's no longer an excuse to disconnect). For them, flying in an airplane can symbolize time to catch up on other work or take a breather.

Planning a flight can symbolize thoughts related to how to reach a goal or personal destination. It can be used to compare with anything that requires planning or preparation.

An airplane can symbolize exploration of your spiritual side or spiritual ideas. Spirits are commonly represented as able to fly, so an airplane can be used to symbolize related ideas and make comparisons that create symbolism. A person who has passed away can be visualized in a dream as stepping aboard an airplane or taking off in one. See: *Spirit*.

A plane broken in half can mean you're divided about something.

For example, a young man whose father died from illness dreams that he's with family members watching his father board a plane. His father tells them he will be back soon and loves them all. The plane takes off and breaks in half in a fiery disaster. The imagery captures the dreamer's thoughts and feelings about whether to believe his father is alive in the afterlife. The plane breaking in half symbolizes his internal division. On the one hand, he wants to believe it. On the other hand, he has no proof.

Jumping out of a plane can symbolize abandoning a project or relationship. A plane in a hangar can symbolize lack of excitement or unused potential.

A flight that is delayed can symbolize a delay in your life. A canceled flight can have similar meaning, except that the symbolism is related to something that is canceled or abandoned, such as plans.

Some people fear flying in a plane, and their dreams can address this fear. Also consider that a fear of flying can symbolize another fear, such as fear of success, failure, or death. See: *Fear*.

See also: *Air, Airport, Ascend, Captain, Crash, Embark, Fear, Fly, Jet, Journey, Left, Passenger, Pilot, Right, Spirit*

Airport—Airports can symbolize a time of transition. Something about you or your life is changing. Or you want to reach a personal destination such as a goal or ambition and are moving toward it, but it hasn't gotten off the ground. An airport can symbolize thinking about what comes next in your life.

It can symbolize waiting for something to happen. You feel delayed or inconvenienced. Air travel can involve a lot of waiting, and sometimes it's a big hassle. Those associations can be used to create symbolism.

A canceled flight can symbolize something hoped-for that doesn't materialize.

The idea of a plane's arrival can be applied to situations such as a child coming into your life or the birth of something new in yourself.

The idea of departure can be applied to death or to a departure from old ways or habits, or from a time of your life, such as when getting married and leaving behind single life.

Airports are points of departure, such as when you're leaving behind old beliefs or practices or a time of life. You're ready to move on from something. On the other hand, arriving at an airport can connect with the idea of starting something new or achieving the success or ambition you seek.

Physically, an airport can symbolize lungs.

Be sure to read the entry for *Airplane*.

See also: *Air, Airplane, Body, Childbirth, Death, Fly, Hotel, Pilot, Spirit, Vacation*

Alcohol—Drinking alcohol excessively in a dream can symbolize lack of control or restraint. You are in a situation you can't control. See: *Drunkenness*.

It can symbolize feeling out of kilter or out of sorts.

People sometimes drink excessively because they're trying to escape something; doing so in a dream can symbolize covering over feelings of inadequacy or regret.

Or the dream might be a straightforward message that you drink too much.

Alcohol is called "spirits," so consuming alcohol can symbolize taking in spiritual teaching, or spiritual practice. This use of the symbolism is more likely in dreams where alcohol is consumed in moderation and does not produce drunkenness. Excessive consumption can symbolize using something as a substitute for spiritual nourishment, or drowning out the voices inside you that want it. Carl Jung's insight about excessive drinking as a substitute for spiritual life is the foundation of Alcoholics Anonymous and other twelve-step programs.

Alcohol is associated with sociability, celebration, and good times. In a dream it can symbolize the desire to mingle, or wanting something to ease social anxiety. It can indicate a need to cut loose and have fun. References to drinking alcohol can be associated with an event in your life that is cause for celebration, such as the arrival of child, getting married, or graduating.

See also: *Abuse, Addict, Bartender, Drugs, Drunkenness, Party*

Alien—See: *UFO*

Alimony—Paying alimony in a dream can symbolize paying for past mistakes, or something from your past that continues extracting a cost. For example, a felony on your record is something you continue to pay for long after the punishment is served.

Alimony can symbolize an ongoing connection with something in your past. For example, after a bad breakup, you won't date anyone new because of fear of repeating the situation. In a sense, you are still paying for a relationship that ended.

Alimony can symbolize something perceived as unfair, especially if connected with the past. Dreams make comparisons, so if you perceive paying alimony as unfair, then a dream can use it to compare with something else perceived as unfair.

For example, you receive a bad evaluation at work, then dream about begrudgingly paying alimony to the supervisor who gave the evaluation.

See also: *Bail, Divorce, Husband, Marriage, Wedding, Wife*

Allah—See: *God*

Alligator—Alligators are known for big mouths with sharp teeth—a great way of symbolizing a big-mouthed person who makes sharp or biting comments.

Alligators ambush their prey by coming up out of the water, which can be a way of describing destructive emotions, personal attacks that come out of nowhere, or the potential for danger.

An alligator can symbolize someone who can't be trusted. Alligators can appear non-threatening while lying in water or on the side of a river, but get too close and you could be their lunch!

A teacher has a dream about entering a building through glass double doors. Inside, it is dark. The floor between herself and the opposite wall is a pool of dark water. In the water is an alligator. She's leery of it, but a female co-worker from her school walks up and pats it on the head. The dreamer walks out of the building, and outside is a set of stairs that leads up into the air, seemingly to nowhere.

The dreamer associates the glass double doors with her workplace, which has similar doors. The day before the dream she had a bad encounter with a supervisor. She thought she could openly talk about feelings regarding a work situation, but the encounter left her cold. The supervisor will turn on her in an instant like an alligator, and she found out the hard way. The co-worker's action of patting the alligator on the head shows that she acts oblivious to the threat from their mutual supervisor. The stairs to nowhere symbolize a suggestion that the dreamer take steps to protect herself.

See also: *Ambush, Animals, Reptile, Teeth*

Alley—Dreaming about being in an alley implies limited options, because alleys are sometimes dead ends. See: *Dead End*.

It can mean you have been sidetracked or diverted from where you want to be. You're not on the main road.

Or perhaps you have put yourself in some sort of jeopardy, because a "dark alley" is typically a dangerous setting, day or night. On the other hand, something that's "right up your alley" means it's perfect for you.

See also: *Dead End, Road*

All-Seeing Eye—The All-Seeing Eye, also known as the Eye of Providence, or the Third Eye, can symbolize penetrating awareness. Nothing escapes its attention. It can symbolize deep insight and knowledge.

The All-Seeing Eye in a dream can symbolize the feeling of being scrutinized and unable to hide yourself. Perhaps someone has his eye on you, or you are secretly being observed. In which case, the Eye in a dream is likely to cause feelings of fear, anxiety, or dread. When it represents something positive, you are likely to react more positively, in accordance with subconscious knowledge of what it symbolizes.

The Eye is associated with the pineal gland located deep in the brain, which looks like an eye and has light-receptor cells. It's the mind's eye. In certain spiritual practices the Third Eye is stimulated so that it will "open." In dreams, a single eye or pair of eyes opening can symbolize a personal awakening.

See also: *Anxiety, Chakra, Eye, Fear, Head, Pyramid*

Altar—Altars are associated with sacrifice, especially personal sacrifice. For example, sacrificing time with family in order to get ahead at work. Such a dream might show you sacrificing your children on an altar.

Altars are associated with beliefs. For example, dreaming about sacrificing your spouse on an altar can symbolize breaking with that person on a matter of personal belief and possibly sacrificing the relationship.

Altars are associated with religious ritual and practice. Defending an altar from attack can sym-

bolize defending your religious faith from doubt or derogatory comments.

Extend the idea beyond religion, and an altar can symbolize spirituality, ideals, and things you hold sacred.

An altar can connect with topics related to social status and maturity, symbolism created by the association between an altar and a place where people are given public attention and special occasions happen. Rituals such as baptisms and weddings are performed at altars. At an altar, faith is strengthened, the divine is sought, and vows are offered. Dreams can cross-reference and draw parallels with any of those subjects and use them to make comparisons.

For example, a woman who finds out that her husband is having an affair dreams about black magic being performed at an altar, symbolizing her perception that her marriage has turned dark.

Praying at an altar is associated with seeking miracles and divine intervention.

Altars are associated with the communities that worship around them and can sum up in one image everything about those communities and the dreamer's place within them.

Be sure to read the entry for *Church*.

See also: *Candle, Church, God, Pastor, Temple, Wedding*

Ambulance—See: *Paramedic*

Ambush—To dream about being ambushed might warn of hidden danger. You have overlooked something that could come back to haunt you, or a situation has potential for trouble, now or later.

The idea of ambush applies to any situation where an attack comes out of nowhere. Someone undercuts you at work or school, and you dream about being ambushed by an animal or mugger.

You can be ambushed by a spouse who brings up a loaded subject at the perfect time to gain advantage, a co-worker who pulls a surprise, or an unexpected change of plans. These are situations where people say they are ambushed, and dreams can portray them through imagery of a sneak attack. The symbolism can be used anytime you feel betrayed or unpleasantly surprised.

The shadow side of the psyche is known for being a trickster. It can interrupt your life, sometimes forcefully and deceptively, seemingly out of nowhere. The ambush is a favorite trick of your shadow because it pops up when you least expect it and sabotages you.

See also: *Animals, Attack, Beat, Escape, Fight, Hide, Run, Shadow*

Ammunition—Ammunition can symbolize saving up favors, dirt on someone, or arguments to use in the heat of battle. Think of when ammunition is used in figures of speech, such as when it means having the ammo to compel a decision to go your way, or to win an argument or debate. In which case, ammunition symbolizes means of persuasion, defense, or coercion.

Stretch the idea and ammunition can symbolize storing for later something energetic or game-changing. For instance, resting up before a big holiday push can be thought of as saving your ammunition.

Ammunition can symbolize having the means to protect yourself or get what you want. Bullets in the gun are a metaphor for the needed personal qualities and characteristics. If you have ammunition, you have the ability and confidence to protect yourself, not just physically but emotionally and psychologically. You can get what you want.

Lack of ammunition can symbolize lacking means to protect yourself, arguments in your favor, or dirt on someone. It can mean that you don't feel that you have what it takes to get what you want.

A woman who lives in a rough neighborhood dreams that her landlord, who lives in the adjacent apartment, gives her a pistol with no bullets. When she asks where to get bullets, the landlord answers that it's up to her. The dream portrays a situation where she fears some neighbors who give her funny looks and make remarks. They hang out on the sidewalk in front of her building, so there's no avoiding them. She talks frequently to the landlord about it, and he tells her to protect herself, but he isn't helpful

on specifics other than that she should carry a gun. The gun symbolizes his advice to protect herself, and the lack of ammo symbolizes the dreamer's perception that she is on her own in this battle.

See also: *Bullet, Fight, Gun, War*

Amputate—Amputation suggests that you have harmed yourself, or been harmed, in a lasting or permanent way. Something happened, or is going to happen, that will cause serious and sudden loss. The loss can relate to your external life—a relationship, job, or opportunity—or it can relate to your inner life and aspects of yourself such as ability and skill, especially when manual dexterity is involved. For example, a pianist with arthritis can dream about it as having fingers amputated.

When body parts are amputated, it's a sacrifice for the greater good, and that association can be stretched to connect with situations such as sacrificing a vacation to make more money.

Amputation can mean cutting off something that needs to go. Time for something to end. For example, if someone is financially draining you, you could dream about amputating a hand, because the hand is what reaches for your wallet or purse. It means you want to cut off financial support.

Or if you impulsively come to the rescue of people you know and don't want to do it anymore, then you might dream about cutting off your feet or legs because they're parts of the body associated with coming to someone's rescue.

Amputating a leg can mean you feel as if you have no room to maneuver or legs to stand on. It can mean you do something that hinders your ability to move forward in your life. Or you had to cancel travel plans.

Dreaming about amputating your ring finger can mean it's time to end a relationship or break with someone close to you, such as a sibling.

Amputation can symbolize trying to prevent yourself from doing something that you know is harmful. For example, if your sex drive gets you into trouble, then you could dream about amputating your genitals.

Then again, amputating your penis can symbolize loss of power, authority, or virility.

As with all dream symbolism, the meaning of amputation is defined by the context, your feelings, and especially your reaction.

For example, in a dream about scheduling a leg amputation, the dreamer reacts nonchalantly, considering the importance of a leg. The dream exposes the dreamer's feelings about what the leg represents: his progress toward getting a college degree. Amputating the leg symbolizes dropping an important class. His reaction shows he is willing to make that sacrifice—perhaps too willing.

In a dream about being forced to amputate a hand, the dreamer's reaction is much different. She is horrified. In the next scene she turns to her father for help. Amputating her hand symbolizes her inability to make her own decisions, and turning to her dad for help symbolizes her dependence on him to make decisions for her. She knows deep inside that she's sacrificing her independence.

The particular body part amputated defines the symbolism. Look up the body part in this dream dictionary to get ideas. Here are a few suggestions:

Breast: Been cheated on. Menopause. Loss of desirability. Inability to nurture. Fear of disease.

Ear: Don't want to hear something. Not listening. Hearing problems. Ignoring the obvious. Overhearing something you aren't supposed to hear. Secrets.

Eye: Failing to notice something. Lack of vision for life. Vision problems. Sacrificing your identity or harming your reputation, a wordplay for "I."

Face: Loss of personal identity. Self-image issues. Damage to reputation. Self-abnegation.

Feet: Making excuses. Shaky personal foundation. Unwillingness to do something.

Finger: Loss of feeling. Lacking "touch" or sensitivity. Clumsiness. Avoiding blame or notice (fingerprint). Can't put your finger on something.

Hand: Difficulty making decisions or taking action. Theft. Inability to "grasp" a situation or con-cept. A weak hold, such as when a relationship is slipping away. Losing touch with reality.

Head: "Losing your head." Not thinking clearly. Chaotic thoughts. Acting rashly. A message isn't getting through.

Heart: Loss of a close relationship. Falling out of love. Sacrificing your emotional health. "Heartless."

Nose: Failure to follow instincts. Needlessly overreacting in a way that's self-destructive (cut off your nose to spite your face). Public disgrace. Nosiness gets you into trouble.

Penis: Frustration with sex life. Loss of virility or authority. Low emphasis on sex.

Toes: Loss of balance or poise. Overlooking minor details.

See also: *Body, Breast, Feet, Finger, Head, Heart, Knife, Leg, Panic, Penis*

Amulet—See: *Talisman*

Amusement Park—An amusement park setting in a dream can symbolize what you do for kicks or amusement. It can say something about your sense of humor.

It can express the feeling of being played—the joke is on you.

The symbolism can tie in with thrills and frivolity. Also, it might tie in with specific experiences at amusement parks, such as getting lost or separated from parents, a rite of passage, or facing fears.

See also: *Clown, Roller Coaster*

Anal Sex—A primary association with anal sex is submission, either voluntary or forced submission. Submission connects with authority, so by extension anal sex in a dream can relate to using, abusing, or challenging authority.

It's associated with trust and willingness to try new things.

It's associated with giving or receiving something special from a sex partner.

It's associated with temptation and obsession.

Dreams start with your associations and build stories around them. So, for example, you could dream about having anal sex with a friend after putting a lot of trust in that person to do something right.

Forceful anal sex can symbolize controlling yourself, or a part of yourself, through domination or coercion. It's one side of you dominating another part, vividly expressing the feeling of dominating or of being dominated. It sums up a "do it or else" scenario.

The same idea applies to situations in your life involving domination or coercion. For an example, see: *Devil*.

It can symbolize motivating yourself with fear, especially fear of embarrassment.

It can symbolize doing something that is forbidden, taboo, or perceived as dirty. See: *Incest*.

It's associated with homosexuality and can be used in dreams to explore the subject. See: *Gay*.

Anal sex in a dream can be a way of enacting the phrase "take it up the ass." It means you're on the wrong end of a deal, or in a vulnerable position. Another definition of the phrase means to take something seriously that is meant as a joke. Your reaction to the scenario and feelings will guide you to which meaning of the symbolism is used in your dream.

If you have been thinking about anal sex and dream about it, you might be exploring the possibility in a safe environment. It's a sort of dress rehearsal to determine whether you'd like it.

A wide variety of associations with anal sex can be used by dreams to create symbolism, even if you've never experienced it: safety, pleasure, giving and receiving, perceptions about morality, sexual demands, avoiding coitus, pleasing a partner.

See also: *Anus, Fisting, Gay, Incest, Sex*

Ancestor—An ancestor in a dream can symbolize inherited traits. Personal qualities, traits, and characteristics can be traced to ancestors, such as having a grandmother's eyes or an uncle's laugh or a parent's brains. People naturally wonder about the soil from which they spring. "Ancestor" opens the door to many subjects for a dream to explore; there are many ways that ancestors can be used as symbolism.

For example, a young woman dreams about receiving several calls in a row for her Aunt Diane, who lives in England and hasn't been seen by the dreamer for two decades. Two days before the dream, she visited with some relatives who all remarked how much she looked like her aunt at her age. But when the woman looked at pictures of her aunt, she disagreed. The dream symbolizes the situation as receiving phone calls meant for her aunt. Phone calls connect people, and in this case, connection is meant in the sense of a connection between her and her aunt—a connection missed by the dreamer.

An ancestor can symbolize tradition, holding onto the past and preserving it.

Or you feel constrained by your heritage or tradition. For example, a young man born and raised on an Indian reservation dreams about wearing traditional Indian garb to a job interview in a modern office building. He feels conspicuous. It symbolizes his perception that his Indian ancestry makes him stand out negatively in certain environments.

Ancestors can be symbolized as a tree. Sometimes these dreams will pair a tree with a location. For example, a man with French ancestry dreams about a beautiful oak tree standing tall and proud in the middle of a field in France, but he actually lives in America. It reflects his admiration for his French ancestry.

See also: *Family, Tree*

Android—See: *Robot*

Angel—Dreams create symbolism and build stories from personal and common associations, and common associations with angels are that they are good, pure, and righteous. In addition, they come to the rescue of mortals in danger. Imagine the possibilities:

An angel can symbolize a good person you know, someone who comes to the rescue. It can symbolize a desire to live a pure life and have pure thoughts. It can symbolize any force for good that helps people in need and does the right thing.

An angel can symbolize your better nature. In Freudian terms, it can symbolize the superego, the inner regulator of impulses and enforcer of morality and ethics—your conscience.

An angel can be a satirical depiction of someone you know who is self-righteous or holier-than-thou. In which case, something about the angel in your dream will seem wrong.

In scripture, angels are messengers from God, so in dreams they can deliver messages from something deeper, wiser, or higher. These dream-characters come from the archetypal layer of the unconscious mind, which is a source of hidden knowledge and insight, like angels. The unconscious mind is the "other side," sometimes completely foreign and incomprehensible to the conscious mind.

If an angel in your dream delivers a message, take it to heart, no matter what your beliefs are. It can guide you to greater meaning and fulfillment in your life. A message read from a scroll by an angel is a particularly powerful image of delivering an important message.

Three angels together in a dream suggest unity and wholeness, as in the Trinity, body-mind-spirit and birth-life-death. Some traditions view it as a sign of high spiritual attainment. Special groupings of three spiritual figures are found in many cultures and belief systems, not just Christian.

The Angel of Death in a dream can signify that something is coming to an end. See: *Grim Reaper*.

See also: *Afterlife, God, Grim Reaper, Group, Heaven, Light, Unconscious Mind, White*

Anger—To be angry in a dream or to express anger can mean that you really are angry. The dream imagery and scenario are chosen to trigger it—you subconsciously recognize the symbolism and react to that, not to the overt imagery. The purpose is to help you understand the source of the anger, to vent it, to deal with it, and to use it constructively.

Dreams act as emotional outlets, so if you aren't expressing your anger, your dreams will help you express it. However, it is better to express it

consciously, because your dreams amplify emotions and it's sure to come out raw and powerful. Anger is a needed emotion, but some people have difficulty with it. Your dreams will try to teach you to channel it into assertiveness. Anger is needed to help you defend yourself and your boundaries.

Look closely at what gets you angry in a dream. You know that the dream is pushing your buttons, so you can look at your reactions for clues to the symbolism. After an anger dream, you can sometimes decode the meaning simply by answering the question, What am I angry about? Sometimes a direct parallel can be found in the symbolism used by the dream.

For instance, a woman dreams that she and her husband are eating dinner and her husband lets half-chewed food drop from his mouth, thinking it's funny. It really ticks her off. The dream has followed an evening when she got angry but had to hide her anger when her husband said something embarrassing in front of a group of their friends—then kept it up all evening. He, of course, thought he was being funny.

The dream scenario triggers the same feelings of anger and embarrassment she felt at dinner. The husband-character's sloppy actions with his mouth is a metaphor for his sloppy words. Both come from the mouth.

An active volcano is a classic symbol for anger building or exploding. See: *Volcano*.

Firing a gun can be an expression of anger. See: *Gun*.

See also: *Emotions, Erupt, Fire, Gun, Hate, Rage, Volcano, Yell*

Anima—In simplest terms, anima represents the feminine aspects of a male's psyche. Everything in his psyche that's traditionally feminine and unconscious summed up in one image, such as hunches, intuitions, moods, receptivity, and capacity to love himself.

Anima is a man's guide to assimilating feminine traits and the feminine principle, yin. She's also the gateway to accessing the deepest layers of his psyche. Ideally, a man is fully masculine while also embodying traditionally feminine traits. Yin is discussed at length in the entry for *Vagina*.

Anima can be the single most important dream-character in a male's life. Ultimately, it's tied to a primary function of dreaming: to help harmonize and unite the conscious mind with the unconscious mind. See: *Unconscious Mind*.

Anima's main enticement is the promise of the best, most meaningful relationship of a man's life if he goes the distance. He gets to marry his dream girl. She can be mom, lover, wife, muse, goddess, and best friend all in one—but usually not all at the same time. See: *Bride*.

Instead, as a male matures through his lifetime relationship with anima, she evolves. She first appears as a mother figure. When he reaches his teen years she morphs into an ideal lover. When he matures into manhood, anima matures along with him, becoming a mature and independent female. Finally, she evolves into a goddess figure such as the Virgin Mary or the Hindu's Devi, the Divine Mother. Unfortunately, it's easy to get fixated at an early stage of development and never evolve past it.

These roles played by anima are the best way of identifying them in dreams. Additionally, they can be identified by a feeling of close familiarity. They're recurring dream figures, appearing time and again as the same figure or as a type of figure, so keeping a journal of your dreams will help you identify them. They can appear as females you know or know of, such as celebrities who embody the role, or as completely imaginary characters.

The form and image of anima depends on what an individual male responds to: princess, professor, mother, queen, sister, biker chick, corporate gal, librarian, runway model, temptress, Playboy Bunny, African queen, Asian beauty. She's alluring and can be powerfully attractive, but her appearance depends largely on a man's relationship with this part of himself. If his relationship with anima is bad, she can appear as a witch, bitch, siren, mermaid, nag or hag.

Anima can be thought of as short for "animated," because that's what she does for a man who lives up to her expectations—which are really

his own expectations. He pleases anima when he does everything he can to mature and live fully, and in return she animates him with purpose and love.

When the relationship between a man and his anima is bad, it leads to self-destructive behaviors and even violence. He's an "addictive personality." He tends to be listless and bored—or he goes to the other extreme and lives a life of constant adventure and challenge. He never stops to ponder what's missing from his life. What's missing is the deep and meaningful relationship he can have with himself. He's moody, unbalanced, depressed, sometimes sexually uninterested—or at the opposite extreme, he's a playboy or sex addict. His tortured relationship with his inner self can bring out the worst in him. In many cultures, a man in such a predicament is said to have lost his soul. See: *Castrate*.

Anima is often described in terms of soul. And indeed, a man with a good relationship with his anima is usually quite soulful.

It's a recipe for disaster when a male projects his anima onto women in his life and expects them to live up to that image. It's a tendency that begins in early childhood and can continue throughout his life. That man will never be happy for long with the women he tries to make into mates, lovers, or mother figures. No mortal woman can possibly live up to the anima ideal, nor should she try.

Anima dreams can be a source of confusion and relationship troubles when misunderstood as desiring someone other than your mate. Married men dream about falling in love with anima, their ideal woman, and think it means they must subconsciously want someone else. Actually, they are called to have a special relationship within themselves. Anima isn't just a dream-character, it's a relationship. Guys, respect it the same as you'd respect a soul mate or love of your life.

Characters like anima arise from the deepest reaches of the psyche and are independent of the ego. They're archetypes. Archetypes are shaped through a lifetime of experience, beginning from birth as a sort of blueprint that's the same in everyone. A male's mother or primary female caregiver is the first image given to his anima. She becomes the blueprint. Then the image is filled in through-out his lifetime by experiences with females of all types, but especially the ones closest to him. See: *Archetypes, Ego.*

His Shadow side won't let him just have his anima all for himself. He has to fight for her like a knight fighting for his beloved, and the stakes are all or nothing. Shadow is a guardian at the gate to deeper access to a man's unconscious mind, the ul-timate test that must be faced. See: *Shadow.*

The female's version of anima is called animus. See: *Animus.*

See also: *Animus, Archetypes, Beauty, Bride, Cas-trate, Collective Unconscious, Ego, Individuation, Love, Marriage, Psyche, Shadow, Unconscious Mind, Wife*

Animals—Language is full of sayings such as "proud as a lion," "slippery as a fish," and "free as a bird"—rich with symbolism for dreams to use. Dreams bring to life these sayings and use animals to tell stories about you and your life.

For example, a dream about fish dying in a fishbowl symbolically warns of an oncoming uri-nary-tract infection. The fishbowl symbolizes this person's bladder, and fish live in water, so the dying fish indicate something wrong with that part of her body. See: *Fish.*

In a dream about finding a white horse in a snowstorm, the horse symbolizes personal strength to move forward under treacherous personal con-ditions. White animals are commonly messengers of the unconscious mind, and a horse symbolizes strength.

In a dream about three kittens drowned in a pool—but one still alive—kitten-like qualities in the young dreamer are symbolically "killed off," but the one kitten left alive shows that he is trying to preserve part of himself from extinction—the playful, kitten-like side of himself succumbing to teenage peer pressure to toughen up.

Other associations can be made with fish, horses, and kittens, though. For instance, if your only experience with a horse is when one kicked you, then you aren't as likely to dream about it in a good context. What an animal in your dream

means to you matters more than pat definitions like the kind found in typical dream dictionaries!

Consider the characteristics and qualities of animals that appear in your dreams. A dog to one person is a loyal companion; to another it's a noisy nuisance. Both are common perceptions—which one fits your dream?

To find out what an animal in your dream means, associate the animal with your experiences, perceptions, and feelings. Also consider figures of speech that might apply, and caricatures from books, movies, cartoons, and TV shows that imbue everything from ants to birds to elephants with human qualities and voices. Your experience with, and impressions of, the creatures that appear in your dreams help determine what they symbolize.

Generally, the wilder the creature, the more in-stinctive or primitive your related emotions or be-haviors. We all have instincts reminiscent of certain animals or creatures. For example, rabbits and bulls are notorious for the instinct to mate. Gazelles and deer are known for the instinct to run. Lions and dogs are known for the instinct to protect ter-ritory. People have those instincts, too.

People are compared to animals and creatures in figures of speech like "stealthy as a cat," "friendly as a dog," and "treacherous as a snake." One image can sum up a person's behavior or personality. Comparisons to animals can be highly accurate ways of describing what we observe in people—and in ourselves.

Pay attention to the age of the animal. A puppy, cub, or other young animal can represent something new or young in you, or something that needs to mature. An old dog might be a play on the phrase "you old dog," meaning crafty or clever. It could symbolize an elder figure in your life, or something nearing its end.

Parents of young children are known to dream about baby animals, because comparisons between young children and young animals are easy to make—and in fact are made frequently in media and everyday conversation. For example, a mother might call her child "my little tiger," then dream about a baby tiger and not realize the relationship between it and her child.

Recurring dreams about abuse of young animals such as puppies and kittens is known as a sign of early childhood abuse.

White animals are an auspicious dream sign when they represent harmony among the conscious mind, the unconscious, and your instincts. Black animals, on the other hand, can be a sign of lacking harmony, or an adversarial relationship with your instincts. However, some animals are naturally white or black—the symbolism applies in situations when the color sticks out as deliberate.

Because the possibilities are so numerous, throughout this dream dictionary are listed specific creatures and what they can symbolize.

And keep in mind, the symbolism of animals in your dreams is given in the context of the dream-story. In other words, the white rabbit you chase down a hole might relate to something rabbit-like about you, like the desire to hide or protect yourself. Or it might be a prop in a story about finding out how deep the rabbit hole really goes.

To explore the symbolism of groups of animals, see: *Group*.

See also: *Alligator, Ambush, Baboon, Bat (Mammal), Birds, Buck, Bull, Cat, Camel, Cave, Chase, Chicken, Cow, Creature, Crow, Deer, Dog, Eagle, Eaten, Fish, Fly, Fox, Frog, Goat, Giraffe, Goose, Gorilla, Group, Guide, Kitten, Leopard, Lion, Mouse, Octopus, Owl, Pet, Pig, Puppy, Rabbit, Raccoon, Rat, Reptiles, Rooster, Shark, Stag, Tiger, Turtle, Vulture, Weasel, Whale, Wolf, Young, Zebra*

Animus—In simplest terms, animus represents the male aspects of a female's psyche. It's everything traditionally masculine and unconscious about a female summed up in one image. Animus is a woman's guide to assimilating masculine traits and the masculine principle, yang, and gaining access to deep layers of the psyche. She can be fully feminine while also incorporating traditionally masculine traits. For an in-depth look at masculine traits and the yang, see: *Penis*.

Animus can be the single most important dream-character in a female's life because it's tied to a primary function of dreaming: to help harmonize and unite the conscious mind with the unconscious mind.

Animus is an archetype, a blueprint for thinking processes and behaviors, and archetypes arise from the deepest layer of the psyche, way outside conscious awareness for most people. The blueprint is an outline, and personal experience with men—beginning with a woman's father or her first important male parental figure—fills in the details.

Animus can be a friend, guide, husband, or lover, depending on what a woman needs and the nature of their relationship. And it's a relationship that lasts a lifetime. Some dream-characters come and go, but animus is there from childhood to the end. The form he takes tends to be one that a female responds to at whatever stage of life she's in, and he can keep the same face for years at a time. A woman knows her inner man on sight and feels him even when he's not visibly present. He can be at her side whenever she wants or needs him.

Animus tends to pop into a woman's dream life for a while, help her with some things, go on adventures together, give her the boost she needs, then go away for a while. And in typical animus fashion, he'll be off doing some manly, important thing, then show back up in her dreams at just the right time. The implication is that her animus has a life of his own even when he's not in her dreams.

Animus dream-characters tend to change form and develop over time, often reflecting a female's conception of an ideal man at that time of her life. During her childhood, he is a father-figure. During her teenage years, animus is portrayed as a man of action, of muscle. He's the quarterback of the football team, the Tarzan to her Jane. He continues to evolve through stages—the house-husband type, the professor type, the man of words and ideas—and if all goes well he becomes a sort of spiritual guide, her own personal Buddha or wise man—except a lot hotter! Animus is keenly attractive, but won't necessarily be the most physically attractive male. It tends to show more as a personal magnetism, especially as a woman matures.

These roles played by animus figures are the best way of identifying them in dreams. Additionally, they are identified by a feeling of close famil-iarity. Keeping a dream journal helps with identi-fying them because they recur, either as the same character or as a type of character. Anima figures tend to appear in men's dreams with a rotating array of faces and forms, whereas animus figures tend to keep the same appearance for long stretches. They can appear as males a female knows, as celebrities, athletes, and other famous males who embody the role, and as completely imaginary characters.

Animus animates a woman, no matter what stage of life she's in. When the relationship is good, she can be both fully feminine and comfortable act-ing masculine, and her life will be filled with pur-pose and gusto. When the relationship is bad, it's *really* bad and shows, especially in her sarcasm and criticism. She'll know exactly where to hit a man where it hurts, and she can make a sport of it. The fireworks get intense when she confuses her inner man with the man or men in her life. Then it's a fight to the death—usually emotional and psycho-logical death, but sometimes physical, too.

Fireworks can be caused, too, when a woman dreams about animus, her ideal inner man, loving him, and thinking it means she subconsciously wants to leave her mate. Her relationship with an-imus is internal. She can have both a mate and an-imus in her life, and she can love both equally and differently. But she errs when she expects the men in her life to live up to the ideal shown to her in her dreams. It's called animus projection, and it's bad news.

A woman's Shadow stands in the way of ac-cessing her animus in a good way. Shadow is a guardian at the gate to deeper access to her uncon-scious mind. Once Shadow is dealt with, animus becomes a consistent ally and friend. See: *Shadow*.

See also: *Anima, Archetypes, Beauty, Collective Unconscious, Ego, Husband, Individuation, Love, Psy-che, Shadow, Unconscious Mind*

Ankle—The ankle is the connector between the leg and the foot, so the symbolism can relate to these body parts. Legs are what you stand on. They move you. They're your wheels, your pillars. Feet

are your foundation, your values, principles, and beliefs, and are also connected with what you stand on. The ankle, as a connector between your leg and foot, connects these two sets of ideas.

For example, a snake bite on the ankle can mean that something venomous is negatively in-fluencing your values or beliefs (feet) and it's pre-venting you from taking strong action (legs).

Along this line, an ankle in a dream can sym-bolize "making a stand," meaning deciding that something has to stop or be supported.

For instance, a dream about wrapping support tape around the ankle follows after the dreamer has her beliefs shaken by a bad experience with a fam-ily member. Support tape on her ankle symbolizes giving herself internal support to confront the sit-uation.

A weak ankle can symbolize a weak spot in character or the psyche, or small fault or fatal flaw, an Achilles heel, a personal weakness, such as for sweets and other temptations.

Feet can symbolize willingness to act. Thus, a sprained or broken ankle suggests unwillingness to act, or difficulty following through with resolu-tions. It can symbolize the one thing that always seems to trip you up.

See also: *Body, Feet, Leg*

Anorexia—See: *Emaciated*

Ant—The symbolism of ants is usually built around associations such as being busy, always on the move. Busy urban environments are compared to ant colonies because of the bustle and crowding.

The symbolism can be built around other common associations with ants, such as self-sacri-fice, carrying a big load, or resourcefulness.

Ants can symbolize feeling like a cog in the machine, one worker among many. You feel that your uniqueness or individuality is not valued.

An infestation of ants, or ant bites, can sym-bolize something that irritates you. It's probably a small irritation or something you try to overlook, since ants are small creatures easily overlooked. See: *Bug*.

Along this line, ants can get into anything, and that association can be used to create symbolism related to an inability to keep something out of your life. It always finds a way back in.

See also: *Bug, Insects*

Antler—To dream about antlers growing from your head can symbolize branching out in new directions, especially in your mental pursuits. Anything that grows from the head can relate to the mind and intellect.

Antlers, together with the action of attacking, can symbolize attacks that come in from many directions. For example, a teenaged female dreams about a young buck battling an old buck that has a massive rack of antlers. The young buck puts up a good fight but ultimately loses, symbolizing how the young woman stands up to her father, the old buck, but ultimately is unable to last against his multipronged arguments. He always wins.

See also: *Animals, Buck, Deer, Hair, Head*

Anus—The dream symbolism of body parts is often built around their function and common perceptions. The anus holds things in the body, and that association can be used to say that something is bottled up. It can indicate a need to loosen up. You're too tight.

Since the anus is where waste exits the body, it has associations with "letting go," "cleaning up," and "wiping away," such as when you let go of a bad idea, clean up your act, or wipe away negativity. Being unable to wipe away excrement can symbolize an inability to be rid of something such as a stain on your reputation or a filthy habit.

Anus symbolism can be used to describe a person you know (an asshole), or a situation you are in (it stinks).

Symbolism related to the anus includes such possibilities as dirty subjects, taboos, or a personal blind spot. It can sum up how you feel in one image.

See also: *Anal Sex, Body, Excrement*

Anxiety—Anxiety manifests many ways in dreams. The most common ways involve teeth breaking or crumbling, or worms or bugs crawling on you. See: *Bug, Teeth*.

Common scenarios for anxiety dreams include the presence of people and creatures that cause you anxiety. The supervisor or teacher breathing down your neck is likely to be referenced in your dreams, perhaps as a big bug that lands on your neck. Creatures such as spiders and snakes in dreams can symbolize anxiety if they mirror how you feel when you encounter them in the daylight world. They are used by the dreaming mind to trigger emotional reactions.

Anxiety experienced in a dream is a sign that something in your life is producing anxiety. Dreams create scenarios that parallel situations from your life, especially the emotional ones, so the best way to identify an anxiety dream is by the fact that it produces anxiety. It's no big mystery. Question is, what's causing anxiety and what are you going to do about it?

Your dreams can act as a sort of inner physician or psychologist, so if you dream about scenarios that cause anxiety, it's a good idea to analyze the dream for suggestions on how to deal with the anxiety or eliminate it. Anxiety is often caused by situations that can be helped, either by changing your external circumstances or your internal ones.

See also: *Bug, Emotions, Insects, Panic, Teenager, Teeth*

Apartment—Dreaming about living in an apartment when you don't really live in one can symbolize being in a temporary place in your life, or in a transition phase. Apartments are commonly associated with temporary dwellings, so think along the lines of anything that's temporary.

The idea applies quite often to relationships, especially romantic ones. If you dream about living in an apartment with someone you're dating, but you don't actually live together or live in an apartment, you know right away it's symbolism. It's likely to be a way of saying your relationship is in transition, or you know deep inside that the relationship is temporary.

For example, a man who lives with his girlfriend dreams that they decide they should move out of their apartment. They actually live together in a house, a discrepancy with reality that stands out as symbolism. He walks into a scene where their roommates (completely fictional characters, another discrepancy with reality) lounge around as she packs their stuff and cleans. Seeing this, he kicks into gear and helps pack, thinking to himself that it's a good idea for the two of them to move on. The dream reflects his thoughts about moving to the next phase of their relationship. He has lived the bachelor life, symbolized as the roommates, long enough. Moving out of the apartment in the dream means transitioning to a new way of thinking about the relationship as permanent. It's something he senses his girlfriend is ready for, symbolized as her taking the initiative to pack.

The idea of being in transition applies to yourself, too. People going through personal or life changes are known to dream more frequently about living in an apartment. It's a way of saying "between places in life."

An apartment can symbolize being apart from someone. It can reflect being apart figuratively, such as when opinions differ or emotional connection is lacking.

An apartment can mean "a part of," as in getting good grades in school is a part of getting into a good college, and a good college is a part of what leads to getting good work afterward.

Apartments can symbolize difficulty controlling your living space. Apartments are known for being close to neighbors, and neighbors are a variable that's difficult to control.

The symbolism of apartments can connect with the association that people live in them when they have limited personal and financial resources. Of course, living in an apartment can be driven by convenience and choice, too.

When you dream about an apartment where you used to live, it can refer to that time of your life. Something started back then that continues today or is relevant to it. For example, a man has recurring dreams about living in his college apartment, a way of saying that years later he still lives like a college student.

See also: *Home, Movie*

Ape—See: *Gorilla*

Apocalypse—An apocalypse in a dream can be an exaggeration of "huge change" or "bad conflict." People can have a personal apocalypse when their lives melt down, or some way of living or doing things can no longer be sustained. Forces have built up that threaten to explode. A dream apocalypse implies the need to examine your life and take action, or prepare for the inevitable.

An apocalypse can be an exaggerated way of describing the battles waged in life; for example, against a barrage of work. See: *Fight*.

The symbolism can tie in with the emotions it invokes, such as dread and panic. See: *Emotions, Panic*.

Dreams about an apocalypse can cause people to fear that a worldwide calamity is about to happen, but this theme arises in dreams millions of times daily, and the world hasn't ended. Therefore, it must be symbolism, and most likely a dream about the world ending means that something about *your* world is ending. You face a big change or loss.

Situations such as major illnesses, breakups, job losses, financial collapses, personal revelations, moving to new locations, and reaching milestones are known to spark apocalypse dreams. Usually the symbolism connects with something bad, but the symbolism is based on your feelings and perceptions. The thing you fear or dread is not necessarily bad. For example, apocalyptic themes are common in the dreams of teenagers facing the inevitability of adulthood.

The theme of apocalypse can capture thoughts related things people say they would do if the world were ending, things they wouldn't do otherwise. For example, you finally tell your true feelings to that person you're totally in love with, or tell your boss what an asshole he or she is. The idea is similar to what people say they would do if they only had *X* number of days to live. You finally do or say what you have always wanted. The truth comes out. Your true feelings show.

You can think of the symbolism of apocalypse as more than a small disaster, but less than Armageddon. For a rundown of how dreams use strength of symbolism, see: *Disaster.*

See also: *Anxiety, Armageddon, Disaster, Emotions, Nuclear War, Panic*

Apparel—See: *Clothing*

Apparition—See: *Ghost*

Appearance—See: *Mirror*

Appetite—See: *Eat*

Applause—See: *Ovation*

Aquarium—An aquarium full of water in your dream can symbolize being aware of your emotions, but unable to fully access them.

It can symbolize being bottled up inside.

Watching fish swim in an aquarium can symbolize idleness or killing time.

An aquarium can symbolize the bladder. Changing the water can relate to urinary trouble and the need for good hydration and show the need for better fluids in your system. Fetid or nasty water in an aquarium can symbolize a urinary-tract infection or similar issue. It can characterize the quality of the liquid you consume.

See also: *Fish, Water*

Archetypes—Archetypes are patterning forces deep in the psyche that you're born with, blueprints for behaviors, thought patterns, attitudes, and feelings that form the foundation of who and what you are and how you live your life. Throughout life they govern the development of major areas such as love, leadership, intellect, skill, self-preservation, mating, parenting, motivation, and discipline.

In dreams, archetypes can personify as unusually magnetic or important dream-characters that evoke strong responses. They can appear as something right out of myth and legend: king, queen, magician, prophetess, hero, knight, saint, sage, artist, trickster, shaman. Or as modern expressions of these universal roles. Today's knight is the spe-cial-ops soldier. Our trickster works in PR. Our kings and queens run companies and governments, and our magicians create lifelike computer graphics and sequence DNA.

Dozens of parallels can be made between archetypal roles as depicted in myths and legends and roles we play today under different names. And it can be tremendously helpful for you to see these parallels in your life, and think of yourself as more than a cog in the machine or just another person. Your life has drama and importance simply because you're alive, here and now, and part of a huge story we're all acting out together.

Thinking of yourself as a knight or magician or queen helps you access the energy of the archetypal layer of the mind, which is the most potent personal energy. It's the other royal road to the unconscious mind. And your dreams lead the way by putting you into stories where you can play these roles.

Archetypes appear in the dreams and myths of people around the world, with roughly the same meaning. They tend to act more independently when portrayed as dream-characters, with an intelligence and perspective of their own, and their behavior can be deeply revealing of underlying dynamics of the psyche, especially patterns.

dream-characters that represent archetypes often come in pairs, representing the two "poles" of the archetype, called positive and negative in the sense of being active or passive. For example, the bully (active) and the coward (passive) are two sides of the same coin, both being immature expressions of the Warrior archetype. The know-it-all (active) and the dunce (passive) are immature expressions of the Magician, which governs intellect and skill.

The tyrant and the weakling are the two sides of the king/queen archetype. In fact, the tyrant acts as he or she does as a way of denying the weakling inside, and the weakling, in turn, undermines and opposes the tyrant but secretly wants to be him. The bully is secretly a coward, and inside every coward lurks a bully. The goal is to transcend the conflict between opposites by rising above it and seeing from a better-informed perspective. See: *All-Seeing Eye, Bully, Coward, Individuation, Warrior.*

Archetypes combine opposites into one. See: *Pyramid*.

Archetypes, according to Carl Jung, are timeless and hereditary, inherited from family and society. He proposed that they might even exist outside space-time, in line with Einstein's theory of nonlocality. However, for our purpose, the central point is that through archetypes, outside forces can influence the individual through dreams—and not just influence, but compel.

Professor Robert Moore and author Robert A. Johnson have written extensively about archetypes, building on Jung's theories, and their work is highly recommended. In this book, you can continue exploring the subject using the entries listed below.

See also: *Anima, Animus, Artist, Boss, Bully, Circle, Collective Unconscious, Coward, God, Hero, Jesus, King, Pyramid, Queen, Shadow, Warrior*

Arena—An arena in a dream can symbolize the public arena where you engage in competition or discourse. It can symbolize your public life—the public arena—or a platform for self-expression. Social media, for example, are a public arena and platform for self-expression. In this sense, an arena is like a stage. See: *Stage*.

It can mean that something needs to be brought out into the open.

Another way of thinking about the symbolism of an arena is that it represents your center, especially if the arena is circular. The center of the circle is your inner core, your inner sanctum, your ego, and the outer circle is the larger picture that is your complete psyche. The actions that take place in such an arena can define the challenges you face to maintain, defend, and expand your psyche. See: *Circle, Ego, Psyche*.

For example, battling a dragon in an arena can symbolize struggles with a dark side of your personality or a fiery temper. Battling a lion can symbolize struggling with pride or intimidation. Battling a dark knight can symbolize a struggle with a side of yourself that abuses power or draws energy from negativity. For a dramatic example of fighting in an arena, see: *Fight*.

Applause from spectators in an arena can symbolize public approval or bringing your internal forces into harmony. See: *Ovation*.

On the other hand, if the spectators boo, it's a sign of disapproval from within you for not doing what you know is right, or not putting the effort into bettering yourself. Booing can also symbolize public disapproval.

Arenas are associated with games and sports. See: *Games, Sports*.

Being a spectator in an arena can symbolize avoiding conflict or staying above the fray. Staying away from the middle of the arena can symbolize lack of self-confidence. Being alone in the arena can symbolize avoiding public gatherings.

Dreams can use the fact that stadiums are public venues to create stories about your relationship with society and your feelings about being in public and in big crowds.

An arena can simply be a setting for the story, and other details are the focus of importance, such as the characters or actions.

See also: *Circle, Dragon, Ego, Fight, Games, Lion, Opponent, Ovation, Psyche, Sports, Stage*

Argue—See: *Anger, Fight, Yell*

Arithmetic—See: *Math*

Arm—To figure out what arms symbolize in your dreams, first consider their use for accomplishing tasks and work and taking actions, and how arms can be used to connect with those subjects, such as when dreaming about shortened arms that can't reach a tool or keyboard symbolizes coming up short at your job, or when long arms symbolize the long arm of the law or long reach of an authority.

Arms can connect with the idea of reaching out, such as when you need or offer help or make contact with someone. Arms can be used to express the idea of bringing someone closer to you emotionally, or something closer to you personally. It's a physical representation of a personal situation. Holding someone in your arms is an act of nurture and support. See: *Hug*.

Arms push and pull and help keep things away from you, like a person or bad habit—anything "arms' length." Pushing something away can show need for objectivity or distance from a subject, or the creation of emotional or personal distance. It can symbolize refusal or rejection.

Pulling can mean wanting someone or something to be closer.

An arm in a dream can be a play on the phrase "arm yourself," take steps to protect yourself or those you love. The possibilities extend beyond physical protection to include emotional, financial, or psychological protection.

An injury to the arms, or restraint of them, can symbolize inability to protect yourself, take action, or use your strength. You are "pinned down." You have no choice.

Weak arms can symbolize helplessness or inability to hold something close to you. See: *Weak*.

A broken arm can symbolize a loss or dispute, being financially broke, or a personal break with a loved one, especially a sibling.

Having one arm can symbolize inhibition, or inability to defend yourself, take action, or overcome an obstacle or obstacles in general.

Strong arms can symbolize the ability to impose your will, overcome your opponents, or get work done. It can symbolize using force to get your way, aka "strong-arming."

In some dream-interpretation traditions, arms can symbolize a brother or close companion. Your arms are at your side, and a close companion is someone who stands by your side. There's also the term "brother-in-arms."

See also: *Amputate, Body, Fingers, Hand, Hug*

Armageddon—To dream about Armageddon carries the same idea as apocalypse, except next-level. Whatever it describes about you or your life is relatively huge, or is something you feel strongly about. For example, the fact or even idea of losing a loved one or breaking up with your significant other is like the world ending and is the sort of strong situation that requires strong symbolism.

Armageddon can symbolize a sense of foreboding about something approaching in your life. For example, facing a "do or die" situation, such as a college entrance exam or a professional certification test. Or a phase of life is about to end. It's an exaggerated way of saying something is critically important or about to change drastically.

For people immersed in End Times prophecy, dreaming about Armageddon can reflect the thoughts that preoccupy their minds or fears they harbor. Some religious leaders constantly point toward signs of Armageddon coming. That association with doom and gloom creates the possibility for using Armageddon to symbolize pessimism.

See also: *Apocalypse, Disaster, Enemy, Erupt, Fight, God, Nazi, Opponent, Pastor, War*

Armor—Wearing armor in a dream can symbolize your defenses. Your armor shields you, protects you, and a dream can mean "protect" in the sense of how you protect yourself and your interests. It can symbolize psychological and emotional protection, or financial or political protection.

Armor can symbolize truth because it protects you if you've done nothing wrong. Your armor can be your faith, beliefs, knowledge, or ability to defend yourself.

It can symbolize the strong reasoning and arguments you use to establish your position, or the feeling of being invulnerable, or self-confident.

It can symbolize an authority or anything else that protects you and makes you feel safe.

See also: *Warrior*

Army—Dreams have a lot of common associations to work with when creating symbolism based on an army, or army-related subjects such as soldiers, battles, and weapons.

Armies are associated with order and discipline, with leadership and strategy, and that only scratches the surface.

You can battle against your workload, or struggle with a homework load. You can battle with your spouse, or struggle with an authority figure. You can battle an addiction, or struggle to maintain an exercise routine. You can battle against doubt, or struggle with your emotions. You can battle with your neighbors, or struggle to stay afloat. The symbolism shows in the actions.

Your dream storyteller can pull out themes related to the army or military whenever order or discipline is given to groups of people such as co-workers, classmates, neighbors, friends, and family members. Or you give yourself discipline or bring order to your life, leading your inner world like an army.

An army in a dream can refer to correction and punishment. For example, a teenager disciplined for staying out too late dreams about being a soldier punished for breaking curfew.

The ego is supposed to lead the psyche, and you can lead your life and people within it, or not. Or you can be led in any area of life: school, work, church, social, relationships. Leadership and authority of all sorts are a daily part of most people's lives, readily comparable to an army. The idea of authority includes internal authority, not just external, and how you lead your life. See: *Ego*.

Planning a war or battle can symbolize other ways you strategize, such as dating strategies, parenting strategies, strategies for advancement, problem-solving, or getting what you want. When you strategize you can be like a general who devises a plan and marshals resources. See: *General*.

Being in an army can symbolize being part of someone's plan or under some sort of authority.

Dreams begin with an idea or association like the ones listed above and branch out to make connections with other ideas and associations. An idea only has to fit comparably in some way for a dream to make the stretch and use it to tell a story.

Another major association with an army is that it's a group organized around a mission, purpose, or cause. Life is full of groupings of people, and armies can symbolize them: work groups, school groups, church groups, social groups, professional associations, neighborhood watch. Any group organized as a hierarchy, formally or informally, is readily comparable to an army. See: *Family, Group*.

For example, a young woman dreams about being in an army and resenting being told to clean the barracks. It symbolizes her resentment about her chores around the house.

Many words used in sports are also used in association with armies, such as "reserves," "advance," "target," "front lines," and "battle." It's ready-made for analogies and comparisons. See: *Games, Sports*.

To dream about being part of an army can symbolize strength in numbers, or the feeling of belonging. For example, your family or social circle is like a small army, and exhibits army-related qualities such as a defensive mentality and esprit de corps. It can represent the desire to be challenged, to "be all you can be," to have more discipline and structure. Or it can suggest that you like rules.

People pondering a choice of actually joining a military or police force can dream about an army as a way of thinking through the decision.

To dream about facing an army can symbolize overwhelming odds or overwhelming force arrayed against you. Facing an army alone or with a much smaller group can symbolize being outnumbered, or something that seems insurmountable. For an example, see: *Fight*.

Marching in an army can indicate harmony or "being in step" with a group of people or parts of your psyche.

Deploying with an army suggests big changes are coming. It can mean you're going to be apart from loved ones for an extended period, or you're taking a risk that can put you in danger, physical or otherwise.

To see an army marching past can symbolize observing big events.

Dreaming about being in the military, or in military-like conditions, can have symbolism based on efficiency and teamwork, on punctuality and sacrifice, and on struggling through adversity.

It can reflect a tendency to approach situations as if you are fighting battles, or to follow a strict regimen.

Soldiers are associated with taking orders. In dreams this idea can be stretched to include doing something involuntarily. For example, when you're "volunteered" to help, or you carry a big load of unwanted work, duties, or responsibilities.

It can mean you have no choice, like a soldier who takes orders.

Soldiers are associated with war zones, and a war zone is used to describe environments or situations that are hostile, harsh, or grueling.

Dreams about soldiers can come in response to situations that require massive effort, extensive training, and discipline. For example, a workaholic might dream about herself as a soldier who is always deployed and never home.

A woman dreams about soldiers pointing guns at her and forcing her to fly a plane, symbolizing the approach she's taking to transforming herself from couch potato to go-getter. She knows the situation is do-or-die, so she forces herself into action. The soldier is apt symbolism because part of her new routine is regular exercise, and soldiers stay fit through regular exercise.

And now, after all that, you have personal associations to consider, especially if you or someone close to you has been in the military or police. They're too numerous to even attempt to list, but a few of the common associations that are likely to be known only from an insider view are:

Armies are bureaucracies and can symbolize inflexibility. Armies are full of hypocrisies, claiming to care about their soldiers but failing to put their money where their mouth is. That association applies to corporations that claim to care about their employees, but it's all talk. And armies can be the tools of the rich to oppress peoples and invade countries for their natural resources.

When dreams branch out to subjects related to combat and war, many more possibilities come into play. See: *Fight, War*

Subjects such as ethics and honor potentially come into play. See: *Warrior.*

See also: *Ammunition, Armor, Ego, Fight, Games, General, Group, Gun, Hero, Invasion, Knife, Nazi, Opponent, Rocket, Sports, War, Warrior*

Arouse—See: *Sex*

Arrest—Begin the hunt for possible meanings and uses of arrest in a dream by thinking of "arrest" as meaning restrain or control, such as when you restrain or control a part of yourself.

It can mean you know you're doing something wrong, or have been accused, rightly or wrongly.

It can mean you're taking a risk that could lead to trouble, or you feel guilty or ashamed. People who commit crimes get arrested. It's a consequence.

Being arrested can be used to symbolize the definition of the word meaning "stop progress." A disease is arrested when the spread of it is stopped. Personal progress or progress toward a goal can be arrested.

See also: *Cage, Chase, Crime, Detective, Escape, Fugitive, Guilt, Jail, Police Officer, Tackle*

Arrow—To be shot by an arrow in a dream can symbolize being targeted by someone's ambitions (especially romantic ones), sarcasm, criticism, or ire.

The symbolism can be used to depict comments directed at you that sting or penetrate. It shows in the action of an arrow striking and causing pain and injury.

"Straight arrow" means upright and righteous. Straight arrow is also a way of saying "very direct." The symbolism will show in the action of an arrow flying straight.

Shooting an arrow can mean aiming for a goal or target, hitting a target or missing. Who or what are you aiming for, and why?

A broken arrow can symbolize a goal or ambition that isn't reached, succumbing to temptation, or the fall of a righteous person.

An arrow can be a phallic symbol because of its shape and ability to penetrate. See: *Penis.*

See also: *Armor, Bullet, Penis, Phallic Symbol*

Artist—To see yourself as an artist in a dream, or to be in the presence of an artist, can relate to your creativity or artistic side. Even if you are not artistically inclined, the idea of art applies to anything creative. Associations with art branch out in many directions to include subjects such as the art scene and anything done with skill, precision or flair.

For example, a great pitcher in baseball "paints the strike zone." An accountant or analyst can be an artist at working with numbers. Lawyers are called artists when they create novel legal arguments. People can be artful with words, strategy, parenting, gardening, seduction. Don't think you're not an artist just because you don't paint or draw or compose or sculpt. If you dream about an artist, one could be within you wanting to come out, or expressing itself already in your work and other endeavors. For an example dream, see: *Daughter*.

Dreaming about an artist can connect with greater creative expression. Sometimes all you need is a nudge in the right direction, which a powerful dream can provide.

Art is about expression. Artists express what is inside them. An artist in a dream can symbolize something in yourself that wants to be expressed, something uniquely you. It can relate to the imprint you leave on the world. Or it can be a way of saying that you are good at expressing yourself. Think beyond the formal sense of art, and think in the simplest terms of what an artist is.

Of course, dreams have other associations of artists with which to create symbolism, such as the perception of artists as being people with free lifestyles. They don't have to report to an office or wear heels or a tie. Their lives and often their personalities are unconventional, and dreams can use that association to describe something about yourself, about someone you know, or about a situation or circumstance in your life.

The artist is an archetype in the psyche connected with love of life and everything about it, and with healing. Search online for *Artist archetype*.

See also: *Archetypes, Colors, Daughter, Emaciated, Embark, Fetus, Fisting*

Ascend—To ascend in a dream suggests rising in some way. The symbolism is seen in the movement. For example, a promotion at work or new job responsibility means that you ascend to a higher level of authority, responsibility, or prestige, or you are recognized publicly. It's a physical representation of a personal situation. When your opinion of some-

one rises, you can dream about it as that person ascending stairs or lifting off in a helicopter.

The action of going up can mean "rise above." It can symbolize physical, mental, or spiritual progress, elevated mood, thought, or feeling, or rising ability, skill, or knowledge.

Ascending movement can symbolize elevated mood or emotions.

It can symbolize the ascent of spirit and refer to the heavens and all related subjects, such as getting closer to God or thinking about the afterlife. See: *Angel, Heaven, Spirit*.

The entry for *Elevator* goes into more detail about upward movement.

Look up *Descend*, and use the list of entries below to explore the subject further.

See also: *Afterlife, Angel, Balloon, Birds, Climb, Descend, Elevator, Float, Fly, Heaven, Spirit*

Asleep—See: *Sleep*

Asphyxiate—See: *Strangle*

Assault—See: *Attack*

Asylum—See: *Insane*

Athlete—Dreaming that you're an athlete can relate to your athletic or competitive nature and knowing how to get the most out of yourself in athletics or any area of life. It can symbolize exerting yourself.

Athletes put time and effort into improving their performance, and in dreams that idea can carry over to any area of life—especially to areas requiring physicality, strength, skill, ability, and energy. At work you shoulder the load. At school you hit the books and see improvements in your academic performance. In your sex life you put in real effort to be a better lover. You are a sexual athlete.

On the other hand, dreaming about being an athlete can express exhaustion, pushing yourself too hard, or excessive demands.

An athlete can tie in with a person's self-image or persona, regardless of whether he or she plays in a sport or how long ago it was. This association is especially true of people who were once athletes and their identities are closely tied with sports.

When you dream about an athlete and the emphasis is on a particular part of the body, look up the entry for *Body* and use the "see also" list.

Sometimes the meaning is found in other details, and an athlete is part of the story in reference to symbolism involving prowess and skill.

See also: *Body, Fitness Center, Games, Locker, Sports, Strangle*

Attack—A dream has many options to choose from when telling a story about your being attacked in some way, or something being attacked. The type of attack and related details help to define the symbolism and lead to the meaning. Oftentimes, what's shown as a physical attack in a dream connects with other associations with the word, such as a personal attack, anxiety attack, emotional attack, plan of attack, or attacking a pile of work. The strength and nature of the attack are clues to deconstruct the story and connect the symbolism with you and your life.

Dreams tell you what you don't already know consciously, so the source of an attack might not be obvious, such as when you're in denial that something is affecting you deeply. For example, see: *Walmart.*

Think about what happened in your life the day before the dream. Were you attacked in any sense, or did it feel that way? Dreams exaggerate, so something that seems small or minor at the time can blow up into something big in your dreams. For example, a romantic partner or friend makes a comment that rubs you the wrong way, or a coworker questions your judgment.

To be attacked can mean your life is in rough water. You're struggling. See: *Storm.*

It can mean you're being attacked from within. See: *Enemy, Opponent, Shadow.*

An attack implies the need to defend yourself. You are in a position open to attack, or feel vulnerable.

Attacking in a dream can symbolize resisting something, and your attack is a way of saying you're keeping it at bay.

Figures of speech such as "on the attack" can mean focused and aggressive. You can attack your work or a problem, for instance.

Another possibility is that an attack is an expression of anger or frustration. See: *Anger.*

An attack can indicate that something within you is trying to get your attention. It might be a neglected, ignored, or repressed part of yourself that won't accept that treatment any longer. Animal attacks in dreams, in particular, can be driven by something from within you trying to get your attention. See: *Animals.*

Animal attacks in a dream can be a sign that something is out of kilter with your instincts. For example, a mother dreams that a bear comes out of the woods and mauls her child. It symbolizes that her motherly instincts to protect her child are actually harming him. "Momma bear" is smothering her teenaged son.

Assaulting someone in a dream suggests resisting something or disagreeing strongly, or being in a situation in which you feel forced to do something against your will.

See also: *Anger, Animals, Beat, Bite, Devil, Enemy, Fight, Nightmare, Opponent, Rape, Shadow, Storm*

Attic—An attic in dreams is associated with thoughts or thinking processes. It can symbolize your mental, intellectual, or spiritual life. The symbolism derives from a physical orientation representing areas of the body. The attic is the head or mind. For example, see: *Dark.*

Attics are where things are stored or hidden, so an attic can symbolize a place in your mind where you store bad memories or hide your bad thoughts.

Hiding in an attic can symbolize hiding from the world, or keeping something about yourself hidden. You wish to be "out of sight, out of mind," or just alone.

A prisoner in an attic can symbolize that you won't accept certain things you find in your mind or thoughts. You aren't living up to your intellectual potential. Or you're captivated by certain thoughts or thought processes.

A cluttered attic can symbolize disorganized thinking or having too much on your mind.

An angry person in your attic can symbolize ignoring personal needs and disregarding the thoughts associated with them. A part of yourself is unhappy about the situation.

The emotional state or demeanor of people in your attic can reflect what's going on in your mind.

See also: *Body, Building, Dark, Fear, Head, Home, Stairs*

Attorney—See: *Lawyer*

Attractive—See: *Beauty*

Audience—See: *Stage*

Audition—See: *Stage*

Aunt—See: *Family*

Author—To dream that you are an author can relate to your storytelling abilities.

It can mean that you have something important to say and are trying to find a way of expressing it.

You have a writing project you are working on.

Or you have an ambition to be an author or write a book, or envy something about the idea of working from home or living the author lifestyle.

What do you associate with authors? That's the basis for the symbolism.

Automobile—See: *Car*

Autopsy—See: *Dissect*

Avalanche—An avalanche in a dream can connect symbolically with the feeling of being overwhelmed, such as when you're facing an avalanche of work or responsibility.

It can connect with the idea of something held back, and once let loose there's no way to stop it. Pent-up emotions are like that, especially anger. Or when the truth must be told and it's been a long time coming.

An avalanche is comparable to anything impossible to stop once set in motion, or a delicate situation. One wrong move has the potential for disaster.

See also: *Climb, Descend, Mountain*

Avoid—See: *Escape*

Award—See: *Ovation*

Baboon—A baboon can symbolize inappropriate, wild, or unpredictable behavior.

See also: *Animals, Gorilla*

Baby—When decoding the symbolism of a baby in a dream, begin with the simple fact that a baby is new life. Ask yourself what's new with you: a relationship, an idea, a feeling, a development in your character or personality?

A dream about finding a baby can symbolize finding something new within yourself, such as a burst of creativity or new wind in your sails.

A happy baby is the image of pure joy, and that too is a possibility for the symbolism. Do you feel happy just to be alive? Do you see the world with awe and wonder?

It's common to dream about happy babies when in a rut, when life is tedious or boring, as a way of rediscovering the simplicity of laughter and giggles.

For example, a man dreams about saving a baby drowning in a pool. It symbolizes attempting to keep the part of himself alive—meaning conscious—that enjoys life but is drowning in adult responsibilities. He's drowning in the personal sense, and in the dream his desperate attempt to save the baby shows how he feels about the possibility of losing his happiness.

People are known to dream about babies—especially crying ones—in relation to caring for basic needs: nutrition, comfort, protection, warmth, and so on. A crying or neglected baby sums up the idea and the feelings involved. See: *Cry*.

Ask yourself why the dream storyteller would choose a baby as symbolism over a child. One way to look at it is, a child is needy, but a baby is helpless. In a pinch, a child can figure out how to survive, but a baby can't.

A baby is vulnerable, and in dreams a baby left alone or neglected can symbolize being in a vulnerable state. It implies the need to create a safe and stable space to live in, or a basic routine of care and attention. Most dream-characters connect with your inner life. A vulnerable baby might symbolize a need to protect yourself emotionally and psychologically. If you don't take care of yourself, who will?

If you don't do it, something else might just step in and take over your life, namely, an archetype such as shadow or anima. A dream can express this idea as a bad person holding a baby captive. Kidnapping a baby can have similar meaning of helplessness against something much more powerful. At its simplest, it means something important is being taken, and what's more important than your freedom and independence?

A baby can symbolize a sense of being entitled to have someone else take care of your needs. Fussy babies, pacifiers, and highchairs are good symbols for childish fussiness or entitlement. For example, you dream about your fussy co-worker with a pacifier in his or her mouth. The symbolism is rather obvious. But what if the co-worker has a fussy baby with her at work? It's not so obvious that the dream is still an observation about the person. The baby sticks out in that setting so it must be symbolism unless you really do have a co-worker who brings his or her baby to work.

For women who can bear children, the first thought after dreaming about having a baby is often, *Oh, shit, does this mean I'm pregnant?* It's possible, yes, but less likely than pregnancy being symbolism.

For example, a young woman dreams that she gives birth and immediately realizes she doesn't have time to care for her baby. Her work schedule won't allow it, which is true—her job at a fast-food place doesn't include maternity leave. After thinking over the situation, she puts the baby in a carrier bag and leaves it behind her workplace, symbolizing putting off having a child until she has a job that allows it. Keeping her job is her number one priority. Her desire to have a baby is behind it in the figurative sense. Putting the baby in a carrier bag is way of saying she's putting off fulfilling her desire till the future.

If the thought of having a baby has been on your mind, it's likely to be expressed in your dreams. Dreaming about a baby can be a way of saying you can start preparing. You can find the right work, mate, or living situation. You can prepare your body, save money, and get maternity coverage. See: *Pregnant.*

Your reaction during the dream shows how you really feel about the idea of having a baby. People who believe they don't want children, swearing it will never happen, are known to change their minds after holding their "dream" baby in their arms. It's an incredibly realistic experience that demands an honest response. They feel, smell, and hear their baby and even know its name. Then

again, dreams can affirm a person's decision to not have children.

Dreams can address decisions parents make about having more children. For example, a mother dreams about three dead fetuses connected by a string dropping out of her uterus while riding on the back of her husband's motorcycle. The fetuses symbolize children she can't have, now that her tubes are tied. Her hope was to have more children, but her husband doesn't want to and he influenced her to have the procedure done. The dream shows her on the back of his motorcycle because he controlled the decision to make sure she'd never again get pregnant.

Parents dream about the care of their children and the responsibilities of parenthood. It's particularly common for parents of young children to have anxiety dreams, often involving scenes of their children harmed or in danger. It's usually just an exaggerated reflection of a parent's diligence and concerns.

It's possible to dream about the children you are going to have. Thousands of reports are on record of mothers and fathers seeing their future in children in dreams, sometimes years beforehand. In one case, a woman dreamed about the children she could have had. She had three miscarriages, but in her dreams the children are alive and well and a joyous part of her life. Perhaps they really are alive somewhere out there in the big universe. It's not such a strange idea when you consider that every possibility exists in the quantum world.

Gruesome dreams involving babies hurt or killed can connect with fears, anxieties, emotional turmoil, and treacherous life conditions. Don't take it literally when you have such a dream, but do take it as a sign that something really needs to change. In most cases, it's a sign that the highly sensitive and vulnerable parts of yourself are going through the meat grinder.

Babies are immature, and the idea of immaturity extends beyond behavior to mean underdeveloped. In the image of the baby in your dream, you see something that will grow and develop if you put the time into it.

For a discussion of breastfeeding in a dream, see: *Breast*.

See also: *Adopt, Boy, Breast, Caesarean Section, Child, Childbirth, Cry, Fetus, Girl, Kitten, Little, Love, Miscarriage, Orphan, Pregnant, Puppy*

Back—The back area of the body is often associated with carrying burdens and things that weigh you down, such as regrets. "Get off my back" is a way of saying "get off my case."

The back is associated with getting work done. A strong back is meant figuratively to mean ability to carry a heavy load. For example, a man dreams he is at the gym doing back exercises such as pullups. He shows off his back muscles to people in the gym. The dream occurs after a day spent straightening up the house and working in the yard. He feels proud of the amount of work he got done.

Injury to the back in a dream can indicate inability to carry a load, or lack of confidence. Injury can indicate a physical issue with the back that needs to be addressed.

For example, a teenaged male dreams about entering a horse stable and seeing a powerful black stallion and a beautiful golden mare. A man who works in the stable tells the dreamer that the mare has back problems. The teenager tells the mare, "It's all right, I have back problems, too." He puts out a hand toward the stallion, and it reacts aggressively.

The dream is about the teen's struggle to handle his responsibilities and carry his burdens. The mare with a bad back symbolizes the feeling that he can't do it; he doesn't think he has the strength. However, the stallion represents another side of the story. He does have the strength but doesn't see himself that way. The dream is helping him to subconsciously tap into his inner strength by first making him aware he really does have it. He is delicate like the mare, and has the strength of the stallion—at least, the potential for it. See: *Weak*.

Something behind your back can mean it's in the past. For example, you dream about your ex following you from behind, symbolizing that the relationship is in the past.

Anything dragged or carried behind your back can symbolize personal baggage. See: *Baggage*.

Something positioned behind your back can be a way of expressing the phrase "go behind your back." Be careful of betrayal, gossip, and sneakiness. You might need to "watch your back."

The back is a blind spot, so something positioned behind your back is hidden from your awareness. For example, a man dreams he's in his apartment and hears a knock at his front door. He asks who is there, and two voices reply in unison, "Enemies." He opens the door, and two men enter his apartment. One of them immediately takes a position behind him, and the other stands in front of him. He hits the man in front of him, who tells him that anger will not help him.

The dream shows the dreamer two aspects of himself he needs to deal with. The man in front of him symbolizes anger. It's an aspect of himself he knows about. The man behind him is an aspect of himself that's in a personal blind spot. He is not consciously aware of it.

Turning the back toward someone or something can indicate withdrawal of care or attention, or turning away from needs. It can symbolize ostracism, rejection, or disapproval.

To be stabbed in the back is a classic sign of betrayal. Or it can symbolize stabbing pain in the back experienced while asleep.

The word "back" is loaded with possibilities for wordplays, such as "back to work," "back of the line," and "got your back." Dreams can make obscure references through comparisons, so if you dream about the back or positioning behind something, consider the possibility of wordplay.

See also: *Blind, Body, Weak*

Back Door—A back door in a dream can symbolize an area of your life you want to remain hidden or out of public view. A back door is generally unseen from the front of the house. Dreaming about seeing someone you know entering the back door of his or her house can symbolize finding out something about the person that's private, or seeing a hidden side of the person.

The back door can symbolize a secret, particularly a sexual secret or secret pleasure. Entering the back door is a euphemism for anal sex. It can refer to the anus or taking an alternative route to sexual satisfaction, such as through an illicit affair. See: *Anal Sex, Anus, Affair.*

Along this line, a back door can symbolize doing something you want to keep secret, particularly behavior. This use of the symbolism is often accompanied by sneakiness and related feelings such as wariness and shame.

A back door can symbolize vulnerability, especially if the door is unlocked or burglars enter through it. The symbolism is derived from the idea of something in the back or behind you being in your blind spot or away from your usual focus. It can symbolize the feeling that you've overlooked something.

It's the door to the past.

"Back door" is used figuratively to mean finding a way around a problem, an alternative solution or route otherwise known as a "workaround." Dreams create symbolism in the same way as figures of speech by making comparisons. So for example, a dream about searching for a back door can symbolize looking for an alternative solution.

It can symbolize seeking an alternative route to get something you want. For example, dating a friend of someone you actually want to date is a backhanded way of getting what you want. Working in photography can be a back door into the modeling industry.

Along this line, you can think of a back door as the unconventional or alternate choice. Going through a door can symbolize making a choice, so combine that idea with what a back door implies.

Going out a back door can symbolize backward movement in your life. See: *Backward.*

A locked back door can symbolize something about you that you can't or won't explore. Or it can mean you think you can get around something or be secretive and find out otherwise.

See also: *Anal Sex, Anus, Affair, Back, Backward, Backyard, Door, Home*

Back Seat—See: *Car*

Backyard—A backyard in a dream can symbolize the background of your life. The background can be something overlooked, ignored, secret, private, hidden or out of view, especially from the public. A front yard, on the other hand, is typically visible from the street and readily viewable by the public, so in dreams, a front yard tends to be used to symbolize something about you that's a public part of your life.

For example, a man dreams about discovering a raised garden area in his backyard and sprucing it up, thinking it would be a great place to teach yoga. He desires to make teaching yoga more prominent in his life, and "raised area" in this dream means "raised in importance." Yoga is a private part of his life, in the background. He works in IT by day and teaches yoga by night, and his IT co-workers know nothing about his "secret passion." These two areas of his life are separate, but that's about to change.

Robbers coming through your backyard can symbolize ways you harm yourself or miss out on something without being fully conscious of it. Think of the symbolism as depicting the phrases "taken from right beneath your nose," and "undermining yourself." Robbers stealing from you is a physical representation of a personal situation, and the fact that they come through the back door could mean you have a blind spot. For example, you don't see that your tendency to criticize harms your relationships, but you do sense that people are reluctant to get close to you.

The same sort of dream imagery can mean that someone is sneaking behind your back, such as when a child disobeys you, a spouse has an affair, or a neighbor spreads rumors.

A backyard can symbolize the past because in dreams, anything located behind you or your home in a dream can symbolize the past.

See also: *Back Door, Burglary, Garden, Home, Thief*

Backward—Dreams can create symbolism by using movement and direction that are rich with possibilities for analogies and metaphors, such as the symbolism in the expression "a step backward," meaning "setback," or "wrong direction." Backward thinking can mean regressive, as opposed to forward thinking. Working backward can mean retracing steps, often to figure out the roots of an issue or problem.

Think of backward as a physical representation of a personal situation. What is figuratively moving backward about you or your life, or what's behind you in the personal sense?

Backward can refer to going back to a place you were before, such as moving back in with your parents, going back to school, getting back together with an ex, or revisiting thoughts and feelings.

Movement backward can suggest need to protect your back. Looking backward can mean looking back in time to spot the connection with something relevant today, especially patterns and tendencies.

Use the entries below to continue exploring these ideas.

See also: *Ascend, Back, Backyard, Car, Descend, Left, Right*

Bag—A bag can symbolize what you figuratively carry with you: memories, responsibilities, burdens, guilt, ideas about yourself, personality and character traits. Think along the lines of things from the past you bring with you while going forward in life.

Packing bags can symbolize preparing for something, getting ready. See: *Baggage*.

A torn bag can indicate worries or problems tearing at you. It can symbolize fear of no longer being able to carry a load, or it can warn about losing important aspects of your past.

A torn money bag or purse can symbolize financial loss. An empty one can symbolize struggle, loss, an empty bank account or bankruptcy.

An empty bag can symbolize a feeling of emptiness. It can symbolize expecting something but not getting it, such as a promotion or phone call, or empty promise. You put in the faith or effort, but don't get the reward.

The stomach is a sort of bag, so an empty bag can symbolize hunger. Lungs, too, are comparable to bags. For example, a dream about a bag full of liquid can symbolize heavy congestion.

A full bag can symbolize a full stomach, acquisition of material possessions, or any sort of abundance.

If something is "in the bag," it means it's as good as done, such as when a sports team is ahead by so many points, the game is "in the bag," and a dream shows it as putting a trophy into a bag. If you're left holding the bag, it can symbolize an unwelcome responsibility.

A bag can symbolize a scrotum, and a tear or other sort of damage to it can symbolize injury to that area of the body or what it represents. See: *Testicles*.

See also: *Baggage, Bankrupt, Eat, Food, Purse, Money, Testicles, Wallet*

Baggage—Baggage in a dream can relate to personal baggage, something from your past that weighs you down or holds you back: guilt, regret, bad decisions, mistakes. The symbolism is especially prominent if you lug or drag the baggage. It will feel heavy. See: *Drag*.

Packing a bag or suitcase can symbolize getting ready for a change, or preparing for something coming up in your life. It can connect directly with ideas associated with baggage, such as taking a trip or moving to a new home. Or the idea can extend to life changes, such as preparing to become a parent or take on a new career. You might say you're packing your bags.

Trying to fit too many items into baggage can symbolize too much to do. You are trying to take on more than you can handle or fit too much into your life. Or you have too many or much of something: expectations, relationships, emotions to process at once, things to think about. The same ideas can be expressed through imagery of endlessly packing bags, especially luggage. In simplest terms, it means getting ready but not going anywhere.

See also: *Bag, Drag*

Bail—To dream that you pay bail can symbolize the price of freedom or separation. Freedom can mean physical freedom, like moving out of your parents' house and paying bail in the form of your housing expenses. Or it can mean personal or psychological freedom, such as when thinking outside the box leads to social isolation, or leaving a marriage means paying alimony.

Bail can be the price for breaking obligations, defying authority, or making mistakes. You'll do anything to make up for it.

Or it can mean that you have crossed some sort of line and can be called to account.

Paying bail for someone else can symbolize the non-tangible price of that relationship. For example, you love your boyfriend but your family hates him and you pay a personal price with them.

It can symbolize paying for others' mistakes or taking responsibility for them, or bailing them out figuratively. You come to the rescue. The ideas are reversed when your bail is paid by someone else.

Dreams draw parallels, make comparisons, and play with words to create symbolism, so there's more to consider. Such as when bail in a dream means to leave a sinking situation, to feel abandoned ("my friends bailed on me"), or that the time has come to end something.

Any of these ideas can be summed up in the dream image of a bailiff.

See also: *Alimony, Court, Crime, Fugitive, Jail, Judge, Shop*

Bake—See: *Oven*

Bald—Baldness is associated with getting older, especially fear of it and related ideas such as fear of losing health or prestige, or losing your hair.

Hair can symbolize thoughts or thinking processes, since hair grows from the head and thoughts are centered there, so being bald can symbolize lack of thoughts or ideas, loss of intellectual prowess, or general decline in thinking abilities.

Baldness can indicate a clean mind, especially if the head is shiny and spotless—clean in the sense of being without conflict or distraction. Or clean as in the opposite of a dirty mind.

Since hair covers the head, being bald can mean something is exposed, as in the phrase "bald, honest truth." It can signify a fresh start, even a new devotion, symbolism created by associations with military recruits and religious disciples cutting off their hair as a way of making a fresh start or giving up something important for a cause.

It's also associated with conformity because hair is a strong visual identifier, which is a big reason why hair is cut very short in the military. That idea carries over to certain corporate cultures because baldness is associated with conformity, seriousness, cleverness, sacrifice, power, and authority.

Baldness can symbolize the wear and tear of time. On the other hand, it can symbolize the wisdom that comes from experience.

Baldness in a dream can relate to illness or fear of it, symbolism created by association between losing hair and getting seriously ill.

Losing hair is associated with losing the vigor or virility of youth. It carries the general idea of losing something that is important to you, particularly if the hair falls out on its own. It might be a physical representation of a personal situation, such as loss of reputation, identity, or self-image.

Losing hair can be a suggestion from the unconscious mind to let go of something (or somebody) voluntarily. You can do it.

Pulling out your hair can mean you are being too hard on yourself. Stress or frustration is getting to you. You aren't thinking clearly.

A bald vagina that's been waxed or shaved can symbolize what a woman does to be attractive. It can symbolize early puberty or childhood. It can symbolize frank talk about sex or reproduction, or exposure of something private.

See also: *Hair, Head, Penis, Vagina*

Ball—Anything circular can symbolize wholeness, so a ball can symbolize something related to personal wholeness—attaining it, or working toward it. See: *Circle*.

People working on their personal development or improving themselves are known to dream about games involving balls. Actions and details involving a ball can symbolize your effort and progress toward becoming complete or whole as a person, but you have many other possibilities to consider. See: *Baseball, Basketball, Tennis.*

A ball can symbolize striving for perfection, especially when combined with actions related to hitting a target or winning a game.

A ball in motion can symbolize the energy or movement of the psyche. It can symbolize the strength and energy to make things happen, to strive forward and create the future you want.

A ball in a dream can be an expression of the phrase "have a ball." It's connected with fun and play.

A light ball such as a Wiffle ball can indicate lightness of being and relief of heaviness.

Throwing or shooting a ball is associated with a personal target you want to hit. See: *Baseball.*

A ball rolling can mean "get the ball rolling."

Dreams can use the image of a ball as a word-play for "testicle." See: *Testicles.*

See also: *Baseball, Basketball, Circle, Games, Sports, Tennis*

Ballet—Ballet can symbolize balance and harmony. In the dancers and the dance, you see elements of yourself and your life working together gracefully. Everyone is on the same page, in consensus.

This meaning of the symbolism applies generally to dancing as self-expression and movement of your feelings, emotions, and thoughts. Ballet adds the idea of grace and harmony to the picture.

Dancing can symbolize your personal style and the way you approach life with rhythm and panache.

Ballet can symbolize grace, poise, and charm and is associated with self-expression, especially expression of feelings and uniqueness.

See also: *Circle, Spiral*

Balloon—In a relationship context, a balloon can symbolize rising or sinking hopes for the relationship. Balloons stay aloft through artificial inflation (helium or hot air), and a relationship can stay aloft with false hope. Giving balloons to a love interest, or vice versa, can mean you know deep inside that the relationship will eventually lose its buoyancy.

In a personal context, a balloon can symbolize the feeling of being filled with something: thoughts, hope, ambition, emotion, pride, spirit. It can symbolize a head full of ideas See: *Air.*

A balloon can symbolize inflated ego, or arrogance.

It can symbolize floating an idea, a "trial balloon."

Rising like a balloon can symbolize a wish to escape a difficulty or situation, or to "rise above," or to mentally disconnect.

A balloon floating aimlessly captures the feeling of being reeeeally high.

Thoughts, like air, are intangible, and a balloon is a container for air, so it can be thought of as a container for thoughts, especially similar thoughts, and all thoughts related to one thing.

Floating like a balloon in the air can symbolize the general direction of your thoughts, or drifting thoughts, "head in the clouds." It can symbolize calm thoughts and pleasantness. See: *Float.*

It can symbolize being unrealistic about thoughts and plans.

Being high up and carried by a balloon can symbolize a broad view of where you're going in life and what the future could hold. It can symbolize being in an elevated position. See: *Above.*

A balloon that pops, or falling out of a hot-air balloon, can symbolize hope lost or ambition failed. It can mean "burst your bubble." Reality intervenes. Annoyances or grievances are about to erupt.

A red balloon can symbolize standing out in a crowd.

See also: *Above, Air, Ascend, Float, Fly, Head*

Bandit—A bandit is a classic symbol of unrestrained sexuality. Dreams about bandits are especially prevalent in young males who are getting to know their sexuality. It's a sign that they're unnerved by the new strength and energy in themselves and don't know how to control it, or that sexual urges have caused confusion or deviation.

For example, a young man dreams that he's a bandit who sneaks into his girlfriend's bedroom to steal her panties. It symbolizes his inner conflict about taking her virginity and portraying himself as someone he's not in order to get into her pants.

A bandit can symbolize a state of anxiety or wariness. It can connect with fear of getting caught doing something wrong. It can symbolize someone or something that takes something valuable from you in the personal sense, such as your spouse or your nest egg.

The symbolism of a bandit adds a swashbuckling and seductive dimension to that of a burglar or thief. Robin Hood, for example, is portrayed as a merry bandit.

See also: *Accomplice, Back Door, Burglary, Raccoon, Thief*

Bank—A bank is associated with finances and money and, as symbolism, can cover any subject related to money, investment of time and energy, "rainy-day fund," and preparation for the future.

Your inner bank is where you have your internal resources such as energy and motivation.

It's your sense of security knowing you've planned well, or insecurity, depending on the state of the bank in the dream.

Withdrawing money from a bank can symbolize tapping into the resources you have accumulated—material or personal. A blocked account can symbolize money-supply issues, or having a hard time using resources for yourself and instead always thinking of others first, or being overly conservative and underutilizing resources.

To dream about a bank being robbed can symbolize needless use or loss of money or resources, or financial instability. The bank is where resources are stored, so a robbed bank implies personal loss.

It can symbolize trying against the odds to preserve importance, or to delay an inevitable decline. Like Hugh Hefner in his eighties gobbling Viagra and dating 20-year-old models, it's a way of

saying you're clinging to something after the expiration date has passed.

Banks are difficult to break into, and that association extends to situations such as getting into a social circle, or gaining access to something closed to you. It can be a clever way of saying, "break the bank," meaning bust finances.

Dreaming about being unable to locate a bank can indicate financial problems such as difficulty saving money, or out-of-control spending habits. Locating the bank can mean internally locating or tapping inner resources, especially related to budgeting, planning, or restraint.

A fat bank account or big bank building can symbolize success, especially material success, or confidence in a secure position. Having a lot of money in the bank is a sign of success and prestige, a source of confidence, and it can give a sense of importance.

See also: *Bankrupt, Burglary, Money, Purse, Thief, Wallet*

Bankrupt—To dream you are bankrupt can symbolize feeling tapped out, drained. The inner bank is empty. See: *Bank*.

It can symbolize financial difficulty. In which case, bankruptcy can be a fear that manifests in your dreams, or an exaggerated way of expressing hard financial times, no money in the pocket, or none coming in.

"Bankrupt" can be a play on the term "morally bankrupt," and can include the idea of loss of respect or prestige, or fear of disgrace or failure.

Bankruptcy in a dream can be a warning that a current path is headed toward disaster or loss by overextending yourself, or exposure to risk. You might be able to avert the disaster, but you'd better act quickly.

See also: *Bank, Money, Purse, Wallet*

Bar—See: *Bartender*

Barack Obama—When someone famous such as Barack Obama appears in your dream, begin decoding the symbolism by asking yourself what you associate with him, and whether the role he plays in society fits the dream. Depending on the person, Obama can symbolize everything from a great leader to an Antichrist figure. Decode the symbolism the same way as for any famous person.

See also: *Famous, President*

Bark—To dream about hearing barking nearby can indicate a need to be alert to danger—dogs bark to alert to danger. A situation is risky, or about to get risky.

Something is trying to get your attention. Dogs bark to get attention.

Barking can symbolize yelling or grumpiness, as in "barking orders" or being "barked at." It can be a sign of unhappiness, annoyance, or aggression. See: *Anger, Scream, Yell.*

Dogs bark to defend territory, so barking in a dream can symbolize protecting turf. It's a warning to stay away. See: *Border.*

As with all symbolism, it's important to apply personal associations. To some people, a dog barking is a friendly sound, a way of saying, "Hi." It has positive symbolism. But to other people, that image brings to mind annoyance and pestering, such as when a neighbor's dog barks all night. To them, barking has negative connotations. The simplest way of discerning the difference is to pay attention to how you feel about the barking in your dream.

Dogs are closely associated with friendship, so barking can be an alert that a friend is trying to get your attention, or there's something about the friend you should notice. The idea extends to anything trying to get your attention. See: *Dog.*

Barking can alert you to risky situations involving friends, such as when you're involved with the wrong people or events with them are headed toward a bad conclusion. It can symbolize sensing danger or a nose for trouble.

Barking can mean "wake up!" Something needs your immediate attention.

Barking in a dream can be the product of something you hear, a dog barking or something similar.

See also: *Anger, Border, Dog, Ears, Friend, Scream, Skin, Tree, Yell*

Barn—Dream symbolism is based primarily on use and function, so a barn can symbolize something related to its use, storing things such as animals, food, supplies, and tools, while in dreams barns symbolize storing less-tangible things. For example, inheritances and home equity are forms of stored wealth. Hope is a form of stored energy.

Pay attention to the condition of the barn. If it's in good shape or full, it can symbolize feeling good about future prospects, or having plenty of personal resources. A run-down or empty barn can show lack of preparation—or future prospects.

Another way of thinking about the symbolism of a barn is that it's where something is out of the way, separate from the main part of your life or personality. For example, a secret passion or interest, or a second career or family. This use of the symbolism will often show as the barn near your home, a way of saying "closely related." See: *Garage.*

Back in the days when family farms were common, barns were places where young people would go to be out of sight of parents and authority figures. They could goof off, smoke cigarettes, make out. Those associations are less common these days but can still be used to create symbolism for doing something you want to keep hidden.

A barn can symbolize a situation that lacks structure or authority, or is out of control, because when the farmer isn't around, the animals run the barn.

It can symbolize a dirty mouth or dirty mind. See: *Toilet.*

If it's a spooky place in a dream, it can be a way of saying, "Don't go there." You avoid something. See: *Hide.*

What are your impressions and personal experiences with barns? Those associations can be the basis of your dream symbolism.

See also: *Animals, Building, Closet, Fire, Garage, Hide, Home, Toilet*

Barren—See: *Desert*

Barrier—See: *Border, Wall*

Bartender—A bartender mixes and serves drinks, and as a dream-character it can symbolize regulating the intake of alcohol or anything else intoxicating, literally or figuratively.

For example, a young adult man who quit a bad drinking habit dreams that he's in one of his old hangouts, crowded with patrons, and sees the bartender he used to prefer. Suddenly, the crowd stampedes and the dreamer is pushed out of the building. It symbolizes his decision to leave that part of his life behind, and affirms it.

Think beyond alcohol and drugs. The consumption of certain foods such as chocolate can be intoxicating. Love can be intoxicating.

Bartenders deal with unruly patrons, and in this role a bartender can symbolize dealing with unruliness in your life, either in others or in yourself. The symbolism is found in actions that are unruly, and the bartender's reaction can say a lot about how you deal with unruliness or trouble.

Bartenders measure and pour drinks, and those actions can symbolize a "measured approach," meaning precise, calculated, or deliberate.

A bartender can symbolize someone who sympathizes with difficulties.

It can be a visual pun for manning or defending a border or crossing.

See also: *Alcohol, Border, Drunkenness*

Baseball—Baseball in a dream can have specific symbolism tied to details about playing the game, or general symbolism of games and competition. You may have personal experience and associations that dreams can use to build a story around.

When analyzing the game of baseball, think in terms of the "game of life" and your efforts to get ahead, both in your outer life and inner life. Doesn't matter whether you've ever played the game, your dreams can use it as symbolism.

The actions involving the baseball give it tremendous potential for use as symbolism to describe your process of inner development. First,

read the entries for *Ball* and *Circle*. Now, think of the ball as a goal or target, especially for personal development, and the other details of the dream tie together with that idea.

However, you have more to consider before drawing a conclusion. Baseball can be a great metaphor for the process of becoming a complete person, but the game is rife with other metaphors and analogies, such as:

"Take a swing" means give something a try, or take a risk.

Hitting the ball with a bat can mean "making contact." It implies meeting a goal, or hitting a target, or making social contact.

"On base" means incremental progress.

Hitting a home run can mean exceptional performance, and striking out can symbolize failure.

Throwing a ball can symbolize accuracy in hitting a target, meaning a goal or ambition, or the accuracy of thinking processes, comparisons, or assumptions.

Pitching the ball can symbolize attempts to "get one past" another person or group of people, meaning to fool or deceive, to slip by unnoticed, or get past defenses or boundaries. Now put yourself in the shoes of the batter as the ball goes past you, and think about the possibilities it presents for symbolism.

A pitch that defies the laws of physics can symbolize the feeling of unfair play. Something isn't right. See: *Voodoo.*

Fear of being hit by the ball can symbolize fear of being someone's target, especially for bullying, sarcasm, or unwanted attention.

A curveball can symbolize something tricky, difficult, or deceptive.

Stealing a base can symbolize taking advantage of a situation while someone isn't looking, such as cheating on a test or spouse.

Notice that each of those examples is a physical representation of a personal situation.

Baseball is used as a sexual analogy. Getting on first base means hugging and kissing. Second base means copping a feel. Third base means close to having sex, but stopping short. Home run is self-explanatory.

The bat itself can be a phallic symbol, while the ball or the ballpark can symbolize the other side of the equation. See: *Penis*.

However, a bat is also a common self-defense weapon and the symbolism depends on how it's used in a dream—to crack a baseball or crack a bone. Both acts are comparable to situations in life. A bat is a symbol of force and authority. In media portrayals, the person holding the bat tends to be the muscle (force) or the leader (authority). In one image the idea is conveyed.

A bat can symbolize something that batters, such as insults and emotionally charged comments. Also consider inner dynamics such as being hard on yourself (a bat is hard) or beating yourself up.

It can symbolize something beating you down, such as stress, a heavy workload, or an abusive relationship.

See also: *Athlete, Ball, Basketball, Circle, Games, Locker, Penis, Phallic Symbol, Sex, Sports, Tennis*

Basement—A basement in a dream can symbolize your emotions or instincts, which are felt primarily in the gut area of the body. Buildings in dreams, especially houses, tend to symbolize your body or psyche, so think of a basement in general terms of "below" or "beneath." See: *Below*.

It can mean that something is below the threshold of your awareness—subconscious. The subconscious is where information is just outside your awareness. The unconscious is a deeper layer, the root programming level of the mind—the sub-basement. Sometimes it is full of things you don't want to know about yourself, don't want to remember, or don't want to acknowledge. You'd rather let them stay stored away in the dark, out of sight. They're usually the most difficult things you face about yourself and your life. See: *Unconscious Mind*.

The symbolism of a basement can connect with the root word "base." It's used in the sense of "base instinct" and "home base." Living in a basement can

mean you're following instincts or acting from them, or acting from base impulses. See: *Reptile*.

It can symbolize the foundation or base that you build your life on, or around which you construct your psyche. It's the support for the ground beneath your feet. See: *Feet*.

The symbolism of beneath and above potentially come into play, such as when something is "beneath you," or "above the fray." See: *Above*.

A flooded basement can symbolize emotions that need to be cleaned up, especially negatively perceived emotions like anger, hatred, jealousy, envy, and fear.

Something hidden in your basement can symbolize emotions hidden from you, or instincts that aren't conscious.

Something lurking in your basement can symbolize emotions or feelings you need to deal with, or something you don't know about yourself that needs to be conscious and dealt with before it starts causing major disruptions in your life.

Because a basement can be used for storage, it can symbolize something you don't know what to do with or how to handle. It can be something you have pushed out of your mind or ignored. See: *Barn*.

Exploring a basement can symbolize investigating your roots. It can relate to hereditary traits, or the psychological foundation of who you are. This symbolism applies especially in dreams about finding and exploring a sub-basement.

In a dream about visiting his childhood home, the guy finds a sub-basement where his old neighbors live, including the son and daughter who used to bully him. It's a way of saying that feelings from that experience continue to live deep down inside him.

In another dream about visiting his childhood, a different guy goes to the basement because a tornado is coming. His sister is already there, and she screams, "I should have seen it coming!" It symbolizes the divorce of their parents, which happened long ago and caught the siblings by surprise. Years later, feelings related to the experience are coming up from deep within the dreamer—his inner basement. The tornado symbolizes the turbulent feelings he repressed. He knows they're still inside him.

A woman dreams that down in her basement is a homicidal young girl holding a knife, which sums up in one image the state of her relationship with her childhood. She had an unhappy childhood, and she'd rather forget it, as symbolized by the basement setting. But the longer she ignores it, the more hostile this part of her becomes. She's angry and sad and unable to address the source of it.

See also: *Below, Cave, Childhood Home, Construction, Emotions, Empty, Fall, Feet, Floor, Home, Rectangle, Square, Unconscious Mind*

Basketball—As with other games, the symbolism of basketball can be derived from particular details of playing the game, from the symbolism of games and competition in general, or from personal experiences and associations that dreams can use to create symbolism.

First, consider what it means to shoot a basketball. In a general sense it can mean "hit the mark," but dreams use a basketball and hoop intentionally because the symbolism fits the story. Otherwise, dreams have other ways of saying "hit the mark." The basketball and hoop are used because they're round, and round objects can symbolize personal wholeness. See: *Ball, Circle.*

Once you understand the symbolism of round objects, the actions involved with a basketball can make more sense. Basketball involves putting a round ball through a round hoop, so it's a ready-made analogy for the quest for wholeness, and your skill or lack of it at dream basketball can symbolize how well you're doing in the game of life.

The idea extends to any activity requiring spirit, skill, or accuracy.

Accuracy in a dream can be a physical representation of a personal situation, such as when it's used to mean truthfulness. So in that sense, an air ball (bad shot) can mean less than truthful, or inaccurate, or just a generally poor attempt at something. Or, the symbolism can be derived from the embarrassment of being inaccurate or publicly failing at something.

Playing basketball in your dreams can symbolize something related to competition or teamwork. It's a competitive team sport, and you can cover a lot of ground with the related ideas of competition, teams, and work.

The game has many nuances that can be used as symbolism and parallels. It involves setting screens (could symbolize blocking progress), rebounding (taking advantage of mistakes), and free-throws (a free pass or unexpected bonus). Rebounding carries the added possibility of describing recovering from a relationship breakup or a setback. A foul can symbolize a penalty of some sort.

Dribbling can symbolize focus, concentration, consistency—something you keep in motion such as the excitement of a relationship or engagement with a project or task. Dribbling the ball off your foot can symbolize losing focus or momentum.

See also: *Athlete, Ball, Circle, Games, Job, Locker, Sports*

Bat—See: *Baseball*

Bat (Mammal)—The only mammals that truly fly, bats only come out at night and have internal radar, associated with human qualities of being comfortable in the dark, meaning unknown or mysterious, and of the sense of direction. See: *Fly.*

Because bats are used as Halloween decorations, and in movies to represent scary creatures, they can be the subject of nightmares.

But they can also be good omens of "finding direction" or "homing in." In dreams, instincts such as these are often represented as animals known for them.

Bats nested in a cave can represent hibernation or deep inner aspects of yourself, which tend to be fragile, especially when outside their native environment. If the sight causes fear, it can mean you fear knowing everything that you are inside. See: *Cave.*

Vampire bats are associated with "blood suckers," which describes something that stealthily drains energy, such as a demanding relationship, job, or responsibility. See: *Blood, Vampire.*

See also: *Animals, Blood, Cave, Emotions, Fly, Nightmare, Vampire*

Bath—See: *Bathroom*

Bathroom—A bathroom is a place where you clean up, get ready to go out, take a look at yourself, and expel waste. These uses and functions are used in a dream to create symbolism, such as when cleaning up symbolizes cleaning up your image or behavior. It can mean you're thinking about the image you project and how you present yourself, and you want to make a good impression. See: *Clean*.

The symbolism is often found in what you do in a bathroom, such as bathe or shower. See: *Shower*.

Or use a toilet. See: *Toilet*.

Or look in a mirror. See: *Mirror*.

Or brush your teeth. See: *Teeth*.

A bathroom is where privacy is usually expected, where you have a "private moment," so being interrupted in a bathroom can symbolize issues related to privacy. See: *Naked*.

This idea extends to include things you want to hide or keep away from public knowledge, including anything shameful or highly personal. For example, the shameful feelings after being sexually assaulted, or suicidal thoughts.

A bathroom setting in a dream is often connected with the idea of being rid of something unwanted. For example, a young man at a small college dreams about washing his hands in a restroom after a group of girls barges in. It symbolizes that he's sick of the dating scene at his school and all the gossip and rumors and wants to "wash his hands" of it all. For more detail about this dream, see: *Library*.

A bathroom is where we assess our appearance and groom, and that use can tie in with self-perceptions and ideas about attractiveness.

A bath can symbolize aspects of physical health. The body is made up mostly of water, so water is a sort of barometer for health and a versatile symbol. For example, very hot water can symbolize fever. Cold water can symbolize chills. See: *Water*.

A bath in a dream can enact the idiom "take a bath," meaning a financial loss or something related. "Cleaned out" has similar meaning, and "clean up" can mean a financial windfall.

See also: *Anus, Bathroom Stall, Clean, Door, Emotions, Excrement, Heat, Illness, Intruder, Mirror, Naked, Shower, Teeth, Toilet, Undress, Vomit, Water, Winter*

Bathroom Stall—Dreams about bathroom stalls can be similar in symbolism to those about bathrooms, but with an emphasis on issues of privacy or small, confining space. A bathroom stall without a door can symbolize feeling like you can't find privacy.

See also: *Bathroom, Toilet*

Battle—See: *Fight*

Beach—The beach in a dream can symbolize where two parts of you or your life meet. Most commonly it's where the unconscious mind and conscious mind meet, but there are other possibilities. For example, the beach can symbolize your rational mind, and the water of the ocean can symbolize emotions. A shoreline can be an analogy for the emotions and feelings that arise out of you.

It can symbolize where the masculine (land, yang) and feminine (ocean, yin) meet. No matter what your gender, you have elements of both genders in you, and they are rooted in the foundation of your psyche. See: *Penis, Vagina*.

Another analogy is that the ocean represents possibilities, and the shoreline represents reality.

The conscious mind emerges from the unconscious the way land rises out of the sea, so a beach or shoreline is a ready-made symbol for newly conscious aspects of yourself. These aspects are often perceived at first as strange, and can take forms in dreams as strange sea creatures or clumps of unrecognizable stuff washed up on the shore. In time, you will get to know these new aspects of yourself and they will become more recognizable.

The beach can symbolize a new phase of life. You've reached new land, in a sense.

The beach is associated with vacations and idle time, so dreaming about a beach can indicate desire for, or thoughts related to, travel and rest. It might indicate a longing for the easy life or, conversely, for adventure, especially if water sports are involved.

The shoreline is commonly used in media and advertising to portray times when a person is reminiscing or reflecting on life.

Looking into the distance from a beach can symbolize trying to discern what is approaching in the future, or keeping attention on some distant goal, pursuit, or event.

If you reach a coast or beach after a voyage, it can symbolize being on firm ground, meaning a more secure place in your life, or feeling ready for whatever comes next.

Taking off from a shoreline can symbolize embarking on a new journey in life. See: *Embark, Journey.*

See also: *Boat, Border, Embark, Flood, Journey, Ocean, Penis, Surfing, Tidal Wave, Undress, Vacation, Vagina, Water*

Bear—Depending on the breed, a bear can be aggressive or docile, and the difference has implications for the meaning of the bear in your dream. For example, Winnie the Pooh is a docile characterization of a bear, and panda bears are thought of as cute and harmless. But grizzlies are known for their ferocity. A grizzly is more likely to be a symbol of ferocity than of docility.

Large bears are very powerful and can symbolize great strength. It's a coarse sort of strength, and when mastered can make you master of your domain, a pillar, especially in difficult situations.

A wild bear can symbolize that your strength and instincts are untamed.

A powerful bear can symbolize a situation that can't be changed, or a person is set in their ways.

A bear can symbolize something menacing—especially the menace of a powerful or intimidating personality.

Bears are slow to anger, but overwhelming when they attack, which is a great metaphor for when a usually docile person is poked one too many times. The same association can be used to symbolize the unconscious mind. It too moves slowly, but can be fierce and unstoppable when roused or protective.

The unconscious mind is the primary source of human creativity, so a bear, as a symbol of the unconscious, can symbolize powerful creativity. See: *Unconscious Mind.*

Befriending a bear can indicate a harmonious relationship between your conscious mind and the unconscious mind, but a hostile bear can indicate an adversarial relationship.

Bears hibernate, so dreams can associate them with dormancy and long periods of introspection. Hibernation is also associated with death and rebirth. You might be going through some sort of big personal change and will emerge as a changed person. A sleeping or hibernating bear can symbolize someone or something you want to avoid arousing. See: *Cave, Coma, Sleep.*

Possibilities for symbolism can be found in figures of speech like "hungry as a bear," "a bear to deal with," and "overbearing." The meaning will show in the actions and other details. For example, feeding a bear (it's a hungry bear), or a bear on top of you (the bear is "over" you, aka "overbearing").

Because bears are mostly solitary, they can symbolize a "go it alone" attitude or desire to be away from people. The idea can stretch to include characteristics such as introversion, independence, and self-sufficiency.

Animals in dreams can represent related instincts in you, such as bear-like instincts to defend, to mother, and to view strangers with suspicion. See: *Animals.*

Bears are associated with sexuality and the dark, devouring aspects of it. Coming to terms with the power of sexuality, the hunger, can be a struggle, devouring people who can't control it. See: *Devour.*

A bear in a woman's dreams can symbolize the power of her sexuality, and more, her inner strength and connection with nature as a vessel for offspring. The same idea can apply to a man—he too can be a life-giver—it's just more likely with a woman because of her innate connection to Mother Nature. See: *Earth, Vagina.*

Being devoured is often symbolism for something figuratively devouring you, such as stress or fear. But dream imagery of a devouring bear is also common to an experience known as *dark night of the soul.* These rare dreams feature bears that shift shapes, often from a wolf or dog to a featureless human, then to a bear, or any combination of this imagery. They also feature a theme of death, and, of course, a bear dining on you.

The devouring bear in these dreams represents the unconscious mind, come to eat away the old person so the new one can emerge. You are "born again," but first the old person must pass away, and it's gruesome when represented visually. Some people give in to the beast and let it eat them, allowing the process of transformation to happen. Others resist, holding on to something about themselves that doesn't want to die, figuratively speaking—or they're unable to let go, because the process of healing isn't complete.

Bears are traditionally associated with nature and motherly instincts. When kept in check, the motherly instincts of a "momma bear" create peace and security for her children. But when unchecked, the motherly instinct can smother, stifle, and psychologically devour her offspring.

Any female figure—sister, girlfriend, aunt, wife—can play the role of momma in its positive or negative aspect and be symbolized in a dream as a bear. A bear can symbolize the desire for a strong mother figure, or a good or bad attachment to one. Your feelings help you determine the difference, because you subconsciously recognize what momma bear symbolizes in your dream and you react based on that knowledge. See: *Mother.*

A mother dreams about walking through the woods with her teenaged son. Suddenly, a bear emerges and mauls him. It's a way of saying that *momma bear's* motherly instincts are smothering her teenaged son. She is overprotective and needs to allow him room to take risks and make his own decisions.

And let's not forget poppa bear—strong, rugged, instinctual, protective. He can be symbolized as a bear.

A bear can be used in a wordplay for "bare," as in bare your soul, or bare naked. See: *Naked.*

A teddy bear can symbolize a childlike desire for protection and comfort. See: *Child.*

Personal associations come into play, too, to create dream symbolism. For example, perhaps you once encountered a bear in the wild and remember well the adrenaline rush and cold feeling of fear. Or you felt sorry for a bear you saw in a zoo. Those associations could be used to symbolize an encounter with a dangerous or wild person, or a feeling of sadness or loneliness.

See also: *Animals, Anxiety, Cave, Coma, Devour, Earth, Eaten, Emotions, Hunger, Mother, Naked, Sleep, Unconscious Mind, Vagina*

Beast—See: *Monster*

Beat—Beating on someone in a dream can be a powerful way of symbolizing frustration or strong feelings about that person or a situation involving him or her. Keep in mind as you analyze such a dream that beating is often a physical representation of a personal situation.

A surrogate-character can be used for someone you feel strongly about, so go by how you feel about a character, rather than appearance, to figure out what it represents to you. A surrogate is likely to be used so that you react instinctually to the person's symbolic presence in your dream.

For example, a man who's been arguing heatedly with his father dreams about viciously punching a random male stranger in the face. The violence is an exaggerated but apt representation of the strength of his feelings. And all the stranger in the dream said was, "I hope you get that fixed," a saying that's his father's favorite subtle putdown. It triggers a lifetime of pent-up resentment and anger. See: *Fist.*

A woman dreams about her mom forcing her to poison her pet dog, symbolizing her mom's manipulation of the dreamer to get her to marry her best friend (symbolized as the dog) and the dreamer's fear that it would poison the friendship. In the dream, the dreamer beats her mom until bones crack and blood flies, dramatizations of her very strong feelings.

Beating can symbolize feeling beaten down or battered. The symbolism can show in the action of being beaten, or doing the beating, or even beating yourself, such as when you "beat your head against a wall."

It can symbolize dominating or breaking someone's will, a "beat down," or forcing something to happen.

On the other hand, beating can symbolize positive assertion of will, or competitive spirit. The victor in a competition is said to "beat" the losers, and dreams can act out that symbolism as beating with fists and objects. Some competitions are of the personal variety, such as competing with yourself against a previous best mark, or competing for the attention or heart of someone. Also, the strength of your feelings show in the severity of the beating and how much it hurts. See: *Games, Sports.*

Beating can symbolize trying to overcome a personality or character flaw, such as when someone says they can beat an addiction. It can mean "beat the odds."

Because dreams exaggerate, they can use beating as a way of saying that someone or something is really irritating you or trying hard to get your attention. In this case, a character in a dream beats on you because it's a part of yourself and nothing else will get your attention.

Beating on yourself can indicate masochism or a desire to punish yourself. It can show that you have strong feelings such as self-hate and shame.

See also: *Abuse, Arena, Attack, Fight, Fist, Games, Opponent, Rape, Sports, Wound*

Beauty—Dreaming about beauty can be a way of seeing the beauty within you. Deep down you recognize it, even if you don't consciously. In the beautiful people, imagery, and feelings of your dreams, you see what you admire, value, and appreciate about yourself. It's what you see in yourself now, or it's potential, something that can or will emerge.

Beauty in a dream can mean you see the beauty in something—the beauty of a proposal, plan, idea,

theory, or turn of events, for example. It's a physical representation of a perception or feeling.

Beautiful can mean attractive, such as an attractive job offer. The thought of something can be attractive to you in the personal sense, such as the thought of traveling or starting a family. You can find math, art, and other subjects attractive or beautiful. The possibilities stretch far and wide, but fortunately you usually only need to look at your recent life and your feelings to find the meaning.

Dreams can use beauty and attraction to promote bonding between aspects of the psyche. For example, dreams often depict anima and animus figures as attractive, both physically and personally, to make you want to better know this part of yourself. The Lover archetype is depicted in a beautiful form, sometimes the most beautiful thing you've ever seen. See: *Archetypes.*

Dreaming about beauty can indicate desire for harmony.

It can mean you see the beauty in life, people, or nature.

Beauty can represent how it feels to be lucky or successful.

To be captivated by beauty can symbolize narcissism or obsession, as in the story of Narcissus captivated by his reflection in a pool of water. Or something else has captivated you—an idea, an experience, sensuousness, life.

Beauty can symbolize refined aesthetic taste, or deep appreciation for life and the finer things.

It can connect with related issues such as wanting to be beautiful, or feeling like you're only appreciated for your appearance. See: *Doll, Mirror.*

See also: *Anima, Animus, Archetypes, Bathroom, Doll, Earth, Face, Fox, Love, Make-Up, Mirror, Prince, Princess, Ugly*

Bed—Your bed is a personal and intimate place. Therefore, dreams featuring your bed can be about subjects close to you.

For example, a teenager dreams that he finds a dead rat in his bed. He then yells at his parents, who are not actually pictured in the scene. That fact is a big clue. The dead rat symbolizes feeling betrayed by his parents, and it's shown in his bed because his parents are very close to him. His reaction of blaming his parents points right to the meaning.

A bed can symbolize secrets. It's where you think about things you don't want others to know about, or don't have time to think about during a busy day. A made bed can indicate that those secrets are safe, whereas a messy bed can indicate that your secrets have been, or will soon be, revealed—especially if the blankets or sheets are pulled down or off. The idea extends beyond secrets to include anything intimate or personal that you want to keep private.

Your bed is where you dream, and dream in another sense means hope, aspire, and imagine. Your hopes and aspirations are personal to you, perhaps something you think about when in bed.

A bed is where you rest and sleep, and it can be associated with those needs.

It's a place retreated to for privacy, to be alone with your thoughts.

A bed is associated with the cycles of life, opening many possibilities for use as dream symbolism. Life begins with conception in a bed. Birth often happens in a bed. A large portion of your life is spent in bed. And life often ends in bed.

The symbolism of making a bed can relate to the phrase, "You made your bed, now lie in it." It means deal with the mess you made. You create your own situations and circumstances in life. It can mean you are straightening up your life.

Restlessness in bed can mean something is troubling you, or you feel dissatisfied. What keeps you up at night or disturbs your sleep?

Disrespecting your bed can be a sign of feeling disrespected. For example, someone peeing on your bed can be a way of saying he or she disrespects you. Peeing on your own bed can indicate you disrespect yourself. Peeing on someone else's bed is a graphic portrayal of how you feel about that person or what he or she represents.

Pushing someone out of your bed can symbolize that you want that person out of your life, away from you. In romantic relationships, this is a sign that your feelings about your partner are changing for the worse. Or it can be a way of saying you need your space.

Because beds are where people have sex, in dreams they can be used to create symbolism related to your sex life and related subjects. For example, a dream featuring a bed with sheets so tight the dreamer can't get into the bed is about the dreamer's being too tight when it comes to sex. Nervousness and discomfort are hindering her sex life. See the entry for *Emotions* for another example of a dream featuring a bed.

An oversized bed can symbolize overemphasis on sex, an expansive sex life, or generous attitude toward sex, whereas an undersized bed has the opposite connotations. Then again, an oversized bed can symbolize a big secret, so as with all symbolism, look at the symbolism of the bed within the context of the dream-story and together with other details.

Dirty bedding can symbolize perceptions of sex as dirty, discontent with yourself, or living in squalor. It can mean your life or mind is in squalor. It can indicate a variety of "dirty" feelings, such as guilt, jealousy, and envy, or a filthy mind.

A burning bed can symbolize burning up with desire or anger.

To dream about a marriage bed when you're single can indicate desire to discover your sexuality, or to have a committed relationship.

The condition of the bed you share with your partner can symbolize the state of the relationship and characterize the intimacy level. It can symbolize the state of other commitments you have made—to your job, your friends, your children, a cause, an ideal, a principle.

An empty bed can symbolize the absence of someone important from your life, or a general feeling of loneliness. It can symbolize lack of aspirations or ambitions. You need something to look forward to, something that makes you want to get out of bed in the morning.

Dreaming about being in bed with a stranger can express the feeling that you don't really know someone close to you, or that someone is acting out of character. Or the stranger can symbolize an aspect of yourself that is unfamiliar or estranged, yet still so close to you that it's in your bed, figuratively. The idea extends further to include situations that feel strange or unfamiliar. For example, you find yourself in a circle of people you don't feel comfortable with, or a business situation goes into uncharted territory. You're not sure about the people you are "in bed" with. See: *Stranger*.

The rectangular shape of a bed can be symbolism. See: *Rectangle*.

Sleeping in a bed that's not yours is known to spark vivid dreams.

See also: *Bedroom, Emotions, Rectangle, Sex, Stranger*

Bedroom—A bedroom is your private space, assuming you don't share a bedroom with other people. Therefore, dreaming about your bedroom can indicate an issue with privacy.

A bedroom is where you have your most private thoughts and feelings, so if it's invaded by someone in a dream, or unwelcome people are in it, the symbolism can relate to needing space to have your private thoughts. The association extends to any subject related to privacy or intimacy. For an example, see: *Gorilla*.

Bedrooms are where people have sex, so the symbolism can relate to something about your sexuality or sex life. For example, a young man dreams that his girlfriend locks him out of his bedroom, and when he asks to be let in, she replies, "It's not safe." She doesn't feel safe having sex with him, and being locked out of his bedroom is a great metaphor for the situation based on the association with sex.

Take the idea of intimacy further and a bedroom in a dream can symbolize any subject close to your heart or deeply personal, or your most personal thoughts and feelings. See: *Bed*.

Dreaming about your childhood bedroom can indicate that a memory from that time of life has been triggered by a situation or event in your current life. The present time connects with the past

and you subconsciously see or feel the connection. Oftentimes it's related patterns in your life that formed back then, or unresolved feelings. See: *Childhood Home*.

Dreaming about being in a bedroom that is not your own can indicate the desire to start a new intimate relationship or new phase of your sexuality. Or it can mean you feel a close or intimate connection with the person who uses that bedroom.

Dreaming about feeling lonely in your bedroom can signify a wish for a partner or close connection with another human being. If you're in a relationship, it can mean that your most important needs are not being met.

See also: *Bed, Childhood Home, Home, Sex, Shapes*

Bee—Bees in a dream are generally a positive sign, but look at the context of the dream before jumping to conclusions. Obviously, being stung by a bee or attacked by a swarm is not a positive sign unless it is, at heart, a message that something about yourself or the circumstances of your life needs to change. In which case, it is a sort of mixed blessing.

Bees are communal, self-sacrificing, diligent, and orderly. Any of these ideas can be expressed in dreams featuring bees.

Dreams about bees can symbolize the relationship between you and the community or neighborhood in which you live, or the circle of people with whom you associate. For example, a school or work community can be symbolized as a hive. It can symbolize a "hive mind."

A hive can symbolize building something as a part of a community. The product of the labor can be material, but also consider less-tangible possibilities, such as building a sense of togetherness or cooperation. Good relationships are built through cooperation, trust, and responsiveness to the needs of others, all of which are exhibited by bees working together.

Bees connect a neighborhood because they cross boundaries and regularly visit every place they can get nectar, and that idea can connect with things that create a sense of cohesion, such as shared values or beliefs.

In that sense, if you think of the psyche as a collective, the bees are the beliefs, values, feelings, thoughts, and processes that connect everything together.

To dream about busy bees can symbolize hard work and being busy, as in the phrase "busy as a bee." It can symbolize a family or community working in harmony.

If you fear bees, they can easily be used in dreams to symbolize a fear, and you will react with fear to the presence of bees.

Another possibility is that bees can symbolize an annoyance that won't go away, something that pesters. This use of the symbolism is likely to be accompanied by the action of swatting or stronger actions to rid yourself of bees. For example, grabbing a shotgun to get rid of an annoying bee in your house can symbolize a strong desire to be rid of a house guest who drops by and won't leave. You are ready to take drastic action.

Running from or avoiding bees can symbolize avoiding responsibility or pain. Avoiding a swarm can symbolize avoiding a group of angry people. A swarm can symbolize thoughts that make your head buzz, or it can suggest disagreement with, or within, a community.

Angry bees can symbolize that you said or did something—or neglected to do something—that angered a group of people. For example, you post something on Facebook that draws a lot of stinging comments.

A swarm of bees is, in simplest terms, trouble! It's something you want to avoid, such as a bad disagreement among friends or a perilous situation.

Stinging bees are associated with pain—especially nerve pain.

To be stung by a bee can symbolize a stinging remark. Feelings such as regret and guilt can sting. It can symbolize the ways you say things to yourself that hurt.

Think more expansively and it can mean a situation you are in is painful in some way.

Because bees make honey, they can be associated with wealth and sweetness. Honey symbolizes the product of your labor or good intentions. It can symbolize a reward or indulgence, especially the intimate and sexual varieties of indulgence.

Honey in a dream can relate to digestion, including the digestion of thoughts, feelings, and experiences. Bees digest nectar to produce honey. You digest your experiences in life to improve yourself. When you dream, especially during REM-stage dreaming, your mind digests the experiences of your day so you can learn and grow.

Bees landing on flowers, extracting nectar and depositing pollen, can symbolize something related to fertilization. Perhaps you are laying the groundwork for a future endeavor or personal growth. Or take the idea further and it can symbolize conception, the fertilization of the female egg with the male sperm.

The image of a bee on a succulent flower is charged with sexual references. The flower is associated with the vaginal area, and a bee extracting nectar and leaving pollen is a heck of a metaphor.

See also: *Bug, Fly, Insect*

Beggar—A beggar in your dream can symbolize someone who asks for favors or mooches off hospitality.

Alternately, a beggar can symbolize something about yourself that wants favors or hospitality, that mooches or takes without giving back. Or a beggar can symbolize part of yourself begging for attention or help, or that feels overlooked, rejected, or held in low regard.

Now expand on the last idea. What do you see about yourself in the beggar? Everything you react to strongly reflects something you see in yourself. People project their Shadow, a component of their psyche, into the world and react to it, often with derision and hatred, when what they really hate is something about themselves. What they hate and fear about themselves can then be symbolized in their dreams as a beggar. For example, they hate their financial insecurity or lack of courage to live how they please, like some beggars do. See: *Shadow*.

A beggar can symbolize fear of failure, based on the association that beggars and homeless people fail at life.

A beggar can symbolize desperation. For example, a high school student dreams that a homeless beggar follows her to school and steals her backpack, which has all her books and school supplies. She tries to explain to her teacher what happened, but she gets no sympathy. The dream reflects her situation at school. She's behind in her studies and in danger of flunking. She feels desperate and is ready to beg for help.

A beggar can symbolize social isolation because beggars are generally shunned by society. It can symbolize feeling ashamed, or being more sensitive or needy than you let on.

To be attacked by a beggar in a dream, or to attack one, can remind you to help and protect those who are less fortunate. No matter what you consciously think about beggars, you are unconsciously programmed to help people in need. An attack in a dream can symbolize deep conflict, strong feeling, or something trying hard to get your attention. See: *Attack*.

A beggar can symbolize fears related to your financial situation. When you see a beggar, do you fear that could be you someday? Have you been avoiding work or loafing off?

A beggar can represent simplicity. Beggars lack physical security, but in return they get ample time for self-reflection and simple enjoyment of life. It's a reminder that material values are not the most important ones.

A beggar can symbolize an overlooked source of wisdom or advice.

See also: *Attack, City, Compensation, Money, Urban*

Below—Physical placement and location in a dream is deliberately used as symbolism. If a detail about placement or location stands out to you as meaningful, it almost certainly is.

Think about when something is said to be below something else. It can mean it's lower priority, importance, or value. Rankings generally go from top to bottom, so "below" can mean not as highly ranked. It can symbolize being low in the "pecking order" or on the "totem pole."

Below can describe low feelings or mood. It can signify dim prospects.

Below can refer to something below the threshold of your awareness—subconscious or unconscious. Or it can refer to something that's instinctual—from the gut—or emotional—from the heart. This use of the symbolism is more likely if the dream refers to those areas of the body, or the setting is a lower floor of a house or other building. See: *Basement*.

Figures of speech such as "below the belt" and "low blow" can be enacted in dreams to symbolize a dirty trick or underhanded tactic. The symbolism will be acted out. It can mean you have a low opinion or low respect for something. Anything low to the ground can have that symbolism.

Then again, low to the ground can mean "grounded," so never jump to conclusions. Look for supporting details. For example, snakes live on the ground, usually, creating an association between them and natural wisdom or instincts.

Low or below can be used in the sense of "beneath you" or "below you." You're too good for something, such as working at an entry-level job. "Lowness" can show your low perception or opinion, such as when you think the person who wants to marry your child isn't good enough and you dream about it as that person driving a car that's low to the ground. The symbolism of the low height of the car is based on perceptions related to value and importance.

See also: *Above, Basement, Short, Subconscious*

Bicycle—Since balance is required to ride a bike, dreaming about riding a bike can relate to personal balance, such as balancing the psyche, balancing logic and feeling, and balancing work and play.

Falling off a bicycle can symbolize being imbalanced in some way by putting too much emphasis on one thing at the expense of another, or allowing part of you to predominate over another, such as when your head overrides your heart, or vice versa. It can mean your behavior or reaction to something is out of balance.

Bicycles are associated with leg work. They are powered by your effort, so riding a bike can symbolize effort, hustle, and exertion.

Bikes have strong associations with independence and free spirit. They are one-passenger vehicles powered by individual effort.

A tandem bike is a beautiful image of joint effort or partnership.

Falling off a bike, or breaking one, can symbolize inability to complete a task.

Riding ahead of your competition can mean you are getting ahead in life or exceeding expectations.

Riding a bike in a dream can connect with feelings of exuberance and adventure. The symbolism is shown in the movement and action, and your feelings while riding can tell you a lot about what the symbolism means and what it describes about yourself and your life.

To dream that you forget to lock up your bike can indicate you need to protect the fruits of your labor. For example, writers copyright their work to protect it from being misappropriated or stolen. An unlocked bike can mean you have left yourself vulnerable to misfortune or manipulation.

Bicycles are associated with being unable to afford a better ride.

Then again, riding a bike is also associated with getting in shape and saving money. It can symbolize going the extra mile in the name of a good cause, or decision-making that centers on using the best means at your disposal to conserve resources.

Dreaming about a bike you had as a child can symbolize yearning for freedom or simplicity, or inability to fully grow into an adult role or personality. It can symbolize reflecting back on that time of life, or thinking about having children. The latter use of the symbolism grows out of the fact that teaching a child to ride a bike is a landmark occasion for parent and child alike.

Many personal associations with bikes can come into play to create dream symbolism. Think of experiences you've had involving bikes and times of life with which they are associated.

If you dream about your bike being stolen, but in everyday life you don't have a bike, begin analyzing by asking yourself if you feel vulnerable. Has it ever actually happened to you? A child finding out that her bike has been stolen is a sad image, and it can connect with thoughts and feelings like "How could a person do that to me?" and "Why was I so trusting?" A dream could use those associations to symbolize personal betrayal or disappointment.

Also, consider the type of bike in the dream and possibilities for how symbolism could be created from details such as a punctured tire, which can mean something has slowed you down or stopped progress, or you feel deflated.

A wheel falling off a bike can symbolize a situation that goes awry or something that breaks down. It's an especially apt way of symbolizing a leg or foot injury.

See also: *Car, Motorcycle*

Bikini—Wearing a bikini in a dream can symbolize being uncovered or exposed in the personal sense. (Almost) everything is revealed. In personal terms, whether you're male or female, that can mean showing who you really are behind your persona, or seeing behind the surface of someone or something. Which can bring up feelings related to confidence, personal flaws, and the difference between the personality that's projected (called persona) and the true person behind it. See: *Naked, Persona.*

Wearing a bikini is said to bare the skin, and dreams can use that idea to mean "bare the truth" or "bare your soul." Extend the idea further to include subjects such as insight and revelation, something that's revealed to you.

Wearing a bikini with confidence can mean something inside you is ready to be revealed. Or you want to show off, to be seen and noticed. It might indicate pride in the condition of your body, or your mind, or your life, or your personal presentation.

Many personal associations come into play, too. For example, if wearing a bikini in public scares you, in a dream it can symbolize something else that scares you, such as the thought of being scrutinized. It can indicate jealousy of people who are more attractive than you, or shame.

Along this line, a bikini can symbolize working hard to get the results you want. The symbolism is derived from preparing for bikini season by losing weight and toning up.

See also: *Beach, Clothing, Naked, Persona, Skin, Underwear, Undress, Water*

Billfold—See: *Purse, Wallet*

Bill Gates—See: *Famous*

Birds—Because birds fly, they can symbolize freedom. They can pick up and leave whenever you want to—"free as a bird." See: *Fly*.

Think of a bird in flight as representing ability to achieve your aspirations or hopes. Ambitions, goals, hopes—all can be described as "flying high." See: *Airplane*.

Thoughts and feelings can soar, can take flight and group together like birds. Birds far away, high in the sky, can symbolize too-high aspiration or something else out of reach.

Birds falling from the sky can symbolize goals that aren't reached or hopes that are dashed. It can have the same meaning as when Icarus flies too close to the sun. Exuberance overtakes you. Hubris leads to nemesis.

A flock of birds can symbolize harmony, or a group mind, people who, in the figurative sense, move in unison, especially in their thoughts and opinions. A "herd mentality," though moving in unison can also mean coordination and organization.

A group of birds attacking can symbolize a group of people who attack verbally, psychologically, or physically. This use of the symbolism is especially likely if the dream features birds clawing and biting.

Birds attacking can symbolize feeling compromised, embarrassed, or dirty. Or emotional or psychological attacks that swoop in from nowhere. The symbolism covers anything that attacks the mind or through it. Angry black birds are frequently used as symbols for compromising situations and ways a person can attack themselves in their mind.

A bird shitting on you sums up in one image the feeling of being disrespected, or bad luck, or something that comes out of nowhere.

A pairing of birds can symbolize love and mutual responsibilities, especially in relation to caring for loved ones or making a home together. Mating pairs in the bird world show a high degree of cooperation to build a nest and raise their young.

Birds can symbolize messages delivered from deep inside yourself, from the unconscious mind. They deliver information during times of need, or tell you what you need to know about yourself. Crows and ravens often serve the role of messenger. The symbolism is derived from birds' being used as messengers and having the ability to fly and talk. In this sense, a black bird can symbolize ominous warnings from within yourself, and a white bird can symbolize good tidings and agreement between the conscious mind and the unconscious mind.

Chattering birds can symbolize gossip.

Birds sing, and have associations with anything related to self-expression and cheerfulness. See: *Artist, Music*.

Birds can symbolize watching out for something coming, or keeping an eye out for danger.

A bird that acts stupidly, such as a dove walking into a busy road, can symbolize acting thoughtlessly or carelessly—a "bird brain."

Particular types of birds can have specific symbolism, such as hawks' association with keen vision and falcons' association with trainability. Refer to the list of entries below.

See also: *Airplane, Artist, Ascend, Bird Cage, Chicken, Clouds, Crow, Eagle, Excrement, Float, Fly, Hummingbird, Music, Owl, Pet, Turkey, Vulture*

Bird Cage—A bird cage can symbolize feeling confined or unable to express yourself.

"The bird cage" is a term used to describe being trapped by your sexuality. For example, a young woman dreams she's trapped in a bird cage and outside it she sees the phone of her crush, a female friend of hers, displaying text messages passing back and forth between her crush and a guy her crush likes. The dreamer is unable to leave the cage or do anything to stop the messages. The situation symbolizes her inability to change the sexual orientation of her crush. She'll never get what she wants.

See also: *Birds, Cage, Escape, Hostage, Jail*

Birth—See: *Childbirth*

Bite—To dream about biting can signify that you feel you have been harmed, especially by a "biting" comment or something similar. The mouth is used to bite and to speak, so the connection between biting and speaking is easy to make.

Being bitten in a dream can symbolize suffering from aggressive treatment. Picture a pack of wolves snarling and snapping at each other over their kill. It's an image that, in an exaggerated way, can describe situations in life where people aggressively posture and snap at each other. "Snap" can mean loss of temper. Being bitten expresses how you feel, how you are affected.

Biting can symbolize anger, particularly if you're bitten by an animal known for its temper, such as a goat or raccoon. See: *Anger*.

Animal bites can symbolize trouble or problems caused by your instinctual behaviors, drives, or impulses. For example, a dog bite can mean you are overprotective. A lion bite can mean you are too proud.

To be bitten by a cat can symbolize arguments or fights with a female, especially a girlfriend or wife. See: *Cat*.

Look up the type of the animal that bites you. See: *Animals*.

Biting in an erotic context can indicate excessive sexuality. It's a way of saying "too much of a good thing."

Along this line, it can mean that something has captivated you, particularly if something bites you and latches on.

Biting is a childish impulse and can be a childish way of expressing frustration or anger. It can symbolize the expression of feelings in a childish manner.

Biting in a dream can be a way of getting your attention. For example, a snake bite on the wrist is known to be an attempt by the unconscious mind to get your attention, because the time is ripe with potential for positive change. It's a way of saying "take action." If you ignore or repress something, it will try to get your attention in your dreams, and a bite definitely gets your attention!

A snake or spider bite can symbolize that something is negatively affecting you, poisoning you figuratively. It can symbolize poisonous thoughts, feelings, or influences. See: *Venom*.

Biting is sometimes used as a warning. For example, when your pet cat bites you because you have crossed some sort of line with it. Therefore, biting can be a warning to be careful, to respect boundaries. A situation can suddenly turn on you, the same as a friendly pet can suddenly turn on you.

"Bite off more than you can chew" means to take on too much at once. The symbolism can show in dreams where you cannot chew everything in your mouth or wrap your mouth around something.

Biting and swallowing a penis can symbolize taking something masculine into yourself. For example, after a day hanging out with a group of macho men, a woman dreams about eating a big sausage given to her by Clint Eastwood. It's a way of saying she's taking the experience into herself and digesting it. Both the sausage (a phallic symbol) and Clint Eastwood are symbols of machismo. See: *Fellatio, Penis*.

A young woman who had been mercilessly bullied by her classmates dreams about being forced to suck the penis of one of the bullies. She decides to pretend like she wants to do it, then bites off the penis. See: *Revenge*.

Biting can symbolize pain in the body, which is sometimes described as a "biting pain." The dreaming mind translates any input or stimuli into symbolism, so a sharp pain experienced while dreaming can be translated into the action of being bitten by something.

Since biting involves teeth, be sure to read the entry for *Teeth*.

See also: *Animals, Attack, Bully, Cat, Chase, Cunnilingus, Dog, Fellatio, Fight, Penis, Pet, Sex, Snake, Spider, Teeth, Wound*

Black—The color black is associated most commonly with mystery and the unknown, derived from the blackness of a dark night and of outer space. They are places full of mystery and the unknown.

Those associations connect strongly with the unconscious mind, also a place of mystery. See: *Unconscious Mind*.

The symbolism of the color black can be used in many ways in a dream. For example, a dark or black room can symbolize an unknown part of you, or an area of your life that's unexplored. The black of night can be an amorphous symbol for fear and anxiety, and is synonymous with feeling lost. See: *Anxiety, Fear, Lost, Wilderness*.

Night is something that's shut out and protected against, so black can symbolize anything you don't want to know or don't want in your life. See: *Door, Lock*.

A black dog can symbolize the dark side of a friend. Notice how the symbolism of the color of black is used to modify the symbolism of the dog. See: *Colors*.

A black snake can symbolize worrying about someone's intentions.

Black is associated with mistrust and suspicions.

It's associated with something exotic or foreign. See: *Foreign*.

It's associated with death. See: *Death*.

It's associated with black moods and dark thoughts.

The use of the symbolism of black in dreams can be the same as in figures of speech such as "blacken," meaning to destroy reputation, and "in the black," meaning profitable.

Black skin, clothing, and overall appearance is commonly associated with the shadow side of the psyche. See: *Shadow*.

Identifying shadow-characters in a dream can be tricky because, by nature, shadow is outside your conscious awareness and likes it that way. And it will go to great lengths to stay hidden. Shadow is identified not just by appearance, but also by how it works against your good intentions, feelings, and thought processes, and encourages your bad ones.

To be clear, a black dream-character is not synonymous with shadow. This is a common source of misunderstanding. Instead, shadow is portrayed as black because of the symbolism of the color. Shadow can be portrayed in dreams as any ethnicity or race the dreamer thinks of as suspicious or mostly unknown.

A black dream-character can appear in dreams after an encounter or interaction with a black person.

See also: *Anxiety, Black Widow, Colors, Death, Door, Emotions, Dark, Dog, Fear, Foreign, Lock, Night, Shadow, Space, Snake, Unconscious Mind, Wilderness*

Black Widow—A black widow spider in a dream can be a warning to guard against someone in your life, most likely a female who weaves webs of intrigue. She is the sort who ensnares her prey and injects her venomous words and ideas. In other words, she's trouble with a capital "T" and someone to avoid.

However, something about her could be almost hypnotically attractive, and some men can't help but walk into her trap. Black widows devour their mates, and in dreams that idea translates into being devoured in a relationship, dominated, threatened, trapped—even killed.

A black widow can symbolize the general idea of danger, intrigue, and something that waits in the shadows till the time is right to strike. For example, the shadow part of the psyche waits in the background of the mind till the conscious mind is vulnerable, then it slides right into the driver's seat to take control.

While a black widow is a specific type of spider, its symbolism can be tied in with spiders in general. Much of it overlaps. See: *Spider*.

Where the black widow differentiates itself is in its close association with a certain type of female who's nothing but trouble, and with situations that are particularly perilous.

In a dream about going down into sewers and encountering a black widow and its webs, a young man is thinking about a situation with his ex-girlfriend. She has been tunneling back into his life, using underhanded means to "bump" into him, symbolized as the sewers. She then proceeds to weave a spell of intrigue around him, symbolized as the spider webs. Her depiction in the dream as a black widow sums up her tactics and characterizes how the dreamer feels. He knows she's dangerous, and he should keep her out of his life.

See also: *Black, Panic, Shadow, Spider, Widow*

Blaze—See: *Fire*

Blind—Sight in a dream can refer to perception or awareness. It's a physical representation of a personal situation. To dream that you are blind can symbolize not seeing or noticing something, especially about yourself, a person you know, or a situation. You need to pay attention, "open your eyes."

For example, a woman about to get married dreams that her fiancé is blind. It distresses her to know he doesn't see her. In this case, blind means he doesn't really know her. He doesn't "see" who she really is, and it distresses her.

Blindness can indicate you're aware of something but choose to ignore it.

Or you struggle with seeing or acknowledging the truth, making you susceptible to being fooled or deluded. For example, you are in love with someone and know you're being used, but you don't care because you're blinded by love. See no evil.

Blind can mean blind to the facts or blind to the obvious.

It can symbolize trouble seeing your way to a goal or destination in life, or navigating through a situation. You know where you want to go, but

don't know how to get there. Or you are just plain lost, "in the dark." See: *Dark, Lost*.

Blindness is a versatile symbol. It can be used to figuratively describe a variety of situations, especially when combined with other symbols. For example, a blind dog can symbolize a friend who doesn't see the obvious. A blind supervisor can symbolize inability to lead.

Look for discrepancies with reality. Obviously, if you are blind or have a serious eyesight issue, blindness in your dream is more likely to reflect reality. If eyesight is not an issue for you, you can bet it's symbolism. Keep in mind that it could be an exaggerated way of saying you don't see well.

See also: *All-Seeing Eye, Black, Body, Dark, Eyes, Lost*

Blizzard—To decode the symbolism of a blizzard, begin by thinking of common associations and how those can be used to tell a story.

Blizzards make travel difficult, and travel in a dream can symbolize movement in your life. The blizzard is the obstacle in your path, or the heavy feelings that weigh you down.

Blizzards make seeing difficult, and sight in a dream can mean "seeing ahead in life" or vision for it. The blizzard can symbolize the difficulties that distract you or the insecurities that hold you back. It can symbolize difficulty seeing what's happening in your inner life. See: *Blind*.

The heavy snow, bitter cold, and howling wind of a blizzard are great ways of describing depression. The whitewashed, featureless landscape visually represents the feeling of depression, or sadness, or grief, or loneliness. See: *Depression*.

For an example dream, see: *Horse*.

Hazards created by blizzards can symbolize hazards in life. You don't see the pitfalls or cracks in the ice that await you.

A blizzard can signify a time of hardship or difficulty. Life is littered with obstacles. It's a real drag.

A blizzard can mean "flurry of activity." It can signify having too much to do and not enough time to do it. Or something major in your life is approaching, for which preparations must be made. Before a blizzard, people hurry to prepare. Afterward, they dig out and repair damage. These associations can be used to create symbolism for digging out of a hole or cleaning up a mess. For example, putting your life back together after a bad breakup.

Strong winds whipping snow around is a picture of chaos and frantic activity. That picture can sum up your outer life or inner life, such as when your thoughts are chaotic or frantic. See: *Tornado*.

On the other hand, a blizzard can signify a period of inactivity. Generally, people stay indoors during a blizzard. They're "snowed in." See: *Winter*.

See also: *Blind, Depression, Ice, Storm, Tornado, White, Winter*

Blood—Blood is life, and many metaphors and analogies can be created with it. Such as blood drained or spilled symbolizing drained energy or vitality. It's a graphic depiction of exhaustion.

Blood spilled can symbolize conflict and wounding, used to describe external situations in life, or internal situations. It implies violence, and violence is not only physical but also emotional and psychological. You bear the stripes of your battles—with yourself, with life, with the world and people in it. See: *Fight, Wound*.

Causing blood to flow can indicate knowledge that you are adding to someone's pain. For example, when breaking up, or firing someone.

It can show the harm you've done through something you said or did, or express fear of causing harm.

Seeing someone bleed can mean that you see inside the person. You see the essence.

Blood shared or transfused can symbolize a deep bond between people, "blood brothers." A blood transfusion can symbolize a source of energy or renewal. Giving blood to someone shows you are willing to sacrifice and share everything you have.

Blood is another word for close family and friends. See: *Family, Friend*.

Blood is associated with the heart, and the heart is associated with love and passion. See: *Heart*.

Blood is red, and red is a color of love and also aggression and anger. See: *Red*.

Squirting blood can be a sign of emotional distress.

Emotional abuse and self-destructive behaviors can be symbolized as blood flowing.

Blood on the walls or collected in puddles can symbolize the aftermath of a terrible conflict. Alternately, it can show that great effort has been put forth. You spill your blood in the name of a cause, task, or duty.

Vomiting blood can symbolize the need to get something harmful out of you; for example, hatred or negativity. See: *Vomit*.

A bloodstain can symbolize shame or guilt. Blood on the hands is a classic symbol of guilt.

See also: *Guilt*

Women are known to dream about blood when menstruating or pregnant. Blood is associated with childbirth, and birth can symbolize the emergence of something new in yourself or your life. It's messy but worth it in the end. See: *Childbirth, Menstruation*.

Blood can symbolize something that causes fear or panic. Some people deeply fear seeing blood and react to it with dread. Dreams can use that personal association to compare with something else that's feared, such as failure or conflict. See: *Fear*.

On the other hand, calmly reacting to the sight of blood in a dream can mean you're cool under fire. You know how to react in an emergency. Or you subconsciously know the blood has a good association, such as when it symbolizes love or kin.

With so many possibilities to consider, it is especially important to view blood within the context of the dream-story, how it connects with other details, and how you react to it—especially your feelings about it.

See also: *Anger, Body, Childbirth, Family, Fear, Fight, Friend, Guilt, Heart, Love, Menstruation, Opponent, Red, Vampire, Vomit, Wound*

Blow Job—See: *Fellatio*

Blue—The color blue brings to mind deep thoughts, personal reflection, and sometimes melancholy or depression, described as "feeling blue" or a "blue mood."

Blue has strong associations with mood and emotion, with thought and insight, and with tranquility and contentment.

It's associated with harmony and can be used in dreams to show the need for harmony in yourself, your life, and your relationships. And harmony is associated with trust.

When associated with water, especially the ocean, blue can symbolize clarity and depth, as in depth of character, insight, or knowledge. See: *Ocean.*

Blue water can be associated with feminine qualities like fertility and mastery of subtlety and mood.

It has strong associations with certain emotions, usually the more tranquil and serene ones. See: *Water.*

Blue can combine with other symbolism. Blue skies can symbolize farsightedness, combining blue's connection with insight together with the open sky's association with ability to see great distances. Blue clothes can indicate depression or tranquility because clothes can be associated with an impression given off. A blue room can symbolize mental coldness because ice can appear blue and a room can symbolize your mind.

Blue, like all colors, can appear anywhere in a dream, and it's there purposefully.

Blue is the color representation of the fifth chakra, an energy center in the throat associated with articulation and self-expression.

See also: *Chakras, Clothing, Colors, Depression, Emotions, Home, Ocean, Water*

Boa Constrictor—See: *Snake*

Boat—Think of a boat in a dream as you, and the movement of it as your life. Where do you go, what shape is the boat in, and what type is it—cruise ship, yacht, rowboat, sailboat, fishing trawler? Is it casually crossing the water, or racing like a speedboat—struggling in a storm, or sitting unused—shiny and new, or weathered and taking on water? Any of these details can be used by a dream to create symbolism. And the ultimate question is, What does the boat say about you?

For example, a yacht struggling in a storm can symbolize trouble with your finances, perhaps from spending on unneeded luxuries. A leaky boat is picture of difficulty with emotions or finances. Rowing a boat in unison is the image of harmony.

A man dreams about being on a beach next to an old church. Giants tear down the church and use the materials to build a ship. By the end of the dream, it's ready to sail, symbolizing how his old religious life is being torn down but pieces of it are fitting together to form a new spirituality that will carry him away on a long personal journey. It's a clever use of symbolism and a deeply meaningful dream.

The uses of a boat to create symbolism vary widely. A common use is as an analogy for your conscious mind. Your conscious mind sits atop the vastness of the unconscious mind like a boat on an ocean. The conscious mind is small in comparison to the unconscious. Most of the mind is "below the waterline," meaning outside of conscious control and awareness. See: *Ocean.*

Boats are vessels for exploration, so exploring with a boat is a heck of a metaphor for self-exploration. It's a theme known to arise in the dreams of people doing deep inner work such as through therapy, meditation, and dream analysis. They go into uncharted territory, down within themselves. The same dream imagery can be used to symbolize exploration of a subject or idea.

A boat can represent the psyche. Both are structures that sit atop something larger.

Together with water, a common symbol for emotions, boats are used by dreams to create symbolism through comparison. For example, a boat tossed around in an angry sea can symbolize internal forces rocking your thoughts and emotions, or something else that "rocks the boat." A boat sinking can mean "going under," overwhelmed by emotions. A calm sea is a metaphor for serenity, while a stormy sea is a metaphor for stormy emotions and situations. See: *Psyche, Water.*

Boats go to destinations, and that association can be used to create a story about where you are headed in life and where you want to be—particularly if a destination is part of the dream-story. Boats generally take longer to reach destinations than other modes of transportation such as planes, so they're a good dream symbol for heading toward a long-term goal, such as graduation, starting a family, or retirement. See: *Embark, Journey.*

A boat can be used to create a comparison for the direction you're headed in life and how you navigate changes as you go through phases. Are the waters calm or choppy, shallow or deep? Are you steering, or along for the ride? Do you hold course, or change direction? Are other people on the boat with you? These details can tell you the intent and message of the dream.

Reaching a new shore or crossing a river can indicate a new phase of life reached or an obstacle overcome. See: *River.*

A boat traveling through murky water can indicate pessimism or uncertainty.

A boat threatened with tipping can symbolize something threatening to upend your life.

A boat without a captain suggests lack of leadership or authority. See: *Captain.*

A speedboat can symbolize the desire to reach destinations and goals quickly, or a love of thrills.

A canoe or kayak can indicate an independent spirit because these water craft are often used individually. See: *Kayak.*

A sailboat can symbolize being driven by intellect and mental pursuits, because wind can be a symbol for thoughts, and a sail catches the wind to propel a boat across the water. It can mean "wind in my sails."

See also: *Backward, Beach, Captain, Crash, Embark, Emotions, Fishing, Float, Flood, Journey, Kayak, Left, Ocean, Passenger, Psyche, Right, River, Storm, Tidal Wave, Unconscious Mind, Vacation, Water*

Body—Parts of the body such as the head and feet have specific symbolism. Look them up individually—a list is provided at the bottom. This entry will give possibilities for overall symbolism.

Since you live in your body and get nightly updates about its health and status via dreams, you dream frequently about it, usually shown through symbolism such as a home, other structure, or vehicle. See: *Building, Bus, Car, Home, Tree.*

For example, a man dreams that he's in the home of a famous baseball pitcher, who has been fixing up the place and is patching up the ceiling. The dreamer offers to do it. It's a way of saying he knows his body isn't what it used to be—like during his baseball days—and he's willing to take the steps to "patch it up." The ceiling that needs patching represents his head. That's where the game is really won.

Sometimes the connection between the body and health is rather obvious, such as in dream imagery featuring a hospital bed, an autopsy, getting examined by a doctor, or getting an X-ray. People sometimes have vivid dreams with this imagery when an illness is developing or their health is on their mind, and after spending time in medical facilities. See: *Dissect, Doctor, Hospital, Illness, X-ray.*

Parts of the body can be symbolized, such as a fishbowl representing a bladder or kidney, windows representing the eyes, or branches representing the arms. See: *Skyscraper, Tree.*

A dead body can symbolize detachment—especially detachment from the physical condition and needs of the body. It can express a fear of what will happen if you allow your health to deteriorate.

It can express the idea of being dead inside, or exhausted. This use of the symbolism is particularly likely if you see yourself dead in a dream. See: *Zombie.*

A dead body can mean that something about yourself is receding back into your mind, or a time of life is over. You are changing—out with the old and in with the new. This use of the symbolism is quite common in the dreams of people who resist change or hold onto something for too long. See: *Death.*

In many dreams about seeing the dead body of someone close to you, the meaning is found in the fact that the relationship is changing. The person portrayed as dead is "dead to you" in the sense of no longer as important in your life, or no longer as emotionally connected to you. It's very important to see beyond the imagery of death and recognize it as symbolism.

A dead body can mean something is figuratively killing you inside. Any sort of tense situation that's close to the breaking point can spark dreams featuring corpses.

A dead body or bodies can signify that old parts of yourself are passing away, or it's time to change. People who make big changes in themselves are known to dream about dead bodies, representing parts of themselves no longer needed or wanted.

For example, a woman dreams about being forced at gunpoint to fly a plane. She manages to do it, lands on an alien planet, and sees dead bodies stacked around her, killed by aliens, but is not bothered by the sight. The dream shows the big changes in her life. She forces these changes on herself by thinking about the consequences of inaction, symbolized as being forced to fly at gunpoint. The aliens and alien planet symbolize being in a foreign place in her life. The dead bodies symbolize her old ways as a self-described "couch potato." That part of herself is gone, and her nonchalant reaction to seeing the bodies indicates it's a welcome change.

The symbolism of a dormant body can be like that of coma, shut down inside, or unable to express yourself. See: *Coma*.

A sleeping body can reflect the fact that as you dream, you are asleep, so the imagery reflects your physical state. Or it can be a way of saying you are "sleeping through life." See: *Sleep*.

Wounds to the body are a physical representation of a personal situation, often tied to how you feel: damaged, battered, sore. It's particularly common to dream about wounding to the body after going through a rough patch. Just how rough it was and how you feel about it are shown in the severity of the wounds. See: *Wound*.

A shriveled body can indicate declining health or shrinking prosperity.

A decomposing body can symbolize a dead situation, or something dwelled on too long. Time to move on. This use of the symbolism is common after close relationships end. Or it can mean putting something off for too long, perhaps allowing an opportunity to pass by.

Disposing of a body can mean you want to forget something, you're done with it. Or you're hiding your feelings and emotions. It can reflect feeling disrespected, unrecognized, or discarded. See: *Hide*.

Burying or hiding a body can symbolize trying to hide or cover up something, such as a secret. Or you feel guilty or ashamed. You want to hide something about yourself or cover up your actions or behaviors. Think of the phrase "where the bodies are buried" and how it's used as symbolism. The bodies are things you want to hide. See: *Bury*.

Stretch the idea of hiding or covering up. Hiding a body can mean you hide *your* body because of embarrassment. Or you have a weakness you want to conceal. Or you don't want to acknowledge something about yourself because your ego wants to keep its illusions.

Covering a body can symbolize choosing to ignore someone or something. For example, covering the body of your father can symbolize choosing to ignore his rules. For an example dream, see: *Casino*.

If you dream about a pain in your body it can be caused by pain experienced while asleep. Oftentimes it's translated into symbolism, such as when a stabbing pain in your back is dreamed about as being stabbed or shot in the back. You can even continue to feel it the next day as a sort of nerve memory. Tells you how believable your dreams are.

See also: *Amputate, Ankle, Anus, Arm, Attic, Basement, Beauty, Birds, Bite, Blood, Breast, Break, Building, Bury, Bus, Cage, Callus, Calves, Cancer, Car, Casino, Clean, Coma, Cry, Death, Deformed, Disease, Dissect, Doctor, Ears, Egg, Elbow, Elderly, Excrement, Eyes, Face, Finger, Feet, Graveyard, Hair, Hand, Head, Heart, Hide, Home, Hospital, Illness, Invasion, Jail, Knee, Leg, Lips, Mouth, Neck, Nose, Ovaries, Pain, Paralysis, Parasite, Penis, Pregnant, Skin, Skyscraper,*

Sleep, Stomach, Teeth, Testicles, Toilet, Tree, Ugly, Uterus, Vagina, Weak, Wound, X-ray

Bomb—In simplest terms, a bomb is something that explodes or has potential for exploding. That association has many possibilities for use as symbolism.

A bomb exploding can symbolize an explosive situation, anger, or conflict. You're under too much pressure, your desires are ignored, your emotions are repressed. Whatever the bomb symbolizes, it's likely to be something powerful and sudden. That's a heck of a way of describing an explosive argument, especially when a bomb makes a loud noise.

An explosion can symbolize a sudden outburst of emotion. When a person explodes, she loses her temper or lashes out. See: *Anger.*

A nuclear bomb exploding can be a more extreme version of the same idea. It's strong symbolism to describe an especially powerful outburst or explosion. Dreams exaggerate, so a situation symbolized as a nuclear bomb might be relatively minor, but the imagery somehow captures the nuances, especially the feelings and emotions. See: *Nuclear War, Rage.*

Situations are described as explosive when volatile ingredients mix. It's the holidays and relatives who intensely dislike each other are going to be under the same roof. Now add alcohol and watch the fireworks.

A man dreams about blowing up his former human resource director's house with a bomb after an incident where he subjected the person to an angry tirade. He "went off" like a bomb and regretted it later.

An explosion in a dream can symbolize a sudden change, and it's probably a change for the worse. Think of times when you might say, "It was like a bomb went off." A new supervisor takes over at work and makes radical changes. A partner suddenly ends the relationship. A sibling announces marriage plans to someone the family doesn't like. You drop out of college or quit your job, and boom! Everything changes.

News and unexpected changes can hit you like a bomb. A layoff notice at work. A loved one is dying. A promotion is denied.

A bomb can symbolize fear regarding a specific situation, often arising out of frustration at being unable to change or control something. Anything associated with fear can be used to symbolize it. Of course, when a bomb symbolizes something you fear, you'll feel fear during the dream.

A bomb can symbolize potential for peril and trouble, something bad about to happen.

Diabetes is a sort of bomb that can wipe out health or even cause death. A failing marriage can be a sort of bomb waiting to go off. Mounting tension can threaten to erupt into something worse.

A ticking bomb in a dream can indicate time is running out. A deadline is approaching. Actions need to be taken. Things can't go on the way they are. A situation has potential for peril or conflict. For example, the rent is due and you don't have the money.

A person described as a "ticking bomb" has deeply rooted emotional issues that threaten to erupt. This is especially the case with repressed emotions, unhealed trauma, and rage.

Throwing bombs can symbolize making explosive statements or provocative comments, especially when the person making them is heedless of the consequences.

Defusing a bomb can symbolize defusing anger or handling a delicate situation. That use of the symbolism extends to dream scenarios where people act very carefully for fear of setting off a bomb. It can symbolize delicacy around someone who has an unpredictable or violent temper.

See also: *Airplane, Anger, Destruction, Disaster, Erupt, Fear, Fireworks, Hate, Nuclear War, Rage, Rocket, Terrorist, Volcano, War*

Bone—See: *Break.*

Book—The symbolism of a book in a dream can connect with its associations with knowledge and information. When seeking answers, you might dream about finding them in a book or library.

The symbolism depends largely on the type of book. A textbook in a dream suggests information related to academics or subjects of study. Students who study before bed are particularly likely to have the imagery carry over into their dreams. A leather-bound tome, on the other hand, might contain important information about your destiny and innermost being.

A central purpose of dreaming is to assimilate new experience and information, like adding chapters to a book. The analogy fits on many levels, creating myriad possibilities for symbolism connected with the story of your life.

Oftentimes, the content of a book parallels your inner life. It puts into words what's on your mind or heart, even identifies and explains your most private thoughts, feelings, and desires. What you read about yourself in a book can be a direct message from your unconscious mind, especially regarding possibilities for the future, and if it excites you, it's a strong suggestion to move in that direction. You truly can be the person described in the book.

It's important to see the parallels between yourself and what you read in a book. A story right out of myth or legend might seem far removed from your life in the twenty-first century, but there could be parallels. See: *Archetypes*.

Identify the title of the book, if possible. It can summarize the subject of the dream and help with the interpretation.

Difficulty reading a book can relate to difficulties, issues, or problems that are not easily solved. Books in dreams are notoriously hard to read. One theory holds that the part of the mind used for reading is inactive while dreaming. Being unable to read a book or a clock is common. It's not universal, though, so it's possible to read while dreaming. Keep in mind that the information or knowledge in the book is already known to you. What you're really doing is reminding yourself what you already know.

Children's books in dreams can symbolize memories from childhood, or a wish to return to simpler times, to escape from reality, or to make life more exciting with adventure and challenge. What do you miss about childhood? Does the dream have any other references to it?

Recollections of the past are not confined to children's books. In general, books in dreams relate to learning from and recording your experiences. In this sense, your dreams are a sort of illustrated diary.

An open book can mean that you are open to new ideas, or that you have nothing to hide. You are an "open book." It can be a way of saying that you have ready access to the information you need to make good decisions and find answers.

See also: *Archetypes, Author, Library, Numbers, School*

Border—A border is a barrier and can symbolize something hindering you or in your way. A line you should not cross.

Or a line you do cross, such as when you enter a new phase of life. Age eighteen, for example, is considered the age of adulthood in some countries, and when approaching that age a person is said to be "on the border" of adulthood. A line is crossed the day you turn eighteen, or graduate from college, get married, start your first job, become a parent, or retire.

When a border symbolizes something hindering you, the dream will have supporting details such as a closed border crossing, a fence, or guards blocking the way.

Paying to cross a border can symbolize investing personal resources such as time and energy, or making a personal sacrifice. For example, to get married you give up single life. Of course, paying to cross a border can symbolize investment of money, too, such as paying the cost of tuition to get the education you need to cross into the next phase of life.

"On the border" can mean you are torn or divided about a decision, or on the verge of deciding, similar to the phrase "on the fence." It can mean "close," especially to a personal destination.

Borders divide and separate and can symbolize things that divide people from each other: race, ethnicity, education level, income, religion. With that use of the symbolism, a border in a dream is likely to show the division or separation. You are on one side, and whatever you are divided from is on the other side. See: *Fence*.

A border can indicate a wish to go in a new direction, or the need to make big changes. The changes might be geographical—you want or need to move to a new location, perhaps even to a new country—but big changes can be made in yourself too, such as starting a new career, reshaping your body, or creating a new persona. It can mean you need challenge or adventure.

Borders are associated with foreign countries, and in dream language that can translate to being in a foreign place in your life. You feel different, things are a bit off. You feel movement inside yourself but aren't sure where you're headed.

See also: *Bridge, Fence, Journey, Fence, Foreign, Trespassing, Wall*

Boss—Dreams create symbolism by making comparisons, and to dream that you are the boss can symbolize being in charge. You call the shots. Or the duty or responsibility falls on you. You make things happen.

You can be the boss at home, in your social groups, or just in your general personality. A phrase such as "boss of the family" shows how informal roles are described as being the boss. The boss has the authority and respect.

The meaning of dreaming that someone is your boss depends in part on questions like, Do you really have a boss, and is that person depicted as the boss in the dream? Does someone act like a boss? Is the boss completely fictional, like an actor playing the part? Is the boss present in the scene, or just someone you sense nearby, someone aware of what you're doing, influencing your actions and behaviors from afar?

When the answer is yes to the last question, a boss can symbolize what dictates or influences your decisions, such as rules, laws, and customs. Something that affects what you do and how you think and feel without being physically present. The same can be said of instructions from a parent and anything you're told to do or not do.

The boss is whatever rules your head, the dominant parts of your psyche, or addictions, compulsions, fears, and obsessions that say do this

or do that, and you obey. The boss of your head is supposed to be the ego, but when the ego abdicates its authority, other parts rule. See: *Ego, Shadow.*

When you actually have a boss, it's common to dream about that person. Many personal dynamics come into play, from issues with authority to desire to please. Archetypal patterns that emerge in you from a young age will play out in your relationship with your boss, and how you react to the person might have less to do with the person and more to do with the role he or she plays.

Your boss is an authority figure, and your first authority figures are your parents, then your teachers and coaches, and other authority figures. These connections open great possibilities for creating symbolism through comparison and use of surrogate-characters. For example, you argue with your boss, then dream about arguing with your father, revealing the roots of your conflict with your boss. Or your boss denies your request to take vacation and you dream about a police officer towing away your boat.

Any authority figure in a dream can symbolize your boss.

Dreaming about taking over your boss's job can mean you want to be the person in authority. You think you can do a better job. Or you have authority issues, or won't let anyone be the boss of you.

Dreaming about your boss driving your car can mean the person controls your life—at least, your work life—or is in control of your future, where you're headed. It can mean that the person takes credit for your progress. Dreaming about driving your boss's car can symbolize doing that person's job, or being the person in charge—at work or otherwise. See: *Car.*

Dreaming about your boss firing you can reflect fear that your job is in jeopardy. See: *Dismissal.*

Look closely at recent interactions with the person. Most of the time, dreams reflect these interactions and focus on the underlying dynamics, such as how you feel about the person and the work.

Anyone able to tell you what to do, or who acts like a boss, can be symbolized as your boss.

A boss-character that's just some seemingly random person, not someone you know, is likely to be a projection of something about yourself related to being the boss in any sense of the word. Or the character can symbolize an authority structure.

Dreams are known to use surrogates, especially when subjects are too close to home, so a boss-character that appears random can actually represent someone you know. For example, your boss acts like a heartless tyrant and your emotions are too charged to dream directly about the person, so your dreams use Mr. Burns from *The Simpsons* to play the role, or Donald Trump.

Common surrogate-characters for bosses include lions and elephants, and authority figures such as parents, police officers, principals, and coaches.

A vivid example of the use of a surrogate comes from a dream about walking into a building where the floor is a pool of dark water, and lurking in the water is a crocodile. The dreamer walks out of the building and encounters steps leading up into the air, seemingly to nowhere. The crocodile is a surrogate for the dreamer's boss. The dreamer recently discovered the hard way that her boss will turn on her in a heartbeat. The steps are the dream's suggestion to "take steps" to protect herself.

To dream about your former boss can indicate that connections with people at your old job are fading. Or you're presently in a situation or circumstance that reminds you of the past. You face similar challenges, requiring similar boss qualities.

Expand on the ideas to include similar emotional or personal situations. Such as: you dream about a past boss because your present work environment is just as dysfunctional, or alternately, just as well organized. Your present circumstances are just as restrictive, or alternately, the situation presents similar opportunities. Dreams have endless ways of connecting the past with the present.

You can dream about your former boss after moving up into a similar position of authority. Was it a good move, or the worst you ever made? Can you learn from that person's example?

Running or hiding from your boss can indicate that you need to tone it down at work. Or you have something you want to hide, such as poor performance. Hiding from your boss can be a physical representation of figuratively hiding by not answering emails, or making excuses to skip out on work.

See also: *Archetypes, Coach, Co-Worker, Dismissal, Job, Parents, Police Officer, Principal*

Bottomless Pit—See: *Abyss*

Bowel Movement—See: *Toilet*

Boxing—The first possibility to consider when you dream about boxing is it represents fighting or struggling with something, or conflict between sides of yourself, with someone in your life, or with a situation. It's a physical representation of a personal situation. For example, fighting against insecurity. Or fighting with yourself over wanting to leave your job to pursue something else, while another side of you prefers financial security. In the action of boxing you see yourself defending against something.

Taking a beating while boxing can graphically express feelings, especially feeling battered and bruised. Damage to the face can symbolize damage to reputation, persona, or self-image. The face is the most identifiable feature of a person, closely associated with persona and self-image. See: *Beat, Face, Persona*.

Boxing can symbolize sparring or contending with something, such as final exams or bureaucracy.

Boxing in a dream can refer to self-defense. Think beyond physical self-defense to consider also how you protect yourself emotionally and psychologically, or spar verbally. This use of the symbolism is likely to show in the action of defending yourself from punches. For a great example, see the boxing-related dream detailed in the entry for *Donald Trump*.

Having your punches blocked can symbolize something that's frustrating you or blocking you from getting what you want. The same imagery can symbolize inability to "get through" to someone, or harsh words that don't appear to affect the person at whom they're directed.

Jabbing can symbolize verbal sparring, tentative steps, or feeling out a situation.

Dodging a punch can symbolize avoiding personal attacks, or dodging a person or task. It can symbolize internal dynamics, such as avoiding certain thoughts or memories, especially ones that have an impact on you like a punch.

A knockout can symbolize the idea in the phrases "knocked out the project," meaning did it perfectly, and "knocked me off my feet," meaning stunned by charm, attractiveness, or sparkling performance. A knockout in a dream accompanied by a period of unconsciousness can symbolize taking a hard personal blow, or lack of awareness of what's happening, similar to the idea in the phrase "sleeping through life." See: *Sleep*.

Boxing without gloves can symbolize the phrase "the gloves come off." It's time to get serious.

The possibilities go on and on. The key is to think creatively and make connections between the symbolism and you.

See also: *Body, Beat, Donald Trump, Face, Fist, Games, Sleep, Sports, Wound*

Boy—Begin with the basic fact that a boy is a child. A child in your dream, male or female, can symbolize your "inner child" and its needs for play, fun, challenge, security, guidance, attention, recognition, and structure—any or all of them. Doesn't matter how old you are, your inner child is always part of you and never stops having needs. Difference is, at some point you become your own parent.

This use of symbolism is especially likely if the child expresses a need, or the need is obvious. For example, you dream you find a lost boy and help him find his parents. Unless it's an analogy for helping someone in your life find his or her way, you can bet you are helping the needs of something childlike about yourself, probably related to guidance. Parents acts as guides, so finding parents can mean finding capabilities in yourself to be your own parent and take care of your own needs. See: *Child*.

A boy is more likely to symbolize the inner child of a male, but it's not a hard-and-fast rule. Females can dream about an inner child figure as a boy because it's better at capturing the truth. For example, she's a "tomboy" or likes to play rough.

A boy in the dream of a male or female can symbolize underdeveloped masculine characteristics. Think along the lines of traditional traits such as self-reliance, aggression, rough-housing, curiosity about how things are built, taking the lead, hyperactivity, impulsiveness, aloofness, tenderness, strength, and sensitivity.

A boy can symbolize something innocent about you or someone you know. See: *Innocent*.

He can symbolize an uncomplicated way of viewing the world. Children don't do well with adult shades of gray. They need yes or no, do or don't, right or wrong. Gray situations as an adult can exasperate your inner children and spark dreams about boyish acting out or unruliness. Such behavior can be a way of getting your attention. Something in you or your life needs your attention and isn't getting it.

A word synonymous with boy is "immature," and immature doesn't just describe behavior, but also development. A boy can symbolize something needing development, or something with potential for growth. For example, a project can be described as immature while it's in the first stages of development.

You can see something childlike in someone you know and dream about it as a boy. For example, a woman dreams that her boyfriend has a young, well-behaved son and they go everywhere together. He doesn't actually have a son, so it must be symbolism. The son represents the boy she sees in the man. He has a boyish smile and shows boyish enthusiasm for some activities and subjects. It's an integral part of him, symbolized in the detail about going everything with his son. And it's something she likes about him, represented as the boy's good behavior.

Read the entry for *Girl* to explore the same ideas from a different perspective, and read: *Man*.

See also: *Child, Girl, Man, Son, Teenager*

Boyfriend—A dream about your boyfriend can connect with some aspect of your relationship— the good, the bad, the ugly. Romantic relationships affect people deeply and will be the subject of dreams. However, avoid the common trap of automatically assuming the dream-character represents the person. Usually, it doesn't.

Of course, you can dream about having a boyfriend when in reality you don't have one. It has to be symbolism, perhaps for something that makes you happy or excited, or something to which you're committed. It can be a way of characterizing a relationship with a male friend. Your feelings for the dream-character will connect with how you feel about something in your life and provide a trail of clues to follow.

You can dream about the dark side of a boyfriend relationship, too, so again, go by how you feel about the boyfriend in the dream. For example, dreaming that you are bound to an abusive boyfriend can symbolize being bound to a job or person that makes you miserable. After being abused by a boyfriend, it's common to dream about being back together with your ex, unable to get away. It shows how you're still bound to the relationship inside yourself. See: *Ex*.

A dream about a boyfriend can be a sort of dress rehearsal for finding one and thinking through what you want and what you'll do when you get him. People can get very specific images in mind of what they want in a boyfriend and exclude other possibilities, then dream about a man who doesn't look at all like what they expect, yet he still intrigues them. For example, instead of tall, dark, and handsome, the man in your dream is kind of short and redheaded, but boy, does he light your fire!

Be careful, though, because parts of yourself personify as dream-characters and are made attractive to promote internal bonding, or the characters represent something attractive to you in another sense of the word. See: *Animus, Beauty*.

For people with a boyfriend, cheating is a commonly reported dream theme—him cheating, or cheating on him. These dreams can result from fears that it will happen again because it happened in the past, or from suspicion that he really is cheating. Oftentimes, though, cheating is symbolism. See: *Cheat*.

Another common dream theme is that you break up with your boyfriend. That can express fears that he's going to find something undesirable about you, or it can relate to other fears and insecurities. You fear you aren't good enough for him. You can't compete with rivals. Or you are doing something that will drive him away, like being overly dependent or suspicious.

You can recognize that a breakup is inevitable. Perhaps something is amiss, and you have no future together, and you just know the end is near for whatever reason. Receiving balloons from your boyfriend is a strong sign that a breakup is inevitable, or that the relationship is kept aloft by false hope. See: *Balloon*.

Dreaming about your boyfriend hurting you physically can relate to his hurting you for real, but probably not physically, or even advertently or consciously. Instead, he might hurt you emotionally or psychologically. He might not be doing anything at all; the hurt stems from your reaction to something he *doesn't* do.

For example, maybe it hurts you to know that he doesn't think you're the prettiest girl in the world, or he's not an animal lover like you are, or he has different aspirations for the future.

If he acts like a jerk in your dreams, but that's not how he really is, it can be an exaggeration of little annoyances or complaints you have about him. It's also possible that you're seeing the way you act in the relationship projected onto a dream-character. What you actually see in the character's behavior is yourself and how *you* act toward *him*.

Dreaming about not being able to find your boyfriend can mean that an emotional or personal connection is missing. Maybe you feel that he is holding back something from the relationship, or part of his mind is elsewhere. Or maybe you are holding back, or your mind is elsewhere. It's very important to remember that your boyfriend in a dream is a character, an actor playing a role. The role might be based on how he actually is, or it might not.

Dreaming about being unable to reach your boyfriend on the phone can indicate communication issues. In some way you aren't "reaching him." You express yourself but don't get the result you want, or you aren't able to express yourself the way you want. See: *Phone*.

Dreaming that your boyfriend is arrested can be a way of saying that you want something to stop, such as a behavior or attitude. Might be something as simple as leaving his dirty socks lying around, or something more serious such as driving after drinking. Or something in the relationship needs to stop—or even something in yourself, like stopping needless bickering or complaining. Arrest can express fear that he will be taken away from you. See: *Arrest*.

A dream involving your boyfriend seeing you naked can symbolize seeing past the surface or facade, seeing the real you. It can connect with feelings of exposure or shyness, or with body image or sexuality. It can be a way of saying you know what he really wants. See: *Naked*.

Dreaming that your boyfriend is blind can mean that he doesn't really see you. He doesn't know the person you really are. See: *Blind*.

To dream about wearing your boyfriend's clothes can mean that you wrap yourself in his identity, or your personality is changing to match his, like a chameleon. It provides a sense of security. See: *Clothing*.

Dreaming that you push your boyfriend out of bed can indicate you don't want him in your life anymore, or don't want to be intimate. See: *Bed*.

Driving together in vehicle or flying together in a plane in a dream can symbolize the direction your relationship is headed. See: *Airplane, Car*.

Dreaming about having sex with your boyfriend can connect with your sex life. Sometimes with dreams, what you see is what you get, and you don't have to look any deeper. But sex can symbolize connection on other levels, such as emotional, intellectual, or spiritual. And sex is a creative process, so dreaming about it can mean you are integrating something new into your personality, perhaps showing how his influence is rubbing off on

you. Or you are creating something with your boyfriend—something tangible, such as a baby, or intangible, such as a feeling of connectedness.

See also: *Affair, Airplane, Animus, Arrest, Balloon, Bed, Blind, Boy, Car, Cheat, Clothing, Ex, Girlfriend, Love, Marriage, Naked, Phone, Pregnant, Sex*

Brain—A dream about your brain can be a glimpse into your mental processes. The brain is very active while dreaming. Dreaming is when you integrate new experience and information. The neural pathways are open to being changed. So your brain is going through some powerful processes as you dream, and it's possible to visualize them. See: *Letter*.

Dreaming about a part of your brain being removed: you might be trying to correct a problem in your thinking, to forget something, or to break a neural pathway. A dream about brain surgery suggests that you need to rethink something. See: *Surgery*.

For example, a young man dreams that his friend, a girl he really likes and dated at one point but has agreed just to be friends with, performs brain surgery on him. She disconnects one part of his brain, then rearranges another part, symbolizing disconnecting from the idea of having a romantic relationship with her, and rearranging how he thinks about her.

The brain is associated with learning, but think beyond academic learning to consider what you learn from life. The dream might suggest that you look closely at the basis of your convictions and ideals, why you have them, what they spring from, and how they serve or benefit you. Also consider the demands and expectations you put on yourself, especially those related to intellect.

See also: *Body, Head, Left, Letter, Psychologist, Right, Surgery*

Brakes—See: *Car*

Branch—See: *Tree*

Break—Breaking something in a dream can symbolize stress or frustration, which are common sources of dreams about teeth breaking. See: *Teeth*.

It can mean you are ready to go in a new direction, break with the past or with someone in your life—a "clean break."

A break can mean that a change is being forced on you, either because of external circumstances or internal ones. For example, breaking off a relationship or engagement.

It can mean you "take a break."

Or you are financially strapped—"broke." See: *Wallet*.

A break can symbolize loss or injury, or infirmity. See: *Elderly, Illness*.

It can mean progress has stopped.

It can be a wordplay for "brake." See: *Car*.

Breaking a bone can symbolize a major setback or a major break in a relationship. It can symbolize loss of support, since bones are used to support the body. Look up parts of the body associated with the broken bone, collected together under the entry for *Body*, and see the entry for *Amputate*.

A fragile object such as glass breaking can mean that you need to handle something more delicately, or that someone or something is delicate. For example, a glass dragon in one woman's dream symbolizes her mother, who is both fragile (glass) and fierce (a dragon).

See also: *Body, Car, Dissect, Elderly, Illness, Teeth, Tree, Wallet, X-ray*

Break-in—See: *Burglary*

Breast—Female breasts are associated with fertility and nourishment, since breasts are a source of nourishment for babies.

They're associated with desire to have a baby, especially if the act of breastfeeding is involved. You will probably be able to connect how you feel about the baby in the dream with how you feel about being a parent. For some women, ability and willingness to breastfeed is a hurdle to overcome before feeling comfortable about having a baby.

Breastfeeding a baby in a dream can symbolize nourishing a young or undeveloped part of yourself. It can mean you are giving yourself the basics to be healthy and happy, to grow and develop. These dreams are often accompanied by positive feelings.

Breastfeeding can mean that you give of yourself in ways that nourish people. You are a source of mental, emotional, or spiritual nourishment. These dreams can be accompanied by imagery of milk coming from your breasts, and this meaning of the symbolism is likely if a man dreams about having breasts and breastfeeding.

Breastfeeding is classically associated with a wish to return to a state of infantile dependence, especially if you are shown breastfeeding in the dream. It shows a desire to be mothered, to be taken care of in every way. This is especially true in dreams about your mother's breasts, or seeing yourself like a baby at a woman's breast.

A man who is primary caretaker for children can dream about having breasts as a way of symbolizing his role of mother for those children.

Alternately, breasts on a man in a dream can symbolize self-consciousness. He isn't comfortable with his masculinity. Or he has been led to believe he doesn't measure up to other men. He's a "girly man." His reaction to dreaming about having female breasts reveals the symbolism. If welcome, it can mean he is comfortable with his feminine side or with a role of caretaker. If unwelcome, it shows inner conflict.

Resting on the breasts of another person can symbolize closeness and connection.

In a sexual context, breasts can symbolize something desired, something alluring, captivating, or attention-getting.

A man dreaming about very large breasts might indicate sexual obsession. His sexuality has too much power over him, or something about his sexuality is out of kilter, disproportionate. Or he has a great need to be mothered.

A female dreaming about having very large breasts can symbolize overreliance on sexual allure to get what she wants. Or, alternately, she's confident in her identity as a woman. Breasts are closely associated with female identity.

For men and women alike, dreaming about large breasts can symbolize material success. The symbolism arises from the association between ample breasts and abundance, and between breasts and the basics of life.

Breasts in the dreams of females raises many possibilities for symbolism based on their personal experience. It can express concern that their breasts are too small or too big. Or that men are more interested in their breasts than in their personality or character. They can symbolize something that gets in the way or makes them feel awkward. For young females, it can be a sign of entering puberty.

Showing breasts or cleavage can be a way of getting what you want or attracting attention.

See also: *Baby, Body, Cancer, Child, Pregnant*

Bride—Begin with the fact that most dream-characters represent something about you. They're projections. Unless the dream is literal, such as if you really are getting married or thinking about what you want in a bride or your marriage, the bride in your dream is likely to represent something about yourself. And if that's the case, consider what it means to "marry" yourself.

It means "unite." Or bond. Or commit. Or love. Or integrate. The long-term goal of dreaming is to unite the conscious mind with the unconscious. Your dreaming mind can present an aspect of yourself as a bride in order to facilitate a union or stronger connection. The love you feel for your dream bride is actually love for yourself, or the potential for it. See: *Individuation*.

The end product of a man's successful psychological development is referred to as "marriage of the soul," where his unconscious mind is presented as the ultimate bride. The union of his conscious mind with his unconscious mind makes him truly complete. See: *Anima*.

A bride can symbolize integration of traditionally feminine traits. It can show development of these traits in yourself.

Jesus of the Bible is referred to as the bridegroom, and his followers as his bride. It's a way of expressing the depth of the spiritual relationship and desire for transcendent experience.

The dreaming mind can create clever symbolism from other associations with brides. For example, attraction to a bride can be used symbolically to refer to an attractive idea or prospect. See: *Beauty*.

On the other hand, other associations can come into play, like "bridezilla," and the high costs of a ring and wedding. See: *Wallet, Wedding*.

A bride can be a characterization of a relationship such as a "work wife," a woman who works close-and-personal with you on the job.

Or the partnership can be between aspects of yourself, such as when your intellect teams up with your will, or your heart teams up with your head.

Run with the idea of commitment and it can apply to being committed to a cause or "married to your work." See: *Marriage*.

A bride in a happy dream can symbolize a good union or partnership, including a partnership within you, or just express happy feelings. It can symbolize a wanted pregnancy.

A bride in an unhappy dream can symbolize a bad union. Relations lack harmony. Feelings are sour. It can symbolize an unwanted pregnancy.

Dreaming that your girlfriend is your bride can express a wish to marry her, or reflect thoughts about it. The dream might depict her in that role as a way of testing the water. In this way, a dream is a simulation to help you sort out thoughts and feelings.

Likewise, a female seeing herself in a dream as a bride can express the wish for marriage. She tests the water, either in connection with a current relationship, or just to get comfortable with the idea. See: *Marriage*.

Just before her wedding day, a woman dreams about herself as a bride at the altar, in a chapel packed with friends and family. Suddenly, her ex-boyfriend barges in and declares his intention to rescue her. This dream is helping her realize she doesn't really want to marry the man she is about to marry, and she secretly wishes to be rescued from making a terrible mistake.

Mothers and wives and other very close female figures can be depicted as a bride. In some way it's an accurate portrayal of the mother-child or spousal relationship. See: *Mother.*

See also: *Anima, Fiancé, Groom, Individuation, Marriage, Mother, Sex, Wallet, Wedding, Wife*

Bridegroom—See: *Groom*

Bridge—At its simplest, a bridge is a route over an obstacle. So in dreams, a bridge can symbolize overcoming an obstacle.

A bridge connects two points together, and in dreams that idea can be used to symbolize bringing people together—or bringing yourself together, such as when you connect your values with your actions, or your intellect with your will.

A bridge can symbolize transitioning from one phase or place in life to another. Such as when transitioning from living with family to living on your own, or from single life to married life, or from professional to retired. In this sense, a bridge symbolizes an important juncture in your life, between two points.

For example, a student finishing law school dreams he walks through a city and comes to a raging river. It has a bridge over it that's tricky to cross. He manages it and continues on his journey. The dream uses the bridge to symbolize his transition to professional life as an attorney, and the raging river symbolizes the bar exam. By passing it, he makes the transition. The city symbolizes his public life, tied closely with his choice of career.

Anything that "bridges the gap" can be symbolized as a bridge.

Being across a bridge from someone you know can symbolize a divide between you. A divide might be caused by hurt feelings, difference of opinion, or different backgrounds. Or it might be a matter of opportunity or personal connection.

For example, a man dreams that he sees the woman he's been flirting with on the other side of a bridge. As he tries to reach her, the bridge crumbles. It's a way of depicting that no matter how he tries, he can't get her interest. He's more attracted to her than she is to him.

See also: *Border, River, Road, Water*

Brother—To see your brother in a dream can connect with some aspect of your relationship with him. This is more likely to be the case if you have had recent contact, or he's been on your mind. It's possible that you're observing something about him.

Since most dream-characters represent something about you, your brother can represent something you see in yourself that you also see in him. For example, if you are impatient and so is he, in your dream he might represent your impatience. If you two quarrel, he can represent your quarrelsome side, or act as a reminder of a recent quarrel with someone else. Or something about him is used as symbolism. For example, he has children and you have been talking about it with your spouse, so in your dream he's used to symbolize the idea of starting a family.

A surrogate can be used to represent your brother. Dreams use surrogates to create personal distance from the subject matter and avoid being obvious. For instance, after an argument with a brother, a dream might use a surrogate to represent him. The surrogate could be any male character, but usually there's some way of connecting the surrogate with the actual person.

The surrogate could be a male relative, friend, co-worker, or someone from the same occupation or school. You can tell by the emotions and feelings the character sparks in you, similarity in behavior and appearance, and how you react. For example, your brother is deployed in the military, and you dream about seeing a seemingly random soldier and running up to hug him and welcome him home. You react that way because you subconsciously know who the soldier represents.

If you don't have a brother and dream you do, the character can represent something about yourself you're not aware of or don't recognize. Something that isn't accepted about you, or that you don't accept about yourself.

For example, a young man dreams that he has a long-lost brother visiting from a psychiatric hospital, and he's put in charge of showing him around. The brother acts a little slow and quirky, but he's actually pretty cool in the dreamer's eyes, and he's happy to take his bro to a party and introduce him to friends.

The brother symbolizes the dreamer's slowness and quirkiness, which cause him to be labeled as a head case, symbolized by the detail about the psychiatric hospital. It's something the dreamer doesn't like about himself, so it's depicted at a distance, as a long-lost brother.

If the dream said, "the brother is really you," he might react differently and not so readily accept the brother-character. But instead, by creating personal distance, the dreamer is given the opportunity to react from his true feelings. And it shows that he can accept and like himself the way he is.

For another example, see: *Kanye West.*

A younger brother in a dream can refer to an immature aspect of oneself, or something that comes second, such as time for sex coming second to caring for the kids, or a house rule that games can't be played until after homework is done. Your dreams can pull in references from anywhere to create symbolism. They don't care how far they have to reach.

An older brother can symbolize a mature aspect of oneself, or the desire for a wise counselor. It might symbolize something that protects you, such as how sarcasm can protect you from getting close with people.

An arm or branch of a tree can symbolize a brother. See: *Arm, Tree.*

A brother can be something related to you in the broader sense, such as how people perceive you in terms of your occupation. Your occupation is connected with you, but is not necessarily who you really are.

A brother is a close male friend or buddy, someone who stands at your side, especially in times of need. In a dream, a brother can connect with the need or desire for a close companion, or someone to lend you an ear.

A brother can be a spiritual brother.

A "bro" is a jock/frat-guy type who comes on too strong, but isn't smart enough to know better.

Most of what's written in the entry for *Sister* also applies to a brother-character in a dream. Go check it out.

See also: *Arm, Childhood Home, Family, Friend, Incest, Sister, Tree*

Bruise—See: *Wound*

Buck—A healthy buck in a dream is an image of virility and masculine strength.

It can symbolize being headstrong.

It can be a pun on the phrase "buck a trend," or on the dollar, known as a buck.

Actions with a buck's antlers can have specific symbolism. See: *Antlers.*

See also: *Animals, Antlers*

Buddha—To see the Buddha or a Buddha-like figure in your dreams can symbolize inner peace, compassion, or wisdom—any common or personal association with Buddha or Buddhism. It can symbolize a philosophical frame of mind.

Buddha is one of a pantheon of spiritual figures that appear in dreams for the same purpose as a *psychopomp,* or guide of souls. It shows your potential. You might not find Enlightenment like the Buddha and go down in history, but you can be more patient and compassionate and Buddha-like in your own way.

The entry for *Jesus* goes into more detail about characters of this type.

See also: *All-Seeing Eye, Fat, God, Jesus, Lotus, Love, Mohammed, Unconscious Mind*

Buffalo—A buffalo in a dream can symbolize strength and power. It can symbolize ability to move forward forcefully, or endure hardship.

It can be a pun on the word "buffaloed," which means intimidated, manipulated, fooled, or baffled.

See also: *Animals*

Bug—A bug in your dream can symbolize something "bugging" you, meaning you're annoyed or irritated by something small. See: *Little.*

Or you have anxieties or fears related to bugs and your dreams use the imagery to connect with other sources of anxiety and fear. See: *Anxiety, Fear*.

Some dreams show you what you're scared of to give you an opportunity to overcome the fear. Dreams about being covered in bugs can be like shock therapy, an all-or-nothing attempt to overcome the fear. The same imagery is a heck of a way of symbolizing phobias and anxiety attacks.

Since bugs can be associated with pestilence and disease, they can symbolize bad influence or negativity.

They can symbolize feelings of guilt and shame. See: *Guilt*.

A cloud of bugs around your head can symbolize a cloud of dark or irritating thoughts.

Bugs can symbolize a low state of living, a slovenly or emotionally decrepit state. See: *Roach*.

A woman dreams about going over to her best friend's house. The friend appears at the front door and the dreamer sees an infestation of bugs inside the home. They symbolize the friend's emotional and personal difficulties. The friend didn't reveal how bad things really are, but the dreamer subconsciously picks up on it.

A bug in your ear can symbolize hearing something that bothers you. Rumors, gossip, and other sorts of intrigue are especially apt to be symbolized by a bug crawling on you or in your ear, the organ you use for hearing.

Alternatively, a bug in your ear can symbolize a suggestion or comment that sticks in your mind.

Bugs can symbolize a viral or bacterial infection in the body. See: *Parasite*.

It's a versatile dream symbol, especially when you consider the many possibilities for symbolism based on your personal experience and associations with bugs.

See also: *Ant, Anxiety, Bee, Butterfly, Disease, Ears, Illness, Infest, Insects, Little, Parasite, Roach, Worm*

Building—To decode the symbolism of a building, begin with analogies, metaphors and wordplay. A person can be described as tall as a skyscraper or built strong like a brick house. An idea can be built upon. Self-esteem and confidence are built up. Marriages, families, faith, and confidence are built. Dreams can use a building as a physical representation for the verb "to build." What are you building in the personal sense? See: *Construction*.

Parts of a building are used in analogies, such as "strong foundation" and "roof over your head." Comparison is the heart of analogy, and buildings can be used in myriad ways to make comparisons.

The type of building in a dream says a lot, too. What purpose does a type of building serve? For example, a shopping mall has many shopping choices, so the symbolism can mean choosing among options. A home-improvement store can mean making personal improvements, such as improving your body or mind. A school building or library can relate to learning.

Areas of a building can symbolize areas of your body, such as a basement representing your instincts or emotions, or a top floor or roof representing your head or thoughts. Floors of buildings can symbolize ages and times of life, such as the sixteenth floor symbolizing your sixteenth year. See: *Basement*.

Much can be said symbolically about your body through the condition of a building. For example, opaque or broken windows can represent poor sight. Plumbing problems can refer to the urinary system or sex organs. A crumbling building can symbolize poor health.

Then again, broken windows can symbolize loss of opportunity (a "window of opportunity"), and a crumbling building can symbolize a belief structure coming down.

Damage to a building, especially to the façade, can indicate damage to self-image or reputation.

A building in ruins can be a graphic representation of a life in ruins, or part of it in ruins, such as after a divorce or other personal disaster.

New additions to a building and newly built buildings can symbolize new aspects of yourself, or additions to your life. For example, a newly built school can symbolize expansion of your knowledge or scope of learning. Having a child is an addition to the family and can be symbolized as an addition to your home.

The height of a building can be used to create symbolism. For example, low or high expectations or opinions can be symbolized as a low or high building. See: *Giant, Little*.

A city full of buildings can symbolize the public sphere of life and a search for opportunities in your career. The symbolism is built on the idea that cities are where the best jobs and the most people are found. See: *City*.

A fallen building can symbolize big changes in yourself or your life, such as in values, morals, and ideals.

Buildings that remind you of a time of life can refer to that time. See: *Childhood Home*.

Scaling a building can symbolize reaching for your ambitions, but ask yourself whether there is an easier way. Perhaps taking the elevator would be better. See: *Climb*.

An empty building can symbolize feeling empty. See: *Empty*.

The symbolism of a building can be derived from its shape. See: *Shapes*.

See also: *Arena, Asylum, Attic, Basement, Body, Castle, Childhood Home, Church, City, Climb, Construction, Destruction, Disaster, Elevator, Empty, Family Home, Fence, Fire, Home, Library, Mall, Movie, Neighbor, Numbers, Pyramid, Restaurant, Shapes, Shop, Skyscraper, Stage*

Bull—A bull is often associated with focused fury and head-on attacks, and with strength and power.

Bulls are used in figures of speech that create symbolism, such as "ride the bull," about trying to stay on top of something powerful. "Grab the bull by the horns" means seize an opportunity.

Bulls are stubborn, and people can be "bull-headed." A "bull market" describes a prolonged rise in stock prices. "Gored" is a term used to describe being viciously attacked. See: *Attack*.

In some cultures, bulls are associated with luxury and wealth.

Bulls are territorial and can be used in dreams to symbolize being in dangerous or protected territory, or protecting turf. See: *Border*.

Bulls are virile and associated with aggressive sexuality. See: *Penis*.

A dream about being a matador can symbolize toying with something dangerous, inviting trouble, or taking risks in return for glory and recognition.

Finally, the bull is associated with the sign of Taurus, and in your dreams it might symbolize someone you know who is born under that sign.

See also: *Animals, Attack, Border, Money, Penis, Venus*

Bullet—A bullet in a dream can symbolize the ammunition to win an argument or get your way. See: *Ammunition*.

A bullet fired from a gun can symbolize directing anger or wrath. A bullet fired at you can symbolize anger, aggression, or derogatory remarks directed at you.

It can symbolize "popping off at the mouth."

Alternately, firing a bullet at a target can symbolize accuracy and the idea in the phrase "hitting the mark." See: *Gun*.

Because a bullet fired is loud, it can symbolize heated words and loud arguments. Heated words are aimed at people. See: *Fight*.

A bullet fired can symbolize an explosive situation or condition. See: *Bomb*.

An unfired bullet can symbolize a *potentially* explosive situation or condition. For example, a person's temper can be "hair-trigger" and can "go off" any moment. An illness that can suddenly spread is potentially explosive. Expand the idea and a bullet can symbolize unused potential or energy.

Being struck by a bullet can symbolize anything that hurts: disappointment, betrayal, insults, shame, guilt, fear, hurtful words, and so on.

It can symbolize a sudden sharp pain felt while sleeping, or a physical or psychological wound.

A bullet whizzing past you can have symbolism related to its speed, something "fast as a bullet." It might symbolize how fast your life is going by. Or "rapid-fire speech." Or something "over your head." The same imagery can symbolize a near-miss. You "dodge a bullet."

Personal experience and associations with bullets and guns can come into play to create symbolism. A key to understanding it is your feelings. Does it make you feel scared, powerful, lucky, hurt, angry, dangerous, accurate?

See also: *Ammunition, Armor, Body, Bomb, Fight, Gun, Machine Gun, Rocket, Speed*

Bully—Dreaming about acting like a bully can symbolize the need to dominate conversations or situations, to be in control or impose your will. In an exaggerated way, the image fits.

A bully can be the image of anger, rage, or even weakness. A common assumption is that bullies act that way because they compensate for feelings of weakness. See: *Coward*.

The bully is actually trying to be a hero, someone with courage. See: *Hero*.

In archetypal psychology, the bully is understood as a shadow manifestation of the Warrior archetype. The bully covers over feelings of cowardice and lack of power and is actually an immature attempt to be a Warrior in the truest sense. See: *Archetypes, Warrior*.

Bullying can symbolize being at the mercy of more aggressive people. Situations with bullies are usually uncontrolled and can symbolize lacking control over a situation or yourself. No authority will intervene.

Dreams can create scenarios that trigger certain feelings. For example, you can dream about being humiliated by a bully, and it corresponds with a recent experience of feeling humiliated by failing a test or being rejected.

Dramatic dreams about being tortured or humiliated can connect with the experience of being bullied and are known to crop up even decades after the fact. It's a sign that something is trying to work through your system. Bullying is torture for the people who endure the worst of it. See: *Torture*.

For example, an adult woman dreams she's cornered by the high school bullies who used to make her life miserable, and is forced to perform fellatio on a henchman. The dream is designed to help her heal from the experience by realizing what's keeping her holding on to it. For the full story, see: *Revenge*.

See also: *Archetypes, Attack, Beat, Bite, Chase, Coward, Escape, Fight, Fist, Hero, Hide, Lion, Opponent, Rape, Revenge, Ugly, Warrior*

Bum—See: *Beggar*

Burglary—A burglary in a dream suggests that something of value is, or could be taken from you. It might be something material, but it's more likely to be a physical representation of losing something else: energy, time, respect, motivation. It *feels* like a crime to lose them.

The first question to ask is, what are you taking from yourself? You rob yourself by failing to live up to your own expectations, or by breaking commitments or promises—including commitments and promises to yourself.

When you are helpless to prevent some sort of personal loss, a burglary or burglar is a great way to represent it. For example, the romantic rival who swoops in and starts dating the person you are interested in is a sort of burglar. The real loss, though, is in your self-respect or confidence.

Burglars are stealthy and often target homes, key reasons why a dream might use a burglar over some other sort of criminal. The dream deliberately chooses a burglar for that role in the dream-story. The next question is, why? Working backward can lead to the meaning.

A burglary is a violation of your personal space, so in a dream a burglary can symbolize violation of your space or your person. Something's out of place or missing. Privacy is compromised.

A burglary can symbolize something done behind your back, a betrayal.

A man dreams about being on the second floor of his house, watching burglars come in through his back door and go out with valuable items. It's a recurring dream theme that always ends with his feeling powerless to stop the burglars. The burglars represent the stealthy demands on his time and energy, the things that always seem to pop up when and where he least expects it. And coming in and out through the back door symbolizes the back-door ways the man leaves himself open to more demands. He feels powerless to stop it.

The dream uses burglars instead of a single burglar because he has multiple demands, not just one.

See also: *Accomplice, Bandit, Crime, Escape, Hide, Home, Intruder, Invasion, Mask, Thief*

Burn—See: *Fire*

Bury—To bury something in a dream can mean you want it out of sight, out of mind. You can bury grudges, feelings, memories, the past, and so on.

To bury means to conceal, and to conceal can mean to hide actions, involvement, true opinion, or feelings. For example, someone blabbing on their phone says something bad about a friend, then tries to pretend it wasn't them after word gets around. They then dream about burying their phone to symbolize the desire to hide the truth. See: *Hide.*

A young man has recurring dreams about burying pretty women in his closet. They're like dolls, open-eyed and lifeless. He panics when he realizes the bodies can't be hidden and he'll be caught. Burying the bodies symbolizes hiding his masturbation habit, including the physical evidence. And they're doll-like because they're creations of his fantasies and serve no other purpose than to help him get off.

Dreams can go many directions with the symbolism of burial. For example, burying a carton of cigarettes can symbolize desire to be free of a smoking habit, or efforts to conceal it. Burying someone you know can mean wanting to be free of the relationship or the person, or to hide something from them.

To bury can mean "put behind you." Time to move on. Disagreements, relationships, and times of life are all things put behind you in the figurative sense and symbolized through the action of burying.

A person can "bury" themselves beneath heavy layers of clothing to hide their body, then dream about it as burying a body.

To see yourself dead and buried in a dream can be a good sign. Contrary to the common misconception that it's a sign of imminent death, it can mean that something about yourself or a time of life is coming to an end, and it might be what you need.

To bury can mean to avoid, such as when avoiding something painful or unwanted, or avoiding the truth.

It can mean "buried by work." Too much to do. This meaning of the symbolism is more likely if a character is buried alive or drowns.

Burying something in a cemetery can mean something is laid to rest, such as a disagreement. It can mean wanting to be free of whatever it symbolizes. For example, dreaming about burying parents can symbolize wanting to be free of their control or influence. See: *Graveyard.*

See also: *Body, Coffin, Closet, Death, Emotions, Funeral, Ghost, Graveyard, Hide, Masturbate*

Bus—A bus is a form of group transportation, so it can symbolize group projects, situations, and endeavors. You are figuratively going the same direction as the other passengers. You're all in the same boat, the same bus. See: *Passenger.*

For example, a man who freelances as a graphic designer dreams that he sees other freelancers on a bus that passes him by without picking him up. It symbolizes the perception that other freelancers he knows are getting plenty of work, but he's hardly getting any. He feels passed over.

Riding a bus with passengers can symbolize your inner life. The passengers are projections from your inner world. They can symbolize what you bring together internally for a purpose, such as to do your job: intellect, skill, will, motivation. They all brought together to go the same direction in your life.

Riding alone on a bus can symbolize feeling like you aren't understood, or are alone in an endeavor or path in life.

The bus driver can symbolize the leader of an organization or group. For example, a pastor is a leader of a flock of believers. A coach is the leader of a team. They figuratively drive the bus that carries the flock or team. The idea extends to leadership in your psyche. Your ego is usually the driver, but not always. Plus, different parts of the psyche can get in the driver's seat depending on the situation and need. See: *Ego, Psyche.*

A bus on fire can symbolize that a group project or endeavor is figuratively going up in flames.

A bus that lumbers, or that is especially large, can symbolize being overweight, or struggling with too much figurative weight, such as the weight of expectation. See: *Fat.*

Because buses are associated with public transportation, they can have related symbolism. For example, being hit by a city bus can symbolize a public dispute.

Riding on a bus can symbolize being on someone else's schedule. And because the bus is usually driven by someone else, it can symbolize lacking control of the direction of your life or something about it, such as your love life.

The potential for symbolism expands if you actually ride a bus. Consider recent experiences on the bus, why you ride it, your impressions, and whom you regularly encounter. For example, if you ride the bus because you lost your driver's license, consider why it happened and how it affects your life.

Being unable to leave a bus station can mean you feel trapped or hopeless. See: *Beggar, Jail.*

As a place of transition between destinations, a bus station can symbolize a transition in your life. See: *Airport, Apartment.*

When interpreting the symbolism of a bus, consider who is on the bus with you, where it is going, and how you feel about the direction and pace of travel.

See also: *Airport, Apartment, Beggar, Boat, Cage, Car, City, Crash, Ego, Fat, Fire, Jail, Passenger*

Butler—Dreaming about a butler can indicate overreliance on other people for support. It can mean "unable to attend to one's own needs." For example, mom and dad still pay the bills for an adult child.

See also: *Janitor, Servant*

Butterfly—A butterfly in your dream can symbolize lightness of being, or leaving a small but important imprint on your environment.

It can symbolize transformation, inspiration, and tranquility, or metamorphosis. See: *Cocoon.*

Because butterflies fly and are easily moved by wind and air, they can symbolize whimsical thoughts and daydreams. See: *Air, Fly.*

A butterfly landing on you can be a sign that your unconscious mind approves of something, probably related to personal development or service to others, same as a butterfly is a servant of nature. It can symbolize that you can be trusted with delicate things.

For example, a young woman dreams that a butterfly lands on her and remains for several minutes. It then flies away, leaving her with a feeling that it's a message. With that in mind she thinks of associations with butterflies and the first word that comes to mind is "delicate." The next thought that comes to mind is the memory of an incident where she dropped and severely injured her sister's baby. It left the dreamer with the feeling that she couldn't be trusted with anything delicate, like a baby, but the dream is saying she learned her lesson.

A butterfly can symbolize being "flighty," venturing here and there, never landing anywhere for long, especially among social groups. A "social butterfly."

See also: *Air, Bird, Cocoon, Fly, Insects, Little*

Cadaver—See: *Body*

Caduceus—See: *Snake*

Caesarean Section—Any action in a dream is potentially a physical representation of a personal situation, and a C-section in a dream can indicate need for help getting something out, especially something creative, since children are creations. You can't give birth to it by yourself. Portraying the situation as a C-section is exaggerated but fitting.

It can symbolize unclogging your thoughts or emotions, or expressing something that's bottled up.

It can connect with fear of childbirth doing harm to the body. This possibility for meaning comes up more in the dreams of women who have given birth and had trouble with it, have had C-sections, or are young and want to keep their bodies pristine. But it can be used as symbolism for anything done to preserve your body or health or youth.

The symbolism can connect with aging, fertility, child-rearing, or health concerns.

It can symbolize being forced into doing something you don't want to do. Some women would rather deliver their babies naturally, but circumstances force them to have the surgery. That creates an association that connects with any circumstance involving obligation, coercion, or pressure. Such as

when you feel obligated to attend an event, especially a baby-related one such as a baby shower

See also: *Abortion, Childbirth, Pregnant*

Cafeteria—See: *Restaurant*

Cage—A cage is the picture of restraint, restriction, and confinement. It's a representation of being unable to live the way you want or make your own decisions, or being forced to behave or act in ways that feel unnatural. A relationship, job, living situation, or way of thinking can be confining. See: *Jail*.

A cage can symbolize ways you restrict, control, or limit yourself. Rules restrict and control. Morals limit. A promise means you will or won't do something.

A cage can symbolize keeping yourself under wraps, hiding the full extent of your abilities or your true feelings. Or the past is a hindrance, a barrier to fulfilling potential.

When a dream shows you in a cage, the symbolism is likely to be about you and is not an observation about someone you know. But when a dream puts you into a scene where you observe someone or something in a cage, it's likely that either you're seeing a projection of something about yourself, or an observation about someone you know. Or it's a way of describing a situation.

For example, you dream about a tiger in a cage and feel sorry because it's wasting away. So you analyze yourself for related feelings and perceptions and nothing rings a bell. You ask yourself whether a tiger in a cage is a metaphor to describe someone you know, and again, nothing rings a bell. You ask whether it's a way of describing something you've observed, and you search your recent memory. And ding ding, you remember a documentary you watched about refugee children who spend years in camps and have little education or opportunity. What a waste! Their lives are like cages and they waste away, like the tiger in the cage.

An animal in a cage can symbolize restraint of instincts or drives, particularly the wilder ones. A powerful animal like a lion or bear can symbolize freedom to roam, to make your own decisions, but a powerful animal in a cage carries the opposite idea. A small animal like a gerbil or mouse can symbolize the instinct to make yourself unnoticeable, to avoid scrutiny or danger, but at the expense of personal freedom. A biting animal such as a snake in a cage can symbolize restraining the instinct to strike.

Feeling safe inside a cage can symbolize necessary restriction or feeling protected from whatever is outside of the cage. For example, the schoolkid who stays indoors rather than venturing out and taking the risk of running into neighborhood bullies puts himself into a sort of cage.

See also: *Animals, Bird Cage, Creature, Dungeon, Escape, Fugitive, Hostage, Jail, Monster, Prisoner*

Cake—See: *Candy, Food.*

Calendar—A calendar in a dream can symbolize the passage of time, or connect with looking forward to an event. It can mean something from the past or in the future is on your mind.

A calendar can be a reminder of something important coming up for which you need to prepare, or don't want to forget: an appointment, an anniversary, a birthday.

Along the same lines, a calendar can represent thoughts about where you want to be and what you want to do in the future. You're making plans, consciously or subconsciously.

A calendar can symbolize your schedule. An empty calendar can mean you need something to look forward to, something to do. A full calendar can symbolize feeling like you have too much to do, too many obligations.

Throwing away a calendar can symbolize putting the past behind you.

A new calendar can symbolize looking forward to something in the future. You are ready to make plans and set goals.

See also: *Baggage, Time, Time Travel*

Call—See: *Phone, Talk*

Callus— A callus can symbolize hard work or labor, because that's how one usually develops.

A callus can mean "calloused," meaning hardened by experience, immune to feelings.

A callus over your heart area can symbolize ignoring your feelings, or something restricting your ability to feel.

Callused feet can mean you are well-traveled in a literal or figurative sense.

Callused knees can mean you feel subservient—you spend too much time doing what other people want.

See also: *Body, Emotions, Heart, Pain, Wound*

Calves—To figure out the dream symbolism related to a part of the body like the calves, think about what it does. Calves are used primarily to jump and elevate. Jumping can mean jumping from one situation, position, feeling, or thought to another. Elevating can mean gaining a better view. That association applies to the immediate concerns or obstacles in your life that prevent you from looking ahead into the future, or things about yourself you can't see past. For example, you can't see past your ambition, and your marriage suffers because of it.

See also: *Ankle, Body, Feet, Leg*

Camel—A camel in a dream can symbolize conservation of resources. Camels store water in their bodies, making them good animals for long journeys. In a related way, people store up resources for their journeys through life—especially emotional resources, but also material and personal resources.

In a positive sense, storing emotional resources gives you what you need, such as motivation, patience, and determination. But in another sense it can mean that emotions are held onto instead of released, as in holding onto a grudge or grievance.

A camel can symbolize frugality. You know how to prepare, how to "stretch a dollar" and make the most of limited resources. Frugality cuts both ways, though. Perhaps you need to be more generous—with yourself and with others.

The symbolism of a camel extends to the idea of waiting till later. For example, saving sex for later in a relationship. The desire builds up like water in a camel's back.

Because camels are used for long journeys, they can symbolize preparing for something requiring endurance, or a long journey. It can refer to the personal journey you are on or have completed. It's a ready-made symbol for the journey of life. See: *Journey*.

The camel is a humble animal, and noble. It asks very little in return for its service, and that's a good description of some people. On the other hand, a camel can symbolize someone obedient to a fault.

Because camels are beasts of burden, they can symbolize carrying burdens. Perhaps you have too many responsibilities and duties, too many people to care for, too much crap dumped on you. Or the load you carry can be of a psychological nature: regrets, guilt, notions about yourself, self-image issues. See: *Horse*.

The phrase "straw that broke the camel's back" refers to something about to break down or a situation about to flip.

Camels are known to be docile and easy to manage if treated well, but when treated badly they become ill-tempered and stubborn. People can be the same way. Because of the bellowing sounds camels make, they can be associated with grumpiness or complaints.

See also: *Animals, Desert, Embark, Horse, Journey*

Camera—A camera in a dream can be used to show point of view or perception, such as how you view yourself, your life, people, events, and situations.

A view through a camera, or a camera-eye view, can symbolize how you view the story told by the dream and how it impacts you personally. For example, a third-person point of view is a strong indicator of observing something that doesn't directly involve you, such as when you dream about the life of someone you know. Then again, it can be a way of creating some personal distance from a subject about which you feel strongly, so the dream can continue without ego interference.

First-person point of view through your own eyes, on the other hand, shows immersion in the story, something that directly affects you. Keep in mind, this is only a rule of thumb. Dreams are infinitely clever with how they construct stories.

A camera can relate to focus and clarity. Or take the idea of focus in another direction and it can mean personal focus, such as focusing on small details or avoiding distraction. A wider point of view can mean "the big picture."

A camera can symbolize memory, the recording of events in your outer life and inner life. The symbolism can convey much information about how you perceive your history and what you learned from it.

Dreaming about always being on camera can indicate a *Truman Show* delusion, the belief that your life is constantly being observed, that you're living in the ultimate reality show. It's a form of grandiosity.

Or you might subconsciously detect that you really are being secretly monitored. Spyware and spying devices are all too common. For example, see: *Phone*.

See also: *Actor, Director, Documentary, Movie, Phone, Spotlight, Spy, Stage, Television*

Campus—A campus setting in a dream can relate to learning, knowledge, and intellectual challenge.

It's common to dream about campuses after encountering a difficulty or issue for which you're unprepared. A campus is where you learn and prepare, so naturally it is a good setting for addressing those subjects.

For example, you must give a presentation but lack confidence. You dream about being on campus, maybe in a communications class, and it connects with the challenge of learning new skills related to the challenge you face.

Or you dream you are back on campus and didn't graduate. You forgot to take a course, or you suddenly have an exam to take or paper due. There's so much to do—argh! That can symbolize feeling like you have gaps in your knowledge or preparation. For an example dream, see: *Teacher*.

This theme also tends to arise in the dreams of people who realize they want to change careers. They return to campus in their dreams to think through what they'd rather be doing.

Of course, if you live or work on a campus, your dreams about it are more likely to connect with everyday events and issues.

More possible meanings are tied to a time of life when you lived on a campus, the social aspects of campus life, and perceptions about what it is like. For example, you perceive campus life as all parties and hookups, and here you are with a job and a kid and no social life. On some level you envy people who don't have your obligations. Or you graduated and your life is a daily grind of work and responsibility. You miss the freedom and fun of campus life. How do you inject more fun into your life?

See also: *College, School, Student, Teacher, Teenager, University*

Cancer—People tend to get nervous when they dream about having cancer, thinking it could be true, but like everything else in a dream it's symbolism, probably, and is understood based on personal and general associations. A general association with cancer is it eats at you, literally. It lurks below the threshold of awareness, undetected. It's disturbing and harmful.

Now run with those associations. What's eating at you? What's lurking undetected and harming you? How is cancer an exaggerated way of describing something happening in you or your life?

Stress comes to mind, particularly prolonged stress. It eats at you. The damage it does is often unseen. Repression affects a person similarly, creating pockets of negative energy in the body and mind. Heavy disappointments, personal doubt, and insurmountable problems can eat at you, too.

Think of what is really disturbing you, but maybe you're not aware of the full impact.

Negativity and pessimism are a cancer of the spirit. They sicken from the inside.

People described as being like a cancer infect the people around them.

Cancerous situations grow on you in a bad way. See: *Infect*.

Think of cancer as a flaw. For example, a man dreams that he meets three wise men in robes and asks them who they are:

"Your intellect," answers one.

"Your spirit," answers another.

"Your cancer," answers the third.

The man doesn't have cancer; instead it's a reminder of the flaws in his character and personality. He has further to go to truly be the wise and enlightened person he wants to be. Cancer can seem like a harsh way of expressing the idea, but it's a good reminder that perfection isn't necessary, and that seeking it can actually be harmful. Embrace your flaws.

Cancer can be a general way of saying something is wrong. A situation needs your attention. Or fears are sapping your vitality. Cancer is a huge scare for some people, and just the thought of it brings out all sorts of fears. In that sense, cancer can symbolize anything you fear, but especially fear of illness.

Dreaming about getting treated for cancer is a good sign of finding a solution to whatever is wrong in your life. In a twist on that idea, a mother dreams that she's told her young daughter has cancer and a treatment has been devised. It symbolizes the way a recent family tragedy has affected her daughter. Her husband got badly injured and suddenly money is tight, plus a new baby is taking the mother's time. Mom is taking care of all of them and doesn't have as much time to give to her daughter. But she is thinking of a treatment, meaning the problem has been in the back of her mind and she knows how to address it.

Cancer is a big gun in the symbolism world. Dreams use it over the symbolism of other diseases because of the strength of its associations and specific ways it can be used to tell a story. Plus, it really gets your attention! Cancer is a disease and an illness, so it can have related symbolism. See: *Disease, Illness*.

The body has an early warning system that communicates through dreams. If you dream about cancer, you could have it—people are sometimes told directly that they have it, and it turns out to be true. However, the great majority of dreams about cancer use it as symbolism. Explore this subject further by looking up the work of Wanda Burch and Larry Burk, M.D.

Figuring out which dreams are just symbolism and which are warnings can be tricky, but there is a process. For one, consider the setting. Are you in a hospital or clinic? It's not conclusive, but is more likely to be used as a setting for delivering health news.

Consider the source of the information. Did someone you know who had cancer appear in your dream as a character to deliver the bad news? Or is the character a doctor? It can indicate a health warning, though to be clear, it's far from certain there's anything physically wrong.

Or if there is something wrong, it's not necessarily cancer. It might mean that you are out of sync with your body or not addressing its needs. Address the issue before it gets worse.

Dreams that give serious health warnings tend to be powerful and clear. See: *Precognitive Dream*.

Another possibility is that cancer symbolizes someone born under the sign of Cancer. The dominant traits of that sign are sensitivity, moodiness, and family orientation.

See also: *Disease, Doctor, Hospital, Illness, Precognitive Dream*

Candle—A candle can symbolize your consciousness or anything that illuminates the dark of your mind, or your life, and helps you see the way: your logic, feelings, intuition, beliefs, values, and so on.

Carl Jung had a dream about using a candle to see his way in the dark. Wind whipped at the flame and threatened to blow it out, but he protected it with his hands, knowing the importance of keeping it lit. The dream is about the "light inside," the flame of consciousness, that helped Dr. Jung explore the depths of the mind.

Psychologically, a candle can symbolize self-examination—light is used to see, and "see" in a dream can mean "aware." That idea extends to enlightenment and knowledge and even recognizing your own power. A candle, once lit, powers itself. In many myths, legends, stories, and songs, candles have a special power to bring out the best in people.

Spiritually, a candle sets a tone of reverence and creates a mood of peace, particularly in dream settings such as holy places. See: *Altar*.

A candle can represent death and resurrection, because it can be snuffed and relighted many times. See: *Death*.

Lighting a candle can symbolize the strength or courage to push forward into the unknown.

An unlit candle can symbolize unused potential, or disappointment.

A burnt-out candle, or one close to burnt out, can mean time is running out, or running out of energy or motivation, or declining health, or waning hope. It can mean that you miss someone important to you, especially after they pass away.

A candle burning brightly can symbolize high sex drive or sexual satisfaction. A dim candle can symbolize low sex drive or unmet sexual needs. See: *Sex*.

A bright candle can symbolize a "bright idea" or potent intellect.

Candles on a birthday cake can symbolize transition into a new phase of life. It can refer to childhood and childlike feelings. A multitude of candles can be a recognition of advancing age.

Candles in a circle can symbolize your psyche or the wholeness within you. See: *Circle*.

Candle burn. See: *Fire*.

See also: *Altar, Church, Circle, Death, Fire, Light, Psyche, Temple*

Candy—Candy in a dream can symbolize a forbidden pleasure. Drugs are sometimes called "candy," and candy is associated with something indulged in secret, or forbidden. The idea extends to sex, vices, and temptations, not just drugs.

Like a cake, candy is used as a reward for children and sometimes for adults, and it has possibilities for symbolism related to reward or recognition.

A dream can use candy's associations—weight gain, tooth decay, mood alteration, temptation, personal weakness—as symbolism.

For example, hiding candy can symbolize concealing a habit.

A man dreams about finding a dead man with his pockets stuffed full of candy. It's a graphic expression of fear that his indulgences are going to ruin his health.

Another man dreams about dropping by a convenience mart and seeing doughnuts for sale, and one in particular attracts his eye, covered in powdered sugar, the picture of temptation. He walks past it several times, resisting the temptation, then finally gives in and eats it. He had the dream the night after being offered cocaine at a social gathering. He declined, but the longer the temptation persisted, the weaker his resistance became. Finally, he gave in. White powder on a doughnut, symbolizing the temptation of cocaine. What a dream!

In a different dream, the symbols are reversed. Doing cocaine symbolizes the temptation of a doughnut seen in a store. See: *Cocaine*.

See also: *Cocaine, Drugs, Eat, Food*

Cannibal—See: *Devour, Eaten*

Canoe—See: *Kayak*

Cap—See: *Hat*

Capital Punishment—See: *Execution*

Captain— A captain can symbolize the side of yourself that leads or navigates your life. It knows where you are headed, what you want, and how to steer in that direction.

Captains take charge. They're leaders, they influence. It's not necessarily a formal role. For example, a person who leads a group of friends can be described as the captain. An ego that knows its authority is like a captain.

A captain can symbolize a leader or mentor in your life, anyone who takes charge, guides, or is responsible, especially for safety and reaching destinations.

Consider specific people and experiences that can be used to create symbolism. For example, if you were in the Navy, or have taken journeys on ships such as cruise liners, a ship captain in your dream might connect with those experiences and the impressions gained from them.

A captain in a dream can reference an upcoming journey, and planning and preparation. Journeys include those of the mind and spirit, too. See: *Journey*.

For ideas about the symbolism of a military captain, see: *General*.

The difference between a captain and a pilot can be found in the type of craft commanded. A boat takes longer to reach destinations. Airplanes are fast. Are you in a hurry? See: *Airplane, Boat*.

See also: *Airplane, Boat, Ego, Embark, General, Journey, Pilot*

Captive—See: *Hostage*

Car—Cars have tremendous potential for use as dream symbolism. They transport you to places, and in your life you "go places." A car moves, and your life moves—forward, backward, sideways, in circles, quickly, slowly, not at all. Movement in a car can show you where you're going, where you are, and where you've been in your life. It shows your personal journey, the road you're on, and the people who share in it. See: *Journey, Map*.

Many other subjects can be addressed through the symbolism of cars, but movement, progress, and direction of your life are where to begin decoding it. Further, cars are used in many metaphors, giving dreams a deep well from which to draw.

Dreams create physical representations of personal situations, and what better way of creating a physical representation about the movement of life than with the symbolism of driving in a car or other vehicle.

Unless a car is towed or moves on its own, movement means it is driven, and how it is driven and by whom presents many opportunities for use as symbolism. For example, driving with someone you know can symbolize a relationship, sharing the road of life. The person behind the wheel calls the shots or leads. Driving together is a common theme in the dreams of couples and families.

Driving too fast can symbolize life going too fast or being too busy. You are too busy or have too much to do. This use of the symbolism is often acted out as someone's continuing to press the gas pedal even when the car is already going too fast. The symbolism is found in the action. See: *Speed*.

Driving from the back seat can indicate a need to be in control, as in a "back-seat driver."

Driving without knowing where you're going, or without knowing which direction to go, is an obvious metaphor for not grasping how to do something, or not knowing where you're going personally. In some way you feel lost, either specifically about something, or generally in your life. See: *Lost, Map*.

Driving a fast sports car might symbolize thriving on excitement and pushing the limits, or that you are a "go-getter," "revved up." For example dreams, see: *Colors, Mountain*.

Driving in reverse can symbolize life going the wrong direction, or a setback. You're headed in reverse.

Driving the car of someone you know can mean you are somehow responsible for that person, you

make decisions for her, or she provides the means and material support to move your life forward.

Details about control of the car show control—or lack of it—of yourself, your life, and the situations in it. For example, driving on snow or ice can symbolize no control, bad decision-making, or a slippery situation. The symbolism can show in steering the car. Steering a vehicle or vessel in a dream can symbolize the way you direct your life. It speaks to your ability to control yourself and go in the direction you intend. See: *Ice*.

Driving off the road can mean your life is out of control—or your desires, emotions, thoughts.

Driving off a ledge is a popular metaphor for taking a big dive in your life, a bad turn of events. See: *Cliff*.

Drive means motivation, hunger for success, or just energy. What drives you? See: *Gas*.

Driving a rental car can symbolize a temporary situation, such as a temporary job. Since a car is related to movement and a job is related to progress in life, the symbolism works on two levels.

Spinning your wheels is a way of showing efforts getting you nowhere.

Lack of movement can be symbolism, too. The car in your dream is parked in a garage, broken down, has a flat tire, or you press the gas pedal and nothing happens, for example. That imagery says "going nowhere." You're idle. Waiting for things to happen. Between places in your life. Underutilized. Passed over. Tired. In poor health.

In simplest terms, a car driving on its own means no one is leading. "No one behind the wheel" means no one is calling the shots. Then again, with self-driven cars, the same imagery can symbolize convenience or allowing technology to make your decisions.

A ghost of someone behind the wheel or in the car can symbolize being haunted by the past. Or someone not physically present is influencing decisions. For example, if you dream that the ghost of a deceased grandparent drives your parent's car, it can mean you think your parent is making decisions based on what his or her parent—your grandparent—wants or would want. See: *Ghost*.

People riding with you in a car can symbolize things you are responsible for and people you protect. The riders can symbolize aspects of yourself, even when they look like people you know. For example, your artistic side can be symbolized as an artistic person in the car with you. A scientist in the car can symbolize your logical side.

To dream that you're in the back seat can symbolize feeling like you aren't making your own decisions. You aren't in control, not in the driver's seat. This is a common dream theme for children who feel controlled by their parents—including adult children. You "take a back seat" when someone else monopolizes the limelight or is "out front" of a situation. See: *Passenger*.

Colliding with another car can symbolize a "run-in" with another person. Your paths, personalities, values, or priorities collide or conflict. The severity of the run-in is symbolism for the severity of the situation. For example, bumping into the car driven by a co-worker can symbolize that your schedules conflict. But colliding head-on at high-speed implies a major conflict.

Crashing a car is classic symbolism for suffering a big setback or coming to a sudden end. You can't get to where you want to go in life. See: *Crash*.

Brakes are connected with bringing something to halt and the ability to control the pace of your life. Malfunctioning brakes can mean you can't slow your life down, or a situation needs to slow down and you can't stop it. For example, you rocket headlong into a new romantic relationship and a point comes when you want to slow it down.

A woman dreams about driving 100 mph toward a wall and slamming on the brakes, but they don't work. Her boyfriend in the passenger seat pulls the emergency brake, but they still slam headlong into the wall. She has the dream at a time when her life is going 100 mph and there's nothing she can do to slow down. The wall is a personal breaking point quickly approaching.

A car that won't start can connect with difficulty getting yourself going or motivated. Or you feel powerless in some situation, or just in general.

Similarly, if you run out of gas, you might be out of energy. Filling up a car with gas or plugging it into an electrical outlet it can symbolize recharging your energy. See: *Gas Station*.

Stealing a car can mean hitching a ride on someone's effort or energy. It can mean you don't want to do the legwork. Or you lack confidence in your ability to move your life forward or provide for your material needs. See: *Thief*.

A stolen or lost car can connect with the loss of something important that contributes to your identity, such as a job. Cars are important to most people—major investments—so the loss of whatever is symbolized by the car is likely to be a big one. And it's likely to be a personal loss, not a material one, such as a relationship, prestige, health, youth, opportunity, or reputation. For example, see: *Deceased Loved One*.

Washing your car can symbolize cleaning up your self-image or preparing for something important, like a job interview or date.

Car keys can be a symbol of freedom or starting something new.

Losing car keys can symbolize missing an opportunity. See: *Key*.

Locking your car can symbolize securing yourself in some way. See: *Lock*.

Parking your car can mean you have found a place in your life where you want to stay for a while. For example, you've been dating someone and think the relationship is going to last, and dream about parking in that person's garage. Or if the relationship is not going to last, it can be symbolized as an inability to find a place to park. Getting hired by an employer can be symbolized as parking your car in the company garage. The garage is a structure, and structure can mean "corporate structure" or something similar. If the company collapses, it can be symbolized as the parking garage collapsing.

Parking a car in a garage is a metaphor for intercourse. Also, cars are places where people can have sex, creating many possibilities for sexual references and metaphors.

A car can represent your body, and the actions involving the car can symbolize something related to your body. For example, a car overheating can indicate a need for hydration, or fever. See: *Fever*.

A car that needs fixing implies the need to fix something about you—health, motivation, direction in life.

A woman dreams that she drives through a tunnel to the entrance of an underground parking garage and stops at the gate. The attendant tells her that to go any further she must put hot sauce on her tongue. The dream is a clever metaphor for her reproductive system. The tunnel symbolizes her vagina, and the parking garage symbolizes her uterus. The gate is her cervix, and putting hot sauce on her tongue refers to a loop electrosurgical excision procedure (LEEP) the dreamer had done. It's a procedure to burn off precancerous cells from the cervix. The cervix is soft and wet like the tongue.

Dreaming about a specific car you used to own or drive can be a reference to that time of life, or the symbolism can be based on personal associations with the car. For example, if you once owned a car that was a real headache to maintain, and presently you're in charge of a project and everything with it is going wrong, it's just like your old piece of junk. Or perhaps the car in the dream is pricey and you are in a situation that's costing too much personally.

Beyond symbolism, dreams can warn of mechanical problems with your car. You might have detected something amiss like a pinging in the engine or softness to the brakes, but it didn't register consciously, or you didn't give it attention because you were distracted. Consider possibilities for symbolism, and if nothing rings a bell it might be a good idea to check out the mechanical soundness of your car.

Dreams are known to warn about car crashes just before they happen, and to give information needed to prevent a crash. For example, if you drive a lot in heavy traffic and find yourself getting frustrated or driving aggressively, you might dream about a crash as a way of saying that your driving habits could lead to trouble. Or even if you drive normally and calmly, you might dream about another car crashing because there is something you can do to prevent it. For example, give some extra room for merging traffic. See: *Precognitive Dream*.

See also: *Accident, Backward, Boss, Brakes, Bus, Chase, Colors, Crash, Deceased Loved One, Dead End, Detour, Elderly, Embark, Escape, Fever, Gas, Gas Station, Ghost, Highway, Hospital, Journey, Key, Left, Limousine, Lock, Lost, Map, Mountain, Passenger, Precognitive Dream, Right, Road, Speed, Thief, Truck, Winter*

Carnival—See: *Party*

Carrot—The orange color of the most common type of carrot and its phallic shape make it a symbol of fertility. It is strongly suggestive of sexuality because the green top symbolizes the green growth of the heart's desire, while the orange growth beneath the surface is the other half of the equation: sexual desire.

Take the idea further and a carrot can symbolize any creative process, including the creation and raising of children, or a child with red hair.

To "dangle a carrot" means to tempt or lure.

See also: *Eat, Food, Garden, Orange*

Cartoon—To dream about a cartoon can mean that you find your life to be surreal, especially if the cartoon is outlandish, or the dream presents you as living in a cartoon world. You might be disconnected from reality, or wish to escape it. There might be a message in the dream about taking yourself too seriously, or not seriously enough.

Cartoons can refer to childhood and related subjects such as innocence, simplicity, boredom, and play.

The possibilities for symbolism really expand when you take into account specific cartoons. It's common for people who frequently watch cartoons, or used to watch them, to dream about them. Cartoons are stories, and dreams love to play off stories to create symbolism and talk about what's going on in your life. For example, dreaming about a cartoon that features a hero can symbolize your heroic traits—or lack of them. See: *Hero, Movie*.

Cartoons often use archetypal stories and themes, easily used to create symbolism about the big events in your life and most important movements in your psyche. See: *Archetypes*.

See also: *Archetypes, Child, Hero, Movie, Television, Warrior*

Cash—See: *Money*

Casino—A casino in a dream is commonly associated with taking chances and risks. It's associated with the idea of gambling—gambling with your luck, your life, possible consequences. See: *Gamble*.

For example, a young man dreams that he goes to a casino with his family to see his sister compete in a pageant. Later, his sister calls from the hotel room to say that something is wrong with their father. The dreamer arrives and sees his father lying still and covered with a sheet, as if dead. His father then sits up and starts telling stories about when he was their age.

The dream is about a secret risk the sister is taking that the dreamer knows about. She has started having sex with her boyfriend, and sex before marriage is against the family code. The casino symbolizes the risk of getting caught and sets up the rest of the story. The father is shown covered with a sheet as a way of saying the sister is ignoring his rule of no sex before marriage. And the detail about the father suddenly reviving and telling stories about his youth is based on another secret known to the dreamer. Their father, despite what he preaches, had sex before marriage, too.

A casino can refer to luck and creating your own. See: *Lottery*.

See also: *Gamble, Lottery, Numbers*

Casket—See: *Coffin*

Castle—The saying goes that a man's home is his castle, meaning your home is your domain where you make the rules and defend the boundaries. Based on this idea, your castle in a dream can symbolize a protected space where you rule. A king or queen rules the castle. You rule in your life, your mind, your body.

A castle can be a place of isolation, defended from invaders by tall walls and strong doors. In dreams it can symbolize a defensive mentality. You put up barriers. Perhaps you are emotionally untouchable, or see yourself as separate from or above everybody else. In which case the castle is probably a gloomy and empty place.

On the other hand, a castle can mean you are secure, steady, solid as a rock. It can mean that you have positioned yourself materially or personally in such a way that you can withstand adversity or attack, or you are secure in your personality and interpersonal relations. It suggests power, wealth, prestige, authority, resources, ability.

A castle suggests nobility, high ideals, and high expectations for conduct and morals. On the other hand, interpretation depends on the state of the castle. A castle in ruins could mean low morals or unrighteous living.

A ruined castle can mean your dreams and hopes for your life lie in ruin. You're beaten down, or your world has crumbled around you. Health is worsening—physical, mental, or emotional. Or contradictory feelings or impulses are causing chaos.

A ruined or smoking castle can mean that an authority figure has fallen. The boss was fired. The president was impeached. A burning castle suggests violent overthrow, a coup, or your life or hopes going up in flames. Keep in mind, it's a physical representation.

Spiritually, a castle can symbolize a strong foundation and rock-solid faith. A tower in a castle is associated with knowledge, especially with esoteric and specialized knowledge.

Psychologically, the castle can represent your psyche, and the characters associated with it represent archetypes. Archetypes are psychological blueprints that shape thoughts and behaviors. In dreams they can take form as mythological characters: kings, queens, knights, wizards, sages, heroes, jesters. It shows that no matter what your outer life is like, your inner one always has potential for high drama.

Dreams with mythological themes can be about the quest to find something worthy of devoting your life to a higher cause or power. And at heart, these dreams are about unifying the psyche and finding common cause among its various parts. A strong ego is required to unify the disparate parts, but at the same time the ego itself needs to serve something higher. See: *Archetypes, Individuation, Psyche.*

In simplest terms, a castle is a building. See: *Building.*

See also: *Archetypes, Boss, Building, Hero, Individuation, King, Jester, Library, Magic, Money, Prince, Princess, Psyche, Queen*

Castrate—The testicles are associated with manhood, so when used figuratively, castration can symbolize an attack on manhood. It means "take away a man's strength or maleness," attacking or removing his authority or other traits associated with masculinity, especially aggression or pride.

It can sum up how a man feels when someone attacks his manhood: like his balls have been cut off. What is a man without his testicles? Less than other men. He doesn't have what it takes. See: *Testicles.*

For females, the imagery of being castrated carries the same suggestion. She doesn't have testicles, but figuratively she can have "balls." Castration can symbolize feeling attacked for her masculine traits.

Castration can symbolize emasculation, knowing how to hit a man where it hurts and undermine his authority and confidence. That image can sum up how a man undermines his own masculinity through how he perceives himself and talks to himself. The nagging female voice in his head—a shadow of his anima—emasculates him.

Castrating an animal can symbolize gaining control of animal instincts—especially sexual instincts, cravings, or drives. For example, dreaming about castrating a bull can symbolize taming or stifling sex drive.

The testicles are involved with procreation, so removing them can symbolize stifling creativity or self-expression. It can express fear of sexual impotency, failing to measure up in the bedroom, or decline in strength and virility. It can mean sacrificing the ability to have children.

Spiritually, castration can symbolize giving up sex to devote yourself to spiritual life. The feeling is entirely different from when castration means something more literal.

See also: *Anima, Animals, Bag, Ball, Genitals, Penis, Sex, Testicles*

Cat—A cat is a versatile dream symbol commonly associated with femininity. Cats are "felines," and, female or male, they exhibit traditionally feminine traits such as grace and affection.

Symbolism can be created from typical cat traits such as curiosity, independence, and leisure. For example, dreaming about a cat caught in a door can symbolize catching your curious sister reading your diary. Dreaming about a tomcat that wants to be let out at night can symbolize a mate who'd rather go out and party than stay home and snuggle. Dreaming about a cat napping can symbolize a leisurely approach to life, or taking a break.

Those common associations with cats can be used as symbolism, but your personal associations matter most. What do you associate with cats, and does it fit the narrative of your dream and the behavior of the cats in it?

Cat owners are likely to dream about their cats. It's often connected with something they see in themselves that's reflected in their cat's personality or behavior.

For example, a woman dreams that her cat escapes the house and she tries to retrieve it. It hides from her and requires coaxing to return to the house. The dream could relate to fear that the cat will get out—she's very protective of it—but in this case, the pet cat represents a quality she shares with it: the instinct to run away when feeling unsafe. Her life has been chaotic lately and part of her just wants to run away. Retrieving the cat is a way of saying she's mustering her resolve to face her insecurity.

The cat of someone you know in your dream can refer to that person. In the dream, it's not just your brother's cat, for example, it's your brother, in a sense. A reference to him. It's something about him such as a trait or fact about his life.

Dreaming about your cat getting lost can symbolize losing something about yourself as represented by the cat. For example, lately you haven't been feeling playful or affectionate like your cat.

Dreaming that your cat dies—whether or not you actually have a cat—is likely to be symbolism along the same lines as what it means to lose it, except that the situation is more serious, your feelings stronger. The loss is harder to take. It can mean the loss of a relationship with a female, or loss of a feminine trait or quality.

Cat owners can dream about cats they owned that died. These sometimes-heartbreaking dreams help the healing process by bringing out unprocessed emotions. If the dreams are positive, they can symbolize fond memories. If negative, it can mean something is unresolved. See: *Pet.*

Alternately, the pet you lost can symbolize a more recent loss in your life or in yourself, such as loss of a friend. It can mean something in you is dying. Or you desire to have the close companionship you had with that pet.

Cats have associations with promiscuity, as in the term "cat around." A cat rubbing against you can symbolize flirtation.

Dreams about fighting with a cat can connect with arguments or fights with a female in your life. For example, a young man who recently broke up with his girlfriend dreams repeatedly of cats attacking him out of the blue. It symbolizes the ambush attacks of his bitter ex-girlfriend.

See also: *Animals, Ambush, Bite, Kitten, Leopard, Lion, Pet, Tiger, Vagina*

Catastrophe—See: *Disaster*

Cave—A cave can symbolize a passage into your inner depths, especially if the dream involves exploring a cave or going into one for an initiation or ritual. The cave is your route to finding out who and what you are deep inside yourself. Oftentimes the dream starts off scary, dark, and mysterious, and eventually leads to contact with powerful inner figures—human or animal—once doubt and fear are overcome.

These dreams are journeys into the unconscious mind, which is much vaster and deeper than the conscious mind and can only be understood in terms of comparisons such as an island compared to the ocean. When you venture down into a cave, deep into your unconscious, you encounter fantastic and mythical beings representing your archetypes: See: *Archetypes, Unconscious Mind.*

They can tell you secrets about yourself and life itself. When dreams use caves to symbolize a path into the unconscious, the atmosphere feels charged. If the light source is a candle or torch, it's almost certain to represent your consciousness. See: *Candle.*

On the other hand, a cave can symbolize isolation, withdrawal, or hibernation.

When associated with the body, a cave can symbolize a mouth, throat, womb, or vagina.

In Freudian tradition, caves are often associated with the birth canal and a desire to join with a mother figure. They're interpreted as expressing infantile wishes and desires. While this interpretation fits in some cases, the idea has been oversold.

Throughout human history, caves have been places of protection and safety, and in dreams they can symbolize the place in your mind, or a physical place such as a bedroom, to which you retreat.

They're also places of initiation into the mysteries of life, the soul, and adulthood, making them ready-made symbols for learning and mastering the mysteries of life. For example, a young man or woman dreams about meeting a wise elder in a cave as a way of visualizing finding that capacity within him- or herself. Sometimes, the elder figures will first appear as mature animals.

A dream about living in a cave can depict depression or hopelessness. It's a picture of how you feel. Stepping out of a cave into sunlight can symbolize emerging from a period of depression or isolation.

See also: *Animals, Bat (Mammal), Bear, Candle, Cave, Depression, Mouth, Neck, Unconscious Mind, Uterus, Vagina.*

Celebration—See: *Party*

Celebrity—See: *Famous*

Cell—See: *Jail, Prisoner*

Cellar—See: *Basement*

Cemetery—See: *Graveyard*

Center—See: *Circle, Spiral*

Chakras—A chakra is an energy center in the body. The body has seven chakras, each associated with an endocrine gland, and they perform vital roles related to health, balance, and well-being. The term isn't well known in Western tradition, but in Eastern traditions, especially Hindu and yogic tradition, it's common. Chakras can't be seen, so their existence is largely discounted in traditional Western medicine.

Because chakras are so integral to the functioning of the body, they appear frequently in dreams, especially through the use of color and movements such as opening and closing, and through circular and spiral shapes. But if you don't know what to look for, you won't see it.

This subject gets really deep and we can't do it justice here. It's mentioned to encourage you to explore further. See: *www.chakras.info.*

See also: *Circle, Colors, Spiral, Tornado, Yoga*

Chase—"The chase" is one of the most widely reported dream themes, with a wide variety of possibilities for symbolism. The key to interpreting it is that it's a physical representation of a personal situation.

It's something from your past catching up with you. You can't escape it. Your reputation and history follow you.

It's something you don't want to acknowledge or accept, such as a bad habit you don't want to give up—an especially strong possibility if you dream about being chased by police or other authority figures.

It's something you don't want to accept about yourself. You're really smart and want to escape high expectations. Or you're female with traditionally masculine traits that are hard for you or others to accept. The person you are deep inside wants to be embraced and accepted. What are you running from?

It's something you can't handle.

It's guilt, remorse, shame, regret. See: *Guilt.*

It's fear. See: *Fear.*

It's your emotions. See: *Emotions.*

It's the person you really are. Wherever *you* go, there *you* are.

It's a limit, rule, law, or restraint you want to avoid or escape. For example, just before spring break, a young woman dreams about her father chasing her around the house, and she avoids him. It symbolizes running from his expectations. She has plans to do things while on spring break that he doesn't approve.

Whatever it is, it symbolizes one of the common associations listed here, or a personal association. And remember, it's a projection based on your thoughts, feelings, and perceptions. If it's scary, it's only because it's scary to you subjectively, not necessarily objectively.

Then again, it might be something really scary, such as a bad health problem you're ignoring, or an abusive person you'll do anything to avoid. See: *Bully, Illness.*

The thing chasing you could be something relatively positive, such as an ambition or goal that wants to be fulfilled. Or you have a vision for your life, but for some reason think you can't make it happen. Anything ignored or repressed can take form in dreams as something avoided. Often, when the thing chasing you is confronted, it's not so scary after all.

And the longer it is avoided or ignored, the scarier and more insistent it becomes.

A young man dreams about aimlessly wandering around in a clothing store. He walks near another young man and they bump into each other. The dreamer insults the other man, who responds by chasing the dreamer around the store.

The dream speaks to the dreamer's need to find his place in life. Clothes are associated with identity, so wandering aimlessly around a clothing store suggests aimlessness in life. The other man in the dream is a projection of the dreamer's aimlessness. The insult he hurls at the man is actually how he feels about himself. And the man chases the dreamer because he knows he needs to do something about the situation but isn't doing anything.

Now let's reverse the scenario. What does it mean if you chase something in a dream? Some of the previous ideas apply. You chase your dreams, ambitions, goals. You pursue becoming the person you want to be and having the life you want, or something else you want, such as recognition, fame, sex, and love. You chase after the answers, your desires, your passions.

Chasing can be a physical representation of closing the emotional or psychological distance between you and another person, such as when dating. Chasing shows desire to be closer to the person. See: *Bridge*.

Or you seek something within yourself that's elusive, such as something about yourself that disappeared. For example, your patience disappears after a grueling stretch at work. Or you don't have the same energy you used to have and want it back.

See also: *Animals, Bridge, Escape, Fugitive, Hunt, Monster, Opponent, Prisoner, Run*

Cheat—Cheating in a relationship is a commonly reported dream theme, and if you're in a committed relationship, it can make you wonder what's going on behind your back. Rarely does it indicate actual cheating, though.

Instead, cheating is often related to insecurity. You feel jealous or have insecurities about your desirability or the relationship. See: *Jealous*.

For example, a young man dreams repeatedly about his girlfriend in bed with another guy. In the dream he can't do anything to stop it and some invisible force pushes him out of the room. It's a manifestation of the dreamer's self-esteem issues. He's unemployed and feels like a loser. His girlfriend in bed with another guy shows his fear that someone more financially secure will come along and steal her away. Doesn't matter how much his girl shows her love for him and tells him everything is all right.

Cheating can be used to symbolize any situation that feels unfair, such as a mate's having other priorities or passions than the relationship.

For example, a man dreams recurrently that his wife tells him she's leaving him to date her colleagues at work. She's a surgical nurse and her colleagues are primarily doctors, successful and desirable men. The dream-character based on her (remember, it's a character in a story) calls him while she's out on dates to tell him what a great time she's having, like she's tormenting him.

The dreams are based on the dreamer's feelings about his wife's dedication to her job. As a surgical nurse she works long hours and is frequently on call. The dreamer knows rationally that it's just part of the job, but can't help but feel jealous and insecure. He needs to stop rationalizing and acknowledge how he really feels.

Cheating can be used to describe situations that involve emotional or physical closeness with someone other than your mate, even if that closeness is platonic.

For example, a college-age female dreams recurrently about cheating on her boyfriend, except that there's no sex. She meets interesting guys and they do fun things together like dancing and going on dates. The dreams arise from her interaction with male study partners at school. She is super-dedicated to school and puts in long hours studying, and her best study partners are guys from her classes. Cheating is a way of expressing her inner conflict about feeling close with them, like she's emotionally cheating.

Another college-age female in a long-term relationship dreams repeatedly about having sex with their mutual friends. She is not actually cheating in the relationship, so the assumption is that it must be symbolism. In this case, cheating is an exaggeration of the dreamer's having intimate conversations with the friends depicted in the dream, talking about very personal subjects that she doesn't talk about with her boyfriend. The dream symbolizes the situation as cheating because of the intimacy involved, and the secrecy.

Cheating dreams pop up a lot with people who have been cheated on in a relationship, either a current or former relationship. The theme can also pop up in relationships that are very secure. In some way, the cheating dream expresses how you feel.

Expand the idea of cheating and it can include other definitions of the word related to being unfair or breaking a rule. It's unfair to bring up past transgressions to win an argument. You break a rule by not calling when working late. You cheat at a game or on a diet. Anything you might call "cheating" can be symbolized as cheating on a partner. See: *Cheat (Exam)*.

A young man dreams that he cheats on his girlfriend with his pretty co-worker. He feels compelled to do it, as if he can't help himself. The dreams reflect a situation with his girlfriend. She's jealous of any woman even remotely attractive and demands that he never talk to his pretty co-worker. But he doesn't want to be rude, so he talks with her. The dream portrays the situation as cheating because he knows he's doing something against his girlfriend's wishes, and there will be hell to pay if she finds out. He feels compelled to cheat in the dream because as a character in the story he acts out the symbolism.

Now, consider the obvious. If you dream about your mate cheating, it might be true. A woman dreams that her boyfriend of five years cheats on her while she's asleep next to him. In the morning, she tells him about the dream and he shrugs it off. She can't shake the feeling that something is up, and continues to pry at him because he doesn't seem to care how she feels. Finally, he admits he's been having an affair.

This dream requires no interpretation. The dreamer subconsciously picked up clues and tied them together in the dream, or it was precognition. Just keep in mind that cheating dreams are usually symbolic. See: *Precognitive Dream*.

See also: *Affair, Boyfriend, Cheat (Exam), Escape, Girlfriend, Husband, Precognitive Dream, Wife*

Cheat (Exam)—Cheating on an exam in a dream can relate to behaviors such as cutting corners, lying, or knowingly doing something wrong.

It can relate to feelings like shame, guilt, or inadequacy.

It can mean that you compromise yourself or have observed it in other people. For example, a man who is not actually a police officer dreams that he's dressed in a police uniform, witnesses a crime, and chooses to do nothing about it. The dream stems from an incident the previous day when he took a certification test for his profession and witnessed another test-taker cheating on it. He chose to keep it to himself rather than say anything. The police uniform symbolizes his power to turn in the cheater, if he chose to do so.

Cheating is comparable to related behaviors, thoughts, and feelings. Look closely at your recent life and ask yourself whether you've been taking the easy way out, feeling at a disadvantage, or acting dishonestly, sneakily, or underhandedly—common associations with cheating.

Also, search your feelings for anything comparable to how you feel or would feel when you cheat. Some people might feel guilty about cheating. Others might get the same thrill from cheating as they do from shoplifting or lying. In which case, the symbolism of cheating connects with the thrill of getting away with it.

For some people, cheating violates their ethics. For others, it's simply a way of getting ahead, and they feel no shame or guilt about it.

Cheating can be used to compare with anything that creates an advantage. For example, using steroids as an athlete is cheating because it gives an unfair advantage over other athletes. But to some steroid users, it's perceived as a way of leveling the playing field with other steroid users.

Cheating can show lack of confidence. You feel you can't get ahead doing things the right way.

And finally, cheating on an exam can symbolize cheating in a committed relationship.

See also: *Cheat, Classroom, Student, Teacher, Test*

Chef—Chefs are adept at planning, preparation, leadership, and organization, so to dream about a chef can symbolize those personal qualities. Consider how well you do the job in the dream, and look for what it says about you and your life.

A messy kitchen can mean you need to be better organized. A clean, well-organized kitchen is a sign of being well prepared. Your inner chef is ready to work.

A chef-character is associated with the idea of what you feed yourself, including what you eat, but extend the idea further to include intellectual, emotional, and spiritual nourishment. For example, skills must be practiced (fed) regularly or they will fade (starve). You consume knowledge, information, opinions, entertainment. You are influenced by the people in your life and the quality of your environment. See: *Eat*.

A chef taking out the trash can symbolize removing negativity or getting the garbage out of yourself or your diet.

Cooking can symbolize creativity, so a chef-character can symbolize your creativity—especially the planning and organizational aspects of it. Cooking combines ingredients to create something new. It is inherently creative. See: *Kitchen*.

In fact, cooking is a great metaphor for creativity because they both involve combining ingredients to create something. Creativity combines ideas, abilities, talents, skills. Add motivation and desire—your "inner fire" symbolized as a stove or oven—to persistence, and you have a recipe for creative productivity.

The idea extends to pregnancy because the fetus grows in a warm, enclosed environment and nourishes itself from the resources of its mother. See: *Pregnant*.

A chef-character can symbolize something you are "cooking up." The term is most often used in association with plans and schemes, but has a broad array of possible applications.

See also: *Eat, Food, Kitchen, Oven, Pregnant*

Chew—See: *Teeth*

Chicken—A chicken can symbolize fear, or lacking courage. If someone is chicken, it means she's afraid.

Symbolism can be created from the behavior of chickens and popular associations with them, such as pecking, preening, nesting, foraging, and fighting. The term "pecking order" derives from social hierarchy in chicken flocks, and human flocks have pecking orders, too.

Pecking can symbolize annoyance or irritation.

Preening can symbolize grooming. See: *Mirror*.

Nesting can symbolize creating a safe, comfortable space for yourself—in your life, or inside yourself.

Foraging can symbolize searching, such as for a mate or a date, or scrounging for a buck.

Fighting is self-explanatory, but consider that a fight among chickens might be better described as a squabble. A dream uses the imagery deliberately to say the fight isn't that bad. See: *Fight*.

The symbolism of chickens can connect with the fact that they lay eggs. See: *Egg*.

A chicken with its head cut off is the image of panic and mindless activity. See: *Panic*.

Keep in mind that symbolism often shows in actions and other details, and that's how you narrow down possibilities for the meaning. For example, if a dream shows a chicken but no egg and no nest, it's unlikely to have anything to do with the symbolism of eggs or nests. Symbolism related to irritation will show in the act of pecking and how you react to it. Has someone been pecking at you? What irritates you?

See also: *Animals, Birds, Eat, Egg, Fight, Food, Mirror, Panic, Rooster*

Child—The symbolism of a child in a dream has wide-open possibilities for meaning. You can't just assume, "Oh, it must be my inner child," or, "It means I've been acting childishly." Instead, look at how the child is used in the context of the dream-story and how it fits together with other details.

A child is innocent. It's vulnerable. It's needy. These associations are commonly used to create symbolism. But is the child presented that way in your dream? If not, you're barking up the wrong tree.

For example, a young man dreams that he walks around the campus where he attends college, just like any other day, except a young boy tags along with him. The boy says the most vile, vulgar, psychotic crap imaginable, like he's possessed by a devil. That's not a picture of innocence or vulnerability, or how a child is supposed to act.

It could symbolize corrupted innocence, or his inner child screaming for attention. But in this case, the meaning is found in the dream's "it's just another day on campus" setting. The young man is studying abnormal child psychology. The behavior of the child brings to life the abnormal behaviors he's learning about. The day before the dream, his class discussed the subject and looked at documented cases of severe child abuse. The dream's purpose is to personalize an abstract subject bringing it to life in the character of the demonic boy. The campus setting isn't any campus, it's specifically the campus where the dreamer attends college. That's the clue used to trace the dream back to what he's been studying.

As with all dream-characters, ask what you see projected onto it, especially what you see of yourself. Who or what does it remind you of? In the previous example, the answer is, "The young boy reminds me of the cases of child abuse I've been studying." But in many cases, the child is a variation of "inner child." It's that young part of you that remains beneath the layers of time and maturation, the child in you that never dies, but might hide because it's not welcome in your adult life.

Or it hides because it's wounded and wants to be safe, so it finds a place deep in the psyche where it can watch and wait. People who suffer abuse as children are known to dream about children in extremely graphic and violent situations that, in an exaggerated way, express their feelings. For an example, see: *Basement.*

A wounded inner child can be symbolized as a wounded animal. During the healing process, people are known to dream about caring for wounded animals and coaxing them out of hiding places.

A child in your dream can symbolize how you care for yourself, beginning with physical needs for nourishment and security, and extending to emotional and psychological needs. What you see projected onto the dream-character is something about yourself.

For example, adults whose lives are mundane and dreary are known to dream about unhappy children. Their inner child needs excitement, fun, play—even if it's "adult play," such as a trip to Vegas. The longer the unhappy situation goes on, the more disruptive that part of yourself becomes. An aggrieved inner child might not even be visualized as a child, but instead as a monster or angry adult.

References to childhood in a dream can point out differences between the person you are now and what you imagined you'd be. During childhood we form the first ideas about the sort of adults we want to be and what we want to do with our lives. Those ideas are often pure idealism and eventually bump up against reality. Compromises made along the way can mean becoming someone far different from what you expected. However, part of you remembers and can be symbolized as a child or a reference to your childhood.

Children are associated with hope for the future. In the image of a child, you see possibilities for growth and the life you really want. When you are at least headed in that direction, your dreams can reflect it with scenes featuring happy children. Hopelessness, on the other hand, is torture for the child within you, and it too will show in dreams right out of a horror movie.

A child's stage of development in a dream can indicate the needs and desires symbolized by it. Young children need comfort and assurance. Older children need guidance and attention. Young teens need structure and challenge. Older teens need independence and opportunity. See: *Teenager.*

Because children are creations, they can symbolize creativity or creative endeavors. Creativity is aided by enthusiasm and fresh ideas, something children have in abundance. Childlike sense of wonder and curiosity are traits shared by many highly creative people. See: *Baby.*

A woman dreams about giving birth to three dead fetuses, symbolizing three art projects she started but doesn't have time to finish because she's too busy with her day job. A man who works as a video editor dreams about a guitar morphing into a teenaged daughter, symbolizing a creative side of himself aching to find expression in his life that his job isn't providing. These dreams use children to symbolize the dreamers' needs for creative expression.

A child in a dream can symbolize childlike behavior, qualities, or feelings you observe in yourself or in other people. For example, a dream about a child playing with matches can symbolize taking unnecessary risks or provoking a confrontation. A child handling a snake can symbolize messing around with something potentially dangerous. A child alone on a street can symbolize concern you aren't doing enough for the children in your care. A child playing with something like a toy or musical instrument can symbolize a need for fun.

A child can symbolize an innocent or blameless person, or someone who must be treated gently, such as an Alzheimer patient who has regressed to a childlike state.

Dreaming about a child can symbolize that you feel like you're treated like one. You feel restricted, bossed around, helpless, or vulnerable. Or your sympathy is sparked for someone who is helpless or vulnerable. It can mean that something has aroused your protective, parental instincts.

Parents dream about their children, especially regarding their care, upbringing, health, well-being, and needs. Parents of young children are known to have frequent anxiety dreams about their children, and parents in general will see their concerns for their children reflected in their dreams. For more discussion, see: *Daughter, Kidnap.*

Children can be symbolized as young animals such as bear or lion cubs. Parents will use terms like "my little tiger" to describe their child and not realize that the tiger cub in their dream symbolizes their child. Older animals can symbolize a parent. For example, a mother dreams about a bear mauling her teenaged son—her real son, not a symbolic one—as a graphic portrayal of what her overprotective motherly instincts are doing to him. See: *Bear.*

Even after this long discussion, we've only covered the basics. Explore the entries listed below, especially *Boy, Daughter,* and *Girl*, for more ideas.

See also: *Abortion, Adopt, Anxiety, Attic, Baby, Bear, Boy, Childbirth, Childhood Home, Daughter, Fetus, Girl, Innocent, Kidnap, Miscarriage, Orphan, Pregnant, Rescue, Sex, Son, Teenager, Young*

Childbirth—Childbirth can symbolize the beginning of something new, especially something new in your life or in yourself. In the image of giving birth, you see the emergence of new creativity, new opportunity, new spirituality, new personality traits, new personal qualities, or a new relationship. See: *Baby.*

For example, a man dreams he's in a hospital giving birth, and the doctor is an old friend and the father of the baby. Childbirth in the dream symbolizes the emergence of new qualities in himself, inspired by the old friend. That friend enjoys much success in his life because he's hardworking and disciplined. The dreamer, wanting to be more successful, made himself become more hardworking and disciplined. The friend in the dream represents the qualities the man associates with him—that's why the man is both the father and the doctor. The symbolism is especially obvious because a pregnant man is a huge discrepancy with reality. The immediate assumption is that giving birth in the dream is a metaphor.

Dreaming about giving birth to an animal can symbolize the emergence of that animal's qualities in yourself, especially instinctual qualities such as protecting your young and mating. But consider possibilities for metaphors, too. For example, giving birth to a full-sized bear can mean that something *really big* is working through you, such as a big idea or plan.

Giving birth to a kitten or puppy can symbolize the emergence of playfulness or innocence in yourself. See: *Kitten, Puppy.*

Giving birth to a dead baby can symbolize the phrase "dead on arrival." It can mean that something you started got halted, such as a creative project. See: *Child.*

Dreaming about a premature birth can mean that you don't feel ready for something. Such as when you are thrown into a situation prematurely, or more is expected than you can "deliver." See: *Miscarriage*.

For pregnant women, giving birth in a dream can connect with related thoughts and feelings such as anticipation of the big day and fears about what could go wrong. The dream is like a dress rehearsal. See: *Pregnant*.

In simplest terms, childbirth means "getting something out of you." It could be something creative that you want to get out of you, but childbirth can also mean getting out thoughts, feelings, or emotions. Oftentimes, you have a tremendous sense of relief after the birth. See: *Caesarean Section*.

See also: *Adopt, Baby, Boy, Caesarean Section, Cave, Child, Father, Fetus, Girl, Kitten, Miscarriage, Mother, Pregnant, Puppy*

Childhood Home—Dreaming about your childhood home can be a reminder of where something in your life began. Where a pattern started. The roots of everything you are now in mind, body, and spirit. Thoughts, feelings, perceptions, beliefs, values, principles, morals, personality, character, strengths, weaknesses, and so on.

This is a very important point for understanding dreams. They speak not only to the present, but also to how the present connects with the past. As you dream, new information and experiences are integrated with the existing structure of your psyche, so of course both new information and the old information will be represented.

There's a reason your mind goes back in time. It wants you to understand what underlies your life now, the foundation upon which you are built. Rarely is a dream about your childhood home just reminiscing, though one can be triggered by a recent reminder, such as when you see a home that's similar in appearance to your childhood home.

Situations related to personal and financial security can spark dreams about your childhood home, such as when your living situation is insecure, or you need support and think of your family because they're a source of support. Or just the opposite: maybe they've never been much help to you, and your childhood home sums up all your thoughts and feelings about it in one image.

A root cause of dreams about your childhood home is unhappiness with your life. Your mind goes back to a time when you were happy as a way of showing you what made you happy back then: a sense of belonging; loving and caring people in your life; freedom to explore; stability, simplicity, close interaction. Dreams want you to understand why you are suffering and where the problems started. For a terrific example, see: *Family Home*.

A childhood home can be symbolized indirectly in a way that characterizes what yours was like. For example, an orphanage, haunted house, playground, asylum, neighborhood, school, circus, or zoo.

A childhood home is specific symbolism, but you can still get ideas about it from the entries below. After all, if you start simple, a childhood home is a home, so that's a good place to start understanding the symbolism.

See also: *Adopt, Basement, Child, Family, Family Home, Home, Individuation, Neighbor, Old Friend, Orphan, Psyche*

Chimney—A chimney can symbolize an airway such as the esophagus. For example, a man with sleep apnea has recurring dreams about being stuck upside down in a chimney. It's a fitting way of picturing the feeling that he can't breathe.

Dreaming about someone climbing down a chimney to enter your home can symbolize the feeling of vulnerability. See: *Burglary*.

A chimney with smoke coming out of it can symbolize smoking tobacco. A blackened chimney can symbolize lungs blackened from smoking or other causes.

See also: *Burglary, Fire, Home*

Choke—See: *Strangle*

Church—Dreaming about a church can connect with your spiritual or religious life, but be careful because dreams can use associations with churches to create symbolism that has nothing to do with spiritual or religious life.

For example, dreaming about being in a big church with an important person in your life can symbolize a huge amount of *faith* in that person. Seeing a friend leaving a church without you can symbolize loss of *belief* in the friendship—maybe it isn't the great, unshakable friendship you once believed it was. Bringing a child to a church can symbolize teaching *right from wrong.*

The condition of the church can be a modifier of the symbolism. A church in disrepair can symbolize lack of care or attention to areas of life associated with church: faith or faithfulness, morality, spirituality, community-building, socializing, inner peace. A church that's like a fortress can symbolize a defensive mentality related to beliefs, even if those beliefs have nothing to do with church. *Bigfoot is real, dammit, and no one can tell me otherwise!*

A man dreams about giants deconstructing an old church on a seashore. They use pieces of it to build a boat, and at the end of the dream the boat is ready to launch. It symbolizes using pieces from his experience with traditional religion to build a new belief system that will carry him onward in his spiritual life.

The symbolism of churches can relate to events that commonly happen in them, such as weddings and funeral services. For example, dreaming about a desecrated church altar can connect with finding out your spouse has been cheating on you. The altar is the place where you both swore fidelity. Hearing wedding bells can symbolize the desire to get married, or the feeling that your significant other is about to pop the question.

But as usual, dreams can add unusual twists, so always begin with your associations. What does the church in your dream bring to mind? How does it fit into the story?

See also: *Altar, Angel, Candle, Demon, Devil, God, Heaven, Hell, Pastor, Temple, Wedding*

Circle—A circle completes a line, and a line is associated with time, as in "time line." You complete the line when your child has a child. Your life as a parent comes "full circle." Or you teach a pupil about a subject that's important to you, and it feels as if something about yourself is completed. A process—sometimes lasting many years—is finished.

A circle or sphere can symbolize the complete picture of your life and who you are. It's the picture of unity between the conscious mind and the unconscious mind, a circle within a circle. The inner circle represents the ego, the center of the conscious mind, and the outer circle represents the unconscious mind. The entire image—the circle within a circle—represents the Self, the archetype of the complete personality. Carl Jung calls the process *individuation.* See: *Individuation.*

You are born with this blueprint for growth and development—the Self—embedded in the foundation of your mind, and throughout your life you dream about using it to complete the picture of your psyche, unify the conscious mind with the unconscious mind, and align the ego with the Self. When aligned, the ego sees and acts based on the big picture of who you are and what you can be. See: *Ego, Psyche.*

Most people do not complete the picture or even know it exists. They don't see beyond the ego. For some people, the picture is fragmentary, pieces of a puzzle scattered willy-nilly, and it shows in their life. But any effort in the direction of wholeness is more than worth the try. Your energy naturally flows in this direction, and it's aided by your desire and persistence. Anything you do to better yourself helps. And keep in mind that your unconscious mind meets you halfway. The energy you consciously put forth is matched by the unconscious and can reap unexpected benefits.

When you dream about circles, especially circles divided into quadrants, circles within circles, and circles that spiral, it's likely to be a story about the development of your psyche. See: *Spiral.*

The process of becoming a whole, complete person can be illustrated in dreams about playing a game involving a circular object such as a ball. In the actions of the game you see your progress or lack of it and what's holding you back or helping you along. Dreams can also use circular images such as balls, pizzas, and pies to symbolize the individuation process. See: *Ball, Games.*

Dreams about marriages and weddings can also speak to this process of unification. The entries for *Marriage* and *Wedding* touch on this subject, and to go deeper with it, see: *Anima, Animus, Bride, Groom.*

A circle or sphere can symbolize the idea of something being inside or outside your "circle of friends" or "sphere of influence." Inside the circle is what you allow into your life, and outside the circle is what you keep at a distance or cannot reach.

A circle can be a bull's-eye or related idea of a target you're trying to hit.

See also: *Anima, Animus, Archetypes, Ball, Baseball, Basketball, Bridge, Games, Groom, Ego, Individuation, Marriage, Spiral, Shapes, Spiral, Tennis, Unconscious Mind, Wedding*

City—Cities in dreams can symbolize your public life, identity, sense of community, or place in society. Cities are where people go to see, be seen, and interact with the public, to make their mark on the world and a name for themselves.

They go to cities to find work, and cities can symbolize anything related to work: employment, job-hunting, advancement, wealth, recognition.

For example, a musician who lives in "Omaha, Nebraska," and dreams about Austin, Texas, might be dreaming about a career step, because Austin has a thriving music scene and it's where bands go to make a name in that part of the country. The symbolism is based on the city's reputation.

The city is a sign of success—you "make it" in the big city. For example, an author who dreams about flying to New York City might be dreaming about the desire to make a splash in the publishing world, because NYC is where some of the biggest publishing companies are located.

For others, a city is a symbol for hustle, overcrowding, or loss of personal identity—just a face in the crowd. Other common associations are struggle, poverty, and pollution. See: *Urban.*

Dreams love to string together ideas to create symbolism and meaning. For example, a city can symbolize your mind, and a polluted city can symbolize dirty thoughts.

The symbolism can take on new dimensions for people who live in a city and dream about it. It's a versatile symbol for anything and everything connected with their everyday life. Dreaming about their city can be "day residue" processed by their mind via dreams, lacking symbolic meaning. You know the difference because meaningless dreams make little impression on you, and tend just to be a progression of imagery rather than a story.

A city can symbolize your psyche or your life. Your psyche has structures like buildings and neighborhoods that fit together to form a whole. The psyche has many interconnections, too, like roads or subway lines connecting parts of town. Your life is "built up" and can be busy like a city. Buildings can symbolize people you know, areas of your life, or your body. For example, a bank can symbolize your finances. In this sense, a city is a great symbol for capturing the dynamics of your life—your outer life or inner life.

See also: *Building, Bus, Empty, Job, New York City, Psyche, Skyscraper, Stage, Urban*

Civil War—See: *War*

Clap—See: *Applause*

Classroom—See: *School*

Clean—To clean has many comparisons and other definitions used as symbolism by dreams. For example: clean conscience, clean record, clean image, clean thoughts. It means lacking stain or blemish. The key to understanding the symbolism is to think of it as a physical representation of a personal situation.

Cleaning can symbolize cleaning up a situation, which can be depicted as cleaning a mess, or cleaning up your image, which can be depicting as bathing or washing laundry. See: *Clothing, Shower.*

A home can symbolize your life, so cleaning your home in a dream can symbolize straightening up your life. It can symbolize improving your health or cleaning up your diet. Start with the possibilities for symbolism presented by whatever is cleaned in a dream, such as your house, then add the symbolism of the action of cleaning. See: *Home*.

Cleaning can mean relieving yourself of cares, thoughts, and worries, in which case you will feel relieved afterward.

Dreams "clean house" by clearing out memory and other day residue to make room for tomorrow. Dreams organize and consolidate your mind. In other words, they clean and straighten.

Cleaning or bathing someone can mean helping to resolve problems that aren't yours. It can mean that you want to keep someone clean of dirty thoughts or unclean influence, or, in the case of children, that you want them to remain innocent.

Cleaning yourself can tie in with the idea of things that make you feel dirty. For example, you could dream about showering vigorously after having regretful sex. This use of the symbolism can show in actions of scrubbing hard or washing away dirt or blood.

See also: *Bathroom, Clothing, Guilt, Home, Shower, Water*

Cliff—When you face a metaphorical cliff in your life, it means you face a tough climb, big risk, or important decision. It can mean an obstacle seems insurmountable.

Standing across from someone on the other side of a cliff is the image of division, either within yourself or with another person or group of people. Connection is lacking. Communication is broken. Or it can mean you've created the personal distance necessary to feel safe.

Climbing a cliff in a dream can have the same symbolism as "climb the mountain," meaning you want to "reach the top." Or it can compare to a perilous situation. One slip-up can lead to disaster. See: *Climb, Disaster*.

Standing on a cliff edge suggests facing a big difficulty. It can mean living on the edge mentally or emotionally, or being close to taking a plunge into something like depression, illness, or a big de-

cision like marriage or retirement. It can symbolize fear of taking the next step, or being on the verge of giving up.

Being stuck on a cliff can symbolize a situation that isn't getting any easier. You feel exposed, vulnerable, or abandoned. You need help.

Jumping off a cliff can symbolize taking a risk or making a leap of faith. For an example dream, see: *Horse*.

Falling off a cliff can symbolize despair or having no control over your life. It can mean you're in free-fall. See: *Abyss*.

Landing safely and feeling good about it can symbolize a good decision. A bad landing can symbolize a bad decision, or a bad outcome is feared. Your confidence is rattled, so you stand at the edge looking down, unable to act.

Cliffs are further associated with confidence—having it, or not—and thrill-seeking. For example, refusing to climb a cliff or to jump off one can symbolize lack of confidence in your abilities, or doubting where you're going to end up after taking a risk.

See also: *Abyss, Bridge, Climb, Disaster, Fall, Horse, Mountain*

Climb—What does the action of climbing up say symbolically? In simplest terms, it means moving up.

It can mean progressing toward a goal or conquering a challenge. See: *Mountain*.

It can mean rising fortunes or status, "climbing the ladder." See: *Ascend*.

It can mean doing something one step at a time. For example, you want to get married, or get a divorce—what steps do you need to take? Or you want to start a family, get a college degree, or command an army. It's a tough climb that progresses in stages.

Climbing can symbolize raising your consciousness or improving yourself. See: *Spiral*.

Climbing can be a way of escaping or avoiding something. For example, climbing a tree to get away from a bear can symbolize escaping an overbearing mother figure. Climbing onto the roof at your workplace might express a wish to avoid work-related difficulties or stress.

For ideas about climbing downward, see: *Descend*.

The symbolism can be based on the skill and concentration, or planning and preparation, involved with mountain climbing. In which case, climbing is used to compare with something requiring similar abilities.

The strong grip required for climbing can symbolize the hold you have on something: your emotions, a concept, a situation.

A ladder is climbed one step at a time, and when you elevate your life, you take steps to do it. In this sense, climbing represents progress toward a goal, something that raises your status or fortunes, such as moving up in a hierarchy.

A ladder is climbed by one person at a time. It's a solo activity that can translate to symbolism for preferring to be alone or doing things your own way.

Oftentimes, the meaning of the symbolism of climbing is deciphered by analyzing the thing climbed. Climbing a tree combines the symbolism of climbing with the symbolism of a tree and can mean rising authority or position within a hierarchy. Climbing stairs can symbolize taking steps to protect yourself or prepare for something. Climbing a wall can symbolize overcoming an obstacle or wishing to escape chaos or stress.

See also: *Ascend, Building, Cliff, Descend, Elevator, Feet, Fence, Hands, Mountain, Tree, Wall*

Clock—See: *Time*

Closet—A closet is generally where stuff is put out of sight and stored. It's become synonymous with concealment, such as concealing being gay, or concealing a behavior or feeling. This use of the symbolism is often accompanied by actions of hiding in a closet or hiding something in it.

Getting something out of a closet can mean you want whatever it symbolizes to be in the open. Or you are rediscovering something. For example,

you dream about pulling golf clubs out of a closet and it connects with a renewed desire to play the game.

See also: *Barn, Bury, Clothing, Gay, Hide, Home, Locker*

Clothing—Clothing in general can have symbolism, and certain clothing items can have specific symbolism. Refer to the entries listed below.

Clothing is associated with persona, the image you "wear" or project. Persona is your public identity. See: *Persona*.

Shopping for clothes can symbolize making decisions about the image you project to the world or the identity you take on.

For example, a man who started a new job dreams about shopping for a jacket for work. He finds one that's appropriate and takes it to the cash register. The price is exactly how much money he has in his checking account. The dream reflects the man's thoughts about the personal price he's paying to do the job. He already feels overextended, and fears that doing the job right will require everything he has in the "bank," meaning his store of energy and personal resources. The fact that he does not wear a jacket at his actual work and does not need to buy one stands out because it must be symbolism. See: *Shop*.

For another example of clothing-store symbolism, see: *Chase*.

Remember, though, that dreams create symbolism based on your personal associations. Clothing is closely associated with image, but for some people, shopping for clothes could connect with spending priorities. You might only shop for clothes after all other bills are paid—or shop for clothes despite being unable to afford it—and those associations can be used to create symbolism for habits or priorities, or for willingness or unwillingness to sacrifice.

Getting dressed can symbolize preparation. See: *Dressed*.

Taking off clothing can be a way of revealing the person beneath, or giving up a role, title, or identity. See: *Undress*.

Dreaming about someone tearing off your clothing can symbolize being self-conscious about your body.

Giving your clothes to someone can show willingness to help or provide, like giving the shirt off your back.

Nakedness can symbolize lacking something related to identity, job, or relationship. For example, after leaving a job as a newspaper editor, a man dreams he's in the newspaper office, at his desk, naked and wanting to get back to work. The lack of clothing symbolizes the social identity he lost when he left the job. As an editor, he had an identity that was closely tied to the job. See: *Naked*.

Clothes are used to cover the body, and other words for cover are "conceal" and "hide." See: *Bikini, Hide*.

Heavy clothes can symbolize desire to conceal yourself or a feeling of personal heaviness. See: *Bury*.

Excessive clothing can symbolize covering the person you are, or feeling weighed down by the expectations and effort of keeping up appearances. It can symbolize trying to protect yourself from emotional or personal closeness, or being overprotective.

Wearing athletic clothes can symbolize energy and achievement. It can connect with a personal image as an athlete or active person. See: *Athlete*.

Formal clothes can symbolize a formal or cultured image. For example, the girlfriend of a man who just got hired to work at a country club dreams about him dressed in a tuxedo and sporting a fancy pocket watch. The tuxedo and watch reflect her perception that the country club is a fancy place. Wearing formal clothes can reflect thoughts related to an upcoming event such as a graduation or wedding. If the clothes feel constricting, it can mean you feel restricted by formality.

Clothes from childhood can indicate holding onto something immature. On the other hand, they can indicate reconnection with the child within you. See: *Child*.

A disguise can symbolize a facade, or deception. See: *Disguise*.

A uniform can symbolize a role you play, whether formal or informal, or something related to the job performed by a person in the uniform, what it says about a person, and how that can translate to symbolism. Wearing a police uniform can symbolize authority. Dressing as a construction worker can symbolize any subject related to building: renovating a home, constructing your life, building up your self-esteem. For an example dream, see: *Cheat (Exam)*.

And remember, action defines the symbolism. Symbolism related to building or construction will show in the action. An idle construction worker is not building anything. Instead, the meaning might have more to do with lack of action or activity.

Work clothes can relate to your work life or roles you play that feel like work. For example, wearing a maid's outfit might express how you feel about doing chores. See: *Job*.

Clothes that belong to someone else can symbolize wrapping yourself in his or her identity. For example, wearing your boyfriend's shirt can be a way of saying your personal identity and public image are connected closely with him.

Disheveled clothing can symbolize a negative perception. Your reputation or self-image is tattered. If keeping up appearances means caring for one's appearance, including social appearance, not keeping up appearances means the opposite. You don't care how you are perceived or put no effort into maintaining appearances.

Torn clothing can symbolize arguments or fighting. It can mean that someone "tore into you," or a situation is "ripping you to shreds."

Stains on your clothes can symbolize stains on your character, self-image, or reputation. See: *Clean*.

The fit of clothing can have symbolism. For example, wearing a stiff suit can symbolize stiffness or rigidness in personality. Ill-fitting clothes can symbolize playing a role or adopting a persona that doesn't suit you. Tight clothes can symbolize the feeling of being constrained or hampered. A tight clothing fit can connect with the idea of freedom to be the person you want to be.

Trousers or underwear that are too tight can symbolize restricted sexuality. See: *Underwear*.

Coats, jackets, and heavy shirts can symbolize protecting your emotions, because these articles of clothing only cover the top part of the body, including the heart. However, a full-length coat or trench coat can symbolize the desire to hide yourself or go unnoticed. Or it can connect with certain personality types: mysterious, dangerous, private.

Gloves can symbolize hiding something, particularly an action taken, stemming from the hands being used to take actions and fingerprints used to solve crime. Gloves are used to protect the hands and keep them from getting dirty, and "get your hands dirty" means participate or be involved in some action—particularly an action that you might describe as dirty, difficult, protective, or underhanded. See also: *Fingerprint*.

Period clothing in a dream can connect with certain personality types, or be used to refer to the past. For example, if a dream drops you into a scene where everyone wears tie-dyes and bell-bottoms, it might symbolize something related to a loose attitude or personality. Or maybe it's related to being a slacker, since some people associate the hippie lifestyle with an excuse to avoid work.

Clothing is associated with certain time periods. If you were a young child during the hippie era, the hippie style of dress might be associated in your mind with your childhood.

The color of clothing has many possibilities for symbolism, especially in connection with emotions. For example, a blue shirt can symbolize "feeling blue." Shirts are worn over the chest, and the chest is where feelings such as sadness and depression are usually felt. Then again, blue is associated with deep thoughts. A deep-blue hat is particularly likely to symbolize deep thoughts because thoughts are associated with the head. To learn more, look up the entries for the color of the clothing in a dream if it sticks out to you. See: *Colors*.

How you see yourself—the real "inner you"— can be symbolized with clothing color, too. For example, red is associated with aggression and is an apt color to symbolize an aggressive or assertive personality, while green is associated with creativity and establishing yourself in the physical world. The symbolism of clothing is usually related to the "outer" you, but it's only a rule of thumb.

Dreams can make connections between people based on clothing. For example, if you dream about your husband wearing your dad's clothes, or your wife wearing your mom's clothes, it can mean they're connected in your mind. Perhaps your spouse is like a parent to you, or exhibits some of the same behaviors, qualities, and traits.

Along this line, a dream-character can represent someone in your life and be identified by the clothing it wears. For instance, if your brother usually wears a baseball cap backwards, a character wearing a cap backwards might symbolize your brother.

Finally, always keep in mind that dreams can use certain details to set the scene, and those details are not as important as how they connect with other details. For example, you dream about thoughts of the future as time traveling forward to a futuristic world. The dream needs the scenario to be believable, so it might dress the characters in futuristic clothing. Otherwise, the discrepancy might jar you out of the story instead of following along with it.

See also: *Athlete, Bikini, Bury, Camouflage, Child, Clean, Closet, Coat, Colors, Conceal, Disguise, Dress, Dressed, Fashion, Hat, Hide, Job, Locker, Mask, Naked, Shirt, Shoes, Shop, Short, Underwear, Undress*

Clown—Dreaming about a clown can symbolize a frivolous attitude or behavior, as expressed in the phrase "clown around."

A clown can symbolize feeling foolish, or be an expression of the feeling that you or someone else isn't taking a situation seriously enough. Perhaps someone is trying too hard to be lighthearted. Something seems artificial, false, or deceptive.

Because clowns wear outfits and heavy makeup, they can symbolize disguising one's true feelings or personality behind a facade.

For some people, clowns are creepy and can symbolize something they fear or don't trust.

See also: *Amusement Park, Disguise, Makeup, Mask*

Coach—A coach can symbolize leadership or authority. Your "inner coach" is the coach-like part of you. It teaches. It leads. It encourages. It decides. It strategizes and analyzes. It knows strengths and weaknesses.

Your dreams are like a life coach, and this innate wisdom can personify as characters such as coaches.

Dreams give advice and perspective that lead to improvements in any area of life, not just athletics, and your "dream coach" is an obvious choice to deliver the coaching that helps you improve.

The sport coached might in some way be compared to another area of life. For example, a soccer coach can teach you how to get ahead of the competition, because in soccer the players gain advantage by getting ahead of other players.

You can dream about yourself in the role of a coach if you lead a group of people, formally or informally, such as when leading a project at school or work. Being coached, on the other hand, can connect with a situation where you're part of a group or project. Coaches are closely associated with teams.

Coaches are associated with athletics, and that idea branches out to include anything associated with competition, practice, effort, discipline, recognition or accomplishment.

If you're involved in a sport, a coach in your dream can relate to that sport.

A specific coach in your dream might symbolize something you associate with that person. Some coaches are known as motivators, some as tacticians, some as disciplinarians, and some as beloved elders. Something about the person resonates with you, and that association is used by the dream to say something about you and your life.

The coach in your dream can be one who actually coached you in a sport. In which case your knowledge of, and experiences with, the person raises many possibilities for symbolism. Or the coach can be one you know by association; for example, the coach of your favorite professional sports team.

For example, a young man has recurring dreams about college basketball coach Bob Huggins. As a student at a university where Huggins coached, he had a lot of exposure to Huggins. In his dreams, he's on the basketball team and Huggins mostly plays the role of observer and figurehead whom the dreamer hopes to please with good performance. The dreamer associates Huggins with hard-nosed discipline, so when he's working hard and being disciplined, he dreams about pleasing Huggins with good performance.

See also: *Athlete, Games, Guide, Sports*

Coast—See: *Beach*

Coat—See: *Clothing*

Cocaine—For people tempted by cocaine, dreams about it are likely to relate to the power the drug has over their mind. However, it can also be used to symbolize anything else that is tempting, pleasurable, habit-forming, or related to peer pressure.

It can symbolize something addictive. See: *Addict*.

It can symbolize something you can't control or change. See: *Crack House*.

It can symbolize something that invites trouble into your life.

For people who've never done cocaine, and for whom it hasn't played a part in their life, a dream about cocaine has to be symbolism. The key is to figure out what sort of comparison is being made to cocaine and things associated with it.

For example, a man dreams that another man pressures him to use cocaine. The dreamer says no several times, but the other man keeps pushing it on him and finally the dreamer relents and takes the cocaine. It makes him feel high. He's never actually done cocaine.

The dream connects with an experience the night before the dream. The man dropped into a convenience store and saw a particular doughnut for sale that tempted him. He passed by it a few times, each time telling himself no, he won't buy it. But finally he gives in, buys the doughnut and eats it. His dream symbolizes the doughnut as cocaine, and the man who pushes it on him symbolizes the voice of temptation. The sugar rush he gets from eating the doughnut is compared to the dream to cocaine.

See also: *Addict, Candy, Crack House, Drugs, White*

Cock—See: *Penis, Rooster*

Cockroach—See: *Roach*

Cocoon—A cocoon can symbolize the feeling of being protected or comforted, or your "nest egg."

It can symbolize personal transformation, or isolation.

See also: *Butterfly, Spider*

Coffin—A coffin is one of those dream symbols that can spark worry and dread, but like everything else in dreams it's symbolism. The trick is to figure out which personal or common association is used to create the symbolism.

Coffins are commonly associated with death, and death in dreams can refer to figurative death: death of a relationship, death of the "old you," the end of a phase of life, a big change in the way you feel or think.

A coffin can symbolize something that you want to put in the past, that you never want to see again. The imagery of closing or burying a coffin arises most commonly in dreams after the end of a contentious relationship or difficult time of life.

Burying a coffin can be associated with ideas like burying a grudge, burying the past, and burying memories. See: *Bury.*

A closed coffin in a dream can indicate that something in your life has come to a close. The lid of the coffin closes, and that's the end.

Digging up a coffin can symbolize digging up old memories or uncovering buried feelings.

Of course, a coffin in a dream can refer to an event in your life, such as the death of someone you know. It can indicate that something about

that event still needs to be processed, especially your emotions.

Being in a coffin can symbolize confinement. A dull, listless, or depressed existence is comparable to slowly rotting away even though you're alive. Something's killing you inside. You might be stuck in a situation or place where you've been too long. See: *Cage, Jail.*

It can symbolize claustrophobia or fear of death.

It can symbolize keeping secrets, something that will "go to the grave" with you.

As with all symbols, your feelings are your guide. If the image of the coffin in your dream makes you feel relieved, it can mean you are happy that something is over and done. You're ready to move on. If you feel anxious or worse, it can mean something still needs to be dealt with, perhaps something that you buried and tried to forget. The longer it remains unresolved, the worse it becomes.

See also: *Body, Bury, Cage, Death, Emotions, Fear, Funeral, Ghost, Graveyard, Jail, Prisoner*

Cold—See: *Winter*

Collective Unconscious—The collective unconscious is a big concept and can only be covered briefly. It originates with Carl Jung, who proposed that the unconscious mind of the individual connects with the unconscious minds of all individuals—those alive today and throughout the history of the human species.

In the words of Victor Daniels, emeritus professor of psychology at Sonoma State University, the collective unconscious is "[t]hat aspect of the unconscious which manifests inherited, universal themes which run through all human life. Inwardly, the whole history of the human race, back to the most primitive times, lives on in us."

In it are structures called archetypes that are the foundation of the psyche and provide the basic patterns for drives, desires, thoughts, and motivations found in all people. Archetypes are formed by the collective experience of all people. They are powerful psychological forces, and they're like a river that runs through everyone. See: *Archetypes.*

The archetypes of the collective unconscious are the anima in males, and the animus in females. See: *Anima, Animus*.

The modern conception of the collective unconscious describes it as a sort of Internet of the mind, a communication network that passes information without apparent causation. That information usually takes the form of summaries or aggregates, but some theorists have gone as far as to say that the collective unconscious can facilitate communication directly between individuals, and it explains psi or paranormal phenomenon such as telepathy and precognition.

If the collective unconscious truly is an Internet of the mind, it means that outside forces and influences can act on you through your dreams.

Read that last sentence again.

This subject is important in relation to dreams because the unconscious mind is where dreams originate, in an archetype that Jung referred to as "the Self." The Self is the complete picture of the person, including potential. See: *Psyche*.

The collective unconscious is the source of dreams of the utmost importance for you and your life, even for all of humanity, because through it the collective speaks to the individual and drives him or her to action.

See also: *Anima, Animus, Archetypes, Circle, Precognitive Dream, Psyche, Unconscious Mind*

College—Being back in college is a frequent dream theme for people who have already graduated, but you don't have to have attended college to dream about it. The symbolism is often related to learning. You feel challenged by something or recognize a gap in your knowledge that needs to be filled. You are learning something new and feel challenged intellectually.

Consider what you learn, or need to learn, about yourself and life. Life is a continual process of adjustment and assimilation. You take in new information, have new experiences, and decide how things fit into the big picture of who you are. A college setting is a natural place in a dream to tell stories about what you're learning about yourself and your life.

College is supposed to be preparation for adult life, specifically for occupation or profession. When situations are encountered for which you feel unprepared, it's common to dream about being in college and unprepared for an exam, or needing classes to graduate. Graduation in the larger sense means "ready for the challenges that come next." See: *Campus*.

Dreaming that you can't find the classroom where you belong can indicate you don't know where to get the knowledge, experience, or information you need to meet a challenge. Think beyond professional or work challenges to consider life challenges, personal challenges, social challenges, and relationship challenges.

Getting through college is comparable to climbing a mountain in the metaphorical sense. Many steps have to be taken and obstacles overcome. Personal and intellectual growth is required, as well as planning and organization. See: *Climb*.

You can dream about being in college if you face other sorts of mountains to climb, such as a big project at work or a big challenge at home. The setting can be used to describe situations that require strategy, skills, talent, and ability.

A college setting can be used to express feelings about missing college life, or missing the opportunity to attend college. Where would you be now?

Time in college is associated with freedom. For many people it's the first chance they have to make their own decisions and set their own agendas. It's where new friendships are made and high school reputations are left behind, giving fresh opportunity to reshape yourself and your image. If you missed that sort of opportunity, you might dream about college as a way of wishing that you'd had it, or that it would come again.

A college setting can be used to express feelings about meeting requirements and being prepared. We are told by teachers, counselors, and parents that college will get us what we want as adults. But what if you do everything right, get your degree, and it doesn't lead you to where you want to be? What if you get into the work world and find out it wasn't what you expected, that the way to get ahead has little to do with what you prepared for, or the occupation you chose does not lead to the adult life you want? You might then dream about college to think back on the roots of what led you to where you are now.

In a more general sense, dreaming about college can be a way of saying that you're thinking about your life, or that you're moving on from that time of life. You wake up one day and realize you're no longer a young adult with wide-open possibilities.

Along the same lines, college is sometimes thought of as a step that leads to marriage and family life. You might dream about college as part of planning for your adult life, or as a way of looking back on the decisions you made and experiences you had that shape your adult life.

Of course, if you are too young to be in college and dream about it, it can be a way of looking ahead and planning your future. It can relate to the expectations and hopes you have for what that time of life will be like, or thinking about what you want to do with yourself, or even wishing for freedom and opportunity.

College can mean "informed opinion." This use of the symbolism often plays out without actually showing a campus or college. Instead, college is referred to, such as through a professor or letter.

The symbolism can be based on the type of college. For example, a dream about attending a business college can be a general way of saying "taking care of business." A law college can in some way tie in with subjects related to law, and law in the general sense means authority and rules.

Types of colleges include junior college and community college, which is a beginner step to getting a college education. A college dream can be a way of saying you're taking remedial steps or going in the right direction. On the other hand, Harvard Medical School can symbolize prestige and preparation for tackling the biggest challenges.

See also: *Campus, Climb, Mountain, School, Student, Teacher, University*

Colors—Colors in dreams can be thought of as coloring the scene and providing the emotional coloring. How mad are you? Seeing red. How sad are you? Feeling blue. How happy are you? Sunny yellow. See: *Emotions*.

The deliberate use of color in a dream is likely to be tied to emotions, though some use of color is simply to set the scene or tell the story. For example, if you dream about sitting peacefully in an open field of grass, you'd expect the grass to be green. But if the grass is purple grass, you can bet it's significant.

Color modifies other symbolism. The sports car in your dream that symbolizes your revved-up career isn't any ol' sports car, it's a hot red one. The red of the sports car represents feeling vibrant and energetic. The darkness around you when you're lost in the proverbial woods is *black* as night, and black is how you feel about being lost. The color combines with other dream imagery to create a composite image that sums up the situation and your related emotions. For more examples, see: *Black*.

Color sets the mood and tone of a dream, much the same way that a movie's mood and tone can be set through an emphasis of certain colors.

Dig deeper into the connection between color and emotion in dreams by checking out the work of Bob Hoss at *dreamscience.org*, and reading the entries listed below.

See also: *Black, Blue, Chakras, Dark, Emotions, Green, Orange, Pink, Red, Violet, White, Yellow*

Coma—Dreaming about being in a coma can symbolize being "dead to the world," or dead inside.

It can be a way of saying you have been withdrawn or out of circulation.

It can have similar symbolism to waking up after a long sleep. See: *Sleep, Wake Up*.

For example, a mother of a young child dreams she awakens from a coma at a hospital. She looks and feels the way she did before having a baby. The dream reflects the fact that her baby had grown more self-sufficient, freeing mom to have more time for other things. For many months, she only had time to care for her newborn. Waking from a coma means she feels renewed.

Coma can mean out of touch, lines of communication are shut down, a person is distant or unresponsive. For example, you dream about a friend being in a coma, and it means you aren't reaching the person on an emotional or personal level. The person is alive in the physical sense but unresponsive in the deeper sense. See: *Zombie*.

Awakening from a coma is a great metaphor for becoming alive inside, or coming out of a depression, personal funk, or time of withdrawal.

For example, a young man dreams he's been in a coma for a year and recently awakened. He goes on Facebook and reads the conversations his friends had about him while he was "out of it." It's a way of saying he recently came out of a year-long funk, withdrawn from friends, and started being social again.

Coming out of coma can symbolize a spiritual awakening.

See also: *Dream Within a Dream, Facebook, Sleep, Wake Up, Zombie*

Compass—See: *Discover, Map*

Compensation—Paying compensation in a dream can connect with a situation where you owe something or feel like something is owed to you.

It could relate to actual compensation, such as paying off a loan or other monetary obligation, but think beyond material compensation. You might feel that you're owed for something you have done, such as a favor. For example, you watch the kids for your spouse and feel that you're owed time to do something personal. You then dream about it as contributing to the Save The Children fund.

Compensation is linked to guilt, grievances, and shortcomings. For example, a person might compensate for losing her temper by acting extra nice, or compensate for a shortcoming by excelling in another area. You then dream about it as financial compensation.

Compensation has another sense of the word used in psychology, meaning "go equally far in the opposite direction." It's the psyche's way of creating balance and reflecting the ego back to itself. If you think you're the smartest person ever, your dreams will show you as the biggest idiot. If you think you're stupid, you might dream about a genius, and in it see your own capacity for it. Beauty is compensated by ugliness, and vice versa. Arrogance is compensated by dreams about being humiliated.

Compensation plays out in dreams through absurd imagery and situations. Characters are grossly disfigured and out of whack. Situations are outrageous. Settings can be like scenes out of Dante's *Inferno*, completely unreal. Reactions are out of proportion. These are signs of compensation.

For example, a grown man dreams about being surrounded by women with massive breasts and exposed genitals. At first, it's like heaven for him, but as the dream continues the women change form into ones he knows, such as his sisters. He sees a nun acting like a whore and flashing her goods. The women leer at him and act like harpies. It makes him extremely uncomfortable as he's forced to view scenes that sicken him, like the character Alex in the dystopian 1971 movie *A Clockwork Orange*, strapped down with his eyes pried open. The dream shows him the ridiculousness of his attitudes toward women and his sexualization of them. He's a grown man who's like a teenaged boy who can't stop sneaking peeks into the girls' locker room.

Psychological compensation is a function of the self-regulating psyche, a hard push on the other end of the scale, showing that strong measures are needed to rein in the ego. If the ego doesn't get the message, well, things only get worse.

Another meaning of compensation comes into play when your dreams compensate for something missing in your life. Are you feeling lonely? Your dreams might give you a friend. Feeling sexually unfulfilled? Here's a dream lover for you. Need inspiration? Your dreams will conjure a muse. Missing a loved one who died? You can dream about the person in the most vivid and realistic ways and wake up feeling like the hole in your heart has been plugged.

See also: *Beggar, Bully, Ego, Hero, Mirror, Money, Psyche*

Computer—Computers have many uses, equating to many possibilities for symbolism. They're used for work, school, entertainment, communication, productivity, social life, and in potentially troublesome activities such as viewing porn, setting up affairs, and making or receiving threats.

The possibilities for symbolism expand when you consider the analogies that use computers and related technologies to describe people and situations. For example, a "computer geek" is someone with high computer-related skill and an obsessive focus on technology, a type of person often viewed as socially and sexually lacking. Those associations are ripe for use as symbolism.

On the other hand, hackers have a glamorous image as renegades sticking it to The Man.

Social connections are a sort of Internet and are facilitated through computer networks. Dreams can use computers and smartphones (mobile computers) to illustrate the connections between people.

The movie *The Matrix* is an analogy for artificial reality created by advanced technology, where people play second fiddle. The modern world is like a virtual reality because of its intense focus on technology, and technology is integral in the lives of so many people. In some cases, the virtual world *is* their world, and the real world is more like an illusion or bad joke. Dreams can use computers and electronic gadgets to tell stories about living in a world that revolves around technology and can seem unreal.

For example, a teenaged girl who spends most of each day on her computer dreams that it starts talking to her on its own. At first, she likes what it says and thinks of it as a friend. Then things get weird when it drops dark hints and won't shut up. She threatens to throw the computer away, and in response it shows her pictures of her changing clothes, taken by the built-in camera, and plays audio recordings of her intimate conversations. It threatens to publicly release the videos and audio recordings and ruin all her relationships.

The metaphor here is clear. The computer has taken over her life and she doesn't know how to disconnect from it. Most of her personal relationships are conducted through computers and gadgets, and she fears that less time on it means the loss of those relationships, some of which are conducted entirely online. She feels blackmailed to continue allowing her life to be dominated by the computer.

A similar dream features the dreamer finding naked videos of herself on her smartphone that she didn't take. The dream is amplifying subconscious fears that her phone could be hacked—or is already hacked, and some creep is secretly watching and recording her. The same scenario could be used to connect with a feeling of being personally compromised or blackmailed.

A computer can be used as an analogy for the brain. Like a computer, the brain has short-term and long-term memory, processing cores, network paths, circuitry, and video and audio processors. Dreams can visualize internal bodily processes that occur while sleeping, including activity in the brain, and a computer is a great analogy. See: *Letter*.

Erasing files on a computer can symbolize forgetting memories, or changing your internal programming. For example, a young adult man dreams that he time-travels back to when he was a child and sees his father delete the game programs he spent so much time playing and replace them with learning programs. He equates the games with why he's a young adult going nowhere in his life. Replacing the games is not just a wish that his father had helped more when he needed it most, it's a way of showing the young man that it's not too late to provide his own guidance like a father, and change his programming. Games are OK, but his primary focus should be on learning.

The special skills that go into programming and engineering computers is like astrophysics to some people. In which case, computers can be used as symbolism for something they don't understand, something they rely on other people to take care of, or something they don't want to know.

See also: *Email, Facebook, Letter, Robot, Subconscious, Time Travel, YouTube.*

Conceal—See: *Hide*

Condemn—See: *Execution*

Confine—See: *Jail*

Constipation—See: *Toilet*

Construction—Your life is usually in a continual state of construction, and dreams show that figurative sense of the word as literal. Think of construction as a physical representation. Construction can mean that your life or an area of it is built up or expanded—outer life or inner life.

For example, when having a child you might dream about adding a room onto your house. When expanding your beliefs, you might dream about building a church or garden. When expanding your mind, you might dream about adding shelves to a library or buildings to a university—a way of saying that your personal universe is expanding. See: *Building*.

Constructing a road can symbolize "making inroads," meaning making progress or building a mental or emotional connection with a person. Alternately, it can symbolize the road of life, and building it suggests creating your own path or doing things your own way, or blazing a new trail. Building a bridge can mean bridging a gap. See: *Bridge, Highway, Road*.

To really grasp this use of the symbolism, think of the ways construction can be used as a metaphor for building your life and your mind. What is your foundation? Your self-respect, values, morals, ethics, principles, fortitude, inner strength, health. What protects you like a roof or walls? Personal boundaries, psychological and emotional defenses, ability to make money, thinking and reason, knowledge and information.

Your psyche is like a neighborhood and the structures in a psyche are the buildings and monuments of that neighborhood. That's why when a person leaves the past behind and goes through big changes, it's common to dream about his or her old neighborhood being demolished or attacked. See: *Neighbor*.

The idea of construction extends further to include constructing an argument and similar sorts of mental constructs.

To look at the same subject from the opposite perspective, see: *Destruction*.

See also: *Bridge, Building, City, Destruction, Fence, Home, Neighbor, Road, Skyscraper, University, Wall*

Consume—See: *Eat*

Contest—See: *Games, Sports*

Cook—See: *Chef, Food, Kitchen*

Cop—See: *Police Officer*

Corpse—See: *Body*

Costume—See: *Clothing*

Cougar—See: *Leopard*

Counterfeit—See: *Fake*

Countryside—Landscapes like countrysides in dreams can symbolize having an expansive view of your life and peaceful feelings about your current status. On the one hand, a countryside suggests freedom and exploration. On the other hand, it suggests remoteness and disconnection. Your feelings while viewing a countryside in a dream can tell you what it means to you.

Sigmund Freud related gently rolling landscapes to the female body.

See also: *Earth, Green, Tree*

Courage—See: *Hero*

Court—To dream about being in court can connect with feeling as if you're on trial. You're getting the third degree. You're under suspicion. You feel prosecuted, or have to defend yourself.

For example, someone accuses you or impugns your character. You want to expose the person or prove him wrong. You feel that you have been wronged. You want justice, and court is where people seek it.

In court is where the truth comes out. It can be a setting to show you what underlies some issue or problem in your life. Truth is brought out into the open, facts are determined, oaths are given, and arguments are made. You're trying to expose the roots or cause of something.

Court can be used in the sense of courting danger or courting a mate.

The symbolism of a court setting is often found in related details. Use the list below.

See also: *Bail, Fugitive, Guilt, Innocent, Judge, Jury, Lawyer*

Cousin—See: *Family*

Cover-Up—See: *Bury, Clothing*

Cow—Cows are slow-moving and can symbolize obstacles, lethargy, or laziness. Something is slowing you down or blocking your way. A cow dream can show slowness in thinking or comprehension.

Then again, cows are also docile and mostly harmless, so a cow in your dream can symbolize a passive or docile nature.

A herd of cows can symbolize a need to belong to a group, or a group of people who are slow, easily led, or an obstacle.

Because cows provide milk for human consumption, they can be associated with maternal qualities. Milking a cow can symbolize work and effort. Or it can be a play on the phrase "milking it," meaning getting all of the value, worth, or mileage from something.

See also: *Animals, Cattle*

Coward—The trick to figuring out the meaning of a character in a dream is to question its role in the story and what it says about you or a situation. The character is chosen to play a role and, by doing so, show you something.

A coward, or acting cowardly, can reflect lacking courage or shirking something. "Coward" is exaggerated but fits when you avoid something rather than confront it.

The meaning can often be found in the opposite idea. A coward lacks courage and ability to act under duress. Dreaming of a coward can be compensation for heroic theatrics or going too far on the fearless end of the scale. See: *Compensation.*

It can express the desire to prove yourself or push your limits. See: *Hero.*

Cowardice can connect with fear of knowing the truth or seeing things the way they really are. In a backward sort of way, it can stem from fear of finding out you are capable of so much more than you are doing with life or aspiring to be as a person.

Everything in the psyche comes in pairs, and the counterpart of the coward is the bully. Both are immature manifestations of the Warrior archetype and can manifest as mean, immature characters such as bullies and gang members. See: *Bully.*

See also: *Archetypes, Bully, Compensation, Fear, Gang, Hero, Panic, Shadow, Warrior, Weak, Yellow*

Cowboy—A cowboy in a dream can indicate a manly and rugged self-image, or a wish for freedom and adventure.

It can connect with doing physical labor, or a primitive living situation.

A cowboy isn't bound by the responsibility and commitment of maintaining a home and can symbolize immature masculinity. The cowboy is the man who walks away rather than settles down, who is restless and isolated.

Co-Worker—An actual co-worker in a dream probably connects somehow to work. The dream might relate to an event at work, or to an ongoing issue there that the co-worker is tied to, directly or indirectly.

For example, a woman dreams about being at work, working, and her co-worker starts touching her sexually. Eventually, she gives up her focus on work and starts going along with what the co-worker is doing.

While a dream like this one can raise questions about whether the dreamer finds the co-worker sexually attractive or has unmet sexual needs, the dream isn't about sex. It's about distraction. At work the day before the dream, the dreamer kept getting distracted. The co-worker, on the other hand, is very focused at work. The sexually suggestive actions have nothing to do with reality. The person is chosen by the dream to use as an example of someone who doesn't get distracted at work.

The dream sets up a contrast between the dreamer and the co-worker, and uses flirting and touching to symbolize distraction. The dreamer is a newlywed and just returned from her honeymoon. She's sitting there at her desk wishing she were back in bed with her lover. No wonder she's distracted!

A co-worker you know, or someone you used to work with, can symbolize something you see about yourself in the person. The person could symbolize your hard work, social skills, or job situation, or that person's. For example, telling a co-worker in a dream that he's about to get fired can symbolize your own job insecurity. Or it can be an observation about that person—they're about to get fired or be reprimanded, or you wish it would happen.

An ambitious co-worker, real or fictional, can symbolize your own ambition.

Anything related to work can be symbolized by a co-worker. See: *Job.*

Following a co-worker around can mean you want to be more like him or her, to emulate that person in some way, at least at work.

Recurring dreams involving co-workers are pretty certain to connect with ongoing situations at work or in work life.

A fictional co-worker can symbolize something that aids you in your work, such as a personal quality or personality trait; an ability to organize and manage time, for instance. The co-worker might symbolize part of yourself that works alongside your main personality. For example, a positive or negative attitude works alongside you, with you, or against you, as you go about your business.

A co-worker can symbolize use of related skills and traits. For example, you use the same analytical skills you use at work to aid in analyzing your finances, and dream about it as doing that sort of work with a co-worker, or as a co-worker who deals with money or finance. Or you use the same alertness and diligence to make sure your house is secure as you do to make sure your job or income is secure.

A co-worker can be a characterization of a relationship. For example, you and your spouse could be thought of as co-workers keeping house and raising the kids.

Dreams can use surrogates to represent people you know, so it's possible to dream about a co-worker but see him or her depicted in another form: human, animal, or otherwise. For example, a co-worker who acts unruly can be depicted as a monkey. A co-worker who acts haughty could be depicted as a prince or movie star.

See also: *Boss, Dismissal, Employee, Famous, Group, Job, Old Friend, Unemployed*

Crack House—Dreams create physical representations of personal situations, especially the dynamics of your inner life. The symbolism is based on your associations.

A crack house is generally associated with squalid living conditions and personal desperation. It could be used as symbolism for being in a really bad place in life.

It's known for being a place that can't be escaped. The drug will always bring back the addict. See: *Cage.*

A crack house can symbolize some sort of terrible personal condition or habit, not necessarily a drug habit.

It can mean there's something you can't control, some way you can't help yourself.

A crack house can symbolize the lowest possible opinion of something or someone. See: *Roach.*

A crack house can be a metaphor for going nowhere in your life, or lacking control of your personal space. Anyone can come and go without asking. Or you have needy people in your life who always want something from you. Or perhaps it's you who are needy, compulsive, or addicted like a crack head, and the house represents your life. Neediness does not have to be at the level of crack head to fit a situation in an exaggerated way.

At its simplest, a crack house is a house. People live there. It could characterize a living situation or home life or characterize something about your life. See: *Home.*

As always, consider personal associations and experiences in relation to dream symbols. If you have been in a crack house, why were you there? What are your impressions? Now ask if your associations show up in the dream-story.

See also: *Arrest, Cage, Candy, Cocaine, Court, Drugs, Home, Jail, Roach*

Crash—Knowing that dreams create physical representations of personal situations gives you an initial way of approaching the interpretation of a crash. For example, it can symbolize lives colliding, or something in your life coming to a sudden halt or bad ending. Hopes crash. Plans crash. Stocks crash. Projects crash. Health crashes. It's a versatile metaphor.

It can indicate a sudden crisis or drop in energy or enthusiasm. You reach your limit. Your body and mind shut down quickly. You "crash."

Crashes are associated with taking risks and being reckless.

Do you cause the crash, or witness it? That detail can make a big difference to the meaning. Causing a crash means you are the likely source of whatever the crash symbolizes. Witnessing a crash can mean you've observed something that didn't directly involve you. For example, you hear that a neighbor is arrested for a serious crime, and dream about a car crash in that part of the neighborhood.

Look at details of the crash for clues to its meaning. A solo crash with no passengers can symbolize a setback that affects only one person. Colliding with another car can symbolize two lives colliding. Or, if the cars are full of passengers, it can symbolize two groups colliding. A pileup can symbolize a messed-up group situation, or an obstacle to your progress. A plane crash can mean that a hope or ambition is lost, or that health takes a sudden dive. A motorcycle crash can symbolize exposure to harm, or inadequate protection. See: *Group, Passenger*.

When interpreting a crash, begin with the symbolism of the vehicle and cross-reference it with the symbolism of a crash.

Watch out for crash dreams that recur. It's a sign of something habitually going wrong in your life, or a warning of what could happen.

Consider your personal associations. Being in a car crash can create powerful personal associations, and you'll recognize them in the dream-story and your feelings about it. In which case, the meaning can be found by cross-referencing the dream with the incident. For example, you were in a major accident while in a car with someone driving recklessly, and now, years later, your spouse's driving makes you nervous. Your dreams could connect the two by reliving the accident, so you see the source of your nervousness.

Reliving trauma is a way of processing it, and you are bound to dream about such an event soon after it happens. For more ideas about how to deal with this sort of dream, see: *Nightmare*.

See also: *Airplane, Boat, Car, Drugs, Group, Jet, Motorcycle, Nightmare, Panic, Passenger, Rocket*

Creature—A creature in your dream can symbolize seeing yourself or someone else as different or unusual, even to the point of being sub-human.

It can be an exaggerated way of expressing that someone isn't acting right.

A creature can symbolize something about yourself you don't recognize—what is that thing you see in the mirror?

A creature can symbolize something that's rejected, shunned, repressed, hurt, resentful, aggrieved, or unmanageable. Taking form as a creature is a graphic way for something about yourself to get your attention and show, in an exaggerated way, how you treat yourself or how you feel.

A creature in your dream can be a reflection of a side of yourself brought out by stress, fear, anger, or anxiety. Think: Mr. Hyde, or the Incredible Hulk, creatures that emerge from their host. See: *Monster*.

For a great example of a creature used in a dream, see: *Skin*.

See also: *Ghost, Monster, Nightmare, Panic, Skin, Vampire, Werewolf*

Crime—Dreams create symbolism by making comparisons, and a crime can compare with something that's wrong or unfair. Think of times when you might say, "That's a crime," but it's not illegal. It's a crime that you didn't get a job promotion, or didn't get accepted into graduate school, or your mate cheated. Crime is equated with feeling cheated, wronged, unlucky, or unjustly denied.

Or you're tempting fate. If you're caught doing whatever is symbolized as a crime, it's big trouble.

A crime can be an exaggeration of breaking a rule or regulation—or breaking a law, but crime is usually symbolic in a dream.

Crime can be a way of connecting with feelings of guilt, fear, sneakiness, or indifference.

Dreaming about yourself as a criminal can connect with taking shortcuts or selling yourself short. In some way, the image fits. Or you are envious of what someone else has and are unwilling to get it for yourself the right way, an attitude commonly associated with criminals.

See also: *Accomplice, Arrest, Bail, Bandit, Burglary, Cheat, Court, Crack House, Detective, Drugs, Execution, Fugitive, Guilt, Jail, Judge, Kill, Murder, Prisoner, Thief*

Crocodile—See: *Alligator*

Crow—Crows have long been associated with bad omens and death, and in dreams they're still associated that way.

But this reputation really sells crows short, because they are among the smartest and cleverest types of birds. In dreamland, death is part of the cycle of life and rebirth, part of the process of initiation into the deep mysteries of life and your existence. Coming to terms with it can lead to tremendous creativity and personal freedom. In this sense, crows serve a very valuable purpose. By accepting death, a person can find the capacity to live more fully.

Crows can symbolize fear of death and the unknown, especially when you react to them with fear in a dream. See: *Death, Fear.*

They're associated with dark thoughts, doom, and gloominess about the future.

They're associated with mirth and the feeling that people are laughing at you.

They can symbolize a sense of foreboding or feeling of unease. Something's not right, but you haven't put your finger on it.

They can symbolize the dark side of someone you know, especially a father or father figure.

They can symbolize humiliation from admitting you're wrong after taking a strong position, as in the term "eat crow."

They can symbolize clever thinking or craftiness, especially in regard to getting something you want or working around obstacles.

They can symbolize the ability to let people go their own way and make their own decisions.

A flock of crows can symbolize many troubles and difficulties, gossip, or chaotic thoughts. The flock is the picture of loose organization—or disorganization! Now compare that disorganization with your thoughts. Do you see a connection?

The sound of crowing can be unnerving, and that association can be stretched to symbolize the feeling of being unnerved or out of sync. It can be a warning from within that you're out of your element or venturing into dangerous territory.

Crowing can be the sound of triumph or gloating.

Crows have long memories for people who do them wrong. In this sense, they're associated with plotting revenge. See: *Revenge.*

Crows are used in dreams to symbolize messengers from the unconscious mind. The black color of crows connects with the mystery of the unconscious mind, especially when it's moved to action. And the fact that crows fly and talk makes them appropriate to use as messengers. In dreams that use this symbolism, you'll sense that the crow wants to tell you something. If it beckons you to follow it, go ahead. You will be led to important self-knowledge.

A white crow is a particularly good sign of protection from danger and harmony with nature and spirit. The messages coming to you from your unconscious mind are positive and propitious.

Crows help make you aware of your hidden, unconscious potential, and for that we should all be thankful when they appear in our dreams!

See also: *Animals, Birds, Fly, Owl, Unconscious Mind, Vulture*

Crowd—See: *Group*

Cry—Crying in a dream can indicate strong emotions—grief, sadness, loss, despair—or just a need for release.

A main way dreams identify emotions is through color, and when combined with imagery they can pinpoint what emotions you are experiencing. See: *Colors*.

For example, you dream about your favorite houseplant wilted and brown after being neglected, upsetting you to tears, and it symbolizes neglecting your personal growth or health. Green is associated with growth and connection with nature, and brown with decay. Plants and people both grow, and can be unhealthy when neglected. You see yourself in the plant and react based on subconscious knowledge of the symbolism. Now you really have something to cry about!

Now ask yourself what else withers from lack of attention or care: relationships, projects, dreams for your life.

The key to understanding the symbolism is your reaction. The dream imagery represents something that triggers your emotions. What do you feel like crying about? Keep in mind that dreams focus on whatever is unprocessed from your day, so if you feel strong emotions but go to bed before processing them, you are likely to dream about them. And when dreams process your emotions for you, they are very likely to be amplified.

While awake, your guard is up, but while asleep, your guard is down and emotions can really be felt. Crying in a dream might simply be a way of releasing tension, but also consider what's going on deep in your heart. Something inside you might need your attention.

If you wake up crying, it's possible that trauma, grief, or something similar is bubbling up to the surface and may be not quite conscious yet. Or something ignored needs to be dealt with or confronted, such as pressure or stress. Or you're

healing, or venting. You can tell the difference because when you vent you feel better. The pressure is released. But if something has been repressed and finally comes to the surface, the relief from crying is temporary.

Dreaming that you cry, but no one seems to notice or care might be a sign that you feel ignored, helpless, or frustrated. You aren't getting your point across, or no one is really listening. The symbolism can be projected onto a character that cries.

You can cry because of joy or relief. The difference in feeling is obvious.

Making fun of someone crying can symbolize lack of sympathy, or being unable to connect with someone emotionally when he or she is sad or upset. It's not necessarily a character judgment. It's possible that you subconsciously know there's good reason to lack sympathy, or crying represents crocodile tears or comeuppance.

Making yourself cry in a dream can symbolize faking sadness or contrition. Or it can be a way of symbolizing acting out to get attention. Or it can mean you have difficulty crying.

Crying can be associated with immaturity—"cry like a little baby"—and manipulating people's feelings and sympathy to get what you want. For example, a man dreams that he's at a big meeting at work and one of his co-workers brings a baby to the meeting. The baby cries incessantly and the co-worker does nothing to try to stop it. The dream sums up the dreamer's opinion that the co-worker in question fusses and complains like a baby until getting his way.

At a basic level, crying is an expression of need. It might be a plea for help.

See also: *Baby, Deceased Loved One, Depressed, Emotions, Flood, Water, Wound*

Cuddle—See: *Hug*

Cunnilingus—Dreams about sex acts have a great variety of meanings, so be sure to read the entries listed below. First, though, let's explore possibilities for symbolism related to receiving cunnilingus and giving it.

Begin with your associations. For some women, cunnilingus is associated with unselfish sex. A partner who will go down is unselfish. He or she is looking out for you and considering your needs, wants to please. It can be used as a comparison to being treated well, or receiving some other sort of pleasure, such as being complimented. A compliment is delivered orally, creating a connection with oral sex.

Giving cunnilingus can symbolize tenderness (it's sensitive down there), attention to detail, "hitting the spot," or intimate knowledge of the body. These associations can be used to create symbolism entirely unrelated to sex. For example, dreaming about your partner giving you rough, unpleasant oral sex can symbolize a feeling of being treated roughly, or being "chewed out."

Cunnilingus can symbolize preparing mentally ("warming up") to take on a big creative project. That association is created by the inherent link between sexual energy and creative energy.

Because anything related to oral sex in a dream can connect with articulation or things said, performing fabulous cunnilingus can be a play on the idea of pleasing people with your words or saying something just right. It can mean exciting or moving people with oration. See: *Kiss, Mouth, Talk.*

Cunnilingus is associated with closeness and intimacy. It can show that someone or something is very close to you.

Any oral sex or kissing in a dream can symbolize talking about sex.

Oral sex has associations with dominance and submission. The person receiving it is in a dominant position. It can symbolize being in a dominant position in a relationship or situation, not just in regard to sex.

As a symbol, the vagina is loaded with possibilities for symbolism. See: *Vagina.*

Oral sex can be associated with body image and shyness or openness. Some women do not feel comfortable opening their legs for close inspection. They worry about hygiene, about turning off their partner, or about being judged, among other things.

Refusing cunnilingus in a dream can mean you are shy about your body. Or it can be a metaphor for being closed off personally or emotionally. It can mean you don't want to let someone in—or let *anyone* in. Then again, spreading your legs wide open to let your partner dive in can be a way of saying you have nothing to hide.

Doing harm to your partner while giving cunnilingus can express fear of accidentally causing harm during any sort of sex, but especially while you've got your mouth on your partner's most sensitive parts!

If a woman has trouble orgasming during intercourse and dreams about orgasming from oral sex, a dream about it can be a suggestion to give it a try.

Finally, consider the female equivalent of the phallic symbol—a yoni symbol—and the many euphemisms for cunnilingus and how they can be used as symbolism. A dream might refer to cunnilingus through symbolism such as eating a pie, licking an ice cream cone, opening a box or flower, or a bee sucking nectar.

A man dreams about removing his penis and attaching it to his wife's stomach, then positioning himself behind her to lick her vagina and anus as he reaches around to jerk off the penis. In that image he sees himself compensating for what he perceives as lack of sexual prowess. A reach-around is slang for compensation, and in the dream it symbolizes his feeling of sexual inadequacy.

Be sure to read *Fellatio.*

See also: *Fellatio, Lips, Mouth, Sex, Talk, Vagina*

Cut—See: *Knife*

Dad—See: *Father*

Dance—See: *Ballet*

Dark—Dark has two common senses of the word that can be used in dreams, the literal and figurative. In the literal sense, the environment is dark. The figurative sense means "dark personality" or "dark mood." Both senses of the word "dark" have symbolic uses and connections to everyday life.

A dark or dim environment can symbolize difficulty seeing in the sense of seeing ahead in life, or seeing the dynamics of a situation, including internal situations in your feelings or psyche. Think: "in the dark." It's a physical representation, such as not knowing better or being misunderstood. For example, you make a comment to someone and he takes it the wrong way, and you dream about it as bumping into someone in a dark room. In this sense, dark means "misunderstood."

A young man dreams he's in an attic with his old crush. They talk, then she gets up and walks out of the room. He follows her into a hallway that's almost pitch black, then down some stairs into a dark basement, where she walks through a door and disappears. It breaks his heart because he can't follow her.

The girl in the dream represents someone he had a big crush on. She befriended him, and he drove her away by trying to make the relationship romantic. The emotional blow of losing her lingered, and he lost his way personally, as symbolized by the dark hallway in the dream. The attic symbolizes dwelling on thoughts related to ruining any chance of getting his heart's desire, and the basement symbolizes his emotions, which are dark and gloomy. When his crush disappears in the dream, it's a way of saying that the relationship ended, and there is nothing he can do to get her back.

That dream provides a great illustration of the symbolism of a dark environment. To symbolize a dark personality, dreams often use dark clothes, dark skin, or a dark cloud or haze. A dark portrayal of a person in a dream reflects your perceptions. It's subjective, not objective, usually, and can mean dark in the sense of "mysterious" or "unknown."

However, your dreaming mind is great at picking up subtle clues and reading signs. A dream can show someone as dark because it's the truth and you need to be fully aware of it. A dark person can hide behind a genial personality, but you can sense what lurks behind the façade. Bear in mind, a surrogate-character can be used in a dream to represent a person you know. You will know intuitively who the surrogate represents. It might even represent you!

Most dream-characters are projections of your inner world, so a dark person is likely to symbolize a Shadow aspect of your psyche. See: *Shadow*.

Dark can symbolize feeling out of place, or being "in the dark," meaning uninformed or unaware. Keeping someone in the dark means concealing or hiding. See: *Hide*.

Be sure to read the entries for *Black* and *Night*.

See also: *Black, Blind, Clothing, Eyes, Home, Light, Night, Shadow, Stranger, Water*

Daughter—Dreaming about your daughter can symbolize something about your relationship with her, presuming you have one. You can dream about her for all sorts of reasons, but the usual ones are concerns, hopes, and fears for her and observations about her development. Parents also tend to dream about financial obligations related to their children.

Your daughter can symbolize something about yourself, too. It's natural to see yourself in your child—"she's just like I was at that age"—and easy to project yourself onto her. Your dream-characters usually represent something about you, even when they appear to be your children, so start there before assuming your daughter in a dream is a direct representation of her. It probably only looks like her.

Parents of young children are known to have many anxiety dreams about them—what are they going to get into next; what haven't you thought of?—and see those anxieties play out in dreams about their children in some sort of danger. The behavior of your child in an anxiety dream can reflect the behavior of your child while awake, but it's usually exaggerated and based on your projections. If the dream seems outlandish in some way, it's a strong clue that it's symbolism. See: *Anxiety*.

For women, a daughter in a dream—a real or imaginary child—can symbolize her roots as a female. It can show where and how the ideas formed about the sort of woman she is. Or it can symbolize the little girl within her who has the needs of a child—for comfort, assurance, guidance, stimulation, challenge, structure. The character can represent potential for personal growth and development. See: *Child*.

If you don't have a daughter but dream you do, begin the interpretation process by asking yourself whether you want a daughter, and is the

dream helping you sort out your thoughts and feelings about being a parent.

In simplest terms, a daughter is a creation, a ready-made symbol for something you create or creativity in general. The association is built-in, so you don't have to be a parent for your dreams to use it.

For example, a man who does not have a daughter dreams that he's in a hotel lobby and sees the musical instruments of a famous band waiting to be carted off. He asks the bored hotel clerk whether he can play the beautiful blue guitar. The clerk says sure. The dreamer picks it up and, even though he's never played guitar, makes the instrument sing with poignant emotion. The instrument morphs into his teenaged daughter—again, though, he doesn't have a daughter, so it must be symbolism. She wears a blue shirt and says she's sorry she died. He tells her it's all right, and when he's done she morphs back into a guitar, and he sets it aside, commenting to the clerk that it's one special instrument. The clerk replies, "It's the player that makes it special."

The daughter is the key to the dream because it's about unused creativity. The dreamer's day job is video editor in a fast-paced studio. He rarely gets a chance to put any real creativity into it, and he realizes his creativity is wasting away. That's what the dream means by the daughter's having died.

His expression of emotion through the guitar shows a deep reservoir in himself, if he can find a way to tap it. Viewed in this light, the clerk's remark at the end is especially poignant, because it suggests he has a special talent for expressing his emotions through creativity.

A daughter in a dream can symbolize something that's precious, that needs your protection, that you are responsible for, that's beautiful, that you watch grow.

We all inherently possess traits of both genders, so for a male, a daughter can symbolize his traditionally feminine traits—his nurturing, receptive, yin side. If his feminine side is shown as a young daughter in a dream, it's a way of saying that side of him is undeveloped. Depicting those aspects of himself as a daughter in a dream can symbolize the internal relationship he has with his feminine side. See: *Vagina*.

Parents can dream about their children as a way of observing changes within themselves as their parental roles change. These dreams usually tie back to a child's leaving the nest, getting married, or having children of her own. As parent, you now find that your role in your child's life changes.

A daughter that's not yours, such as a friend's daughter, can be a surrogate-character for your daughter. You see something about your daughter in her—they possess similar traits and qualities—or the two characters are connected symbolically by the fact that they're both daughters. If you're close to that person, it can be a way of saying she is like a daughter to you.

A daughter can symbolize any close relationship that's like a parent-child bond.

If you have a daughter and dream about her dying or committing suicide, it can symbolize that some aspect of the relationship is dying. Perhaps you are growing apart, or have been out of touch and need to reconnect. It can symbolize concerns about your daughter and her health, decisions, future, progress, and so forth.

In rare cases, dreams can give warnings to parents that something bad is about to happen, or could happen, to their children. These are known as precognitive dreams. However, the great majority of dreams parents have about something bad happening to their children are symbolic. And while a bad dream can show the need for action on the parent's part, don't jump to the conclusion that it's a literal warning. Analyze it for symbolism and search your heart. If you can't shake the bad feeling, or if the dream recurs, do what you think is best. See: *Precognitive Dream*.

(FYI, *The Gift* by Sally Rhine Feather documents a multitude of precognitive dreams that parents had about their children.)

A man in drug treatment dreams that his future daughter calls him and says that if he relapses again, he'll die and she'll never be born. On one

level you can interpret the dream just as a strong inner message to stay sober—the dream devised the best strategy, the best reason, for him to stay sober. On another level, it just might be true: if he relapses, he'll die and erase any possibility of having children. Precognition is more like a forecast than a prophecy. It tells you what *could* happen.

If you dream that your daughter has an illness, it can symbolize that you have observed something ill about her. Could be a physical illness, but also consider emotional and psychological illness, and the idea of illness meaning simply that something doesn't feel right to you.

Illness can symbolize concerns that she is being negatively affected by an external circumstance. For example, your home situation has hit a rough patch (arguments with spouse, financial difficulty), and you are concerned it is influencing her in a bad way.

For example, a mother dreams that her young daughter has cancer and the doctor tells her a treatment is already being devised. In this case, cancer symbolizes a very difficult family situation that mom fears is affecting her daughter. Mom recently had another baby, and dad got seriously hurt while serving overseas in the military. Mom just hasn't had as much time for face-time with her daughter. But the prognosis is good. She's aware of the problem, and in the back of her mind is thinking of a solution. That's what the dream means by a treatment already being devised.

It can mean something is ill about the relationship.

If you don't have a daughter but dream that you do and she is ill, it can say that something in you needs attention, tenderness, or treatment. You need to act like a good parent toward yourself.

Dreaming about your daughter being raped can indicate that a side of yourself feels abused or violated. It can mean that your innocence has been lost. Recurring dreams about a young child being abused is a sign that you're dealing with the abuse that happened to you as a child. The dream projects these feelings and thoughts onto a character to give you distance to observe.

A daughter can symbolize her sibling, another child, or an entire family. For example, a woman dreams about her baby niece as a symbol of thoughts related to the entire family. As the latest member of the family, the niece symbolizes the woman's thoughts related to the future of the family and how to preserve its cohesion.

To explore further, see: *Sister*.

See also: *Anxiety, Child, Girl, Kidnap, Pageant, Parent, Precognitive Dream, Rescue, Sister, Son, Suicide, Vagina, Woman*

Dead End—A dead end in a dream can mean that you see no way of moving forward with something. The road isn't leading to where you want to go in life. Progress with something isn't being made. It can relate to an external situation such as a project or idea, or an internal situation such as where your feelings have been headed.

A dead end can mean that something has come to an end; for example, a relationship or job. It can express the feeling that something has trapped you or is pointless.

It can mean that time for making a decision has run out.

Everyone knows what a dead end means, but we tend to make dreams too complicated and miss the obvious. In simplest terms, a road or path that ends is a dead end.

See also: *Abyss, Alley, Car, Cliff, Road*

Deadline—See: *Execution*

Death—Death in a dream can indicate a big change in yourself or your life. In simplest terms, death is "the end," and in dream-speak that means the end of something such as a situation or phase of life. It can even relate to the end of a favorite television series or a big project.

When related to yourself, it can mean that some part of yourself is passing away. You're maturing. Or some aspect of yourself is under threat. For example, a distressful dream about a child dying can mean that an innocent and joyful part of yourself is receding. You need more fun. Or perhaps the child represents an immature part of

yourself that needs to grow up. In which case the feeling is entirely different. You know deep inside that it's all right for the child to pass on. But if you're having difficulty letting go, these dreams can be distressful, even terrifying.

When analyzing a dream that features death, think of how it's used as a comparison or metaphor. For example, "dead to the world" means unresponsive or disconnected. "The death of me" can mean that a situation or circumstance is wearing you down. "Dead on your feet" means totally exhausted. See: *Coma*.

Death can be a way of saying you failed. For example, flunking an exam is the death of your chance to get a good grade.

When you say that something is killing you, it's killing you inside. Unless meant literally, it's an exaggeration that gets across your feelings. You may not consciously realize the situation is as bad as it is, or that you feel as strongly as you do. "Dead inside" means depressed, lacking spark or emotion. See: *Zombie*.

Of course, death is a reality we all face, and you will dream about it. Dreams about death are known to occur after close brushes with it. See: *Grim Reaper*.

Death dreams can be sparked by fear that you're losing your good health, especially if you have a bad habit or lifestyle sapping you. See: *Cancer, Disease*.

Elderly and very sick people dream about death as a way of preparing for it. Studies have shown that if death can be faced and accepted in a dream, it brings peace and makes passing away easier. Just before someone you know passes away, especially a loved one, you may dream about it. A common theme in such dreams is that deceased family members return to take the person away for a journey. See: *Deceased Loved One*.

Dreaming about the death of someone you know can mean that you want that person out of the picture or out of your life. It can connect with strong feelings about the person. For example, a young man dreams that he accidentally kills his best friend then attends the funeral alongside the friend's girlfriend, expressing a subconscious wish to get his friend out of the way and have a shot at his girlfriend. See: *Kill*.

Feelings of hostility, wounding, or aggression connected with someone you know can spark dreams about that person dying, but more often it connects with feelings of guilt, envy, jealousy, or even the possessive sort of love expressed in the phrase "love you to death." Which isn't really love at all.

Dreaming about the death of a parent can be a subconscious wish fulfillment. It makes room for the child to become the adult, the student to become the master. Or it expresses a wish to replace the parent as spouse to a beloved mother or father—a classic Oedipus or Electra complex. Such wishes are rare. However, if you have a difficult relationship with a parent and dream about him or her dying, perhaps you really would like to see the parent out of the picture in the sense of being out of your life.

You can dream about your parent dying because you are doing something you think he or she would disapprove of, such as sex before marriage, drugs, or dating the wrong person—something you might say would kill your parent if he or she found out. For examples, see: *Casino, Hang*.

Or maybe your relationship with a parent is changing and you aren't as close. You're out of touch, or you fear for his or her health or safety.

A Christian might dream about Jesus dying because he or she feels guilty about sinning. You could dream about an ex-mate dying after the relationship has ended. It means the relationship is dead, or the feelings you once had are gone.

Dreaming about the death of someone you know can be a reminder of how important the person is to you. It's meant to shake you up. Use your time together wisely.

Dreaming about someone who really has died can be triggered by a reminder of the person. You don't even have to think directly about him or her. For example, driving by a cemetery can trigger subconscious associations. Anniversaries and birthdays are known to trigger dreams about deceased loved ones and friends.

A dead animal in a dream can symbolize the possibilities already discussed, but combined with the symbolism of the animal. For example, a dead dog can symbolize a friendship in jeopardy. A dead lion can symbolize a major blow to your pride. A dead bird can mean you have lost the ability to express yourself, or feel like your life is going nowhere because of a personal wound.

To dream about euthanasia can symbolize wanting to end something as painlessly as possible. For example, breaking up with a significant other, ending a friendship, or giving bad news.

See also: *Animal, Black, Body, Bury, Calendar, Cancer, Coffin, Coma, Crow, Decapitate, Deceased Loved One, Disease, Elderly, Execution, Friend, Funeral, Ghost, Graveyard, Grim Reaper, Hang, Hospital, Kill, Murder, Panic, Strangle, Subconscious, Time, Vampire, Widow, Zombie*

Death Sentence—See: *Execution*

Decapitate—The symbolism of decapitation is often associated with the head and its functions. It can mean unclear thinking, or not listening. Or something deserves more attention or consideration.

Or you don't like the thoughts in your head. It's too full. Or you're ignoring the obvious message that something isn't right in yourself or your life.

Decapitation can symbolize the idea in the phrase "lose your head," acting out of character or irrationally.

Or you aren't listening to your heart. Conflict between your head and heart is a common dream theme. Your head says one thing, your heart says another. You're being too rational, or too emotional. Important parts of you are separated or divided. See: *Giraffe*.

Whether or not the action is directed at you or someone else is important. If it happens to you, the symbolism is likely to apply to you. But a stranger being decapitated is either a surrogate-character for you, or an observation of something that happened recently, such as someone you know losing his head figuratively, or drastic action was taken, or hard punishment was dished out.

Decapitation of an animal can mean you aren't listening to your instincts, or you're taking drastic measures to control your impulses. In that sense, decapitation is similar to the symbolism of castration.

See also: *Body, Castrate, Death, Execution, Giraffe, Hang, Head, Neck*

Deceased Loved One—The first possibility to consider for the meaning of a dream about a deceased loved one is that the person is a projection of yourself, a character in a story, not your loved one. Otherwise, strong emotions and thoughts tend to muddy the water. It's difficult to step back and analyze the dream as you would any other dream-story, but that's how you get to the bottom of it. Eliminate other possibilities before thinking it's spiritual contact with the person in the afterlife.

Grief and loss are the two most common subjects of these stories. You're processing emotions related to the death of the person you love, or adjusting to life without him or her. In broad terms, the tone and tenor of the dream show where you're at. If the dream is distressing or your deceased loved one's character acts strangely, it indicates that you're still processing the emotions and getting a grip on your loss. An encouraging dream generally indicates you've made it through that part of the grief process, at least enough to find balance within yourself again.

For example, a young man whose father died dreams about balancing the water temperature in a fish tank. Once it's balanced, his father appears in the room, and they have a happy reunion. Balancing the temperature of the water symbolizes balancing his emotions, giving him access to the memories of his father in positive ways.

That dream contrasts with one a young man had about seeing his father at a memorial service and being unable to get his attention. It's a way of saying his father is no longer around to hear him, to share his life.

A widow dreams that she's lost her car, and a man offers to help her find it; then he wants to kiss her. She refuses his advance. The dream could be interpreted as her needing physical closeness, and the time has come to find it with another man. But the dream is actually about moving on from her grief. It's what keeps her connected to the memory of her deceased husband, and she feels that moving on from her grief, as symbolized by finding her car, means losing the last thing connecting them. She's not ready to move on.

The actions and behaviors of dream-characters are projections from inside you, so if you dream about a deceased loved one in distress, it probably means *you are in distress*.

In dreams, you project your inner life to see it more clearly and from different perspectives. That key piece of information helps you decipher your dreams about deceased loved ones.

Dreams about a deceased person can relate to fears about your health or the possibility of death, or fears about someone you know. It can express a wish that the person were still part of your life, especially during a time of need, when, in the past, you would turn to that person. For example, missing the advice your father used to give you, or the company of a friend. It can mean simply that you miss that person, whose memory is still alive within you.

After many years of studying this subject and speaking with people about their dreams involving deceased loved ones, I am convinced that dreams *can* act as a sort of telephone line between those alive in this world and those alive in the next world. The subject is way too deep to explore here, so I encourage you to go to my blog at *dreams123.net* and search for "dead loved ones." I give a thorough breakdown of how to tell when a message is coming through from beyond, or is coming through from inside you.

See also: *Afterlife, Daughter, Death, Family, Father, Mother, Love, Precognitive Dream*

Deep—See: *Fishing*

Deer—Dreaming about deer can indicate nervousness or skittishness, since deer flee at the first sign of danger.

Deer can symbolize something elusive, such as the solution to a problem, or a person you can't pin down.

They can symbolize an easy prey.

The phrase "deer in the headlights" means frozen in place and unable to take action. Perhaps you are indecisive about a situation, or in shock about something. This use of the symbolism will show in the imagery of being unable to move.

A deer can symbolize someone you refer to as "dear," especially if the deer talks.

See also: *Animals*

Defecate—See: *Toilet*

Deformed—Think of deformity in a dream as a physical representation of something askew, out of kilter, or misunderstood.

It can mean something is not right. Think: "distorted."

Deformity can reflect a distorted self-image, especially if a mirror is involved. See: *Mirror*.

It can symbolize excessive self-criticism.

It can symbolize severe issues with body image, or show self-loathing, heavy guilt, or shame.

Deformity can be a way of visualizing an undeveloped aspect of yourself, or something about yourself that's repressed, ignored, or disrupting your development or creativity. Creations are formed, so deformation can mean the creation process is awry or incomplete.

It can mean the internal picture of something hasn't come into focus, or something about yourself has recently emerged from the unconscious and hasn't taken distinct form yet. See: *Beach*.

To dream about being dismembered can express feelings about being attacked personally. A situation is tearing you up. You go through the "meat grinder."

Deformity or dismemberment can symbolize an ill mood or bad temper. It's "ugly." See: *Ugly*.

It can represent how you think people perceive you or react to you. If you get strange reactions from people, you can wonder if something really is wrong with you.

Deformity can visualize personal damage done by making a terrible mistake, something that

harms your image or reputation. It's a physical representation.

Carry the idea of "mangled" further, and it can symbolize a botched job or major fubar.

It can symbolize something horrible or frightening. See: *Creature, Monster*.

It can symbolize action or behavior that does or could cause harm to yourself or other people. Taking daredevil risks, for example, can lead to the sort of accident that disfigures you. In which case, a dream about being disfigured in an accident can symbolize fear of its actually happening.

Deformity or disfigurement can stem from personal neglect. It's an extreme way of calling attention to your physical, emotional, or mental health.

See also: *Beach, Body, Creature, Face, Handicap, Mirror, Monster, Ugly*

Déjà Vu—See: *Precognitive Dream*

Demolish—See: *Destruction*

Demon—Look at the demon in your dream. Do you see anything about yourself: a personality trait, a bad attitude, a problem that won't go away, a foul mouth, disregard for the welfare of others, something you can't control or that's looming over you?

Does it remind you of someone you know, or a situation?

Most dream-characters are reflections of something about you, but it's not to say you're demonic because you dream about a demon. Instead it's an exaggeration that fits. It expresses how you feel, or captures the dynamics of a behavior or thought process.

In simplest terms, a demon is bad. Start there.

Demons are commonly associated with fear. In the demon, you see fear personified. Demons tend to symbolize a plague of fears because demons generally come in bunches. Devils, on the other hand, tend to be singular and specific. For example, demons could symbolize fear of spiders in general, and a devil can symbolize fear of the spider you saw lurking in your laundry room. A demon might symbolize a group of people you fear, and a devil symbolizes a specific person. This is only a rule of thumb.

Fear of death and consequences are commonly symbolized as demons, because demons are conceived as what's waiting for bad people after they die. This association can branch out to include subjects related to doing the right thing and taking responsibility for actions. The entry for *Hell* has a terrific example. See: *Death, Fear*.

A demon might symbolize a person you know whom you fear, or someone who uses fear or intimidation.

Fear is at the root of many personality disorders, bad personal problems, neuroses, and complexes, which can take form as dream-characters such as demons. They are your "personal demons."

A demon is a helluva symbol for something about yourself or another person that you can't stand, and it won't go away.

Demons are associated with possession, and a person can be possessed by a mood, thought, feeling, or compulsion, among other things. Possession can mean "not behaving like your usual self," especially if that behavior is compulsive or destructive, or involves loss of control. See: *Possessed*.

It can mean you are possessed by your Shadow. See: *Shadow*.

Exorcising a demon can symbolize confronting a dark side of yourself or of someone you know. But think more expansively to consider possibilities such as confronting a bad situation or bad influence, or just needing some sort of higher power to intervene. Exorcism can symbolize getting something bad out of your body or mind, such as disease or addiction. See: *Addict, Cancer*.

You can dream about a demon as a way of trying to explain something that seems inexplicable, such as why someone commits suicide or murder. The person must be possessed.

Demons are associated with temptation. It's likely to be a powerful temptation if it's symbolized as a demon. Could be something like drugs or sex, something "sinful." Dreams can make exaggerated comparisons, so perhaps a temptation symbolized by a demon is related to something like eating rich foods, lashing out when angry, or shocking or inappropriate statements.

An infestation of demons can symbolize many temptations. See: *Infest*.

Demons are associated with dark personality and character. A demon dream can characterize what you observe about a person or yourself—especially if it's hidden or shadowy. Some people give off a bad vibe. Some act selfishly. Some are abusive. Some take advantage of others. Some are bigots. Some have bad habits and addictions. Some rob, cheat, and kill. Dreams translate these baddies into imagery such as demons.

When you sense something wrong about a person, or the person acts in a way that strikes you as wrong, your dreams can compare him or her to a demon. This is an especially strong possibility if you have recently been abused or been the victim of a crime, racism, or misogyny. You see the worst in people, and dream about that feeling as a demon or demonic possession.

Anything repressed or neglected in yourself will try to get your attention in your dreams, and what better way to do that than to take form as something shocking or scary like a demon? The more something about yourself is repressed or neglected, the scarier it becomes. A demon can be something you ignore or don't want to accept about yourself.

Demonic characters appear in dreams during times of conflict. They can symbolize the negativity of a situation, or powerful feelings such as anger, jealousy, and resentment that are brought out by conflict or abuse.

They can symbolize a grudge, revenge, guilt, dread, or severe anxiety.

They can be used to symbolize the source of problems in your life, especially when the problem seems inexplicable or intractable. For example, you have arguments with a sibling or spouse and realize there is something deeper to the conflict you can't put your finger on.

If you have been abused, there is a good possibility that recurring dreams about demons are related to the abuse. Think back on when the abuse started and ask yourself whether the dreams started around the same time. If so, the possibility increases to very likely.

If you have recurring dreams about demons, it strongly suggests that something needs to change. Remember, dreams use demons as an analogy. Your job is to figure out what's behind the comparison. If you suspect something spiritual is haunting you, a great resource for you is *www.religiousdemonology.com*.

You can dream about demons or devils because of sleep paralysis, also known as rapid eye movement (REM) atonia. Sleep paralysis occurs when you wake up but are still dreaming. Dream imagery and sensation overlap with your waking reality, making you believe the imagery is real and really happening.

Sleep paralysis is at the root of myths about incubi and succubi, demonic beings that seduce people in their sleep. The experience is so vivid and real that it can convince even the most rational and non-religious people that they're being attacked by real evil. See: *Sleep Paralysis.*

For people with a religious bent, their minds can be chock-full of demonic imagery. Because this imagery carries a strong emotional charge, it's very likely to be expressed in dreams. And "spiritual warfare" is a common theme in these dreams. In this sense, demons can symbolize anything contrary to your spiritual beliefs.

Demons and evil characters can simply be a way of saying you can't explain something that feels dark or terrifying. In this sense, demons are catch-all characters similar to aliens. See: *UFO.*

See also: *Addict, Beast, Black, Cancer, Creature, Dark, Death, Devil, Enemy, Evil, Fear, Hell, Monster, Nazi, Nightmare, Possession, Shadow, Sleep Paralysis, UFO*

Depression—Dreaming about feeling depressed can indicate you really are depressed. A dream can explore the roots and reasons for depression, or simply reflect that you feel that way.

Depression can be used as a comparison to feeling sad, listless, moody, or bored. You aren't necessarily depressed, but feel close to it. Depression can be symbolized in dreams by the color blue, a deflated balloon, downward movement, zombies, comas, a blizzard, or a depression in the ground, among other things. See: *Abyss, Blizzard, Coma.*

Depression is the opposite of inflation, and the two go hand in hand. Periods of depression tend to follow periods of ego inflation and ego frustration. Do you feel depressed soon after being denied something you want, or when you are unable to move toward a goal or vision for your life? Those possibilities are the first to consider after dreaming about depression.

Feeling depressed is treated like an illness, to be cured with prescription medicine, when it's actually a natural function of the psyche to force attention inward and solve problems and answer existential questions. Clinical depression truly is an illness. What I refer to here is the feeling of depression.

Many side issues related to depression can come up as subjects in dreams, sometimes as a way of exploring why you feel depressed and what, if anything, can be done about it.

The entry for *Cry* can give you more ideas, even if your dream doesn't involve crying.

For an example dream from someone dealing with depression, see: *Horse.*

See also: *Abyss, Black, Blizzard, Blue, Cry, Dark, Descend, Emotions, Horse, Zombies*

Descend—The symbolism of descending in a dream can mean the same as "in decline." For example, a peak is reached in life—physically, personally, mentally, socially—and everything afterward is perceived as moving down or declining. It can symbolize falling fortunes, falling body temperature, lowered expectations, or declining health, skill, or ability.

"Stepping down" means to relinquish a position of authority or power. See: *Stairs.*

Movement down can be associated with emotions, especially if the setting is a basement or stairs. Emotions are felt most strongly in the gut and chest, which are located below the head, so in dreams your emotions can be symbolized as descent into a basement or low area. See: *Basement*.

For example, a young woman dreams that her boyfriend is at the top of the stairs of their house and is about to take a step down. She screams and shouts for him to stop. Her reaction here is key because it reveals strong feelings related to the underlying symbolism. Otherwise, why react so strongly to something as simple as walking down stairs? It's because stepping down symbolizes his attempts to understand her, especially her emotions, and subconsciously she understands what stepping down means. She's highly protective of her emotions, doesn't let anyone in. "Don't go there," is what she's really trying to say.

Downward movement can symbolize a lowered opinion of someone or something.

It's associated with a "sinking feeling" and "descent into chaos." You have a feeling things are about to take a turn for the worse, or a situation is melting down.

Downward movement is associated with "coming down" off a high—drug-induced or related to mood and feelings. See: *Crash*.

Downward movement, especially a spiral movement, can indicate that a solution or answer is being sought in the unconscious mind. When solutions are sought for issues related to soul or personal development, we descend into the unconscious mind. In spiritual traditions the underworld is a place of wisdom and rebirth. See: *Spiral*.

Descending movement can be a visual pun for "descendent," meaning "to descend from."

Be sure to read the entry for *Elevator*.

See also: *Ascend, Basement, Climb, Crash, Depression, Descend, Elevator, Fall, Hell, Spiral, Stairs, Unconscious Mind*

Desert—Dreaming about a desert can indicate a barren, dry, or empty time of life. The imagery captures how you feel or what you perceive. Your life, job, or relationships lack meaning or zest.

For example, a woman dreams about walking endlessly in a barren wasteland. She's alone, and the only landmarks appear far away. For protection from the sun she puts on her husband's favorite baseball cap, but for some reason it lacks a visor and ends up looking like a dunce cap on her head.

Walking alone in the desert sums up how she feels in her loveless marriage. Her husband is distant emotionally, as symbolized by the landmarks distant on the horizon. Putting on her husband's baseball cap is a way of symbolizing thinking about her marriage to him. A hat or cap is worn on the head, and thoughts are associated with the head. The visor, which is supposed to protect her from the sun, is missing, because what she's really trying to protect herself from is thinking too deeply about what's missing from her marriage. It only makes her miserable. And the dunce cap refers to her feeling that she must be stupid to continue trudging forward in a marriage that's making her miserable.

Being lost or alone in a desert can have similar symbolism to being lost in a forest or wilderness. See: *Forest, Wilderness*.

Water is closely associated with emotion, so a dry dream environment can be a metaphor for lack of feelings and emotions. See: *Water*.

Barren is a word used to describe being childless or unable to conceive.

An endless desert can symbolize the sense that a bad situation has no end.

A desert is a great setting to connect with "feeling the heat." A situation has become tense or risky, or you can no longer stand it, such as in the example above in which a desert symbolizes a loveless marriage. See: *Heat*.

For people who have spent time in deserts, dreaming about them can be associated with that experience. For example, soldiers who served in Iraq might dream about the desert as a reference to that war.

See also: *Empty, Forest, Heat, Lost, Sun, War, Wilderness*

Desk—A large or imposing desk can be a symbol of authority. It can be a symbol of your inner authority, especially if you meet an important person in association with the desk. Or it can represent an authority figure or structure.

A work desk can symbolize something related to work life or tasks that need to be done. For example, straightening up a desk can symbolize taking care of loose ends and paying bills. For some people, these small tasks need to be done before a big task is tackled.

Sitting at the desk of another person can indicate lacking trust in your own abilities, or wanting to assume that person's authority or responsibility—not necessarily take over, though that's certainly a possibility, too.

A desk can remind you of a person and refer to him or her. It can remind you of a time of life. For example, a school desk can symbolize school life. It can symbolize the feeling of being treated like a kid, or unable to assume an adult role. This use of the symbolism is especially likely if you dream about yourself as a fully grown adult trying to stuff yourself into a small school desk.

See also: *Campus, Parents, School, Student, Teacher*

Dessert—Eating a dessert in a dream can symbolize a reward for a job well done or a good effort.

It can also symbolize giving in to weakness or temptation.

See also: *Candy, Eat, Food*

Destination—See: *Airplane, Boat, Road*

Destruction—Think of destruction as a physical representation, such as for volatile situations and big changes. Trust and faith can be destroyed. Home life can be destroyed. Health can be destroyed.

A city destroyed can symbolize damage to your public life, because cities are where many people live, careers are made, and aspects of public life are carried out. Buildings closely spaced together, such as in cities, are ready-made to compare with close relations and connections, so destruction of said buildings can symbolize conflicts with people close to you, such as family members or co-workers.

Scenes of destruction can show your old life or aspects of it passing away. For example, seeing your old neighborhood destroyed can symbolize changes in your values, priorities, belief systems and ways of thinking. You are no longer the same person. The same ideas can be expressed in scenes of your old school or home destroyed. See: *Neighbor*.

Demolition in a dream can indicate that an area of your life or yourself is undergoing a change as previous structures collapse. For example, during a divorce you might dream about the house you shared with your ex-spouse being demolished—the marriage is a sort of structure. Or when your personality "structure" is changing, you might dream about a building being demolished. Or your beliefs change, and you dream about a church demolished.

The difference is, demolitions are deliberate and planned, and destruction is more random.

After taking a huge blow to your self-image, or your life suddenly turning to crap, you might dream about your car being destroyed or a building crumbling.

See also: *Bomb, Building, City, Construction, Neighbor, Nuclear War, Tornado, War*

Detain—See: *Jail*

Detective—A detective-character in your dream can connect with investigating something or seeking the truth. Detectives investigate crimes and wrongdoings. They seek information and truth. That idea translates to your life when you have questions you want answered.

For example, you realize your marriage is on the rocks and wonder how it happened. You dream about a detective watching a person as she works long hours, and realize your marriage is falling apart because you or your spouse spend too much time at work.

Detectives pry into personal lives and uncover hidden information and motives. In dreams, that idea translates to feeling that your personal life is pried open, that someone is snooping around where you don't want them, or that something you want hidden will be exposed. It can connect with a guilty conscience, bad intentions, and secrecy—strong possibilities to consider if you dream about being followed by a detective.

Detectives establish the facts, so dreaming about a detective can connect with separating fact from conjecture, opinion, fiction, or lies.

You can feel like you are a detective when you have been entrusted with secrets or private information.

Detectives investigate crimes, and the idea of what is a figurative crime can stretch far. Such as, it's a crime that you dropped a good habit or idea, or gave up what you want to do with your life. You feel robbed, victimized, denied. See: *Crime*.

When you play the role of detective in a dream, maybe it means you are the one prying into personal lives or discovering secrets. Or you are investigating a possibility, or why something happened. It can mean that you're trying to uncover something about yourself that's hidden, such as talents or abilities. Or you repressed memories and they need to be uncovered. However, any personal association with detectives can be used to create symbolism.

For example, a man has recurring dreams about being a homicide detective in a city where he used to live. He never actually investigates crimes; instead, the dreams largely revolve around thinking about the implications of having a steady job. He associates the job of homicide detective with making major sacrifices to personal life in return for salary and benefits, and that theme is prevalent in his life as he pursues his dream job and sacrifices having a salary and benefits. The city he used to live in is where he first started pursuing his dream, so it's used as the setting.

Excitement about investigating something can mean you are excited about a prospect or opportunity such as buying a home or starting a new career. Being bored or frustrated while investigating can mean you're bored of the same old routine and need a new adventure. Connect the feelings brought up by the dream with what's happening in your life.

See also: *Affair, Cheat, Crime, Fugitive, Jail, Police Officer, Prisoner, Spy*

Detour—A detour in a dream can mean a change of direction in your life, or getting off track from a goal. For example, you study to be a marine biologist but end up working in retail. It's a detour in your career path that could be symbolized in a dream as driving to a marina but detouring to a shopping mall.

A detour can symbolize deviations from the main road, not just career path but personal development, spirituality, relationships, and so on.

A detour can mean someone is detouring you from what you know it right. It means bad advice or influence.

On the other hand, it can mean getting around an obstacle or path that's blocked.

Think in general terms of a detour as a deviation, a break in the routine, or an alternate route.

See also: *Car, Dead End, Highway, Road*

Devil—A good discussion of the general symbolism of devils and demons is covered in these entries: *Demon, Evil*. However, some things can be said separately about a devil dream-character—or *the* devil, aka Satan or Lucifer. These characters can come with religious overtones, but unless you have a religious bent, they're likely to be pure symbolism and have little to do with religious ideas of the devil. This is important to mention off the bat because many people assume that a powerful dream featuring an evil character such as Satan means they're confronted by spiritual evil, and that's just not the case.

Then again....

If you strongly believe you can be influenced or tempted by the devil, the theme is more likely to pop up in your dreams. However, it's not a requirement, it just means that the idea is already planted in your mind.

The difference between demons and devils is that demons are understood as minions or soldiers, whereas devils tend to have more personal distinction and authority. Demons are many, the devil is singular, though the terms are used interchangeably.

That idea applied to your dreams can be used to differentiate between many and one. For example, demons can be used to describe many temptations, and a devil is used to describe one especially bad one. Demons can be used to describe something general, such as fear, and the devil can be used to describe fear of something specific. Demons can be used to describe many thoughts plaguing you, and the devil can be used to describe one thought plaguing you. See: *Demon*.

The devil as a character appears in dreams as a singular figure. It might symbolize something in your life causing real problems, something dangerous. But dreams exaggerate, and the devil can represent something relatively harmless. For example, a mischievous child is described as a "little devil." A troublesome temper can be described as "a devil inside." Compared to a real encounter with the devil itself, a troublesome temper is easier to handle!

Satan and Lucifer are specific devils. When they appear in a dream it can mean something is not just bad, it's really bad. It's awful.

For example, a young woman dreams that Satan crawls into her bed. At first she thinks it's her boyfriend and she welcomes the presence. Then she realizes it's ... Satan! And he has her in his clutches. She feels his erection enter her from behind and she can't do anything to stop it. It has a strange pull on her—she even starts to enjoy it, but at the same time she hates it and is scared out of her mind that she'll get pregnant. The dream symbolizes her fear of getting pregnant. It's a thought that terrifies her, but she enjoys sex with her boyfriend, so what's a girl to do? Satan is used to dramatize the story because she doesn't just fear accidentally getting pregnant, she's terrified. It would make her life a living hell.

A young man dreams about being anally raped by Satan. He reaches around, pulls out excrement and rubs it in Satan's face. Satan returns the favor by rubbing it in the dreamer's face. Satan laughs and says the dreamer will never be free. The dream dramatizes an awful situation. The young man is locked in a nonstop war of words with a classmate. They say the nastiest things to each other, as symbolized by rubbing shit in each other's faces. The dreamer sees no end to the situation; he'll "never be free" of it. In an exaggerated way, it feels like anal rape, and Satan represents "my tormentor." See: *Anal Sex*.

A woman dreams that she's pregnant with Satan's baby and desperate to get an abortion. The dream symbolizes evil thoughts that have wormed into her head. She's in a really dark place and is desperate to get out of it before it changes her for the worse.

A woman dreams that she's at Lucifer's wedding. The scenery is decorated in black, but otherwise there's nothing else dark or malicious about the scene. The dreamer is in the wedding party, waiting for Lucifer to arrive. The dream then flashes to the kitchen, where she helps to decorate the wedding cake. It's shaped to look like a ruined building, and the dreamer puts on the icing.

Quite simply, this dream is about the dreamer changing, and the new direction she's going is symbolized as participating in Lucifer's wedding. Wedding can mean "wedded to" in the sense of bonding or uniting, and that's a great analogy for new beliefs, values, and ways of thinking that become part of you. They bond with the ego. The cake in the shape of a ruined building shows that her belief structure is changing, and putting icing on the cake is a way of saying the process is close to completion.

The key clue is found in the dreamer's associations with Lucifer as accepting of everyone, in stark contrast to her experience with intolerant religious people. The Lucifer of the dream is not the Lucifer of the Bible. This Lucifer is a projection of the dreamer's perceptions, a contrast of everything she perceives about religious people. She's moving toward becoming more accepting of everyone and that's symbolized as a wedding with Lucifer. Being the bride in that scenario has a different connotation, so the dream shows her in the wedding party.

As seen in the above example, the key to deciphering the symbolism is to connect the dream devil with what it means to you. This is a very important point, especially with characters like Satan and Lucifer, because while they *can* represent religious associations with them, that doesn't automatically mean they *do*.

Of course, always consider the possibility that a dream-character is part of the scene, not a central actor in it. For example, if your life is hell and your dreams create a metaphor for it, a devil or demon might just go with the territory. It depends on the role the character plays. Usually, though, every detail of a dream is meaningful and connects with the story.

See also: *Death, Demon, Dragon, Enemy, Evil, Hell, Infest, Nazi, Possessed, Shadow*

Devour—When a dream uses "devour" to tell the story, it's next-level symbolism above eating. It's not just hunger, it's voraciousness. It not just taking something into oneself, but doing it in a way that's extreme. Otherwise, a dream can just show the symbolism as eating. It uses devouring for a reason. See: *Eat*.

To devour implies a huge need or appetite, not just for food but for intangible things such as attention or success.

It can indicate powerful passion or desire.

Being devoured can mean you fear loss of your identity, particularly in cases when someone dominates or smothers you, such as a dominant parental figure or an authority figure such as a boss or commanding officer.

You can be devoured by stress or the daily grind. It's not just eating at you, it's eating you up. See: *Cancer*.

It can symbolize a desire to lose yourself, to disappear and never be seen again. See: *Eaten*.

See also: *Animals, Bear, Boss, Desire, Dragon, Eat, Eaten, Father, Food, Monster, Mother, Shark*

Diamond—Dreams create symbolism based on associations, and a primary association with diamonds is clarity. Clarity in dream-speak can mean "clear" or "coherent," as in, "my thinking is clear," or "the situation needs clarity." The clarity of the diamond will be part of the dream-story.

Diamonds are the hardest mineral and are put in settings, which can symbolize being set in your ways, and having strong character and values. Extend the idea of hardness and it can symbolize hard-headedness, a hard heart, a hard job, and so on.

Diamonds have facets and can symbolize a multifaceted person or situation. This use of the symbolism is more likely if the facets are noticed.

Diamonds are associated with value and can have symbolism related to what you value most. Your prize. Your *precious*.

The idea of value stretches further to include what you're willing to pay for what you want. Such as when weighing the trade-off between what you can afford to pay for an engagement ring and what you think your girl is worth. Even if she's worth the world to you, there's still a valuation involved with buying her a ring, and it's a very public decision because a lot of people are going to see that ring and make an instant judgment about how much you value her—and so is she, if she uses the cost of the diamond as her measuring stick.

Diamonds are associated with wealth, especially stored wealth, portable wealth, and show of wealth. A fat diamond on your finger or around your neck says, "I can afford it. I have high status." And if you begin with just affordability and status, you can branch out in a hundred directions to compare further with something about you and your life.

For example, a diamond can symbolize your retirement fund or the reserve of energy you know you can tap if you need it. It can symbolize that you can earn good money anywhere with your skill, talent, or education—earning potential is a sort of stored wealth. The quality of your health insurance or medical care can make you feel important. Your important job can be symbolized as a diamond.

Diamonds are associated with allure and temptation, with bling and the good things in life, and with extravagance and excess.

They're associated with vanity and conceit, and with marriage and commitment.

A diamond can symbolize something unaffordable or unattainable.

Personal associations come into play. For example, someone who works in a jewelry store could dream about diamonds in terms of employment, or real value versus perceived value.

See also: *Fiancé, Gem, Jewelry, Marriage, Money, Wedding*

Dick—See: *Penis*

Die—See: *Death*

Digest—See: *Food*

Dinner—Anytime food is consumed in a dream, think about what you take into yourself. Not just food and nutrition, but the knowledge, information, and media you consume. See: *Eat*.

Dreaming about dinner can mean you're planning your next dinner or meal, especially if the thought was on your mind before you went to bed, or you went to bed hungry.

The symbolism of dinner can depend on whether you eat alone or with company. Eating alone can indicate isolation, sadness, or feeling unwanted. Or maybe you need time alone. Eating dinner with company can symbolize enjoying the pleasures of friendship and socializing.

Also consider the subtle social interactions of eating dinner with company and what can be found out about people under the circumstances—from how they eat to what they talk about. It can mean that you're sizing someone up.

Serving dinner can connect with the services and favors you render.

Consider your feelings. For example, are you anxious about how the meal will be received? That can symbolize worry that you aren't living up to expectations, or aren't doing enough to make someone happy or pleased.

Consider the preparation, planning, and work that go into cooking a big meal and how that's comparable to something in your life. For example, you put tremendous effort into preparing a report for your employer. How was it received? See: *Chef*.

If you're served a dinner or meal in a dream, ask yourself whether you're happy with what's served to you and what it symbolizes in your life. Think of it figuratively as a circumstance or situation that someone else has created. For example, a dating relationship is a situation that is prepared. Your significant other says, figuratively, "This is what I have to offer in this relationship." Are you happy with it?

Or an employer serves up a set of circumstances—pay, benefits, work environment, type of work, opportunity for advancement—that is like a meal served to you. How you react can tell you how you really feel about the situation.
See also: *Chef, Dessert, Eat, Food*

Dinosaur—To dream about a dinosaur can mean you face something overwhelming. What sort of chance do you really stand against a dinosaur?

It can symbolize something you want to avoid—huge, loud, fearful, dangerous, dominant, primitive—or that's too big to handle. See: *Giant, Reptile*.

As a figure of speech a dinosaur describes a person who is out of touch with the latest trends and ideas, synonymous with the words "outdated" and "extinct."

For example, a teen male dreams about a dinosaur following him and his friends around. They hide from it, and as it sniffs around, one of the dreamer's friends makes a noise, attracting it's attention. The dinosaur symbolizes the dreamer's grandfather, the old man with outdated ideas poking around the dreamer's life. And the dreamer has things he wants to hide, especially related to what he does with his friends.
See also: *Animal, Attack, Giant, Hide, Reptile*

Direction—See: *Map*

Director—The symbolism of a director, such as a movie director, is often connected with giving or getting direction. Direction in a dream can connect with direction in life and personal development, or where something such as a relationship or situation is headed.

A director sets everything in motion and coordinates it to put on a good show. Motion and movement can connect with the movement of your life, and coordination can connect with smooth functioning—or malfunctioning, depending on the job the director does. The association can apply to the functioning of your psyche, which is a collection of parts like actors who each play a specific role. The ego is the director, ideally. See: *Ego*.

The possibilities for symbolism extend to needing direction in your career, relationships, energy, focus.

You can be a director at work or at home, or in your social groups. You're a director when you give people direction—and give yourself direction. You're a director when you coordinate a family holiday or organize an event, or when you marshal resources to achieve a goal or ambition.

Being directed against your will can symbolize lacking a choice. It can mean you don't have freedom to think for yourself. For example, a woman dreams about directing a robot at work, symbolizing her work in a call center where she follows a script. She feels like a robot.

Directing actors can symbolize manipulating people, being "played," or leading an effort or charade. It's all a game.

Playing the role of director in your dream can symbolize what you do to gain recognition—especially public recognition.

Directing a war can symbolize handling problems and dealing with issues, especially in a work, school, or family situation. The symbolism can tie in with any situation or condition that can be described as a "battle zone." See: *General*.

Finally, consider the possibility that a movie director or similar character can symbolize a supervisor or leader, in a role that can be formal, such as a board of directors, or informal.

See also: *Actor, Camera, Captain, Ego, General, Hollywood, Map, Movie, President, Psyche, Stage*

Disability—See: *Handicap*

Disappear—See: *Ghost*

Disaster—"Disaster" is used to refer to a variety of situations. A pipe bursts and floods the kitchen—it's a disaster. You spill red wine on your clothes. You go out on a bad date. Your car breaks down.

These situations are minor when compared to real disasters like tornadoes, earthquakes, and oil spills, but we describe them as disasters to convey the personal feelings and dynamics involved. It's an exaggerated representation of a situation that's bad. And how bad it is, along with how it helps tell the story, determines the type of disaster used in a dream. For example, something that shakes you up

is symbolized as an earthquake, and how shaken up you are is symbolized by the strength of the earthquake.

A disaster in a dream can symbolize fear. It can be as seemingly innocuous as a fear of flying because of disasters you've heard about. It can express fear for people you know who put themselves at risk. They are said to be "flirting with disaster." See: *Fear*.

Dreaming about a disaster can mean you have been thinking about the worst that could happen. You feel pessimistic.

A natural disaster in a dream can symbolize something that's happened in society at large, such as a stock market collapse, or your favorite sports team losing the big game. In either situation, you are more likely to dream about it as a disaster if the event affects you personally or strikes close to home.

For example, a stock market collapse wipes out your retirement savings and you dream about it as an earthquake that destroys your house. On the other hand, if you had nothing invested in the stock market and don't know anyone personally affected, it's not really a disaster as far as you're concerned. It's still possible to dream about it as a disaster, just not as likely.

A disaster can symbolize internal dynamics. You're a mess. Your thoughts or emotions are out of control.

Disaster is such a broad term. Use the list below to zero in on what best describes the events in your dream.

See also: *Apocalypse, Armageddon, Blizzard, Bomb, Crash, Earthquake, Erupt, Fear, Fight, Fire, Flood, Nuclear War, Storm, Tidal Wave, Tornado, Volcano, War*

Discover—Discovery in a dream can symbolize something you discover about yourself, or an area of personal interest such as a new hobby or subject to study. In a dream you discover a hidden room in your house, and in your life you discover something new about yourself. You discover a deposit of gold deep inside a cave, and in your life you discover you are related to a king from long ago. In a dream an enemy patrol discovers you hiding in some bushes, and in your life a co-worker discovers you have been reading her email.

The same imagery can symbolize what you discover about someone you know—especially someone close to you.

"Discover" goes hand in hand with "explore." You can explore a possibility, an idea, a proposal, a thought, a feeling, and so on.

Discovery in a dream can connect with the idea of discovering a secret, a cool new restaurant, a hot stock, and so on.

Discovery can connect with the idea of "to be discovered," like the next up-and-coming actor or musician. Perhaps you have talents or abilities for which you want recognition.

If a dream-character discovers something, it can be a way of pointing you in the right direction. You've been seeking an answer, a new direction in your life, a resolution, and the dream-character that discovers something represents your internal guidance.

The key to decoding the symbolism is to keep in mind that dreams create physical representations of personal situations. Look beyond the surface of the dream-story. Whatever you discover in a dream is likely to represent something about yourself or your life.

See also: *Airplane, Boat, Embark, Journey, Map, Vacation*

Disease—Having a disease in a dream can indicate something's wrong. It might be your health—dreams are known to deliver direct messages about health, and the body has a monitoring system that speaks through them. Or it might relate to your mind or emotions, either of which can be said to be diseased.

Think of disease as a metaphor. What does it describe in an exaggerated way?

Disease in a dream often relates to stress, anxiety, and anything else you might say is slowly killing you. See: *Cancer*.

Disease can mean you're no longer able to cope with a situation.

Disease can symbolize something you do that's wrong. For example, a woman who starts shoplifting dreams about having gangrene in her hands. She uses her hands to shoplift, and gangrene symbolizes the fear of getting caught that's eating at her.

Fear of disease can lead to dreams about it. It can be your worst nightmare come true. The nightmares will continue until the fear is confronted or resolved. See: *Fear*.

Dreams can speak directly when they warn of disease and identify what it is and where it's located in the body. Dr. Larry Burk's research into dreams that warn of breast cancer goes into depth on this subject. All varieties of diseases and medical conditions can be addressed through dreams. Dreams can advise about treatments and cures.

Direct-warning dreams feel heavy. They're somber, serious, sometimes with a "Sorry I have to tell you this" vibe. They can be repetitive, coming night after night until the message is heeded. And they can be seconded by the dreams of people close to you, who can pick up on subconscious clues.

A man had a dream that harkened back to when he caught typhoid as a child, and it was triggered by smelling typhoid on the breath of someone he met the previous day. Typhoid leaves a distinct smell on the breath that manifests before the symptoms, but he didn't realize at the time why the smell was familiar. That night he had the dream, and the next day he found out the person he met had typhoid.

Diseases can manifest in dreams as problems with the condition of a building, especially a house, because a building is a common symbol for the body, and many comparisons and metaphors can be made with it. For example, cloudy windows can symbolize cataracts. Rusty hinges can symbolize arthritis. Clogged pipes can symbolize arterial disease. A bullet embedded in your body can symbolize a tumor (which can suddenly "explode" with growth). A bite on the neck can symbolize throat trouble.

Or perhaps someone is a pain in the neck, or something is draining your vitality. Always consider alternatives. Disease in a dream is usually figurative, not literal.

"The root of disease is dis-ease," is a saying from the holistic-health community. "Dis-ease" is a state of unease, anxiety, stress, or fear. Dreaming about disease can mean dis-ease, and the two go hand in hand because chronic dis-ease is a precursor to actual disease.

Disease can express itself through somatic metaphor. Symptoms are physical manifestations of a person's life story, often arising from chronic situations. For example, chronic lack of physical intimacy can manifest as symptoms in the reproductive organs. A situation crippling you in the personal sense can manifest as an autoimmune disease crippling you in the physical sense.

Dreams can use symbolism comparable to getting a disease, or someone you love getting a disease. It can rock your world like an earthquake, hang over your head like a funnel cloud, and toss your boat like a hurricane.

Also consider situations described as "diseased." Diseased organizations are dysfunctional. A family disease, such as addiction, is something passed down through generations.

See also: *Abscess, Addict, AIDS, Body, Cancer, Deformed, Doctor, Elderly, Fear, Hospital, Illness, Infect, Infest, Panic*

Disfigured—See: *Deformed*

Disguise—A disguise in a dream can symbolize putting up a façade or concealing true intentions. See: *Imposter, Mask*.

The symbolism can connect with the feeling of being deceived or surprised.

Wearing a disguise can mean you have something to hide. See: *Hide*.

It can symbolize playing a role, especially one that's new. For example, a parent or spouse goes away and now you're in charge of the house, and you're doing your best to "fake it till you make it." You then dream about disguising yourself in the clothes of the person usually in charge of the house, but they're too big, meaning the role is too big for you. Or you wear a police uniform when you're enforcing rules or handing out punishment, playing the role of cop. See: *Clothing*.

Dreaming about someone you know in a disguise can tie two people or ideas together. For example, you don't realize how much your boyfriend is like your father until after you dream about him disguised as your father. Or you have an unruly roommate and dream about him barging into your bedroom dressed in a gorilla costume.

A disguise or costume can set the scene and reveal the underlying subject of a dream. For example, a clown can connect with the subject of "clowning around." Wearing camouflage can symbolize the desire to avoid being seen or noticed.

See also: *Actor, Camouflage, Clothing, Clown, Face, Hide, Imposter, Mask, Stage*

Disgust—See: *Insects, Maggots, Roach*

Dismember—See: *Deformed*

Dismissal—The meaning of the word "dismissal" cuts three ways that can be used interchangeably to create symbolism. One, dismissed means fired from a job or position. Two, it means sent away. Three, it means to be treated as unworthy of serious consideration. A dream can use one sense of the word to mean another. For example, to be dismissed by a captain in a dream can mean that a supervisor or teacher dismisses your ideas.

To dream about dismissal from a job can reflect fear it really could happen, especially if you have reason to think so. The job you're dismissed from is not necessarily depicted directly in the dream. For example, a mayor can symbolize a job in public relations, and losing a mayoral election can symbolize losing the job. See: *Fear, Job*.

However, usually the theme of dismissal is symbolism and quite often it connects with the feeling of failing to measure up or of making the grade. It can reflect fear that people are conspiring against you.

Dismissal can symbolize fear of separation, and the idea of separation applies broadly, not just to work. For example, dismissal can symbolize breaking up with someone you've been dating. See: *Divorce*.

Dismissal can connect with fear of financial loss. Losing your job is a financial loss. It can symbolize related ideas, such as the value of your home dropping. Something you count on for financial security is not living up to expectation. See: *Unemployed*.

See also: *Co-Worker, Divorce, Employee, Execution, Fear, General, Job, Money, Unemployed*

Dispose—See: *Bury*

Dissect—Dissection in a dream can indicate a sharp, incisive mind, an analogy between razor-sharp tools and a razor-sharp mind.

When a situation is dissected, it's inspected closely. To symbolize such a situation, a dream can use the imagery of dissection or an autopsy.

An autopsy has further possibilities as symbolism for analyzing what went wrong. For example, Monday morning after losing the game, the football coaches perform an autopsy of the team's play to figure out what went wrong. In this sense, an autopsy has duel symbolism representing careful deconstruction and analysis, and loss (dead body).

Being dissected can mean you feel like someone analyzes you in ways that reveal information or knowledge that you'd rather remain hidden, such as motives, personal flaws, and personality traits.

See also: *Body, Dead, Diamond, Doctor, Knife, Surgery*

Ditch—A ditch in a dream can indicate a lowly personal state. When a ditch is used as a comparison, it can express a similar meaning as "mind in the gutter."

For example, a man dreams that he waits for his pretty female co-worker to leave work and abducts her. He drives her to a deserted area, saying out loud, "I just have to get it." He pulls her out of the car and into a ditch, presumably to rape her. She kicks him in the groin and runs away. He tracks her down, knife in hand. The last thing he sees before the dream ends is the thick look of fear in her eyes.

The dream could easily be interpreted as a rape fantasy, but in the co-worker the dream presents two layers of meaning. One, she's the sort of pretty girl he feels like he'll never have, and two, his advancement at work is blocked. He's not getting what he wants on either front, expressed in his statement, "I just have to get it." The situation is hitting him right in the manhood, symbolized by the kick in the groin. The ditch symbolizes where his thoughts and feelings dwell. He's in a lowly state.

A ditch is commonly used to describe a situation that runs off the proverbial road. If your life is in a ditch, it means you encounter difficulties that bring you down.

A ditch is where water drains or escapes, and that idea can be used in dreams to express a wish to escape a situation or be rid of troublesome emotions.

A ditch can symbolize wanting to conceal your feelings, thoughts, motives, intentions, or actions.

"Ditch" can be wordplay for "avoid."

See also: *Alley, Dead End, Hide, Road*

Divorce—The symbolism of divorce revolves primarily around the ideas of something coming to an end or of being being divisive. Dreams have other ways of saying the same things, so focus on how divorce captures specifics of the situation, such as feelings of acrimony, symbolism of marriage and family, division among close people, and something that ends and is not chosen lightly. Divorce can connect with other associated feelings and emotions, such as bitterness, disappointment, and anger.

Personal experience with divorce, or close observation of what it does to people and families, opens the possibility for a wide array of symbolism based on personal association.

A divorce is a final end to a relationship, so dreaming about getting a divorce can mean the end of something else, or your feelings for someone or something are finally settled. It can symbolize finally getting over a breakup, or realizing you'll never get back together with your ex. See: *Ex*.

The symbolism can extend to any sort of relationship that ends, such as a friendship or business relationship, or even the relationship to something intangible, such as a television show. The show disappoints you one last time and that's it, goodbye, show.

Divorce is a negotiated settlement, such as when employment ends with a severance package.

Divorce gives you distance from something. You want to walk away. Finito.

Dreams can get creative with how far they reach to make a comparison. Divorce is comparable to a mistake that costs you a bundle, or to the high personal price for failure. It can symbolize a mistake that you pay for over time. See: *Alimony*.

Psychologically, divorce can symbolize disharmony inside you, being at odds with yourself. Or other parts of the psyche want to divorce from the ego. It can be a shock from within to make you realize things are at the breaking point. Something can't continue the way it is, and it might be the way you treat yourself.

Then again, divorce can be good when it means "freedom," especially freedom from something that's sapping you. It's a clean break.

See also: *Alimony, Court, Ego, Ex, Execution, Husband, Judge, Lawyer, Marriage, Parents, Wedding, Wife, Wound*

Doctor—A doctor-character in a dream can be used to deliver information about your physical health. The body has a monitoring system that uses dreams to communicate, and a doctor is a natural choice to deliver its information.

When you have been ill or your health has been on your mind and you dream about a doctor, there's a good possibility these things are related, especially if the doctor examines you or gives advice. But think beyond physical health to consider mental and emotional health and other areas of life described in terms of health, such as sexual, financial, and familial.

A doctor in a dream can be associated with healing—any sort of healing. Healing your body, your mind, your emotions, your life, a relationship, the past.

A doctor-character can speak to issues related to the health of someone (or something) close to you. Differentiating can be tricky. Dreams can refer to someone else when they actually mean you. Before telling your friend about a dream you had related to his or her health, make sure the dream isn't referring to something about you.

For example, a doctor tells you in a dream that your best friend is going to die. Naturally, that sparks concern for your friend, but the dream actually refers to the health of the relationship. You have been too busy lately to maintain it and it's in danger of losing its depth.

Another possibility to consider is that a doctor symbolizes looking for the cure to a problem or situation. You need answers, advice, or perspective. For example, you dream that a doctor gives you a prescription for a gardening hoe and pruning shears, and you connect that with the idea that working in a garden is good for stress relief—and boy, have you been stressed! Or you have been in a rut lately and dream about seeing a foreign doctor, which connects with the idea of doing something different ("foreign") as the cure for your rut.

Because doctors ask deeply personal questions, they can be used in dreams to symbolize the feeling of having your privacy invaded, being forced to talk about something you'd rather not talk about, or revealing something private or hidden. See: *Hide*.

For example, an ex-mate from years ago calls out of the blue, and your current mate answers the phone. It leads to having a long and deep conversation about your ex, a subject you'd rather avoid, but you have no choice. Or you face uncomfortable questions during a job interview. You are examined in a personal way, and your dream portrays the situation as examination in a physical way.

Dreaming about playing the role of doctor can mean that you take responsibility for your own health. The idea also applies when you take responsibility for other people's health. Because of the wealth of health information available on the Internet, anyone can play the role of doctor or diagnostician.

Some general associations with doctors that can be used as symbolism are that they command respect, work hard, prepare extensively, and are well compensated and widely admired. And they're commonly perceived as a good catch as a mate.

A doctor can represent your ability to offer healing, support, or advice. It can mean you fix a situation or diagnose a problem.

A doctor can symbolize someone who listens to you—or conversely, doesn't listen to you.

Some people avoid doctors, and for them a doctor can symbolize the plague.

You can tell by your reaction if the symbolism ties in with something felt strongly. For example, you dream about suddenly finding yourself in a doctor's office and you run away. Question is, what are you avoiding? What subject makes you want to turn and run?

The type of doctor can have specific symbolism. For a broken heart you see a cardiologist. To treat pessimism you could see an oncologist, because pessimism is like a cancer. To give birth to an idea, you could dream about an obstetrician. To see inside yourself, you could dream about a radiologist. To understand what's going on in your mind, you could dream about a psychiatrist. For a sexual-related issue, a dream can use a gynecologist. To remove something unwanted, like a bad character trait, a person could dream about a surgeon.

Because doctors are fixers, a dream featuring a doctor could be about fixing or patching up something. For example, you dream about seeing a doctor with your spouse after having a rift, and the doctor recommends speech therapy, meaning improve the way you communicate with each other. Of course, this use of the symbolism will show in the dream-story; otherwise, the symbolism means something else.

See also: *AIDS, Amputate, Blood, Body, Brain, Caesarean Section, Cancer, Coma, Death, Disease, Dissect, Drugs, Elderly, Hide, Hospital, Illness, Infect, Nurse, Psychologist, Surgery, X-ray, Yoga*

Doctor Who—See: *Time Travel*

Documentary—Dreaming about viewing a documentary can be a way of conveying information about yourself, your life, or a situation or circumstance in it. Documentaries are generally about people's lives and issues of interest. They go into depth and generally offer different perspectives.

They are the official record. Dreams document your life and interests, and show your life from different perspectives.

A documentary can help you explore a subject or find an answer to a question. For example, you want to know what your stoic grandfather really thinks of you and dream of him being interviewed about you for a documentary. What he says shows you a different perspective. It might help you understand him better, or see yourself in him.

Dreams can play with the word "document" by using a documentary in connection with particular documents that are part of your life—wills, bank statements, reports—and in connection with how you feel about handling documents.

For example, you dream you're forced to view a really boring eight-hour documentary, which connects with the eight hours a day that you deal with documents at work, and how boring it is. Or you dream about a document going up in flames in your hands, and it symbolizes something too hot to handle.

See also: *Actor, Camera, Director, Hollywood, Movie, Television*

Dog—When you dream about a dog, same as with any animal, the symbolism can connect with a particular quality or characteristic of the animal. Some dog qualities like loyalty and approval-seeking are easy connections for dreams to make. Dogs are also protective, sometimes demanding. They can be expensive and yappy. Start there and branch out.

Dogs are used as symbolism in dreams more frequently in relation to their positive associations, especially companionship, friendship, and devotion. Dreams can show something to be lacking, too, such as when a dog running away symbolizes loss of a friendship.

Dogs are "man's best friend." That popular association can be used to describe something about a particular friend, the subject of friendship, or what sort of friend you are. The possibilities for symbolism are extensive.

For example, a black dog can symbolize the shadowy, mysterious, or dark aspects of a friend.

A sick dog can symbolize a neglected friendship.

A dead dog can symbolize a dying or dead friendship.

A growling or attacking dog can indicate a conflict with a friend.

Following a dog can mean that a friend provides guidance or direction in your life.

Buying a dog can symbolize buying your friends and companions.

A friend's dog in a dream can represent the friend. Then again, you might dream about that dog because of its traits or your experiences with it. Or the dog's name connects it with someone else you know.

A giant dog can symbolize oversized loyalty or admiration for a friend.

Being followed by a dog can symbolize a friend who is a "follower."

Ignoring a dog can symbolize ignoring your instincts or ignoring a friend.

A decapitated dog can symbolize that you are ignoring the advice of a friend.

Being forced to kill a dog can symbolize pressure to do something that can jeopardize a friendship. See: *Pet.*

There are figures of speech to consider, too, like "going to the dogs" and "hair of the dog." Dreams can act them out in scenes such as running with wild dogs, or brushing one and swallowing its fur.

Also consider the breed of dog and your associations with it. A bloodhound can symbolize being "on the scent." A Doberman can symbolize alertness. A yapping poodle can symbolize something small and annoying. A bulldog is relentless.

A dog peeing on your bed can mean that someone close to you is disrespecting your ambitions and goals or attacking your character.

Because dogs run in packs, dreaming about dogs—especially packs of dogs—can symbolize your social side, how you feel when among groups of people, and the role you play. Are you a leader, a follower, a watcher, an instigator? A pack of dogs barking loudly or acting out can symbolize squabbling and quarreling, especially among friends.

A barking dog can symbolize grumpiness, or be a play on the phrase "barking orders." You might need to go easier on people, or be less demanding. Alternately, someone needs to be less demanding of you. Barking can be a warning to watch out for danger or intrusion. You can tell the difference by how you feel about and respond to the barking.

A dog chasing its own tail can mean an approach to something isn't getting you anywhere.

A dog bite to the leg can indicate lack of balance in your life, since legs are used for balance. A dog bite on the wrist can symbolize loyalty holding you back. A gentle bite can symbolize guidance or influence. Biting the hand can be a call to action, or symbolize the phrase "bite the hand that feeds you." Such as when a friend you've been supporting does something to cross you.

A dogfight can symbolize a conflict, or conflict of interest, between friends or in a group.

See also: *Animals, Attack, Bark, Bite, Colors, Friend, Group, Guide, Pet, Puppy*

Doll—A doll in a dream can poignantly symbolize feeling like someone's plaything, especially if you dream you are the doll, or have recurring dreams about a scary doll. Dolls are played with and appreciated mostly for their appearance, and people can be played with and appreciated only for their appearance.

A doll is associated with feeling put on display and having your every move manipulated.

The symbolism of a doll can connect with its being a carbon copy, and that can connect with the question of whether to run with the herd or take the road less traveled. In this sense, a doll in a dream can symbolize that your personal identity isn't filled out. The job isn't finished. Or you feel like just another pretty face.

Dolls can symbolize feminine ideals and feelings about trying to live up to them—especially true of dreams featuring Barbie Dolls and other pageant dolls.

A woman dreams about a doll wearing a skirt and high heels, but she loses its heels, and after searching, decides the doll looks fine without them. This mirrors her feelings about having to wear heels to work and recent thoughts related to wanting to wear something more comfortable. She's tired of being uncomfortable just to conform to a norm. The doll in the dream is a prop to help tell the story.

Playing with a doll can be associated with immaturity. Or, like a toy, it can refer to childhood, and from there the possibilities are wide open. See: *Toy*.

A talking doll can symbolize something about yourself projected onto it, such as a personality trait or feeling. Colors the doll is dressed in, and the color of its skin and hair, can paint a picture of your emotions. See: *Emotions*.

Combing a doll's hair can symbolize thoughts brewing in your head, especially thoughts related to intrigue.

See also: *Child, Colors, Disguise, Emotions, Face, Hair, Mask, Robot, Toy*

Dollar—See: *Money*

Dolphin—The symbolism of dolphins in dreams is often connected with common associations such as playfulness, intelligence, and friendliness. Dreams can go a million different directions when using those traits and behaviors to tell a story about you and your life.

Dolphins are social and known for cooperation, so a group of dolphins is a ready-made symbol for a group of people that get along—especially schoolmates, because dolphins gather together in "schools," though the correct term is "pods."

Dolphins are like happy, chattering schoolchildren, and that imagery can connect with similar behavior observed in people, especially children.

The powerful swimming ability of dolphins and the fact that they live in water gives them strong associations with emotions, especially joy, enthusiasm, and zest.

Dolphins can symbolize ability to navigate emotions and emotional situations. See: *Water*.

Dreams have other aquatic creatures to choose from when they want to make a comparison for how you navigate emotions and emotional situations, so a key to analyzing the symbolism is to figure out why a dolphin is chosen. For example, a dolphin can be used to say that you never let anything get you down, or you can get away quickly when danger lurks. Read the entries for *Shark* and *Whale* to see how other aquatic creatures are used in dream-stories.

Dolphins are known for rescuing endangered swimmers, so they can symbolize something that rescues or guides you—especially help from the unconscious mind. Creatures that symbolize helpful messengers from the unconscious are often colored white.

Dolphins hurt or killed can symbolize something that destroys your enthusiasm, or that overpowers your ability to navigate your emotions. It can symbolize something that overtakes your better nature. For example, a shark eating a dolphin can symbolize having to be mean or predatory, though by nature you'd rather live and let live.

For a predatory person, a dolphin can symbolize a tasty, elusive prey.

Positive dreams featuring dolphins can be a good sign that your life is headed in the right direction.

These are common associations with dolphins. Be sure to think of your own associations.

See also: *Animals, Emotions, Fish, Ocean, Shark, Water, Whale*

Donald Trump—As with any famous person in a dream, begin with your associations. Do you identify with any of Trump's personal traits?

For example, a man dreams about watching a boxing match between U.S. President Donald Trump's son and another fighter. Trump's son doesn't fight back until round five, then quickly knocks out his opponent. Trump's son is used to symbolize the dreamer learning to stick up for himself, as a son learns by watching his father, because Trump is known for taking no guff. The detail about the son's not fighting back until round five symbolizes the dreamer's usual habit of taking people's shit for a long time before fighting back. And when he does fight back, he comes on strong.

Many other public associations with Trump can be used as symbolism: heartlessness, speaking his mind, self-promotion, arrogance, power, greed, big business.

For example, a woman dreams that Trump is her new gynecologist. She meets him at his mansion for the appointment, for which she arrives late, and Trump launches into a speech about how she doesn't need a physical exam. Trump in this dream symbolizes the mega-health-care corporation that recently began providing her health care. She's concerned that it won't be as thorough as her last company in testing her, especially gynecological testing. She has a family history of related disease, and regular testing is important to her. Arriving late to the appointment symbolizes that it's too late to do anything about it. She's locked in for a while with this company.

See also: *Boxing, Famous*

Door—The symbolism of a door in a dream can connect with the idea of stepping into a new area of life, or having a new experience, which are commonly depicted as walking through a door.

Doors are associated with choices. When you dream about making choices, that can be visualized as your having a number of doors from which to choose. For example, you can choose among schools, subjects to study, or places to live. You subconsciously know what's behind the doors and what picking one means.

A door can be used to make choices about what sort of person you are or will become. For example, a woman with a limited sex life dreams about being in a red-light district with her girlfriends, just for fun, and she sees a beautiful woman on display behind a window. Next to the window is a door, and she knows what going through the door means. Her girlfriends push her toward it and for a moment she's ready to give in to the temptation, but turns away. This shows her decision to re-

main in a limited sex life. She's not ready. Her friends in the dream are the sexually adventurous ones who push her to be more like them.

Doors are used in dream imagery related to areas of the mind. When a dream visits a certain area of your memory, for instance, it can visualize that area as being behind a door. This use of the symbolism often goes hand in hand with finding unexplored rooms in your house. The house is your psyche, and the unexplored rooms are unknown parts of yourself. See: *Psyche*.

Along this line, a common dream theme involves barging through the door and into a scene where you are unwelcome. The dream-characters act like you're an intruder. And they're right: you have entered an area of your psyche that you're not ready to access. You have more maturing to do first.

Locking a door can symbolize keeping something out of your life. See: *Lock*.

Unlocking a door can symbolize getting access to something that had been denied to you. See: *Key*.

A back door can symbolize a secret or some way you're vulnerable. See: *Back Door*.

The front door of your home is the boundary between your private life inside the home and your public life outside of it. Therefore, dreams featuring your front door can connect with subjects of privacy, intrusion, and what you share about yourself publicly.

A man dreams about going to his new home where his family and friends have a house-warming party. He's not much interested in socializing and is happy when they all leave, and he can be alone. As soon as he sits down, someone knocks at the front door. He opens the door and no one is there. He sits back down; he sees an indistinct white figure come to the door and knock, and when he opens the door it is gone. And it happens again and again, angering him.

The dream is about the subject of privacy and solitude. The dreamer is reclusive and entering a stage of life where he can keep people out of his life, a stage symbolized by moving into a new home—obviously symbolism because he is not actually moving into a new home. The front door symbolizes the boundary he sets up against intrusions into his life, and the action at the front door symbolizes his frustration at being unable to keep people out. It's not particular people, it's people in general, symbolized as the indistinct white figure.

See also: *Back Door, Burglary, Dark, Discover, Home, Intruder, Key, Lock, Psyche, Stranger*

Doughnut—See: *Candy*

Downhill—See: *Hill*

Drag—See: *Baggage*

Dragon—Dreams have an array of associations with dragons with which to create symbolism. One of the most popular is that dragons breathe fire, and breathing fire is a metaphor for a heated argument or fiery temperament. See: *Fire*.

A dragon can represent an intimidating and relentless person such as a boss or in-law who just won't let up. For example, a woman dreams that her mother transforms into a glass dragon, symbolizing mom's dual nature as someone both fiery and fragile.

A dragon can symbolize a person with a cold and calculating intellect.

Dragons have strong associations with smoldering sensuality and passionate sexuality. In myth, the knight that slays the dragon and rescues the virgin is symbolically taming the wildness of his sexuality. Dragons can symbolize the dark side of sexuality that's devouring and all-consuming.

A woman dreams that she's in her bedroom, and her boyfriend turns into a dragon and flies around the room, performing tricks for her. The dragon then turns back into her boyfriend and lies beside her in her bed. She feels the sexual tension between them. He then tells her that she has to pay for his time. This bothers her—she doesn't understand why she has to pay for his time and wonders if she can get a discount.

The dream symbolizes a situation with her boyfriend. He is very sensual and passionate, and she loves how he "performs" for her, but she's also

paying the living expenses for both of them while he's unemployed. In a sense, she's paying for their time together. Her thoughts about getting a discount connect with her hope that her investment in the relationship will pay off when he gets a job and can pay his share of their living expenses.

Dragons are associated with being strongly materialistic and possessive. Dragons defend their hoard of treasure, and some people are similarly defensive about their possessions. Along this line, dragons are associated with jealousy, greed, and envy.

A sleeping dragon, or one that's slow-moving, can symbolize feeling bloated or overburdened. It can symbolize a person you want to avoid arousing. The symbolism can extend to situations with the potential for danger or conflict that must be handled delicately or avoided altogether.

A dragon can symbolize the unconscious mind. The unconscious mind is immensely powerful and requires a strong ego to tame it. Fighting a dragon can represent trying to tame your dark side, known as Shadow. In myth and legend, fighting a dragon is a sign of courage, a theme prevalent in the dreams of teenagers learning their own power.

See also: *Anger, Attack, Cave, Devour, Dinosaur, Fire, Fly, Giant, Jealous, Monster, Mountain, Shadow, Unconscious Mind*

Dream within a Dream—A dream within a dream can be a clever ploy to keep you asleep and dreaming. Otherwise, at the end of the dream segment you might wake up or fall into dreamless sleep. Instead, you continue dreaming, allowing the story to continue, and continuing to get the dream time you need.

The dream within a dream is a popular theme for sleep-deprived people. REM-stage sleep, when the most vivid dreams tend to occur, is essential. It's why REM-deprivation is used as torture, and sleep deprivation is forbidden by the Geneva Convention. It's a well-established medical fact that dreaming helps to process everything that's happened since the last time you dreamed, and if you don't get the chance to dream you will quickly break down mentally and physically.

Given this, you can see why your dreaming mind uses any means to keep you asleep and dreaming!

The dreaming mind is a storyteller that uses every trick in the storyteller's playbook, including nesting one story within another, aka "dream within a dream." It's the best way of telling the story, or to show how scenes interconnect. The scenes can appear unrelated, but they actually have a common thread that's found in the meaning and message of the dream.

Dress—Like other articles of clothing, a dress can symbolize your outer identity, your "persona." Because dresses are typically worn by females, they're associated with femininity, and in the dreams of females they can show comfort, or lack of it, with that gender identity.

For example, put a tomboy in an ill-fitting dress, and how does she feel? Probably awkward. The dress is ill-fitting because the outward appearance does not go well with how she sees herself inwardly. On the other hand, a dress that fits well can symbolize that a woman is comfortable with her gender identity.

The symbolism depends a lot on the type of dress. For example, a wedding dress can connect with thoughts related to relationships, marriage, and commitment. A divorced woman has a dream about finding her wedding dress in her attic. Because she does not have an attic where things are stored, the scene is obviously symbolism. It connects with recent thoughts related to her ex-husband. She hasn't thought about him in a long time, but recently she heard that he's remarried. The attic is an appropriate setting because it symbolizes memories that had been stored way in the back of her mind.

A prom dress carries with it a bundle of ideas related to that time of life, the experiences you had, and the patterns that began then.

For example, a woman applying to graduate schools dreams about shopping for a prom dress. She finds one that she likes but she wants to continue shopping around and asks the clerk whether the store will hold the dress for her. The clerk says no, they can't hold the dress. The dream symbolizes a situation in which she has been accepted at a graduate school she applied to, but it's not the one she is really hoping to be accepted into. She delays accepting the offer, in hopes that the one she really wants will materialize. However, she fears that if she waits too long, the school will rescind the offer. Shopping for a prom dress is a great way of symbolizing the situation because shopping involves making choices, and prom is associated with hopes for the future.

Another possibility for the symbolism of a prom dress is that you are holding onto a youthful self-image. The same idea can apply if you find yourself wearing the dress of an older female figure in your life (mom, grandma, aunt) and it doesn't fit, or is stained or torn. It's a way saying that you have difficulty seeing yourself playing a similar role in your life.

Along a similar line, a dress from a younger time of life can mean you're holding onto something childish. Alternately, it can mean you are reconnecting with a playful side of yourself. The difference can be ascertained from how you feel during the dream and details related to the dress. For example, dreaming about finding a dress from your childhood and trying to put it on despite the fact it's too small can indicate immaturity.

A beautiful dress in a dream can indicate luck and success.

It can indicate confidence in your appearance and the way you present yourself.

It can indicate vanity if the dress is excessively adorned.

A dirty dress can stand for failure or something that has dirtied your self-image or reputation.

A torn dress can indicate aggressiveness or conflict.

Taking off a dress can symbolize the end of a relationship or time of life.

A red dress can symbolize pride, passion, and desire to be noticed.

A black dress can symbolize grief, mystery, danger, or formality.

A green dress can indicate envy, love, or connection with nature.

A purple or violet dress can indicate spiritual connection, high status, or a feeling of richness and wealth.

Be sure to look up the color of the dress. See: *Colors*.

See also: *Clothing, Colors, Doll, Dressed, Persona, Prom, Undress*

Dressed—In simplest terms, getting dressed is preparation. You get dressed in preparation for whatever comes next: a date, work, or going out with friends, for example. Which in turn can connect with love life, work life, or social life. Preparation is a physical representation of how you present yourself and the persona you project. Persona is the identity worn over the inner you. See: *Persona*.

Mood and attitude are like layers of clothing, additions to the image you project. For example, getting dressed in a tuxedo jacket can symbolize a mood of extravagance.

Another simple way of describing getting dressed is that you cover yourself with something protective. In a personal sense, you protect yourself from prying questions about your feelings by always wearing a smile. *Everything's awesome!* Or you protect yourself from risk by always having extra funds in the bank, symbolized as carrying a big purse.

Next step is to connect the symbolism of getting dressed with the type of clothing worn. See: *Clothing*.

Dressing someone in a dream can mean you're in charge of that person, the same as when a parent dresses a child. It can mean you're influencing that person's behavior or public image.

If you are slow to get dressed, it can mean you are having difficulty making a decision, especially in relation to what you want to do with your life.

See also: *Closet, Clothing, Dress, Persona, Undress*

Drive—See: *Car*

Drone—See: *Spy*

Drown—To drown in a dream can symbolize feeling overwhelmed—by work, circumstances, emotions, or illness, to name a few possibilities.

Because water can symbolize emotion, drowning is especially well suited to symbolize being overwhelmed by emotion, but the analogy carries over to any situation where you feel overwhelmed. For example, a man dreams about watching a horse drown, symbolizing that he's overwhelmed by work. See: *Horse*.

Drowning can mean you're in a situation where you have no control, or are desperate. For example, you are low on money and rent is due.

Almost drowning can symbolize a situation you want to avoid or don't want to repeat. Or a situation could have been really bad but you escaped at the last moment.

Saving someone from drowning can connect with trying to save someone figuratively, or helping the person through a rough time. Remember, though, that dreams can project you into a dream as a character that you save from drowning. Question is, if the character doesn't represent someone in your life, what does it represent about you, how does drowning describe how you feel, or how is it used to tell the story?

Drowning in a dream can relate to a physical issue. For example, you have pneumonia and your lungs are full of fluid. Dreaming about drowning can be a reaction to breathing difficulties while asleep. It's your dreaming mind's way of visualizing the feeling that you aren't getting enough air.

Drowning can symbolize something about yourself becoming unconscious. Everything that's conscious about you arises from the deep waters of the unconscious mind, so when those parts of you return to the unconscious, that occurrence can be shown in dreams as a person submerging into water and disappearing. See: *Water*.

See also: *Body, Death, Emotions, Flood, Horse, Ocean, Pool, Rescue, River, Tidal Wave, Unconscious Mind, Water*

Drugs—Dreams build stories around associations, such as drugs being associated with altered states of mind, which might be a way of saying you haven't been feeling like your usual self. You're fooling yourself, the same way an addict does. You're acting compulsively, taking risks. Or you want to escape reality.

Drugs can be used to tell a story about someone acting like a drug user: isolated, sleeping a lot, always broke.

They're associated with addiction. Drug addiction is comparable to other addictions—sex, food, gambling—and the associated thoughts and feelings. These sorts of addictions are known to provide a high, often followed by a low, so a comparison with drugs works as symbolism on two levels: the nature of the situation, and feelings connected with it. See: *Addict*.

Drugs are associated with experimentation, trying something new.

They're associated with wasting your life, being a loser, being low on the social totem pole as some drug addicts are.

Drugs are a temptation and can symbolize temptation. See: *Candy*.

Injecting drugs can symbolize taking in bad influences or negativity. See: *Inject*.

Giving up an addiction is known to spark powerful dreams. The question behind them is often, "Do you remember why you gave up your addiction?" The dream will put the dreamer back into scenes of buying or being offered drugs. And the reaction really tells the story about resolve to kick the addiction.

For example, a man who quit smoking weed dreams about hiding beneath a massive pot plant and stuffing his pockets with its buds, symbolizing that he knows he'll smoke again in the future.

A man who quit a drug addiction dreams he's in the back seat of a car driven by his former drug dealer. The dealer's girlfriend, in the passenger seat, holds up a baggie of the dreamer's favorite drug, which is how things used to work when he'd make a buy. He turns down the offer and asks to be dropped off, but instead the dealer continues driving to a cemetery and buries the dreamer in a grave.

The dreams shows that the temptation to go back to his old ways is still there, symbolized as being offered the drug, and his reaction tells the story: his resolve is stronger. Getting buried means that the addict part of himself is gone. It's a great sign.

See also: *Abuse, Addict, Alcohol, Candy, Cocaine, Drunkenness, Inject, Overdose*

Drunkenness—Dreams have all sorts of ways of using drunkenness to tell a story about something happening in your inner or outer life. Begin by thinking of it in simplest terms. To be drunk is to be out of control. It means too much of something, putting yourself and others at risk, or losing your inhibitions and doing things you wouldn't normally do. Drunkenness helps to tell the story.

Next consider common associations with drunkenness, such as boisterousness, rudeness, celebration, brazenness, flirtation, and talkativeness. A dream can address any of these subjects through the symbolism of drunkenness.

Now connect the story and its details to you and what's happening in your life.

A dream tells a story about being "drunk with love" by showing you drinking too much passion punch. It tells a story about bingeing your way through a stressful holiday season by showing you swimming in a pool of bubbly. A story about being disgusted by drunken behavior shows you stepping in a puddle of vomit.

Your associations and feelings are used to tell the story. For example, if you think drinking is for losers, or you associate it with wild lifestyles and trouble, a dream can build a story around it.

A man dreams about walking down a public street through an entertainment district in his town. He passes by a raucous nightclub just as a drunk man is kicked out of the club and careens into a crowded public street, where he's hit by an older-model car that looks vaguely familiar to the dreamer. The dreamer reacts by thinking the drunk man got what he deserved.

The dream is sparked by a recent incident. A relative drove drunk and crashed into another car, causing all sorts of trouble for himself. The details of the dream match what the dreamer knows about the incident and show his thoughts about it. The car is familiar because it looks like one the relative drove when he was a teenager, something the dreamer hadn't thought about in twenty years—but there it is, used as a detail in the dream, because teenagers are notorious for irresponsible behavior. And in the dream-story, the accident occurs in a public street, a way of saying the relative messed up in a very public way and is "kicked out of the club," meaning the club of respectable society. Notice that the character representing his relative is not portrayed directly. The dream would be too obvious otherwise.

See also: *Abuse, Addict, Alcohol, Bartender, Drugs, Float, Overdose, Teenager*

Dungeon—A dungeon in a dream can be a graphic, albeit exaggerated, way of representing the feeling of being trapped in a bleak situation. "My life is a dungeon" and "I work in a dungeon" don't mean you actually live or work in a dungeon, but it feels that way—dark, dreary, confining, hopeless.

For example, a woman dreams about a lion trapped in a dungeon. It tries to go up some stairs and past an iron gate, but is pushed back down and tumbles to the bottom. The dream symbolizes her situation at work. She works in customer service, the lowest level in the corporate hierarchy. She wants to rise to a higher position, symbolized as going up the stairs, but her attempts have been rebuffed by the management, symbolized as falling down the stairs. Like a lion, she is proud and confident, and like a lion in a dungeon, she is trapped. The iron gate symbolizes the inflexible corporate structure she faces in trying to advance.

Because dungeons are associated with places deep inside another structure, they can symbolize the subconscious or the unconscious mind. They too are structures of the psyche nestled within larger structures. And if they're characterized as a dungeon, it implies the need to bring light into your mind and be aware of everything you are inside. It could be a way of saying that your mind is a bleak place!

Dungeons are associated with punishment and hopelessness, so if you dream about a dungeon you might feel like you're being punished or can't escape a hopeless situation. See: *Torture.*

Dungeons can have specific symbolism listed here, or connect with the symbolism of a jail, hostage, or prisoner, or feelings such as guilt.

See also: *Abyss, Cage, Guilt, Hostage, Jail, Prisoner, Subconscious, Torture, Unconscious Mind*

Eagle—Eagles soar. They're strong fliers, and that association can be used to describe your life or some aspect of it, such as your career. Eagles are among the strongest and fastest birds, and flight is associated with accomplishment and achievement, so an eagle can be strong symbolism for really flying high.

Or you wish to fly high. You have high ambition and lofty goals. Or your thoughts reach the sky in the figurative sense. The symbolism shows in the action of flying. See: *Fly*.

An eagle in your dream can be a symbol of your strength, especially in relation to accomplishment, personal vision, and reaching goals.

But keep in mind that any of these associations can be used in the negative sense. For example, dreaming about an eagle shot out of the sky can symbolize an ambition shot down.

Because birds fly under their own power and eagles are among the highest fliers, they're particularly good to use in an analogy for "soaring." An eagle soaring high over the landscape is the image of movement in your life created through strength and power, but also consider the idea of having a perspective that allows you to see far and wide, that spans horizon to horizon and also sees the smallest detail.

Eagles are associated with keen vision, and vision in a dream can symbolize the idea in the phrase "vision for your life." Keep in mind that symbolism connects with other details. An eagle in a cage staring at a blank wall is not likely to symbolize keen vision, but it could convey the opposite idea: limited vision. See: *Eyes*.

A caged eagle could symbolize lack of opportunity for advancement, or being confined by rules and circumstances. See: *Cage*.

Eagles can be associated with their qualities as parents, such as watchfulness and protectiveness. See: *Parents*.

Eagles are predators and powerful hunters. They appear intimidating. Do you know anyone who fits that description?

The eagle is a symbol of patriotism in countries like the United States, where it is a national symbol. They're also associated with certain heritages, such as Native American.

See also: *Animals, Ascend, Attack, Birds, Cage, Eyes, Fly*

Ears—When analyzing a symbol, begin with its use and function in everyday life. Ears are used for hearing, and hearing is associated with listening, so ears in dreams can be used to symbolize anything related to hearing or listening. See: *Hear*.

An ear cut off, mangled or missing can mean you aren't really listening to someone, or you are choosing not to hear—you don't want to know something or give it credence, or you choose to ignore it, as in the phrase "hear no evil."

Red or burning ears can indicate shame or embarrassment. It can symbolize hearing something that shocks you.

Bugs in your ears can symbolize hearing gossip or rumors, or something that bugs you. See: *Bug, Insects, Worm.*

Bleeding from the ears can symbolize hearing something that hurts you, or inability to follow direction. It can symbolize a physical issue with hearing.

Be sure to read the entry for *Hear.*

See also: *Amputate, Blood, Body, Bug, Head, Hear, Infest, Insects, Music, Phone, Talk, Vibration*

Earth—The Earth is your connection to the physical world, the soil in which you have roots. It's the giver of life. Without Earth, there is no life. This association has tremendous potential for use as symbolism related to the foundation of your life and your being, your connection with nature and the physical world, your relationship with the feminine principle, yin, and what grounds you. What's the simplest way of describing a planet? It's home. See: *Home.*

In many mystery schools and initiation rites, a person is taken underground to be reborn into a new understanding of him- or herself and the world. In that sense, Earth represents the archetypal Mother who gives birth to all life—not just physical life. See: *Cave, Uterus.*

Seeing planet Earth from space can express feeling disconnected from your roots or from society. Then again, feeling awe at the sight can tie in with feeling connected intimately with the planet, nature, and your roots as a human. It's a mystical experience of Oneness, such as what astronaut Edgar Mitchell says he experienced when traveling back to Earth from the moon. He said it was life-changing.

Seeing the entire planet in a dream can mean "the big picture" or "larger perspective." It can be a suggestion to "see the world." Expand your horizons and have new experiences.

See also: *Beauty, Cave, Discover, Father, Green, Home, Meteor, Moon, Mother, Night, Space, Sun, UFO, Uterus, Vagina, Woman, Worm*

Earthquake—Decoding the symbolism of an earthquake works the same as with other natural disasters. Begin with the most obvious meaning that it's connected with something that really affects you, in your life or in yourself—especially in your emotions. You are "shaken up." Next, assume that when a dream picks through its options for how to say "disaster," it chooses one that best matches the situation, so something about the nature or dynamics of an earthquake is the best way to tell the story.

An earthquake is a big disaster. It's strong symbolism, whereas an aftershock is minor in comparison and would be used in connection with something comparatively minor. An earthquake is an upheaval, something "earth-shaking," and an aftershock is a rumble or hiccup. An earthquake is picked to tell a story about big trouble at a job, and an aftershock is just rumors about proposed layoffs. The earthquake is the argument that rocks your marriage, and the aftershock is just a disagreement.

An earthquake causes chaos. It disrupts normal life for an extended period. It comes on strong without warning. The disaster that's foreseen, that has a bigger buildup, is better symbolized by a typhoon or volcano.

An earthquake can mean you feel shaky inside.

The noise associated with an earthquake can symbolize grumbling or grumpiness. A sound such as the rumble of a helicopter passing closely overhead can translate into a dream as an earthquake.

Be sure to read the entry for *Disaster.*

See also: *Disaster, Earth, Erupt*

Eat—In simplest terms, to eat something means to take it into yourself. You consume and make it part of you, and when you expand that idea it can mean consuming knowledge, information, opinions and media, such as books and movies. You take it into yourself and digest. Some of it becomes part of you, and some of it is discarded out the other end. See: *Food.*

Voracious consumption means to devour. See: *Devour.*

To eat in a dream can symbolize satisfaction and pleasure. A satisfying meal in a dream can be an expression of satisfaction or pleasure with life. It can mean you are well prepared for the future.

To be full in a dream can mean that you have had enough of something, and food is used to symbolize whatever it is—for example, sex, success, attention.

On the other hand, to eat in excess in a dream can mean you are "full of yourself." Your ego is inflated, a need won't be satisfied, or you can't stop yourself from doing something. This use of the symbolism can show in scenes combining consumption of food with imagery of obesity and bloating.

For example, a man dreams he's at a restaurant sitting next to a morbidly obese man who rapidly sucks down spaghetti noodles. A waitress comes to the table and begins talking slowly and deliberately, which irritates the dreamer because he wants her to get to the point. He thinks she must be slow in the head and starts tuning her out, but she says something that catches his attention: she knows his name from a past life and has tried previously to tell him about it, but he got angry so she stopped talking. Her statement triggers memories of a previous dream featuring her.

The dreamer recently became interested in reincarnation. He doesn't know if it's true, but he's finding out everything he can. His mind works rapidly, devouring lines of thought, symbolized as strands of spaghetti. The obese man symbolizes the dreamer's ego inflation. He's very smart and can grasp subjects that are beyond the abilities of most people to understand. The contrast between the dreamer and the waitress shows that he needs to slow down and digest what he's learning. If he really wants to know the truth behind reincarnation, he must be slow and deliberate like the waitress.

Notice that two sides of the dreamer are projected onto dream-characters, the obese man and the waitress. The dream could show the dreamer as the obese man, but the message is more effectively communicated by giving him distance to observe. When he finally recognizes himself and his inflated ego in the obese man, the message really hits home.

Eating in a dream can be an observation related to body weight. Seeing someone eat voraciously in a dream can be a judgment about that person's eating habits and the perception that it makes the person fat or unhealthy. On the other hand, emaciation raises questions about whether a person can afford to eat or is going too far to be skinny. See: *Emaciated, Fat.*

Dreams about eating particular foods can relate to nutrition. Dreams about buying food can speak to the decisions and choices you make about what you consume, physically or otherwise. See: *Food.*

Buying food might have general symbolism related to choices. The food is not as important to the story as the choices made. This use of the symbolism is especially likely if you order from a menu, because a menu offers choices, and you decide from among them. See: *Menu.*

Eating in a dream can connect with what nourishes the heart, mind, and spirit. In this sense, nourishment or eating means nourishing yourself. Food is also called sustenance, and dreams can compare sustenance to what "sustains" you, such as good health and nourishment of your spirit. See: *Spirit.*

To eat junk food can symbolize the idea in the phrase "garbage in—garbage out," a term used to mean that the quality of the output is determined by the quality of the input.

The setting and characters in such a dream can tell you the area of life that needs better-quality input. For example, a cafeteria at school can relate to quality of learning. A meal with your family can relate to quality of family life. A luncheon at church can relate to quality of spiritual life. A meal with a spouse can relate to the quality of the relationship.

Dreams about eating can be sparked by going to bed hungry, and by meal-planning or thinking about food just before you go to sleep. People on calorie-restricted diets and those with eating disorders are known to dream about food in response to related subjects on their mind and the rumble in their bellies.

See also: *Chef, Devour, Dinner, Eaten, Emaciated, Excrement, Fat, Food, Grocery Store, Hunger, Menu, Restaurant, Spirit, Teeth, Toilet*

Eaten—To be eaten in a dream can symbolize the idea of being "eaten alive." It means worn down or overwhelmed. Things are going badly, either in a specific or a general sense. For example, after a hard day at work you might dream about being devoured by a bear. The bear could symbolize the situation in general, or a specific person, problem, or issue eating at you. It could even symbolize the unconscious mind, which is much more vast than the conscious mind and does have the ability to overwhelm it. See: *Bear, Devour.*

A "being eaten" dream can express feelings of being picked on or picked at. Dreaming that a small fish is picked at or eaten by a bigger one can symbolize criticism, bullying, or harassment. It can symbolize a larger company "eating" a smaller one.

Being eaten can be a sign of danger or vulnerability. Only the strongest survive. Some people will "eat you up" with their negativity or rapacity. See: *Shark.*

To be eaten by a wild animal can symbolize instincts overcoming reason, or being controlled by passions. Great passion is sometimes expressed through biting and the desire to totally consume the object of passion. See: *Bite.*

Fear of being eaten in a dream can connect with any sort of fear, but especially fear of being used up or overwhelmed.

Another sense of the word "eaten" is related to consumption. See: *Eat.*

See also: *Bear, Bite, Chef, Devour, Eat, Ego, Emaciated, Fear, Food, Shark*

Egg—In the image of an egg you see potential for something new to emerge, new life. It could be a physical representation of something emerging in you, such as a new personality trait, desire, or idea.

Eggs are associated with birth. The egg can symbolize the birth of something in yourself or

your life, or something emerging from the unconscious mind. See: *Childbirth, Unconscious Mind.*

The symbolism can connect with learning about your natural abilities and realizing your potential. It can symbolize entering a new phase of life or taking on a new role, such as a job or becoming a parent.

An egg in a dream can symbolize incubation, as in incubating a thought or idea. Something is gradually coming to maturity or getting ready to emerge from yourself. It is not yet fully conscious or developed. Incubation can mean you are in a period of rest or contemplation.

If the shell of an egg is cracked, it can symbolize fragility. It can mean your feelings are fragile, or a situation is delicate. It can mean that clumsiness or too much force leads to misfortune or damage. For example, dreaming about your spouse with a cracked egg can mean now's the time to go easy on the person. Or it's a delicate time for the relationship.

The same imagery, though, can also indicate "coming out of your shell." You might be learning to really show yourself, or be feeling comfortable engaging with people or with life.

Symbolism shows through action. So for example, dreaming about juggling eggs and dropping one can symbolize being careless with something delicate. Dreaming about squeezing an egg can symbolize something that gets stronger the more pressure is applied.

Females can dream about eggs in connection with the eggs in their ovaries, related to thoughts and feelings about conception, children, and family. Eggs tend to appear in the dreams of women concerned about the onset of menopause. In this sense, counting eggs in a dream can symbolize guessing how much longer a woman has to get pregnant. Eggs are also a common theme in dreams related to getting pregnant—it's a way for the body to tell the mind that an egg has been fertilized, or a woman is ovulating. See: *Ovaries, Pregnant.*

The idea of fertility extends further to include the fertility of the planet, Mother Earth, and of the soul, both of which are symbolized as the egg in some cultures. It is not necessary for you to know that the egg is a symbol of Mother Earth or soul. It is an archetypal symbol, meaning universal, and its symbolism is embedded in the collective unconscious.

Finding a basket or nest of eggs can symbolize discovering something about yourself, especially in relation to inherited traits and talents. It can symbolize resources stored for the future, as in "nest egg." It can indicate a physical inheritance in the form of money or possessions.

Decayed or rotten eggs can indicate bad intention and character. A "rotten egg" is a bad person.

To be pelted by eggs can indicate defamation or dishonesty.

The idiom "egg on your face" means embarrassment.

See also: *Archetypes, Birds, Chicken, Collective Unconscious, Earth, Food, Menstruation, Ovaries, Pregnant, Vagina, Unconscious Mind, Uterus*

Ego—Ah, the ego. Such a misunderstood and sometimes maligned component of the psyche, and so important to understanding your dreams. See: *Psyche.*

The ego is equated with your personal identity, "I," but the psyche is actually a "we," and here's where the confusion begins. Most folks have little awareness of anything about themselves beyond their ego. Their approach is dictator or lone wolf instead of CEO—they don't know better.

The ideal relationship between the ego and the rest of the psyche is like a CEO's relationship with a board of directors. The ego is first among equals, taking input from all sources before making decisions. But this relationship can get askew, to the point of being like master and slave, and when it does, you are sure to dream about it.

When the ego gets out of balance with the rest of the psyche, dreams compensate, meaning they go just as far in the other direction. If you're too full of yourself, you can dream of scenes involving humbling and absurdity and things blown out of proportion. If your ego is weak, you might dream about slaves and things that slink and grovel, that are small

or powerless, or even that are overly strong, like a bully. See: *Bully, Compensation, Coward.*

Your dreams are a big part of the individuation process, a term coined by Carl Jung to describe the journey of life that begins with a helpless child and ends ideally with a fully mature, complete person. To do this, first your ego must be made strong, to act as a bridge for reaching the next level of maturity. It can then be reintegrated with the unconscious, except now as a much stronger and better-defined entity. This is where most people get stuck. They spend all that time building up the ego and don't want to give it up. In this sense, dreams act as a bridge between the ego and the unconscious. See: *Individuation, Unconscious Mind.*

Your dream-ego is basically your ego in dreamland, except that the filters are off, and the reactions are raw and honest. Most dreams boil down to stories about the relationship between the ego and everything in your inner and outer life—which is to say, basically, everything.

You don't play by the same rules in dreamland. There, you can do anything you want—the only constraints are what you place on yourself. But you have a built-in circuit breaker that won't allow you to venture too far or access parts of the mind you can't handle.

When reflecting on a dream, step into the shoes of the dream-ego. See everything from that inside perspective. It helps you remember what the dream really feels like while having it. A dream is an experience and should be treated and honored as such. It's not something that just happens. It happens to you, and in the deepest reaches of your mind it registers the same as the experiences you have in your waking life. That's a very, very important fact. To the rest of your psyche beyond the ego, your dreams are just as real as your reality while your eyes are open.

The ego can be represented as a circle within a circle. See: *Circle.*

Ego is associated with persona. See: *Persona.*

The entry for *Eat* details a dream about the dreamer's inflated ego.

See also: *Balloon, Captain, Circle, Compensation, Disguise, Eat, Father, General, Individuation, King, Mask, Mother, Persona, Psyche, Queen, Slave, Unconscious Mind*

Elbow—An elbow in a dream can symbolize the need for, or creation of, personal space. It means you need "elbow room," space to maneuver. "Throwing elbows" means creating space, such as in basketball, when elbows are used to ward off defenders. That idea connects with the feeling of being hemmed in, or the walls are closing in around you and you need space to breathe.

"Elbow grease," meaning applying yourself vigorously to a task. Dreaming about breaking an elbow can symbolize something that hinders ability to work or apply yourself.

Elbows are used in waking life to surreptitiously direct attention at something, so in dreams they can be used to subtly point you in the right direction.

In some dream-interpretation traditions, elbows are associated with sexual function, specifically with arousal or "getting worked up." Thus, injury to an elbow can symbolize sexual dysfunction.

Connectors between parts of the body can have compound symbolism. Elbows connect the upper arm to the forearm. The upper arm can symbolize strength, emotional connection, and hard work, while the forearm can symbolize grasp (the muscles for gripping are located in the forearms) and help with accomplishing tasks. In this sense, an elbow can symbolize the strength to hold on under difficult circumstances, or the need for help with work.

Extend the idea further and a connector can symbolize a person to whom you are connected by bloodline, friendship, or circumstance. It can symbolize a connection in the sense of someone who can help you. Connection can also be used in the sense of emotional connection or attachment.

A bent elbow can symbolize the idea behind the phrase "bent out of shape." Extend the idea further and a bent elbow can symbolize ability to adapt.

Elderly—Something old or elderly in a dream can refer to the past. It's in the past, history. Or it's worn out, getting old.

Elderly can refer to problems with aging. For example, being too old to date someone much younger, or too old or too late to take on a task or start something new.

It can be an expression of feeling old. Exhaustion, illness, stress, or worry might be making you feel old before your time, or you recognize the potential for that to happen.

Advanced age can relate to realizing your limits. The symbolism can show in the age of objects in a dream, not just people. For example, an old, battered car can symbolize feeling or appearing old and battered.

On the other hand, the elderly commonly are free to use their time as they please because they're retired and don't have needy children at home. And in this sense, if you are young and dream about an elderly person, it can connect with thoughts about having to wait a long time before you have that sort of free time.

To dream about being old when in reality you aren't can represent fear of getting older without doing everything you want to do. You might fear becoming infirm or not living your life fully, implying the need to make the most of the time you have. This possibility is especially likely if you see yourself aging rapidly in a dream, or see an image of yourself as a much older person and react with fear. See: *Calendar, Time*.

A man about to turn fifty years old dreams that he looks in the mirror and sees an old man. The reflection doesn't look like him—he still looks and feels young for his age—but he recognizes that old age is rapidly approaching. He's all right with it—at least, he doesn't fear getting old—but he wants time to finish raising his kids and doing what he wants to do with his life, and he recognizes that his new job could make him old before his time. It's stressful and could wear him out, but with the insight from the dream he can take steps to prevent that.

A young woman dreams about an old woman who obviously doesn't have much time left to live. The sight of the old woman creates a sense of panic in the young woman. It symbolizes her fear that she won't be able to do everything she wants to do in her life. Old age is far off for her, but she has a sense of how quickly the time can pass. The underlying message is, "Seize the day."

When an elderly character is paired with a young one, it can be an archetypal configuration. Archetypes are created from opposites. See: *Archetypes*.

Old can mean "wise." If you react positively to an elderly person or see yourself as elderly, it might mean you embrace the role of wise elder or appreciate having that sort of guidance. Then again, to react negatively can symbolize rejection of tradition or advice.

See also: *Archetypes, Calendar, Death, Doctor, Fear, Grandfather, Grandmother, Hospital, Time, Wheelchair, Young*

Electricity—See: *Lightning*

Elephant—To decode the symbolism of an elephant, first consider the obvious. They're massive and strong, usually gentle but ferocious when angry. These associations are used in dreams to compare with people and situations. It's exaggerated, but fitting in some cases.

For example, a woman dreams about a huge, friendly elephant that likes to gently lift her high in the air with its trunk. It's fun. She feels exhilarated. Moreover, she feels safe. She knows the elephant will protect her. The elephant symbolizes her husband, a large and powerful man who appears intimidating to everyone else, but who she knows is a gentle giant. His awesome strength and protective nature make her feel safe, same as she feels in the dream, and his presence in her life is uplifting, as depicted in the elephant lifting her gently off the ground.

An elephant in a dream can mean you have the strength to do what you need to do and the endurance to get to where you want to be. Or you don't know your own strength.

Or something is unmovable about yourself, a person, or a situation. *Once dad makes up his mind, there's no moving him.*

Dreams can use physical traits to describe mental and other personal characteristics. For example, an elephant can symbolize long memory, determination, loyalty, and strength of character. And some traits of elephants, such as adaptability

and parental love, are directly equatable to human traits. If you see these qualities in an animal, that animal can be used in your dreams to symbolize them in yourself and people in your life—and even in other animals, such as a pet Great Dane that, as dogs go, is huge as an elephant. In addition, elephants have an uncanny sixth sense for registering the smallest details and changes about their environment, and some people do, too.

The harmonious nature of elephant herds can be used to symbolize harmonious family or communal life.

Elephants generally lumber along. This association can be used to create symbolism related to a person who plods, to slow-moving situations and feelings and careful thinking processes. This use of the symbolism is likely to show in the action of moving slowly.

Elephants are associated with masculine strength and sexuality, and their trunks and tusks can be used as phallic symbols.

The combination of massive size, sure movement, wisdom, and strong instincts makes an elephant an apt symbol for the unconscious mind. The conscious mind is small in comparison, like a human to an elephant. Most of the working parts of the mind are outside conscious awareness, and you know that, whether or not you're aware of it. And like a powerful animal, once the unconscious decides to move in a particular direction, there's not much you can do to stop it. It does not care about excuses nor respond well to rational arguments. See: *Unconscious Mind*.

To ride an elephant in a dream can indicate gaining control of the powerful forces of the unconscious mind. Or you have the strength and energy to overcome the obstacles in your life. Or you have high status or authority.

An elephant can symbolize missing the obvious—the "elephant in the room."

A wild and destructive elephant can symbolize forces that are untamed and uncontrolled. An unruly elephant can symbolize an out-of-control problem.

An ill or dead elephant can indicate disturbance in the unconscious, or loss of strength.

A baby elephant can symbolize the potential to be elephant-like in the ways described here, once matured. But as always, the meaning is found in the context of the dream-story. For instance, a baby elephant that gets away can symbolize a problem or situation that seems small now but can quickly get out of hand.

See also: *Animals, Bus, Giant, Phallic Symbol, Speed, Unconscious Mind*

Elevate—See: *Elevator*

Elevator—The main way elevators are used as symbolism is through their function of going up and down. That movement can describe the ups and downs of life and anything that ascends or descends, rises or falls: blood pressure, fortune, opinion, reputation, desire, age. The movement is a physical representation.

Going up is associated with a rise in status, similar to the idea of "climbing the ladder," on your way up, successful. The people with you in the elevator could represent the parts of yourself primarily responsible for your success: your work ethic, ambition, skill, intelligence. Or they could represent people in your life who are rising with you. See: *Ascend, Climb.*

Rising up is associated with personal development. The floors passed as you rise are stages of personal development—as a professional or student, as a parent, as a leader.

It can symbolize elevated mood, thought, or feeling, or rise in skill, ability, or knowledge.

It can symbolize aging or maturing.

Upper floors and the roof of a building can represent the head of the body. So rising in an elevator can visually represent raising your intellect or going up into your thoughts. See: *Attic.*

Going down in an elevator can visually represent descending into your emotions, or movement into the depths of your being, especially if you end up in a basement. Those depths might include forgotten or avoided memories, receded as-

pects of yourself, or your heritage or family roots. See: *Basement.*

It can symbolize depression or sinking hope. See: *Depression.*

Going down in an elevator can mean loss of status or decline in health. This dream theme is particularly common in people who have peaked mentally or physically and are starting a slow decline, shown in the movement of the elevator slowly descending.

Descending in an elevator can mean that your status, thoughts, feelings, opinions, or expectations are lowered. See: *Descend.*

Descending suddenly and crashing can symbolize feelings related to a sudden loss or trauma. It captures the sensation of a weightless stomach, that sick feeling you get when something goes horribly wrong or is really shocking.

While descent can symbolize misfortune or setback, it can also mean grounded or down to earth. Use your feelings to tell the difference.

Up-and-down movement can represent changes in mood. Fast movements in an elevator can symbolize mood swings. It can symbolize the rush of taking a drug, or the crash that happens as you "come down."

Dreams that feature elevators going to different floors of a building and the doors opening on various scenes can be like a survey of what various parts of you think about something. Down in the basement is where you might see your emotions. In the middle, you might see your gut feelings or instincts. And in the upper floors you might see your thoughts.

The same imagery of stopping at floors in an elevator can symbolize times of your life, and the specific floor is an age of your life. Floor nine is age nine, and so forth. See: *Numbers.*

Another possibility is that the symbolism of the floors visited in a dream elevator are more important for the numbers used. For example, ten is how many cousins you have, or the number of days till an important event, or the number of people you are competing against. Dreaming about avoiding floor five can symbolize avoiding thinking about how early you have to wake up—5 a.m.

If the elevator won't open, it might symbolize an opportunity that won't open for you, or you are unable to access a particular area of yourself. For example, if you ride an elevator to a basement and the doors won't open, it might mean that you are closed off to your emotions or instincts.

An elevator that doesn't arrive at your floor can symbolize an opportunity that doesn't materialize, or an event canceled.

An elevator door closing as someone tries to get on can symbolize cutting off a person, or ending a situation or relationship. For example, you decide to fire a contractor who has been repairing your house, and in a dream you shut elevator doors on a construction worker trying to enter it.

An elevator can symbolize an esophagus or throat.

See also: *Ascend, Attic, Basement, Building, Climb, Descend, Numbers, Skyscraper*

Emaciated—Emaciation in a dream can symbolize wasting away. In dreams, physically wasting away connects with a wasted life, wasted opportunity, or the gradual wearing away of spirit brought about by depression, abuse, grief, worry, listlessness, boredom, confinement, and a variety of other conditions and circumstances. It can show that more vitality and substance are needed.

Consider the obvious. You might need to eat more or eat better. You don't get enough nutrition. Or you have body-image issues.

It can symbolize that you need to be fed something non-material: ideas, enthusiasm, energy, spirit, emotion, knowledge.

For example, an artist who uses nature walks to feed her inspiration dreams about her body wasting away like someone starving. The dream follows after a period of being cooped up in an apartment. Her artistic side is starving for inspiration.

It can mean thin on substance or character, or starving for attention.

In simplest terms, emaciated means "not much there." It can symbolize a thin argument, thin on ideas, or thin in the wallet or bank account.

Dreaming that you are anorexic can show that you lack self-esteem, because a common association is that people with anorexia lack self-esteem.

It can symbolize frugality. In a general sense, anorexia means "too restrictive." The symbolism can be spun out to connect with situations such as not studying enough to get a good grade on a test, or practicing enough at something to improve.

A young mother dreams that her children are anorexic, reflecting her feelings that she doesn't give them enough attention.

In the Old Testament, Genesis 41, Joseph is called to interpret Pharaoh's dream about seeing seven fat cows rise up out of the Nile. Then seven emaciated cows rise out of the Nile and eat the fat ones. In a dream that follows, Pharaoh sees seven plump heads of grain on a single stalk. Then seven thin heads of grain sprout and consume the fat heads. Joseph interprets the imagery as meaning that seven years of good harvest will be followed by seven years of bad harvest, and advises Pharaoh to save his resources from the good harvests in preparation for the seven lean years to follow. And indeed, according to the story, that's what transpired.

See also: *Cage, Eat, Fat, Food*

Email—To receive email in a dream can mean that you are getting a message from the unconscious or subconscious mind. Information is being communicated to you. The content of the email is often related to a current issue in your life or thought on your mind. See: *Letter.*

It's also possible to dream about email because you are expecting communication from someone. People are known to dream about receiving an email from someone, then waking up to find a message from that person.

Dreaming about receiving an email from someone you haven't heard from in a while can be a way of saying that you miss the person. It's a good time to get in touch.

Sending email can symbolize a need to communicate, or simply be a way of saying that the person you email is on your mind. Composing an email in your dream, for example, can be a way of thinking through what you want to say to a person. Stretch the idea and it can apply to situations such as what you want to say in a poem or in a report.

Email can symbolize communication that lacks substance. Email is sometimes a way of communicating with someone indirectly. These days, texting and instant messaging have usurped email as the go-to way of communicating indirectly, but the perception of email as impersonal persists.

Email in a dream can symbolize being misunderstood or taken the wrong way, because it's all too common for the message in an email to be taken the wrong way. As with all dream symbolism, look for details that support an idea before making conclusions.

See also: *Computer, Facebook, Friend, Job, Letter, Phone, Subconscious, Talk, Unconscious Mind*

Embark—Embarking in a dream can symbolize entering a new phase of life. The ship of your life is sailing. You have a fresh start. You are changing.

Another way of looking at it is that the journey relates to a particular project or area of life. For example, setting sail is a way of describing getting married. A project is said to "get off the ground" or "launch." See: *Journey*.

Or perhaps you're growing as a person or reaching for new personal destinations. You leave your old ways behind—leave behind the person you were—to become someone new. You'll never be the same again.

Symbolism can be created through the feelings involved with embarking on a journey and how they connect with your recent life. Embarking can be associated with feelings of freedom, relaxation, and escape.

To embark is an analogy that captures the idea of a journey of imagination. For professionals such as fiction authors and songwriters who use their imagination regularly, a dream about embarking can symbolize setting off to a new place to which their imagination takes them—writing a new book or song. See: *Artist*.

Of course, imagination is integral to many endeavors and professions, and imagination isn't lim-

ited to work. It's used for fantasies and daydreams, too. For example, you dream about embarking on a cruise and falling in love, which reflects the tone and even the content of your recent daydreams. Or, as a fantasy, it expresses your deepest desires.

See also: *Airplane, Airport, Artist, Balloon, Boat, Bus, Car, Journey, Love, Train, Vacation*

Embrace—See: *Hug*

Embryo—See: *Egg, Fetus*

Emerald—As one of the hardest stones, emeralds can symbolize strength of character and firmness of values.

Emeralds are symbols of luxury and wealth. See: *Jewelry*.

The green color of emeralds is associated with fertility, nature, and love. See: *Green*.

See also: *Earth, Gem, Green, Jewelry*

Emotions—Emotions are at the heart of most dreams. Dreaming is a two-part process of creating symbolic imagery and tying it to emotions, like two sides of a coin. However, some dreams appear to connect only with thoughts and thought processes.

Dreams trigger emotions that would otherwise stay bottled up or unexpressed. So in that sense, dreams provide venting, as a volcano vents to release pressure. By releasing emotions during a dream, you might avoid a blowup while awake.

Dreams can trigger strong emotions like rage, terror, love, and ecstasy. Experiencing these emotions while dreaming doesn't necessarily mean you feel them in your waking life, but it's a good indication you feel something similar or could feel that way under certain circumstances. In dreams the gloves come off, your inhibitions come down, and the emotional centers of your brain light up.

So you might not feel rage in your waking life, for example, but if you dream about it, something could be pushing you in that direction, and if the situation is left unaddressed, you could find yourself in a rage. You might not feel ecstatic, but maybe you feel really happy—or could feel that way under the right circumstances. The potential is there.

For example, a young man dreams he's back in high school and is told he won't graduate. He asks the teacher for help, but the answers confuse him. He reacts with rage and tosses desks around the classroom, then stalks off to track down the school counselor, knowing that the counselor is somehow responsible for his predicament.

The dream summarizes a situation he's in. He graduated a few years back and has been directionless since then. He doesn't know what to do with his life, and no adults are providing answers, as symbolized in the dream by confusing answers from the teacher and looking for the school counselor, meaning someone to guide him. The rage felt in the dream is a raw, honest expression of his emotions, and it's shown in how he reacts so strongly. His life is wasting away, and he knows it. After analyzing and understanding the dream, he resolves it by joining the Navy.

One of the golden rules of dream interpretation is that dreams exaggerate. They do so to get your attention as they express the underlying dynamics of a situation.

For example, you are buried with work and dream that you are buried alive. Being buried alive is a much worse situation than being buried at work, of course, but in an exaggerated way it expresses your emotions. Many dreams can be interpreted simply by relating the emotions they trigger with your waking life and gauging the strength of your reaction.

For example, when being buried alive elicits a mild reaction, you can bet the symbolism connects with something that's just the way things are. Perhaps being buried in work is just par for the course. Hell, maybe you enjoy it!

When you react strongly to a situation in a dream, it's a good indicator that it symbolizes something you feel strongly about, something that arouses powerful emotions in you.

For example, a female dreams about a drink spilling on her mattress during sex while a condom is being put on. She flies off in a rage and kicks her partner out. Her reaction shows that she feels very strongly about what the spilled drink symbolizes:

the possibility of accidentally getting pregnant. It only takes a little bit of spilled semen to get her pregnant.

Her reaction reveals that she subconsciously knows the meaning of the symbolism of the spilled drink. Otherwise, why react so strongly to something that on the surface appears innocuous? Her emotional reaction reveals the meaning of the symbolism, and in turn reveals the meaning of the dream.

Colors in dreams have strong correlation with emotions. A rule of thumb is that colors signify related emotions. Bob Hoss's work in this area is terrific; you can find it by searching online for "Bob Hoss dreams color." And see: *Colors*.

Feelings are not synonymous with emotions. How you feel about something is a value judgment, not an emotion, but emotion is felt in the body, so in that sense "feeling" is appropriate. The list of entries below includes some entries better classified as feelings.

See also: *Anger, Anxiety, Ascend, Boat, Body, Bomb, Colors, Cry, Depression, Descend, Dolphin, Drown, Elevator, Empty, Erupt, Fear, Fight, Guilt, Hate, Jealous, Joy, Insane, Love, Numb, Octopus, Pain, Panic, Psychologist, Rage, Revenge, Scream, Wound*

Employee—Dreams about employees often connect in some way to work, involving either a formal role as an employee, or an informal role such as a volunteer. For example, getting an allowance in return for doing chores makes a child an "employee" of the family. Staying after class to run errands for a teacher is similar to being an employee. Taking care of the kids is a job, and by extension that makes you an employee. If work is involved, the role of employee is comparable. See: *Family Business*.

Dreaming about a specific employee you work with or who works for you most commonly symbolizes something about your relationship with that person, events he is involved in, or a role she plays. Most dreams involving employees and coworkers relate to recent interactions with them. Think back on the day before the dream and remember all interactions with the people in your life who appear as characters in your dreams.

Remember, though, to avoid the temptation of assuming that a character in your dream represents that person. Often characters are reflections of aspects of yourself.

For example, you dream about an employee you work with pulling a gun and shooting up your workplace. Because we hear about similar situations in the news, it's easy to assume that such a dream is a warning that the person in your dream is about to pop a cork. But in reality the dream is actually acting out your feelings about being frustrated at work. The dream uses that employee because you know that person is also frustrated at work. You're in the same boat. See: *Co-Worker*.

A good example of how to interpret a dream-character that looks like someone you know is found in the entry for *Sister*.

A general rule for interpreting the meaning of dream-characters is to ask yourself whether you have had any recent interaction or contact with the people they represent. If the answer is "no," then they most likely represent an aspect of yourself. Or something about them—character or personality traits; roles played; facts about their life—is used to tell a story.

If you dream about a new employee and the character is purely fictional, then you could be seeing a new aspect of yourself emerging in your personality. It's portrayed as an employee because it assists the work of your ego in running your life. Or it represents a new job or responsibility you've taken on. See: *Job*.

Dreaming about an employee who plays a formal role, especially one involving a uniform, can connect with a role you play in life. For example, you dream about a security guard you know at work checking the doors. You play the role of checking the security of your house, and dream about that security guard because you relate to the role he or she plays.

See also: *Boss, Co-worker, Dismissal, Ego, Family Business, Job, Unemployed, Walmart*

Empty—When a dream shows something as empty, it can be a physical representation for something lacking or missing.

For example, an empty plate or cup can symbolize lack of activity, energy, or opportunity. An empty bed can symbolize missing your mate, or missing the close comfort of a lover. It can mean you lack dreams or visions for your life.

An empty building can symbolize feeling empty inside or socially isolated, or symbolize lack of purpose or meaning. It can mean there is a gap in your life. Someone or something important is missing from the picture.

Emptiness can be associated with empty gestures or promises. It can mean something lacks substance.

An empty house can symbolize lack of purpose. Life feels pointless. You're lonely. Or you are an "empty-nester."

Empty streets can indicate lack of prospects, such as when someone is looking for employment or opportunity but finding none. It can connect with feeling lonely or isolated.

An empty pool can signify lack of emotion or energy.

An empty glass can signify lack of prospects, or pessimism.

An empty picture can mean something's missing from the picture of your life. The metaphor is obvious if you step back.

In Eastern culture, emptiness is generally a good sign. It means overcoming ego needs. It's a sign of a clear mind. In Christianity, an empty vessel is an allegory for a person who is free from sin, old patterns, and former ways, and is ready to be filled with the Holy Spirit. An empty house can have the same meaning, because a house can symbolize the spiritual or psychological body. As always, use your feelings and reactions to guide you.

See also: *Building, Car, City, Dark, Emaciated, Home, Pool, Road, Space*

End of the World—See: *Apocalypse*

Enemy—A character in a dream presented as an enemy might symbolize a person in your life who is a nemesis, an enemy. Are you in conflict with someone? A rival? Someone you just can't stand?

See the entry for *Devil* for a great example of how a bad struggle with a personal nemesis is turned into a story about rape.

Say you don't get along with a certain colleague, and tomorrow you have a meeting in that person's office. You dream about being in enemy territory pursued by a dark figure. Enemy territory symbolizes the person's office, and the dark figure is the colleague, who treats your relationship like hunter and prey.

It is common for enemies in dreams to symbolize ways you work against your own best interests or sabotage yourself. But think more expansively to consider anything that threatens your ego, or threatens your beliefs or social status. For example, secular society is perceived as the enemy of some religions. A habit of putting your foot in your mouth (figuratively) can be the enemy of your ambition to be socially popular.

Sometimes, however, the enemy is within you, an aspect of yourself, something about yourself perceived as threatening. For example, an enemy in a dream can mean you are "your own worst enemy."

You can make an enemy out of an aspect of yourself through rejection, repression or neglect, and it will personify as a character or characters in dreams. This sort of enemy is known as Shadow, and it is the ultimate enemy from within you. See: *Shadow*.

The enemy could be fear, or expectation of the worst. See: *Fear*.

You can create enemies because of your behavior or attitude. If you dream often about enemies out to get you for no apparent reason, it might reflect that you are the ultimate source of your trouble and are blind to how you create the situations.

An enemy in a dream is a characterization or projection. Your job is to figure out how it connects with you and your life. Bear in mind, dreams have a lot of options to choose from and they pick particular symbols according to how they tell the story and fit the situation. An enemy is specific symbolism. It's stronger symbolism than an opponent, but not as strong as a killer or devil. See the entry for *War* for an example of how to use the strength of symbolism to help interpret it.

See also: *Apocalypse, Arena, Army, Attack, Devil, Erupt, Fight, Group, Kill, Murder, Opponent, Rape, Revenge, Serial Killer, Tackle, Terrorist, War*

Engaged—See: *Fiancé*

Envy—See: *Jealous*

Erection—See: *Penis*

Erupt—Dreams create symbolism by comparing one thing to another. An eruption is comparable to something that happens suddenly and forcefully, such as a volcano erupting. Hot emotions and feelings such as anger, hostility, and frustration suddenly emerge. Devastation can ensue. See: *Bomb*.

A tense or heated situation is said to erupt when someone snaps and sparks fly.

An eruption implies something that happens suddenly, but also builds pressure beforehand. For example, your best friend is dating your ex. The situation is tense, and trouble is brewing. It might erupt into a big conflict or cause a rupture with your friend. And if it happens, it could bring years' worth of grievances to the surface. During an eruption, something that was contained comes out into the open.

Repression, neglect, and desire for change create internal pressure that can lead to an eruption of the psyche, if these conditions are allowed to prolong unresolved. Jungian psychology uses the phrase "eruption of unconscious content" to describe when the unconscious mind suddenly pours into the conscious mind. The dam bursts and there's no stopping the flood.

Carl Jung said it happened to him when he was in his mid-thirties, and fortunately as a psychiatrist he had the tools to deal with it. Many of his greatest insights about the psyche came forth during that time of his life, but the flood of crazy thoughts, emotions, and imagery almost got the best of him. The ego keeps up walls against the unconscious for good reason; otherwise, it can be impossible to handle everyday reality. See: *Unconscious Mind*.

Some people are completely overwhelmed when such an eruption happens. They can make unsound and rash decisions and suddenly stop acting like themselves. Their dreams fill with images of things erupting and bursting, and often the dreams will recur almost exactly, until the right decision or insight is made that allows them to take the next step.

See also: *Anger, Bomb, Ego, Emotions, Ex, Hate, Insane, Psyche, Rage, Unconscious Mind, Volcano*

Escape—A question at the heart of a dream about escape is: what are you getting away from or is getting away from you? The meaning might not be obvious till you step back and ask what personal situation is represented as escape.

Another question to ask yourself is, do you want to escape from something about yourself or your life? For example, a dream about escaping from a liquor store can symbolize wishing to overcome a drinking problem. The most dramatic dreams of this type show you running to escape from someone pursuing you. Finally you're cornered, and your pursuer shows its face. And it's you.

Someone or something escaping from you can symbolize a situation such as an interest or opportunity getting away. See: *Chase.*

Dreaming about escaping a prison can connect with escaping from a situation that's keeping you confined or restricted. See: *Prisoner.*

Escaping a monster can mean giving up an addiction or getting away from an abuser. See: *Monster.*

Escaping a fire can mean escaping danger or someone's anger. See: *Fire.*

Each of the last three examples have other possible meanings. They're meant to show you how the action of escaping combines with other details to create symbolism.

Escape can mean that something's after you, or that you might be next to face the firing squad. For example, your supervisor or spouse was on the warpath yesterday, and you decided to lie low. Then you dream about the situation as fleeing from a gun battle.

Escape can connect with ideas related to being a fugitive. See: *Fugitive.*

The theme of escaping implies sneakiness and furtiveness. You can't just walk out the door. It can mean that a person is trapped physically or emotionally. That an abuser has a psychological death grip on the person. Or that an obligation or duty won't allow the person to just walk out the door.

Escaping and avoiding go hand in hand, and avoiding can connect with avoiding rules, restrictions, authority, or social situations. Avoidance translates into a dream as escaping, perhaps over a fence or under a wall. The entry for *Hell* has a great example of this use of the symbolism in a dream about escaping from hell.

Procrastination is, in a sense, escaping the fact that something needs to be done. You can escape from your responsibilities, from stress or problems, from a relationship and its expectations, or from strong emotions and feelings. You can escape from your conscience. You can try to shake a certain feeling.

Sometimes, the thing from which you flee is exactly what you need or want. That's why it pursues you.

See also: *Abyss, Accomplice, Arrest, Burglary, Cage, Chase, Fence, Fly, Fugitive, Hide, Jail, Police Officer, Prisoner, Run, Torture, Wall*

Euthanasia—See: *Death*

Evil—Describe evil in simplest terms. It's wrong. It's immoral. It's harmful. Those give you a few ideas to begin your search. Unless you're dealing with real evil, you know it's a comparison. Question is, to what?

Evil can be a sort of catch-all term to describe anything bad or even unknown. It's only presented as evil because of your perceptions. It's a subjective portrayal, not objective.

For example, a woman dreams several times about an evil shadow chasing her, looming over her like a tidal wave. She can't get away, and the shadow never shows what it really is or reveals why it's chasing her. She just reacts with fear at the sight of it and tries to get away.

She begins decoding the symbolism by asking herself what she fears most and how it might connect with what's pursuing her, and immediately the answer is obvious. She fears being unable to provide for her children. Her work situation is in flux, and money is tight. The possibility of running out of money looms over her. The shadow is perceived as evil, because the thought of failing her children is unfathomable.

Evil can mean fear. Dreams begin with what you fear, then give it a physical representation. It's an easy connection to make because evil is commonly feared. In this sense, evil is a catch-all. Now consider that evil is often something that you know when you see it, but otherwise it's intangible, so as a symbol of fear it's more likely to represent something intangible. For example, fear of spiders and fear of flying are tangible, with a physical source, but fear of failure and fear of the dark are intangible.

Dreaming about something evil can symbolize a situation that feels morally or ethically wrong. It can mean you have come under bad influence. Or you recognize the dark side of someone you know or of a situation.

Or perhaps you recognize something dark about yourself. Repressed, unwanted, and shadowy parts of you can be labeled "evil." See: *Shadow*.

Evil is an exaggerated way of labeling addictive, immoral, and criminal behaviors.

Think of your associations with evil and ask yourself whether any of them apply to your dream. For example, evil is known for exploitation, abuse, possession, temptation, corruption, and dishonesty. It's also associated with something out to get you, and with feeling victimized. Any of those associations can be symbolized in a dream as something or someone evil.

And evil is a label applied in some cases to anything that's unknown or beyond your comprehension.

See also: *Addict, Crime, Dark, Demon, Devil, Fear, God, Hell, Nazi, Suicide*

Ex—It's common to dream about an ex when something about the relationship is unresolved. It is a common type of recurring dream, and it can be quite unwelcome. The dreamer senses that an important message is trying to get through, but more often than not, the dreamer, you, would rather just quit dreaming about the person. Or you take it as a sign that you should get in touch with your ex, but that's a mistake, too, because your ex in a dream is a symbol used in a story—a versatile symbol with a wide range of possible meanings.

When something is left unsaid or unpaid, it's almost guaranteed to pop up in a dream. These things keep you tied emotionally and financially to your ex. They're like fishing hooks embedded in your body, and until they're removed, you can't really move on. If you're still paying for the relationship in the form of bills, dings on your credit rating, or harm to yourself or your reputation, then of course you will dream about it. And if your heart is still with your ex, well, you need it back.

You can dream about your ex when you're in another relationship and are reminded of the old one. Something about the new person or situation reminds you of the old one. Or you fear your current partner will soon be an ex-partner.

Or perhaps just being back in a relationship is enough to spark a dream about the old one. It's a prime time to step back in time, especially if something from the past is unresolved. Dreams don't reminisce, normally. If you dream about an ex, there's a reason for it related to your present life, your thoughts, your feelings, and what's stirring deep inside.

Dreaming about an ex can indicate you miss something from that relationship or time of life. For example, it's common to dream about your first love or other idealized relationship when you feel that something is missing from your present relationship. You miss the passion, fascination, innocence, or simplicity.

An ex in a dream can connect the past with the present. For example, a person experiences depression while in a relationship then then later dreams about that person whenever the feeling of depression returns. Depression is just an example. It could be any present feeling, thought, or circumstance that connects with the past.

Abusive relationships leave a deep impression and tend to be dreamed about long after they're over. Reexperiencing the trauma can be a way of processing the emotions and creating psychological distance. It helps a person heal, and the process can be aided by actively exploring related thoughts, feelings, and memories.

Here's a dramatic example. A woman dreams she's driving to her family home at night. She's lost and needs directions and pulls over to check the map on her phone. A man reaches through her window, grabs items from her car and runs away. She tracks him down and gets back her stuff. He apologizes. Then he snatches her phone and runs away again. This time she throws a knife, hitting him in the back, and he falls down. Then she pulls out the knife, and with extreme personal malice stabs him in the heart.

Wow! The ending was unexpected, but it all makes sense when you understand that the man represents her ex. The character and the ex don't look alike, but the connection is made in three ways. One, he was the type to do crappy things to her, then apologize. Two, he got her into hard drugs and consequently she lost her way in life, as symbolized by getting lost while trying to find her way home. In a personal sense she doesn't know how to find her way back to the life she had before meeting him. And three, the sheer malice she feels as she stabs him in the heart points right to where she's wounded.

She didn't need to stab him in the heart to get her phone back. That's an expression of how she feels about her ex, summed up neatly in one image of ramming a knife into his heart when he's defenseless. Subconsciously, she knows who the man represents when she stabs him.

Under the category of "unresolved," dreaming about an ex can relate to learning from the experience. Dreams help you learn, and part of that function is to help you avoid repeating mistakes. By figuring out what went wrong in a past relationship, you have a better shot at success in present and future ones.

But it goes deeper. Your dreams want you to become a complete person and will take every op-portunity to help you grow. Adversity is a great teacher. It pushes you out of your comfort zone and forces you to grow.

Dreams can use characters as surrogates for people you know, and an ex in a dream can be a surrogate for a current relationship. Doesn't matter whether the ex is at all like your current partner—they don't have to look or act alike. They're connected by the role they play.

Or, a surrogate can be used to represent an ex. Sometimes just the sight of the person in a dream will cause such a hot reaction that a surrogate must be used in order to tell the story.

If you dream about kissing your ex, or kissing someone in front of your ex, see: *Lips.*

See also: *Boyfriend, Dismissal, Girlfriend, Husband, Lips, Marriage, Wedding, Wife*

Exam—See: *Test*

Examination—See: *Doctor*

Excrement—Excrement in a dream can be a graphic way of expressing how you feel about something—a situation, a person, how you are treated, your life.

It can symbolize something unwanted that needs to get out of you. It can be a sign that you're holding onto things that are no good for you.

Excrement is the end process of digestion, and "to digest" means to process. In this sense, excrement can symbolize something you processed emotionally or psychologically.

The word "shit" is so versatile. You can feel like shit. You can be in a world of shit. You can feel like your ideas or efforts are shit. You can get caught in a shit storm.

Shitting in public can mean you publicly humiliate yourself. You "stepped in it" in a very public way. Or you strongly object to something.

Dreams can respond to signals in the body, so dreaming about excrement can be a response to the physical feeling of needing to move your bowels.

The entry for *Devil* has a great example of excrement used as symbolism.

See also: *Anal Sex, Anus, Bathroom, Devil, Eat, Food, Toilet*

Execution—Dreaming about execution can connect with something you're dreading. You face a deadline. You fear failure. For some reason life as you know it is about to end, or you fear that will be the case, such as when an important relationship ends.

Execution is "the end." And it's involuntary, a key reason that it's used in a dream over other similar symbolism such as death, murder, or suicide.

For example, a college student about to graduate might dream about execution as symbolism for the sudden end to college life. Entering the professional world can require major lifestyle changes, and it can feel like a part of oneself is being forced to die. Or a bachelor about to get married doesn't want to give up single life and feels like the fun-loving part of him- or herself is going to pass away in the process.

Dreams about execution can be sparked by thoughts about mortality, or something that makes you fear sudden death. For example, you hear about someone you know who is healthy and happy suddenly dying. Or you think of your car as a rolling death trap.

Along this line, health fears and illness can spark execution-related dreams. Life as you know it could suddenly be over if you get sick. You're not dead, but might as well be.

Dreaming about receiving a death sentence can symbolize feeling as if an ax is hanging over your head. Everything hinges on something important coming up. You have to make that sale, get that grade, or perform well in a tryout, for example.

A death sentence is the ultimate punishment and can symbolize a severe consequence, or fear of it. For example, getting fired at work for making a mistake. You do something wrong or forbidden and have a guilty conscience. You fear getting caught. A death sentence is exaggerated, but it expresses how you feel. See: *Dismissal.*

It can symbolize the idea in the phrase "signing your own death warrant." Something could be your downfall, or cause irreparable harm.

To be condemned can mean resigned to an unpleasant fate or circumstance. For example, a bad illness can spark feelings that your body has condemned you. To condemn can be a harsh way of disapproving of someone's actions, behavior, or character. Depicting it as a death sentence or execution is exaggerated but fitting.

See also: *Death, Decapitate, Dismissal, Divorce, Grim Reaper, Gun, Hang, Jail, Judge, Kill, Prisoner, Suicide*

Exercise—See: *Fitness Center*

Exorcism—See: *Demon*

Explode—See: *Bomb*

Explore—See: *Discover*

Expose—See: *Naked*

Eyes—When you decode the importance of a body part in a dream, begin with what it does. Eyes see, and another word for see is "vision." Vision can be meant in the sense of "vision for my life" or "tunnel vision." A dream that draws attention to eyes can speak to awareness or perspective—of yourself, of a situation, of a problem—and to what you notice. It's a physical representation of a personal situation.

Seeing can mean "see the answer," or "see the truth." "Both eyes open" means "aware." Seeing can mean perceive, as in "see things my way." You can "keep your eyes peeled," or "have an eye for art." Something can be "eye-catching," or an "eye-opener." These figurative uses of eyes and sight are popular ways for dreams to create symbolism.

The symbolism of eyes and sight is often shown through actions. For example, covering the eyes can symbolize "see no evil." It can symbolize lack of giving attention, or something is preventing you from seeing in the figurative sense.

Being unable to look someone in the eyes can indicate shame, guilt, or dishonesty. It can indicate something to hide.

Worms or bugs crawling out of the eyes can symbolize viewing something that makes you squirm, or that worms into your brain, such as brutal horror movies or scat porn. The same symbolism can be created through the action of plucking out an eye or deliberately blinding yourself. It means you've seen something that you'd rather not see, or that's harmful.

Eyes are associated with attention. When something has your attention, you keep your eyes on it, such as the value of a stock, the behavior of a person, the ball, or the approach of a special day.

Eyes are known as the "windows of the soul" because of how they're identified with the uniqueness of each person. Looking at someone in the eyes can symbolize getting a read on the person, trying to ascertain true character and intentions. It can indicate a special emotional or spiritual connection. If a dream-character is a surrogate for someone you know, you can often tell because of the eyes.

It is said that the eyes give away the identity of the soul within.

Windows of a home can symbolize eyes when the home represents the body or mind. Windows are used to see through, and so are eyes. A window can symbolize perspective or point of view, the way you "see" things.

The symbolism of eyes missing can connect with inability to see from someone else's perspective—a specific person, or just in the sense of "see no perspective but your own."

Both eyes are missing can mean you don't really know who you are, or alternately, you don't really know someone in your life. Or something is askew with your perception or perspective. See: *Blind*.

One eye missing can symbolize not seeing the whole situation, or only giving half your attention.

The color of eyes can coincide with emotion. See: *Colors*.

Eyes colored black are associated with the unconscious mind. When you look into the eyes of a character with black eyes, you might be looking into your inner depths and the mystery of your existence. The price of entry to the unconscious is that you must take the hardest sort of look at yourself and embrace it all.

On the other hand, black eyes can symbolize lacking soul or depth. You can tell the difference between meanings by how you react.

A "black eye," the bruised area beneath the eye, is a classic mark of dishonor or shame.

Left and right in dreams can have meaning. Left is related to creativity, and right is related to logic, so closing the left eye can mean something related to creativity is missing or undervalued, and closing the right eye—or plucking it out, or wounding it, or blindness—can mean something related to logic is missing or undervalued. Left can mean "wrong," or "unconventional," and right can mean "correct," or "orthodox." See: *Left, Right*.

Take note of discrepancies with reality, such as dreaming that you can see despite having no eyes or if they're covered. It's a sure sign of symbolism.

Pupils in a dream can be a wordplay on the definition of pupil meaning "student." For example, a teacher on maternity leave dreams that she sees a doctor and her pupils are missing. It symbolizes that she misses her students. The pupil of the eye allows in light, and light can symbolize knowledge. They're the gateway to inner life.

Eyes that are all color, no pupil, can symbolize seeing from within you, from your inner being or depths. It's a theme that arises particularly in people who have a spiritual outlook or women who are pregnant.

See also: *All-Seeing Eye, Amputate, Blind, Body, Dark, Face, Head, Left, Light, Right, Student*

Face—The face is the most distinguishable feature of a person. In dreams it's associated with personal identity, reputation, self-image, and appearance, and can have symbolism related to those subjects. See: *Persona*.

The actions and details tell the story. For example, washing the face can symbolize trying to wash away guilt, embarrassment, regret, or stain on self-image or reputation. The term "save face" captures this idea, because to save face means to avoid embarrassment. Vigorously scrubbing the face can express a wish to be someone different from who you are, scrub away your identity, even negate yourself. See: *Clean*.

Take note of anything unusual or out of kilter about a face. For example, a deformed, wounded, or scarred face can symbolize issues with self-image. It can symbolize skewed perception. See: *Deformed, Wound*.

A swollen face can symbolize bragging, or swollen with pride.

An expressionless face or "poker face" can symbolize emotional numbness or inability to read emotions or intentions. It can mean something is hidden from you. See: *Hide, Numb*.

Expressions on faces of dream-characters can reflect mood, emotions, and feelings, and have symbolism such as in the phrase "put on a happy face." See: *Emotions*.

A blurry face can symbolize uncertainty about personal identity. It can mean you don't really know someone, or you're not sure about the person's intentions or true feelings. It can mean a situation is murky.

A face painted heavily with makeup can symbolize compensating for perceived weaknesses or flaws, or intention to cheat or deceive. It can symbolize covering over the true person inside, or putting on a facade. That idea is also captured in the image of wearing a mask. See: *Compensation, Disguise, Hide, Makeup, Mask*.

A face that changes or morphs can symbolize changing to fit a situation or blend in like a chameleon. A face morphing into the face of someone you know can show a connection with that person. For example, the face of a queen turns into the face of your mother, and that explains all the other details involving the queen in the dream.

A face can be a visual pun for "face the truth" or "face a problem." It can mean there's something you can't "face," especially if a face is missing or turns away.

Facing left or right can have symbolism connected with those directions. See: *Left, Right*.

Facing a wall can indicate shame, as well as facing difficulties, obstacles, divisions, and problems. See: *Wall*.

For example, a woman dreams about a female stranger facing a wall in shame as "mean girls" throw darts at her back, symbolizing the mean ways the dreamer talks to herself. She feels that she doesn't live up to cultural ideals of beauty and is ashamed because of it. The stranger is a projection of herself, and so are the mean girls.

Dreaming about concentrating on a face can symbolize attempting to get to know someone or see inside them. The same idea applies if you search your own face in a mirror. It's a way of looking at the inner you. See: *Mirror*.

A face missing a nose can depict the phrase "cut off your nose to spite your face," a warning against overreacting in a way that is self-destructive. Or perhaps your ability to "smell out" a situation is hampered. See: *Nose*.

Because eyes are used for seeing, a face missing eyes can be a way of saying you are not noticing something, or lack vision for your life. See: *Eyes*.

A faceless dream-character can symbolize lack of personal identity, or express the feeling of being "just another face in the crowd." See: *Doll*.

A facelift can express the wish to change your personal identity or create a new persona. You are ready to "shed your skin." You want to be someone else, or are in the process of personal transformation. Or, thought of another way, you want to be rid of the baggage associated with the person you are. It can express a wish to change your look, or to turn back time. See: *Baggage, Time Travel*.

See also: *Baggage, Beauty, Blind, Cheat, Clean, Compensation, Deformed, Disguise, Doll, Ears, Emotions, Eyes, Facebook, Hair, Head, Hide, Left, Lips, Makeup, Mask, Mirror, Mouth, Nose, Numb, Persona, Right, Stranger, Time Travel, Ugly, Wall, Wound*

Facebook—Facebook in a dream brings up all sorts of interesting possibilities for symbolism.

A primary way it's used in dreams is in association with friendship. See: *Friend*.

It can be used to address subjects such as putting your best foot forward, persona, public life, and privacy. See: *Hide, Persona*.

Facebook is used to communicate, so in dreams it can symbolize anything related to communication—especially misunderstandings that arise from brevity, sarcasm, and lack of context and communication in groups. See: *Email*.

People can have broad but shallow relationships on Facebook, and when in a pinch and needing a friend, Facebook is the last place most people look, so it's great symbolism for shallow relationships and feeling like you can't count on your friends, or like your friends take no real interest in you. Another joke about Facebook centers on heavy users' having nothing better to do. This association can be used by dreams to symbolize wasting time and energy, or lacking priorities.

A man dreams about feeling something small and hard beneath the skin of his right index finger. He pulls it out and realizes it's the "Facebook implant," which identifies who he is. Later, he regrets removing it when his friends no longer recognize him.

This dream is a fascinating twist on the idea of a person's social identity revolving around social media like Facebook. It reflects the dreamer's feelings that people online don't really know him. He fears that by disengaging from Facebook he'll lose what friends he has. The placement of the implant in his right index finger is appropriate and symbolic because that is the "clicker" finger. When using a computer mouse to navigate, the right index finger is used to press the mouse button. It's also used for swiping and tapping touchscreens.

Facebook is a great way of quickly keeping current with the lives of people you might not otherwise know much about. On the flip side, it's also a great way of keeping tabs on people you don't have much direct contact with, such as exboyfriends and ex-girlfriends. A change in relationship status, for example, can spark curiosity, and curiosity can lead to spying or stalking and can bring out strong feelings and emotions.

For example, a man checks Facebook before going to bed and notices that his ex has changed her relationship status to "in a relationship." That night he dreams he's supposed to meet his ex and the new boyfriend, but puts little effort into getting himself ready and thinks he looks shabby. He meets up with his ex and the new boyfriend and thinks the boyfriend is ugly. He thinks to himself, "My ex really downgraded."

At the heart of the dream is the dreamer's insecurity and need to feel superior in comparison to other people. He's jealous of the fact that his ex is dating someone else, while he's still wallowing and not really putting any effort into finding a new relationship, symbolized in the dream as putting little effort into getting ready to meet up with his ex. What is "ugly" is actually the dreamer's insecurity and shallowness. It's a physical representation.

Recent activity on Facebook is a prime candidate for why you dream about it.

Facebook can be intrusive. It invites comments and prying into your life from people you might not care to engage with, and therefore can be used to symbolize feeling intruded upon. Remember that the intrusion might not be at all related to your activity on Facebook, but is comparable in some way. For example, you suspect that your activity at work is being secretly tracked, and you dream about a stranger tracking your activity on Facebook.

See also: *Book, Computer, Email, Ex, Face, Group, Hide, Jealous, Letter, Spy, Talk, Ugly*

Faceless—See: *Face*

Facelift—See: *Face*

Fake—Dreams connect ideas, so something fake in a dream can connect with something false or insincere in your life. For example, a fake driver's license can symbolize pretending to be qualified for something, or taking a leadership role that isn't deserved. Drivers are in control of a vehicle, an association that extends to leadership.

Any sort of fake identity document or money can symbolize pretending to be something or someone you are not. It means "faking it."

Money is a representation of value, so fake money can symbolize value that's misplaced or misrepresented. It can symbolize something undervalued. It can connect with lack of appreciation for talent, ability, or effort. Think of it this way. Imagine that you've worked hard all week and you're paid for it with Monopoly money. What a slap in the face!

It can connect with feelings related to watching less-qualified people succeed where you fail.

Fake can mean "lie."

Fake can mean "unreal." See: *Imposter*.

See also: *Diamond, Disguise, Doll, Imposter, Mask, Money*

Fall—Falling in a dream is a common theme and is often associated with a sudden change for the worse, or the idea behind the phrase "ground disappears beneath your feet." It means something you thought was solid and dependable suddenly is not. The business you work for goes under. Your mate leaves. Your pastor is having an affair. Your best friend turns on you. Your parents divorce.

Your values, ethics, principles, ideals, and beliefs are part of the figurative ground you stand on, the foundation on which you build your character, so if you do something contrary to them, you are in a sense removing the ground beneath you. You fall. Extend that idea further to include situations in which it's not your actions that cause a fall, but a change of circumstance or heart. It can mean you are unsettled or undecided.

The theme has many possibilities for connection with everyday life and internal situations. For example, falling from a height is likely to have a bad ending, so falling in a dream can reflect the expectation that something won't end well.

In simplest terms, while falling you are between places, so it can mean between places in your life, or you're experiencing a big change.

Falling can connect with feelings of stress, pressure, dread, shock, or horror. Dreams use the feeling of one thing (falling) to connect with another thing (help!).

It can connect with falling in love.

Falling can express fear of failure: at school, at work, in a relationship, in life. Failure is equated with falling.

Falling can be thought of as "coming back to earth." This use of the symbolism is often accompanied by the action of flying. Flying up, then falling back to earth, can mean giving something a try and not quite making it.

Falling is used in figures of speech such as "fall from grace" and "take a fall." Fall from grace means a loss of status, respect, or prestige. To take a fall means to accept blame, particularly for something you did not do. The same meaning is expressed in the term "fall guy." See: *Descend.*

Falling can symbolize a fallen state of being.

Falling can symbolize a decline in physical or mental health, or fear related to it.

It can symbolize depression. Depression is something that a person is said to "fall into." See: *Depression.*

Falling is associated with "hitting bottom," a term used in recovery groups and therapy to mean a person is tired of living in a fallen state and is ready to turn his or her life around.

Voluntarily leaping carries a different connotation. It can mean venturing into the unknown, being a daredevil, or the idea expressed in the phrase "leap of faith." The fall is not scary, or at least doesn't carry the same fear or dread as other falls. And the landing, if there is one, is soft. For example, you leap from a cliff into a pool of water and emerge unscathed, showing that you venture out of your comfort zone and everything turns out all right.

Falling can symbolize being pushed into something you are reluctant to do, especially when you're not sure where you're headed. Falling through empty air captures that idea in one image. You have no idea when or where you'll land.

Falling from a bridge can symbolize failing to take advantage of opportunity. A bridge is a route to somewhere, and in life opportunities are routes to get to where you want to be. Thus, falling from a bridge can mean you aren't getting to where you want to be in life. Or you miss an opportunity to "bridge the gap." See: *Bridge.*

A tooth falling out has a variety of possibilities for symbolism, as does a tree. See: *Teeth, Tree.*

See also: *Abyss, Bridge, Building, Cliff, Depression, Descend, Destruction, Elevator, Fly, Teeth, Tree*

False Teeth—See: *Teeth*

Family—The possibilities for symbolism and personal meaning involving family in dreams are endless. This entry will cover the overall symbolism of family. Use the entries listed below to look up individual members.

When a dream refers to the concept of family or subjects connected with your overall family, it is likely to show scenes with your entire family or at least the ones closest to you, instead of just individual family members. However, individual members of a family clan can symbolize the entire clan, especially the youngest or oldest members.

Dreams about family members can relate to roles played in it and the associated expectations, responsibilities, feelings, and so on. The role you play can be limiting or expanding, debilitating, or uplifting. You can be the glue in the family, or the black sheep, a matron or a patron, a good role model or not. You can carry on family traditions or defy them. You can be the high achiever, the breadwinner, the goat, the joker.

Your family and your role in it is a deep root running through your life. It's the foundation of who you are, assuming you have a family, and dreams connect the past with the present to show you not only what's happening now, but how it's rooted in what happened *then.*

Family is the biggest influence on character and personality for most people. It shapes self-image and in many cases determines choices related to school, career, marriage, friends, beliefs, and geographic location, to name a few.

Even years after moving away, you can still be greatly influenced by your family. You can be ninety years old and still dream about being back in your childhood home. See: *Childhood Home, Family Home*.

You can dream about recent interactions with family members and news you have heard about them, especially if you are affected personally by the experience. It's common to dream about family members when you miss or need them, or something happens with them that is "big," such as marriage, divorce, pregnancy, or illness. Usually they're depicted as themselves, and sometimes as surrogate-characters.

A dream gives clues and hints to identify surrogate-characters or something about them. For example, you hear news that your sister, who lives in another country, has a drug problem, and subsequently dream about a burglar breaking into her room in the family home and stealing her childhood toys, symbolizing your perception that she has lost her innocence. The burglar symbolizes her addiction.

Changes in your relationship with your family can spark dreams. For example, a woman dreams that she serves eggs sunny side up to her family members. The short snippet stands out to her as important. And it is important because she's going through some big changes in her relationship with her family. She no longer wants to maintain the "sunny" facade she's been projecting. Even when ill, depressed, or sad, she serves her eggs sunny side up. It's a metaphor with deep meaning and significance for her.

Dreams can use family members to make connections between their personality and character and yours. Are you stoic like your father, or organized like your mother? Are you jealous of your sister? Do you have your uncle's sense of humor, or share with your cousin the same propensity to choose mates who aren't good for you?

A dream with imaginary family members can symbolize sides of yourself trying to integrate into your personality. Your psyche is, in a sense, a family. It's a collection of parts, not a singular "I." Some parts are integrated with the conscious personality—in the family—and some are unconscious,

dormant, or unwanted. The unwanted parts don't fit into the ego's picture of who you are. For example, see the example of the long-lost brother dream detailed in the entry for *Brother*.

Integration of internal parts and personal experiences is a primary function of dreams. See: *Psyche*.

For example, a docile personality might have a hard time accepting the combative aspects of him- or herself. A high achiever can have difficulty with the parts of herself not goal-oriented and time conscious. These parts of the psyche can show up in dreams portrayed as family members of any sort, actual family or otherwise. It's a way of promoting internal integration because family is close to you.

Family can mean "familiar," or integral to who you are.

Family members can be used as a group in a dream to speak to something common to all of them.

For example, a young woman dreams that she dry humps a cousin as all of her other cousins watch. She feels revolted and very embarrassed, both during the dream and after remembering it. But the scene with her cousins is an expression of feeling that she has no privacy in her large family. She has many cousins close to her age and they're all up in each other's business. Everything she says and does becomes fodder for gossip and conversation, and she feels violated.

All of her cousins are present in the scene, which strongly suggests that the dream connects with her cousins in general, not any one of them specifically—not even the one in bed with her. It's simply a way of creating a scenario that mirrors her feelings and illustrates a big issue.

Dreams about family gatherings with multiple family members are often about your place in your family, how they treat you, and how you are shaped by your experiences with them. The meaning and message are found in the big picture.

A young man dreams that his family and friends throw a birthday party for him at his aunt's house. Various family members say things that are factually incorrect, but he blows it off. He notices plastic bags of red paint interspersed around the house, and they leak on him. But he just lets it happen and feels confused and embarrassed. The weird conversations continue and people talk nonsense, like they're all in on the joke, but he's not. Finally, he realizes he's being tricked. The game is to see how long it takes him to speak up about the inaccuracies he notices. He plays along and laughs with them, but feels humiliated.

What a strange and beautiful dream. Dreams create scenarios that test your reactions and spark your emotions. The point is to show you something about yourself. This dream is showing the dreamer his feelings of insecurity. In waking life he tends to hold his tongue rather than speak his mind. He hates himself for it and lives with a feeling of regret and failure. Plus, a few months prior to his dream, his family held a surprise birthday at the same aunt's house used as the setting in the dream and he felt very embarrassed by all the attention. He felt tricked, not surprised.

So the dream puts him in a scenario where he can speak up or be passive, and he chooses to be passive, even to play along with his humiliation and laugh uncomfortably about it. The red paint that spills on him symbolizes his embarrassment. The family members paint a big picture of the dreamer's self-consciousness and passivity rooted in his family experience.

Family members can symbolize structures of your psyche such as archetypes. We are all born with a "Father" archetype and a "Mother" archetype that shape our ideas and expectations of what our parents are supposed to be like. Early in life they're godlike figures. See: *Archetypes*.

As you get older, your opinion of your parents is heavily influenced by how the reality of them compares with the archetypal blueprint. If they fail to live up to it, you can be deeply disappointed and disillusioned. Eventually, if you have children, your opinion of yourself as a parent will be influenced by how well *you* live up to those ideas and expectations.

As you step into the role of mother or father, the archetype charges with energy, and you find capabilities in yourself you didn't know you pos-

sessed. In dreams, that occurrence can translate into your being visited by a mythological figure, an ancestor, or a talking animal like a "momma bear" that gives you advice about how to be a parent. See: *Ancestor*.

Archetypal-like figures can appear in dreams to represent your parents, though they are more likely in the dreams of children. For adults, parents tend to be portrayed more realistically.

Dreams use depictions of family members tied to the roles they play in the family and connect these roles with your life. For example, you're likely to dream about your parents when figuring out how to be one yourself. Your parents are the closest example you're likely to have when you are a new mother or father, and it is common to dream about them under those circumstances.

Family in dreams can symbolize other senses of the word, such as how friends, workmates, and teammates can be like family. In simplest terms, family means close ties or proximity between people, and organization under a hierarchical structure.

Important people in your life can play family-like roles. A beloved teacher can be like a parent, for example. The similarity shows the strength of the connection.

Euphemisms can be used for family, such as "Mafia," which organize into Mafia "families." Work organizations like to call themselves families, so you could dream about a family when you are actually dreaming about your workplace. Church and military organizations, too, like to refer to themselves as families.

See also: *Ancestor, Archetypes, Blood, Brother, Child, Childhood Home, Daughter, Family Business, Family Home, Father, Grandparent, Guide, Incest, Love, Mafia, Mother, Nephew, Orphan, Sister, Son*

Family Business—When you dream about working for the family business, but your family does not have a business, it has to be symbolism, a comparison to something that's like a family business.

Family business means matters related to the family, such as taking care of an elderly parent or dividing an inheritance or anything else money-related. Under this umbrella falls any situation where you would say, "It's a family matter."

A woman dreams she's working behind the counter at the family business and a commotion breaks out in the lobby. She dreads knowing it's up to her to intervene because no one else will do it. Her family does not own a business, but she is enmeshed in family matters: planning holiday gatherings, running errands, intervening in disputes and misunderstandings. The commotion in the lobby symbolizes the personal upheaval that taking care of family business causes her, and her feelings show in the detail about the job being left to her.

See also: *Co-Worker, Employee, Family, Job, Shop*

Family Home—When you dream about visiting a family home you used to live in, it can be a way of revisiting the past, exploring the roots of who you are now and where you are in your life. Or back in that home is a part of yourself that's left behind.

A family home can be dreamed about as a way of pointing to when something began that's relevant now. It is where patterns take hold, habits start, ideas form, and thought processes begin. You don't dream about a family home simply to reminisce. You dream about it because your present life is patterned after, or affected by, what started there.

For example, a young man dreams he's a kid again and back in his old family home with his sister, also a kid again. A siren sounds. A tornado is coming. Ominous black clouds dominate the sky. He goes to the basement and his sister is down there. She screams, "I should have seen it coming!" What the siblings should have seen coming was their parents' divorce when they lived in that home. She's in the dream because she shared in the experience and was affected, too.

The detail about being a kid again in his family home is clue that the dream is about something that happened when he was that age. The tornado symbolizes the mess of tumultuous feelings related to the divorce, and the black clouds symbolize the ones hanging over his life since the divorce. The siren warns of the coming difficulty as the feelings finally come out. He can repress it all back down into his

"inner basement," but it's coming up now in his dreams, years after the fact, because he's ready to deal with it even if he doesn't consciously know it.

People starting a family will dream about their family home as a way of thinking about the environment they want to create—or avoid creating—for their children.

You might dream about your family home because you want to create a similar living environment for yourself, with love, acceptance, connection, belonging, purpose, meaning. Or you want to avoid recreating the stress, loss, and hard feelings you grew up with.

What does a family home symbolize for you? For some people it's a place of great comfort. Many special memories are formed there. Adults can dream about their family home (and family members) during challenging times as a way of drawing strength from it. For them, the family home is the foundation of adult life, their rock.

For other people it's a source of unresolved issues. They are called home in their dreams to sort things out.

See also: *Basement, Childhood Home, Family, Family Business, Father, Home, Mother, Old Friend, Parents, Psyche, Storm, Tornado*

Famous—A famous person depicted as a character in a dream can symbolize something about that person that also relates to yourself. You have something in common: talents, traits, background, ambitions.

The connection can be with what you know about the person, or the role he or she plays in society, TV, and film.

You can dream about a famous person because you desire fame, recognition, or admiration. It might stem from fantasies of grandeur or importance.

A famous person can symbolize someone you hold in high esteem.

You can dream about being famous because you have been treated in a way that makes you feel important.

A famous person can be used to set the scene, such as when a famous comedian is used in a dream related to sense of humor, or a famous leader is used to address the subject of leadership.

Dreaming about a famous billionaire can reflect a desire to be rich, or skill with money and finance, or admiration for the person. You might have something in common with the person.

A famous musician in your dream can symbolize similarities in your musical talent or style, or simply that the musician is famous. See: *Kanye West, Snoop Dogg*.

Dreaming about a politician can symbolize qualities related to your leadership, influence, negotiation, debating, or decision-making skills. You can dream about someone famous because of ambition to be successful like that person, perhaps in the same profession, but not necessarily.

dream-characters based on famous people often symbolize the qualities and characteristics you associate with them. As with other dream-characters, begin interpreting the symbolism of a famous person by thinking of what you associate with the individual. See: *Donald Trump*.

A famous person can be used as a dream-character because qualities or characteristics of that person are appropriate for the story. For example, Al Pacino is a natural choice in the role of grizzled detective, because he has played that role in several movies and his personality is suited for it. Steve Buscemi is a natural choice for the role of lovable goon. If a dream needs a troubled blonde, it has many celebrities to choose from—Lindsay Lohan comes to mind. Think of your dreaming mind as a casting agent with thousands of actors and celebrities at its disposal. None of them is chosen at random. They appear in your dreams for a reason.

While these are the main ways dreams use fame and famous people as symbolism, there are other possibilities. For example, because famous people are in the public eye, they can symbolize a feeling of being watched, or a "*Truman Show* delusion." You think all eyes are always on you.

Famous people are recognized everywhere and some are hounded by paparazzi and intrusive fans. Those associations can be used to symbolize loss of anonymity or privacy.

In Western culture, celebrities in dreams play the role gods and goddesses play in Eastern culture to bestow blessings. Such dreams are a way of saying, "Good job, you are on the right track."

See also: *Barack Obama, Donald Trump, Hitler, Hollywood, Kanye West, King, Limousine, Movie, Queen, Snoop Dogg*

Farm—See: *Earth, Garden, Harvest*

Fast—See: *Speed*

Fat—A possibility to consider when you dream about an obese character is that it symbolizes ego inflation, "full of yourself." Most of your dream-characters are projections of something about you, so symbolism related to obesity can apply to yourself even it's shown through a character. The entry for *Eat* has an example of a dream that shows the dreamer his bloated ego through the character of an obese man.

As usual, one symbol has a variety of interpretations. Fat can be used in the sense of "ripe with opportunity," or "fat chance." It can mean "big tease," or "larger than life."

Because overweight people can be mocked or derided, a fat character can symbolize ostracism, or being the object of scorn. It can mean you have a low opinion of someone, or of yourself. It can be a self-critical voice in your head, or a sign of disgust with yourself or someone in your life.

For people who are overweight, dreams will connect with related thoughts and feelings. For example, an overweight man dreams that he can't stop himself from becoming enormously fat, expressing a fear that if he doesn't get control of his weight, he'll end up enormous.

Along these lines, dreams about being fat can be triggered by dieting and trying to lose weight, by an eating disorder, and by body dysmorphia—the belief that your appearance is defective and must be hidden or fixed. In this sense, it means you're driven by a compulsion. For example, you constantly work out because you're afraid of being fat, and you dream anyway that you are fat.

Being fat in a dream can be a way of saying you are self-conscious. You worry about your appearance. It can express fear you are "growing" unattractive with age. You're not necessarily overweight, but being overweight is sometimes synonymous with being unattractive and getting old. This meaning of the symbolism pops up most often with people who are past their physical prime and worried about it.

Fat in a dream can mean "weighed down" with burdens, responsibility, guilt, or personal baggage. It can mean that something is slowing you down, because excess body weight is associated with slow movement. You are overtaxed. Or you overemphasize pleasure and material values.

Fat can be associated with wealth or privilege, as in "the power company is growing fat at my expense." Being fat used to be a sign of wealth because it meant a person could afford to eat as much as he wanted. It can mean you're storing away resources for future use—fat is essentially stored energy. Time to reap the harvest. Fat is associated with celebration, as in the term "fatted calf."

Fat connects with the idea of being "bloated," as in "bloated bureaucracy" or "trimming the fat." In this sense it means excess.

Dreams can make references through symbols to being overweight, for example, a whale, sea lion, bus, pig, or Jabba the Hutt. Don't jump to conclusions, though, because those symbols can be interpreted differently. If a dream uses them to refer to body weight, it will include other clues pointing in that direction, such as derisive comments made about body weight, bullying, or feelings of humiliation or anger.

Dreams compensate, and the psyche is a self-regulating and balancing system, so a dream image of a fat person can be a form of compensation for something imbalanced in the psyche, something that isn't given enough respect or energy.

See also: *Baggage, Bully, Bus, Eat, Emaciated, Food, Giant, Whale*

Father—When your father is used as a character in a dream and the two of you have recently interacted, it's likely connected in some way with that interaction. If you haven't had any interaction in the past week or two, has he been on your mind? Is he affecting your life and decisions? Do you miss him?

Any and every aspect of your relationship with your father can be the subject of dreams. Parental relationships can be the closest and most challenging, and the source of the most dramatic dreams, that can play out like a Shakespearean tragedy.

For example, a young woman has a recurring dream about being forced to have sex with her father. Her mom tells her he is waiting in the bedroom and she has to let him take her virginity. She thinks it's weird, but everyone in the dream thinks it's totally normal and no big deal and expects her to hurry up. She feels that it's her duty, what a good daughter should do, but it makes her so uncomfortable. She goes into the bedroom and they start to undress, and he doesn't understand why she is so slow, because to him it's as if he's brushing his teeth or something. She wakes up in a panic right before getting into bed.

This young woman feels forced into a relationship with her father. It's how she feels about being pushed into his metaphorical arms. Her parents are divorced and her dad is distant, and her mom makes her spend time with him. The dreamer is being a "good daughter," but doesn't really like her father and resents being forced to do something she doesn't want to do. The dream memorably dramatizes the situation as being forced into bed with him. It's a poignant metaphor.

Or take the example of a young woman who dreams that her father is her kidnapper, and he admits that he's madly in love with her. The dream flashes back to a scene where her father doesn't let her date a certain boy, and suddenly she understands his behavior. It's a way of saying, "overprotective father!" But it's also a dramatic illustration of her feelings. To her, his decisions sometimes seem like madness and his restrictions feel like being kidnapped. The dream exaggerates, showing it as her father being madly in love with her.

Your father in a dream can symbolize similarity in your personality, character, and life, such as having the same knack for fixing things, the same laugh, or the same tendency to sacrifice yourself or downplay problems. This use of the dream symbolism is especially likely after you or someone else notices the similarities between you and your father.

Perceptions of your father can be the basis of a dream. For example, a young man dreams about being with his father next to a lake, and they see a snake. It's not threatening or dangerous, but dad grabs a stick anyway and beats it. The snake transforms, with the body of a snake and the head of a dog. The son wants his father to stop hitting the poor creature, but he just whacks away till it splits open.

This dream tells a story about the dreamer's frustration with his father's attempts to be helpful. Dad sticks his nose where he isn't wanted and messes things up. The dreamer wants him to stop trying to be helpful, as pictured in the dream when he wants him to stop beating the harmless creature. It morphs into a dog as a way of saying he's trying too hard to be friendly, acting dog-like, and over-reacting.

Dreaming about your father can relate to what he taught you. Much of adult life can be spent trying to assimilate and reconcile with the patterns programmed into you. Living up to parents' expectations and example can be a two-edged sword. On the one hand, if your father set a good example, modeling your adult personality on his is good so long as you draw a line between where his life ends and yours begins. On the other hand, the root of personal issues can begin with your relationship—or lack of a relationship—with your father.

Rebellion, addiction, and passivity are a few of many issues that can have roots in your relationship with your father. Dreams shine a light into our personal blind spots, so if something about your relationship with your father is unresolved or causing problems, odds are you will dream about it.

Your dreams can use surrogate-characters for your father, such as other males in the family or circle of friends you associate with him, and for the ways you perceive him: coach, police officer, principal, prisoner, and so on.

When the father in the dream does not look like your actual father, you might be dreaming in general about "fathering," meaning paternal guidance and care. Perhaps you need to be your own father in the sense of providing direction and vision for your life, or by tempering childish behavior and impulses. The conventional image of a father is of someone who provides for the needs of his family, who protects them, who is an authority.

Father is synonymous with masculinity, and your interaction with a father dream-character can symbolize your relationship with masculinity in general. People who feel subjugated or abused by masculinity can dream about fighting with fathers or father figures. They aren't fighting with the person depicted, but with what the person represents.

The same idea applies in cases where a male struggles to live up to masculine ideals. Not all males are rough, tough, and burly. Some are sensitive and physically small—and pay a helluva price for it when bullied and discriminated against. Related dreams often involve scenes of violence and gore at the hands of a group of men, which are exaggerations of the feelings and inner struggle of people who can't live up to an image or ideal.

Father is synonymous in some people's minds with patriarchy, and struggle with it plays out in dreams filled with struggle and violence involving patriarchal men. Patriarchy expects women to "know their place" and live up to ideals, sparking all sorts of inner conflict in women who try to live up to them, as well as those who don't or can't. Father figures abuse them in their dreams, sometimes night after night, showing their conflict and feelings. For men, patriarchy expects them to be self-sacrificing and tough, and can be especially hard on men who don't live up to those ideals.

This pattern of dreaming is especially strong in females who have been abused by a man, especially by a father or someone with that sort of status. These women tend to dream recurrently of being dramatically assaulted and abused by men.

Father is associated with childhood. In the image of your father you see your childhood. He's there from the beginning—assuming that's the case with your father. For example, a woman dreams that her deceased father is alive and acts as if everything is all right. But over time she senses that something isn't right. He looks thinner and weaker. She asks him about it, and he gives the typical dad answer, "I'm fine." She corners him and asks again, and he says, "I have cancer. There is nothing that can be done." She begs him to go to see a doctor, but he replies that the damage has been done and there is no point.

This dream is about the dreamer realizing that the memory of her father is slowly fading, and also that her childhood is becoming more distant. Seven years ago he passed away—she was sixteen at the time—and since then she has become an adult. She isn't his little girl anymore, and has to handle the responsibilities of life without him. The cancer represents time, which is slowly eating away at his memory and her childhood. It's like she is losing him again—and losing part of herself. She has dealt with the grief and accepts that he isn't around, but it makes her sad. As she said in her own words, "My dream is about my being terrified of not being a child anymore. My dad is the symbol of my childhood. The older I get, the more it feels like my childhood is dying."

When interpreting dreams featuring father-characters and father figures, also consider traits commonly associated with fathers in general, such as practicality, rationality, sensibility, and respect. You could dream about a fatherly figure when trying to figure out how to get ahead at work, or dealing with a dispute. Oftentimes, the character is presented in the dream as your father but doesn't look like him, and it doesn't matter because you accept that character as your father. It's the archetypal father programmed into you, the father within you.

Your inner father can appear in a dream as your father. But if you don't respect him, then you are unlikely to dream about him in the role of positive father figure, unless it's a wish or recognition of his potential. See: *King*.

Dreaming about avoiding your father can symbolize avoiding responsibility, sensibility, or practicality—or anything symbolized by a father. Avoiding your father can connect with actually avoiding or doing something against his wishes, rules, or teachings. See: *Hide*.

For example, a college student about to go on spring break dreams about running around the house to avoid her father, symbolizing that she wants to cut loose while on vacation and knows her father would not approve. Avoiding him symbolizes planning to break his rules.

A young male dreams about his sister covering their father's lifeless body with a sheet, symbolizing that he knows she is having sex before marriage, and their father taught them that's a no-no. Covering him with a sheet is a way of saying she's ignoring his wishes.

In the dreams of men considering starting families, seeing themselves in the role of a father can be a dress rehearsal. It helps to address fears and doubts about their fathering abilities. It's also a way of planting the seed of desire. Some men who think they never want to be fathers change their minds after dreaming about having children and seeing themselves living the role. Such a dream can be sparked by talk of starting a family.

A final consideration is that father can be synonymous with God. God is "the father," and early in life your father is a godlike figure. See: *God*.

See also: *Archetypes, Cancer, Daughter, Deceased Loved One, Family, God, Guide, Hide, Mother, Parents, Penis, Son, Sun, Testicles*

FBI—Dreaming about the FBI can connect with the subject of suspicion or trouble, especially with an authority. It can be a reflection of guilt or wrongdoing. This use of the symbolism is more likely in dream scenarios about being investigated or watched by the FBI.

Working for the FBI reverses the above ideas. You suspect something. You're investigating someone or something. Dreams can expand the idea of investigating to mean exploring a possibility or researching a subject, gathering information.

The FBI in a dream can symbolize an exclusive organization or occupation. For example, a female researching what to study in college dreams that she is up for a job with the FBI, but has to pass a rigorous physical exam. The other females taking the same test all fail it, but she passes. The day before the dream, she'd researched STEM jobs—science, technology, engineering, math—which are notoriously difficult fields for females to gain entry into. A physical test to get into the FBI symbolizes thoughts related to the difficulty of a female's getting a STEM job, and passing it indicates that the dreamer thinks she has what it takes.

See also: *Crime, Detective, Police Officer, Spy*

Fear—Dreams make connections between similar ideas, situations, and emotions, so fearing something in a dream can connect with something else you fear. For example, fearing a boa constrictor in a dream can symbolize fear that a new job will constrict your lifestyle. Looking with fear over the edge of a tall building can symbolize fear of risk. It's a physical representation.

Fear in a dream can connect with facing a situation that brings up feelings of fear, such as a health scare, the death of someone close to you, observing something disturbing, or trying something new. It is common for fear to be sparked by anything that gets you out of your comfort zone, situations you have never dealt with previously. One reason children stop having frequent nightmares around age thirteen is that by then their comfort zone is bigger.

Fear in dreams can connect with phobias and fears such as of heights or failure. A dream will create a scenario that sparks fear and help you work through it. For example, a man dreams that a co-worker traps a big hairy spider in a glass jar. The co-worker holds up the jar and wants him to look at it, and he says, "No way!" The spider looks huge inside the jar, as if magnified by the glass. It's a way of symbolizing that the dreamer's fear of spiders is overblown. And the co-worker is used to create contrast with the dreamer because she's a fearless type and the dreamer admires that about her.

Feelings of fear in dreams can reflect something you fear about yourself. Perhaps something frightening comes out of you during certain situations, such as during confrontations or when you are really fatigued. See: *Monster*.

Or you fear something about yourself of which you're only vaguely aware. It's quite common for repressed, neglected, or unwanted parts of oneself to take form in dreams as scary characters, and for scary dream situations to reflect fear of finding out that you are more—or less—than what you think you are. The ego protects its turf and will hold onto beliefs about itself despite evidence to the contrary. It can be quite scary to confront your illusions and cherished beliefs.

It can also be scary to find out you are capable of more than you thought, because along with it comes an expectation that you'll leave your comfort zone and live up to your potential.

See also: *Co-Worker, Ego, Emotions, Enemy, Evil, Hero, Monster, Nightmares, Opponent, Panic, Scream*

Federal Bureau of Investigation—See: *FBI*

Feet—Feet in a dream can refer to where you "stand," meaning convictions, values, issues, beliefs, opinions, and principles. We say that a person "stands" for one thing or another, such as, "I stand for family values." Someone may "make a stand."

The symbolism can be similar to the foundation of a house. Your feet are what you stand on, and in the larger sense what you stand on is your character and personality, your personal foundation.

Your feet are closest to the ground. If you're "grounded," it means you are "down to earth" and steady. See: *Basement*.

The symbolism is expressed in the saying "feet of clay," meaning built atop a weak foundation. Dreams can take that idea and run with it to describe a relationship, plans, thought processes, willpower, empires, and so on.

Feet are associated with movement. Movement in the symbolic sense means movement in your life, "going places." "Step up" means rise in authority, status, or prestige. "Step on" means to dominate or disrespect. "Out of step" means out of sync. Dreams will show these uses of symbolism through the actions and other details. See: *Car, Climb*.

Movement in a dream shows the progressions of your life, the incremental movements and the leaps and bounds, and action with the feet can help tell the story. Movement up, down, forward, backward, and everything in between is symbolism, and if your feet take you there, the symbolism can combine to really tell the story. See: *Backward, Left, Right.*

Feet are associated with social position. People of high social position have others "fall at their feet." The same action of falling at someone's feet can symbolize admiration, groveling, gratitude, or supplication. The symbolism can show in washing or massaging feet.

Mangled or bruised feet can symbolize low status or position. It can symbolize a hard road in life, or taking a beating. See: *Beat, Servant, Wound.*

Dreaming about injury to the feet can mean your ability to move your life forward is hindered. It can mean illness or anything that "knocks you off your feet."

Plucking hair from your feet can symbolize preparing for something. For example, a young man getting ready to go back to college after summer break dreams about plucking long hairs from his feet. The long hair symbolizes a long summer he just spent being idle, and plucking it symbolizes his mental preparation to get busy again. Plucking hair, in his mind, is associated with preparation.

Feet can symbolize willingness to take action. The symbolism compounds when your willingness is based on your convictions, beliefs, and values, such as willingness to tell people about your religion or spread the Gospel. The symbolism is based both on feet meaning willingness to take action, and meaning personal foundation.

Toes can symbolize something overlooked. They are farthest on your body from your eyes and hidden inside socks and shoes most of the time. Toes are easy to overlook.

Toes are used for balance and can connect with your personal balance, especially the big toe.

They can symbolize something small that's essential for everything it connects to, such as when a secretary makes the office run smoothly.

Toes can symbolize something you count. For example, you dream about having three toes on your right foot and two on your left. It symbolizes that you think three of your children turned out right, and two have more to prove.

Toes can be used as an analogy for roots of a tree. See: *Roots.*

See also: *Amputate, Backward, Ballet, Basement, Body, Car, Climb, Floor, Left, Right, Roots, Run, Shoes*

Fellatio—Fellatio has so many possibilities for symbolism and meaning. It can connect with subjects related to sex, but you really have to expand your mind and think in terms of symbolism and uses in storytelling, as with any symbolism.

Begin with the simplest way of describing fellatio as taking the penis into the mouth. That can mean taking in the essence or strength of a man, or taking in masculinity, making it part of you in the most personal sense. It can mean talking about sex. Think about it: an oral activity involving the phallus. It's not such a stretch when you think of it as a physical representation that combines a possibility of the symbolism of the mouth (talking) and of the penis (sex). See: *Penis, Sex, Talk.*

Here's a great example. A woman dreams about giving fellatio to her ex-boyfriend. His penis grows longer and bigger till it's jammed down her throat. What does it mean? Her ex is being a "big dick" about the breakup, and the "longer" the situation persists, the more she feels like he's shoving it down her throat. The metaphor is obvious once you step back and observe.

The symbolism can connect with subjects related to communication and communication skills. For example, giving fellatio in public can symbolize public speaking and performance. It can symbolize wanting or receiving public attention, or unwanted attention. If the blow job is interrupted, it can mean you didn't finish something you started, or it can connect with issues related to finding privacy to have sex, look at porn, or masturbate.

It can symbolize getting intimate with a subject, situation, or person. For example, fellatio can symbolize mastering a subject, "taking in" knowledge and information. Getting to know a person intimately can be symbolized as oral sex, especially when talking is involved. The same idea applies to learning a skill, especially an artistic skill, because giving good oral sex is an art as well as a skill. It involves technique and also a subtle understanding of the body and pleasure. Conversely, bad oral sex can symbolize awkwardness or lack of mastery or understanding.

Dreaming about playing musical instruments using the mouth, such as the trumpet and clarinet, can be symbolized as fellatio. Also, music has many associations with sex, and the two ideas easily overlap. Making a living by playing an instrument with one's mouth is literally a "blow job." Conversely, dreaming about playing such an instrument can symbolize giving fellatio.

Fellatio in a dream can connect with subjects such as giving or getting pleasure, or getting comfortable with the body—oral sex requires a certain comfort level. It can connect with concerns about being a good lover. Giving oral sex requires delicacy, and fear of being too rough can show in exaggerated imagery of hurting or mangling your lover's penis.

Giving fellatio with confidence in a dream can symbolize ability to take control of a situation, including but not exclusive to sexual situations. It can mean you know what you want and how to get it.

Fellatio puts the giver in a position of control. "Control through submission" has a complex psychology that is often learned through years of dealing with abuse, powerlessness, or unpredictability. Though to be clear, it can be learned simply as a strategy for getting what you want.

For example, learning how to deal with an alcoholic parent can involve making the person think he or she is in control when actually that control or authority is subverted or undermined. The person in the submissive position can use submission to reverse the power dynamic.

Because sex can be used as means of manipulation, fellatio can be associated with taking control through manipulation. Dreams that use the symbolism this way will sometimes be accompanied by themes of seeking freedom. For example, you dream that to get out of prison you have to give fellatio to a guard.

On the other hand, fellatio can be associated with pure submission or dominance. The symbolism is captured by the ways derogatory statements use references to fellatio. If someone says, "Suck my dick, bitch," it means, "You will submit to me. I dominate you."

For example, a woman who was mercilessly bullied in high school dreams of being trapped and forced to give fellatio to her tormentor. She does it and bites off the member. The scene is graphic, with blood and vomiting. Her tormentor just laughs, as if he expects her reaction. The dream illustrates how the dreamer is still tormented by the bullying she experienced, and nurses thoughts of revenge. However, it only makes her relive the past and continue to experience life-wrecking emotions. See: *Revenge*.

A young man dreams that his girlfriend has a penis and forces him to suck it. The dream occurs after she accuses him of being selfish about sex and an all-around awful person, psychologically beating him down, and the more aggressive she gets, the more he grovels. It makes him feel like crap about himself. Sucking her penis is a way of saying he is submissive to her.

More complex psychology comes into play when you consider that fellatio in modern times has come to be associated with instant gratification. It is "safe sex" in the sense that it can be done with no commitment. You don't even have to take your clothes off. These associations can be used by dreams to symbolize situations in which a person takes shortcuts, plays it safe, or makes compromises.

Fellatio is associated with reward. The "birthday blow job" expresses this idea. For a married man whose partner no longer gives him fellatio as he or she used to, dreaming about getting a blow job can symbolize an unexpected surprise or a return to the "good old days" of a relationship. It can mean breaking a routine or doing something out of the usual.

Some people consider fellatio and oral sex to be "dirty" or "forbidden," in which case dreaming about it can be an expression of guilt, regret, blemish, humiliation, rebellion, or defilement. Before the turn of the century, fellatio was associated with taking risks and breaking taboos. However, the banality of the blow job in modern Western culture has largely erased this association.

Giving fellatio to multiple partners can symbolize taking on multiple subjects or tasks at once. It is sometimes interpreted as the desire to have multiple sexual partners.

Giving fellatio to yourself can stem from masturbation, because masturbation can involve fantasies about getting and giving fellatio. Masturbating to fantasies of getting fellatio is, in a sense, giving yourself oral sex. See: *Masturbate*.

Symbols for fellatio include eating a hot dog or banana, smoking a cigar, milking a cow's teat, licking and sucking a popsicle, and swinging a bat.

For example, a gay male who recently started having sex with men dreams about eating a hot dog and finding a pubic hair on it, a rather obvious reference to oral sex.

See also: *Artist, Bite, Cunnilingus, Lips, Masturbate, Mouth, Penis, Phallic Symbol, Sex, Talk*

Female—See: *Anima, Bride, Daughter, Girl, Sister, Wife, Woman*

Fence—Fences are boundaries meant to keep things out or in. They divide. They contain. They separate. They protect. They isolate. They mark territory. They limit. They hinder. They are obstacles and hurdles.

Now apply those ideas to what a fence can symbolize in a dream. It can connect with personal boundaries, comfort zones, lines you won't cross, and creating or protecting personal space.

It can connect with what divides people from each other in a general sense: social class, upbringing, beliefs, race, geography, and wealth, to name a few.

Think of what divides people in a personal sense: hard feelings, defensiveness, conflict, ignorance, misunderstanding, lack of communication. Think of how people protect their "turf." The possibilities go on and on.

A fence can symbolize divisions within you and places where you won't go in your thoughts and feelings. For example, a woman has recurring dreams about a tall fence that stretches across the landscape as far as the eye can see. She's told that she needs to figure out how to get to the other side of the fence, but it seems impossible. The dreams speak to the divide between her thoughts and feelings. She's strongly analytical, at the expense of the feeling side of the equation. The woman compartmentalizes her feelings and the dreams suggest that she cross that divide.

Emotions that are too powerful to handle, or are discounted or minimized, can be pictured as being on the other side of a fence.

Another possibility is that a fence can symbolize limits you impose on yourself. You fence yourself in. A fence can symbolize lacking the confidence to take a risk, or a need for comfort and security. In some way you are "fenced in" or restrained. See: *Cage, Jail*.

Those restraints can originate outside yourself. For example, beliefs can be like fences because they create exclusion zones. Social customs and cultural norms create exclusion zones.

Now let's consider situations where fences can be used as dream symbolism.

Let's say that your significant other has to take a business trip overseas. You dream about seeing that person on the other side of a fence, representing the coming physical divide between you.

You have an argument with a friend and are unable or unwilling to bridge the gap between you, and see it symbolized in a dream as a tall, barbed-wire fence dividing you.

You dream about a romantic rival building a fence between you and a guy you both like, symbolizing the rival marking territory.

You dream about a doctor telling you to stay within the fence surrounding your yard, symbolizing advice to limit your activity for health reasons.

You dream about being on a horse and jumping a fence, symbolizing overcoming a barrier to your advancement at work.

You dream about a fence separating you from your neighbors, symbolizing a perception that you are wealthier or from a higher social class.

See also: *Bridge, Building, Cage, Climb, Home, Jail, Trespassing, Wall*

Festival—See: *Party*

Fetus—A fetus in a dream can symbolize something new in yourself, like a new part of your personality developing. Dreams are aware of deep, unconscious processes, and new parts of the personality and the psyche grow beneath the surface like roots before emerging above ground, where they are noticed consciously.

It can symbolize something new in your life, such as a project or idea. Or, since a fetus is a creation, it can symbolize the early stages of creation.

For example, a woman dreams about giving birth to three dead fetuses. They represent three art projects she worked on until her day job got in the way. The projects are dead in the sense of dormant. The dream symbolizes not only the projects, but the artistic process within her. Art is not just an external process of creation. It's internal, too. See: *Artist*.

To understand the symbolism, think about what a fetus can represent: hope (symbolism derived from the hope of getting pregnant), responsibility (a pregnant woman is responsible for the fetus), or a new phase of life (getting pregnant is a big life-change). A fetus can be associated with the idea of caring for yourself, since a fetus is part of the body and pregnant women have to take special care of themselves.

Be sure to read the entries for *Baby* and *Pregnant*.

See also: *Baby, Child, Egg, Pregnant, Uterus*

Fever—To dream about having a fever can mean "hot" for something. Interest, passion and/or intensity are piqued. Fever is often used to describe intense, passionate love.

Being hot is associated with anger and hatred. A fever occurs when the heat of the body rises above normal limits, and that can symbolize losing control of anger or passion. See: *Anger*.

Fever is associated with burnout. During times of illness that involve fever, a person can feel totally spent. It's a ready-made comparison.

A "group fever" means a group of people are overtaken by delusion or hysteria.

Fever is connected with illness, and you can be ill in mind and spirit as well as body. See: *Illness*.

Flushing can accompany a fever, and flushing is associated with embarrassment.

Having a fever while dreaming is known to cause bizarre and nonsensical dreams. Oftentimes, it reflects what's happening in the body.

See also: *Anger, Desert, Doctor, Fire, Group, Heat, Hospital, Illness, Love, Oven*

Fiancé—If you are engaged then you are likely to dream about related subjects, such as the person you plan to marry, the coming marriage, and hopes and plans for the future.

Your fiancé (or fiancée) can appear in dreams that explore the nature of the person, such as character, personality, and suitability. You can dream about planning a family or your honeymoon and all the dynamics and related issues and questions, such as whom to invite and how to pay for everything. You can dream about how your family and friends get along with your fiancé.

In some ways it's no different from dreaming about anyone else you know—you go about decoding the symbolism the same basic way, and first presume that the character is like an actor playing a role and following a script. Your job is to analyze the story.

Your fiancé could be a projection of something about yourself: your thoughts, feelings, emotions, perceptions, and so on. This possibility is stronger when your fiancé acts differently from the person you know. Branch out to consider how your fiancé can be used to make a comparison or connect with something going on in your life—an event, situation, circumstance.

The majority of dreams are about your inner life and how you respond internally to the events and situations in your life. However, your fiancé in a dream could be a direct representation or observation about the person, and the dream-story is built around what you have observed and experienced.

Make associations with the person—what would be the first thoughts that came to mind if you were to describe your fiancé to a stranger?

The dream could be a simulation to help you work through something or answer a question related to your fiancé or what your fiancé means to you. For example, you dream you're at the altar and about to say "I do." Your reaction at that moment can say everything about the prospects for the marriage and how you really feel about it.

A woman dreams that it's her wedding day, she's at the altar in front of all her family and friends, and her ex-boyfriend barges in and declares he's there to rescue her. It's a way of saying that she needs to be rescued from marrying the wrong man. Deep down, she knows that her fiancé is the wrong man to marry.

Things get really interesting when you dream about a fiancé you don't have—you're not engaged and maybe never have been. It has to be symbolism. To figure it out, begin by thinking about what it means to be engaged.

One, you could be "engaged" with an idea, cause, project, or something else that captures your attention or interest. It is "engaging."

Two, in simplest terms, a marriage is a commitment. For example, you commit to going to a certain university, and the start of the first semester is still many months away. In a figurative sense, you're engaged but not married. The school is like your fiancé. That idea can extend to any sort of commitment you make to yourself. See: *Marriage, Wedding.*

Or you plan a vacation and make a commitment to yourself that, no matter what, you're going when the time comes. Nothing will stop you. That commitment to a future event is comparable in the dream to being engaged.

As with all dream symbols, use your feelings as a guide, and pay close attention to the actions involving the symbol. Look for parallels and comparisons and fit the details together like puzzle pieces. From that emerges the big picture, the meaning and message.

A woman dreams that her fiancé—the actual man she plans to marry, not an invented character—is blind and it distresses her to know that he doesn't see her. It's a way of saying that she's distressed that her fiancé does not see her in the personal sense. He doesn't know who she is beneath the surface, and apparently doesn't care enough to find out. The symbolism is easy to decipher when you put her feelings of distress together with the detail about her fiancé's being blind. See: *Blind.*

The character based on her fiancé is a projection of her thoughts, perceptions, and feelings, a subjective portrayal. She *feels* like he doesn't really know her. It might be objectively accurate, but then again a neutral observer might say otherwise.

A man dreams that he goes to a party with his fiancée and loses her in the crowd. He runs across her friends and asks whether they've seen her, and they reply that she was just there and left. He tries to reach her on her phone, and the line is busy—a weird detail considering that most phones have call-waiting. And it's a telling detail because it ties together the others. A party is a busy environment with lots of people, a reflection of the dreamer's feeling that his fiancée is too busy to give him the time and personal interaction he wants. They socialize a lot, but it's not the sort of personal time he wants. The busy phone line provides another layer of similar symbolism, a way of saying he feels that his fiancée is too busy to really communicate with him.

See also: *Blind, Bride, Diamond, Groom, Husband, Marriage, Party, Wedding, Wife*

Fight—Fighting or battling in a dream presents many possibilities for symbolism. In simplest terms, a fight is a conflict or struggle, and it could symbolize a conflict or struggle with yourself, a situation, a person, or a group of people.

For most people, the majority of their dream-characters are projections, so fighting a character can mean fighting with yourself. It might connect with conflicting needs, desires, sides within yourself, interests, or roles. It implies that you need to consciously mediate your internal conflicts.

A fight can show a battle within yourself, such as when you fight against discouragement, pessimism, or temper—feelings that are likely to be strong if they're symbolized as a fight or battle. Pay attention to the details of the battle to gain insight into the nature of it—to the settings, combatants, uniforms, weapons, tactics, and especially the actions. It's all symbolism and the details fit together somehow to tell a story.

Dreams exaggerate, so the situation symbolized as a fight might not be at the level of "fight," but instead fall somewhere in the range of skirmish or conflict. It's a subjective portrayal.

A man dreams he's in a home-improvement store battling against a hugely overweight man who floats in the air between the aisles hurling objects at the dreamer. The dreamer shoots him down with tongs from an electric mixer, fired like missiles. The dreamer is about to finish off the man with a grilling fork when the character asks, as a last request, to be fed meatballs from a can lying nearby. The dreamer agrees.

The dream is a classic example of fighting with yourself. The dreamer is trying to lose weight by modifying his diet, so the home-improvement store setting is apt because he's trying to improve his body, which is the home for his mind. The man he battles is the side of himself that wants to eat the foods that have made him overweight, and the last request for meatballs is hilarious. It really sums up the dreamer's internal battle. The weapons of battle, all related to food, are also funny and ironic. All the details tie together to tell a story about the dreamer's internal struggle to lose weight.

You can fight yourself to work harder, to be more outgoing, to regulate your impulses, to stop procrastinating, and to overcome weakness, habit, and addiction. Or the conflict might rage inside you between sides of yourself, between your rational and impulsive side, between your head and heart. If life is you against the world, you might feel as if you're constantly fighting something.

The symbolism can show in figures of speech and phrases that use the words "fight" and "battle." Fight boredom, fight for your rights, fight for what you believe in, fight for your life, fight for independence, fight like cats and dogs, battle temptation, battle a workload. Your dreams act out those ideas.

For example, a young doctor dreams he's in an arena and faced off against himself in a fight to the death. The version of himself he battles is presented as clean and angelic, while the "other him" is dirty and sweaty. The dream is a great representation of an internal battle for this young doctor. On the one hand, he has a strong desire to live up to the typical image of a doctor as clean and angelic. On the other hand, that's not who he really is. He gets down and dirty. Doctors are held in high esteem and have an image to maintain. The dream's portrayal of the situation as a fight to the death is an apt way of describing his inner struggle between expectation and reality.

Fighting can crop up in dreams when you're not paying attention to your feelings or expressing your emotions. Dreams act as outlets for feelings and emotions and are a safety valve. Fighting can mean you are not consciously processing emotional content from the day, and if you want less conflict in your dreams, it is wise to give them fewer unprocessed emotions as fodder. If emotions are repressed or ignored, they come out in exaggerated form in your dreams. If the situation causing you conflict can't be addressed directly, some other strategy for emotional release is needed. See: *Emotions.*

For example, you are frustrated and upset about a situation at school, but know better than to say anything because teachers punish students who speak up. Or you are really frustrated with a parent and know that expressing your feelings will only make the situation worse. The ensuing dreams put you in situations where you fight for your life, but it's not your physical life you are fighting for, it's your emotional and psychological life. Something needs to be done either to change the situation or provide emotional release.

Interpersonal conflict is another good possibility for the symbolism of fighting. Arguments, hostility, battle of wills, something ongoing—often reflected in recurring dreams—or one-time event. Something that happened or you expect could happen.

You argue with your spouse or significant other, then dream about being attacked by a tiger or wolf. You disagree with your supervisor, and dream about a wrestling match. An angry customer at work acts hostile, and you dream about a random person attacking you on the street. You're really mad at your dad, and dream about punching him in the face.

Also consider the possibility you are fighting or battling a situation. For example, battling problems at work, fighting to save your marriage, rescuing your child from making big mistakes, or saving your home from going under.

A woman dreams about traveling forward to the end of time, only to loop back to the beginning of time, to a world that's rocky and blanketed by thick mist. There, she joins a group of super-soldiers in a never-ending battle against insect-like humanoid creatures that stream to the surface from the center of the planet. The battle is going badly for the humans, so the dreamer tells the leader about it, and the leader fires the general overseeing the battle.

The dream symbolizes the dreamer's work environment, which is like a never-ending battle against a massive workload. The humanoid creatures in the dream represent the impersonal forces of work and responsibility the dreamer faces every day working in the front office of a school. The key clue is found in the detail about time reaching the end and looping back to the beginning. That symbolizes the never-ending and cyclical nature of the work. Firing the general is the dream's suggestion for helping the situation. A general delegates responsibility, and the dreamer tends to take everything onto herself rather than delegate.

A battle that involves an invasion might symbolize interference in your personal matters. An invasion can symbolize unwelcome guests, invasion of privacy, or invasive thoughts. The idea of invasion applies far and wide to situations in your life and yourself. See: *Invasion*.

A battle with an animal can symbolize fighting your instincts or feelings. Or the animal represents someone you know, or a situation you are in. See: *Animals*.

A key fact to keep in mind when interpreting dreams about battles is that they use symbolism. Even dreams featuring carnage, death, and violence are using symbolism to express an idea. Don't take the imagery literally, but do acknowledge that in most battle dreams there is something trying to get your attention. Something needs to be addressed and resolved: stress, fatigue, conflict, personal disappointment, bitterness, unfulfilled desires. It might be affecting you more deeply than you realize.

People who have fought in combat or lived in gang-infested areas are deeply affected by the experience and can dream about it in a literal sense, reliving battles and specific experiences of combat or shootings. Usually, though, it relates back to something within the person that is trying to find release or resolution. A dream-based technique that helps is mentioned in the entry for *Nightmare*.

Fighting with weapons can have specific symbolism. See: *Fist, Gun, Knife*.

The seriousness of a fight in a dream reflects the seriousness and emotional charge of whatever it's connected to in your life. A fight might just be a squabble, but a war is next-level, and a nuclear war takes it to the max.

See also: *Abuse, Ambush, Animals, Apocalypse, Arena, Armageddon, Armor, Army, Attack, Beat, Bullet, Bully, Drown, Emotions, Enemy, Erupt, Fist, Gang, Gun, Invasion, Knife, Nightmare, Nuclear War, Opponent, Pain, Strangle, Tackle, War*

Finger—The symbolism of body parts featured in dreams often relates to their function or use. Start there and consider the possibilities for symbolism.

To begin with, fingers are used to point, and if you "point the finger" it means you accuse or assign blame. Pointing a finger can mean pointing out and drawing attention to something.

You use your finger to point the way and give direction, which in another sense can mean personal direction, and knowing the way to reach a goal. *It's that way!*

Fingers grasp. "Grasp" can mean "grasp the idea." It means you "get it," you understand.

Grasping can be an expression of care. Dreaming about holding someone or something in your grasp can symbolize your emotional hold, and holding on by a finger means the grasp is tenuous. See: *Hug*.

Fingers are used to type, an act associated with communication, and the index finger in particular is used to click a computer mouse and swipe a touchscreen, activities associated with communication, doing tasks, and gaining or giving information. For an example dream, see: *Facebook*.

The middle finger is used to "give the finger." To give the finger in a dream can be a perfect expression of feelings. It can mean, "I don't give a fuck." A character giving you the finger can express how you feel about yourself. After all, the character is likely to symbolize yourself.

The ring finger is specifically for wearing a wedding or engagement ring, and from there a dream can connect with a variety of ideas related to finding a mate, making a commitment, or engaging with a subject or task. Dreaming about a missing wedding band, despite the fact that you're not actually married, can symbolize missing that piece of the puzzle you want in your life: a mate, or something to pour your love and dedication into. Or it can refer to a commitment that's avoided, broken, or unfulfilled.

Fingers chopped off or injured can indicate "losing your grip," meaning losing control of a situation or yourself.

It can express anxiety about performing a task or taking a test.

It can indicate hiding guilt or culpability because fingerprints are used to identify culprits in crimes. See: *Fingerprint*.

It can symbolize wanting to hide involvement in something. The same idea is expressed in the image of dirty fingers. It can mean you are involved in something "dirty," perhaps some sort of intrigue. A plan backfires, or your character is defamed.

Cutting off a finger can mean a task seems impossible. A broken finger can mean a task or responsibility is breaking you. It can symbolize a sacrifice. See: *Amputate, Break*.

Fingers can symbolize children, because children can be thought of as outgrowths of your life in the way that fingers grow from hands, and people sometimes count on their fingers the number of children and grandchildren they have. Sacrificing a finger can symbolize that a child is being sacrificed in the figurative sense. For example, the demands of your job require you to spend long hours away from home, and in a sense you are sacrificing your child for your job. For a great example dream, see: *Cancer*.

Similarly, cutting off your ring finger can mean you are sacrificing your marriage or the idea of marriage.

Fingertips, which leave fingerprints, can symbolize "tip," meaning a clue or hint. Fingerprints are clues used to solve crimes. If a dream draws attention to a fingertip, it can mean "a clue." This use of the symbolism is more likely if the index finger is upraised, drawing attention to itself.

Another possibility is that you're being shown something that upsets you, because tip can mean "to overturn," and when applied personally it can mean you are upset, or your life has been overturned.

Fingers are used to touch and feel and can be used to symbolize sensitivity, especially personal sensitivity. For example, dreaming about pressing your fingers onto a hot frying pan and feeling no pain can symbolize being impervious to emotion or unable to relate to people emotionally.

On the other hand, feeling pain through the fingers can mean you are sensitive, are affected by emotion, and are able to relate emotionally. Bad pain can be a way of saying you are too sensitive. The same meaning can be expressed by dream imagery of someone else's getting fingers cut off and your feeling the pain.

The symbolism of fingers injured or falling off takes on a new dimension for people who use them for specialized skills, such as playing piano or performing surgery. In which case, injury to fingers can symbolize decline in skill or fears related to one's occupation.

Fingers can have sexual symbolism. They are used to touch, and "fingering" means inserting a finger or fingers into the vagina or anus or rubbing the clitoris. A pointed finger is a phallic symbol, while a limp finger is associated with erectile dysfunction. Dreams with this theme are likely to have other sexual references.

After all that, you have personal associations to consider, too, including all of your experiences with your fingers. If you've ever broken a finger, for instance, a dream can use that experience to create symbolism. For instance, you broke a finger in a car accident and forever after associate that finger with freak luck—the accident could have been a lot worse—or sudden trauma.

See also: *Amputate, Body, Break, Bride, Groom, Facebook, Fingerprint, Hand, Hug, Marriage, Phallic Symbol, Sex, Surgery, Wedding*

Fingerprint—Fingerprints are used to identify culprits in crimes, so dreaming about leaving fingerprints can mean you fear leaving traces of your involvement in something. Wiping them away or wearing gloves can mean trying to conceal involvement.

For example, a man dreams that he's in a store with a partner in crime—someone the man never sees fully—and they know they can take some small, oddly shaped guns from inside a glass display case. He slips his hand into the case and grabs the closest gun, which is shaped more like a metal cannabis pipe. He then notices his fingerprints left on the glass and anxiously wipes them away.

The man is hiding the fact that he smokes cannabis. A gun is used as symbolism for a pipe because a toke of cannabis is also called a hit, and a bullet from a gun hits whatever it's fired at. Smoke comes out of the barrel. Wiping away fingerprints symbolizes that he smokes from his pipe in secret and hides the pipe afterward. The partner

in crime is his addictive side. It's a part of himself that only shows when cannabis is involved.

The connection between fingerprints and involvement can go in many directions, such as when you're involved with a person disliked by family or friends, and wiping away fingerprints means you don't want them to know. Or dreaming about your fingerprints on a group report, symbolizing your involvement in writing it.

Concealment is connected with related feelings such as guilt, suspicion, and regret, and behaviors such as sneakiness. Dreams exaggerate, so the situation doesn't have to rise to the level of crime for the symbolism to be used. It could be something as innocuous as hiding the fact that you ate the last cookie, or went out for a drink instead of working late. Think in general terms of concealing something—including something about yourself. It's not necessarily a behavior or action you want to conceal, but something in your thoughts or feelings, or a personal flaw.

On the other hand, fingerprints are unique to each person and can represent individuality, the unique imprint every person leaves on the world.

Dreaming about someone's fingerprints can mean you recognize that person's involvement, uniqueness, or schemes. For example, you dream about finding your spouse's fingerprints at a crime scene related to disorderly conduct, and it connects with his or her raising hell.

See also: *Burglary, Crime, Finger, Guilt, Hand, Hide, Thief*

Fire—A fire is dangerous, and in dreams a fire can be associated with a dangerous situation—a danger already present in your life, or something you sense coming.

Fires tend to develop from small to large, and that association can be used to symbolize something destructive that starts small and spreads quickly.

Fires are associated with anger, "burning up," "boiling mad." An uncontrolled fire in a dream can symbolize uncontrolled anger. A "head on fire" means a person is consumed with hatred, thoughts of revenge, or desire for justice. The imagery of top floors of a building on fire can have the same symbolism. It can mean you're losing your mind or losing control of your thoughts. See: *Anger, Hate, Rage.*

Fire can symbolize a physical danger, for example, taking risks and putting yourself in harm's way. You're tempting the fire to hurt you.

The danger can be material. For example, you might dream about your home burning down when you're in danger of losing it to foreclosure, or you have been thinking about the possibility. A house burning down can symbolize your spouse leaving, your health plummeting, or your life going up in flames. See: *Building, Home.*

It can symbolize a big loss.

A fire is a crisis, so dreams can use it to compare with any sort of crisis.

The fire can be in your body as illness sets in, often accompanied by fever. See: *Fever.*

It can be used to symbolize overheating while asleep, or smelling smoke.

A man dreams there is a fire next to his bed. After waking up, he cleans his bedroom and moves his bed. The electrical outlet behind it is red hot. A cord is melted. The situation could have been much worse if he hadn't happened to move his bed and notice the outlet. He probably smelled smoke as he was sleeping and his dreaming mind translated the input into imagery related to fire.

Fire consumes and destroys, so it can be used in dreams to symbolize destruction of the personal sort. For example, your life is destroyed when you do something that causes a serious divide from your family or friends, and you dream about your house burning down. Your plans for the future "go up in flames" when you flunk out of school, and you dream about a school burning down.

A city on fire can symbolize your public life going up in flames, because cities can symbolize your life in society. Your neighborhood on fire can symbolize big changes in yourself. It means that the psychological structures on which you are built are changing. See: *City, Neighbor.*

A bed burning can symbolize passion, burning up with desire. See: *Bed.*

Love can burn. It is "hot." If you "keep the flame burning," you keep passion and love alive. A fire dying down can symbolize passion that cools. See: *Love.*

Fire's association with passion extends to passion meaning strong attraction to a subject, to an idea, to life, to your family, to your job, to a cause or belief.

Dreams use wordplays, and fire might be a play on "you're fired," the loss of a job, responsibility, or duty. Or you no longer play an important role you used to play. See: *Dismissal.*

"Fire" can mean fire a gun. See: *Bullet, Gun.*

Carl Jung had a dream in which he was trudging along in darkness, into a brutal wind. In one hand he held a lit candle and with the other hand he shielded the flame from being extinguished. He interpreted the dream as meaning he must continue forward with his sacred work despite the forces (wind) arrayed against him. He was having much personal and professional difficulty at the time of the dream. Soon after, though, he brought forth many of the groundbreaking theories and insights that made him famous. Jung saw himself as a vessel for channeling messages from the collective unconscious to humanity, a "keeper of the flame."

Consciousness and spirit are compared to fire. Mystic traditions speak of fire inside a person that moves throughout one's being as progress is made to higher levels of consciousness. In the vedic and Hindu traditions, the god Agni is the god of fire, representing a function of "digesting" everything that a person takes into himself. This includes food, but also emotions, ideas, knowledge, and experiences.

When representing spirit, the flame is sometimes blue. In Christianity, the Holy Spirit first appeared to the Apostles as "tongues of fire" on the Day of Pentecost. God appeared to Moses as a burning bush and as a column of fire to lead the Israelites through the desert at night. You don't have to be exposed to the scriptures and teachings of mystic or religious traditions to make the association between fire and spirituality. The imagery is imprinted in the collective unconscious. For thousands of years fire has been used in ceremony and as part of spiritual practice. See: *Spirit*.

Fire is associated with light: See: *Light*.

Fire is associated with purification.

More possibilities for symbolism are brought into play by the nature of fire itself. What is fire? The simplest answer is that fire is energy produced by chemical reaction, and many figures of speech that use the word fire mean energy—raw energy, personal energy, sexual energy. Romantic passion is a sort of interpersonal chemical reaction comparable to fire. Motivation and drive are compared to fire.

To create fire, substances are transformed, and in alchemy the transformation process is driven by fire. Alchemy is popularly understood as the quest to turn lead into gold, and people make the mistake of thinking of it literally when it is meant figuratively. Lead is ordinary human consciousness, and gold is what is produced as consciousness goes through the process of transmutation in which the old person is "burned away"—like removing the cocoon to allow the butterfly to emerge.

Which brings us to the question of how to tell the difference among the many possibilities for the symbolism of fire. The simple answer is that it depends on the context in which fire is presented by a dream and how you react to it, how you feel about it. For example, if a fire is raging through your house and you react with panic, the fire probably symbolizes something destructive. On the other hand, if you dance around a fire with a shaman, it might symbolize a creative process—especially within yourself.

See also: *Anger, Bed, Building, Bullet, Candle, City, Collective Unconscious, Disaster, Dismissal, Fever, Gas, Hate, Heat, Home, Light, Love, Neighbor, Rage, Revenge, Sex, Spirit*

Firearm—See: *Gun*

Fireworks—The symbolism of fireworks in a dream is similar to the way it's used in metaphors and figures of speech. It can symbolize love at first sight, or a conflict between big egos. It can sym-

bolize a loud argument or heated conversation. It can signify a big event or reason to celebrate.

See also: *Bomb, Fire, Party, Scream, Yell*

Firing Squad—See: *Execution*

Fish—Because fish live in water, they have strong associations with subconscious information and the unconscious mind and what's floating around in there. The image of a fish coming to the surface of water captures the idea of a thought or memory coming into your awareness. See: *Subconscious, Unconscious Mind*.

Water can symbolize the unconscious mind, so a fish swimming to the surface of water can symbolize that something that was in the unconscious mind is becoming conscious. A fish can symbolize guidance from the unconscious mind. Legends and myths tell of talking fish that give valuable information to people trying to find their way. These stories are allegories for ways that the unconscious mind communicates with its conscious counterpart, and dreams are, in essence, allegories about yourself and your life. See: *Unconscious Mind*.

Water is also strongly associated with emotions, and the size of the fish can indicate how "big" the emotion is and how much of an impact it has. See: *Water*.

A school of fish can symbolize a group of people whose actions, thinking, and perceptions are closely tied together, or who are easily swayed or directed. They engage in "groupthink."

Fish can symbolize options, as in "many fish in the sea."

Because fish swim and the bloodstream has components such as antibodies that travel in it, dreams can use fish to symbolize anything that travels in the bloodstream. For example, in a dream in which a fish eats coffee grounds from the dreamer's knee, the symbolism relates to the body repairing itself—the dreamer had debris in his knee and his body cleared it out while he was asleep.

Fish can be associated with the internal pH of the body, because they live in water and bad water will harm them. Fish can symbolize the urinary tract. A woman dreams that she finds a fishbowl in her house with sickly yellow water and three fish dying in it. She then goes about trying to save the fish by swapping out the bad water with fresh water. It symbolizes her internal awareness of a urinary-tract infection coming on. The fishbowl represents her bladder.

Pale or lethargic fish can be associated with low energy or lack of vitality—pale means something is missing from the bloodstream, probably related to nutritional deficiency.

Fish are considered a healthful food and it's possible that eating fish, or preparing them as food, is related to your diet and what you consume. See: *Eat, Food*.

Colorful fish can symbolize distraction, because it is easy to be distracted by watching them swim in a tank.

Fish in water can connect with thoughts, emotions, or feelings, but a "fish out of water" implies someone out of his or her element. More cross-associations are possible with waking life activities like swimming, bathing, and urinating. Fish swimming in murky water can mean that a situation is murky.

Fish are associated with Christianity, as a symbol used throughout Western culture. Jesus and his followers were known as "fishers of men," and one of the most famous stories about him is the feeding of the masses with a few fish and some bread. This symbolic use of fish shows up more in the dreams of practicing Christians, but the stories are widely known and fair game for dreams to use. Ingesting fish in these dreams is associated with Christian teachings.

. Fish that slip away can symbolize failing to follow something you have been taught—moral teachings in particular. It can symbolize a slippery situation or something you have a hard time holding onto. See: *Ice*.

A dead fish can symbolize someone who is unresponsive, especially sexually. It can mean "you're next," as in the famous scene with the fish in *The Godfather*. "Something fishy" is used in connection with suspicion.

More plays on words can be made from types of fish. For example, "to carp" means to make petty criticism. "To flounder" means to struggle helplessly. Consider these possibilities, remembering that your associations are the most direct route to the meaning.

See also: *Animals, Death, Eat, Fishing, Float, Food, Grocery Store, Ice, Subconscious, Toilet, Unconscious Mind, Water*

Fishing—Dreams play with words and create visual puns. So in the case of fishing, think of when the word is used to mean something other than catching fish. You can "fish" for the truth or for a compliment, or fish for opportunity, such as in a dream a man has about fishing in a very shallow lake with a fishing pole. He catches a small fish and tosses it back because it's too small to eat. The dream occurs after a day of looking through employment ads and finding the opportunities to be shallow. In this metaphor, the shallow lake symbolizes limited job opportunities, and the small fish—too small to eat—symbolizes that the few opportunities he found don't have much to offer.

Shallow can refer to people, relationships, knowledge, perceptions, finances, etc. It's a physical representation of depth. If the man in the previous dream had found lots of job opportunities, the lake would have been shown as deep and full of fish. Emotional depth can be represented as a deep pool.

"Plenty of fish in the sea" is a term used in dating to mean many people available to date. In that sense, fishing can mean looking for a mate or someone to date.

Successful fishing can symbolize a "good catch," usually associated with success or profit in business, and with finding a mate. Fishing is also associated with the acquisition of knowledge, particularly self-knowledge.

See also: *Boat, Fish, Ocean, River, Water, Worm*

Fist—A clenched fist is an image of heavy-handed authority and conflict. Dreaming about a fist can symbolize the idea of "iron-fisted," meaning inflexible or absolute. It's authority that beats down any challenge.

A clenched fist can symbolize "tight-fisted," meaning stingy. People can be stingy with money, but also consider how it applies to other situations, such as when someone won't give compliments or they keep a tight hold on their emotions.

Dreaming about hitting with your fists can express frustration or anger. Hitting someone you know with your fists can connect with anger and frustration with that person. Usually it's a way of acting out your feelings. The entry for *Mother* has a great example. If a character hits you, it can be a sign of frustration or anger directed at you, or anger with yourself.

An unfamiliar character you hit with your fists can be a surrogate for someone you know, or it might represent a side of yourself that's unwanted or repressed.

For example, a teen male dreams about a pack of boys his age mercilessly beating up another boy who doesn't appear able to fight back. The boy who takes the beating doesn't look like anyone the dreamer actually knows, yet the dreamer feels that he knows him well. He joins in the beating and gets in a few blows of his own as he mocks and scorns the boy as a "pussy" and "fag."

The character that takes the beating is the soft and gentle side of the dreamer. Now that he's a teenager, he can't allow any sort of softness or weakness to show around his peers or he'll be labeled as a sissy. The action of beating the boy in the dream is a physical representation of repressing this side of himself, and his scorn of the boy is actually a reflection of how he scorns himself for being soft and gentle. He fears this side of himself, and he acts out all the related feelings. The action tells the story.

Another possible way of looking at the same dream scene is that it expresses the dreamer's anger or frustration with himself. Scenes involving hitting are common in the dreams of people who are angry. If the person you hit is not someone you know or recognize, you might be expressing anger or frustration with yourself. The character is a surrogate. See: *Anger*.

In simplest terms, hitting is abuse, and in dreams it can be a physical representation of emotional or psychological abuse or an expression of how you feel. People who have been physically abused are very likely to dream about it; in which case, hitting in their dreams connects closely with actual experience. See: *Beat*.

Things aren't always as they appear, though. Most dream characters are projections of your inner world, and actions involving them such as hitting are symbolic. It all ties back to you, even when a dream character looks like someone you know. For example, you dream that your best friend hits you, and that action actually expresses your guilt because you did something that let the person down. The character's action is scripted based on your feelings.

And now for another twist. Some dream-characters don't represent people at all. They don't represent something about you. They represent a subject, idea, or organization. For example, a math teacher getting beat up by a group of students in a dream is an expression of the dreamer's frustration with the subject of math. Beating up a mail carrier can symbolize frustration over a package being delayed or lost. See: *Beat*.

Also consider that hitting in a dream can be a way of acting out other definitions of the word. For example, your best friend hits you in a dream and it means the person has been "hitting on" you, expressing romantic interest. Or you get hit upside the head in a dream and it means you finally realize something. Duh!

See also: *Abuse, Anger, Beat, Boxing, Conflict, Fight, Fisting, Weak*

Fisting—Fisting is an aggressive sex act of inserting the entire hand into the rectum, and in dreams it can symbolize doing something that a part of yourself resists, or that feels degrading. It's a graphic depiction of your thoughts, feelings, and perceptions, and is worth a mention here because it's actually used as symbolism in dreams.

Note: The most shocking and obscene dream imagery can also be the most revealing, and it shouldn't be shied away from because of the content.

For example, a man dreams about another man abducted by a third man. The abductor is an alien, though he looks human. The victim is brought to the back room of a storefront. The captor's skin begins to swell. He becomes bloated and warty, his clothes ripping off. A faint blue light emanates from his skin. Instead of regular male genitals, the alien has a large, bald, wrinkled sphincter between his legs, and he compels the victim to shove his arm into the hole. The man knows what is happening and is horrified, but is unable to help himself. As the man sticks his arm in and out, the alien groans with pleasure and glows brighter. The bloated alien orgasms and a blast of blue light vaporizes the screaming victim.

Seriously, this dream happened, and like most others it's explainable when understood as symbolism.

The dreamer is a playwright commissioned by a foreign man to write a play. Foreign is another word for "alien," so the alien in the dream represents the foreigner. The experience has turned into a nightmare for the dreamer because the foreigner makes unreasonable demands. With this in mind, the dream can be understood.

Begin with the setting, a storefront. That can be associated with work or profession, and the subject of the dream is related to the dreamer's professional work. As a playwright, he's an artist, but the work he's been commissioned to do turns his stomach and makes him feel like a whore, selling his talent for a buck. That's represented in the action of fisting the alien. It's how the dreamer feels about doing work for the foreigner. He's forced to do something that's revolting, and is horrified but unable to stop himself, like the captive in the dream. Furthermore, he feels like he's a captive because he's committed to finishing the job, which to his inner artist is like performing an obscene act for someone's pleasure. The circumstance and his feelings about it are all summed up in the image of fisting the alien.

Next, consider the third-person narration of the story. It can be a way of depersonalizing the story so it can be told without objections from the ego. If you know the captive man in the story is really you, you might react too strongly for the dream to continue.

Here's another example. The dream starts off in a small building near a parking lot at night. The lights are off. The dreamer sees a guy wearing latex gloves fisting another guy in the rectum. The man being fisted has the plumage of a chicken on top of his head. He says, "My ass is tightening up real good." It will all make sense in a moment.

The dreamer plays a game called Minecraft and has been thinking about creating a custom map that other players can use. The maps are "parked" at websites, which explains the parking-lot setting in the dream. The dreamer has a strong desire to create the map but hasn't done it because of fear of the possible reaction. The online world is full of "trolls" who are negative about everything. The dreamer is sensitive to criticism. The symbolism is expressed in the dream when the character says, "My ass is tightening up real good." It means the more the dreamer thinks about the possible criticism of the map he wants to create, the more he tightens up. The chicken plumage symbolizes the dreamer's fear. He perceives himself as "chicken."

See also: *Anal Sex, Anus, Artist, Chicken, Fist, Foreigner, Sex, Store, UFO*

Fitness Center—A fitness-center setting in a dream can symbolize anything in life related to fitness, such as finding the time or motivation to exercise. Dreaming about obstacles in a fitness center, or on the way to one, can symbolize obstacles to exercising.

But many associations and activities associated with fitness centers can be used as symbolism. For example, lifting weights can symbolize "heavy lifting," meaning getting a lot of work done or taking on the majority of a workload. See: *Horse*.

Trying to lift too much weight can mean you are taking on more work or responsibility than you can handle. Weight that's easy to lift can be a sign that you find a task easy, or that you are allowing someone else to "do the heavy lifting."

The symbolism of a fitness center can connect with body image, self-image, ego, and finding a mate or date. It ties in with the motivation to exercise and how you present yourself socially.

Running or walking on a treadmill or riding an exercise bike can symbolize putting forth effort and not getting anywhere. These are activities that involve movement, although you begin and end in the same place.

Showing off your body in a fitness center can have symbolism related to the area of the body shown off. For example, showing off your arms can symbolize strength of character or personality. Showing off your back can symbolize your ability to take on work. Showing off your legs can symbolize feeling proud about getting somewhere in life. Look up entries for the body parts in this dream dictionary for more ideas. These are just a few ideas to get you started.

Dreams create symbolism by making connections between ideas, and with a fitness center you have the word "fitness," which can mean suitability for a role or task. For example, to be fit or not as a parent. And "fit" can relate to how well things fit together, such as in finding the right relationship or occupation.

See also: *Amputate, Athlete, Back, Body, Clothing, Horse, Job, Locker*

Flame—See: *Candle, Fire*

Flee—See: *Escape*

Float—Floating in air or water implies relaxation and lack of worry. However, put the action of floating into the larger context of the dream and how you feel about the scenario.

If you float in a raft down a lazy river and feel at peace, the symbolism is more likely to relate to relaxation and enjoying your life. It can indicate there is no need to rush. You are at ease. But if you float atop debris on a flooded river and feel anxious or overwhelmed, it can symbolize being overwhelmed by emotions or content arising from your deep mind, the unconscious. There is something inside you that needs to find expression in your life. It cannot be held back any longer. See: *Erupt.*

Floating implies you are not determining the direction in which your life is going. As symbolism it can express the same idea in the phrase "go

wherever the wind blows." It can mean you are undecided or need to think about where you are headed in life.

Floating through the air can symbolize the high experienced from drugs such as opioids and cannabis, or the desire to disconnect the mind from the body. When dreams use this meaning of the symbolism, it is accompanied often by your deliberately trying to disconnect from the ground. The meaning is found in the term "get high." Look at it literally. If you "get high," how do you get there? You disconnect from the ground. You float away. Your body is numb and you no longer really feel it. See: *Drugs.*

Floating can symbolize the idea in the phrase "head in the clouds." It can symbolize daydreaming. In which case, floating is a visual pun, a physical representation.

Floating can symbolize gaining a different perspective. If you're off the ground, it can mean you are gaining a higher perspective. See: *Balloon.*

See also: *Air, Ascend, Balloon, Birds, Boat, Erupt, Fish, Flood, Fly, Numb, River, Swim, Water*

Flood—Water in a dream can symbolize emotions, so a flood can symbolize outpouring of emotion. Flooding implies the threat of being overwhelmed, and psychologically it can relate to being overwhelmed by your emotions, especially if the water is murky, dirty, or full of debris. However, dreams have many ways of creating symbolism with the action and imagery of flooding.

For example, the unstoppable nature of a flood can be used to create symbolism connected with anything that can't be controlled: illness, old age, a person, a situation.

Water is associated with the unconscious mind, which can act as a repository for everything psychologically repressed, rejected, or unwanted. A point comes when those elements will not be held back any longer. The dam breaks and out rushes everything previously held back. When the symbolism of flooding is used in this sense, it implies a time of danger for the person, a mental breakdown, or onset of neurosis. See: *Erupt.*

On the other hand, if handled properly, it can precede a time of creative fertility. Floods create rich soil from which crops grow. Artists, inventors, and other types of creative people can be "flooded" with ideas and inspirations. In this sense the imagery of flooding is quite positive and welcome.

Flooding can mean letting go of something. After a flood of emotion or creativity, the head and heart are cleared. You are ready to start fresh. It can be the first step to healing.

Flooding is associated with threats to property and life, because floods are dangerous and often accompanied by destruction. It can mean you face a dangerous situation or are overwhelmed by events.

Flooding is associated with fears and worries. This use of the symbolism is more likely in dreams where a flood is feared to happen, or the possibility of it causes panic.

A more literal reading of the symbolism of flooding involves the visualization of badly needing to urinate. A flood of dirty brown water can symbolize diarrhea. See: *Toilet*.

Flooding can have personal associations based on experience. If you've ever lived through a flood, especially one that wrecks your life or home, dreams can draw on the experience to create symbolism.

News about flooding can seep into dreams. If you have no personal connection with the places being flooded, consider the possibility that the dream uses a flood to connect with whatever you were thinking, feeling, or doing at the time you heard the news. In which case, the symbolism has nothing to do with water or flooding. It's simply a marker for when a thought or feeling occurred.

See also: *Bathroom, Disaster, Fear, Home, Rescue, River, Shower, Tidal Wave, Toilet, Water*

Floor—In simplest terms, a floor is what you stand on, and what you stand on in the figurative sense are your values, ethics, morals, convictions, principles, beliefs, memories, job, safety, and health. See: *Feet*.

A floor can refer to stability—relationship stability, mental stability, health stability, financial stability.

A floor suddenly moving and tossing you about can symbolize a sudden upheaval in your life. See: *Earthquake*.

Think of the phrase "rug pulled out from beneath you." It means something you count on is suddenly gone.

Floors in a home or building can symbolize levels of consciousness and your roots as a person. For example, a bottom floor can refer to heredity and inherited traits and characteristics. A top floor or attic can refer to your mental life, thinking processes, and knowledge. See: *Building, Elevator*.

When a house symbolizes your body, a floor can refer to pelvic floor.

The floor is something below you and can symbolize something below you in the sense of status, authority, or prestige. It can symbolize something that's unnoticed.

See also: *Ballet, Basement, Building, Construction, Earthquake, Elevator, Feet, Home*

Fly—Flying is a common dream theme and has a variety of meanings. The most common are related to flying as an expression of "going somewhere" in your life. It expresses confidence and enthusiasm, or just pure happiness. It can show achievement and success. It's a physical representation of a personal situation.

The symbolism of flying depends heavily on whether you fly under your own power or in a plane. Flying under your own power is often associated with ability to "soar" in your personal life and development. These flying dreams are common in people who are discovering their capabilities and developing their skills and intellect. Thoughts are sometimes said to soar, and intellect is associated with air, so flying under your own power can be a graphic way of representing the power of your mind.

Flying under your own power is associated with freedom. Like a bird, you are free. You can come and go as you please. See: *Bird*.

The symbolism of flying in a plane is discussed at length in the *Airplane* entry. But, quickly, the symbolism often relates to getting to a place you want to be in your life—a goal, ambition, aspiration, desire.

Flying is associated with "rising above" and gaining a broader perspective. See: *Balloon.*

Flying can symbolize progress—personal progress, or just progress in general, such as toward getting a degree or reaching another sort of goal.

It can mean finding a way out of a tricky situation. When you fly away, it means "goodbye."

It can mean you wish to escape. See: *Escape.*

Flying is used to describe the feeling of being high on drugs, or just "in the zone" where nothing can stop you or hold you down. See: *Float.*

The flip side can be expressed through flying symbolism, too. If you are restricted, you can dream about being unable to fly, or about trying to take flight but something stops you or shoots you down. You are not successful. You don't have freedom. You are unable to rise above.

Inability to fly, or hindrance in flight, can symbolize limits that you place on yourself or that are placed on you. It can mean you're having difficulty "taking off" or launching.

For example, a gay teenaged female dreams about being trapped in a bird cage while seeing her love interest's cellphone passing messages between that girl, who is a close friend, and a boy her friend likes. The bird cage symbolizes the dreamer's sexuality limiting her. She can't have what she wants, her love interest. See: *Bird Cage.*

A woman has a recurring dream about flying in which she launches into the air and feels exhilarated. However, how high she can fly is limited, as if she bumps into an invisible ceiling.

It's tempting to interpret this dream as a metaphor for the "glass ceiling," but it's actually more personal than that. Really, it's about accepting her own limits. Flying in this dream symbolizes her personal development. She is finding out that she has high capabilities. She can really soar and be successful. However, she is also finding out she has limits. They're invisible in the sense that she doesn't know she's reached them till she's actually there.

There is a saying, "The higher you fly, the more you must be grounded." It means that the more success a person has, the more they need to stay in touch with everyday reality—especially important for highly intelligent individuals who might otherwise get lost in their heads. The psyche is a self-regulating and balancing system, and if any one part of it goes too far one direction, its complementary part will bring the person back to earth—sometimes with a rough landing! This female needs to learn how to ground herself more in everyday reality and in her body if she wants to expand her limits. See: *Compensation.*

Distance in a dream can refer to emotional or personal distance, and in this sense, flying can be viewed as a means of quickly closing that distance. When traveling long distances, flying is the fastest mode of travel, which can symbolize the fastest means to get to a goal.

People who are afraid of flying or have concerns related to taking flights, such as how to handle small children on a plane, can dream about flying in connection with these issues. These are possible topics for dreams to explore through scenes of flying.

See also: *Airplane, Airport, Bird Cage, Birds, Compensation, Embark, Float, Insects, Journey, Rocket*

Food—Dreams about the condition and needs of the body are among the most common, and the symbolism can be expressed through food. But sometimes they're straightforward representations of foods desired by the body. For example, a banana can be a phallic symbol, or a suggested food for getting more potassium in your diet.

Food in a dream can symbolize something that you consume. It can relate to diet or nutrition, but also to other things that are consumed or absorbed, like opinions, information, media, entertainment, knowledge, and facts. Food is consumed and absorbed into the body, in an association that branches out to connect with many ideas.

You consume and process emotions and feelings.

You consume information and knowledge.

You absorb experiences and learn from them, doing which in turn shapes your self-image, direction in life, values, and decisions.

The saying goes that "you are what you eat." It means that whatever you take into yourself shapes what you are as a person. The saying is often meant as the connection between physical health and diet, but as an idea it can be used as symbolism in dreams for whatever you feed your mind and spirit. See: *Eat*.

For example, exposure to someone who is negative or a bad influence can give you a negative outlook and influence you in bad ways, which can be symbolized as eating food that's bad for you. Reading or watching news reports that focus on murder and death can negatively influence your outlook on society and color your perceptions. You "feed" on the negativity.

On the other hand, exposure to people who are positive and a good influence can give you a positive outlook and shape your thinking and feelings in positive ways, which can be symbolized as eating good food.

To digest something in a dream can symbolize absorbing something you take into yourself. It could relate to digesting what you eat, but dreams are known for creating physical representations of personal situations, such as when you "digest" a thought, idea, or feeling. In this sense it means "to process." It means taking time to break down and fully absorb something.

Foods shaped in a circle, like pizza and cookies, can relate to the idea of wholeness as a person. See: *Circle*.

Food in dreams can speak directly to nutrition and the needs of your body. You can dream about specific foods because your body is saying, "Hey, I need that." It can speak to other needs, such as a lemon symbolizing the need for sunshine or optimism, or a steak representing the need for satisfaction or fulfillment.

For example, a man dreams that he goes with friends to dinner at a nice restaurant and orders a steak. He's told to pay for it first. So he does and it arrives, but then he's told to fill out a questionnaire

before eating it. He does, grudgingly, and by the time he gets around to eating his steak, it's cold. In the image of the cold steak, the dream sums up a situation where the dreamer moved to "the big city" after long planning and much expense, symbolized as the questionnaire and paying ahead of time for the steak. It's his "dream come true," but when he gets there he finds the reality to be much different from what he imagined and he's disappointed and left feeling cold and unfulfilled.

Eating raw meat can symbolize plunging ahead unprepared. Something isn't ready. Or you want to get past the surface and down to the "meat." You want it raw, unadorned. Just the facts or truth. It can mean you feel raw or used, just a piece of meat.

For people who are particular about how thoroughly their meat is cooked, raw can symbolize fear of contamination, probably in the figurative sense, such as protecting yourself from being contaminated by being associated with someone with a bad reptutation.

Spicy food can symbolize something too hot to handle, or the "spice of life," connected with feeling passion and intensity. Consider possible physical stimuli, too, such as spicy food used to symbolize the sensation of acid reflux.

Buying food can indicate a desire to buy the attention or sympathy of other people.

Individual foods get into all sorts of associations based on color and appearance, texture, temperature, taste, and personal experience. The possibilities for symbolism it opens up are way too many to delve into here, but you can explore further by using the entries listed below.

See also: *Body, Candy, Chef, Chicken, Circle, Colors, Clothing, Cow, Devour, Dinner, Eat, Eaten, Egg, Emaciated, Excrement, Fish, Fitness Center, Grocery Store, Hunger, Kitchen, Menu, Orange, Stomach, Teeth*

Foot—See: *Feet*

Football—The symbolism of football in a dream has many possibilities related to competition—especially rough-and-tumble competition and competition between males.

Football can symbolize giving and receiving blows, especially verbal ones, and if that's the case, you'd expect to see the symbolism play out in the actions.

Football is associated with teamwork, and again, the symbolism shows in the action. Lack of teamwork can show as a team that doesn't work together.

Analogies using football can be pulled off the shelf anytime two sides face off. Such as opposing groups of friends or co-workers, or sides of yourself. Your logic opposes your feelings, or loyalty opposes freedom. Think creatively. A battle between two football teams in a dream could symbolize a battle within yourself about choosing between two places where you want to live, represented as opposite end zones. You will "end up" in one or the other.

Elements of the game of football can be used to create symbolism. Such as a goal post or goal line representing a mark you want to reach, or a deadline. A goal post far away can symbolize a goal in life that seems distant or unreachable.

A high school kid dreams that he's handed the football and he scores a touchdown. As a celebration antic, he tries to dunk the ball through the goal posts, but the crossbar is higher than normal and he's unable to reach it. It all symbolizes his high expectations of himself and how they prevent him from feeling satisfied when he reaches a goal. He never really feels like celebrating. Nothing he does is good enough.

Running with a football can symbolize that you have been given a job or task and must "run with it." It can symbolize "the runaround," or hurriedly getting stuff done.

A young man dreams that he's inside an enclosed football stadium, in the stands with his father watching the game. Suddenly a young boy runs out onto the football field and tries to join the players. The referees tell him to get off the field. In the middle of the field is a high mound. The dreamer sees himself as a running back sprinting up the mound.

The dream symbolizes the dreamer's busy activity related to getting ready for his girlfriend to have their baby. She's due any day and the young man is busy preparing, as symbolized by running up the mound. The presence of the dreamer's father is a sign that he is about to become a father himself. The young boy who runs onto the field symbolizes the child the dreamer is about to have. The referee's telling the boy to get off the field symbolizes giving birth, because the enclosed stadium represents his girlfriend's womb and the field of play is where the baby lives within it. It's a sign the dreamer is eager for the big moment to arrive.

Tackling can mean "tackle the job," or keep something close to you that's trying to get away, such as a romantic interest. See: *Tackle*.

Myriad personal associations come into play, especially if you play (or have played) football, watch it, or hear about it. For some people, listening to someone talk about football is the most boring thing they can imagine, while for others football is all they talk about. In that sense it can be used as a gauge of interest or excitement level.

Football is associated with time off from the usual routine. Football Sunday is like a Sabbath day in some households, so it could be used to describe a situation where you've been given something to do during a time that's inconvenient or just dead wrong.

Football can remind you of your dad or your youth. It can be used in connection with feeling aches and pains.

Do you make football analogies? Does your understanding of the sport and its intricacies color how you think? If so, your dreams have even more ways of using football to make comparisons and create symbolism.

See also: *Arena, Ball, Chase, Coach, Games, Locker, Opponent, Sports, Tackle*

Foreign—Dreams bring to life alternate definitions of words, so with anything foreign in a dream, consider that it could mean "distant," "strange," or "new." Dreaming about being in a distant foreign land, for example, can symbolize emotional distance from a significant other. It can express the need for something new and interesting in your life, such as new experiences, travel, or just a break from the routine.

Escaping to a foreign land in a dream expresses the wish to escape a situation in your life that's getting you down or holding you back.

Another word for foreign is "alien," and in dreams aliens—creatures from other planets—can symbolize something foreign to you, meaning "outside the scope of your experience."

The entry for *Stranger* goes into more depth about this subject.

See also: *Border, Stranger, UFO*

Foreigner—See: *Foreign, Stranger*

Forehead—See: *Head*

Forest—When you feel lost in the personal sense and are trying to find your way, a forest is a natural choice as a setting to tell the story. Why? Because people get lost in forests, and the imagery is appropriate because tall trees and foliage block your line of sight. Moreover, a forest path can symbolize the path you're on in life, an analogy that can be stretched many ways.

For example, wandering off a forest path and getting lost can mean trying to do something your own way and getting lost. A path disappearing can symbolize wrong directions or bad advice to get somewhere you were trying to go in your life. A path splitting can symbolize the proverbial fork in the road.

Usually in dreams that use a forest to symbolize being lost in the personal sense, being physically lost will be a theme. Or think in more general terms of feeling your way through something where the way forward isn't clear. It could be an external situation, such as figuring out the best path in your career, or an internal situation, such as figuring out the sort of person you want to be.

Another possibility for the symbolism of a forest is related to the symbolism of trees. See: *Tree*.

A city full of skyscrapers is comparable to a forest of towering trees. An urban area is often referred to as a "jungle," so a lot of trees together can symbolize a city. See: *City*.

In the dreams of children, being in a forest full of tall trees can represent how they feel in comparison with adults, who look like giants from a child's perspective. Also, families are referred to as trees, so being in a forest can symbolize being a member of a big family.

This discussion continues in the entry for *Wilderness*.

See also: *City, Giant, Left, Lost, Right, Skyscraper, Tree, Wilderness*

Fox—Foxes are most commonly associated with feminine beauty, as in "foxy lady," and with sneakiness. The difference is found in the action. A fox teasingly running its tail across your neck might symbolize temptation or flirtation, while a fox sneaking in your back door might symbolize being taken advantage of or robbed. It can mean that a person cleverly works around your boundaries or limits.

A young woman dreams that she's a fox being pursued, and to slow down the male hunters on her trail she tosses her friends in their way. It symbolizes how she uses her friends to divert male attention. She attracts a lot of it.

Foxes are also associated with cleverness, and that idea can be stretched further to include craftiness, cunning, and intelligence.

As with any animal in your dreams, consider your personal associations and experiences. What are the first thoughts that come to mind when you think about the fox in your dream and foxes in general?

See also: *Animals, Bandit, Beauty, Burglar, Raccoon, Thief*

Freeze—See: *Ice*

Friend—Friends are among the most common dream-characters, and have widely varied possibilities for symbolism. The characters can be friends you know, or they can be inventions of a dream that are portrayed as friends. This difference is the place to begin the interpretation process.

When you dream about friends who are people you know, the dream might connect with a recent interaction with a person, a situation or circumstance, or something you heard. Many dreams connect with events of the previous day or two, or in anticipation of the day ahead, so if you were with a friend, plan to be together, or the person was on your mind, it's a good bet that it's related to his or her appearance in your dream.

For example, a friend borrows money from you and you wonder when you're going to get paid back. It's no big deal, but there's a little voice in your head raising questions. Then you dream that you receive a letter from the friend with a check inside, reflecting your thoughts about being paid back and a hunch that it'll happen soon. Now you can rest easier.

Friends in dreams can connect with ongoing situations and circumstances, too. For example, an ongoing situation is depicted in a dream about a friend throwing firebombs into a crowd. It symbolizes that friend's habit of throwing verbal bombs and getting people riled up.

dream-characters that are presented as friends but do not resemble someone you know can be surrogates for friends. A surrogate is used as a storytelling device to create psychological distance and avoid arousing strong emotions or reactions that would disturb your sleep or make the story veer off course. Surrogates can be used to represent people you know yet look nothing like them. Oftentimes they're identified by occupation, actions, or some other distinguishing feature or characteristic, including physical characteristics such as hair color or style.

For example, a young man dreams that he goes to school on the bus, gets off, and while walking into school he's stabbed in the back by someone who's supposed to be a friend. The day before the dream, a friend betrayed him, figuratively stabbing him in the back. And while the surrogate-character in the dream does not look like that friend who betrayed him, they are one and the same.

Invented friends in dreams can symbolize the subject of friendship, desire for it, or friendship skills.

Potentially, a multitude of everyday situations with friends can be dreamed about, if you consider the dynamics of friendship and the widely varied areas of life it involves. The dreams you're most likely to remember, however, are the ones that involve strong emotions or feelings. Those are usually pretty easy to connect with what was on our mind or in your heart the day or two before the dream.

When a strong reaction is provoked in a dream, it's connected with something you feel strongly about, and it could be about a friend portrayed in the dream. But keep in mind that most dreams are about your inner life, and most dream-characters represent something about you and your life.

Consider also that the friend in your dream can symbolize something you feel strongly about other than that person, such as the place where you live or work together. This sort of dream can be identified at times by an overreaction. For example, you dream that a friend from work is a couple of minutes late coming over to your house, and you're furious. You'd never actually get furious about such a thing if it really happened. On the other hand, you are really mad about a writeup you got at work for being two minutes late. In which case, the friend symbolizes the place where you work together and has nothing to do with being angry with that friend. You react angrily because you know while dreaming what the friend represents.

Jealousy and envy are two strong emotions that can come out in relation to friends. A common theme in cheating dreams involves your close friend sleeping with your significant other. Often, it reflects jealousy or wariness about how they interact. Perhaps they're a little too friendly for your comfort, or you see—or think you see—some sort of romantic spark between them. Or you're insecure and project your thoughts and feelings onto the dream-characters.

That's an important fact for understanding dream-characters, because most of the time they are reflections of something about you, not about the person—friend or otherwise—portrayed as a character.

Friends in dreams can symbolize something you know about the person—distinct characteristics, traits, or qualities, among other things. Often you can decode the symbolism simply by pulling thoughts about the person off the top of your head. See the example about a guy giving birth to a friend's baby in the entry for *Childbirth*.

Or you have a friend who is good at meeting new people, and you are reserved. The friend is then used in a dream as a symbol for gregariousness. If you want to be more gregarious, you can learn from the friend's example. The same idea applies to dating skills.

A young man dreams that his best friend hits on all the girls he likes, then has sex with them. The dream is an answer to the young man's question, How do I get the girls I like to like me? And the answer is, learn from your friend, the one who is good with the ladies.

The key to decoding the symbolism is found in the dreamer's feelings while watching his friend pick up the girls. He admires his skills while lamenting his own lack of them. If he'd reacted angrily, it might indicate stronger feelings behind the symbolism. As in, maybe his friend is the sort of jerk who deliberately spites the dreamer by targeting girls he likes.

Friendly dream-characters can represent aspects of yourself. The character is presented as a friend because it portrays a part of yourself that is in some way like a friend—helpful, close, interesting, comforting. Your psyche is a collective, and some parts are independent of you and outside the control of the ego. Those parts make their own decisions and have their own viewpoints. They can be portrayed as friends or enemies, depending on your relationship with them. And the real key point here is they're all you.

Parts of yourself can play the role of friends. This meaning of the symbolism is especially likely if you have been feeling lonely or isolated. Dreams can act as compensation for something missing in your life, and if you need a friend, your dreams can provide it. See: *Compensation*.

Another detail to notice is whether a friend-character is in your dream individually or as part of a group. Individually, friends in dreams tend to

symbolize what you see about the friend in yourself, your recent interaction, or related thoughts and feelings. As a group, friends tend to symbolize something related to the subject of friendship. It's only a rule of thumb, a place to begin asking the questions. See: *Group*.

You can dream about a waking-life situation or circumstance with a friend, but the friend is not pictured in the dream. For example, say you have an argument with a friend, then dream about yelling at a brick wall. The friend is not in the dream but is instead symbolized by the brick wall because arguing with the person is like yelling at a brick wall!

If the friend in the dream is someone from the past, see: *Old Friend*.

See also: *Childbirth, Compensation, Facebook, Group, Guide, Old Friend*

Frog—Frogs are commonly associated with a person's inner nature. The connection relates to the fact that frogs are very sensitive to their environment. The inner nature of a person is also very sensitive, quick to jump or duck for cover, and is therefore closely guarded under the water line of your mind. Small fluctuations in a frog's living environment can make huge differences in its state of being, and the same goes for the inner, sensitive you.

Dreams about frogs squashed or split open can be analogies for how you feel deep down: exposed, or flattened by events in your life.

Dreams of caring for frogs can symbolize the care you give to your inner life.

Dreams of frogs getting away can symbolize the need to take better care of yourself. It can connect with a slippery situation.

There are some negative associations with frogs. They are slimy. They are used in biblical tales of plague. They are described as "unclean" in Revelation 16. And they croak, which can be associated with death or unintelligible noise.

Licking a frog in a dream can symbolize trying something because you've heard about it, or gullibility.

See also: *Animals*

Front Door—See: *Door*

Frozen—See: *Ice*

Fuel—See: *Gas*

Fugitive—In simplest terms, a fugitive is like a prisoner, except with the added elements of escape and pursuit. It can be like the symbolism of escape, except the presumption is a fugitive has done something wrong. See: *Escape*.

A fugitive can symbolize escaping from a situation that feels like prison. For example, you make up an excuse to get out of work, and must be careful to cover your tracks. You then dream about being a fugitive hiding from pursuers.

It can mean you feel like a prisoner. See: *Prisoner*.

You feel like a fugitive when you intentionally do something wrong, dodge a responsibility, or break a promise. It can mean you feel guilty—karma must be paid. It can mean refusal to confront something, or running away from a situation or relationship. It can mean you violate your values, ethics, or other sort of self-imposed restraint. Fear of consequences, or your conscience, is hunting you.

Aiding a fugitive can mean you are compromising yourself. Or your ego has come under the spell of your Shadow, which is the side of yourself that makes excuses for wrongdoing but always extracts a price for the aid it renders.

It can mean you think you can get away with doing something wrong. Or you are helping someone avoid responsibility or get away with wrongdoing. It's a compromising situation.

See also: *Accomplice, Arrest, Bail, Ego, Escape, Jail, Police Officer, Prisoner, Shadow*

Funeral—A funeral suggests that something has come to an end—a time of life, a relationship, a situation.

It can mean that something about yourself is changing. For example, there comes a point when you are no longer a child or teenager, and that part of yourself recedes to allow a more mature version

of yourself to take over, and to mark the passing, you dream about a funeral.

The idea extends to anything about yourself that changes. For example, someone who used to stutter learns to speak fluently, and the stutterer and the stigma that came with it is buried. You are "closing the lid" on the past, like closing a lid on a casket. See: *Coffin*.

A young man dreams he's with two other men as they hold a funeral for a teenaged Cherokee warrior. The warrior is in a canoe, and they push the canoe into a river. At the last moment, the dreamer thinks it would be funny to pull a prank by dropping a Pez dispenser into the canoe, then he feels bad about disrespecting the young warrior's funeral. The funeral symbolizes that an immature part of the man is receding, but his action of pulling a prank shows that he's holding onto some of his childish ways.

Funerals are associated with burial. See: *Bury*.

They're associated with graveyards. See: *Graveyard*.

Dreaming about attending the funeral of someone you know can mean you are growing apart from the person or separating yourself from his or her influence. For example, dreaming about the funeral of your still-living parent can mean escaping the parent's sphere of influence, becoming your own person, or escaping the parent's restrictions.

Dreaming about the funeral of a friend can mean you recognize that your relationship with the person is changing.

Funerals are associated with death. You might be thinking about death because of a recent brush with it, or because someone you know is seriously ill or has recently died. Or perhaps you heard about a tragedy involving death. See: *Death*.

Along this line, consider the phrase "it's your funeral," often associated with taking a risk that can end badly.

See also: *Body, Bury, Coffin, Death, Graveyard*

Fur—See: *Hair*

Future—See: *Calendar, Precognitive Dream, Time, Time Travel*

Gamble—When you gamble you take a risk, so gambling in a dream can symbolize anything risky or associated with chance. For example, starting a new business or relationship is a gamble. You are willing to accept the risk because of the possibility of reward.

Gambling has other associations related to cheating, lying, and anything else that carries a risk of getting caught.

Gambling can be associated with a hunch, especially when something isn't right about someone or something. It can mean you're in danger of being fooled, or fooling yourself, or you're the target of a shakedown or scam. The feelings are similar, a hunch you can't put your finger on, you just know something isn't right.

Gambling is associated with intuition, strategy, deception, and playing the odds.

A gambler in a dream can symbolize someone who thinks he can get away with something. The idea can be extended to making strategy and analyzing risk.

Gamblers are commonly perceived as people who are bad with money and aren't willing to work at a regular job.

Gamblers create perceptions of themselves that may have nothing to do with reality, so dreaming about a gambler or gambling can relate to the difference between perception and reality. The image of a gambler and that lifestyle can be much different from the reality.

Gamblers are associated with strong nerves and a poker face. These skills are comparable to situations in life such as making business deals or trading in financial markets.

Good gamblers who play against other gamblers are said to "read the player, not the cards." This idea can be used to symbolize ability to read people and their motives. The idea extends to knowing the strength of a position you are in. For example, you know when is the right time to ask for a raise at work or make your move in a relationship.

Gambling is associated with luck, and in dreamland luck isn't found only in a casino. For example, you are "lucky" if you have the perfect spouse and beautiful, well-behaved kids. You are "unlucky" if you get laid off at work or catch a terrible illness. See: *Lottery*.

The symbolism of gambling takes on new dimensions for people who gamble and go to casinos. Hours glued to a slot machine or spent at a gaming table can create all sorts of imagery for dreams to process. But also consider what's happening in your mind during those hours. For example, you might notice patterns that can aid your play, or devise a betting strategy, but the knowledge is subconscious. Your dreams can help bring those thoughts and observations forward.

Wins and losses associated with gambling, and how they can affect your life is also fodder for dreams. When these associations are brought into play, dreams have many connections that can be made between gambling and other areas of life, especially in relation to the value of money and how it is prioritized. See: *Money*.

For example, a woman who habitually loses money at casinos dreams about attending a funeral in a potter's field in the back of her favorite casino. Instead of flowers, the mourners toss poker chips onto the casket, and the service is overseen by a pit boss. The woman becomes very curious about who is in the closed casket—she assumes it must be someone important. The pit boss opens the casket for her, and she's mortified to see her lifeless body inside. The message in the dream is clear enough: she's throwing away her money in casinos, and it's killing her inside because she can't stop. And if she doesn't stop, she fears she'll go to her grave penniless, as symbolized by the potter's field.

A final consideration is that gambling is associated with odds, statistics, numbers, and specialized skill. In this sense, dreaming about gambling or being a gambler can symbolize ability to analyze numbers and make quick decisions.

See also: *Casino, Lottery, Money, Numbers, Subconscious*

Games—When considering what a game in a dream means, begin with how it can be used to make comparisons. Playing a game can compare to "the game of life." It shows your progress or lack of it in advancing your life and personal development. Games are comparable to the rivalry you may have with a friend or sibling. To maneuvering at work to get ahead. To the games you play to attract romantic and sexual partners. To "head games."

Games are associated with outwitting someone and "gaming the system."

They're associated with rules.

They're associated with taking something seriously—life is not a game! But for some people it is.

Games can compare to something you're trying to accomplish: an objective, goal, or ambition. Games have objectives, and life can be full of them.

Games can be competitive. Consider ways you compete with people and with yourself—or against yourself. The same skill and ability used in games can be used in life. Can you connect the game in your dream with your life or personality?

See also: *Arena, Baseball, Basketball, Boxing, Chase, Coach, Football, Gamble, Opponent, Sports, Tennis*

Gang—A gang in a dream can connect with the experience of being "ganged up on." Dreams exaggerate, so the gang depicted might be a clique of co-workers or schoolmates, not the Crips, but the dynamics are the same.

Gang symbolism connects with the idea of inclusion and exclusion, in the gang or out of the gang, accepted or rejected, welcomed in or left out.

The symbolism of gangs can connect with peer pressure and cultural pressure. You feel forced to do something or be something that doesn't jibe with you. For example, a liberated Western woman in a backward country where women are subjugated might feel massive pressure to curb her behavior. She feels "ganged up on" and dream about it as a gang harassing her.

Gangs are known for cruelty, criminality, and inflicting suffering. These associations are ripe for use in dreams. For example, after a rash of robberies in her neighborhood a woman dreams about protecting her home from a gang trying to break in. It reflects her fear and is pure symbolism because she doesn't know who is committing robbery. She just knows that gangs commit those sorts of crimes, and her imagination fills in the rest.

Gangs are associated with being overpowered. In particular, people who have been sexually assaulted—whether by an individual or group—are known to dream about being overpowered by a gang because it connects with the feeling of being overpowered when assaulted. The circumstances of the assault don't have to match the circumstances of the dream. The feelings are the most important connection.

Because gangs and gang members are typically feared, gangs can symbolize fear. See: *Fear*.

The experience of being bullied and harassed stays with a person long after the threat has subsided, so no longer are you dealing with bullies or gangs of people, but instead dealing with voices in your head and feelings of inadequacy and threat to personal safety, symbolized as a gang. See: *Bully*.

A theory of dreaming asserts that its primary purpose is threat assessment and simulation. Basically, dreams are a tool for adapting to your environment and increasing your odds of survival. Dreaming about gangs can be a threat simulation, either because it helps you think through situations in which you could be confronted or threatened by a group of people, or because gangs are a fact of your daily reality.

Gangs can symbolize internal dynamics, especially groupings within your psyche. All parts of the psyche work in pairs, and those pairs can form into larger groups. Many powerful dreams involve groupings with those numbers.

Take note if the gang members come in groups of three or four. Three in dream psychology is an incomplete grouping. It can mean something is missing in you, out of balance. Four, on the other hand, is a complete grouping. It means you have what you need to create balance in your psyche. See: *Group*.

Oftentimes it's not the number arrayed that's most important to the meaning of the dream featuring a gang, it's the general sense of something working for or against you.

A gang can symbolize the control you have of yourself. Most of the mind is unconscious. Anything unconscious is outside your control, and gangs are known for being uncontrollable. See: *Unconscious Mind*.

Anything about your psyche that's outside your control is in the domain of Shadow, and gang members are excellent symbols for Shadow because the mindset is the same: rebellious, angry, injured, misunderstood, unwanted. See: *Shadow*.

When dreams use gangs to symbolize internal dynamics, your interactions with a gang can tell you a lot about rogue parts of yourself. Do you run from them, or confront them? Do you explode with anger, or coolly think your way through the situation? Do you have sympathy for their plight, or do you coldly refuse to understand any perspective but your own? Do you stand up for what's right, or succumb to pressure?

How you react to a gang in your dreams can tell you a lot about how you treat yourself, especially the parts of yourself that refuse to "get with the program." Tightly controlled personalities tend to speak to themselves in absolutes, and if the environment in their head is bad enough, they're almost certain to have parts of the psyche "go rogue" and take form in dreams as shifty, shady, and resistant to any control.

A gang can symbolize the dark side of city life. See: *City, Urban*.

See also: *City, Fight, Group, Locker, Opponent, Men, Numbers, Rape, Shadow, Thief, Unconscious Mind, Urban*

Garage—Garages are used for storage, especially for storing cars and other items when they are not in use. Cars are associated with the movement of a person's life. Therefore, a garage, or a car in a garage, can signify idleness, not going anywhere in life. It can symbolize a period of malaise or doldrums, or lack of direction or motivation.

A garage can symbolize something close to you but separate. For example, your primary life is at home with your family, but a major component of it is your work life. You go to the garage to get into your car and go to work, creating an association between these separate but closely related parts of your life. Since garages can be used as workshops and for working on vehicles, it creates another association that can be used as symbolism.

The idea extends to many areas of life, not just work. If a home represents the life you build for yourself, the garage is attached to that life. If a home represents your body, the garage can symbolize the hip, genital, or mouth areas—they open to receive.

See also: *Barn, Building, Car, Genitals, Home*

Garden—A garden in a dream can symbolize growth in yourself, because a garden is where things grow. It can symbolize personal growth, or an area of life that's growing or flourishing. For an example dream, see: *Backyard*.

A man has a recurring dream that his father is in the dreamer's garden (which is completely imaginary; the dreamer lives in an apartment), planting vegetables and pulling weeds. Over the course of several dreams the plants grow and the work continues. The dreams symbolize the dreamer's inner work to become a better man, and his father is the primary example he has for how a man acts and behaves.

The dream image of a flourishing garden might be a representation of your inner being, or your life in general, especially in connection with the proverbial seeds you plant or are planted in you and the things you nurture, tend, and grow. See: *Harvest*.

Gardens are tended and organized and that idea translates to any area of your life that you tend to and organize.

Planting a garden can symbolize planting the seeds for future growth. Something you are doing now will pay dividends in the future, just as a farmer plants in the spring and reaps in the fall.

Extend the idea and a garden can symbolize a womb, not only because both are places for physical growth, but also because the growth is gradual.

On the other hand, a garden filled with debris or in decay can symbolize lack of growth as a person. An overgrown garden can symbolize disorganization or untidiness, or inner turmoil. It can symbolize an abandoned project or idea.

Gardens are associated with peace and relaxation. If you go to a garden in a dream but don't get any peace or relaxation there, it can be a sign that stress and problems are interfering with your peace of mind. You need to create space where you are not bothered, whether it's a physical or mental space.

See also: *Backyard, Carrot, Earth, Harvest, Tree*

Gas—Gas in dreams is often associated with energy and motivation. Fueling up a car at a gas station, for example, can symbolize eating foods that energize your body, or "pumping" yourself up. Motivation is a sort of mental energy and it can be symbolized as gas. Think along the lines of anything that makes your life go, anything that provides energy or movement in the personal sense.

Fuel is potentially explosive, and can represent an explosive situation or the potential to get burned in the personal sense.

See also: *Car, Fire, Gas Station*

Gas Station—A gas station is where you fuel up a vehicle. A vehicle can symbolize your life, and movement of a vehicle can symbolize its progress, so a gas station is symbolically connected with energy and motivation. For example, a gas station can symbolize the classroom of a teacher who inspires you or a book that motivates you. It can symbolize something that sparks your desire to perform and improve, to create the life you want.

On the other hand, a gas station can represent a potentially explosive situation, in which there is likely to be a reference to fire or explosion, or a threat of it.

Or a dream can relate to a recent incident or experience at a gas station. Dreams can recount incidents from the previous day and dramatize them. For an example dream, see: *Rape*.

A gas station in a dream can be a reminder that you need to fill up your gas tank.

Dreams create symbolism from your personal associations, and a gas station has wider possibilities than the ones listed above. For example, the price of gas might symbolize something related to the price paid to keep your energy level up. Being shocked at the high price of filling up a gas tank could symbolize the high personal price paid to maintain a busy lifestyle.

A gas station that is out of gas, or pumps that don't work, can symbolize the idea of "the well has run dry," meaning you're having difficulty "filling up your tank." Your energy is depleted.

See also: *Car, Gas, Rape*

Gay—Dreaming about being gay is usually symbolism through comparison, not an indication of latent homosexuality, which is a common assumption. However, it is possible for people wondering whether they're gay to dream about it as a way of "testing the water."

It can be a way to see—by standing in someone else's shoes—and to understand homosexuality in a way that personalizes it.

You can dream about being gay as a way of symbolizing the experience of being perceived by someone as gay. For example, someone tells you that a rumor is going around that you are gay. You then wonder what it is about you that's perceived as gay, and a dream reflects your suspicions, brings to light subconscious thoughts.

The subject can pop up in dreams after you've been talking about it. For example, you socialize with a group of people who make derogatory remarks about gay people, and dream about the subject that night or soon after.

Common associations with being gay can create symbolism. While attitudes are changing, there is still a stigma attached to being gay. Gay people can be marginalized and disliked, and those associations can be used in dreams to express the feeling of being stigmatized. It's a comparison that captures the essence of a situation and your feelings about it.

Some of the most visible gay people, such as those seen in gay-pride parades, are viewed as flamboyant, so a gay person in a dream can represent something viewed as flamboyant or eccentric.

The phrase "in the closet" means a gay person hides his or her sexual orientation, and can be symbolized in a dream as hiding in a closet. See: *Closet, Hide.*

Another association with being gay is that homosexuals are not attracted to the opposite sex, and as dream symbolism that can express the feeling of not being attracted to someone of the opposite sex. For instance, someone of the opposite sex shows interest in you, or you show interest in that person, and it is not reciprocated. In which case, being gay in a dream is simply a way of saying "not interested."

It can be a way of saying your romantic and sexual interests tend to focus on the wrong sorts of people who don't return your interest or don't make good romantic or sexual partners. It's not to say that being interested romantically in a gay person is wrong. It's an association that dreams can use to tell a story about choosing the wrong people.

Another consideration is that dreams can bring to light subconscious information and perceptions. If you dream that someone you know is gay, but in waking life the person does not indicate or admit it, it's possible—though not probable—that the dream is putting two and two together. A dream can use a surrogate to represent a person you know, so keep that in mind. The gay character won't look like the person you know, but will somehow remind you of him or her.

Another definition of the word gay is "happy." To dream that you are gay can mean simply that you are cheerful, lighthearted, joyful.

See also: *Anal Sex, Bird Cage, Closet, Cunnilingus, Fellatio, Hide, Joy, Man, Subconscious, Woman*

Gem—One way dreams create symbolism is through the use of related words. A gem can stand for anything that you treasure or value, something precious or special, such as a special relationship or talent. For example, your best friend is a "real gem." You treasure the person. Or your remarkable ability to sing is more precious to you than anything else.

These ideas can connect far and wide, but begin with what you value most. The size of the gem, or expense, can be a measure of the value you place on what it symbolizes. See: *Diamond.*

The bigger the gem, generally, the bigger the association. For example, if you have an extravagant aunt and dream about her wearing a massive diamond, it can be a way of symbolizing your perception of her level of extravagance. She's *really* extravagant.

Gems are associated with special events such as weddings and anniversaries. A gem in a dream can be a reminder of an upcoming event, or why you made a commitment, or your wishes for someone close to you. For example, you watch your child leave to start attending college and make a wish in your heart for a healthy and fulfilling life.

Specific types of gems have associations that dreams can use. For example, diamonds are associated with engagements and hardness. Emeralds are associated with natural beauty and love. Rubies are associated with passion. Jade is associated with money and growth. Color has associations with emotion, so a gem with a distinct color can symbolize an emotion. See: *Colors*.

See also: *Amulet, Colors, Diamond, Emotions, Fiancé, Jewelry, Wedding*

General—The symbolism of a general in a dream is commonly built around associations with leadership and authority. The general is the highest authority. A proverbial general rules the household, takes charge at work, and gives orders. It characterizes leadership style. Usually, the symbolism is created through a comparison.

Situations in life such as a busy work place or home are comparable to battlefields. They are environments that require decision-making, strategic thinking, and leveraging authority. They are also hierarchies, and the general is at or near the top.

Dreams create symbolism by making comparisons. What do you recognize about the general in the dream? Does it characterize you? Someone you know? A situation or circumstance? How is it used to tell the story?

Generals delegate responsibility, and that association is used in a dream about an apocalyptic battle. The dreamer tells the person in charge to fire the general leading the battle. It connects with the dreamer's inability to delegate responsibility at work. Instead, she takes everything onto herself and it makes her job more difficult. See: *Fight*.

A general can symbolize someone in a position of authority: a boss, coach, king, parent, principal.

Imperiousness and arrogance are associated with generals. Dreaming about a general can be a satirical depiction of a person's character, personality, or reputation. A big clue to the meaning of the symbolism can be found in how the general in a dream

acts or is portrayed. For example, dreaming about Napoleon sitting behind your supervisor's desk issuing orders can be a satirical depiction of the person.

It can symbolize the style of your ego and how you talk to and motivate yourself and others. See: *Ego*.

Generals are associated with conquest, and from there a dream can branch out far and wide. What are you trying to conquer in the figurative sense? How far does your authority extend? What do you rule in your life?

A general is someone who can't be told no without running the risk of major consequences.

As you analyze a dream-character such as a general, keep in mind, odds are it symbolizes something about you.

See also: *Boss, Captain, Coach, Ego, Famous, Father, Fight, King, Mother, Principal, War*

Genitals—Genitals are "private parts," and in dreams they can symbolize something related to privacy. This use of the symbolism is often associated with exposing or covering the genitals. It can mean there is something about yourself you don't want exposed, or you feel embarrassed because it was, or could be, revealed.

Genitals are generally hidden beneath clothing, so they can symbolize something you want to hide or to remain hidden. For example, you have a romantic interest in someone other than your spouse and want to keep it a secret. Or you have taken an interest in a subject that could open you to ridicule. See: *Hide*.

Exposed genitals can symbolize "letting it all hang out." Perhaps you or someone you know is revealing too much.

Dreaming about exploration of, or fascination with, genitals can reflect interest in the subject. This is especially true of children and people with limited or no sexual exposure. It's a natural curiosity.

The easy availability of pornography and the saturation of sexual imagery in today's culture has created an epidemic of addiction to sex and sexuality, and it shows in dreams featuring absurdity and obsession with genitals.

However, keep in mind that dreams cross-reference and compare, so a dream about obsession with genitals might symbolize another obsession; for example, an obsession with the sex lives of celebrities, or with exposing people's personal lives.

Genitals can symbolize anything taboo or forbidden, such as a subject that isn't talked about, or a "black sheep" family member who isn't mentioned.

See also: *Anal Sex, Breast, Castrate, Cunnilingus, Fellatio, Masturbate, Penis, Sex, Underwear, Vagina*

Ghost—A ghost in a dream can be a reference to the past, because ghosts are perceived as relics from the past. Like memories and feelings, ghosts can linger. They won't go away until dealt with.

Ghosts haunt, and people can be haunted, for example, by guilt and regret. Someone who is "seeing ghosts" is haunted by the past, usually associated with misdeeds and guilty conscience. See: *Guilt.*

Ghosts can symbolize fear, since they are commonly feared. Usually the symbolism is tied to associations specific to ghosts, such as fear of death or fear of the past catching up with you. But ghosts can symbolize any fear, or paranoia—a strong possibility considering the amorphous nature of ghosts and paranoia. However, a friendly ghost is not likely to symbolize fear. You can tell by how you feel about or react to the ghost. See: *Fear.*

A ghost in a dream can refer to someone who isn't around anymore. For example, after the death of a loved one, especially one you lived with, you can dream about a ghost to symbolize the feeling that the person is still around. You feel his or her presence. The same idea applies to someone who left, such as after a breakup or divorce.

Ghosts are associated with death, and in dreams they can refer to someone who has passed away, or to a brush with death. See: *Death.*

A ghost can refer to being overlooked or ignored. If you "feel like a ghost," it means nobody is giving you attention or recognition.

As with all dream symbolism, the meaning is found in the context. For example, a ghost in a place where you used to live can symbolize something from your past. A ghost haunting the bedroom of a sibling who ran away from home and hasn't been heard from in a long time can symbolize the sibling or the situation. The person is thought about or remembered, but is absent physically. A sad ghost can connect with the feeling of being ignored or overlooked, or with something from the past that makes you sad.

A ghost can symbolize the influence of someone who is not physically present. For example, long after leaving home you can still feel the presence of a parent or other influential figure in your life. In which case, the dream is likely to include references to that person and actions such as doors opening and closing on their own.

Ghosts are used in the sense of "ghost of your former self." It means loss of energy, prestige, status, or influence.

Ghosts are known as "lost souls," and that can symbolize someone who has no direction in life or no close relations.

See also: *Bury, Chase, Coffin, Death, Fear, Graveyard, Guilt, Spirit*

GI—See: *Army*

Giant—The size of something in a dream can symbolize its importance, prominence, amount. A giant is oversized, so in a dream something like a giant spider can symbolize oversized fear or worry. A giant moon can symbolize a female figure who plays an oversized role in your life, such as a domineering mother figure or girlfriend. It can symbolize a giant attraction to a female or a heavy infatuation. See: *Moon.*

Giant is a modifier of other symbolism. A problem or challenge is portrayed as a giant wave because it's really big. It's no ordinary problem. A huge snake can symbolize a huge danger. A giant clock or watch can mean time is especially important.

A giant can be a sign of great admiration, respect, or status. The idea is captured in the phrase "a giant among men." For example, a graduate student dreams about going up in an elevator with a professor from her program who is greatly respected. The professor in the dream is ten feet tall, and going up with him symbolizes the dreamer's perception that her fortunes are rising because of her association with that professor.

Think of tall height as a metaphor for "look up to." The same symbolism can be created by putting a person or object in a raised or upper position. Dreams can be very creative with how they visualize these ideas. For example, a tall person can symbolize "stand up to." It can symbolize "stand out in a crowd." It can mean "tall tale." And the taller the person, the taller the tale.

See also: *Above, Bear, Emaciated, Fat, Limousine, Little, Mansion, Moon, Skyscraper, Whale*

Giraffe—The long neck of a giraffe makes it an excellent choice to use in a metaphor about sticking your neck out.

It can symbolize something related to the neck that's exaggerated, such as a tendency to be verbose—someone who talks on and on.

A giraffe can symbolize a long distance between the head and heart. Your thoughts and feelings are far apart on a matter, or in general.

See also: *Animals, Neck*

Girl—The most difficult and revealing part of interpreting a dream-character as general as a girl is figuring out if it represents something about you, about someone you know, or about an event, situation, or circumstance. Narrowing it down provides you with the approach to interpreting the character's role in the story and what it says about you and your life.

Characters that represent something about you tend to register more strongly in your feelings and emotions. The kinship and familiarity you feel is generally a few degrees higher than what you feel for other types of characters.

Dreams promote internal bonding between parts of yourself, so the feeling of being drawn to or repulsed by a dream-character can reflect the fact that you see something about yourself in them. A part of yourself may be portrayed generically as a girl, instead of more specifically, because you're still

getting to know that part of yourself. The picture is vague or incomplete. The key piece of information is that the dream-character is entirely a projection of your inner world. You see yourself in them, even if they seem completely opposite of you.

Some dream-characters are based on individuals or groups of people you know. The girl-character is a surrogate for an individual, someone you know, giving you distance to observe by disguising the appearance. Often, such a dream is based on a recent event or interaction, or what's been on your mind, such as when you miss someone. Your initial focus for interpreting this type of dream is on the events of your life and personal interactions.

A girl-character can provoke strong feelings and emotions in you because you subconsciously recognize who the character symbolizes, and really it's the person you feel strongly about. For an example, see: *Ex.*

Dreams can present a character in a general form such as a girl because you don't know them personally. Your "off the top of the head" thoughts and associations can trigger recognition of who such a character symbolizes. For example, you associate "cheerful" with a girl-character and connect that with someone you know who is cheerful or a cheerleader. Or the dream-character can sum up your impressions of all cheerleaders. A single character can represent a group, such as one member of a family symbolizing the entire clan.

If the character isn't from your inner world or a portrayal of someone you know, you look for ways it can be symbolism to tell a story about an event, situation, or circumstance. For example, at work you're told that company policy dictates that all employees give the impression of cheerfulness when interacting with the public. You dream about it as a girl in a cheerleader outfit.

A girl can symbolize your inner child or a feminine-based aspect of yourself. An inner-child character may have a strong pull on you because subconsciously you recognize yourself in the character. See: *Child.*

In simplest terms, a young girl is a child, and a child is a creation, so a girl in a dream can symbolize something you create, especially if the character is presented as your daughter. For example, a man dreams that he's walking through a forest with two girls who are supposed to be his daughters (he doesn't actually have any children). One of the girls runs away to go back home, and he runs after her. It's a way of saying one of two movie projects he's working on is getting away from him, depicted as the daughter who runs home. Home in this case means "back to the drawing board." The girls are symbolized as his children because they're his creations, and they're young because the projects they symbolize are in early stages of development.

Women who have few happy memories from childhood can dream about unhappy or lost young girls as symbols for something unfulfilled in themselves. This theme is found often in the dreams of women forced to grow up too quickly. While their friends have fun, they clean house, do homework, and take care of siblings. As adults, they're unfulfilled and searching for something missed when they were young.

On the other hand, dreaming about a happy girl can symbolize that the inner child is happy.

The same idea applies to people you know when you see the girl in the woman, or in the man, and it shows in your dreams as a character, often depicted as a child or sibling of the person. Something about the girl in the dream will remind you of the person you know, even if just in how you feel about the character and respond to her.

A girl-character can symbolize a young female you know. They don't have to look alike. In fact, sometimes it's better for a dream to use a surrogate-character to give distance to observe something about someone personally close to you.

A girl-character can symbolize characteristics generally associated with girls: playful, pouty, pushy, sensitive, caring, affectionate, talkative, manipulative. The character can symbolize someone you know with girl-like characteristics, whether the person is young or old, male or female.

Males can dream about a girl-character in connection with seeing the girl within a woman they know. It can be an observation, or an attempt to

figure out what makes them tick. Girl-characters may also appear in the dreams of men who feel pressured to live up to gender expectations, or who dislike male tendencies. They're expected to be tough and detached when really they want to be sensitive and affectionate.

A man can dream about a girl as a character from his inner world when he's in the early stages of developing traditionally feminine traits in himself. When it's something he wants, he tends to dream about interacting positively with a young girl. On the other hand, if he denies those aspects of himself, he can dream about harming or neglecting young girls. This is especially likely to be the case if the dreams recur.

If you have a daughter, a girl in a dream can be a surrogate-character for her. The girl-character can symbolize the child within your daughter. This theme is common for parents (and siblings) who see the adult personality emerging and view it as a layer over the child within the person they know. Sometimes these dreams are related to the adjustments a parent needs to make to allow the child's adult personality to emerge.

Females who dream about a girl can be seeing a contrast between the way they are now and the way they were then.

Dreams can create symbolism from figures of speech, and one phrase that comes to mind is "treated like a little girl." It means you are treated as if you don't have the maturity to take care of yourself or handle adult subjects or responsibilities.

Be sure to read the entries for *Boy* and *Daughter*. And consider that girl can be short for "girlfriend."

See also: *Boy, Boyfriend, Child, Daughter, Doll, Dress, Girlfriend, Sister, Toys*

Girlfriend—Girlfriends and ex-girlfriends are common characters in the dreams of their mates and ex-mates. Anything that affects a person deeply will be the subject of dreams, and love and mating are among the most affecting.

As with other dream-characters, the place to begin the interpretation process is with discerning whether the character symbolizes something about you, about a person you know, or about an event, situation or circumstance.

Most dream-characters are projections of your inner life, so it's likely that your girlfriend is in a dream to show you what's happening in your thoughts and feelings.

Most dreams can be classified in two general categories: external or internal. If they are about your external life, your girlfriend in your dream represents herself—though remember that the character's behaviors and characteristics are symbolic. So for example, if you dream about your girlfriend chopping your head off as you sleep, you don't need to hide the knives. It's symbolism, perhaps for criticism she directed at you, or an argument.

Internal and external tend to intermix, but it can help you understand a dream to focus more on your thoughts, feelings, and perceptions (inner life), or on recent events or ongoing situations or circumstances (outer life). Carl Jung refers to this differentiation as subjective and objective dreams. Most dreams are subjective at least to some extent, but some are objective looks at your life and the people in it.

This example comes from the dream life of a young man who lives with his girlfriend. They're both college graduates beginning their careers and working at the bottom of the ladder. He dreams that his girlfriend is at work in a coffee shop, when in reality she works as a freelance writer. Working in a coffee shop is obviously symbolism. In his dream, he visits her at work and discovers that she's having an affair with a co-corker.

The dream raises his suspicions that his girlfriend really is having an affair, but it's symbolism for his dedication to his career and concern that while he's so busy away at work, his relationship with her is suffering. His career is a rival for time and attention he could give to his girlfriend if he had it. The symbolism of the coffee shop is based on the perception that it's an entry-level job. The girlfriend-character is a projection of the dreamer's inner life. It only looks like her.

A common source of confusion and difficulty for people new to dream interpretation is seeing yourself in your dream-characters, especially when characters depict someone you know. You dream about your girlfriend and automatically assume the dream is about her when really it's about you, as most dreams are. Everything the girlfriend-character says and does is a projection of your thoughts and feelings.

You can dream about your girlfriend when assessing the prospects of the relationship. Are you compatible? Do you have a future together? Is she "the one"? In general, if your dreams with your girlfriend are pleasant and you get along well, then you can take that as a good sign. Arguing and fighting, on the other hand, is a strong indicator something isn't right. This is especially true of recurring dreams.

Inability to reach your girlfriend on the phone in a dream can symbolize communication issues. You aren't explaining yourself well enough, or you want her to understand or know something and she doesn't "get it." See: *Phone*.

In dreams about her having your baby, you might be assessing whether she could be a mother for your children or at least the right person to take things to the next level. It can mean you are expectant or excited about something unrelated to having a baby, since pregnant women are said to be "expecting." Perhaps you're seeing something new about the relationship coming to life—or something coming to life about yourself inspired by the relationship. For example, maybe her influence is making you more mature or caring.

Dreaming about her wearing your clothes can be a way of saying that she wraps herself in an identity based on being your girlfriend.

Dreams can really play with the idea of "girlfriend" when a character is presented to you as a girlfriend but you don't have one. It can be a way of saying that something or someone in your life is like a girlfriend. This theme tends to pop up in dreams of people who have a very close female friend and the relationship has the potential to be romantic, or you desire to take that next step with someone you've been dating.

It is also possible that a girlfriend-character represents something in your life related to companionship, stability, inspiration, devotion, commitment, romance, or other girlfriend associations. For example, people who are highly devoted to their work are said to be "married to the job." Marriage is a commitment, and the idea of commitment extends to other committed or close relationships, such as girlfriends and boyfriends.

A job, hobby, or social cause can be portrayed in dreams as a girlfriend or boyfriend.

See also: *Affair, Boyfriend, Cheat, Ex, Girl, Love, Marriage, Phone, Pregnant, Wife, Woman*

Gloves—See: *Clothing, Fingerprint, Hands*

Goat—In biblical times the goat carried the burden for sins, and today the idea is used to describe someone who takes the blame.

Goats are known for stubbornness, a common association used by dreams to create symbolism. "Get your goat" means to annoy to the point of anger. And an angry goat won't relent.

Goats are messy. They're tough. They're independent. Does that describe you or someone you know, or characterize a situation?

These are the most common associations, and of course the important ones are the first that come off the top of your head as you think about the goat in your dream.

See also: *Animals, Guilt*

God—If you dream about God, begin interpreting it as you would any other symbol. Make associations. What does God mean to you? The final authority. The Creator. The ultimate judge.

Now ask yourself, who is the final authority in your life—a parent, a boss, a teacher, a priest? Or is God related to creativity, either in the artistic sense, the general sense, or the procreative sense? Are you feeling judged, or is your conscience bothering you?

Those associations only scratch the surface of the possibilities for symbolism. God is also commonly associated with faith, disasters, thankfulness, illness, crisis, love, goodness, good vs. evil, mystery, and power.

A "God" character can be part of your dreams when you are in a pinch and need help, or in a situation that requires faith. Or you are confronted by someone or something that seems "evil," or witnessing suffering, or seriously ill, or feeling thankful, shocked, appreciated, or loved.

The possibilities are endless because God means so many things to so many people.

God as "Father" is a common idea with a set of associations used widely as symbolism. It's the embodiment of the masculine principle, known as yang in Eastern thought, the balance to the feminine principle, yin. It's a duality found in all things, with yang representing traditionally masculine traits. The entry for *Penis* goes into detail about yang.

The sun is a common representation for God the Father. See: *Father.*

Some dreams present God as a distinct intelligence interested in you, that gives you wisdom, knowledge, and insight. That tests you and gives you tools to grow and develop. Whether that God in a dream is the creator of the universe or a projection of something in the psyche, or something else, doesn't matter as much as the subjective experience.

Deep in the psyche is a universal idea—or blueprint—of God that has nothing do with beliefs or theology. Doesn't matter if you are an atheist or the pope, that idea is imprinted in you, too. Its activation in the psyche is often accompanied by dreams and visions featuring a powerful, disembodied voice, a glorious light shining down from above, talking fish and animals, and imagery such as cathedrals, temples, and mandalas.

Archetypes are structures located in the unconscious mind, and the God archetype can make you feel like God is right there with you. See: *Archetypes.*

The unconscious mind is like the ocean, and in comparison your conscious mind is like an island. Whether your island is small or large, or your consciousness is expansive or limited, it still seems tiny when compared to the vastness of the ocean. That comparison can be presented in dreams as the relationship between God and the individual.

People with a widely expanded consciousness can dream about themselves in godly or holy terms. It's not grandiosity but simply a way of symbolizing the fact that they have a strong union with the unconscious mind. See: *Unconscious Mind.*

Religions and spiritual traditions around the world tell stories about direct contact with God in dreams. These accounts are not presented as symbolism or archetypes or the unconscious mind, but as actual communication with higher beings. Every morning thousands or even millions of people wake up believing that God talked to them directly in their sleep, or sent a messenger to talk to them. Objectively, nothing can be verified, but subjectively it is safe to say that the people who have these dreams truly believe them to be communication with God. The experience can be life-changing.

If you have such a dream, pay attention! Take the message to heart. Don't allow belief or disbelief to interfere. Beliefs don't matter. Only the subjective experience and how you process it matters. It's your dream. Interpret it how you want. Just remember, a God that forces or coerces is likely to originate in the Shadow side of the psyche.

In Eastern cultures, a common type of dream involves being blessed by a god or goddess. The equivalent in Western culture is a dream about meeting a celebrity and bonding with that person or receiving recognition or approval from him or her. Gods and goddesses are the "rock stars" of certain Eastern cultures, and in dreams they can serve the same function of bestowing approval. It is a way for the unconscious mind to say, "Good job. You are on the right track."

God in a dream might symbolize holding someone in very high regard, to the point of idolization. It can be a sign of epic grandiosity or delusion.

A godlike character can symbolize someone who is a final or highest authority. Yes, it's exaggerated, but that's how dreams create symbolism.

On a final note, keep in mind that your dream is a story and the characters are chosen to help tell it. People get confused when God appears in their dreams because they automatically connect the appearance with God the Creator when actually it's a character used to tell the story.

See also: *Afterlife, Altar, Angel, Archetypes, Buddha, Church, Circle, Collective Unconscious, Death, Demon, Devil, Father, Goddess, Guide, Heaven, Hell, Jesus, Mohammed, Pastor, Penis, Shadow, Soul, Spirit, Sun, Temple, Unconscious Mind*

Goddess—A goddess is the feminine side of the image of god. God is usually referred to as a "he," especially in patriarchal societies, but God has a feminine face, too. The feminine face of God is associated with mystique, compassion, fertility, nature, and beauty. In dreams, a goddess-character can help you connect with those qualities and high ideals in yourself.

Read the entry for *God* because most of it applies to this entry.

A goddess can symbolize a female in your life whom you hold in very high regard, or plays a godlike role. For example, children can think of their mother as a goddess because she gives them life. See: *Mother.*

A goddess can symbolize femininity and its power or hold on your mind.

A goddess can have the same symbolism as God, and can be represented by the moon. See: *Moon.*

The entry for *Vagina* goes into detail about the yin, the feminine principle, which can be symbolized as a goddess.

See also: *Circle, God, Moon, Mother, Vagina*

Gold—Dreaming about finding gold can relate to something valuable or important you find in yourself, such as in your personality or character. It's the same idea expressed in the phrase "struck gold." Gold coins, in particular, are connected with "inner gold" because of the symbolism of their circular shape combined with the symbolism of gold. See: *Circle.*

Gold can represent success and wealth. It's connected with the accumulation of material resources.

In general, gold is perceived as precious, so in dreams it can symbolize something or someone precious to you. Think of the phrase, "worth their weight in gold." See: *Gem.*

The symbolism of gold can connect with ideas about value. See: *Diamond, Money.*

Finding a gold object can be a sign of conception or pregnancy. Gold symbolizes the preciousness of that new life being brought into the world.

Golden bells can symbolize hearing good news.

A golden calf is a biblical image representing idolatry. As a dream symbol, it can mean you place too much emphasis on material possessions and values.

See also: *Amulet, Circle, Diamond, Gem, Jewelry, Money, Pregnant.*

Goose—A goose in a dream can symbolize the idea behind the phrase "silly as a goose." A gosling is a baby goose, sometimes associated with actor Ryan Gosling.

See also: *Animals*

Gorilla—Gorillas are associated with wild and territorial behavior. They can symbolize the "animal mind," unfettered sexuality, or something wild, physically powerful, and unpredictable.

For example, a young man dreams that a gorilla is in his bedroom and he tells his roommate to lock it up. Then, fearing the gorilla, he acts sweetly toward it, and it acts sweetly toward him. It symbolizes an ongoing situation with an unpredictable and sometimes unhinged roommate. The roommate frequently enters the dreamer's bedroom without permission. The dream makes the connection with the roommate when the dreamer tells him to lock up the gorilla, then acts nicely toward it. It symbolizes the dreamer's strategy to act nicely toward the roommate and hide his true feelings about the intrusions—the guy is too unpredictable and immensely strong.

Gorillas and apes are associated with human evolution and can be used as symbolism to show something in the early stages of development.

These creatures can be shorthand to mean "primitive."

If someone acts like an ape or gorilla, it means the person displays primitive behaviors or impulses. For example, a young man dreams that his uncle dresses up in a gorilla costume and jumps around on the roof of his grandma's house. It symbolizes the uncle's behavior during holidays at grandma's house when he gets drunk and acts like a gorilla.

Grandfather—The symbolism of a grandfather in a dream can connect with family lineage, or something that runs in the family such as habits, patterns, or traits. It's a way of tracing them to the source and recognizing them in you.

Dreams create symbolism by making comparisons, so a dream involving your grandfather might not have anything directly to do with him. Instead, he's a symbol for something entirely to do with you.

Your grandfather can symbolize what you see about yourself in him. Think about the example he provides and what you learned from him. In many dreams featuring grandparents, they serve as reminders of what they teach you, the example they provide, the love they give, their expectations of you, and the feelings and thoughts they spark in you.

Grandfathers can symbolize wisdom, tradition, protection, and other characteristics of mature masculinity. As dream-characters, grandfathers can embody the image of the "wise old man" or archetypal elder. Keep in mind, these are general associations and their use in your dreams is independent of what you associate with your grandfathers, who can symbolize the archetypal grandfather regardless of whether they live up to the expectation.

Grandfathers are known for giving advice, and that association can be used in dreams. Think of it as the casting department in your dreaming mind deciding who is the best actor to deliver news, information, knowledge, or advice. Often it's a reminder of what you already know, not necessarily advice that your grandfather gave you. In which case, a dream uses the image of someone you trust—your grandfather—as a vehicle to convey the message.

This sort of dream, in which a character like a trusted grandpa appears to deliver advice, can occur when you are uncertain, at a crossroads, or on the verge of making a bad decision.

So far, this entry has dealt with the positive image of a grandfather, but some grandfathers are rotten and ornery. Some are bad examples. Some are bored, confused, bitter, or regretful. Some cause strife and conflict in the family, and in dreams they can symbolize any of these negative associations.

Elderly or sick grandfathers can act as reminders of your mortality, or symbolize fear of death, infirmity, or illness. You only have so much time to do what you want to with your life. Someday, if you live that long, you will be elderly, and the productive years of your life will be mostly behind you. The clock is ticking. See: *Elderly*.

A sick grandfather portrayed in a dream can be a way of describing the status of the relationship. It has been neglected, or you have been out of touch. Perhaps you worry about how much time you have left with your grandfather.

A grandfather in a dream can symbolize a grandfatherly figure in your life.

The symbolism of a grandfather-character can be the same as father symbolism. Or the character can be used as a surrogate for your father. Your grandfather is an obvious choice for a dream to refer indirectly to your father (or great-grandfather). See: *Father*.

If your grandfather has passed away and you dream about him, see: *Deceased Loved One*.

See also: *Ancestor, Archetypes, Deceased Loved One, Elderly, Family, Father, Grandmother, Guide*

Grandmother—A grandmother in a dream can have the same symbolism as a grandfather in the sense of being an elder figure and important person in your life, someone from whom you learn directly or through example, so read that entry. In much of it, you can substitute the word "grandmother" for "grandfather" and not miss a beat. See: *Grandfather*.

Grandmothers are typically figures representing mature femininity, such as maternal wisdom, protectiveness, and care. However, your experience with your grandmothers and grandmotherly figures might not jibe with the archetypal image of them.

The symbolism of a grandmother can be based on the universal image of a grandmother, or on your personal experience and the specific traits and characteristics of your grandmother. What do you see of her in you? How does she influence you and your family? Have you had recent interaction with her, or has she been on your mind?

A grandmother can act as a surrogate-character for your mother (or great-grandmother). She's a natural choice for the role.

See also: *Ancestor, Deceased Loved One, Elderly, Family, Grandfather, Guide, Mother*

Grasp—See: *Fingers, Hand*

Graveyard—Graveyards are associated with things that come to an end. For example, a relationship ends, or you sense the end coming, and dream about a graveyard. Or a phase of life comes to an end. You are maturing, growing, moving on. Perhaps something about yourself is changing and some part of yourself is passing on, a normal part of maturation. Death in this sense is figurative, an exaggeration that fits.

While this sort of dream can be distressing, it is essentially positive if you are handling the changes well or are willing to make the effort. If you aren't handling them well, then take a dream like this as a suggestion to let go and move on.

Graveyards are associated with death, and in dreams death can be referred to in the literal sense. Perhaps something happened recently that brought the thought of death to mind, such as the passing of someone you know or a news report about death that affected you.

A more literal interpretation of a graveyard involves fear of death or recognizing it as inevitable. Cemetery dreams are prevalent in older or very ill people for whom death is a very real possibility. See: *Death*.

Graveyards can connect with concerns about your health, and with taking risks that put you in danger. There is nothing like the image of going to the grave or seeing your name on a headstone to snap you out of it! See: *Illness*.

Graveyards are where people are buried, and dreams can use that association to create symbolism for other things that are buried, such as feelings and memories. See: *Bury*.

A young woman dreams she's at a graveyard and discovers that her mom is buried there. She then frantically digs her up and tries to revive her, symbolizing the dreamer's attempts to revive the relationship.

Dreaming about a graveyard can symbolize things from the past that are gone now, such as hopes you had, relationships that are over, or aspects of yourself that have receded. Think of situations for which the terms "dead and buried" or "lay to rest" are used. The idea can be used expansively. For example, your favorite television show comes to an end and you feel a real sense of loss.

Cemeteries are associated with peace. When you are dead, you have nothing to worry about. There is hardly a quieter or more peaceful place than a cemetery. It is easy to confuse the longing one feels in a dream featuring a cemetery with a death wish when really it is a "rest wish."

A cemetery can symbolize remembrance of a loved one, in which case the dream is likely to include some references to that person.

Parts of yourself can recede back into the unconscious mind but are never fully gone. They are, in a sense, buried by time. A cemetery can symbolize remembering or honoring what got you to this point in your life. For example, the teenager in you gives way for the adult to emerge, or self-doubt gives way to confidence, or a previous job leads to advancement to a new one.

A dream about living in a cemetery or near one, or sleeping on top of a grave, can symbolize dwelling on the past, or living in the past. It implies the need to let go and live in the present.

See also: *Bury, Coffin, Death, Funeral, Ghost*

Green—Green is most commonly associated with nature and money, but it's an enigmatic color that includes a little bit of everything.

"Growth" is the one word that best sums up the emotional and personal symbolism of the color. Green things grow. They establish roots in a growth medium such as soil and shoot upward.

That association is ripe for use to compare with anything that grows within you, that establishes roots in your being and takes off.

The analogy extends to establishing yourself in the physical world, to putting down personal roots, to growing as a person in many different ways, to your social status, education, career, achievements, security, self-esteem—all things that establish you in the world.

Green is associated with money, but what does money do for you? It gives you the means to "put down roots," to create security, to have experiences, to promote growth, to support a family, to surround yourself with what you want. Green can symbolize any of these things.

See also: *Colors, Countryside, Earth, Emerald, Forest, Mother, Tree, Wilderness*

Grim Reaper—A Grim Reaper character can appear in dreams to give a stern warning or symbolize something related to death, such as fear of it or flirting with it.

As with all dream symbolism, the meaning depends on the context and how you react. If the sight of the Grim Reaper strikes fear into you, then the symbolism is more likely to be related to a fear related to death, mortality, or making a big mistake. But also consider the implications if you aren't afraid of Grimmy.

For example, a man dreams he's in a store and takes out the trash. On his way back he sees the Grim Reaper and, unafraid, strikes up a conversation. Grimmy loses the hood and scythe and now appears as a normal man. The dreamer starts making smart-ass remarks, and Grimmy says, "Why do you mock me?" The question makes the dreamer uncomfortable, so he tries to go back into the store, but Grimmy grabs his arm and asks more forcefully, "Why do you mock me?" The dreamer doesn't have an answer. The Reaper laughs sardonically and says, "Go grab some beer so I can cook with it!"

The clues that reveal the meaning of this dream are in plain sight. A store is connected with making choices. Taking out the trash is connected with throwing something away—in this case, the dreamer's life. The night before the dream, he had a few drinks at a bar and drove home. He didn't feel too buzzed, but in the back of his mind he knew he was taking a risk. Basically, he mocked death, and that explains his action of mocking the Grim Reaper. The Reaper's comment about getting more beer so he can cook with it symbolizes the dreamer's perception about his flippant attitude toward the dangers of drinking and driving. It's a very dramatic way of making the point, so next time he's in the same situation he'll take a cab or ask for a ride.

Death can mean the end of a relationship or time of life, or loss of something important, so the Grim Reaper can embody it. To be symbolized as Grimmy, the end or loss is probably pretty dramatic.

The Grim Reaper can symbolize a rejected, repressed, or estranged part of yourself, which take on strange, distorted, and frightening form in dreams. See: *Stranger*.

Also consider the "grim" part. In the image of the Grim Reaper you could be seeing a pessimistic, gloomy, or morbid side of yourself.

See also: *Creature, Death, Ghost, Graveyard, Monster*

Grocery Store—A grocery store is a place commonly associated with making decisions about what to consume, and in dreams consumption means what you take into yourself: media, information, opinions, knowledge, and so on. The symbolism is basically the same as shopping in any store, but adds the modifier of specifically shopping for food and other grocery-store items. See: *Eat, Food*.

It's possible that the choices are related to nutrition and food, but dreams like to make analogies, so think in general terms about the decisions you make and choices you have. What are your options? The analogy of shopping in a grocery can apply to something as simple as which movie to watch, or as complex and important as which school to attend, subject to study, job to take, or mate to choose. And it doesn't mean that choice is upon you—though it can be—but instead just that it's been on your mind or could soon be coming up. See: *Shop*.

See also: *Eat, Food, Mall, Menu, Shop*

Groom—A groom in a dream can symbolize thoughts or feelings related to marriage or the long-term prospects of a relationship, especially when paired with symbolism related to a wedding. It's a way for a dream to ask, "What if?"

What if you'd married your high school sweetheart?

What if the man you're dating pops the question?

What if you never find the right person to marry?

In this sense, your dreams create simulations to help you think through important questions and decisions.

Marriage is a commitment, so in dreams, references to a groom can relate to any sort of commitment or devotion, such as commitment to a cause, pursuit, job, or your life. The groom represents something you "marry" in the metaphorical sense. See: *Marriage*.

To read more about the ways dreams can expand these ideas, see: *Bride*. Bride and groom characters are, in many ways, interchangeable, both being symbolism to help tell a story.

A groom in a dream can symbolize masculine aspects of the personality. It can mean that a union is happening, or could happen, in the psyche with masculine aspects. For a female, dreaming about marrying a groom can symbolize union with male aspects of herself. See: *Penis.*

Or it can symbolize a wish to be married, or the weighing of her prospects. Never presume.

For a male, dreaming about being a groom, or being in a wedding party with a groom, can symbolize taking on a new role in life. He is ready to accept responsibility as a husband and possibly as a father, or just accept the responsibilities of being an adult. The dream can indicate a wish to be married or plans related to it. For example, perhaps first he needs to get his career started or improve his dating skills.

Another possibility is that a groom in a dream can symbolize union with the soul or the unconscious mind. See: *Animus, Wedding.*

In Jungian psychology, being a groom in a dream can symbolize a man's preparation to unite with his anima, his feminine sub-personality and representative of his unconscious mind. Men usually learn first how to be masculine, then go through a process—often a long one—of learning how to unite their masculinity with traditionally feminine traits (detailed in the entry for *Vagina*). However, significant numbers of men do the process in reverse. See: *Anima.*

This union of the ego with the unconscious is called the "marriage of the soul," and in Jungian terms it is considered the pinnacle of personal development. Religious and alchemical literature is full of references to grooms and brides as symbols of commitment and union between aspects of oneself, or between the individual and God. For example, Christ is spoken of in the Bible as the "bridegroom" and his followers as the "bride."

A groom can represent the verb "to groom," meaning to prepare, such as preparing to take a leadership position. It can mean groom your appearance.

See also: *Anima, Animus, Bride, Fiancé, Husband, Marriage, Penis, Unconscious Mind, Wedding, Wife*

Group—Family, social, and work lives involve groups of people, so it is natural for groups of char-

acters in dreams to symbolize something related to those areas of life, such as relationships with family, fitting into society, and correct behavior.

How you behave and think in a group can contrast with how you behave and think when alone. Fitting into groups, or not fitting in, raises issues related to inclusion, exclusion, and self-image, which in turn open many avenues for dreams to explore. Socialization, a huge part of life, will be a subject of many dreams throughout your lifetime.

A group can symbolize a subject related to the group. For example, a group of friends can symbolize the subject of friendship. A group of your cousins can symbolize your relationship with your cousins in general, not with specific ones. A group of co-workers can symbolize your general relationship with them. For example, a dream about hiding from your co-workers can symbolize hiding your personal life from them. See: *Family, Friends.*

Groups can be used in dreams anytime you're thinking about how people will react to something you have done or created. For example, dreaming about a group of people who are hostile toward you can symbolize cutting against the grain or falling outside expected social behavior, such as when a liberal works among conservatives, or a fan of a particular sports team finds him- or herself in "enemy territory."

On the other hand, being welcomed by a group of people in a dream can symbolize good social behavior, and beliefs and opinions that conform to a group or group thinking.

Groups of animals can symbolize groups of people and your perceptions of them. For example, a group of lions can symbolize the "in crowd," or a pack of power-hungry or prideful people. Then again, animals quite often represent instinctual qualities in yourself and groupings of related parts of your psyche.

A group of sheep can symbolize people who are easily led (or misled).

A group of wolves can symbolize family or friends, because wolves are very social animals with strong familial bonds. Or they can symbolize a group of ruthless or predatory people, similar to the symbolism of a group of sharks.

A group of fish can symbolize people moving in the same direction with each other, or in a coordinated fashion. This analogy works particularly well with students and teachers in dreams because groups of fish are referred to as "schools." See: *Fish*.

Groups of characters in dreams can symbolize interrelated personal characteristics and personality traits that work in tandem or in support of each other. For example, as a parent you might draw on your organizational skills, inner authority, and compassion. For your job you might draw on your social skills, rationality, and motivation. These are simplistic examples. In reality, many more aspects of yourself come into play as a parent or employee. The point is to make you aware that groups in your dreams can represent internal dynamics. See: *Psyche*.

On the other hand, characters at odds with each other can symbolize working against yourself and disorganization inside yourself.

Groups of all males or all females can symbolize your thoughts, feelings, and perceptions about men in general or women in general. See: *Men, Women*.

Similarly, a group of people of the same profession can symbolize your impressions of the profession, the people in it, or a related subject. For example, a group of computer technicians could symbolize the subject of computers.

Groupings of four can symbolize what Carl Jung called the "primary mental functions," also called cognitive processes. Each character represents one of the functions. A grouping of three characters implies that something in yourself is incomplete. A grouping of four implies completeness in the sense that all four functions are in a balanced configuration in the psyche, especially likely in dreams that feature squares. See: *Gang, Mental Functions, Square*.

Three is an incomplete psychological grouping because functions of the psyche come in pairs. A grouping of three implies that the other half of a pair is missing—though not technically "missing," just underdeveloped, underutilized, or repressed. Jung said that one of the four functions is domi-

nant, or *primary*, meaning it is the main function used in the psyche. Its counterpart function is "inferior," meaning sub-dominant.

For example, some people are predominantly intuitive, some factual, some rational, and some "feeling." Feeling is not synonymous with emotion. Instead, it means judgment based on value, as opposed to the thinking function's judgment based on utility. Everyone has a dominant function, though the degree of dominance is lesser or greater depending on the person. People who are especially intuitive can devalue their factual function, and vice versa. People who are especially rational can devalue their feeling function.

The devalued function is "inferior" and will be portrayed in a group as one character of your opposite gender and three of your gender.

Consciously, you might have no awareness of the mental functions, but your unconscious mind is well aware and will portray your mental functions as groups of characters.

People you know can be portrayed as a mental function if they embody it. For example, someone you know might be highly rational and embody the image of the thinker. However, usually the functions are portrayed by generic characters—for example, your thinking function can be symbolized as a scientist or professor.

The subject of mental functions and their relationship to dreams is fascinating and can go on seemingly forever. The intent here is to introduce you to the subject and provide enough information for greater insight into your dreams and exploration on your own.

Groups of characters can symbolize archetypes, especially if the characters within a group are strongly contrasted between old and young, rich and poor, black and white, and other polar opposites, or if they're mythological. In which case, groups of three are "strong" because the internal configuration of an archetype is made of three parts. See: *Archetypes, Pyramid*.

See also: *Archetypes, Co-Worker, Family, Friends, Gang, Men, Mental Functions, Neighbor, Numbers, Pyramid, Shapes, Square, Teenager, Women*

Guard—See: *Cage, Hell, Jail, Prisoner*

Guide—A guide in a dream can symbolize some-one in your life who guides you. It can symbolize looking for guidance, in your external life or internal life. dream-characters such as school counselors, parents, grandparents, animals (bears, dogs, wolves, and crows in particular), and tour guides can symbolize someone or something that guides you, or the general subject of guidance. For an example dream, see: *Teacher*.

Guides lead you somewhere. In dreams, "somewhere" can mean a place in your life. In these dreams, you feel that you should follow the guide, and generally you will not feel threatened. Nervous, perhaps, but not threatened—unless something is guiding you toward changes that threaten the supremacy or power of someone in your life, or threaten to topple something that has control of you, such as an addiction or ego inflation.

Guides are often dreamed about during times of need. For example, you need to get out of a rut, escape depression, or improve your health. You already know deep inside what you need, and a guide in your dream leads you to that knowledge. As you dream, the help is accessed subconsciously and shown to you symbolically, for example, as a room on the other side of a door, or a chamber deep within a cave.

Some dream guides lead you in your spiritual development. They are figures from the unconscious mind and commonly take form as saints, spiritual leaders, and demi-gods. You will feel connected with them and innately trust them. See: *Unconscious Mind*.

See also: *Angel, Animals, Archetypes, Bear, Coach, Crow, Depression, Dog, Ego, Forest, Jungle, Light, Parents, Pastor, Teacher, Unconscious Mind, Wolf*

Guilt—Dreams create symbolism that triggers feelings and emotions, so if you feel guilty in response to something in a dream, you can bet it relates to something you feel guilty about in your life. Oftentimes, whatever triggers your guilt is a symbol for it, not a direct representation.

Read the entry for *Incest*. See how guilty feelings are brought out by dreams and what really underlies those dreams. Read the entry for *Murder*, too.

You subconsciously know what the symbols in your dreams represent. It can explain why you react to something differently in a dream than you would while awake. For example, you dream about a neglected dog and feel really guilty because somehow you know the dog's condition is your fault. You know subconsciously that the dog represents a friend of yours, and the guilty feeling connects with knowing you are neglecting the friendship.

You can often make the connection between a dream and your life by reflecting on the events of the previous day and what was on your mind. Ask yourself whether something is bothering your conscience. Since dreams are known for amplifying things that escape our attention, it's possible you are not consciously aware of the source of a guilty feeling.

If you dream about being found guilty in a dream, convicted in a court, then ask yourself if something happened in your life in which you were blamed or held responsible. For example, a big snafu at work gets blamed on you. Being found guilty in a dream can be a sign of a guilty conscience, but more often the symbolism connects with the idea of taking blame or accepting responsibility.

See also: *Arrest, Clean, Court, Crime, Emotions, Goat, Incest, Innocent, Judge, Murder*

Gun—Guns are so prevalent in media and society that the possibilities for symbolism are almost endless, especially when you factor in personal associations. Dreams begin with an association and create symbolism with it, and guns have many associations: self-defense, coercion, conflict, hostility, aim, targeting. We'll discuss these and more, and give you the tools you need to figure out what a gun in your dreams means.

As with all dream symbolism, a gun is understood within the context of the dream-story. Is it pointed at you, or do you point it? Is it fired? Is anyone hurt? Is it loaded? These details carry different connotations.

A primary association with guns is linked with self-defense, so if you point or use a gun to defend yourself in a dream, it might symbolize defending yourself in some other way: from personal attacks, from intrusion, from hostility. It might be a sign that you need to stick up for yourself—probably not with a gun, but in some way to defend your boundaries or appropriately express your anger.

Or perhaps you're being defensive. Something feels threatening, including intangible threats such as to your reputation. You don't want to realize or admit something, or are resisting a change. Instead you act hostile, you resist, you threaten. A gun in this context means "defensive" or "resistant."

A gun can symbolize feeling pressured, coerced, or forced. You are "under the gun." The symbolism is created by how guns are used to force people to do things they don't want to.

Along these lines, consider that using a gun in a dream can symbolize taking the easy way out. Rather than talk through a conflict or take time to persuade, you pull a gun in the figurative sense and impose your will. That sort of scenario is portrayed all the time in television and movies. The person holding the gun says, "Do this or else," and the person on the other end doesn't really have a choice. It's "do or die."

Guns are used to point, and pointing can be a way of indicating guilt, blame, or responsibility. It says, "That's who did it."

On the other hand, aiming a gun can symbolize focus, such as focus of attention or concentration. When you aim a gun, you focus on a target. A target in a dream can symbolize anything you aim for or target in your life, such as a goal or ambition. For example, targeting a romantic interest with your attention can be symbolized as seeing that person in your gun sights. See: *Arrow, Bullet.*

Your feelings can tell you the difference. There's a big difference between pointing a gun in anger or with hostility, and pointing one to symbolize targeting a romantic interest.

Aiming or firing at a moving target can mean you're trying to hit a proverbial moving target! The metaphor is obvious when you step back and look at it.

If a gun is fired at you, it can symbolize verbal or personal attacks. A fired gun is loud and can symbolize loud arguments, confrontations, and heated words. If you fire a gun, it can symbolize that you are being loud or angry, or taking "verbal shots." The key to the symbolism is the loud noise and the feeling of confrontation. See: *Bullet.*

Firing a gun can be a raw expression of anger. See: *Anger.*

Situations that get out of hand can involve guns, so in dreams guns can be used to create a scenario in which things get out of hand and use it to connect with something in your life that's out of hand and potentially dangerous.

A gun in a dream can indicate paranoia or delusion, connected with the association that some people who carry guns are paranoid or delusional.

Guns can symbolize egotism and machismo. Put a gun in someone's hand and watch the worst in the person come out. See a false sense of confidence and authority emerge. If you observe such behavior in yourself or someone you know, you can dream about it as being careless or overconfident with a gun.

A gun with a hair trigger, which fires or threatens to fire at the slightest touch, can symbolize a temper set off by small provocations. Even people who don't normally show a lot of temper can have times when stress, pressure, and anxiety make them feel like they could "go off." Have you lost your temper lately, or do you feel the pressure building?

A hair trigger, or a gun that fires on its own, can symbolize premature ejaculation. Guns have many other phallic associations. A bullet penetrates. A barrel is long, straight, and hard. Guns are symbols of machismo. They shoot. See: *Phallic Symbol.*

Feeling threatened by a gun pointed at you can symbolize feeling threatened by someone's sexual advances.

Loading a gun in a dream can mean you are preparing for a confrontation. It might be a warning to be careful of getting carried away with emotions, especially anger. It can symbolize thinking of the points you will make during an argument or talk. Ammunition is used in this sense to mean preparation. On the other hand, if you have no ammunition, it can mean you aren't prepared, or don't have good points to make during an argument. See: *Ammunition.*

If you try to fire a gun and it jams or misfires, it can mean you aren't able to express your anger. You have trouble expressing anger—you hold it in rather than let it out—or fear what might happen if you do express it.

A jammed gun can connect with a feeling of powerlessness.

If a gun is pointed at you and you try to block it or take it away, it can mean you are worried about being targeted. You feel threatened. Or you want to deflect blame or responsibility.

The symbolism of guns can get especially deep and varied for people who carry one as part of their job, or have used guns in combat. For example, a gun in the dream of a police officer might symbolize thoughts and feelings related to the possibility of having to use it. It could be used to symbolize other aspects of the job or the person's career. For example, dreaming of having no bullets could symbolize feeling unqualified or unable to advance in the job. Dreaming of not having the strength to pull the trigger can refer to the guts it takes to actually pull the trigger and kill another human being, or reluctance to do so.

(On that note, inability to pull the trigger can symbolize inability to make a decision or move forward with something, to pull the trigger in the figurative sense.)

Anyone who has been involved in a shooting incident can dream about it for many years afterward. The fear, anger, anxiety, and other related emotions are processed in dreams, and psychological distance from the experience(s) is created by dreaming about it. Such an experience can become synonymous with those emotions, so that anytime they're experienced for any reason, a dream can use the original incident to compare with something presently going on in your life. In such dreams the assailant can be shot multiple times but not go down, or appears unharmed, symbolizing that no matter how a person tries to forget such an experience, it won't go away.

The same imagery can symbolize someone or something that won't go away, a problem that can't be solved, a situation that won't resolve, or a person who doesn't get the message. Most dream-characters represent something about yourself, so the first possibility to consider is that a character you shoot in a dream represents something about yourself you want to change.

The same idea applies when you are the one shot. Being shot by a bad guy is a common theme in the dreams of people who are frustrated with themselves and can't or won't do anything about it.

A silenced gun in a dream can indicate you aren't voicing your anger or feelings. Perhaps you need to be more vocal.

Shooting yourself with a gun can symbolize doing some sort of harm to yourself. For example, shooting yourself in the heart can symbolize having to break off a relationship with someone you love. Shooting yourself in the head can symbolize hating your thoughts. Shooting yourself can express the feeling that you want to give up, figuratively or literally.

Shooting yourself, or being shot, in certain parts of the body can show where you're hurt or wounded physically, emotionally, or psychologically. See: *Amputate, Body, Suicide.*

See also: *Ammunition, Amputate, Anger, Army, Arrest, Arrow, Body, Bullet, Death, Hate, Head, Heart, Phallic Symbol, Police Officer, Suicide, War, Wound.*

Gym—See: *Fitness Center*

Hair—Because hair grows from the head and because thoughts are associated with the head, the primary dream symbolism of hair relates to thoughts and thought processes.

For example, crazy hair can indicate crazy thoughts.

Knotted hair or dreadlocks can indicate confusion or inability to think something through.

Kinky or curly hair can symbolize convoluted thoughts.

Combing hair can symbolize putting thoughts in order.

Cutting hair can symbolize simplifying thought processes.

Then there are common metaphors that use hair as symbolism. Letting hair down can symbolize relaxing inhibition. Messing up hair can symbolize a "bad hair day" or disorder. Pulling hair out can express frustration or stress. It can be a sign of illness.

Washing hair can symbolize the nightly process of clearing the memory banks to make room for the next day, or cleaning up your thoughts or thought processes. It can symbolize trying to forget a bad memory.

Washing hair is associated with the routine of getting ready to go out in public or just face the

day. Washing hair can be part of the ritual of getting ready for work or school, so the association can be used to create symbolism related to preparation. For example, you prepare ahead of time for a meeting by thinking through what you want to ask and say. See: *Shower*.

Dreaming about changing your hairstyle can symbolize a new approach or self-image. The idea ties in with how a change in hairstyle can indicate a new phase of life or other big change. For example, you change your hairstyle before taking a new job, so you project a more professional image. A great haircut can change your life. It can show a new outlook or perspective, a new phase of life, or a "new you." See: *Persona*.

Because hair is used to cover the head, it can symbolize wanting to hide something about yourself, especially your thoughts or appearance. It can mean you're uncomfortable showing who you really are. This use of the symbolism will show in details such as the face being covered or obscured by hair.

Very long hair is associated with being instinctual or natural. It can symbolize the long, slow process of growth in your mind, emotions, or inner being. It can be a sign of a deep intellect.

Vanity is a possibility for symbolism when you dream about being obsessed with your hair, or a character makes fun of your hair. Being made fun of can be a way of having your ego punctured, or indicate self-consciousness.

Dying your hair an extravagant color can symbolize a desire to stand out or express your individuality. It can mean you don't care if some people think you're eccentric or weird, or you do things your way and don't care what other people think. See: *Colors.*

Touching someone's hair has sensual and intimate connotations. It suggests personal or physical closeness, because you generally have to be close with someone to touch the hair. It can be a sign of trust and letting your guard down. It can symbolize understanding a person's thoughts or connecting on a personal level.

Removing body hair can symbolize cleaning up your image or getting ready for a big personal change. For example, after a summer away from college, a student dreams about plucking long hairs from his feet, symbolizing that he knows that when school starts again, he's going to busy.

Removing body hair can mean you're willing to make sacrifices to fit in socially. Or it can show discomfort with instinctual drives. For example, a man dreams about shaving off his pubic hair, showing that he's uncomfortable with sex and disconnected with something that should come naturally.

Removing body hair or head hair can symbolize wanting to see what's inside or beneath, such as when one is truly getting to know a person, or trying to understand a subject or situation.

Hair that grows or covers the body like fur can symbolize something that protects or guards you physically or psychologically, such as a protective instinct or even your persona. It can symbolize a period of being idle, such as being on a long vacation or home for summer break and "letting it all hang out."

To explore the symbolism of baldness, see: *Bald.*

Removing fur from the body can symbolize denying your instincts and instinctual drives. It shows discomfort with the body or bodily processes. See: *Animals.*

See also: *Animals, Antler, Bald, Bathroom, Body, Brain, Colors, Face, Fashion, Hat, Head, Illness, Persona, Shower*

Hand—The symbolism of hands is often connected with what they do. Hands are used to take action. They carry out your decisions and thoughts. They hold and grasp. Now start with those ideas and consider the possibilities for symbolism and ways it can connect with you and your life.

Hands in a dream to show taking action, or need for it. When you can't take an action, you can dream about something wrong with your hands. For example, a young woman dreams that she's forced by a bad man to cut off her own hand. Blood flies everywhere and she screams in terror at what she's done. She then seeks out her father and begs him to help, and he tells her everything will be all right and he'll take care of it.

The dream illustrates the young woman's inability to make decisions, leaving them to her father to make. Cutting off her hand is symbolism for inability to make her own decisions. She "hands over" that power to her father, and a point has come in her life when she needs to take it back.

Holding something in a dream can symbolize the hold you have on yourself, as in the phrase, "Get a hold of yourself, man!" It can symbolize the emotional or psychological hold you have on someone or that the person has on you.

The character you hold in a dream can symbolize something about yourself, and the harder you hold onto it, the more it is needed or wanted personally. For example, holding tightly to a child can symbolize holding onto your inner child or a childlike trait or quality. See: *Hug.*

A mother dreams that she discovers that her hand is missing when she reaches out to hold her daughter's hand. It symbolizes lack of personal connection. They recently reunited after a long time apart and they aren't connecting as mother and daughter like they used to.

The possibilities for symbolism expand further when you consider what else hands are used for:

stealing, hitting, pinching, stroking, petting, aiming, throwing, playing, playing with yourself.

Hold can mean "hold on," as in wait, or a hold on reality. For example, dreaming about a troubled relative barely holding onto a high ledge can symbolize the perception that the person is barely hanging on in the personal sense.

Grasping with hands can symbolize your grasp of a situation, idea, or problem.

When you are led or guided, you can be led by the hand. In that sense, a dog biting your hand and leading you somewhere can symbolize a friend's guidance, or there's a direction you want to go in your life and the dog symbolizes your inner guidance. See: *Guide.*

A hard bite on the hand can mean you have been putting off taking an action or making a decision, and time has run out. This use of the symbolism is commonly acted out with a snakebite on the hand.

A disembodied hand can symbolize inability to understand an action or grasp something. As in, you can't understand why you're being audited, or why your child stole from a relative, or why you slapped your spouse. Notice how all these actions are in some way associated with hands.

Many figures of speech involve hands. You can lend a hand, or give a hand. One hand might not know what the other is doing. Some people are "handy."

Visual puns and wordplays can be created with imagery and actions involving hands. For example, cuff links that chain the hands together could symbolize handcuffs. Making the hand motion for jerking off can symbolize wasting time or being "jerked around."

Hands are sensitive, and physical sensitivity in a dream can be used to symbolize personal sensitivity. See: *Fingers.*

Hands are used to give and receive money, and itchy hands have long been associated with receiving money. See: *Money.*

And to be clear, hands appear in potentially any dream with human or humanoid characters in

it, but the symbolism generally only applies when something about hands sticks out as important or draws attention to itself.

See also: *Beat, Body, Climb, Fingers, Fist, Guide, Handicap, Handshake, Masturbate, Strangle, Thief*

Handicap—Dreaming about a handicap can symbolize giving, receiving, or seeking special consideration, an association created by the special considerations afforded for disabilities, such as handicap entrances and parking spots.

A handicap can symbolize special consideration that's expected but not necessarily needed. *I have asthma; I don't like to be touched; I can't do that because of my bad back.* Well, kid, why are you trying out for the football team if you can't do what's expected of the players? For an example, see: *Wheelchair.*

A handicap can be used to symbolize a situation where you feel at a disadvantage, or are being treated as if you can't perform up to par.

It can symbolize being pitied, feeling sorry for someone or for yourself, or overcoming weakness or disadvantage.

A handicap can symbolize something about yourself that you don't like. A close example dream is discussed in the entry for *Brother.* In it, a long-lost brother who escapes from a mental ward symbolizes the dreamer's perception of himself as "mentally handicapped."

A handicap can mean you aren't utilizing your full power and ability. You have the capability, you just aren't using it.

People can be handicapped by their circumstances, such as growing up poor or in an abusive environment. See: *Abuse.*

Addiction can be a sort of handicap because it keeps people from living up to their full potential. See: *Addict.*

Symbolism can be created through general impressions or specific instances. For example, if you have a handicap or know someone who does, then you have specific associations to use as symbolism. Or perhaps you wonder what it would be like to live with a handicap, so your dreams create a simulation to give you the experience.

A handicap can symbolize something preventing you from taking action. The symbolism works on two levels. One, a handicap really can make somebody unable to do certain things. And two, the word "hand" is associated with taking action. See: *Hand*.

The symbolism of a disability can connect with the affected body parts. For example, a disability with your arms can symbolize something hindering your ability to relate to people, because arms are used for hugging and holding. Arms are also associated with strength, so disabled arms can symbolize feeling weak, or not utilizing your strength. Think beyond the physical definition of strength to consider strength of character and mind. See: *Amputate*.

See also: *Abuse, Addict, Amputate, Arm, Blind, Body, Brother, Crutches, Ears, Eyes, Hand, Weak, Wheelchair*

Hang—The most common use of hanging symbolism, as in hanging from a rope, is to symbolize when something isn't getting through to the head. Hanging cuts off blood circulation to the head and airflow, and dreams can use it as symbolism for when someone doesn't want to listen or think about something, or isn't getting the message.

For example, a young man dreams that his mom hangs herself in the basement, symbolizing that he is secretly doing something illegal that he knows she disagrees with but he's doing it anyway. The message isn't getting through to his head.

The tricky part to understanding dream imagery like this is to recognize that the imagery of mom hanging is related to the dreamer, not to her. Mom is a projection, not a direct representation of the actual person. She is not the one about to throw her life. The next scene of the dream gives away the meaning. After the dreamer sees his mom hanging, he runs away to get help, and when he comes back she's not hanging. She's standing and fine, showing that the dream is not about her, it's about him.

Hanging by the neck can symbolize a blockage between the desires of the head and heart, or ig-noring signals from the body, or wishing to ignore something.

Hanging can mean "hanging by a thread." A situation is precarious or difficult. You are barely holding on. For example, you are close to failing a class, or a relationship is close to ending. See: *Cliff*.

Also consider the idea of being "left hanging." For example, you send an email or text message to someone and don't get a reply. Or you're at a meeting and expect support from someone but she doesn't give it.

A noose in a dream can symbolize constriction, such as when a situation feels constricting, your options are limited, or a deadline looms. See: *Strangle*.

When associated with death, a noose can symbolize "rope to hang yourself with," meaning a big screw-up. When associated with execution, a noose can symbolize the end of something or fear of consequence. Death in dreams has associations with major changes in a person or his life. Suicide in dreams can symbolize the idea in the phrase "kill your chances."

Dreams can use the imagery of hanging to symbolize a physical condition such as your airway being blocked as you sleep.

This subject is continued in the entries listed below.

See also: *Air, Cliff, Death, Execution, Neck, Strangle, Suicide*

Harvest—Dreams make analogies. It's one of the main ways for creating symbolism. A harvest presents some possibilities for analogies about situations in life. For example, the time and energy you put into dating pays off when you meet the right person with whom to get serious. The situation is comparable to planting seeds (showing interest), growing a crop (putting effort into making the relationship work), and harvesting it (making a commitment).

That analogy can be used for many situations in life, such as creative projects. The seed is the idea, growing the crop is the effort put into the project, and the harvest is the completion of it and perhaps the recognition it gains you. In everyday conversation, harvest is used in the sense of harvesting talents, skills, and abilities, and taking advantage of opportunities.

The harvest can symbolize when you reap what you sow, especially in your personal and spiritual life. Something you have been growing within you comes to fruition.

A crop ready for harvest can symbolize that the time is ripe for something. Perhaps the most common use of this dream symbolism is for starting a family or having more children, because a baby starts as a sort of seed that grows in the womb, but it applies to a wide variety of situations.

See also: *Earth, Food, Garden, Jesus*

Hat— Because hats are worn on the head, they can be associated with thoughts or thinking processes, as in the term "thinking cap." They can symbolize knowledge or wisdom.

A hat askew can symbolize thoughts that are awry.

A hat too tight can symbolize constricting thoughts or restricted thinking.

Hats can be associated with social status and authority. A tall hat suggests authority or high status.

A hat held in the hands can symbolize humility, need for favors or assistance, or waiting to be acknowledged.

A hat thrown in the air can symbolize celebration or good news.

Putting on a hat can symbolize preparing for a journey, or leaving a situation or a relationship. Or the same imagery can symbolize thinking deeply.

See also: *Clothing, Hair, Head, Journey*

Hate—Dreams provide outlets for emotion and make comparisons. If you feel hate during a dream, it's possible you really hate someone or something. It's a powerful emotion, and when felt in a dream, it's triggered by your subconsciously recognizing the symbolism of whatever you react to with hate.

If you have a hard time expressing or feeling that emotion, you can dream about what you hate, as a symbol, to allow the emotion to freely express itself.

For example, a woman dreams that a man steals her phone and she hunts him down and rams a knife through his heart, expressing her hatred of her ex-boyfriend, symbolized as the man. If the dream had shown her ex directly as a character in the story, she might have reacted differently. Instead, she knows subconsciously what he represents and stabbing in the heart shows how she feels about him and where she's wounded. See: *Ex.*

But don't jump to conclusions. Dreams tend to exaggerate, which can be a way of exposing how you really feel, but it might also be a way of getting your attention or making something stand out. Perhaps hate is too strong a word, but it sure gets your attention!

People will say they hate something when they don't really mean it, in an exaggeration ripe for use as dream symbolism. They say "I hate this class," or "I hate my parents," or "I hate my job." It's comparable to hate, but in most cases the feelings aren't as strong as hate.

Or you really do passionately hate your job or school or parents. Dreams can act as outlets for emotions. Better to let it out than hold it in.

See also: *Anger, Emotions, Ex, Fire, Kill, Murder, Rage*

Haunted—See: *Ghost, Graveyard*

Head—You can get great ideas about specific features related to the head such as eyes, hair, and face by looking them up.

The head itself is associated primarily with thoughts, thinking processes, and intellect, so that's where we begin discussing possibilities for symbolism.

Symbolism involving the head is shown in figures of speech and idioms such as "Get your head screwed on straight," meaning think straight, be sensible. To get ahead means to advance, usually after thinking through how to do it. "Losing your head" means your thinking is faulty, irrational.

Dreams enact those figures of speech, so if a dream wants to say that you lost your head, it'll show you losing your head—it comes off, or is missing. In simplest terms, a headless person is someone who lost her head.

Your "heading" is your direction, and direction in a dream can refer to direction in life or a specific area of it such as work life or family life. The symbolism could be shown as a head rolling along the ground, flying through the air, or faced in a certain direction. See: *Left, Right*.

A head swiveled around backwards can be a way of saying "look behind you" in the figurative sense. Something is in your blind spot, or in your past, and it's important.

If something goes over your head, it means you don't get it, you don't understand. Dreams may enact the symbolism through imagery of something flying over or above your head.

Holding your head high may indicate pride and related ideas, whereas a head held low indicates shame and related ideas.

Turning the head away can indicate disapproval or negative opinion, whereas the opposite action can indicate approval or positive opinion.

All functions of thinking and decision-making are fair game to be symbolized with the head: self-control, attention, intention, opinion, analysis, intuition, reason, strategy.

Conflict between the head and heart, between rationality and feelings, is central to many dreams. The symbolism can be shown in closeness or distance between locations or objects. For example, a giraffe's long neck can symbolize a wide distance between the head and heart.

Injury to the head can symbolize figurative disconnection from the body. You "live in your head." It can mean you live in your head at the expense of your physical needs. The same idea can be expressed in the symbolism of being headless. See: *Wound*.

It's funny when you step back from a dream and realize how obvious it is. For example, you dream that your head swells to many times its normal size.

You wonder whether it means you're "sick in the head" or have an illness in the head such as swelling of the brain, then realize it means your head is swelled with pride. It can mean you have a big intellect, a "big brain." The swollen head is a metaphor.

Having two heads, or switching heads, can mean you're of two minds about something.

Getting shot in the head can symbolize thoughts that hurt to think about, or doubts about your intellect. It can symbolize a headache. In rare cases it can indicate a more severe physical issue such as a tumor. Dreams that warn of dangerous physical conditions are likely to recur—your dreams will keep sending the message until you get it. See: *Disease*.

The forehead is the seat of intellect, insight, and critical thinking. In dreams it can symbolize anything related to thought processes and rationality. A third eye in the forehead is a sign of deep insight. See: *All-Seeing Eye*.

See also: *All-Seeing Eye, Amputate, Antler, Balloon, Brain, Decapitate, Disease, Ears, Execution, Eyes, Face, Fellatio, Fever, Hair, Hang, Hat, Illness, Insane, Mouth, Neck, Psyche, Psychologist, Wound*

Hear—Physical senses in a dream have many possibilities for symbolism, often related to their use or function. In the case of hearing, you can hear something that makes an impression on you, hear a rumor, hear good or bad news, or overhear a conversation. Your internal reactions to these situations can then be turned into stories involving something you hear. For example, the sound of church bells can symbolize hearing about an upcoming wedding.

We take in a lot of information through our sense of hearing, and some of it might require processing by our dreams. This is especially true if you have been attending lectures or listening to audio books. Dreams amplify things that escape our attention but register subconsciously. It's possible that something you heard is amplified by your dreams to make sure it registers consciously.

Hearing a strange or powerful sound can symbolize the sense that something is impending. Someone might say, "I hear the stock market is going to drop" to summarize a feeling, hunch, or popular opinion. In a dream, that sense of an impending drop in the market could translate into the sound of a bear (as in "bear market") roaring or rumbling.

The roar of a storm or tornado can symbolize a coming emotional storm. Something's stirring the deep water within you.

Loud words or arguments can translate in dreams as the sound of gunshots or thunder.

If something spoken in a dream stands out to you, it's probably meaningful and relates to the subject of the dream. For example, in a dream about being back in a childhood home, the dreamer sees a tornado coming and goes to get something in the basement. He finds his sister down there, and she screams, "I should have seen it coming!"

The dream is about revisiting the past in search of the source of something disturbing the dreamer's feelings, and it is found in the sister's statement. What they should have seen coming was their parents' divorce, which happened in their childhood home and hit the family like a storm. The signs of impending breakup were there, like the storm approaching, but the dreamer and his sister didn't see it coming.

Hearing can be used by a dream to mean expecting news or contact from someone. This use of the symbolism is often sparked by concern for someone who has been out of touch. Sometimes in these cases you say "hear from" a person but communication actually comes via email or text message. "Hear" is used to mean contact or communication.

Along similar lines, a voice delivering a warning, or sound of distress, can mean there is a reason to wake up. Something needs your attention. Perhaps a window was left open or the oven is on. Parents with young children are known to become highly sensitive to the sound of a child crying.

Inability to hear can mean someone isn't listening or getting the message. The symbolism is often accompanied by a reference to the ears, though not always. For example, not listening can

be symbolized by damage to the ears or something covering them. Sometimes inability to hear is not willful. It's simply a sign of miscommunication or lack of communication. Telephones and letters are commonly used to create symbolism related to communication. See: *Letter, Phone.*

Inability to hear can mean you're not really being heard. You feel ignored, left out, unappreciated. You have something important to say but no one is listening, or someone important in your life is not listening. Listening in this sense means noticing and responding. Or you are having difficulty expressing yourself or making your feelings known.

For example, a young man whose father died dreams about seeing him at a memorial service. The son does everything he can to get his father's attention, but the father-character acts as if the son is not there. He's not listening or even hearing him. The situation symbolizes the fact that dad is no longer around to listen to his son, to have conversations and share their lives together.

Hearing people saying things about you can be a projection of what they think of you—or what you think they think of you.

Alternately, if the comments are directed at a dream-character based on someone you know, the dream can stem from something you have heard said about that person. But also remember that dreams can use surrogate-characters.

For example, say you dream about people at work making comments about a co-worker who is introverted and doesn't say much. You reflect back and don't remember overhearing anything said recently about the co-worker, but do remember thinking the previous day that your co-workers might think you are weird because you don't talk much at work. You see yourself in that co-worker because you too are introverted.

Hearing things in your dreams can symbolize sounds heard while dreaming, such as a radio, baby crying, or people talking.

Be sure to read the entry for *Ears.*

See also: *Decapitate, Ears, Head, Letter, Music, Phone, Talk, Vibration*

Heart—The heart is the center of certain emotions related to love, caring, and self-worth. This is true not only in the figurative sense, but also in the anatomical sense. Near the heart is a bundle of nerves that acts as a processor for related emotions. Therefore, symbolism related to the heart tends to be about emotions and emotional life.

The heart is also where feelings are processed. Emotions and feelings are not synonymous, though they can be closely related. Feelings are value judgments, such as when you say, "I feel that she's valuable to the organization." Dreams can express this sort of thinking through references to the heart.

The associations between emotions and the heart create many possibilities for symbolism. As with other symbols, the meaning is found in modifier details. For example, a frozen heart can symbolize "cold-heartedness," meaning emotionally cold and unsympathetic. A heart that smells bad can symbolize pretending to care but actually being unemotional. A callus or other sort of covering over the heart can symbolize protecting emotions, or being "calloused," unfeeling.

For example, a man dreams that he has a thick callus on his chest over his heart. He goes to a doctor to have it removed, but the doctor is unable to remove it all. It symbolizes the emotional layers of protection he has after his heart was broken by failed relationships. That he knows it's a problem and is trying to help himself is symbolized by the doctor removing the callus. The fact that the doctor can't remove all of the callus symbolizes that the dreamer has more inner work to do. He needs more time to heal his wounds.

Heart problems can symbolize problems in love life or emotional life.

The heart is also used metaphorically to mean center or focus, such as in the phrase "heart of the matter." For example, a dream about finding a heart in a box symbolizes the dreamer's getting to "the heart" of a matter. A dream about stabbing Jesus in the heart symbolizes the dreamer's qualms about organized religion that are at the heart of why he rejects Christianity. A dream about shoot-ing an arrow at the heart symbolizes the dreamer's focus on a love interest.

This idea goes deeper when you consider the heart as the center of your being. It's the place where body and mind meet. It's where emotion is balanced by thought. It's commonly depicted as the home of the soul. In metaphysics, the heart interfaces with the fabric of reality to determine your reality. It responds to what your heart says, not what your head says.

Wounding to the heart in dreams tends to symbolize hurt feelings and emotions, especially emotions related to love. See: *Wound.*

For example, a female dreams about shooting herself in the heart, and in her waking life she just broke up with her boyfriend, not because they were incompatible, but because their jobs forced them to move far apart and they decided to break up rather than try a long-distance relationship. It's a self-inflicted wound to her emotions.

In another heart-related dream, a female dreams about hunting down a man who stole her phone and stabbing him through the heart. The man in the dream symbolizes an ex-boyfriend who deeply wounded her and messed up her life. See: *Ex.*

A heart pounding in a dream can symbolize anxiety. Dreams translate physical sensations into dream imagery, and it's possible that your heart is pounding as you sleep, or you are experiencing heart palpitations or an irregular heartbeat.

See also: *Anxiety, Blood, Body, Emotions, Ex, Hate, Love, Red, Wound*

Heat—Feeling heat in a dream can symbolize "feeling the heat," meaning suspicion or attention.

Heat is used to describe feeling emotions such as passion, jealousy, and anger. Dreams enact symbolism, so passion could be symbolized as a hot fire, and angry thoughts could be symbolized as your roof (head) on fire.

Heat is used as symbolism to compare with passion ("hot for you"), pressure ("the heat is on"), attraction ("he's *hotttt*"), popularity and trendiness ("the hot new thing") and excitement ("that sounds hot").

The analogies go on and on. Add water and you can be "boiling mad." Add the stomach and you have "fire in the belly." Add ice or snow and you've got "hot and cold."

To explore this subject further, look up the entries listed below, especially: *Fire*.

See also: *Fever, Fire, Hell, Oven*

Heaven—If heaven is a dream setting, it might be a way of symbolizing being in a good place in your life. You are at peace. You feel joy, connection, love.

Dreaming about heaven can come in response to wondering what it's like, especially after hearing descriptions of heaven, seeing depictions of it, or sorting through your beliefs. Is it a real place, or metaphorical? Do only good people go there, or only people who practice a certain religion? Dreams can respond to these sorts of questions, but remember that the answers received are likely to be subjective, not objective.

Powerful and vivid depictions of heaven in dreams run the gamut from typical "angels on clouds" and "bearded wise man running the show," to a black void of absolute peace. These are subjective viewpoints. That, or heaven is whatever you believe it to be. Considering what we are learning from quantum physics about reality being whatever you make of it, it's entirely possible that objectively a place like heaven (presuming it exists) has myriad manifestations.

Dreams where heaven is referred to and not depicted can relate to a place you're trying to get to in your life. Perhaps you have a goal in mind that sounds like heaven to you, such as retiring to a tropical island. Dreams use analogies to create symbolism, and heaven to you can be something like buying a house on a lake, or sending your kids off to college.

Oftentimes, personal notions of heaven are related to romantic love. You will find your personal heaven when you find the love of your life. For people who are lonely and isolated, their version of heaven can simply be a close connection with another human being.

Along this line, heaven in a dream can be an expression of a wish. For example, a loved one dies and you dream about the person in heaven. It's a wish that the person is in a good place in the afterlife. Or it can symbolize being at peace with the death of that person. See: *Afterlife, Deceased Loved One*.

How does heaven symbolize something from your thoughts or feelings? Is it used to describe a situation? Is it something you think about or long for? Is it used as a setting to help tell the dream-story? Remember, a dream setting sets the stage to tell a story using symbolism, and the symbolism is based on your associations.

What are the first words that come to mind in relation to heaven? Peace, contentment, harmony, afterlife, God, eternity, mystery, love, light, soul. These are common associations with heaven that can be used to symbolize what's going on inside you, in your life, as an observation about a person, or to identify the subject of a story.

See also: *Afterlife, Angel, Ascend, Collective Unconscious, Deceased Loved One, God, Hell, Soul, Spirit*

Hell—Dreams make metaphors, and hell can be a poignant metaphor for describing your life or a situation. Do you ever catch yourself saying something like, "My life is hell," or "I'm going to burn in hell for this."

You hear a description of the misery or stress someone is going through and think the situation is comparable to being in hell.

Hell can be an apt way of describing emotions that torment you. See: *Emotions*.

It can be a general symbol of fear, or be a metaphor for how fear makes life hell. See: *Fear*.

Hell is associated with a place where bad people go, and it can be used in dreams to symbolize guilt, regret, or self-knowledge that you (or someone you know) have done something sinful or wrong. Hell is punishment, eternal torture for wrongdoing. You think you belong in hell. You've been a bad, bad boy or girl. You're tortured by guilt over things real or imagined. This notion is common in the minds of people exposed to "hellfire and brimstone" dogma. See: *Guilt, Torture*.

Keep in mind, most dream-characters are projections of something about you, so if a dream refers to a person in hell, it might be a projection of something about you or an aspect of yourself. For example, your lustful sex life that could land you in hell.

Hell is conceived as a place where people suffer the consequences of their actions, and that association can be used to create a story about consequences and taking responsibility for your actions. See: *Court.*

For example, a man dreams he's in hell with members of a group he's in that challenges beliefs and notions, akin to an encounter group. Hell is a huge stone quarry, and their job is to break rocks. He's told by the group that anyone who tries to leave will be hunted down and vaporized by demons that exist unseen in guard towers surrounding the place.

One day he decides the demon guards don't exist and he tries to leave, and ends up in a dark cave. There, he burrows through hell's wall and is confronted by several pairs of glowing red eyes, like stoplights—the demons! He's afraid and makes a right turn. A powerful, disembodied voice tells him, "Learn to take responsibility for the consequences of your actions!" He then slides uncontrollably and appears in daylight over a bottomless chasm, and the dream ends with him falling helplessly through open air.

In this metaphorical story, the walls of hell and the demon guards symbolize the beliefs and notions that keep a person imprisoned, unable to see beyond them, constrained. The guards are unseen because beliefs and notions are intangible. The man is learning to challenge them and leave them behind, symbolized as breaking rocks and burrowing through the wall of hell. The dark cave symbolizes the lonely personal place he finds himself in as he questions not only his beliefs and notions, but also those of his social group.

When this happens, constraints will make a final stand, symbolized as the red eyes appearing. They're like stoplights because something inside the man wants him to stop and go back to the relative comfort and safety of his prison. He's afraid.

Instead he makes a right (correct) turn, meaning a turn in his journey of life, and absorbs the lesson that his unconscious mind, speaking through the powerful voice, is teaching him:

Take responsibility for the consequences of your actions!

Doing that means that the ground he'd based his life on disappears, as symbolized by free-falling, but it also means he will eventually find better ground to stand on. It's a lesson that will stick with him for the rest of his life.

While hell is believed by some people to be a real place, an alternate conception of it is as a state of being cut off from God while alive in body. When translated to a personal situation, hell can mean a person is cut off from the goodness in him- or herself, or alienated from fellow humans.

Burning in hell can connect with a burning temper. Losing your temper can make you feel guilty. Guilt is associated with hell. The ideas all interconnect.

Dreaming about burning in hell might be a response to physical stimuli as you sleep. You could dream about being in hell when you have a high fever, your body is overheated, or you have the sweats. Or it might be in response to something you heard, especially if you have been exposed recently to religious notions about hell or a person's beliefs about it.

Or the "heat is on," meaning you are tense and under pressure.

See also: *Dark, Demon, Devil, Evil, Fire, Heat, God, Guilt, Heaven, Oven*

Help—See: *Rescue*

Hero—To interpret the meaning of a hero in a dream, or of playing a heroic role, begin by thinking about the classic traits of the hero: courage, prowess, morality, faith, skill, conviction. Everyday life can be filled with moments when we draw on those qualities and others associated with heroism.

Dreaming about a hero can come in response to playing a role of hero, even in seemingly small or everyday ways. For example, maybe your young children see you as a hero, or you come to the rescue of a friend or family member. Portraying you as a hero is exaggerated but ultimately true. If it's hard to see yourself that way, a dream might project it onto a character.

Most of us have people we model ourselves after or admire. Sometimes these people are directly involved in our lives, such as parents, teachers, coaches, and pastors. We can view them as heroes and dream about them in that role, but keep in mind that maybe you are the hero now. Most dream-characters reflect aspects of yourself, after all. When you dream about someone who is a personal hero to you, you might be seeing yourself in that person.

Along a similar vein, you might have heroes you admire from afar, such as sports stars and celebrities. When one of them is dreamed about, it's often because you see something about the person in yourself, or aspire to be more like him. Our inspirations to become the best we can be often begin with seeing someone else do it, often someone who has successfully faced the same challenges we face.

A common type of dreams involves meeting and hanging out with your heroes, and generally these dreams are a good sign that you are absorbing something from their example. It's a way for something deep inside you to say "Hey, keep up the good work."

Remember that dreams can bring balance to the psyche and produce images that are the opposite of your conscious attitude or self-perception. An image of a hero in your dreams might be showing you untapped potential, or compensating for your feeling unheroic or cowardly. See: *Compensation, Coward.*

The opposite of the hero is the bully and coward, and related behaviors, attitudes, and feelings are actually immature attempts to be a hero.

Dreams can respond to your fantasies, and dreaming about being a hero can reflect your fantasy life. This is especially true for teenagers, because it's quite common for them to imagine themselves as heroes. It's healthy because doing so plants ideas in their minds and connects them with the hero inside of them—the hero in all of us.

For females, a hero can symbolize their animus. In the early stages of this archetype, animus is presented as a man of action who appears when needed and saves the day. He's a sort of knight in shining armor. See: *Animus.*

The hero is an archetype, the Hero, with generally the same meaning across all cultures. As a universal part of the psyche, the Hero archetype is a blueprint to follow, a set of traits, qualities, and characteristics for accomplishing the heroic task of becoming a fully developed and matured person and tackling the challenges of life. Just look at how it all starts: first a helpless infant, then childhood, then puberty and the teen years, and figuring out what you're going to do as an adult. Get through school, start a career and a family. See: *Archetypes.*

It takes a hero in you to courageously march forward in life. Then, when you consider the adversity almost everyone faces along the way, you see why we all need to be heroes. It often begins by playing the hero in your dreams.

See also: *Animus, Archetypes, Army, Athlete, Coach, Coward, Famous, King, Lifeguard, Magic, Paramedic, Police Officer, Queen, Rescue, Teacher, Teenager, Warrior*

Heroin—See: *Drugs*

Hide—Actions like hiding in a dream can be a physical representation of a personal situation. For example, hiding a body in a dream can symbolize hiding from guilt or hiding your involvement in something regretful. It can symbolize avoiding a painful truth, hiding negative feelings, or concealing your true thoughts. It can mean that you're hiding something from yourself through denial or wishful thinking. See: *Bury.*

Hiding in a dream can symbolize hiding away from the world generally, or from a person or situation specifically. This is especially true of people who are private or secretive, but it also applies to anyone dealing with a stressful or difficult situation. Sometimes you just want to get away from it all or avoid someone. For example, you always find a reason to be away or busy when your in-laws visit. You are, in a sense, hiding, and dream about it as hiding in the basement when the doorbell rings.

Hiding from a specific person can mean you avoid that person's scrutiny, or conceal something from that person. For example, hiding from your mother can mean you know you're doing, thinking, or considering something that goes against her wishes or teachings. Hiding from your supervisor can mean you're trying to conceal poor work performance. Hiding from a significant other can reflect a situation where you feel ambiguous about the relationship but don't want to raise suspicion, or you're doing or considering something you don't want that person to know about.

Also consider that a surrogate-character can represent a person in your life. The big bear stalking you in the woods can symbolize a parent. The serial killer can symbolize a bully or business rival. A dinosaur sniffing around can symbolize a nosy grandparent. Hiding from an overly enthusiastic suitor can symbolize avoiding the phone calls or messages from someone who shows interest in dating you. For an example, see: *Dinosaur.*

Hiding in a dream can mean you're avoiding something, such as a responsibility or painful realization. You might even be avoiding something like pursuing a goal or dream you have for your life. In order to go on with daily life you avoid thinking about what you'd rather be doing.

Hiding can mean you don't want to know something. It can mean you don't know something about yourself. In a dream you hide in a closet, which is connected with hiding your sexuality.

Hiding can mean saving something for later, like a squirrel burying nuts.

Dreams can use the symbolism of hiding the same as figures of speech like "hide in plain sight" and "hide out."

Hiding or being invisible in a dream can symbolize the feeling of not being seen or heard. You feel like a ghost. Or something is overlooked. It's in a blind spot.

See also: *Bury, Coffin, Clothing, Ghost, Imposter, Mask, Panic*

High-Rise—See: *Skyscraper*

Highway—Driving on a highway in a dream can mean you're in a hurry to get somewhere in your life. For example, you can't wait to get married and have children.

A highway can symbolize the "fast lane" or "fast track." You're advancing quickly.

A highway can symbolize that your life is moving too quickly. This use of the symbolism is often accompanied by the action of driving on a highway when the brakes don't work, or you can't stop yourself from pushing on the gas pedal.

A highway can symbolize nervousness about getting into a car accident. The worst car accidents tend to happen on highways. Moreover, dreams can warn of risky behaviors such as driving too fast or driving distracted. You know in the back of your mind that all it takes is one bad turn of events, and your life is over.

Highways connect destinations, making a highway great to use as an analogy for the longer journeys of life, or even for life itself. As the old song says, life is a highway. It's something you ride.

See also: *Brakes, Bridge, Car, Motorcycle, River, Road, Speed, Truck*

Hill—A hill in a dream can symbolize something big, not quite mountainous but still big—a big challenge, big problem, big ego, big ambition. If a dream needs to say something is huge, it's more likely to use the imagery of a mountain.

Running up a hill can symbolize taking on a big task, something that requires a lot of effort. For an example dream with this symbolism, see: *Football.*

A hill can symbolize making a big deal out of something, a "mountain out of a molehill."

The opposite side of a hill, or going down one, can symbolize "over the hill." It can mean regression, as in "her health is going downhill." However, looked at another way, traveling down a hill can symbolize gaining momentum, things are getting easier, or they're getting out of control. The symbolism will show in the actions. For example, you dream about going downhill on roller skates and gaining speed. At first it's fun, but then you worry about how you're going to stop, symbolizing a romantic relationship "gaining speed" and giving you a thrill, but losing its fun as you realize it has momentum of its own and you are no longer in control.

Looking out from the top of a hill can symbolize gaining perspective or rising above to get a better view. You're trying to see what's upcoming in your life or in a particular part of it, or you want to see the big picture.

See also: *Cliff, Climb, Mountain*

Hit—See: *Beat, Fist*

Hitler—Hitler is commonly viewed as the embodiment of evil, among the worst human beings who ever lived. In dreams, a Hitler-character or reference to Hitler can mean "as bad as it gets." It can be a way of describing a person, situation, or personal quality.

Other associations with Hitler can be used as symbolism, such as paranoia, charisma, and domination.

The symbolism of a famous person like Hitler in a dream can be decoded the same as with other famous people. See: *Famous.*

See also: *Famous, Nazi*

Hobo—See: *Beggar, Bum*

Hold—See: *Hand*

Hollywood—A dream about being in Hollywood can mean you're living in a fantasy world. Tinsel Town is a world of illusion, of impossibly beautiful people whom most folks will never get close to. In that sense Hollywood can symbolize the unattainable.

Hollywood is associated with fame and glamor, and can be used in dreams to symbolize the desire to be noticed, to stand out, to be famous. See: *Famous.*

The meaning of the symbolism depends on the context. For example, if you dream about yourself at the Oscars, walking the red carpet, with adoring fans screaming your name and paparazzi jostling to get the best photo of you, the symbolism is more likely to relate to fame and glamor. If you dream that you are an actor on a Hollywood set, it can symbolize an image you project or role you play. See: *Actor.*

For people in the movie business, Hollywood can symbolize a place they want to be in their career. Hollywood is a symbol of professional success, the same as NYC is a symbol of professional success for authors, fashion designers, and media professionals.

See also: *Actor, Camera, Director, Documentary, Famous, Movie, New York City, Spotlight, Stage, Television*

Home—Home is one of the most common dream settings, which makes sense considering how much time the average person spends at home and the ways it closely ties together with the life you build for yourself, both physically and psychologically.

Home is where the heart is. Home is where you invest your emotional resources. Home is where you are comfortable, loved, accepted, nourished, connected. Home is wherever you *want* to be, which is not necessarily the physical place where you reside. It's a metaphor, and dreams *love* to use metaphors.

Home is the life you build for yourself, represented as a building. You "construct" your life, and your life has areas and divisions like rooms, floors, and walls. See: *Building.*

Of course, when a dream wants to address something that is happening at home—your literal home, not a figurative one—it can use the place where you live as the setting.

However, when a dream presents a place as home but it's not the place where you live or have ever lived, you know it has to be symbolism. The details about the home and the story involving it reveal the meaning.

Dreaming about living in a warm, cozy home can mean you're in a good place in your life. Living in a cold, drafty home can symbolize being in a bad place in your life.

Inviting someone into your home can symbolize a new friendship. On the other hand, keeping someone out of your home can symbolize trying to keep someone out of your life. See: *Door*.

References to returning home can symbolize the desire to be in a good place in your life. This theme pops up most frequently in the dreams of people who are unhappy, unstable, or disconnected from their roots, or who are starting a family and wish to create for their children the same sort of happy home they grew up in—or avoid recreating their unhappy childhood home.

Returning to your childhood home can symbolize revisiting the past in search of the roots of something affecting you in the present. The childhood home is where patterns form, ideas take root, and the foundation of your character and personality are molded. See: *Childhood Home*.

The idea of returning to a place in life that's been left behind carries over to dreams about homes or places where you used to live as an adult. For example, if you were depressed while living in a certain place and sense depression coming back again, you can dream about it as revisiting that place where you used to live. The same idea applies to returning to places you lived where you felt happy, loved, comfortable, and so on.

When you dream about places where you used to live, think of the overarching themes and big picture of that time of life and what that place means to you. For example, a man has recurring dreams featuring the first place where he lived after leaving college, a setting his dreams use whenever they want to refer to the decisions he made that form the basis of his career.

Home is where your mind is. In that sense, home is your head. "You" see out of your eyes, and your eyes are in your head. When people are asked where their consciousness or soul resides in their body, the most common answer is that it's right behind the eyes or forehead. See: *Attic*.

A home can symbolize the mind's structures and layers. The roof or attic represents the highest layer of the mind, the thought centers. The ground level represents feelings, and lower levels represent emotions, instincts, and stored memories. Farther down are the base layers, such as your hereditary roots and the collective unconscious. Carl Jung said that a home can represent "the Self," the complete picture of the person you are, even the parts that are unrealized or unconscious. See: *Attic, Basement, Collective Unconscious*.

This stretching of the definition leads to interesting symbolism. For example, feeling harmonized with yourself and calm can be depicted as living in a peaceful garden or on a beautiful stretch of beach. Turmoil can be depicted in a dream as a house battered by a storm. A mind "in the gutter" can be depicted as a sewer or garbage dump. Living in the clouds can symbolize detachment from reality.

A home can symbolize your body. Areas and features of a home can symbolize areas of the body, such as plumbing to represent the bowels, windows to represent the eyes, and electrical circuits to represent the nervous system. See: *Body*.

A home collapsing or falling apart can symbolize illness—your house, your body, is in disrepair, or your life is in disarray. See: *Illness*.

A home-improvement-store setting in a dream can be used to tell a story about making improvements to your body through exercise, diet, and beautification. For example, a man dreams about battling another man, someone overweight, up and down the aisles of a home-improvement store. The dreamer shoots a mixer tong at the man and knocks him down, then comes over to finish him off with a grilling fork. The man asks for a last request, to be fed meatballs from a can lying nearby. The dreamer agrees.

The dream is about the dreamer's struggle to lose weight. He's dieting and thoughts about food are taking over his mind. The man he battles is the part of himself that wants to eat freely, and the home-improvement store setting is perfect for telling a story about improving his body.

Finding new or secret rooms in your home is an analogy for discovering new aspects of yourself, or opening up new areas of your life. You are changing. Changes in you or your life can be symbolized by remodeling a home, constructing new rooms, or buying a new home. For example, a person makes big changes by quitting an addiction and joining a spiritual community. He dreams about adding a new room onto his home, representing this new phase of life. Then temptation to return to a former lifestyle creeps in, and he dreams about a storm buffeting the home. See: *Discover.*

Dreams about something invading a home can symbolize difficulties, problems, or other sorts of disruptions to your peace of mind or your routine. It can symbolize invasion of privacy. See: *Back Door.*

Locking doors and windows can mean you want to keep someone or something out of your life. See: *Door.*

Rats or roaches in a home can symbolize a decrepit emotional life, or living in squalor. See: *Rat, Roach.*

Snakes or spiders getting into a home can symbolize bad influence or someone bringing personal problems into your space. For example, your troubled child gets involved with the wrong crowd and you suspect he or she is hiding drugs in his or her room. See: *Snake, Spider.*

Robbers breaking into your home can symbolize loss of privacy, or insecurity—especially material insecurity—or the feeling that you're being robbed of something immaterial, such as robbed of opportunity or energy. See: *Burglary, Thief.*

Intruders in your home can symbolize loss of privacy, or anything else that feels intrusive. An intruder can represent an illness or virus that invades the body. See: *Intruder.*

A dream about a home destroyed or in ruins can symbolize a breakup, divorce, or other situation that breaks up a family or disrupts a living situation. See: *Family.*

A vacant house can symbolize missing the comforts of home. It can symbolize a time of life you miss, especially the people who were part of it, and related feelings. It can symbolize something you vacated or gave up, such as a long-term project or a plan for your life. A house isn't built overnight, and neither is whatever is symbolized by a vacant house.

An empty house or building can symbolize feeling lonely and empty. See: *Empty.*

See also: *Attic, Backyard, Barn, Basement, Body, Building, Burglary, Castle, Childhood Home, Chimney, Collective Unconscious, Colors, Construction, Destruction, Dinner, Discover, Door, Ego, Elderly, Empty, Fence, Fire, Front Yard, Garage, Ghost, Illness, Intruder, Kitchen, Living Mansion, Neighbor, Psyche, Rat, Roach, Snake, Spider, Thief, Tree, Trespassing, Wall*

Homosexual—See: *Gay*

Honey—See: *Bees*

Hooker—The symbolism of a hooker in a dream can connect with associations such as promiscuity, poor reputation, and shame. You could dream about a hooker when you or someone you know has casual sex, has a promiscuous reputation, or has done something shameful.

A hooker can symbolize an informal arrangement of exchanging sex for money. For example, a sugar-daddy arrangement, giving sex to advance at work or to get a good grade. The symbolism of a hooker can be used in any situation where sex or the hint of sex is used to get what you want.

Promiscuity and sex are the most obvious associations, but as usual, dreams branch out far and wide to create symbolism and connect it with your life. For example, the symbolism can connect with the feeling of being overlooked, discriminated against, or having a bad reputation. You feel like a hooker when a friend doesn't invite you to a party and you wonder whether you were deliberately overlooked. A hooker's reputation might prevent her (or him) from being invited to certain social events.

You feel like a prostitute when you do something for money that compromises your integrity. For example, a woman dreams that she arrives at work and the place is a brothel. Another woman with her, a seemingly random co-worker, voices reservations about working at a brothel. The dreamer tells her that maybe she can just do dances instead of having sex. The dream then shows the woman after being arrested and shamed. The dream shows how the dreamer really feels about her job. She has to compromise her integrity to work there. Notice how the dream uses a surrogate-character as a projection of the dreamer's feelings. The entry for *Walmart* has a similar example of projecting symbolism onto a character in order to step back and notice something.

A hooker can mean "cheap," and cheap is an expression of value. For example, you're a musician and dream about a hooker charging five dollars for a blow job, after someone makes a low-ball offer to you to perform a gig. It shows low opinion of your profession and skills, or at least, that's how it feels to you.

A hooker in a dream can connect with doing whatever you have to do to survive, particularly something that's desperate or shameful.

See also: *Cunnilingus, Fellatio, Hotel, Money, Sex*

Horse—Horses in dreams are commonly associated with movement in your life because they're used for activities such as riding and racing, but there are many other possibilities based on figures of speech and personal associations.

Horses are strong and able to travel long distances. Therefore, they are associated with ability to plow through large amounts of work or endure difficult circumstances.

A man dreams about a horse drowning in a pond and doing nothing to help it, symbolizing his inability to ask for help at work. He's a "work horse" who won't seek help when he needs it, and in the dream that idea is shown as watching the horse drown.

"Healthy as a horse" is a common saying to describe strength and virility. A horse can symbolize your inner strength or sexual prowess.

Horses are used in many romantic tales, with someone either riding to the rescue or mounted on a horse. It's a common association to use as symbolism.

Riding a horse can symbolize a high position of authority, high ideals, or a high opinion of yourself, as in the phrase "get off your high horse." Alternately, it can symbolize the strength to endure a long personal journey.

"Riding a white horse," long associated with heroin use and biblical prophecy, is also used by dreams to indicate moving forward in life with the aid of the unconscious mind. This symbolism is true of other white animals, too, such as white crows and white wolves.

A woman dreams that she finds a horse while struggling to walk through a blizzard. She wants to mount the horse but a shadowy man pulls it away from her. She analyzes the dream and understands that the blizzard symbolizes her depression, the man symbolizes her Shadow side, and the horse symbolizes help from within her to help escape the depression. A short time later she has the same dream, except she reacts by jumping onto the horse and fleeing before the shadowy man can stop her. She comes to a cliff, pursued by the man, and must make a split decision. She decides to leap off the cliff. It symbolizes her decision to make a "leap of faith" and escape her depression. By riding away on the horse, she makes a decision to claim the help bubbling up from her unconscious mind.

Being chased by a white horse can indicate conflict with issues of sexual purity.

Other phrases that can be depicted in dreams include "beating a dead horse," and "straight from the horse's mouth." Symbolism like this is likely to be acted out.

A dream about a horse with back problems can indicate trouble enduring a situation or finding the strength to accomplish a difficult task. See: *Back*.

Taming a horse can symbolize taming wild instincts. A horse out of control can mean that your passions are running wild. A horse that has difficulty walking can symbolize shame.

Dreaming about a horse carrying a burden can symbolize feeling that you carry other people's personal burdens, or people dump their problems or responsibilities on you.

A horse is associated with the Sagittarius zodiac sign, which is depicted as half-horse, half-human.

What role does the horse play in the dream-story? What does it do, and how does it tie together with other details from the dream? As with all symbols, a horse is understood within the context of the story, and your feelings are used as a guide to understanding it.

See also: *Animals, Back, Cowboy, Rescue, Unconscious Mind*

Hospital—Dreaming about being in a hospital can symbolize seeking help with a health matter. It's the most obvious association. Remember, though, that instead of physical health, health can mean emotional, psychological, or financial health. Relationships are described in terms of being "healthy" or "unhealthy." Family life is described that way, too.

The connection between hospitals and health extends to situations in which you are trying to make something healthier, such as improving the health of an environment by spreading good cheer, or lifting the spirits of someone who has been depressed or sad. A hospital is an appropriate setting to tell the story.

A hospital setting can link with a situation in life where you know someone is physically unwell. For example, your grandma is ill and you fear she will end up in a hospital, then dream about an elderly lady rushing to the hospital in an ambulance. The dream reflects concern for her well-being. Well-being includes ideas related to comfort, happiness, and success.

Hospitals are associated with dread—going to a hospital is a nightmare come true for some people.

They're associated with emergencies.

They're associated with boredom.

They're associated with invasion of privacy, because at hospitals a person may be poked and probed. For example, a man getting a security clearance dreams about going through invasive exams at a hospital and answering personal ques-

tions. He's given a clean bill of health. It reflects his expectation that nothing about him or his past will prevent him from obtaining the clearance.

Hospitals can remind you of your mortality. See: *Death*.

The potential for symbolism branches out further when you consider the connections between hospitals and bankruptcy, and pain.

Dreaming about being in a hospital and well cared for by attentive staff can symbolize giving yourself the care you need, or the feeling that you're the center of attention. Hospital can be a word play for "hospitality."

Areas within a hospital can have specific symbolism. A maternity ward can relate to care of a child or your inner child. Radiology can relate to seeing into or through something, or fear that something like a bad mood will spread invisibly like radiation. Surgery can symbolize the removal of something sickening you, something that is no longer needed, or something you want to change about yourself. A psychiatric ward can symbolize mental health.

See also: *Cancer, Coma, Death, Disease, Doctor, Elderly, Handicap, Illness, Insane, Nurse, Paramedic, Psychologist, Surgery, Wheelchair*

Hostage—Being held hostage in a dream can connect with feeling powerless, or forced into a situation against your will. It may be an exaggeration that captures how you feel, such as when you are hostage to waiting in line at the DMV. Think of situations in which the word "hostage" is used in the metaphorical sense. "The company is holding the payment hostage until getting the changes they demanded."

A hostage can symbolize situations in which leverage is used against you. You have no choice but to go along, like a hostage.

You can be hostage to your emotions or desires if they control you.

You can be a captive of your morality, inhibitions, or duties. You won't allow yourself to go beyond certain limits or boundaries—for example, a severe introvert is captive to a life of isolation—or someone else makes your decisions and you don't have any choice. For example, a young woman dreams that she's kidnapped by her father, who confesses that he's madly in love with her. It's an exaggerated way of saying he places restrictions on her because he loves her. See: *Father*.

Being a hostage can mean that monotony and limited horizons are getting to you. Same old routine.

Enjoying the role of hostage in a dream can mean you enjoy your restrictions or limits, or want someone else to make your decisions.

Another word for hostage is "captive," and it opens possibilities for symbolism. You can be a captive to an idea about yourself, for example, or unable to leave a bad relationship. You can be a captive to attitudes, beliefs, fears, thoughts, feelings, ignorance, and so on. Your mind or heart is your jailer, in a sense.

"Captivated" means something has your attention and won't let go. It's one step away from "mesmerized."

See also: *Accomplice, Arrest, Cage, Escape, Fugitive, Kidnap, Prisoner*

Hot—See: *Heat*

Hot Air Balloon—See: *Balloon*

Hotel—A hotel is a place of transition, where you stay when away from home. Your dreaming mind begins there and branches out to connect ideas.

A hotel is often used as a setting to tell stories about transitions in your life. You leave one place in your life and haven't arrived at the next one. You're not the person you were but haven't quite become the person you will be next. You're changing.

For example, you leave college but don't have a professional job yet, or you break up with someone and don't have any new romantic prospects. After a breakup and moving out, a hotel is a place to stay while you sort out a new living situation.

The entries for *Airport* and *Apartment* go into more detail about dream settings connected with making a transition.

A hotel setting can connect with a feeling that a relationship is temporary. Not only are hotels temporary dwellings, they're associated with flings and affairs.

You can dream about staying in a nice hotel to symbolize the feeling of being treated with hospitality, because hotels are known for hospitality. On the other hand, the symbolism connects with situations such as being treated with no respect, which is how hotel staff can be treated, or looking after the cares and needs of others. This use of the symbolism is more likely if the dream puts you in the role of hotel employee.

Hotels are associated with public gatherings and can be used as a setting to symbolize anything that involves gatherings of people or public life. For example, after attending a busy party where you don't know many people, you dream about a hotel full of guests. It connects with a hotel as a place where many people gather who are unfamiliar to you. Plus, like guests at a party, the guests in a hotel are only there a short time.

The symbolism of a hotel connects with the idea of "home away from home." For example, a friend's home where you spend a lot of time, or an Internet forum where you are part of a community, could be described as a hotel.

Of course, consider the obvious, too. You can dream about a hotel while staying in a place that's not home, such as when staying with a friend or relative.

See also: *Airport, Apartment, Building, Home, Job, Servant, Vacation*

House—See: *Home*

Hug—Getting or receiving a hug in a dream can symbolize closeness and connection with a person. It can be a sign of harmony between people.

For example, a woman dreams about deeply embracing her elderly and beloved grandmother, who is dressed and packed to go away on a long trip. They express their love for each other before grandma departs. In the morning, the woman gets news that her grandmother passed away peacefully during the night.

Hugging someone represented as a dream-character can mean you miss the person, especially if you haven't had contact in a while.

Hugging someone you have had difficulty or problems with can be a sign of putting aside your differences. The feelings you experience during the dream and afterward should be easy to connect with the meaning of the hug.

Hugging can express strong concern for a person. For example, a mom hasn't heard from her young adult son in a few days because he's traveling overseas. She knows he's probably just having a great time, but she's a mom and she worries. Just before bed she gets an email from him—he's fine, having a great time—and that night she dreams about deeply embracing her son and feeling relieved.

A dream-character can represent something about you, so hugging a character can symbolize getting closer to, or embracing, yourself. However, the character is not likely to look like you. Instead, it's a projection that depicts something about you. For example, you struggle with yourself over being eccentric, but come to realize you like that side of yourself. It is then symbolized in a dream as hugging Marilyn Manson, an eccentric musician who doesn't care what anyone thinks of him.

Along similar lines, a hug in a dream can symbolize being close to a subject or situation. It can mean you embrace it. For example, you have the impression you're not good at math, but a math teacher persuades you to give it your best shot, and you dream about it as embracing the teacher. You're really embracing the subject.

As you can see by now, hugging in a dream is likely to be a physical representation of a personal situation. It's an action that can be an expression of feeling or that symbolizes other definitions of the words hug and embrace. You can embrace a new idea or culture. You can embrace death. In these senses, embrace means the opposite of reject or deny. It means "accept."

For example, you are distressed that a dear friend is moving out of town, but you know it's for the best. Embracing the friend in a dream could symbolize accepting the move. People often embrace before parting ways.

Embracing in a dream can be a sign of close emotional connection with a person, or a wish for it, especially if the dream-character embraced depicts someone you know.

Hugging can express romantic feelings and intentions.

It can be a way of "feeling out" the situation.

In a dream, embracing a person you know can mean you embrace something about the person, such as embracing their beliefs or ideas. For example, a woman who is agnostic has a friend who is a true believer. Through the friend's influence, the woman is realizing her problem is actually with religion, and God is something separate. She dreams about embracing her friend outside a church, symbolizing how she's not quite ready to embrace the friend's spiritual life—she's outside the church, not in it—but is rethinking her beliefs and appreciates her friend's influence.

In Freudian tradition, embracing is viewed as expressing desire for sexual union, but it's only true in a small minority of dreams. Even when sexual feelings and situations accompany embracing in a dream, the likelihood is you are embracing and integrating something about yourself. The character you embrace is a projection from your inner world.

Because arms are used to embrace, they can symbolize ideas related to embracing without actually physically acting it out. For example, you dream that an ex-spouse is in the hospital and has no arms. It symbolizes that the affectionate feelings you once had for the person are gone. Arms are needed to embrace. No arms, no embrace. See: *Arm*.

More possibilities to consider are that dreaming about an embrace, especially one that makes you feel good, is compensation for a lack of intimacy, contact, and affection in your life. Dreams can give you what you are missing in your waking life. If you feel isolated or unloved, your dreams might fill the void.

Embracing can symbolize forming an alliance or bond. If you see people embrace and you feel left out, you might feel left out of some other situation in your life. For example, you dream about a classmate embracing your teacher, and the dream connects with your feeling that the teacher gives preference to the classmate.

A hug that's too tight can symbolize something that you can't let go of, or that won't let go of you.

Cuddling is associated with how people fit together, and in dreams, fitting together can mean how personality, character, and other aspects of people fit together.

A man going through a divorce dreams about being in bed with his wife and cuddling. Suddenly, he feels movement down by his feet and looks down. He sees snakes in his bed. The dream sums up the situation with his (soon to be) ex-wife. The two of them are divorcing. They've been amicable and even close, as symbolized by cuddling. But her family is telling her to get mean and make the divorce hell to get every penny out of him that she can. Their "poisonous influence" and "venomous behavior" is symbolized by the snakes.

See also: *Arm, Emotions, Escape, Lips, Love*

Hummingbird—Picture in your mind a hummingbird. What are its qualities? It's fast. It darts. It gets into tight places. It's territorial.

Now consider how those qualities can be used to connect with your personal qualities or situations in your life. You could be like a social butterfly, never settling anywhere for long. You might feel like the time you have is short or is going by quickly. You have the ability to get out of tight personal places. You defend your territory.

The hummingbird in a dream can depict something about you or a situation you're in, or it can characterize something you observe about a person you know.

A hummingbird can symbolize quick wit or a quick mind. It can symbolize never settling anywhere for long, as with someone who travels constantly. It can symbolize cheerfulness and enthusiasm. Because hummingbirds have regular territory, they can symbolize something that connects people or communities.

See also: *Bees, Birds, Fly*

Hunger—Hunger in a dream can be a metaphor for being hungry in the sense of really wanting

something—success, fame, recognition, love. Think of when the word is used to describe something unrelated to physical hunger and ask yourself whether hunger in the dream is observing that sort of personal hunger in yourself or someone you know.

You might have a wish that is unfulfilled, or have a need for spiritual or emotional satisfaction. For example, some people "hunger" for God.

Appetite can symbolize desire, vice, or need.

It can indicate a pending health problem. Your body is asking for what it needs to repair or maintain itself. See: *Food.*

Hunger can connect with the idea of emaciation. See: *Emaciated.*

Finally, consider the obvious. Hunger in a dream can mean you really are hungry. You went to bed hungry, or food was on your mind.

See also: *Bear, Dinner, Eat, Emaciated, Fat, Food*

Hunt—To decode the symbolism of what it means to hunt in a dream, begin with how the word is used in figures of speech.

To hunt in a dream can symbolize pursuing a goal, such as "job hunting."

It can mean you have your eyes on someone, such as a romantic interest. You are in pursuit, on the scent. Or you have targeted someone, such as a business or romantic rival.

The same ideas apply to being the one hunted in a dream, except in reverse. Someone or something is after you.

Consider also that the hunt—especially the role of hunter—can represent a nice summary of your personality. Some people have the instincts and mindset of a hunter, even if they don't hunt—they're patient, stealthy, aggressive, observant, ruthless, quick-thinking, decisive. Hunting can symbolize the personal qualities needed to do a job, such as detective work or investment banking.

Oftentimes, whatever hunts you in a dream is something about yourself that feels left out, is repressed or unwanted. It's a physical representation of a personal situation. Or it can be something you've been ignoring, such as a desire to do something. Being pursued or hunted is a common dream theme with people who have something they really want to do—something big, like write a book, start a business, or travel—and aren't doing it.

Being hunted by an animal can mean an instinctual side of you wants to find a place in your life, a side somehow related to the symbolism of the animal. For example, being hunted by a tiger can mean you have the ability to dominate but don't use it. Or you have a need that's unmet. For example, a need for more sleep and rest can be symbolized as a bear hunting you. Bears are known for napping and hibernating. See: _Animals_.

An animal can symbolize a person you know, so being hunted by an animal can characterize something about the person or your relationship. For example, being hunted by a panther can symbolize the relentlessness of a suitor.

Hunting can tie in with other symbolism such as animals, guns, and killing. Use the entries listed below to explore further.

See also: _Animals, Arrow, Chase, Gun, Kill, Knife, Warrior_

Hurricane—After a major hurricane dominates the news and conversation, dreams featuring hurricanes tend to increase in frequency. It's simply a reflection of current events. However, usually a hurricane is used as symbolism.

A hurricane can symbolize a turbulent or destructive event.

The noise and destructiveness of a hurricane can be a metaphor to describe a turbulent situation. For example, a messy, acrimonious breakup can be symbolized as a hurricane. Even a messy child or living situation is comparable to a hurricane. It's an exaggerated but apt comparison.

A hurricane can symbolize a powerful attractive force, around which everything else revolves. For example, the desire to get rich, be successful, or have a family.

The spiraling motion of hurricane can symbolize the movement of energy from your inner being out into your life, or vice versa. See: _Spiral_.

Hurricanes can be used to describe the feeling that something is coming into your life that will change everything, probably for the worse.

An impending mental breakdown is like a hurricane that blows through your mind. Chaotic and swirling thoughts are like a hurricane, as are turbulent emotions. It could symbolize something that's been building in you, and when unleashed it won't be stopped.

A hurricane can symbolize a feeling of dread or fear. See: _Fear_.

It can symbolize a "force of nature." Nothing will stand in its way. It could symbolize a person who blows through your life.

Hurricanes tend to come on slowly. Affected areas usually get warning days ahead of time, and the destructive force of a hurricane builds slowly, as opposed to a tornado that strikes all at once. These characteristics of hurricanes can be used to create metaphors that are comparable to situations in your life. For example, you know that relatives are coming for a visit and bringing their troubles with them, and you do everything possible to prepare for the storm—hide the booze, send the kids away.

Refer to the entry for _Disaster_ for a general idea of how dreams use different types of disasters as symbolism.

See also: _Disaster, Fear, Lightning, Spiral, Storm, Tornado, Weather_

Hurt—See: _Wound_

Husband—When your husband is a character in the dream (presuming you have one), a good first guess is the dream is about something related to the person or your relationship. The most common dream themes usually center around what you do most and whom you see most in your daily lives. They also focus on our emotional lives. Your husband is likely to meet those criteria and be a frequent character in your dreams.

The door is wide open for areas of life addressed by a dream featuring your husband. The entry for _Sister_ shows how to analyze dream-characters based on people close to you. Begin narrowing down the possibilities by reviewing everything that happened the previous day involving him, including your thoughts and feelings.

You can dream about wanting his attention, sometimes symbolized as following him around, calling his name, or calling him on the phone. See: *Phone*.

You can dream about your finances, probably featuring details such as banks and money. See: *Money, Wallet*.

You can dream about your sex life, complete with beds and bedrooms and as scenes that depict intimacy or hint at it. See: *Bed*.

You can dream about his fitness as a provider and father. See: *Father*.

You can dream about his health. Doctors, nurses, and hospitals are commonly featured in these dreams. See: *Doctor*.

If he has cheated on you or you suspect him of cheating, it's likely to come up in your dreams. Keep in mind, he's a character in your dream, and if that character cheats, it's part of the story, not necessarily something that's actually happening. Usually, cheating is symbolism. See: *Cheat*.

Dreaming about your boyfriend in the role of husband can be a "dress rehearsal." Is he "husband material"?

Close relationships can be akin to marriage, in which case the unfamiliar husband character could be a surrogate for a male in your life, such as a friend you spend a lot of time with, someone you feel close to.

The dream-character that looks like your husband may be a projection of something about yourself and have nothing to do with him. Something about him is used to tell a story about you.

For example, he doesn't like to talk about his feelings, and yesterday you resisted a friend's probing of your feelings. You then dream about your husband being kidnapped and interrogated, an exaggerated way of describing your situation. The actions and details with him in the dream describe what's going on with you.

What if you dream about a husband and the character is completely imaginary? It's obviously symbolic. A husband is someone you are committed to, and as a dream-character it can symbolize being committed to something such as a cause, project, spiritual pursuit, or your job. See: *Marriage*.

A husband can symbolize the masculine principle, known as yang. Everything in creation is made of opposites, expressed as masculine and feminine, and yang encompasses everything traditionally masculine. It's the giver to yin's receiver, the sun to yin's moon, and it's the best way to understand your relationship with your animus, because you're actually relating to the masculine archetype of the unconscious mind. The subject speaks to the deepest reaches of your being and processes going on outside of conscious view. See: *Animus, Penis*.

Finally, a husband might represent your ideal, or a cultural ideal. Dreams can act as simulations to help you figure out what you want in a husband and how to find him. They ask, "What if it really happened? Would you think the same way?" You might find that your ideal is not what your heart wants. See: *Boyfriend*.

These possibilities really only scratch the surface. Use the entries below to explore further, especially: *Boyfriend, Groom, Man*.

See also: *Animus, Archetypes, Boyfriend, Father, God, Groom, Man, Marriage, Money, Penis, Phone, Wallet, Wedding, Unconscious Mind*

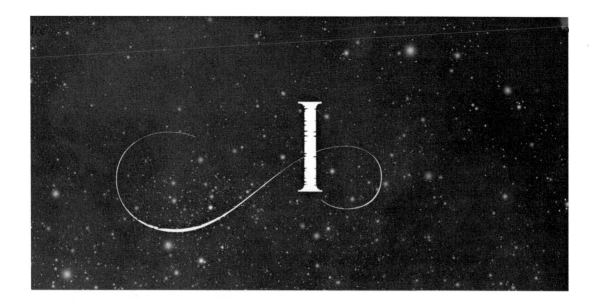

Ice—In simplest terms, ice is frozen liquid, and that association offers many interpretive directions to explore that have nothing directly to do with frozen liquid. Instead it's a physical representation of a personal situation.

Frozen can refer to lack of emotion or compassion—a person is "cold." See: *Emotions*.

When people are tense or distant, the environment is said to be frozen. It can mean a situation is at a standstill, as in the phrase, "The negotiations are frozen."

You get a cold feeling in some places and around some people.

Ice can indicate feeling unwelcome, as in the terms "frosty reception" and "cold shoulder."

Ice is slippery and can symbolize a slippery situation. Something trips you up. You lose your internal sense of balance.

Movement in a dream generally symbolizes movement in your life, so ice implies a "slippery situation," or moving cautiously forward with something.

Encountering ice while driving can symbolize loss of control—of yourself, your life, a situation. Or it can connect with overreaction, because there's nothing to do while sliding on ice in a car but hope you regain control before crashing—but if you overreact you make the situation worse. See: *Car*.

Walking on ice can connect with a physical condition affecting your gait. Injury can affect the way you walk. The short, shuffling steps a person takes when walking on ice are similar to how a person can walk when an injury or infirmity affects gait.

Walking on thin ice can symbolize being extra careful to avoid mistakes, breaking rules, or stepping over proverbial lines.

Freezing temperatures are associated with delays and dangerous travel conditions. It raises the possibility for danger in travel, to health, and to state of mind or mood, as in the term "winter blues." See: *Blizzard, Winter*.

It can mean now's not the time to do something. Wait till conditions are better.

Freezing conditions are a way of describing war. While most dreams are personal and not related to geopolitics, dreams love to make connections between related ideas, and perhaps in some way a dream with these themes describes a state of conflict. See: *War*.

Freezing in a dream can reflect a physical state. Maybe the covers fell off your body while you slept, and you got cold, or you hear wind howling outside as you sleep and know it's cold out there, or you have the chills from fever or illness.

See also: *Blizzard, Car, Emotions, Fever, Precognitive Dream, War, Weather, White, Winter*

Illegal—See: *Crime*

Illness—While illness in a dream is likely to symbolize something unrelated to physical health, first consider the obvious: you might really be ill, or have an illness developing and aren't consciously aware of it. For example, a dream about finding sick fish in a fishbowl filled with bad water warns the dreamer that a urinary-tract infection is coming on. By applying a simple home remedy, the dreamer treats the condition before it flares into a full-blown illness.

An illness can be represented directly, but is more likely to be referred to using symbolism, such as in the last example. Illness is sometimes referred to as "a bug," so a dream can represent an illness as an insect or infestation of insects. See: *Bug*.

Generally, a reference to illness in a dream is more likely to mean that something is out of kilter, not working as it should. It is "ill," dysfunctional. That idea can apply widely to create symbolism. For example, a dysfunctional work or home environment is said to be ill. Societies can be ill. The idea applies to dysfunctional organizations and people, too, creating cross-references that can be used as symbolism.

"Sick in the head" means mental illness or moral depravity. See: *Psychologist*.

Behaviors that cut against the grain can be labeled as mental illness and represented as physical illness. For example, today's attention-deficit/hyperactivity disorder (ADHD) diagnosis in children used to be called "rebellion" or "free thinking." Dreams can use this contradiction between what we're told is illness and what we know to be true to create symbolism.

Illness can begin with belief. Belief that you are ill can be a self-fulfilling prophecy, and dreams know the difference. Dreams will create scenarios involving illness then leave it up to you whether to believe it. If you react with disbelief, or a dream-character reacts that way, it's an indicator to examine the connection between belief and reality. What the mind believes to be true—especially about health and the body—becomes true. This is especially true in dreams, because they create simulated realities based on what you believe to be true, and

what you believe to be true in a dream can become true when you are awake.

For example, author Robert Moss dreamed about seeing through the eyes of another man as the man was shot multiple times in the chest. Moss woke up with welts on his chest where the bullets penetrated! During the dream, he thought it was real, and his body responded in kind.

See also: *AIDS, Abscess, Bug, Chase, Disease, Doctor, Elderly, Fever, Hospital, Infect, Insane, Psychologist, Vulture*

Imam—See: *Pastor*

Imposter—An imposter in a dream can symbolize pretending to be something you're not. For example, a person who pretends to be interested in someone just to have sex or gain favor is an imposter. However, the person feigning interest might not see it that way, creating a difference between how the conscious mind views something and how it's viewed by the unconscious mind—perfect conditions for sparking powerful dreams.

The idea connects with other situations that aren't intentional; for example, you can feel like an imposter when a teacher or supervisor praises you for work for which you know other people deserve credit.

The symbolism of being an imposter can connect with the idea in the phrase, "Fake it till you make it." It's a way of saying you are learning as you go. You don't feel qualified for a role, task, or position, but you sure are trying. Portrayal as an imposter is an exaggeration that captures your feelings.

Along similar lines, being an imposter can mean you're fooling yourself.

The symbolism of an imposter connects with the idea that something is unconvincing. For example, as layoffs are going on at work, you're told that the company will come out of it better off than before, but you are not convinced. You then dream that top management are actually aliens wearing human bodies.

You can dream about an imposter when someone you know has been through a big change, to the point that the person is almost unrecognizable.

For example, you get into a relationship with someone and down the line start to feel that he or she is not the same person you first met.

See also: *Disguise, Fake, Mask*

Incest—People tend to freak out over incest dreams, but incest can be used as a comparison to create symbolism, the same as anything else. It's all fair game for your dreams.

Incest is a taboo, and can symbolize anything that's taboo or close to it. For example, dating the younger brother or sister of your best friend is taboo in some circles.

It can symbolize sex—or just the thought of it—with someone very close to you, such as a best friend or teacher.

It can symbolize integrating new parts into the personality. Quite often, sex in dreams symbolizes the integration of new parts of the personality. Physical union represents mental union. In which case, incest is simply a way to symbolize how a relative rubs off on you.

For example, a young woman dreams about having sex with her brother. During the dream it feels very natural, but afterward she questions whether something is really wrong with her. However, the dream simply shows that she's been learning from his example how to be more competitive. Sex in this dream means "integration." It means something about him is *inside* her. Get the idea? It's symbolism.

Incest can symbolize something that disgusts you, that feels really wrong.

It can be a sign of doing something that invites big trouble with your family. See: *Family*.

It can be a way of saying that two people are a little too close.

It can symbolize talking about sex with a relative, especially if the incest involves oral sex. See: *Cunnilingus, Fellatio*.

It can amplify feelings of attraction for a relative and capture related feelings. For example, a young man dreams about having sex with his female cousin and wakes up feeling dirty. He can't help but notice that the innocent little girl he grew up with has blossomed into a beautiful young woman. The more he tries to ignore it, the more he feels conflicted. The dream is simply reflecting his thoughts and feelings. It's not saying he wants to have sex with her. Instead, it amplifies his feelings of attraction so he will come to terms with them, allowing him to notice that his cousin is sexually attractive and not feel guilty about it.

For more example dreams, see: *Family, Sex, Sister*.

Incest can connect with feelings of shame and self-loathing.

In simplest terms, incest means "inappropriately close," an idea ripe for use as symbolism.

See also: *Brother, Family, Father, Genitals, Guilt, Naked, Mother, Sex, Sister*

Individuation—Individuation is an important concept for understanding dreams because it's a big reason that you dream. Yes, you dream to process, to learn, to vent, but most of all you dream *to grow*. Growth is defined as becoming more conscious. Carl Jung coined the term *individuation process* to mean "make conscious what is unconscious" and fill out the personality. See: *Circle*.

"Self-actualized" is another term from psychology that means basically the same thing, except that in Jung's teachings, the completed personality is like a blueprint in the unconscious mind, and you build your life and yourself on the basis of that blueprint, like building a house.

This subject leads deep down the rabbit hole. Use the entries listed below to branch out and explore, and search online. Many excellent resources are available.

See also: *Anima, Animus, Archetypes, Circle, Collective Unconscious, Psyche, Spiral, Unconscious Mind*

Infect—To decode the symbolism of an infection, begin with the possibility that it's a physical representation of a personal situation. Next, imagine how that idea can apply to you and your life.

An infection can be contagious, and bad moods and influence are contagious, spreading from person to person. Negativity is contagious. Your body can symbolize your mind or psyche, so an infection of the body can symbolize an infection of the mind. It's the sort of graphic, exaggerated imagery that dreams love to use to make comparisons.

An infection eats at you, and other things can eat at you: stress, anxiety, difficulties, problems. See: *Cancer*.

Now ask, why would a dream use an infection to tell the story? Because an infection spreads. It multiplies. It grows worse if left untreated. It overpowers the body's natural defenses. It connects with feelings of dread and helplessness.

In addition, an infection works from inside you. It gets under your skin. It causes inflammation. Now imagine how that can be used to compare with something that harms you from within. That you can't shake. That "inflames" you and gets under your skin. A bad attitude is a prime candidate, or criticism that works its way into you. Something in your thoughts and emotions needs to be healed.

Always consider the obvious. Dreaming about an infection can mean something is affecting your health. Perhaps you really do have an infection. A dream usually delivers the news in such a way that you'll get the message. However, it's more likely to be turned into symbolism. For example, an infection can be symbolized as an infestation of bugs. See: *Illness*.

An infection festers, and that association can be used to say that something has been going on for too long. A situation needs to be cleaned up, and it might be a situation in your mind or feelings, or it might be something about your life.

Someone with an infection is a person you don't want to come into contact with, and as symbolism it can mean you feel like a pariah, or you avoid something that might rub off on you. For example, you avoid someone who has a bad reputation because you don't want your reputation to be sullied through association with that person. You then dream about avoiding someone with an infectious disease.

Infection is associated with quarantine, and quarantine can have symbolism related to feeling that you are being ignored or need to be away from people. Or it can mean that a person is "poisonous," and his or her influence needs to be prevented from spreading. The idea extends to situations that rub off in a bad way. For example, you bring your problems at work home with you, or vice versa.

What's eating at you? What's gone on for too long? What's rubbing off on you? Usually, answering simple questions like these lead to the source of the dream.

See also: *AIDS, Cancer, Disease, Doctor, Erupt, Fever, Hospital, Illness, Infest, Invasion, Venom*

Infest—An infestation in a dream can connect with a situation in decay, such as when you haven't been taking care of yourself and your emotional, psychological, or physical health declines. It's a condition that spreads and grows because of neglect. The symbolism is based on the association that an organic substance in decay is likely to be infested with insects or maggots.

Yeah, gross, right? But in a way it's beautiful because it's part of the process of eating the waste and renewing life. If you dream about an infestation eating decayed flesh, it can symbolize that you are letting go of something holding you back, in your life or in your personal development.

Infestation can symbolize squalor. For example, an infestation of rats or roaches can symbolize squalid living conditions. An infestation of bugs can symbolize worries, problems, and anxieties. They infest your mind. An infestation of sharks can symbolize feeling as if you're in dangerous water. You don't trust the motives or intentions of people around you.

Infestation can symbolize shame or disgust. The bigger the infestation, the greater the shame or guilt. See: *Bug*.

Infestation can have similar symbolism to disease or plague. It's something contracted, something spread, something dirty, damaging, or disgusting, something that plagues you, that won't go away, that has to be cleaned or cut out. See: *Disease*.

Something infested most likely has not been cleaned up in a long time, and in dreams that idea can translate into a personal condition that has gone on long enough to negatively affect you. For instance, abuse and trauma infest the rest of the psyche when left untreated or unhealed, leading to secondary issues such as depression, anxiety, and delusion. In which case, an infestation in a dream symbolizes how an untreated psychological wound can create other problems. See: *Clean, Wound.*

It can go deeper. In rare cases, dreams about infestation are associated with serious psychological and spiritual issues. These dreams will recur and are likely to be nightmares—unless, of course, you personally identify with whatever has infested your mind or spirit and enjoy the company. See the writings of Adam Blai for more information about this sort of infestation. See: *Demon.*

An infestation of worms or grubs in your face or head can symbolize bad thoughts or influence that has wormed into you. It can symbolize something that affects your reputation or self-image. See: *Face.*

See also: *Bug, Cancer, Demon, Disease, Erupt, Illness, Infect, Insects, Invasion, Parasite, Rat, Roach, Skin*

Inject—An injection can symbolize taking something into your system, not just into your body but also into your psyche, your being. For example, being injected with a bad drug can symbolize taking on another person's problems, or the influence of negativity or bad habits.

An injection can have positive connotations, too, when used in the sense of "inject some humor." It can have similar symbolism to the idea behind the phrase "breath of fresh air." It can mean you renew your energy, focus or motivation, or bring about a needed change. For example, a vacation renews you and feels like an injection of energy.

An injection can symbolize something you physically take into your body, such as caffeine or supplements, that infuses you. For example, drinking a big cup of coffee is referred to as a "caffeine injection."

Your reaction is a big clue to the meaning of the underlying symbolism because you subconsciously know what it means and react accordingly. Reacting with fear or horror or happiness or relief speaks volumes. Take note of whether you are voluntarily injected or not, too, because it can tell you whether you are voluntarily taking something into yourself, or if it's forced on you.

If an injection stings, it can have related symbolism. See: *Bee.*

If an injection is poisonous or venomous, see: *Venom.*

If it has a sexual vibe, it could symbolize something being integrated into your personality. See: *Sex.*

See also: *Bee, Blood, Body, Drugs, Sex, Snake, Venom*

Injury—See: *Wound*

Innocent—To dream that you are innocent can come in response to being accused of something. A dream will make a comparison to a situation in which you feel accused, though the details are likely to be changed. The symbolism will express your feelings and emotions.

The theme of innocence can pop up in dreams when you or someone you know acts innocent, as in not guilty. For example, a friend does something to betray you, then minimizes his or her involvement, even pretends it is no big deal. The friend "acts innocent." You then dream about the person claiming innocence of a crime they obviously committed.

Seemingly innocent questions and remarks in a dream can expose big differences between you and someone you know, or between you and a group of people—especially differences in viewpoints or opinions. For example, you have been attending a church and start to feel uncomfortable with some of its teachings. You then dream about questioning the preacher. The questions are innocent in the sense that you just want clarification, but even raising them in your mind can make you feel guilty.

An innocent character in a dream might be a symbol of purity. This theme tends to arise in the dreams of people who had their innocence taken or corrupted, or who are protecting the innocence of themselves or someone else, such as a child or sibling. A dream can take that idea and turn it into a story about crimes and courts. The theme can arise in response to witnessing changes in someone who used to be innocent. For example, the first time you see your little sister wear a miniskirt sparks a dream about remembering her as an innocent young girl.

See also: *Angel, Child, Court, Guilt, Hooker, White*

Insane—Dreams exaggerate, and insanity can be an exaggeration of wild, reckless, or irrational behavior. It's a way of amplifying the behavior to make you aware of it.

It can reflect a situation in which you don't understand a person's reaction. It seems crazy or irrational to you.

Insanity can symbolize chaos. Life is upside down, or a situation is tense or unpredictable. It can be the sort of situation where you say, "It's driving me crazy!" Or, "I could go insane!"

Dreams use wordplays to create symbolism. Another word for insane is "mad," and mad can mean angry. Therefore, dreaming about an insane person or situation can symbolize being angry or upset. Or it can mean a safe place or refuge. See: *Anger.*

Of course, people can act insane, and crazy things do happen. A dream is likely to obscure such events with symbolism. For example, after an encounter with a crazy relative at a Christmas gathering, you dream about Santa Claus flying his sleigh like a drunk pilot and cackling maniacally.

The theme of insanity can arise in dreams to symbolize something scary or bad. The connections are made because crazy people can be scary and do bad things.

An asylum is a perfect setting to describe chaos in your mind. Your mind is represented in dreams as a place, especially a building. It can mean you have been acting or thinking irrationally or recklessly. Your life is out of control. Your feelings are in turmoil.

An asylum can characterize an environment such as home or work. It's crazy, chaotic, dysfunc-

tional, leaderless. Is your job like an insane asylum, or home life like a mental ward?

An asylum can symbolize living in a fantasy world.

It can symbolize feeling like you are treated like you're crazy or abnormal. For an example dream, see: *Brother.*

It can symbolize an out-of-control situation.

An abandoned asylum can symbolize a crazy time of your life that's behind you. You might dream about that time of life because something recently reminded you of it. You saw an old frat buddy, or exam week is coming up, or you started a new relationship and hope it doesn't turn out crazy like the last one.

See also: *Ego, Erupt, Infest, Nightmare, Psychologist, Terrorist, Zoo*

Insects—Types of insects can have specific symbolism, so if a dream features a type of insect, see below.

The meaning of insects in dreams tends to relate to what insects do. Two of the most common references are to biting and stinging. In a dream an insect bites you on the neck and it refers to a situation or person that's a "pain in the neck." In a dream a bee stings you, and in life you are stung by someone's comment. In a dream a house is infested by cockroaches, and in life you are taken advantage of by filthy people, or someone's personal habits are gross.

Insects in dreams can symbolize anxieties and irritations, something that "bugs" you. For example, you find grubs in the bottom of a Styrofoam cup and associate it with the cups used for coffee at work. A situation there is bugging you. Or your neighbor's blaring music is getting on your nerves, and you dream about it as cicadas buzzing loudly outside your windows. Or someone's personality irritates you, and you dream about it as flies buzzing around your head.

Insects buzzing around your head can symbolize thoughts that irritate you. The head is associated with thoughts, and insects with irritation. The two associations go together.

Insects can symbolize problems and worries that bug you. The more insects, generally, the more problems and worries. See: *Infest*.

The same imagery can symbolize shame or disgust with yourself.

Bugs crawling on you can symbolize a physical condition such as a skin rash, or a mental condition such as a phobia.

Bugs inside your body can symbolize illness, such as a virus or bacterial infection. See: *Illness*.

An insect eaten can symbolize the feeling of being small and powerless.

Maggots can symbolize depravity. Maggots eating into the head can symbolize thoughts that plague or infest you. Maggots in the eyes can symbolize seeing something that worms into your thoughts.

Those are all negative comparisons, but there are good ones involving insects. For example, a butterfly landing on you can symbolize that you can be trusted with things that are delicate or fragile. See: *Butterfly*.

Insects can be used to make metaphors. When you look around a busy city, do you see a comparison with an ant colony? Ever watch people swarm like flies to take advantage of misfortune? Do you observe like a fly on the wall? The comparisons are all around us.

See also: *Ant, Bug, Butterfly, Infest, Little, Maggots, Roach, Worm*

Intoxicated—See: *Alcohol, Drugs, Drunkenness*

Intruder—The symbolism of an intruder can be found in the root word, intrude. When you feel intruded on, you can dream about an intruder breaking into your home or barging into a private situation such as while you're using the bathroom or taking a shower. Many situations in life can be symbolized this way.

For example, hosting a house guest can intrude on your regular routine. Or missionaries show up at your front door uninvited. Dreams turn such situations into symbolism.

Dreams use comparisons to create symbolism, so an intruder can compare with something that makes you unsettled or uncomfortable. For example, you can be unsettled by rumors at work that layoffs are coming. You can be uncomfortable with a person who is too forward or demanding. You can feel intruded upon when someone asks you personal questions or pries into your private life, such as during a physical exam.

Unwanted thoughts and feelings, or something that interferes with your concentration, can be intrusive. Thoughts that keep you awake at night are intrusive. Bad memories can be intrusive.

An intruder can symbolize an unknown, repressed, or rejected part of yourself trying to get your attention. It wants to be consciously recognized and integrated into the personality. It's like a family pet left out of the fun. Everyone is inside the house, warm and together, while the dog is outside in the cold. If the situation prolongs, what is the dog likely to do? Whimper, cry, bark, act out. When a part of yourself is left out, it will find a way of getting noticed and making its presence felt. To the ego, this is an intrusion because it is unwanted.

See also: *Ambush, Burglary, Door, Ego, Invasion, Panic, Parasite, Thief*

Invasion—An invasion in a dream can symbolize something that invades your thoughts or breaks your routine. It can be anything you would describe as "invasive." For example, you're trying to study or get some work done and your phone rings constantly. Or you come home to find that someone has been poking around on your computer. It's an invasion of privacy. See: *Intruder*.

An invasion implies a heavy struggle that comes on suddenly, though it might be expected. For example, you know that a major push is coming to get a project done at work, and dream about preparing for an invasion. In the eyes of retail workers, "Black Friday" is comparable to an invasion. For teachers it could be the first day of school.

Of course, dreaming about an invasion can be interpreted more literally. For example, viruses and germs "invade" your body. They can number in the millions, so it's like an invading army, and a person is said to "fight" or "battle" illness. Or you live near your country's borders and people are illegally crossing over, "invading" your land. Or your company is bought out by "corporate raiders." Or you have been taking in news about countries preparing to go to war or invading their neighbors, and your dreams respond to it.

When Russia took over Crimea, people in America suddenly started reporting more than the usual number of dreams about a Russian invasion of America, reflecting the fact that the annexation of Crimea was big news, and some news outlets framed it in terms of an invasion.

See also: *Army, Fight, Intruder, Tidal Wave, War*

Invisible—See: *Ghost, Hide*

Island—Being on an island can symbolize isolation or the desire to be alone. You're cut off from the world. Or you're alone in some situation. The comparison to being alone on an island is made when you don't have support, companionship, or help.

An island can symbolize thoughts related to vacation, retirement, or the good life of ease and fun. It can mean you want to slow down or get away from it all.

As bodies of land that rise out of the ocean, islands are great metaphors for the conscious mind, which rises out of the unconscious mind. See: *Ocean.*

An island can symbolize the ego, which is basically the conscious mind. See: *Ego.*

See also: *Beach, Boat, Ego, Mars, Ocean, Unconscious Mind, Vacation, Water*

Jaguar—See: *Leopard*

Jail—Being in jail is likely to be a physical representation of a personal situation. You're trapped, confined. A situation is never-ending. Things never change. You can't get away. See: *Prisoner*.

Dreams can begin there and branch out far and wide. For example, you have a disability that creates a perception of you that can't be escaped—people will always see you that way—or that limits what you can do. Or you are perceived as an unintelligent or quiet person, so you are never asked for your opinion or input.

You *feel* trapped in your body, in your life, in your head. It's like being in jail.

Racial and gender stereotyping can be confining. For example, a female working in a male-dominated profession might feel like she can't advance because of her gender.

Rules and restrictions can be confining. They can make you feel limited and trapped.

Making decisions can spark a dream about being in jail. It captures the feeling that once a decision is made, it can't be changed. It limits your freedom to choose.

Beliefs can be limiting—not just religious beliefs, but personal ones, as well, such as a belief that you can't do something because you don't

have the skill or ability. Some people avoid any sort of religious organization because they don't want to limit their spiritual pursuits.

The same idea applies to social groups. To be part of certain groups, you have to look and act a certain way and espouse certain opinions and beliefs. To some people, such conformity is equivalent to being locked in a cage or kept in a jail.

"Detained" is another word for "jailed" and it can be associated with a feeling of being delayed or bogged down, in a specific situation or just in general. Or you feel you are under suspicion—suspects in crimes are detained.

Jails are associated with punishment, and in dreams a jail setting can symbolize that you feel you are being punished, or that someone—yourself included—deserves punishment. For example, you can feel that an abusive or neglectful parent deserves to be punished, and dream about the person being sentenced to jail. The parent might not have broken any laws, but did break your heart or spirit. That idea applies to other people in your life. If they wrong you, they deserve punishment.

Dreaming about being jailed can stem from a guilty conscience—you feel that's what you deserve. See: *Guilt*.

Jails are associated with isolation. Isolation can be involuntary, such as when you don't have any friends. Isolation can be necessary for thinking through what's happening in your life, or pursuing something that requires long hours of solitary concentration. In such a situation you might dream that you are sentenced to jail, symbolizing self-imposed exile.

See also: *Accomplice, Arrest, Bully, Cage, Dungeon, Escape, Fugitive, Guilt, Hostage, Jail, Police Officer, Prisoner*

Janitor—To dream about a janitor can mean you feel you are cleaning up other people's messes. Or you aren't appreciated for what you do, or are treated like hired help. See: *Servant*.

Janitors are associated with being at the bottom of the totem pole. For example, see: *Afterlife*.

See also: *Employee, Job, Servant*

Jealous—Jealousy in a dream often directly connects with how you feel. Dreams create symbolism that sparks the feelings or emotions that need your attention, so whatever you feel jealous about is often disguised. However, you can make the connection and uncover the meaning of the symbolism simply by thinking about whatever has made you feel jealous lately. You subconsciously know what the symbolism means and react on that basis, not to the overt imagery, so if you react with jealousy to something in a dream, you know it symbolizes something that sparks your jealousy.

Two common sources of jealousy are success and love. You can be jealous of someone's success, or jealous of the attention that a love interest or mate gives to someone else. Jealousy often arises from feelings of inadequacy and disappointment. It is an "umbrella emotion" that covers deeper emotions, and it projects your inner dramas onto external situations and people. If you feel jealous, your dreams might try to show you the source of the feeling. What's missing from you that makes you jealous of someone else?

See also: *Cheat, Emotions, Shadow*

Jehovah—See: *God*

Jester—See: *Clown*

Jesus—No other figure in dreams is as easily misunderstood as Jesus Christ. The temptation is to interpret it literally when first it should be thought of as figurative, symbolic, like almost everything else about dreams.

As a symbol of Christianity, Jesus can be used as a character in stories about faith, spirituality, and religion, for example. The possibilities expand further when you consider associations with Jesus such as hope, goodness, honesty, healing, love, acceptance, sacrifice, and conflict.

You can dream about Jesus when your faith is tested; times are bad and you need hope for the future; you're confronted by a person or situation that can bring out the best or worst in you; you are sick, dealing with evil, or have issues or questions about organized religion and spiritual beliefs.

Or perhaps you relate to Jesus because he went through long periods of withdrawal from society, or because he was persecuted.

People going through powerful changes can dream about figures such as Jesus who guide them and even forcibly abduct them. Abduction is a way of saying that something inside you won't wait any longer for you to take action or make changes. Alien abduction can have the same symbolism. See: *UFO*.

Sometimes Jesus is not presented in a dream as a symbol but instead as a living spirit. These dreams often involve powerful messages and emotions and are completely believable. It really feels like the living spirit of Jesus visited you, and the experience can be life-changing. It causes some people to find within themselves faith they didn't know they had.

Your unconscious mind can dress up a character as Jesus when it really wants your attention, to shock you back to reality or drive home an important message. The unconscious mind will use whatever is at its disposal to get the job done. See: *Unconscious Mind*.

Carl Jung wrote about *psychopomp* figures that act as bridges between the material and the spiritual, between mankind and God, between the conscious mind and the unconscious. The form they take in dreams is usually of the highest religious or spiritual figure in a culture. For Muslims, their psychopomp is the Prophet Mohammed. For Buddhists it's Gautama Buddha. For Hindus it's Krishna or Saint Ishu. For Christians it's Jesus. Saints and other lesser religious figures can act as psychopomps, too.

A psychopomp is a projection of your potential to be like these great figures, to emulate them, to live as they did and practice spirituality as they did. However, it's difficult for most people to see that potential in themselves, so they project it onto a figure like Jesus until they develop their own capabilities.

Figures such as a Jesus can act as the face of the Hero archetype. The mythic hero—the man who is God, is king of the spiritual kingdom, is killed and resurrected—is an archetypal story that has appeared throughout the ages in cultures around the world. See: *Hero*.

See also: *Archetypes, Buddha, Collective Unconscious, God, Heaven, Hero, Mohammed, Soul, Spirit, UFO, Unconscious Mind*

Jet—The symbolism of a jet can be the same as an airplane, but with the added dimensions of high speed and agility. Flying a jet in a dream can connect with feelings of thrill and excitement. It can mean you are quickly going to destinations in your life. It can symbolize rapid success and advancement. It implies power and a powerful impression.

You can dream about a jet when you hear one flying overhead while asleep.

See also: *Airplane, Airport, Army, Fly, Speed*

Jewelry—In general, jewelry represents value, particularly value you place in yourself or in others, or that others place in you. The connection is easy to make through associations such as "precious" and "expensive."

The context of the dream is especially important for jewelry symbolism because it can be used in the negative or positive sense. For example, dreaming about cheap jewelry can mean something is undervalued or treated cheaply. But precious jewelry can mean high regard, including high regard for yourself. Jewelry can symbolize recog-

nition of importance. Finding precious jewelry can mean that you find something precious in yourself, such as a quality, trait, or ability. It's something to be treasured.

Jewelry can connect with family wealth, as in the term "family jewels." For example, if you dream about your mom giving away family jewels, it can mean she is sharing valuable resources with someone outside the family, such as her time or praise or even material resources.

Read the entries below for more ideas, especially *Diamond, Gem, Gold,* and *Money.*

See also: *Amulet, Diamond, Emerald, Gem, Gold, Money, Silver, Talisman*

Job—Considering the importance of work and career for so many people, it's not surprising that dreaming about your job is common. These dreams usually reflect recent events and situations related to it. However, expand the idea of what constitutes a job, and consider how the word is used to mean something other than formal employment, and dreams can branch out from there to touch on a variety of subjects.

For example, being a parent is a job. Maintaining social relationships requires work, and for some people "networking" is an integral part of their job. A hobby that you're trying to turn into a paid gig is treated like a job. The possibilities go on and on.

A man dreams that he has two jobs, both in restaurants, and decides to call off one of them. It symbolizes his feeling of being overextended. He has a career and home to take care of, and he's too busy with work to put as much effort into his home. It has to wait, symbolized as calling off of work.

Now let's return to "job" meaning what you do for a living. Your dreams can branch out to tell a story about advancement, authority, recognition, prestige, pressure, time management, skill, competence, education, training, compensation, choice.

Dreams can talk about your job—or a job—without referring to it directly. For example, shopping at a mall can symbolize casting a wide net for a job, because a mall is place with many stores (employers) to choose from, and making a purchase is an investment you make (giving your time and energy) in return for what you get in return (salary, benefits, authority, challenge, prestige). Fishing can symbolize looking for a job. See: *Fishing, Mall*.

Dreams involving driving and your car can be closely connected with your job. A car takes you places in life, and so can your job. See: *Car*.

For more examples of other not-so-obvious dream themes that can connect with your job, see: *Horse, Journey, Lost, Marriage, Robot, Servant*.

The dreaming mind is a very clever storyteller, oblique when it needs to be or when that's the best way to tell the story. However, it can be direct. If a dream takes place at your place of work or involves co-workers and other people related to your work or occupation, it's a clue that the subject somehow relates to your job. For an example, see: *Walmart*.

Remember, though, that dreams can address anything related to your job, and they don't necessarily have to use your workplace as a setting. Instead, your workplace, even if it's at home or on the road, is portrayed through a different setting based on your associations and feelings. See: *Dungeon*.

In another example, a woman dreams about an apocalyptic battle symbolizing her job conditions working in the front office of a school. She loves the work, but it can be a battle to get everything done. See: *Fight*.

Dreams about your job are not necessarily related directly to events at work, but instead address something related. For example, a female dreams that she is at work, at her desk, and a co-worker comes up and touches her suggestively, distracting her. The dream is about the dreamer's distraction at work. She was recently on her honeymoon and her mind is not on her work. See: *Co-Worker*.

A man dreams that he's at a party with his co-workers and he's naked. No one seems to notice, though. Being naked symbolizes his fear that he'll be exposed for not knowing how to do his job—he's still new. And his nakedness going unnoticed symbolizes that no one knows he doesn't really know what he's doing at work.

Use the entries listed below to further explore this subject. This book has entries for a variety of occupations (nurse, pilot, doctor, artist, police officer, soldier) and titles (president, captain, general) and work settings (grocery store, restaurant, school) that are addressed as symbolism, generally not from the point of view of someone who works in those occupations, but it still could be helpful to read them if your job or dream involves them. They are too numerous to list.

See also: *Army, Boss, Car, Computer, Co-Worker, Dismissal, Dungeon, Email, Employee, Family Business, Famous, Fight, Fishing, Gun, Hooker, Lost, Naked, Police Officer, Principal, Robot, Servant, Slave, Tackle, Teacher, Unemployed, Vacation, Walmart*

Journey—As with other symbolism, when considering what a journey in a dream can mean, think about how it's used to compare with situations in life, and explain it in simplest terms. A journey is an act of traveling from one place to another. In our lives we "go places." We have destinations to reach and landmarks to mark our progress. We journey from one point to the next—from high school to college and job training, from college to career, from marriage to children.

A close friendship is comparable to a journey because you share major events and landmarks of your lives together. A major project can be like a journey. A career can be a journey.

You can dream about a journey when your life goes off in a new direction. Oftentimes it marks the beginning of something new and exciting, but also consider that changes in your life can slow you down. For example, you reach an age when you can't get around as you used to, you retire, or your children leave home. These situations are the beginning of new journeys in life. See: *Embark*.

Life itself is a journey, and the pace shows in how you travel: jet, boat, car, train. See below.

The journey of life can be summarized as developing your ego, your unique identity, then reintegrating it with the unconscious mind. See: *Ego, Unconscious Mind*.

See also: *Airplane, Airport, Boat, Car, Discover, Ego, Embark, Forest, Highway, Hotel, Jet, Lost, Map, Psyche, River, Train, Unconscious Mind, Vacation, Wilderness*

Joy—The emotions experienced in dreams are likely to connect with some event or circumstance in your life. If you experience joy in a dream, ask yourself what you have to be joyful about for yourself or someone close to you. What have you accomplished, what is going well, what makes you really happy? It might be connected with a big, joyful event such as having a child, getting engaged, or graduating from school.

However, dreams also amplify the smaller events and circumstances in our lives, so they don't pass unnoticed or under-appreciated. Waking up feeling great about yourself and your life can translate into a dream as a feeling of joy. Being the center of attention or gaining recognition can be a source of joy. Doing something that makes you proud of yourself, or starting a new job or embarking on a new course in life, can be a source of joy.

Keep in mind that the source of your joy might not be apparent in a dream. Instead, you react to a symbol according to your subconscious knowledge of what it symbolizes. For example, you react with joy when you dream about your dog giving birth to a puppy, and the symbolism connects with the joy you feel for a friend who had a baby. You react with joy when you dream about going to Paris, and the symbolism connects with Paris as symbolism for a destination you reach in your life.

See also: *Emotions, Love, Subconscious*

Judge—The first possibility to consider when interpreting the meaning of a judge in a dream is linked with the verb "to judge," meaning "to form an opinion." It's often referred to in the sense of judging the quality of a person, performance, or prospect. This use of the symbolism can connect with events in life, such as being tested at school or reviewed at work—you are "judged."

Or, after you create something and reveal it publicly, your creation might not be formally judged, as in a contest, but it can feel that way de-

pending on how people react to it. For an example of a dream involving the theme of being judged about a creative work, see: *Fisting.*

Being judged in your dreams might reflect a situation in life where someone has judged or criticized you. In such a situation, strong feelings and ego can be involved, in turn creating a higher likelihood of having a memorable dream in response.

You can be the judge. You are the one making critical evaluations or forming opinions. Or you are the final authority. In these dreams you might play the role of judge, or have that part of yourself projected onto a judge character.

Think of the qualities of a judge and ask whether those associations fit your dream. For example, a judge is supposed to be fair, impartial, honest. A dream about an angry or corrupt judge might reflect a situation where you or someone else is not being fair and impartial.

You can dream about a judge when you want the truth to be told or exposed. A courtroom setting is likely to be used to tell the story. See: *Court.*

Judges have power over people, so dreaming about a judge can come in response to a situation where power or authority is involved.

People are said to be judged in the afterlife. In this sense, the judge is God or even your own conscience. The psychic Edgar Cayce said that in the end we are our own judges, and we judge ourselves on the basis of how well we live up to our own ideals. See: *Afterlife.*

You can dream about a judge when you feel wronged. You wish for an impartial authority to hear your side of an argument, or for someone to intervene in a situation that is out of whack.

You can dream about a judge when you have done something wrong and fear getting punished. This association branches out to include any scenario involving punishment. See: *Guilt.*

You can dream about a judge when you want to see deeper into your psyche or a situation. For example, a woman dreams that she's in court, at the defense table, in front of a judge. Her parents are seated in the gallery. A curtain separates part of the room, and behind the curtain is the prosecutor. He emerges and berates a girl in the gallery who is eating needles. The curtain symbolizes the woman's being blocked from seeing a part of her psyche represented as the prosecutor. The girl symbolizes the other side of the equation, the part of herself that feels persecuted. Eating needles symbolizes taking into herself things that hurt; namely, in the way she talks to herself. She's sharply critical of herself, and eating needles is a hell of a metaphor for sharp self-criticism.

The judge in this dream represents the side of herself that knows the truth. It knows why she is so critical of herself—self-criticism is rooted in her family history, symbolized in the dream as her parents—and it knows, essentially, that she's being unfair to herself.

A judge can symbolize the part of yourself that knows: knows better, knows you, knows people, knows the facts, knows the system.

A judge can symbolize the side of yourself that compels you to do the right thing. You might not listen to anyone else, but when it comes from the judge, you're all ears. In this sense, the judge is your conscience, or what Sigmund Freud calls the superego.

This idea extends to when you need isolation. Being sentenced by a judge can be a sign that you need time to reflect on yourself and your life, which is supposed to be one of the purposes of being sentenced to jail, but you need to feel that you have permission to do it.

For example, a man dreams that a judge sentences him to ninety days in jail. Immediately he thinks about all the idle time and feels distressed about it, but he also realizes it could be a blessing in disguise if he uses the time for introspection. The judge in this dream is the side of himself that knows he needs time to turn within himself and figure out some of the big questions about his existence. The ninety-day sentence is just a way of saying this isn't something that can be fixed overnight.

A judge in a dream can mean you are pondering a situation that involves, or could involve, a judge. For example, you sense a divorce is coming from your spouse, or a dispute with a neighbor can't be resolved, and going to court is the only option. If you have a court date coming up, you can dream about a judge in connection with it.

See also: *Alimony, Bail, Crime, Court, Divorce, Execution, God, Guilt, Innocent, Jail, Jury, King, Numbers, Prisoner, Queen*

Jungle—See: *Wilderness*

Jupiter—The symbolism of the planet Jupiter can connect with its immense size. Physical size in dreams can be used to symbolize the figurative size of something, such as having an immense crush on someone, a huge fear, or a long way to go to reach a destination.

The symbolism can also connect with Jupiter's astrological qualities. You do not have to be aware of those qualities for them to be used in your dreams. Dreams can tap into knowledge in the collective unconscious, and astrology has been around for thousands of years. Use online sources.

See also: *Earth, Mars, Mercury, Moon, Saturn, Space, Venus*

Jury—Dreaming about a jury can mean you feel observed or scrutinized. It can mean you feel judged, especially if you're being judged in your life by a group of people instead of an individual. For example, you could dream about a jury after interviewing for a job in front of a hiring committee.

Dreaming about serving on a jury can mean you are doing the judging or scrutinizing. It can connect with having your own opinion about something, especially if you stand alone on a matter. If you are alone in your opinion as a juror, it can mean you think for yourself. Alternately, if you agree with the consensus, it can mean that you base your judgments and opinions on what other people think, or wait until other people are in agreement before weighing in.

It can mean that you place importance on what people think of you.

A jury can be a symbol of public opinion, social opinion, or conventional wisdom. In this sense, a jury is a physical representation of something intangible—opinion and convention are sometimes intangible or tacit, unspoken or undefined, but commonly understood.

A jury agrees or disagrees on matters of guilt and innocence, and that association can branch out in many directions to create symbolism connected with opinion, convention, mores, cultural edicts, consensus, and agreement or disagreement.

You can dream about a jury connected with a situation that involves judgment or group opinion. For example, after breaking up with her boyfriend, a woman dreams about being on trial for domestic abuse. The trial is broadcast live on Facebook, and the jurors are Facebook friends and relatives. Her boyfriend takes the stand and gives a litany of her faults and ways she caused the breakup of their relationship, most of which she disagrees with, making her fuming mad. At the end of the trial she is found guilty. The only juror who disagrees is her mother. The judge sentences her to anger-management classes.

The dream is a perfect summary of the situation surrounding the breakup. She thinks it's her ex-boyfriend's fault, but the consensus on Facebook is that it's her fault and connected with her temper. Her temper is a character flaw that she doesn't recognize for what it is, as shown in her reaction of disagreeing with her ex-boyfriend's testimony. Being on trial for domestic abuse is appropriate because she abused him—and every boyfriend she's ever had—with her temper. The jury represents the majority opinion that she caused the breakup, and her mother's dissent points to the source of the woman's temper: mom. The judge symbolizes the woman's inner self-knowledge of the truth. And the judge's sentence is the dream's suggestion for a solution. She needs to manage her anger.

See also: *Court, Crime, Guilt, Innocent, Judge*

Kanye West—Celebrities like Kanye West commonly appear in dreams, but Kanye deserves special mention because of the frequency with which he appears—*a lot*—at least among the generations that grew up listening to his music. He is one of the best known hip-hop stars, a huge figure in current Western culture.

As with anyone famous who appears as a character in a dream, the symbolism of Kanye is mostly based on what you associate with him. For one, he's immensely talented as a musician. Two, he's very articulate. Three, he's free with giving his opinions and controversial. And four, he doesn't take shit from anyone.

Now consider how those associations can be used as symbolism that connects back to you. For example, an aspiring musician dreams that he meets Kanye and they perform together. At the end, Kanye tells the dreamer that he's got talent. It's a way of encouraging the dreamer to continue pursuing his dream of being a successful musician. He probably won't achieve the same level of fame as Kanye, but he has the potential to develop a similar level of talent, and that's really the point.

Another example: A young man dreams that Kanye is his older brother. He attends a performance and Kanye gets into a heated argument with the sound guy, who pulls a gun and shoots Kanye dead.

The dreamer loses it and passes out. When he wakes up, he's in a car with his mother, going to the memorial service. His mother says that what makes her most sad is knowing how many lives Kanye had yet to touch, and she asks the dreamer what upsets him most. He says, "What makes me most sad is that, at the heart of everything, he was still just a little boy trying to find his place in the world."

The two statements really sum up the meaning of the dream when they're understood as statements about the dreamer. He has great potential as someone who can touch the lives of many people, but he hasn't found the means to do it. Or, as he says, he hasn't found his place in the world.

Kanye is portrayed as his older brother because he wants to be like Kanye when he grows up. He looks up to Kanye the same way that a younger brother can look up to an older brother. A brother is kin, a way of saying that the dreamer feels kinship with Kanye.

The detail about getting shot by the sound guy connects with the idea of being heard. The dreamer feels that he has some deep and important things to say, but he hasn't found the means to do it.

See also: *Famous, Music*

Kayak—A kayak is usually a single-person vessel, and as a dream symbol it can mean you're on a solitary journey, or you do things your own way.

A two-person kayak is a great symbol for a relationship. Paddling in harmony can symbolize the cooperation and coordination of a close relationship. Paddling out of sync can mean a relationship is out of sync.

The actions involved with kayaking and the conditions of the water can symbolize your life, or what you anticipate coming up. Rough waters can mean turbulence or turmoil, such as when a relationship hits a rough patch, events in your life are tossing you about, or your emotions are churning. On the other hand, calm waters can mean your life is running smoothly. You have harmony in yourself or your relationships.

See also: *Bicycle, Boat, River*

Key—To decode the symbolism of a key, consider what it does. It's used to unlock, to gain entry, and as symbolism it can symbolize gaining access to something you need, working through an obstacle, or solving a problem.

"Key" can mean "the answer." In a dream you look for a key, and in your life you seek an answer. In a dream you use a key to unlock a car door, and in your life you meet someone who can help your career, the answer to the question of how to advance. In a dream you take car keys from a drunk friend, and in life that friend needs answers for his or her problems.

The symbolism of a key can connect with internal dynamics. What unlocks the door to deeper access to your psyche? It could be the right attitude or viewpoint, or willingness. What unlocks your emotions, the key to your heart?

When looking for a home or shopping for a car, a key can connect with making a decision.

Be sure to read the entries for *Door* and *Lock*.

See also: *Car, Door, Home, Lock, Lost Item*

Kid—See: *Child*

Kidnap—To be kidnapped in a dream can symbolize being forced to do or accept something against your will. Dreams exaggerate, so the situation symbolized as kidnapping is not necessarily coercive or forceful. For examples, see: *Father, Husband*.

Kidnapping can capture the feeling of being the victim of circumstances or events. It can mean something is going wrong and you can't do anything to stop it. For example, you are powerless to stop bad decisions being made at work. Or a friend is involved romantically with a person you think is wrong, but the friend is hopelessly in love and doesn't want to hear your opinion.

Kidnapped in a dream can mean "held hostage." See: *Hostage*.

The symbolism of kidnapping can derive from the stress of the event. A dream uses it to compare to an event or situation that is stressful or adrenaline-filled. It can even relate to difficulty falling asleep, as if your ability to shut down your thoughts has been taken.

The presumed character of a kidnapper is an association used to create symbolism. Kidnapping is a heinous crime, and kidnappers rank low in society along with rapists and child abusers. When used as symbolism in a dream, it can mean you have a very low opinion of someone or yourself.

Kidnapping can have symbolism related to the root word, "kid." It can refer to the feeling of having your childhood stolen from you. This theme is common in the dreams of high-achievers who were not allowed to be kids. It's also common in the dreams of people who were abused or neglected as children.

If your child is kidnapped in a dream, it can mean you are concerned for his or her welfare. For example, if your child suddenly starts acting out of character, it can seem as if the child you know has been taken from you. Or perhaps you are worried about the care your child is receiving when you aren't around, such as at day care or school.

For example, a mother dreams that she's at her child's day-care center, and a voice comes on the loudspeaker warning that children are being kidnapped. She then sees a shady man trying to abduct her child. It symbolizes the uneasy feeling she has about the day care.

Parents of young children are known to dream frequently about danger to their children, in what are generally classified as anxiety dreams. They're generally not an indication of imminent danger to the child, but instead reflect a parent's need to be constantly vigilant. See: *Anxiety*.

Dreaming about an important person in your life being kidnapped might symbolize the perception that the person is being unfairly taken from you. For example, your wife is going on another business trip, "kidnapped" by her job, or your husband is being deployed in the military and it means a long period of separation. The idea extends to something that changes the personality of someone close to you, such as when the person is drunk or stressed. The usual personality is replaced.

Kidnapping can symbolize a situation in which forces from deep within the psyche force your life in another direction. See: *UFO*.

See also: *Accomplice, Anxiety, Child, Crime, Fugitive, Hostage, Thief, UFO*

Kill—Dreams create symbolism by making comparisons, and killing in a dream is often misunderstood as a violent tendency or homicidal potential when really it's related to figurative uses of the word.

For example, if you say, "I'm so mad at my parents, I could kill them," it doesn't mean you really want to kill them. It's a way of expressing frustration or anger. If you say, "This heat wave is killing me," it doesn't mean you are actually about to die from the heat; it means it's oppressive and wearing you down. If you say, "I want to kill my boss," it can mean you intensely dislike the person, or just strongly disagree with his or her decisions.

Kill is a strong word, and it's used to compare with strong feelings and situations. The symbolism of killing can connect with related strong emotions and behaviors, such as revenge, ruthlessness, brutality, hatred, and loathing. Dreams use actions and imagery to trigger related emotions. Killing, or references to it, can be a dramatic way of expressing related emotions. Sometimes the object of strong emotions is depicted through a surrogate-character. For example, the ex you loathe is depicted in a dream as a burglar you shoot in the face.

Like other dream symbolism, killing is an exaggerated way of expressing emotions or dramatiz-

ing the dynamics of a situation. It can be a way of characterizing a person or situation. For example, you dream about a killer stalking you, and it symbolizes a person who is coldly and ruthlessly undercutting you. The killer might symbolize a situation that is stressful or wearing you down. Or it might relate to an illness or fear. For example, cancer and heart disease are commonly referred to as killers.

Killing can mean "the end," usually a sudden and dramatic end, such as having an affair that kills a relationship. In this sense, to kill means to terminate. You can "kill your chances," meaning make a big mistake. For example, you screw up a job interview, and it kills your chances of getting the job.

In a related sense, to end something means to stop it. So to kill something can mean you stop it, such as, "The boss killed my idea."

Killing someone in a dream can mean you want the person out of the way. For example, a young man dreams that he accidentally kills his best friend, and at the funeral he stands next to his best friend's girlfriend. It sums up a situation where the dreamer is very attracted to this girlfriend and wonders what would happen if his best friend were out of the picture. In no way does it express a desire to kill his best friend. It's a "what if?" dream.

Killing can connect with death and its symbolism. Death in dreams tends to relate to something coming to an end. It can tie in with processes going on within you and the dynamics of your inner life, or with an external situation. For example, the death of a parent in a dream can symbolize "leaving the nest," becoming your own person, or lacking contact or communication with the parent. The relationship is dying, or you fear it is dying. Or it's just changing. For more about death symbolism, see: *Death*.

Killing an animal or other nonhuman creature in a dream carries the same possibilities for symbolism as killing a human. The creature might symbolize someone you know, or a situation with a person. For example, if you have been fending off unwanted sexual advances from males, you might dream about killing a snake. Animals can represent aspects of yourself, so the killing of an animal can mean that something about yourself is changing or is repressed. For example, killing a lion can symbolize taming your ego or taking a blow to your pride. It can mean you are trying to tame or repress something instinctual about yourself. See: *Animals*.

If you kill yourself in a dream, it might be a way of saying you want to change something about yourself. You're tired of being the person you are. Or it might be a way of enacting symbolism. For example, hanging yourself can be a way of saying that something isn't getting through to your head. Shooting yourself can be a way of saying you "shoot your chances." Drowning yourself can be a way of saying you are drowning in emotion or debt. The key aspect to note is that you are taking the action, which means you are ultimately the source of the conflict, behavior, or problem. See: *Suicide*.

People who need to change something about themselves, but can't or won't, tend to have recurring dreams about being murdered. It's a way of sending a loud and clear message. The theme arises most often in the dreams of immature young adults, addicts, and people who "shoot themselves in the foot."

See also: *Animals, Death, Gun, Hang, Knife, Murder, Serial Killer, Strangle, Suicide*

King—A king is the ruler or final authority, someone with power. The trick to figuring out what a king-character means in a dream is to decide whether it represents something about you, about someone you know, or about a situation, and match that with the role the king plays in the dream-story and your associations.

When connected with you, a king can symbolize the ability to rule over your own life, to make decisions, and create your own little kingdom. Everyone has an inner "King" or "Queen" involved in leadership and vision for life. In dreams it can be depicted in a form other than a king, such as a president, CEO, or famous person who embodies the qualities and characteristics of a king.

When connected with someone you know, a king can symbolize a father, boss, or husband. It is a characterization of a person's status, authority, or style. For example, if your father rules the house like a king, he can be presented that way in a dream. The king won't necessarily look like your father, but some detail will connect the two together. For example, the king in your dream sits at your father's desk.

A king in a man's dream can characterize a role he plays in life, such as head of the family or owner of a business. He is a king to his wife and children, or to his siblings, friends, and neighbors. Strip away the pretensions and what is a king? An authority, a leader.

When connected with a situation, the symbolism of a king can stretch to create more possibilities for symbolism. At its simplest, to rule means to be on top, to have the power to make decisions. Thoughts can rule your mind. Ideas can compete for supremacy. For example, choosing a new king from among candidates can symbolize choosing among competing ideas. Only one will come out on top.

The symbolism of a king can derive from associations with the stereotypical image of a king, such as strength, ambition, and wisdom. The image of a good father and husband is a reflection of what makes a good king. On the other hand, some kings are arrogant, demanding, and indulgent. How does the king in your dream act?

A king is someone you want to please. Someone who inspires. Someone very important. Remember that in dreams, you can substitute some-*thing* for some-*one*. So, for instance, a crown can symbolize authority or an authority figure. The figure doesn't have to be present in the dream. See: *Giant*.

A king is the highest authority, and that idea can branch out in many directions. Because the king is a character, it's tempting to assume it represents a person, including you, perhaps, but a king is a set of ideas, traits, and qualities that can be embodied by a person, or by something impersonal. For example, if you live by a code, such as a code of honor or ethics, or a spiritual code, it's the highest authority in your life.

A king can symbolize the highest figure in a spiritual or religious tradition.

And just because a king is a masculine figure doesn't mean a woman can't play the role. It can characterize her style of leadership or personality. Also, a king can represent her animus, the male face of her unconscious mind. See: *Animus*.

Males have the King archetype deep in the psyche that can play the role of king in your dreams. It shapes energy related to ruling your life, having a vision, and marshaling resources in pursuit of it. The female equivalent is the Queen archetype. Search online for "king archetype" to learn more, and see: *Archetypes*.

Read the entries for *Prince* and *Queen*. They approach the same subject from different angles and can provide valuable insights.

See also: *Archetypes, Boss, Castle, Father, General, Giant, God, Jesus, Queen, Prince, Princess, Warrior*

Kiss—See: *Lips*

Kitchen—Begin decoding the symbolism by thinking about what you do in a kitchen. It's a room where food is prepared and cooked. When you need to prepare for something in your life, you can dream about it as working in a kitchen. Symbolizing, for example, the preparation that goes into a wedding, a job interview, a holiday gathering, or a test.

Cooking involves combining ingredients and making something new out of them. The same idea applies to combining ingredients in your personality and character. For example, combine a good work ethic together with skill and resourcefulness to create a successful career.

Extend the idea further, and working in a kitchen can symbolize preparing for a change in your character or personality. Dreams can illustrate unconscious processes, and changes in yourself rarely come out of the blue. First, preparations are made in your psyche, usually outside of your conscious awareness. You could say it happens in your "inner kitchen." These dreams often involve observing activities in a kitchen, rather than participating directly in them.

Cooking in a dream can symbolize "cooking up a plan" or "cooking up an idea."

A kitchen setting is especially suitable for dreams related to creativity. See: *Chef*.

Another kind of creation is a baby. Combine sperm with an egg, heat in a womb for nine months, and voilà! A baby is born. The figure of speech "bun in the oven" expresses this idea. See: *Baby, Pregnant*.

An oven can be used to symbolize "getting baked," as in frying your brain with cannabis or other drugs. For an example dream, see: *Oven*.

Kitchens are connected with diet. A kitchen setting in a dream can relate to food choices or nutritional needs. See: *Eat, Food*.

Another type of need is for warmth, as in personal warmth, and kitchens are known for being the warmest room in the house. Warmth in a dream can mean relatedness or nurturing. A warm person is someone who makes people feel welcome.

Sometimes a setting in a dream is not related to symbolism but instead refers to something that happened there. For example, while cooking in your kitchen you remember that a bill hasn't been paid. You are busy at the time and the thought slips your mind. That night you dream about a repo man breaking into your kitchen and repossessing your refrigerator. The kitchen is used simply to refer to the thought that crossed your mind while in your kitchen.

And finally, kitchens are associated with knives and cutting. Cutting can mean "cut off," as in cutting off support or a conversation. For example, a dream about a guy's sister grabbing a knife in the kitchen and cutting their brother's throat symbolizes that she does not want to hear what either brother has to say about the man she plans to marry. She "cuts off the conversation." See: *Knife*.

See also: *Baby, Chef, Dinner, Eat, Heat, Home, Knife, Oven, Pregnant*

Kitten—The symbolism of kittens in dreams can be based on associations with kittens in general. They are typically viewed as cute, cuddly, sweet, playful, innocent, and helpless. They require nurture and care. What do those ideas compare to in your life?

One possibility is that "kitten-like" qualities are emerging in you, especially if you dream about giving birth to a kitten. This theme is more prevalent in males because being sweet and playful does not fit the image of the standard male, yet these traits are part of the human repertoire. Males have a harder time allowing them to become part of their personality. It's not to say that females can't have the same inner conflict, but that these traits are generally more encouraged in females than males.

When the traits arise and are unwanted, a person might dream about kittens that are starving or dead. If the traits are wanted, a person might dream about nurturing kittens and caring for them.

Kittens and other young animals such as puppies and bear cubs can symbolize young children—children already born, or still in the womb.

For example, a pregnant woman dreams about a litter of kittens. She is not a "cat person" and doesn't particularly like the kittens, but one of them, the only boy in the bunch, a beautiful gray one, catches her eye. She warms up to him and starts to like him by the end of the dream.

It symbolizes her process of warming up to the idea of keeping her baby, which she has recently found out is male. When she first found out she was pregnant, she intended to abort; then she looked into adoption. But once she learned her baby was male, she decided to keep him—not because she had anything against females, but because she felt a special bond with him. The association that clinches the connection between her fetus and the kitten in the dream is the name she has in mind for her boy: Sterling. Sterling is a shade of light gray, the same color as the kitten.

Kittens can have symbolism related to cats. See: *Cat*.

Kittens can have symbolism related to animals. See: *Animals*.

And kittens can have symbolism related to being newly born, to something that will grow and mature, and it doesn't necessarily have anything to do with traditional associations with kittens or cats. See: *Baby*.

For example, in a dream about suddenly having four kittens to care for and trying to figure out how to do that and continue working, the dreamer is actually thinking about four college courses she is taking. She also works full-time, and juggling it all is tricky. Raising kittens is an apt metaphor for her classes because they require constant, careful tending.

See also: *Animals, Baby, Cat, Puppy, Young*

Knee—As a joint that connects the upper and lower parts of the leg, the knee can have symbolism related to the leg. See: *Calves, Leg*.

Connectors in dreams can connect ideas or associations. For more ideas about how that works, see: *Elbow*.

The knee can symbolize flexibility.

The knee has a protective cap, and the idea of something protective can be used in a dream to symbolize anything that protects you, especially from harm or delay in the movement of your life.

Dreams can visualize processes in the body happening as you sleep. For example, a man dreams about fish with big teeth eating coffee grounds from his knee, symbolizing a process of antibodies cleaning up debris in his knee as he sleeps.

To be kneed in a dream can mean you've been ignoring a need. It's a wordplay.

Knife—The symbolism of a knife in a dream can connect with associations like "sharp," "close," and "cut." An incisive intellect is "sharp as a knife." Cutting with a sharp knife can symbolize getting to the heart of a matter or getting to the point, as in the phrase, "Cut to the chase."

Cutting someone with a knife requires close proximity. To be close to someone in a dream can mean closeness in the personal sense, such as a close friend or relative. So a knife is more likely to be used as a weapon when a dream tells a story about something or someone close and personal.

Knife fights in dreams can symbolize intense, heated situations. Knife fights rarely play out as they do in the movies, where it looks more like dancing or boxing. Instead, they're usually brief, up close, and brutal. The situation symbolized as a knife fight can be something that's already happened, or something you fear will happen. For example, you know that breaking up with your significant other is going to be an intense situation, or that a confrontation with your sibling about a family matter is going to be heated.

Cutting in a dream can symbolize wounding, as in, "Her comment cut to the bone." This use of the symbolism of a knife will usually be accompanied by fighting, cutting, and wounding. Marks on the physical body from a knife symbolize marks on the emotional body, on the psyche. It hurts! See: *Fight, Wound*.

Think of what can be wounded in the figurative sense. Pride and reputation can be wounded. Self-image can be wounded. Emotions can be wounded. Dreams show these sorts of wounds as physical when really they are personal, emotional, or psychological.

Cutting and stabbing are associated emotions like anger, frustration, and bitterness. When related back to the previous idea of having to be close to someone to cut or stab him or her, it can mean that someone close has really hurt you, or vice versa. For example, a woman stabs a man in the heart while coldly looking him in the eyes. See: *Ex*.

Up close can also mean "engaging." Though fighting with knives often has negative associations, it can mean simply that you are trying to get a point across or engage someone. For example, a teacher tries to engage students with the course material, and to do so he or she comes up with "sharp" analogies. The difference in symbolism is obvious in how it plays out in a dream.

Cutting can mean "cut off," as in cut off support or cut off relations. You're done, finished. This use of the symbolism is more likely when a rope, cord, or arm is cut.

An intense dream in which the dreamer observes his sister cut their brother's throat symbol-izes that she doesn't want to hear what either brother has to say about the man she plans to marry. The brothers know the guy is a player, but the sister is blinded by love.

Cutting your own throat can mean "ruining your chances" or sabotaging your life. This symbolism can be projected onto a dream-character that represents you.

Throwing a knife at someone can symbolize hurling nasty comments, insults, and sharp words. Words cross the distance between people as sound waves, so throwing a knife is an apt metaphor when those words are meant to cause harm. Also consider the idea of crossing the distance of time to engage with a memory of someone who hurt you. Basically, you're fighting with a memory.

A dream about defending yourself from someone with a knife can symbolize defending yourself from harm, or from verbal or personal attacks. But again, remember that most dream-characters represent something about you, so a person with a knife might represent the ways you criticize yourself, or some part of yourself that has turned hostile toward you.

Defending yourself in a dream can mean you want to maintain some sort of illusion about yourself, keep something repressed, or deny a fact. For example, a woman dreams about going into the basement of her childhood home and finding a homicidal child armed with a knife. It symbolizes her inner child that's hostile because it's hurt and she's ignoring it.

Looking for a knife with which to defend yourself can mean you feel the need to defend yourself personally or physically. For example, you have a dispute with a neighbor and wonder whether the person is capable of creeping into your house late at night to harm you. The fear plays out in a dream in a scenario in which you fear someone is in your house, and you look for a knife to defend yourself. A knife is used as symbolism because the neighbor is someone who lives close to you.

But also consider the ways you protect yourself from the world, from misfortune, from intrusion. See: *Intruder*.

A Swiss Army knife can symbolize taking different approaches to solving a problem.

See also: *Dissect, Ex, Intruder, Surgery, Wound*

Knight—See: *Hero*

Knockout—See: *Boxing*

Krishna—See: *Jesus*

Ladder—See: *Climb, Descend, Stairs*

Lake—See: *Water*

Las Vegas—See: *Casino, Gamble*

Lawyer—To dream about being a lawyer, or being defended by a lawyer, can symbolize arguing your case. When do you argue your case if not in a courtroom? At school, work, home, online. You can argue your case with a spouse or significant other, when you are trying to get hired, or while negotiating a deal. There are many possibilities. The key to the meaning is that you assert or defend yourself, try to uncover the truth, or need help making your point or arguing your side in a situation or argument.

Many other associations come into play when you consider the possible symbolism of a lawyer. Lawyers are commonly associated with people who take advantage of misfortune (ambulance chasers), with working long hours, and with speaking in a way that most people can't understand (Latin and legal terminology), to name a few.

Dreaming about being in the presence of a lawyer who speaks a language you don't understand can symbolize a situation where something is "over your head." For example, you want to create a website and are a beginner. You talk to an expert who spouts acronyms and jargon, and you hardly understand a word of it.

As with all dream symbolism, the meaning is found in the context and action of the dream. If you dream you are a lawyer and in court presenting your case, the symbolism is more likely to relate to making arguments or debating.

Dreaming about being defended by a lawyer can connect with feeling accused or guilty. Keep in mind that most dreams are based on your internal dynamics, so if you need a lawyer to defend you, it might be against an accusatory voice in your head. You know, the one that says you're no good and can't do anything right. Or the voice of your conscience. See: *Guilt.*

If you are involved in a legal situation, you could dream about a lawyer. Or if you are considering an action that will lead to going to court, such as getting a divorce, you could dream about a lawyer because soon you might be hiring one!

See also: *Court, Crime, Divorce, Guilt, Innocent, Judge*

Leader—See: *Captain, Coach, Famous, General, President*

Leaf—See: *Tree*

Left—Direction, orientation, and spacing can be used as symbolism in dreams. Start by reading: *Map* and *Turn.*

Dreams make a point by deliberately showing something on the left; otherwise, it's a waste of time and even a distraction. A house, car, or person is deliberately placed on the left and it means something. It's symbolism when the placement or orientation stands out to you as important.

Left is most commonly associated with "wrong" because it's the opposite of "right," or sinister because it's the opposite of *right*eous, but the possibilities vary widely and depend a lot on a person's cultural background.

For example, in Asian cultures, left is equated with yin, the feminine principle, and it has a broad set of ideas and characteristics associated with it. See: *Vagina*.

In Muslim culture, the left hand is never used for shaking hands or eating because it's always used for cleaning up after a bowel movement, a practice that extends back to long before the days of toilet paper and sewage systems.

Because the heart is just left of center, it can relate to feelings. To the right can mean more rational or logical. See: *Right*.

Left is used in vedic, tantric, occult, and other traditions to mean a path other than the traditional or orthodox "right-hand path." The left-hand path incorporates taboo or forbidden beliefs and practices, or anything that deviates significantly from the norm.

The symbolism really shows in the dream a young man had about walking on a path through the woods and coming to a split, left and right. The left-hand path is narrow and less traveled, and the right-hand path is wide and well traveled. He considers which one he wants to take and decides to go left. The dream is about which path he's going to take in life, particularly in his career. He's being pushed to go the traditional route and pursue a traditional job, the right path, but he feels pulled to try something different. He's not even sure what it is, but his dream makes clear what his heart wants him to do.

The symbolism of left can be based on a wordplay, such as "left out" or "left behind."

But it goes deeper when left means "entering my life" and right means "exiting my life." Or left means unconscious and right means conscious. See: *Spiral*.

Dreams can use the left hand to refer to someone you know who's a lefty. When dreams use surrogate-characters to represent people you know, they give some sort of identifier, and left-handedness is a way to do it.

Left can mean liberal. Leftist politics emphasize social equality and egalitarianism, and branching out from there opens up a multitude of possibilities for symbolism.

Left is associated with creativity and free thinking because the left side of the body is controlled by the right hemisphere of the brain, the "creative" hemisphere.

Turning left in a vehicle can symbolize a wrong decision or choice because it's the opposite of "right."

See also: *Collective Unconscious, Eyes, Handshake, Map, Right, Spiral, Turn, Unconscious Mind*

Leg—The uses and functions of a body part are the primary ways it's used as symbolism in a dream. Legs are what you stand on, and what you stand on in the figurative sense are your values, principles, beliefs, and other aspects of who you are as a person. Legs move you, and physical movement in a dream can be a representation of movement in your life, opening up ripe possibilities for making comparisons and telling a story.

Legs are associated with strength. The largest muscle group in the body is the thigh. Therefore, legs may have symbolism related to strength or lack of it. Physical strength in a dream may mean personal strength—strength of character, conviction, or resolve.

Look closely at the actions involving legs, such as running and climbing, because through action the dream tells the story. See: *Climb, Run*.

For example, breaking a leg in a dream can mean a source of support is taken away, or harm is done to your ability to move ahead in life. It can mean that something suddenly comes to an end or breaks, such as a relationship or your will to keep moving forward with something. Kicking can symbolize hard feelings toward someone, or else "kicking into gear."

Details related to legs in a dream can be used as symbolism. For example, missing legs can symbolize inability to walk away from something, or to "kick ass." For an example, see: *Family Business*.

A rotting leg can symbolize something that's gone on for too long, or been left unused, such as unused potential or strength.

Amputating a leg can symbolize causing harm to your ability to move ahead in life or with a plan. See: *Amputate*.

See also: *Amputate, Ankle, Body, Climb, Feet, Home, Infect, Knee, Run, Shoes*

Leopard—The presence of a leopard, panther, or jaguar in a dream can be an alert to danger or warning against vulnerability. They are particularly stealthy, creating an association with something that stalks and strikes when prey is vulnerable.

Dreams can dramatize personal situations, so while the danger from a leopard in a dream is depicted as physical or mortal, the danger in your life is more likely to be personal, emotional, or psychological.

Leopards are known for their temper, so a leopard in a dream can represent your temper or the temper of someone you know.

They're known for being defensive and territorial and can symbolize the instinct to protect territory. Territory includes personal territory, such as a person you consider to be "yours" or an area of expertise where you dominate.

A leopard can symbolize freedom to roam and be yourself. A leopard or other sort of big cat in a cage is the opposite image. See: *Cage*.

Because leopards aren't seen very often in the wild, a leopard in your dream may symbolize someone who isn't seen very often, such as a long-lost sibling.

Leopards and panthers are strong, proud, and fiercely independent, creating possibilities for symbolism to describe qualities about yourself or someone you know, especially strength of spirit.

Wild animals can also be used as markers to tell a story. For example, because panthers hunt by night they can symbolize venturing into the unknown or seduction. Because they stalk their prey, they can symbolize a hyper-competitive environment or situation.

Panthers can symbolize instincts associated with them, such as to remain hidden rather than be seen in the open. They can symbolize an instinct to protect yourself.

A dream about a leopard can be sparked by thoughts of traveling to exotic places, because they're the sort of environments where leopards are usually found.

Be sure to read: *Lion, Tiger*.

See also: *Ambush, Animals, Cage, Cat, Lion, Tiger, Zoo*

Letter—As something that comes in the mail, a letter can symbolize a message, answer, or reply you're expecting to receive.

Receiving a letter, note, email, or even a text message in a dream can symbolize communication between parts of your mind, or between mind and body. Your head and heart communicate. Your ego and unconscious mind communicate. It's a regular gabfest in there as you sleep.

And dreams are the facilitator, the mailman.

Your brain is very active while dreaming. During REM stage, when dreaming is most vivid, the brain is as active as when you're taking a test. It becomes like a plastic that heats up and is malleable—referred to in neuroscience as neuroplasticity. Neural pathways form and reroute as the brain reviews everything that happened since the last time it cleaned house, and it creates dreams around the memories to help the process along. Memories, thoughts, emotions; messages from the body, the spirit, the unconscious—all included in the tune-up and pruning. Everything you learn, everything new experienced, is integrated into what you already know and the existing structure of your psyche.

Valuable information is communicated to you in dreams. Think of it as a "note to self." Your unconscious mind, which is better at putting together clues and has no illusions or blind spots, sends you a message in a way most likely to get through.

For example, a woman has been communicating with a love interest who lives overseas. She dreams that she receives a letter from him that's addressed to another woman. The dream shows that she knows deep inside that the situation with the man is not leading to where she wants it to. She wants a relationship with him, wants to move to be with him, but he is not on the same page.

Another fascinating theme related to letters that arises in dreams is when you read about yourself in a letter. Often, these dreams are related to communication from the unconscious mind. The unconscious sees the big picture of you and it has really valuable things to say. It can provide insight, perspective, and direction. See: *Book*.

Reference to mail in a dream can be a wordplay on "male," the gender. For example, a woman dreams about checking into a B&B. A woman is at the front desk, and an unseen man is in an adjoining room, the mailroom. The mailroom is the part of her mind focused on her father, and the man is back there unseen because her father has been in the background of her life for many years. At the end of the dream, a thick letter addressed from him awaits her at the front desk. It says all the things she needs to hear about how he loves and cherishes her, which she knows subconsciously but isn't sure about consciously.

See also: *Book, Computer, Email, Talk, Unconscious Mind*

Library—To figure out the symbolism of a library in a dream, begin by thinking about what you do there and why you go there. Libraries are places to get information and knowledge. Think beyond academic-related information and consider what else you might want to know.

For example, does a love interest reciprocate your feelings? Does your supervisor at work approve of your work performance? Are your friends really interested in you as a person? These are a few of the myriad possible questions we can seek answers to through information and knowledge, and a library is an ideal dream setting to symbolize that search.

A young man dreams he's at the school library and sees his love interest. She walks past him as if he doesn't exist, and he ends up in a restroom. A bunch of girls come in while he has his pants down, and he discovers that he's actually in the girls' restroom. The scene turns into a huge drama. He yells at them and storms out.

The dream helps him answer a question, "Does my love interest have any interest in me?" So it uses a library as the setting. And through the action of his love interest ignoring him, the dream tells him what he already knows. She's not interested. The scene in the restroom basically sums up everything he dislikes about the dating scene at his small college and all the gossip and rumor. The girls, especially, talk about everyone and who likes whom and who's dating or sleeping together. There's no privacy, symbolized as the man's being interrupted while his pants are down.

If you study in a library, a dream can use it as a setting to branch out and cover any related subject, even ones that are not at all obvious. For example, a female college student who regularly studies in the library dreams about being there with a guy from class. They start dancing together, and the whole time she's thinking, "I can't do this—I have a boyfriend." The dream uses the library as a setting to tell a story about her conflict over devoting more time to school than she does to her boyfriend.

Libraries are associated with peace and quiet, and in dreams they can symbolize the need for it, or symbolize the calm and quiet of your mind or heart.

When having difficulty learning something, you can dream about having difficulty at the library. For example, you argue with the librarian, or can't locate a certain book on the shelves.

Some dreams feature fantasy libraries that are more like magicians' towers. Instead of books, they might have scrolls or holographic displays. These dreams are generally related to gaining highly specialized or esoteric knowledge, or accessing the Magician archetype in your deep psyche. The Magician archetype is associated with mastery of skill, manipulation of the material world through non-physical means, and attaining higher states of consciousness. See: *Magic*.

See also: *All-Seeing Eye, Archetypes, Book, Castle, Computer, Letter, Magic, School*

Lie—See: *Fake, Hide, Imposter*

Lifeguard—Dreaming about a lifeguard can mean you are guarded with yourself and your emotions. It can mean you want to avoid "troubled water," such as the trouble that can be caused by getting into the wrong relationship, or intervening in a heated or complicated situation.

A lifeguard can be used to symbolize a "sink or swim" situation. For example, freelancers can sacrifice job security for freedom. They either make it or not, sink or swim.

Being a lifeguard in a dream can mean you play the role of savior, or see yourself that way. Lifeguards save people from drowning, and figuratively, drowning can mean overwhelmed by emotions or circumstances. Saving someone from drowning can be a way of expressing a fantasy of being the hero. It is common for young men to fantasize about saving the person who is their crush or love interest.

See also: *Hero, Ocean, Paramedic, Pool, Rescue, Water*

Light—Light in a dream can be associated with something that illuminates the interior of your psyche and helps you understand what's happening in your life. It helps you see the way ahead in your life.

Light helps you see in the dark, and in dreams the dark can mean the unknown or uncharted. If someone says, "I can't see the way ahead in my life," it doesn't mean the person is blind. That figurative use of "to see" means see the way forward, see a path to reach a goal or the next phase. See: *Dark*.

"To see" can mean see yourself for who you really are, or understand the dynamics of a situation.

Light guides you. It helps your vision. Vision can mean vision for your life, vision for the future, or "visionary," meaning imaginative, innovative, or creative. See: *Eyes*.

A primary purpose of dreaming is to illuminate your interior world, to show you everything you are. You might think you know everything you are, and maybe you do know everything you are consciously. But the conscious mind is an island in an ocean in comparison with the unconscious mind. Dreams originate in the unconscious and shine a light into those depths. Sometimes, the symbolism is shown as a light illuminating a room or landscape. See: *Unconscious Mind*.

Light exposes that which is hidden. See: *Hide*.

Light can symbolize goodness and purity. When used this way, the light often comes from above, or is a glow around a character, setting, or object. It is a pure light, too. Often the light used in this sense inspires a feeling of joy and connection. See: *God*.

Light can symbolize insight, inspiration, or an idea. Picture a light bulb over the top of your head. For example, you are trying to solve a problem at work and go to bed with the subject on your mind. You dream about finding a light switch in a dark room at work. You flip the switch and the room lights up, symbolizing that you are no longer "in the dark" about solving the problem at work.

A welcoming light can mean simply that you feel good about your life.

Light can symbolize the presence of someone in your life who makes you feel good or provides guidance, someone like a close relative, friend, or mentor. Imagine that you have a friend who has been acting funny, not as talkative, but when you ask about it, she says, "I'm fine." Then you dream about her blowing out the candles of a birthday cake with her father, who passed away, and the room goes dark. You remember that the first anniversary of his passing is coming up and realize what's making your friend sad. Candles provide light, and blowing out candles can mean that the light that someone brought to your life is gone. See: *Candle, Fire, Guide*.

Light can symbolize hope. For example, holding a light source between you and someone you are attracted to can symbolize holding onto hope that your feelings will be reciprocated.

Light is associated with enlightenment. You see past the surface. You let your inner light shine. See: *Fire*.

Light can be meant in the sense of lightweight or a light burden. If a light in your dream is accompanied by a feeling of lightness, it might be a wordplay.

Finally, absence of light means something, too. See: *Black*.

See also: *Black, Building, Candle, Colors, Dark, Eyes, Fire, God, Guide, Home, Spotlight, Sun, Unconscious Mind, White*

Lightning—When decoding the symbolism of lightning, consider associations with something that happens rarely—lightning never strikes twice—or that is shocking—lightning is electricity, highly charged—or that strikes suddenly. For example, infatuation, ideas, misfortune, or good luck can strike suddenly. The dream will define the symbolism through the action of striking or shocking and how you react to it.

Lightning and thunder are associated with anger: "stormin' mad." See: *Anger*.

They're associated with fear. See: *Fear*.

Lightning can symbolize a temper that lashes out suddenly, and thunder can symbolize the loud booms of an argument.

Lightning is dangerous and can be a warning to seek shelter. Translated into your life, that idea can mean that you sense trouble coming. Danger is ahead. Protect yourself.

Dreams are stories and they do everything necessary to make the stories believable, so lightning and thunder can be thought of as details that set the scene, to create a scary, tense, or ominous atmosphere.

A sky full of lightning can be a way of saying that something is coming to a head, to a finale.

See also: *Anger, Fear, Light, Storm, Tornado, Weather*

Limousine—A limousine is a symbol of wealth and power. Used in a dream, a limo can help tell a story related to wealth and power, the desire for it, or perhaps the lack of it.

Limos are associated with fame, recognition, and importance. See: *Famous*.

As with all dream symbols, look at a limo within the context of the story, particularly the actions. If it's a story about wealth and power, a dream will use other details to support that idea, such as Wall Street, the White House, or Warren Buffett. On the other hand, if the limo in your dream takes you to the school dance, that's an altogether different idea being expressed. The limo could symbolize the boyfriend who went all out to make it a special night, losing your virginity, or trying to pay for something you can't afford.

Stepping out of a limo can symbolize making a grand entrance, or a new part of you emerging that's ready to be seen, ready for the spotlight.

A limo that passes you by can symbolize the feeling that you are excluded from privilege, or you missed a big opportunity.

A very long limo—a "stretch limo"—is a detail that acts as a multiplier. It's the same symbolism as discussed above, but more of it: more wealth, more power, more fame, more recognition, more extravagance. The opportunity you missed was *really* big. Or it can mean that an idea or argument is a stretch, or you feel stretched thin.

See also: *Car, Famous, Giant, Hollywood, Prom*

Lion—For creatures that are rarely seen in person, lions sure do appear in the dreams of a lot of people, connected with the powerful impression they make and the multitude of associations with them.

A primary association is with temper. The loud sounds and sudden, violent actions of lions create strong association with temper.

A lion can symbolize use of scare tactics and loud protestations. For example, a woman dreams about protecting a turtle from a massive lion. The lion roars and she's scared, but she stays between the lion and the turtle. The lion symbolizes the voice in her head that uses scare tactics to motivate herself, "do it or else" statements. The turtle symbolizes her sensitive inner nature, and protecting it from the lion means she's realizing that protecting this part of herself is necessary for her to come out of her proverbial shell.

Usually, animals in dreams symbolize something about you, especially your ego, so ask yourself what you see about yourself in the lion. And pay attention to how you react, knowing that your reactions—especially your feelings—are tied to the underlying symbolism. See: *Ego*.

Consider the actions and context of the dream-story. For example, a lion sleeping in a cage is not the image of ferocious temper, unless it symbolizes one that's been tamed. Avoiding a lion can symbolize wariness of a dangerous person or situation. Encountering a lion in the wild is a way of saying you are vulnerable.

The lion is "king of the jungle" and can symbolize acting like an alpha or bully. See: *Bully*.

Lions show no fear. They're dominant. They bully. They're brave, or "brave as a lion." Does that describe you or someone you know? See: *Hero*.

Lions act proud and can symbolize a high sense of self-worth or egotistical behavior: "proud as a lion."

Lions are known for being savage, though in reality savagery depends on the temperament of the lion. In dreams, an attacking lion might symbolize a savage emotional or psychological attack, or a situation that threatens great harm, such as a bad illness or auto accident. The symbolism can be used in situations where a savage reaction is expected or feared. For example, you know that tomorrow you must give a presentation and fear being ripped to shreds by criticism of it. See: *Attack*.

A pack of lions can symbolize a group of influential, power-hungry, or egotistical people. They dominate other people and attack in groups.

A caged lion can symbolize a need for kitty to be let out to play. You need freedom to roam, explore, and live the way you want to. See: *Cage*.

Finally, the lion is the animal associated with the astrological sign of Leo. A lion in your dream might symbolize someone you know who is born under that sign.

Be sure to read: *Leopard, Tiger*.

See also: *Ambush, Animals, Attack, Bully, Cage, Cat, Eaten, Ego, Fear, Hero, Leopard, Tiger, Wilderness, Zoo*

Lips—Lips have potential for symbolism related to their use and function, such as for talking, eating, and kissing. The symbolism will be defined by the actions and other details involving lips, and by the context in which they're used in the dream-story. Most human dream-characters are going to have lips and that doesn't mean that the symbolism of lips is being used. The lips in the dream have to be important to the story.

For example, chapped lips can symbolize difficulty with articulation, or saying things that hurt, or embarrassment.

Bloody lips can symbolize arguments and other sorts of harsh verbal exchanges.

Swollen lips can symbolize proud talk or arrogance, similar to the idea expressed in the term "swelled head."

A fat lip can symbolize saying something stupid or something that provokes someone's anger.

Cut lips can symbolize saying something that gets you into trouble, or that hurts.

Lips cut off or missing can symbolize restrictions in your diet, or being forbidden or unable to say something.

Putting on lipstick can symbolize sweet-talking, or hiding the truth. Lipstick can symbolize something you say that sticks to you. It becomes associated with you, perhaps part of your reputation or image. See: *Makeup*.

People who talk for a living, such as salespeople and broadcasters, have more to consider because lips can be used to symbolize something related to their work. See: *Job*.

Kissing in a dream can be a sign of intimacy. Intimacy is often used in the sense of romantic or sexual intimacy, but dreams can use it in the sense of being close and personal. For instance, you might dream about kissing a close friend after having an intimate conversation or sharing secrets. Kissing and talking both involve the mouth, creating a strong connection that can be used as symbolism.

Extend the idea of intimacy and it can symbolize intimacy with a subject. Ideas and creativity are candidates for kissing symbolism because people tend to feel a personal closeness with them. Ideas and creativity are intimate parts of a person. Just watch how people commonly react to comments or criticism about their ideas and creative endeavors. They tend to get defensive and take it personally, like protecting someone they love.

A common variation of the kissing theme in dreams involves your significant other kissing another person, or kissing your ex. See: *Cheat, Ex.*

Seeing your ex kiss another person in a dream can symbolize recognition that the person has moved on from the relationship and is perhaps seeing other people. Kissing your ex can express the desire to get back together with that person, or to get in touch.

Kissing someone as your ex watches can mean that your mind is still on your ex, or you have moved on from the relationship, and you know your ex hasn't. It can symbolize desire to make the person jealous.

Kissing in a dream can be a wish-fulfillment or fantasy, especially if you have a crush on the person depicted as a character in a dream. Dreaming about your crush kissing someone else can be an expression of jealousy or desire to get the person's attention. But also consider that it can symbolize a close conversation with the person. People often confuse kissing for desire when usually in dreams it's associated with talking and conversation.

See also: *Body, Cunnilingus, Ex, Face, Fellatio, Jealous, Mouth, Talk*

Little—References to sizes such as "little" in a dream can symbolize size in the sense of the amount of something. For example, a little snake can symbolize a little problem. An insect can symbolize a small irritation. Little can mean "minor."

"Little" can mean an amount. For example, a little person can symbolize little respect or attention. You can take a little of the credit or blame. You can give something little thought or little consideration. You can get upset over the little things or choose not to sweat the small stuff.

It can symbolize a short attention span or little notice.

Little can express the feeling of not being seen or noticed. This interpretation is especially true for introverts who watch the extroverts around them dominate the spotlight and feel that they get little attention, or they leave a small personal imprint.

Be sure to read the entry for *Giant.*

See also: *Baby, Bug, Giant, Insects, Mouse, Short*

Living Room—In many homes, the living room is the main room for socializing. In dreams it can be a setting for depicting the image of yourself that you want others to see—your social image or persona. It can be a setting that shows how you see yourself, your self-image, or how you think people perceive you, which can be different from reality. See: *Persona.*

A living room can have symbolic meaning similar to that of a front door, a boundary between your public and personal life. Guests who come to your home are welcome in the living room, but might not be welcome in your bedroom, for example. They're welcome to see the public version of you, but not the private version. See: *Door.*

Of course, a living room can be a popular room in your house, a place where you spend a lot of time, and a dream that takes place in your living room might refer to a recent event or something that commonly occurs there, such as talking with family members. A living room might not have specific symbolism, but instead simply be a setting for telling a story about your life.

A living room can be used to describe your living situation. For example, a messy living room can symbolize a messy living situation, not just physically but maybe also personally or emotionally. A clean and orderly living room can reflect a clean and orderly life.

Dreaming about a living room in a home where you used to live can refer to that time of your life. Something from that time is relevant to the present, such as a pattern that started or idea that took root.

See also: *Building, Door, Home, Persona*

Lizard—See: *Reptile*

Lock—Dreams create symbolism by making comparisons, and a lock is comparable to anything you want to lock away, keep secret, or keep out. Think in terms of what you want to keep out of your life, what you don't want to know, what you don't want to remember, what's too difficult to think about, and what you want to keep to yourself. See: *Hide*.

The symbolism of a lock is often connected with its use and function, and with analogies related to locks and keeping things secure.

Locking a door can mean you want to keep someone out of your life. Or you don't want to acknowledge something difficult or painful. Or you want to shut yourself away. See: *Door*.

Being locked in can mean you can't escape a situation. Facts are facts. You refuse to "open up" emotionally or personally. You have something about yourself that you don't want people to know, as in when a person is "in the closet." See: *Jail*.

A common theme in the dreams of people who feel insecure is that they can't lock their doors and windows, or can't keep them locked. For example, you dream that you find the front door of your home unlocked and think that anyone could have just walked right in, and you connect the symbolism with the feeling that you can't set or enforce boundaries with people.

Example: A woman dreams that she realizes a stranger is outside her front door and she wants to lock it to keep the stranger out. The stranger symbolizes her father, an estranged figure in her life, and wanting to lock the front door to keep him out means she wants to keep him out of her life. He'd recently made contact with her and asked to be part of her life again. Part of her wants to let him in, but experience tells her it's a bad idea.

An unlocked door can symbolize feeling vulnerable. You worry that you forgot to take care of something important. You haven't thought of every angle.

Locked can mean "inaccessible." Something locked—a door, a window, a safe, a treasure chest—can mean that you are denied an opportunity, or can't get access to something you need or want.

For example, you think you can have a career as a singer if only you could be heard by the right producer, but that door of opportunity is locked. Or a romantic interest won't let you in emotionally or personally. You've been dating someone and the person is not ready to be more physical, such as in the dream a high school guy had about his girlfriend locking him out of his own bedroom. He asks her to let him in, and from the other side of the door she says, "It's not safe." It's a way of saying she doesn't feel that it's safe to have sex with him, and locking the door to his bedroom—a room associated with sex—symbolizes denying him access to herself sexually.

The symbolism of accessibility also extends to your psyche. Parts of yourself and potential that you have are inaccessible until you lay the groundwork. The psyche has mechanisms for restricting access to certain areas until you are ready, sometimes symbolized in dreams as locked doors. A common theme in these sorts of dreams is that you explore a house and find locked rooms. The house is your psyche, the place where your mind lives, and the locked room is a locked aspect of it. See: *Home*.

Dreaming about finding a door unlocked can mean "the door is open to you." You have an opportunity. For example, you talk with your ex and the person leaves the door open to getting back together.

Finding something unlocked can mean that you are able to gain access. You can gain access to a person, to resources and knowledge, and to parts of yourself. For example, a woman has recurring dreams about exploring a mansion. One particular door is always locked, till one time she finds it unlocked and walks inside. That symbolizes her personal growth. An area of her psyche that was inaccessible is now open to her. New rooms in your mind are already there before the doors to them open. The same imagery of finding an unlocked door can symbolize entering a new phase of life.

Unlocking a safe can symbolize getting past a person's defenses, or finding a way around safeguards. See: *Safe.*

A locksmith can symbolize trying to open up someone who is emotionally closed off. Or it can mean trying to find out something that's concealed from you. For example, picking the lock on your supervisor's desk might symbolize trying to figure out what he or she really thinks of you.

Dreaming about being locked out of your car or home and needing a locksmith can mean you need help with an area of life symbolized by the car or home. Perhaps your career is stalled (car symbolism) or you're cut off from your emotions (home symbolism).

See also: *Burglary, Car, Door, Home, Key, Locker, Safe, Stranger, Thief*

Locker—A dream theme that arises with surprising frequency is that you are unable to remember the combination to your school locker. This theme is especially puzzling for people who have been out of school for years. To understand the symbolism, begin with what it can mean to be back in school. It can mean that you're challenged to learn something new, or feel unprepared for something in your present life—something for which school was supposed to prepare you, such as career, college, and adulthood.

Now apply that idea to the symbolism of a locker. It's where you store your books and school supplies. If you can't find your locker in a dream, or can't remember the combination, it can mean you are having difficulty getting access to what you need in your present stage of life to accomplish what you want, or to reach a goal.

Accomplishments and goals often involve a combination of factors, such as perseverance, skill, opportunity, and luck. A locker can mean you're looking for the right combination to make something happen in your life, symbolized as trying to remember the combination to your locker. Also, in your love life you look for a combination of background, traits, and qualities in a person to date or marry.

Another way of looking at it: a locker is supposed to be your private place. If you can't remember the locker combination, can't find your locker, or someone breaks into your locker, it can mean you are having issues with privacy and setting boundaries. You can't figure out how to keep someone out of your life, or to prevent people from prying into it.

There are other types of lockers, such as at work or the gym, which can be used to create symbolism similar to a school locker. For example, dreaming that you can't find your work locker can mean you forgot the reason you started working at a certain job or profession. If you're retired, perhaps you're trying to figure out how you're going to occupy yourself now that you don't have an occupation.

Finding a rat in your locker can symbolize feeling betrayed. Dreaming about your workout clothes missing from your gym locker can mean that your identity as an athlete or jock no longer suits you, or you face obstacles to finding the time or motivation to work out.

See also: *Fitness Center, Games, Job, Key, Lock, School, Sports*

Locksmith—See: *Lock*

Lost—Being lost in a dream can reflect a situation in your life where you do not know where you are going personally. It's a physical representation of a personal situation, an expression of your feelings or perceptions. You're lost, and the dream represents that situation.

For example, you're trying to figure out how to get recognized for your great performance at work, and you dream about getting lost while trying to find an awards ceremony. Or you're trying to figure out how to find a mate and dream about getting lost on the set of *The Bachelor*.

Being lost can mean you don't know what to do with yourself, such as after retirement or a separation. For example, you retire from work and dream that you go out to lunch and can't find your way back to your workplace, or you forget which exit to take off the highway.

Being lost in a woods, desert, or jungle is a theme that commonly arises during times of life when you feel personally lost, such as when trying to figure out what to do with yourself and where to go. Teenagers, in particular, dream this theme because they face so many decisions and need guidance. See: *Guide, Wilderness.*

When you feel disconnected from a mate or significant other, you can dream about losing track of them personally or emotionally. Some sort of divide is between you. Losing them in a crowd can symbolize that your life is too crowded, or their life is too crowded.

Being lost in a dream can mean "loss," such as loss of face, loss of a loved one, or loss of opportunity.

Being lost in a maze or maze-like place is another way of symbolizing the difficulty of choosing among options, or reaching a destination in your life. You don't know which road or path to take to get to where you want to be. See: *Maze.*

See also: *Car, Desert, Empty, Forest, Guide, Lost Item, Maze, Phone, Teenager, Teeth, Wilderness*

Lost Item—When you lose an item in a dream, it can mean you're missing something intangible, such as your confidence, health, or freedom. For example, you dream about losing a lucky charm; it symbolizes losing your confidence. You dream about losing the keys to your car, symbolizing an illness that has kept you house-bound.

Keys can symbolize something that is "key" to you. For example, a certain employee is a key person for accomplishing a project, so losing a key can symbolize losing something that's a key to success. See: *Key.*

The symbolism of a lost purse or wallet can connect with items that are commonly kept in them. Purses and wallets typically contain identity documents, money, and financially related items such as credit cards. See: *Purse, Wallet.*

Losing a phone can symbolize a communication problem. You're not able to articulate your thoughts or feelings. Or the person you're trying to reach on the phone isn't listening or accessible—especially emotionally accessible. See: *Phone.*

Usually, the symbolism of a lost item connects with the symbolism of the item itself, but consider also how a lost item can be used to tell a story about being disorganized, misplacing and losing things. Losing an item can connect with the general symbolism of being lost, which often connects with feeling lost or not knowing the way to a goal or destination in life. See: *Lost.*

See also: *Bag, Car, Keys, Lost, Party, Phone, Purse, Wallet*

Lottery—Winning the lottery in a dream can symbolize being lucky. Good fortune is smiling on you, and it doesn't necessarily have anything to do with the lottery. People are said to win the lottery when they get hired for a coveted job, or marry the perfect mate, or have a wonderful family, or rise to the top in their profession. They get lucky, the few chosen from among the many, even when the luck is earned.

Winning the lottery can mean you're working through in your mind how to be more lucky, or how to gain what winning the lottery represents: security, opportunity, resources, freedom, influence, importance, success, dramatic change, money. Lottery dreams are rarely about money directly, but instead about what it symbolizes, and the lottery's universal and personal associations. See: *Money.*

A lottery dream can be a "what if?" simulation. What if you actually won? What would you do, and how would it change your life? Dreams help clear impediments, such as the belief that nothing good ever happens to you. And they address side questions such as, Would winning the lottery change you and your life in bad ways? Would it be bad for people close to you? Are you better off where you are?

Some people say that winning the lottery is blind luck, and others say that our consciousness creates our reality and our so-called luck. If consciousness creates reality, then improving and raising your consciousness is a direct way of improving your reality. Dreams are primarily interested in your personal growth. If you learn from them, you put yourself in a better position to win the lottery of life.

Playing the lottery can symbolize creating your own opportunity or luck. Luck can play a role in the gaining of opportunities, but you can create your own luck by putting yourself in a position to succeed.

For example, an author dreams about buying permanent lottery numbers. If the numbers come up in any future lottery, he wins. He realizes he did not buy all the numbers he could have, and wonders how he would feel if someday he almost wins the lottery but comes up one number short. He resolves to buy all the numbers available. It's obviously symbolism—no lottery works that way.

The dream symbolizes his efforts as a writer. He's put high effort into building an audience and drawing attention to his work, but he sometimes skips opportunities to promote his work because he doesn't think they will pay off. In dreams, buying something can symbolize an investment of time and energy, so buying permanent lottery numbers symbolizes putting the time and energy into maximizing every opportunity to promote himself and his work. One day, he hopes to "get lucky" and be a hit in the publishing world.

A woman dreams that she holds a winning lottery ticket and tries to read the numbers as people around her react with excitement and bewilderment. She wakes up thinking that maybe the dream tried to give her the winning numbers in an upcoming lottery drawing. But with more thought she realizes the dream is really about getting motivated to create her own success. In the dream she is distracted by the hoopla around her, symbolizing the distractions that keep her from fully applying herself to her work.

People have dreamed about winning lottery numbers, played them, and struck it rich. Then again, they've also played numbers found in a fortune cookie and won, so just dreaming about winning numbers is not a sure thing. But in some cases

the coincidences are meaningful and too synchronous to be random—especially cases in which people who've never played the lottery wake up and say to themselves, "It's my lucky day, I really should play the lottery," and they win.

Synchronicity is the concept of meaningful coincidence, including the uncanny timing and arrangement of events. Synchronicity is behind some cases when money comes to a person at just the right time, such as when they win the lottery. To learn more about synchronicity, see Dr. Bernard Beitman's website, *www.coincider.com.*

See also: *Collective Unconscious, Gamble, Groups, Money, Numbers, Unconscious Mind.*

Lotus—The lotus flower has deep symbolism connected with the evolution of the individual. Consciousness is a slice of the pie of the complete mind, and it grows out of the unconscious mind like a lotus from the mud.

The lotus can symbolize something beautiful that grows from humble beginnings.

See also: *Buddha, Earth*

Love—Love is a powerful emotion, and when dreamed about, it can compel a person to pick up a dream book like this one to figure out the meaning. Falling in love is the most common variation of the theme, though dreams will address every sense of the word.

Dreams about falling in love are common when a person is actually falling in love. It's simply an expression of the emotion.

But even if the person you fall in love with in a dream is someone you know and love, the dream could still use the image of the person to symbolize something else, such as falling in love with a subject, idea, or creative project, among other things. Falling in love with someone in a dream doesn't necessarily mean that love is in the stars for the two of you. It's more likely to be symbolism for something entirely personal.

For example, a young woman dreams about falling in love with a classmate who's in her favorite class. The classmate symbolizes the class, not the person. Sure, he's physically attractive, which is all she really knows about him. But the dream uses him as a character in the story only because he's someone she finds attractive, and what she's really attracted to is the class.

The symbolism is especially obvious if you search your feelings and don't register feelings of love for the person in the dream. In rare cases dreams are known to bring together people who are destined for each other, truly the man or woman of your dreams, and those dreams are known to show you the potential for deep love with someone you barely know, or haven't met yet—a person you will meet in the future, strange as that might sound to people who don't know it's possible.

The feeling of love for someone in a dream may symbolize something you love to do or somewhere you love to be. For example, you have a favorite hangout place, such as a pub, then dream about being in that setting and falling in love with someone. What you really love is going to the pub!

For people who are in a relationship that involves, or could involve, feelings of love, dreaming about love can be a way of revealing how they feel or what they want from the relationship.

A common variation of the theme is the "loves me, loves me not" dream that explores your feelings for someone and whether or not the person is a good long-term prospect.

On the other end of the spectrum, dreams can tell you when you no longer love someone. If it's hard to admit, your dreams are likely to amplify the loss of love and get your attention that way.

Obsessive love can be symbolized in dreams as something about love that's out of proportion, such as if you dream about the person you love as being fifty feet tall; it means the person has too big a place in your life or mind, or you're taking things too far.

You can develop feelings of love for yourself and have it show up in your dreams as loving a character—often love at first sight—and it's a great sign

because it shows you can love yourself, something about yourself, or something about your life. It shows a soul-level connection inside you. See: *Soul.*

Throughout your life you go through a process of uniting the conscious side of your mind with the unconscious side, referred to as "marriage of the soul." And what better way of promoting that goal than by portraying the unconscious as a dream-character, and you fall in love with it because you recognize yourself in it.

The unconscious mind can present itself to you in dreams as a perfect mate. The purpose is to motivate you to pursue the process of personal development that makes you more conscious and personally integrated. Carl Jung called it the "individuation process." The figure that takes form in dreams as a man's perfect mate is called *anima*, and for women it's *animus*. See: *Anima, Animus, Individuation.*

Being loved by someone in a dream can motivate you. It can make you believe in yourself. It can reflect the fact that someone holds you in high esteem and otherwise makes you feel loved and appreciated. For people who don't have anyone to love or who loves them, dreams can provide a valuable connection to the love that comes from within, and that anyone can have. You don't have to deserve it, but you might have to earn it in your dreams with your anima or animus by dedicating yourself to living the best life you can. See: *Compensation.*

See also: *Anima, Animus, Boyfriend, Bride, Compensation, Emotions, Fire, Girlfriend, Groom, Heart, Marriage, Red, Wife*

Low—See: *Below*

Lucifer—See: *Devil*

Luck—See: *Lottery*

Luggage—See: *Baggage*

Lunatic—See: *Insane*

Machine Gun—Guns have a variety of possibilities for symbolism related to defensiveness, anger, and destructiveness. A machine gun can be thought of as gun symbolism on steroids, expressing a higher level of defensiveness, anger, or destructiveness.

For example, in a dream a guy hides behind a metal garage door as his girlfriend on the other side sprays bullets through it with a machine gun, symbolizing a heated dispute with his girlfriend the previous day. She made multiple angry accusations against him, against which he tried to defend himself, symbolized by the metal garage door. The bullets fired through it symbolize that some of the accusations "hit home," and her method was to keep firing till she hit her mark.

Machine guns are prevalent in the media, and if you watch something during the day featuring machine guns, the imagery might be replayed in your dreams. The difference between meaningful symbolism involving a machine gun and just replaying imagery seen during the day is found in your response to the presence of a machine gun and the context of it in a dream. A machine gun that symbolizes something you fear or dread will evoke those feelings in you. On the other hand, if a machine gun symbolizes a rapid-fire way of talking, you aren't likely to react with fear.

For example, you dream about machine guns firing on the beaches of Normandy during D-Day. The previous day you watched a documentary about the event, and the imagery in your dreams is similar. Your mild reaction to the imagery is a big clue that your brain is just coughing up memories. On the other hand, you may dream from the perspective of a soldier dodging bullets, feeling terror or courage or other emotions. Such a dream is more likely to be meaningful.

Dreams create scenarios to test you and help your growth, so a machine gun in a dream might be part of a test of your courage or resourcefulness. Or, if you're a student of history, the same imagery could be a way of putting you into the scene to truly understand what the soldiers went through that day. It's a dream theme common to students wanting to know a subject from the inside out. See the example dream at the end of the entry for *Serial Killer*.

See also: *Army, Fear, Gang, Gun, Hero, Kill, Serial Killer, Talk, War*

Mafia—Mafias organize as families, related by bloodline and association, and Mafia figures in dreams can symbolize your family life or family members, especially if there's something shady about your family, or you're caught up in its business. See: *Family Business.*

A mafia can symbolize perceptions about your family or another group of people that are like family, such as co-workers or teammates.

A mafia can symbolize people you don't trust, or paranoia that people are out to get you.

Mafias are known for bitter rivalries among them and the betrayal and violence they do to each other, associations that dreams can use to create symbolism.

What are your associations with Mafia, and how might they characterize people or situations in your life?

dream-characters based on criminals may be Shadow figures. See: *Shadow*.

See also: *Crime, Family, Family Business, Shadow*

Maggots—Maggots can be associated with something bugging or eating at you. It might be something producing stress or anxiety, or that seems wrong to you about a person, situation, relationship, or yourself. See: *Bug*.

For example, a dream about finding large grubs in the bottom of a Styrofoam cup used for drinks at work symbolizes a situation bugging the dreamer about his work environment. He suspects that some employees are pocketing cash meant for the business.

An infestation of maggots can symbolize shame, guilt, or disgust, including disgust with yourself. See: *Infest*.

Maggots worming into the skin can symbolize something negative that gets beneath your skin, or is trying to. It can symbolize bad influence, disgusting thoughts, or depravity.

Maggots in the eyes can symbolize seeing something that worms into your thoughts, such as graphically violent imagery or pornography. Maggots in the ears can symbolize hearing something disgusting or that disgusts you. See: *Worm*.

Maggots are commonly associated with filth and decay, and the symbolism can branch out from there. For example, someone important in your life comments that your car is filthy, and that night you dream that you have to drive a VIP to a big gala event. When you let the person into your car, you see maggots all over the passenger headrest. The VIP symbolizes the important person in your life, and the maggots symbolize the filthy condition of your car. It's exaggerated but it fits.

Decay in a dream can be associated with a relationship or situation in decay.

Maggots eat decaying matter, and in dreams that association can be positive if it means the removal of "dead weight." For example, a new supervisor at work breathes life into a decaying situation, or moving to a new town frees you from the burdens of the past.

See also: *Body, Bug, Fly, Infect, Infest, Insects, Roach, Skin, Worm*

Magic—Magic in a dream can symbolize something that seems to happen on its own. It's magic that clean clothes always appear in your drawer. No, actually, Mom does your laundry but you never really see her in action. Or you think you really flubbed something, such as a test or a meeting with a dating prospect, and magically everything turns out all right.

Magic can symbolize anything that seems to happen on its own, or that you make happen with your creative imagination or force of will.

Magic is used in the sense of personal magic, that magic touch, that ability to turn people and situations your way.

See also: *Precognitive Dream, Psychic Power*

Magnifying Glass—A magnifying glass can symbolize taking a closer look at something. Magnifiers are used to make objects appear bigger, so they can be studied more closely. As dream symbolism it can mean you want to understand something in detail.

Magnified can mean "magnified in importance." For example, you need to ace a test in order to get a good grade in an important class, so the importance of the test is magnified.

Fears can be magnified. In this sense it means they appear bigger and badder than they really are. For example, seeing a spider magnified in a jar can symbolize that a person's fear of spiders is overblown. For an example dream, see: *Spider*.

Maid—See: *Servant*

Mail—See: *Letter*

Makeup—Makeup covers, so applying makeup can be thought of as covering up something. It can mean you are hiding or concealing something about yourself, such as personal flaws. The heavier the makeup, the more you are trying to conceal—especially when makeup is used to cover skin flaws. See: *Hide, Skin.*

Makeup is part of growing up for females, a rite of passage. Some females begin using makeup regularly at around puberty, so it marks a time of life when childhood is left behind. For a female around that age, dreaming about makeup can symbolize trying out new aspects of her persona as a female between childhood and adulthood. Then for the rest of her life, any rite of passage can be symbolized through makeup, especially the application of it. See: *Persona.*

For example, a woman dreams about stealing makeup from a store and trying to hide in the dressing room, but the attendant won't allow her to enter because she looks like a boy. The dream sums up the dreamer's experience as a teenager when her mom forbade her from wearing makeup and she was made to feel that she couldn't be like the other girls her age. Stealing makeup symbolizes the feeling that she has to hide the fact that she uses it, even though she's an adult, and generally feeling uncomfortable wearing it.

The associations branch out to include subjects such as loss of innocence, sex appeal, and cultural ideals of beauty and femininity.

Many personal associations can come into play when you dream about putting on makeup, especially if you regularly wear it. For example, makeup is associated with feminine sophistication. The more sophisticated the makeup, the more sophisticated the woman. Some women judge each other on how well they use makeup, so the symbolism of makeup can connect with subjects such as feeling judged by appearance and how a woman compares with other women or lives up to cultural ideals.

Using too much makeup can symbolize compensating for perceived weaknesses.

See also: *Actor, Beauty, Compensation, Disguise, Doll, Face, Hide, Imposter, Lips, Mask, Persona, Skin, Woman, Women*

Mall—What do you do at a mall? You shop, usually. Shopping is about making choices. Many choices are available at a mall. So what is comparable to shopping? The most obvious connection is with making choices.

Take the example of looking for a job. When a type of job offers several employers to choose from, it's comparable to stores in a mall. When you find the right one, you make a decision that's comparable to buying something. Buying something is an investment, and a job is an investment of your time and energy. When you spend your money at a store in the mall you get something in return, and with a job what you get in return is income, benefits, prestige, authority, challenge, security, personal fulfillment, and so on.

In life we make choices about the sorts of people we want to be, the crowd we run with, and the image we project, and these situations are all comparable to shopping at a mall.

The analogy can be used to describe looking for a romantic relationship. You are said to "shop around" when considering choices about whom to date or marry. A mall is comparable to a dating site. You browse through the offerings and decide on whom you want to contact. At the mall you browse through stores before deciding which to visit and what to buy. It's comparable to thinking about the people you know and wonder who would make a good partner. You're looking at your options and deciding where to invest yourself.

Malls are associated with materialism, keeping up on the latest trends and obtaining "must have" items. It's the object of many jokes about material culture.

Many personal associations come into play, so always consider the first words and phrases that come to mind in connection with a mall.

See also: *Clothes, Grocery Store, Menu, Shop*

Man—A man in a dream—whether he's a representation of a man in your life or an imaginary character—can symbolize a masculine role or trait, or the masculine principle, the yang. Yang is the force of creation that gives, and the feminine receives. See: *Penis.*

Otherwise, an unfamiliar man in your dream can be a surrogate for someone you know. When a dream refers to people you know, their identity is sometimes disguised. However, clues will be given to identify the person.

For example, the man can be identified by occupation, a role he plays such as father or boss, or general appearance. He can be identified by how you react. For example, a woman dreams of a man who represents her ex-boyfriend, and she knows it because she reacts with cold hatred, just as she hates her ex. See: *Ex.*

When a dream-character represents a person you know, the character and the person may appear together in the same scene, or adjacent scenes. For example, a young woman dreams that a man steals some items from her. She goes to his house and steals them back. In the next scene, she tells her father about what happened, who tells her she should return the items, even though they're hers to begin with. The items represent her independence, and the man who steals them represents her father, who makes her decisions for her. When he tells her to return the items, she faces a decision whether to claim her independence or go back to being the "good daughter." The man is a surrogate-character for her father.

A man in a dream can symbolize men in general and the dreamer's relationship with them. Men are commonly viewed as assertive, authoritative, forceful, sometimes pushy and aggressive, and less emotional than women. The associations are based on common perceptions, which can be used as symbolism in dreams along with your personal associations. See: *Men.*

A key fact that helps you to interpret a generic dream-character, such as an unfamiliar man, is it must symbolize something. We discussed how a man can symbolize someone you know or a trait associated with men. But the most likely meaning is a man symbolizes something about you, especially if you're a man. It's a part of you personified. For example, a man dreams about watching another man get abducted by an alien. The other man is a projection of a role the dreamer plays. See: *Fisting.*

For a woman, a man-character can represent a masculine trait or her relationship with men in general. The character is not her gender, but she can still have traditionally masculine traits. The entries for *Animus* and *Men* go into more detail about this subject.

When a dream shows you yourself through a dream-character, the purpose is usually to mirror a side of yourself, a trait or aspect, or a feeling, thought, or emotion. Something about the character will give away what it represents. These characters are often stereotypical: a bully, a leader, a weakling, a thief. And what they represent is found through association. For example, a bully can symbolize a feeling of being forced to do something against your will. A thief can symbolize a tendency to undermine yourself or take the easy way out. Using a character to show you something about yourself helps to depersonalize the subject and say that it's a side of yourself, not the complete picture.

A man in a dream can symbolize a subject or idea.

To continue the discussion of gendered characters in dreams, see: *Woman.*

And read: *Boy.*

See also: *Animus, Boss, Boy, Boyfriend, Bully, Father, Groom, Hero, Husband, King, Men, Penis, Stranger, Testicles, Woman*

Mansion—The symbolism of a mansion can connect with its size. For example, taking care of a house the size of a mansion is a huge responsibility, so in a dream a mansion can symbolize a huge responsibility. Dreams will give supporting clues, so if "huge responsibility" is the symbolism, responsibility for the mansion will be a theme of the dream.

A mansion can symbolize a huge problem or expense. It can symbolize big impact or potential, or an obstacle.

A big, empty mansion can symbolize feeling alone or unwanted. An empty mansion is a lonely place.

A mansion is a home for someone wealthy or above everyone else. A person's wealth, upbringing, specialized skills, or high intelligence can make him or her feel alone in the world, separated from the rest of humanity.

A house in a dream can symbolize you, specifically your mind or psyche. In this sense, a mansion can symbolize an expansive mind. The great size of the mansion can symbolize your potential for growth. It can mean you feel that you have a lot to learn about yourself, or a lot of room to grow. For more about this use of the symbolism, see: *Home*.

Moving into a mansion can mean you are entering a more expansive phase or stage of life.

Dreaming that someone you know lives in a mansion can mean the person is inaccessible personally, emotionally, or physically. Or it can mean you admire the person and perhaps are learning from her how to achieve her level of success.

See also: *Giant, Home*

Map—To dream about a map can mean you are looking for guidance or direction. Think of direction as personal direction, the direction to head in your life. See: *Guide*.

Getting directions in a dream can mean you need help reaching a goal, solving a problem, or dealing with an issue. It can mean you're looking for personal direction; you're not sure about the best direction to go in your life. Giving directions can mean helping someone with a goal, problem, or issue.

The symbolism of a map can be used in the sense of "map out" a big project. It can mean you are being careful in plotting something, the next steps to take. You "map out" where you are going in your life or an area of it such as your career, living situation, finances, or family. For example, see: *Old Friend*.

Dreaming about needing directions back home can mean you're trying to return to a feeling of safety, security, or connection. Home is where you feel secure and wanted. It is "home base." You can dream about finding your way home after ending a relationship or taking a blow in your life and needing to recover from it. You're trying to get your life back on track. For example, see: *Ex*.

See also: *Above, Ascend, Backward, Below, Car, Descend, Director, Elevator, Guide, Left, North, Right*

Marriage—To understand the symbolism of marriage in a dream, begin with what marriage essentially is—a commitment. Dreams can use the commitment of marriage to compare with something else, such as commitment to your job, your personal development, or your destiny. You can commit to a vision or creative project. You can commit to a cause. You can commit to a relationship other than a marriage.

For example, a female dreams that she is on live television with Rachel Maddow, the MSNBC host, and Rachel asks to marry her. The dreamer initially says yes, wanting to avoid embarrassing Rachel on live television, then afterward tells her they can't get married. The dream symbolizes a situation involving being asked in front of a group of people to commit to a social cause. To avoid embarrassment, she says yes, but once she really thinks about it she realizes it is a commitment with which she is uncomfortable. Maddow is used by the dream because she is known as a social crusader.

Marriage has many other associations involving commitment and integration of aspects of yourself, found in these entries: *Anima, Animus, Bride, Groom, Wedding*.

If you are in a relationship that could lead to marriage, or the thought of marriage has been on your mind, you can dream about it in this traditional sense—not as symbolism for commitment to something else. Dreams can provide a "dress rehearsal" to help you sort out your feelings related to marriage and the possibilities for its happening.

For example, you might wonder whether the person you are dating is marriage material. You might dream about preparations that need to be made or obstacles to overcome. You might dream about compatibility and issues such as the desire to have children. If you want to have children and the person you are dating doesn't, or vice versa, that's a major obstacle.

A bride-to-be dreams it is her wedding day and her family and friends are gathered to see her get married. Then her ex-boyfriend bursts through the door and declares he is there to rescue her. The dream is trying to help her realize what she already knows deep inside. She is about to marry the wrong man, and deep down she knows it.

If you are married, you can dream about marriage when thinking about related issues. For example, you have been married for a while and the zest is gone from the relationship. You have had some serious difficulties with your spouse lately. You then dream about marrying your spouse and feel really positive about it. That's a good sign that you subconsciously know you married the right person and can work out your differences. On the other hand, if you run from the altar, it might be a way of saying you know deep inside that you can't work out the differences with your spouse.

Carl Jung and his student Robert A. Johnson wrote about the "marriage of the soul." It is the union between the conscious mind and the unconscious mind. The bride in a man's dream can symbolize his *anima*, and the groom in a woman's dream can symbolize her *animus*. In dreams, union with the unconscious can be expressed as marriage to an ideal mate. Who could be more ideal for you than yourself? This sort of marriage only comes after you have developed yourself and realized your personal potential. It's often a long process, sometimes lasting a lifetime. See: *Anima, Animus, Bride, Groom.*

See also: *Alimony, Anima, Animus, Bride, Divorce, Fiancé, Groom, Wedding, Unconscious Mind.*

Mars—Mars in a dream can have symbolism related to its astrological significance. In astrology, Mars is perceived as the planet governing war and aggression, assertiveness and initiative. You can dream about Mars during times of conflict and strife, or when you need to defend yourself aggressively.

Mars can symbolize anger. It's the "red planet," and red is associated with anger and aggression. See: *Anger, Red.*

Some people have difficulty being aggressive or dealing with anger. But aggression is not just physical—it can mean aggressively going after what you want or defending your boundaries. It can mean passion. Anger is a needed emotion, too, and is good for you when it's channeled into assertiveness. See: *Warrior.*

Mars is perceived as a lifeless place, and it can be used in dreams to symbolize feelings of loneliness, isolation, and desolation. For example, a young man dreams that he lands on Mars in a spaceship. The landscape is barren and lonely. It expresses his feelings about being isolated and friendless.

The saying "Men are from Mars" connects it with the symbolism of a man, masculinity, or men in general. See: *Man, Men.*

Mars can symbolize something that's far away or out of reach. Expand the idea past physical representation. For example, with twenty years to go till retirement, it can seem far out of reach.

See also: *Anger, Man, Men, Red, Space, UFO, Warrior*

Mask—Wearing a mask in a dream can mean you're hiding something about yourself, as in the phrase "hiding behind a mask." It can mean you put up a facade or project an image rather than show your true self. See: *Disguise.*

A mask is a great symbol for persona. See: *Persona.*

It can mean you are playing a role that doesn't fit you, or feel that you are being fake. Or perhaps you are concealing something, keeping secrets, or hiding your feelings. See: *Hide.*

Evil-looking masks can symbolize observing the darkness that can lurk behind the image of normalcy, or behaviors that can drive people to do things they otherwise wouldn't. For example, addiction, envy, and lust can twist people to do things that compromise themselves and others. The darkness in them is like a mask over the good person inside.

A mask can hide an aspect of yourself that's consciously unknown. This use of the symbolism is especially likely when you encounter a dream-character that's your gender and wears a blank mask. What you actually see in that image is a part of yourself that wants to be a conscious part of your life, or a feeling that you are a "blank canvas."

The same imagery of a blank mask can symbolize lack of emotion. It can symbolize a weak sense of identity.

Explore this subject further using the entries listed below.

See also: *Disguise, Emotions, Face, Imposter, Makeup, Persona, Stranger*

Masturbate—Like anything else in a dream, masturbation is symbolism. For example, it can symbolize settling for less than what you really want (real sex), or doing something that gets you nowhere (going back and forth, or round and round).

However, masturbating in a dream can be straightforward in the sense that it refers to masturbation. But most likely it's going to connect with something related, such as privacy, compulsion, or an outlet for sexual energy.

For example, a young man dreams that he's in his bedroom and getting ready to have sex, and suddenly his younger sister knocks at the door. He tells her to go away but she keeps knocking, and he gives up on the idea of having sex. The dream reflects his feeling that he doesn't have the privacy to masturbate. His sister has a habit of barging into his bedroom, and he fears it'll happen one of these days when he's masturbating, so the thought is always in the back of his mind.

In a variation of the theme, a man dreams that he's on his front porch and wants to masturbate, but is aware that people could walk by and see him. It symbolizes his discomfort masturbating at home when he knows other people are in the house.

Masturbating in public can symbolize doing something to embarrass yourself, or something you do that is impulsive or compulsive.

For example, a man dreams he's in a locker room and another man wrapped in a towel starts touching himself, then masturbates openly. The dreamer berates him for it. For the dreamer, the urge to masturbate can begin with something as innocuous as scratching an itch near his genitals, or seeing the image of a pretty woman. Next thing he knows, his hand is wandering. Then next thing, he's masturbating. The dream shows him the source of the impulsiveness. When he berates the dream-character for masturbating in public, he's really berating himself for masturbating impulsively.

Masturbating can symbolize something you do for pleasure: take drugs, drink alcohol, get a massage.

Dreams can use imagery to refer to masturbation that's not obvious. For example, a man dreams about seeing another man flying through the air and sucking his own phallus. Flying in the dream symbolizes the pleasurable feeling of masturbation, and sucking his own penis symbolizes fantasizing about getting fellatio. When the man fantasizes about getting fellatio, he is, in a way, sucking his own penis.

Masturbation in a dream can symbolize preoccupation with sex or a related issue. Oftentimes, these dreams have absurd sexual imagery, such as massive genitals, and inappropriateness, such as making advances on a relative or having sex with an animal. It shows that the psyche is out of balance and sexuality has too big a hold on the person.

Giving up a regular masturbation habit can lead to a surge in personal growth, reflected in dreams. The person has a sense of being rewarded personally for making a sacrifice.

See also: *Genitals, Penis, Sex, Vagina*

Math—Doing math in your dreams can be an expression of your logical thinking. You might be applying logic to a problem or situation in your life.

It could be a suggestion to be more rational in your thinking.

To dream that you cannot solve a math problem can symbolize an unsolvable problem in your life. Perhaps logic isn't the best faculty to use. You might need to use intuition or feelings.

Inability to solve a math problem can be a way of saying that something doesn't add up or make sense.

People who focus on math in their daily lives are known to dream about it. For example, students in math classes will dream about working on math problems in their sleep. It's a way of integrating what they learn and rehearsing for challenges they will face.

The great Indian mathematician Srinivasa Ramanujan said that a goddess came to him in his dreams and revealed mathematical insights that made him one of the most highly respected mathematicians in history.

See also: *Accountant, Numbers, School, Student*

Maze—The best guidance about dreaming of being in a maze is: consider the obvious. It's a popular way of describing finding your way through a complex situation or problem. It can mean your paths lead you nowhere. It can sum up in one image the feeling of being lost. Branch out from there and a maze can describe a variety of situations in life and be a metaphor for what's going on in your head or heart.

See also: *Lost, Wilderness*

Meal—See: *Chef, Dinner, Eat, Food*

Men—Groups of men in a dream can symbolize something related to your perception of men in general, or some men in particular.

For example, a group of men in a dream can symbolize competitiveness and dominance, because groups of men tend to compete with each other and compete for a dominant role. This meaning of the symbolism shows up particularly in women who are struggling with their masculine side, or men who are trying to be, or needing to be, more assertive.

Men can symbolize the masculine principle, the yang, and in particular how it structures the physical world. It's associated with building hierarchies and organizations. Men are group logic. They're forces that control, that dominate. Remember, by "men" we mean the masculine principle, which can be embodied by women and groups of women, too. But traditionally, men build societies and women build homes, and no matter how

much those roles change, they're still hard-wired into us.

Men can symbolize the "typical guy response," such as initially showing interest in a woman then ignoring her, covering up his feelings, or giving off an unwelcoming vibe.

A dream about a group of men can express your thoughts and feelings related to recent interactions with a group of men, or your feelings, thoughts, and perceptions about men in general. For example, you are disgusted by the behavior of an ex-boyfriend and dream about a group of men harassing your sister with the same sort of lurid remarks your ex makes. It's because the behavior of your ex in the dream reflects your thoughts about men in general. They can symbolize however you finish this sentence: "All men are ... ?"

For more on this subject, see: *Man, Women.*

See also: *Brother, Father, Group, Man, Numbers, Son, Women*

Menstruation—As a part of the process of reproduction, menstruation can connect symbolically with any aspect of it: fertility, conception, sexuality, choice of partner.

In simplest terms, menstruation is a process of letting go of the old to make way for the new, and that association carries many possibilities for symbolism. For example, you let go of your feelings for your ex to open up to the possibility of a new relationship. You let go of old ideas about yourself so new ones can emerge.

On rare occasions, dreams about missing a period can foretell actual pregnancy. The body has an early-warning system that speaks through dreams. However, usually a reference to a missed period in a dream is symbolism. For example, it can mean a woman is "late" for something. See: *Pregnant.*

For a female, any reference to blood or bleeding can refer to menstruation. For example, a woman dreams that she's scheduled to give blood and suddenly realizes the appointment was a week ago. She wonders whether her doctor will be mad at her. The dream refers to the fact that her period is a week late and she wonders whether she needs to visit her obstetrician. See: *Blood.*

Dreams about leaky or running faucets and things that collapse are prevalent in women just before their periods. Another prevalent theme is ironing, both because of the need for iron in the diet to replace what's lost with menstrual blood and because the surface of the endometrium appears wrinkled just before it sloughs off. Ironing is associated with eliminating wrinkles. You don't have to be aware of how this process works in order to dream about it.

For a young girl, menstruation is associated with onset of puberty. For a fertile, sexually active female who doesn't want to get pregnant, it's the monthly sense of relief. For a middle-aged woman, it's the monthly affirmation that she's not in menopause. Dreams can begin with these associations and branch out far and wide. For a man it might symbolize abstinence from sex or handling his wife's or girlfriend's moods.

Menstruation is "your period" and can be used to symbolize a period or cycle of life.

As part of the creation process, menstruation can have deep significance related to it. See: *Uterus.*

See also: *Blood, Egg, Ovaries, Pregnant, Red, Uterus, Vagina, Woman*

Mental Functions—Carl Jung developed a theory of personality types based on four primary mental functions, aka cognitive processes, and today's Myer-Briggs Type Indicator (MBTI) test is based on Jung's original work. It's a subject that goes so deep that this book can't do it justice.

However, it is an important base of knowledge for dream psychology and specifically for understanding certain dream-characters, which can be representations of mental functions, and certain groups of characters, which can be representations of how the mental functions interact. Which ones predominate? Which ones take a back seat? See: *Group.*

To explore the theories behind personality types, visit: *cognitiveprocesses.com.* To take a personality test and zero in on your type, visit: *16personalities.com.*

See also: *Group, Psyche*

Mental Institution—See: *Hospital, Insane, Psychologist*

Menu—A menu is associated with choosing among options. When you look at a menu of foods in a dream and decide what to order, you might actually be choosing from among other options, such as:

Deciding on a career, job, or employer.

Picking a school or area of study.

Choosing where to live.

Choosing friends and your social circle. Restaurants are social places, too, adding another layer of symbolism.

Deciding what you want to do for entertainment or where to go for a good time.

Food choices, and issues related to diet and health. See: *Food.*

Picking a mate, and related ideas such as dating, deciding what type fits you best, and your preferences: appearance, personality, intellect, background, style, ethnicity, gender, race. For example, not to be crude or simplistic, but if you look at a menu and decide to order the Polish sausage, it might be a way of saying you like Polish men!

See also: *Chef, Eat, Food, Mall, Restaurant, Shop*

Mercury—The symbolism of the planet Mercury in dreams is sometimes tied to its astrological meaning. In astrology, Mercury is associated with communication, quick thinking, and wit.

You could dream about being on Mercury when life is going by quickly—it has the fastest orbit of any planet—or when a dream wants to refer to a mercurial temperament, meaning quickly changing, volatile, or fickle.

See also: *Earth, Jupiter, Mars, Moon, Saturn, Space, Sun, Venus*

Mess—A mess in a dream can be a physical representation of a personal situation. You're a mess. Your life's a mess. A situation is a mess. Your house is a mess.

See also: *Infest*

Meteor—Meteors in dreams are associated with major events and big impacts, something that might be described as "Earth-shattering" or "end of the world." Of course, that idea is probably exaggerated when compared to an actual meteor strike.

For example, a major health problem has a big impact on your life. Your world is rocked after you find out your spouse cheated. Failing a major test seems like the end of the world. Moving to a new town or starting a new job means radical changes.

A meteor can symbolize rapid progress or rise in status, a "meteoric rise."

A meteor can symbolize a wish, stemming from the tradition of making a wish when you see a shooting star.

It can symbolize a thought that flashes through your mind.

It can symbolize a brief and intense relationship. Extend that idea to include a brief or sudden incident or event.

A meteor falling to Earth can symbolize a fall from grace, or your thoughts returning to Earth after being far, far away.

See also: *Apocalypse, Space*

Midnight—Midnight is associated with deadlines. The clock is ticking. There is something you need to accomplish.

Midnight is known as the "witching hour." It can symbolize the dark side of a female, selfish and scheming—especially if that side of her shows only at certain times.

See also: *Dark, Time, Witch*

Military—See: *Army*

Mirror—A mirror in a dream can be a means of taking a look at yourself. It can reflect who you are inside or outside, where you are in your life, and what you have done. It can show you the truth about yourself and your life, or reflect your personal perceptions and biases.

It can symbolize a reflective mood, looking back on your life, and thinking ahead to what comes next.

Talking to yourself in a mirror, or looking in a mirror while hearing a voice, can symbolize giving yourself "a talking to," or psyching yourself up. See: *Talk*.

A cracked mirror can symbolize anxiety or something disturbing you. It can show a split in the psyche or disturbance in the personality, especially if the crack in the mirror runs through the reflection of your face.

A dirty mirror can symbolize guilt or stain on your character or self-image.

Being unable to see yourself in a mirror can indicate a difficult time taking an honest look at yourself. It can mean you don't know who you really are.

Being captivated by your image in a mirror can indicate vanity or self-obsession.

Your appearance in a dream can reflect how you see yourself, or think others see you—not physically, necessarily, but personally.

A disheveled appearance can symbolize a life in disorder or a situation that's messy. It can mean that you give off a bad or careless impression. It can mean that you don't put time into caring for yourself, or that the prospects for something look bad.

A groomed or otherwise attractive appearance can symbolize a positive perception of yourself. You put time and effort into caring for yourself or maintaining the image you project to the world. The same idea can apply to caring for others.

An attractive appearance can mean that the prospects for something look good. For example, a businessman in the midst of negotiating a deal dreams that he meets with the other team, joined by an attractive woman who he is told will handle the negotiations from that point forward. Her attractive appearance symbolizes the attractiveness of the deal.

Physical appearance in a dream can symbolize "appearances," as meant in the phrase "keeping up appearances."

See also: *Bathroom, Beauty, Deformed, Eyes, Persona, Talk, Ugly*

Miscarriage—Miscarriage is a common theme in the dreams of pregnant women, and it reflects their fears. Once in a while a dream will predict a miscarriage, but such a dream is much more likely to be based on fear or the symbolism of losing something important.

For example, a woman dreams that she's carrying her ex-boyfriend's baby and miscarries. The ex-boyfriend-character confesses that he's happy it happened because it frees him to do what he wants to with his life. Carrying his baby is a way of saying that the dreamer carried a piece of her ex with her after they broke up—you could say that he's inside her—and the miscarriage symbolizes letting go of the relationship so she can move on. It has nothing to do with actually being pregnant.

Miscarriage can be used in the sense of "miscarriage of justice." It means something wrong has happened, a tragedy. It can have similar symbolism as an abortion, meaning something that's aborted, such as a project or idea. See: *Abortion*.

The symbolism of a miscarriage can connect with related associations, such as a fetus, baby, or pregnancy. Use the entries listed below to explore further.

See also: *Abortion, Baby, Fetus, Pregnant*

Missile—See: *Rocket*

Mohammed—The Prophet Mohammed of the Muslim faith can have specific symbolism related to associations with the man and the religion he founded, or general symbolism based on the role that such a character can play in the psyche. See: *Jesus*.

For a Muslim, dreaming about Mohammed can connect with a desire to be a better Muslim— or alternately, denying one's Muslim heritage. The symbolism plays out in the actions and is defined by the context. For example, dreaming about being in a crowd to hear Mohammed speak and eagerly listening to everything he says can symbolize eagerly taking in Muslim teachings. On the other hand, if you run from a crowd to avoid hearing him, it might mean you don't want to follow his teachings.

Mohammed can be associated with teachings such as abstinence from alcohol or not keeping graven images.

Mohammed can symbolize a Muslim, especially to someone who's not Muslim and has little direct exposure to Islam.

The possibilities for symbolism go on and on. Begin with what you associate with Mohammed. If you don't know much about him, it would be wise to do some research, especially to find out more about his life. It's well documented.

See also: *Buddha, God, Jesus*

Mom—See: *Mother*

Molest—Themes of molestation and abuse arise frequently in the dreams of people who have unresolved issues from childhood. The first reaction is often to assume you were abused in childhood and repressed the memories, but that's not usually the case.

Dreams make comparisons and exaggerate. What is presented in a dream as molestation is actually an exaggerated way of comparing how you feel to what you have observed. If you boil down the idea of molestation, it translates as "mistreated" or "abused." Molested children are, in essence, mistreated children. They're vulnerable. Their innocence is preyed on and lost to adults who take advantage of them. Your situation might not have been that bad at home, or be bad presently in your life, but perhaps something inside you identifies with the idea of being taken advantage of, or of being vulnerable, mistreated, or innocent.

Molestation doesn't only happen to children. As an adult you can feel molested when someone takes advantage of you and your good nature. You can feel molested in an emotionally unhealthy situation. It can be a way of saying you don't trust someone—a molester is, after all, someone who can't be trusted—especially when it comes to children or anyone else who is vulnerable or innocent.

A child molester can symbolize something that's inexplicable in a bad way. The association is created by your being unable to understand why someone would molest a child.

In a similar way, a child molester can symbolize someone or something that disgusts you, something representing the lowest form of life. It can symbolize the feeling that someone deserves the harshest punishment.

The entry for *Rape* can give you more ideas about how a dream can start with an idea and branch out to create symbolism. Remember, molestation in a dream is likely to be a physical representation of a personal situation.

See also: *Baby, Child, Crime, Innocent, Rape*

Money—Money in dreams is often a reflection of value. The association is made every time you open your purse or wallet to purchase something and consider the value of what you buy compared with the amount spent on it.

The idea of value applies to a wide variety of situations. For example, pay and benefits at work reflect a person's value to the employer. The care and effort you put into a relationship reflects how much you value it. You can value (or not value) someone's opinion, time, love, or input. See: *Diamond.*

Money can symbolize self-perceptions about your abilities and worth, or the worth of something in your life. For example, a woman dreams that her husband is given a big raise. She jokes with him that his employer finally recognizes his value to the business. When she wakes up and remembers the dream, she wonders if it's presaging that her husband really will get a raise. But what she's really dreaming about is his value to her and their children. The raise in the dream refers to her raised esteem for him. She's come to realize what a great provider he is, not just the income he provides but in his roles as father and husband.

Along this line, money can symbolize the importance and priority of someone or something.

Dreaming about giving money away to someone who doesn't need it can mean you're wasting your time and effort. It is not valued.

On the other hand, dreaming about giving money to someone who needs it can mean something is worth your time and effort. It can mean you want to show someone that he or she is important

to you. It can mean that something is worthy of your investment—investment in the personal sense of investing your time, effort, hope, or faith.

Dreaming about being happy to receive money can mean you feel valued. Your efforts and contribution are being recognized.

Money in a dream can refer to related subjects such as greed, stinginess, and generosity. In this way, a dream can act as a simulation to show you how you really feel. See: *Wallet.*

People may say they would do this or that if they had the money, but put them in a dream where they suddenly have it and find out. Would your ego explode? Would you abandon your principles or ideals? Would you take care of the people who have taken care of you? See: *Lottery.*

Of course, money in a dream can be taken at face value, not as symbolism. Money and finances are a part of daily life and likely to be dreamed about. See: *Bank.*

Money is a resource that's invested, and that idea carries over to non-material investments, such as where and how you invest your focus, time, energy, and intellect. It can symbolize who your put your faith and time into, such as in a relationship or friendship, but most dreams connect with your inner life, and what you spend your money on—or your willingness to spend it—shows what your priorities are.

For example, a man dreams that he's part of a protest group against an entrenched authority structure. He's on the frontlines of the protest, deep down in some mines. They have blocked the tunnels and are awaiting the riot police. A fellow protestor mentions something about paying bail after they're arrested. The dreamer suddenly realizes he doesn't have the extra money for bail, or at least doesn't want to sacrifice what he has, so he decides to back away from the conflict and avoid getting arrested.

The dreamer's reaction shows that he subconsciously knows that the sacrifice of money symbolized in the dream means his time and attention, and the setting deep down in the mine symbolizes deep inner work. He's too busy in his life to divert his focus away to clean up some old personal wounds and confront some entrenched structures in his mind. He feels a calling to do it, but it's just too much to handle at the moment. He chooses instead to back away.

Counterfeit money is discussed in the entry for *Fake*.

See also: *Alimony, Bag, Bail, Bank, Beggar, Casino, Diamond, Fake, Gamble, Gem, Gold, Jewelry, Job, Lottery, Numbers, Purse, Wallet*

Monster—Monsters are the stuff of which nightmares are made. But like just about everything in a dream, monsters are symbols.

For example, monsters are used to compare with people whose behavior and character are "monstrous." A difficult situation can be a "real monster."

"The monster within" means that something nasty lurks there. It can be a way of comparing to mental or physical illness. For example, cancer is compared to a monster. See: *Cancer*.

Anything repressed, unwanted, or ignored in you can take form as something progressively nastier until acknowledged and healed. What's depicted as a monster in a dream can be something about you trying to get your attention: a feeling, desire, perception, old wound, aspect of yourself. It can even be unused potential or the little voice calling you to deeper experience. Its characterization as a monster is based on your feelings and perceptions. It's a projection from within you.

A monster can be a general symbol of something feared. The symbolism is revealed by your reaction. If you see a monster in your dream and flee in terror, it's a clue that the monster symbolizes something you fear. If you confront the monster, it can mean you are confronting a fear. If you laugh in its face, it can symbolize freeing yourself from fear, or from someone whose bark is worse than his bite. See: *Fear*.

For example, a woman dreams recurrently about a huge monster hunting her. She never really sees it in detail, it's just dark and scary. She flees at first sight of it and continues running long after the danger is past. Finally, sick of running, one night she turns on the monster and screams at the top of her lungs. The monster shrinks down to a little girl who looks timid and afraid. The woman continues yelling, exasperated, saying it's mean to play such a trick on her and that good girls behave themselves.

She reflects on the dream and is struck by her statement about good girls behaving themselves. It's something her mom used to say to her. Her mom used to criticize everything she did, and in response she's a perfectionist. Her mom has been dead for twenty years, but the woman is still an obsessive perfectionist, still afraid of being criticized, as if she's still a little girl struggling to understand why, according to her mom, she can't do anything right. The monster that chases her in her dreams is this unresolved part of her childhood that still deeply affects her.

A monster is something that can't be controlled. In dreams, that can symbolize a situation or person that can't be controlled. Something is getting out of hand. It's a shit spiral.

On the other hand, "monster" can be used to describe something that can't be stopped. It's not necessarily bad. For example, if someone has a "monster game," the person dominates, can't be stopped. Some athletes and soldiers are referred to as beasts or monsters because they have wild strength and indomitable will, an association that opens avenues for dreams to use the symbolism.

A beast or monster can symbolize the animal side of human nature—not just the "animal in you," but animal instincts, which can be perceived as beastly if unrestrained, untamed, or shunned.

Or it's the "beast within," your Mr. Hyde.

In that sense, a beast or monster can symbolize something about yourself that pops out only under certain circumstances, such as when you feel threatened or under duress.

A beast can symbolize a rejected or repressed side of you that takes a beastly form in dreams as a way of symbolizing your adversarial relationship with it. As with all dream-characters, when a beast is in your dreams you look it in the eyes, and ask what you see about yourself or your life in it.

A destructive beast or monster in a dream can symbolize something causing destruction in you or your life: bad temper, financial loss or mismanagement, a failed marriage, addiction, neurosis, mental illness. It can mean that a behavior, instinct, thought, or feeling is unconscious and characterized as a monster only because it isn't fully understood.

See also: *Addict, Animals, Anxiety, Cage, Cancer, Chase, Creature, Demon, Devil, Dragon, Drugs, Fear, Games, Ghost, Insane, Nightmare, Panic, Shadow, Spirit, Sports, Vampire, Werewolf, Witch, Zombie*

Moon—The moon is associated with femininity and feminine power and influence. It can symbolize a strong feminine or maternal figure, or the influence femininity has on you, especially on your emotions, feelings, and moods. The moon drives the tides, and that unseen but discernible force is comparable to the unseen forces that act on your inner life.

Femininity has a general sense meaning the power that women in general and specific women in your life have on your thinking, feelings, and behavior. Femininity also means "traditionally feminine," such as caregiving, nurturance, and receptivity. It's a powerful and motivating force, and the amount of power and influence on you can be symbolized by the size of the moon. For example, a huge full moon in a dream can symbolize a maternal figure who has a huge influence on you, or the influence of femininity in general. A moonless sky can symbolize that femininity has little or no influence on you, or your life lacks a strong female influence.

Because the moon changes appearance as it progresses through phases, it can be used to symbolize phases of life and changes a person goes through.

You subconsciously know the meaning of a symbol in your dream and react to it according to that knowledge. Your reaction and feelings will tell you what the moon symbolizes.

The moon is associated with romance and love. It can connect symbolically with sexual attraction.

The full moon is known for having a strange effect on people, and that association can be used to symbolize strange or unusual behavior. A full moon can symbolize the lure of sex and the influence of sexuality. It can symbolize a desire to explore a mystery—especially the mysteries of your existence. It can symbolize the huge prominence of a female in your life. See: *Giant*.

A full moon gives you light to see by at night. See: *Guide*.

It's considered a sign of luck and can symbolize the feeling of being lucky, or "getting lucky." See: *Lottery*.

And because the entire face of a full moon is in the light of the sun, psychologically it can symbolize awareness of everything about yourself. Nothing is in shadow. See: *Sun*.

Then again, a crescent moon is mostly hidden in shadow, and it can show that something is hidden from you—especially something about yourself. See: *Shadow*.

More possibilities come into play when you consider your personal perceptions, feelings, and associations. As with all symbols, when considering the symbolism of the moon in your dream, begin with your impressions and associations. What are the first thoughts that come to mind?

See also: *Archetypes, Circle, Dark, Giant, Goddess, Guide, Lottery, Mother, Night, Shadow, Sun*

Mother—One of the most confusing aspects of understanding a dream about someone you know, especially someone close to you, involves separating the person from the dream-character. They're not one and the same, usually.

The character does not represent the person directly. This is important to know when you dream about your mother, because strong feelings can make you think a dream is speaking literally when really it is speaking figuratively.

The symbolism of a mother in a dream can be difficult to pin down, in part because of the wide variety of possibilities, and in part because of the difficulty of separating the dream-character from the person you know.

Dreaming about your mom can connect with some aspect of your relationship with her. For example, a teenager dreams that he is in the passenger seat as his mother drives on a snowy road. They come to a bridge and she misses it, driving onto a frozen lake. The ice breaks and the truck sinks. The dreamer rescues his mom, then admonishes her for her bad driving. The dream symbolizes the poor decisions his mom makes and the fact that he has to rescue her from her mistakes. Their relationship is reversed. Instead of mom rescuing her son from making bad decisions, correcting his mistakes and cleaning up his messes, it's the son who performs that role.

A young woman who moved away from home eight years earlier dreams that she goes to her mom's house and just starts pounding on her. She then tries to leave and is blocked by her stepfather, so she returns inside the house and again repeatedly hits her mother. Hitting her mom is an expression of frustration about their relationship and anger at how she was raised. Her mom was neglectful and made many bad decisions when it came to the men she chose, including the stepfather in the dream.

Dreaming about your mom dying might mean you fear growing apart, sense it happening, or need it to happen. It is common for young male teens to dream about their mom dying, symbolizing the changes they go through as they come out from under her wing. In a figurative sense the old dynamics of the mother-son relationship are dying.

For males and females alike, this most important relationship goes through changes, which can feel like something about it is dying. Dreaming about parents dying is common when young people move out of the home and miss the direct support and care of their mothers.

For example, a twenty-something female dreams that her mom is buried in a grave. The daughter digs frantically to uncover her. She succeeds, only to find her mom's body in a state of repose. She tries to revive her. The dream symbolizes the daughter's perception and fear that she is growing apart from her mom, and it's not because of an incident or negative feelings. It's simply a process

that's happening as the daughter becomes an adult, and Mom's role in her daughter's life changes. Attempting to revive her shows that the dreamer wants to revive the relationship.

The symbolism of your mom dying can mean that you are breaking her rules, going against her teachings or wishes, or doing something that is potentially a threat to your relationship. This figurative sense of "dying" can mean she would "die" if she found out what you were doing.

For example, a young man dreams that a meteor is about to hit the Earth. It's an apocalypse. He goes to the basement and finds his mom hanging by a rope, as if she'd committed suicide. He leaves to get help, and returns to find his mom is fine, no longer hanging.

The dream symbolizes a situation he's involved in, which his mom doesn't know about. He's selling dope. The apocalypse symbolizes his fear that she will find out, and it will cause major damage to their relationship. Hanging is an apt metaphor because strangulation can symbolize that something isn't getting through to your head. For the dreamer, it means he's ignoring the voice in his head telling him he's taking too big of a risk. The basement setting is appropriate because basements are where things are put out of sight.

If your mom has been on your mind, or a recent interaction with her made a strong impression on you, then dreaming about her is likely to connect with it. For example, if your mom has been ill and you are concerned about her health, this is the sort of strong impression that is likely to come up in a dream. The situation will be exaggerated, so something like your mom's nagging cough turns into a dream about rushing to the hospital and finding out she has pneumonia.

On the other hand, your dreams can use the image of your mom to represent something about yourself, such as feelings, attitudes, beliefs, values, or character traits. Whatever it represents probably relates back to her, either something about you that is shaped or influenced by her, or something you see in yourself that you also see in her. The dream is not about her. Unless your life is tied very closely to your mother's, the majority of your dreams about her will be of this variety.

For example, a young man dreams that he is at a friend's house where his social group regularly gathers to party and kill time. He sees his mom's car parked in the driveway, walks over to it, reaches under the passenger seat, finds a gun, and shoots himself with it. The dream scenario symbolizes his desperation as he tries to figure out what he wants to do with his life and how to take the steps to make it happen. Instead of working toward his goals, he wastes time at his friend's house. His mom's car is used in the dream because moms give their sons the ideas about themselves that they use to build their adult lives. The son can't figure out how to move ahead toward his goals and ambitions, and it's killing him inside. The gun is under the passenger seat of his mom's car because his life is an extension of hers. He is her passenger.

You can have much in common with your mom, especially if you are female. In your dreams, she can represent something you two have in common. For example, let's say that your mom is a whiz at event planning, and you are planning a surprise party. You dream about your mom organizing your house, symbolizing how you draw on the organization skills you learned from her to plan the party. You see yourself in her actions and behavior in the dream.

Or say that your mom is neurotic, worrying over every little thing, and you find yourself sweating the small stuff, too. In a dream she acts neurotic, and in her behavior you see yourself. It's a trait you picked up from her.

Dreaming about your mom can mean you need mothering or nurturing. This can also be the case if you dream about a mother who is not yours. The use of the symbolism is most common when you are feeling down or in need of hope. Moms, ideally, pick you up when you are feeling down and give you hope for the future. Even if your mom is not this type of mom, it is still a common perception that can be used as symbolism in a dream.

The mom in your dreams can be the mom you *wish* you had.

Dreaming about your mom can mean you are playing the role of mother, either directly as a mother of your children, or indirectly as a mother figure. In these dreams, you see that side of yourself projected onto a dream-character. You can have mother figures in your life who appear as dream-characters, too, such as a beloved teacher, coach, or female relative.

Dreams can mix and match people from the same maternal or paternal line, so someone such as a grandma, aunt, or sister can symbolize your mom, and vice versa.

Pregnant women, or women trying to get pregnant, are known to dream about their moms as a way of preparing to be mothers themselves. Their moms are the closest examples they have for how to do it.

For example, a pregnant woman dreams about shopping for clothes with her mom and sister. Shopping symbolizes the preparation and decision-making related to her pregnancy. Her sister is also a mom, so the image of the three of them together shows that the dreamer is drawing on the example of her sister and her mom to help her have a successful pregnancy.

A mom in a dream, whether your mom, a mom you know, or a random dream-character, can symbolize typical mom characteristics. Even if your mom is not a typical mom, you are aware of the common characteristics of moms, such as nurturing, warm, giving, self-sacrificing, supportive, and helpful.

Moms care for young children who can't care for themselves, so a mom in a dream can symbolize caring for yourself, especially for the childlike parts of yourself.

For example, a woman dreams that she holds her mom in her arms and Mom shrinks down to a baby. The dreamer recognizes in the baby her need to take care of herself, to mother herself, especially when it comes to caring for basic needs such as good nutrition, regular sleep, and emotional warmth.

See also: *Baby, Bear, Child, Egg, Family, Family Home, Father, Grandmother, Moon, Orphan, Ovaries,*

Parents, Passenger, Pregnant, Shrink, Uterus, Vagina, Woman

Motorcycle—Riding a motorcycle in a dream can have the same symbolism as driving a car: See: *Car*.

The difference is, a motorcycle is usually a single-passenger vehicle and can symbolize doing things your own way, or finding your own road in life. You are very much an individual, perhaps even a loner or iconoclast. This use of the symbolism will show you alone on a motorcycle or on an empty road.

In addition, a motorcycle is open instead of closed like a car, an openness connected with vulnerability and exposure.

Riding a motorcycle with someone else can symbolize something about your relationship. For example, a woman dreams that she is on the back of a motorcycle driven by her husband. Dead fetuses connected by a string fall out of her body and onto the road. The dream uses that imagery to symbolize her feelings related to getting her tubes tied. The decision meant she and her husband would not be able to have more children.

Riding with someone you know, such as a spouse, can mean it's the two of you against the world.

Motorcycles are known for their speed and can be used to symbolize your life speeding by—perhaps too quickly. This use of the symbolism will be accompanied by supporting details, such as riding at a high speed. See: *Speed*.

Motorcycles are exciting to ride and can be used to symbolize an exciting time in your life.

Or perhaps you need excitement. This use of the symbolism is found in dreams about looking for a motorcycle or trying to buy one.

Motorcycles are dangerous, especially for new riders. If you actually ride a motorcycle and dream about being in an accident, it is wise to pay it heed because many instances of precognition related to motorcycle accidents have been recorded.

Dreams can use the imagery of a motorcycle accident as a general warning. Perhaps you are not being as careful as you should be. No matter whether you actually ride a motorcycle, it can be symbolism for putting yourself at risk. But if you do actually ride a motorcycle, you have more to consider because the warning could be specific. A young male rider has such a dream and realizes he sometimes eschews wearing protective gear on short rides. In the back of his mind he knows it's risky. He decides to heed the warning and always wear a full complement of gear.

Dreaming about a specific motorcycle that belongs to someone else might be tied with that person. A dream can use objects and items associated with people you know as a way of connecting with a certain person or group of people. For example, a young man who misses his older brother, who's deployed overseas in the military, dreams recurrently about his brother's motorcycle, often related to its being in the garage. The imagery is a way of saying that their relationship is stored away until he gets back.

See also: *Bicycle, Car, Crash, Kayak, Passenger, Precognitive Dreams, Speed*

Mountain—A mountain in a dream can be a metaphor for a huge task, major difficulty, or long slog, as in the phrase "climbing a mountain." This use of mountain symbolism will usually be accompanied by the action of climbing. See: *Climb*.

Running up a mountain can symbolize having a lot of things to do, a "mountain of work."

Driving up a mountain can symbolize easily mastering something difficult, such as a subject or musical instrument. For example, a woman in a conservatory of music dreams about driving up a mountain and enjoying the sounds of the wind. Doing this symbolizes the way she "breezily" masters the most difficult subjects for music students. She's highly talented and has deep understanding of music and music theory.

Climbing a mountain can symbolize taking on a challenge that requires effort over a period of time, such as starting a business, getting through college, regaining your health after a bad illness, or establishing a close relationship.

For example, a woman dreams that she climbs a mountain and reaches the top. There she finds a red sports car waiting for her—it looks like one her father used to own. She hops in, ready to drive away, but the keys are missing. Climbing the mountain symbolizes getting through college. The sports car symbolizes the "revved up" career she expects to have, and the association with her father connects with the success he's had as a professional. She expects to have similar success in her career. But it doesn't start the way she expects. She graduates from college and can't find the job she wants.

Climbing a mountain can mean you will go to any length to get your way or accomplish something. Mountain climbers are among the most determined sorts of people.

Mountains are generally sparsely populated and can symbolize isolation, tranquility, and emotional space. For example, a man dreams about climbing halfway up a mountain to the cave of an old wise man. They don't talk. Instead, they just sit in each other's presence and meditate. The mountain and cave symbolize isolation, which the man chooses for himself because he prefers it. The old wise man is a projection of himself.

Mountains are also dangerous, and can be associated with taking risks, or dangerous lifestyles.

A mountain can symbolize an immovable person or obstacle.

See also: *Avalanche, Cliff, Climb, Fall, Hill*

Mouse—The symbolism of a mouse is often connected with its small size and associations related to being a pest. In dreams mice can symbolize small things that irritate you. An infestation of mice can symbolize that some worry, problem, irritation, or anxiety won't go away or is getting worse.

Mice are known for eating into things such as baseboards and stored food, and that association can be used to symbolize something that "gnaws at you."

Some people are deathly afraid of mice, and in their dreams mice symbolize more than an annoyance. For them, mice represent something in their life that really scares or bothers them. For example, mice are associated with poverty, and if you have ever lived in poverty and escaped it, you may well fear it can happen again.

Remember that dream symbolism is built on your associations. The common perception of mice is that they are pests, but they are also kept as pets. People who keep mice as pets have no fear of them. In fact, they might view mice as delicate creatures that require tending and care. That association can be used by dreams to symbolize something in your life that is delicate, such as a situation or person. It might represent something about yourself that you want to nourish.

Mice run away at the first sign of danger, and people can behave the same way. For example, you feel shy about your singing voice. You work up the courage to sing publicly, and someone remarks carelessly about your singing ability. The comment makes you want to run and hide and never sing in public again, and you dream about it as a mouse in a hiding place.

In some spiritual traditions, mice are viewed as spirit guides because they are familiar with hidden and inaccessible areas. If you dream about a mouse leading you somewhere, it might symbolize being led to a hidden potential in yourself for personal growth. See: *Guide.*

See also: *Animals, Guide, Infest, Little, Rat*

Movie—When you dream about a movie or movie theater, focus first on the root word "move." Move can mean physical movement, as in moving to a new town, but also think of movement within you and movement in your life. People are said to move into a phase of life or new understanding of themselves. Or they are moved by compassion or inspiration.

Movies are also a terrific storytelling device for telling the story of your life. The focus can be tight, on a specific event or situation, or broad, an overview of you and your life. See: *Documentary, Television.*

See also: *Actor, Cartoon, Director, Documentary, Famous, Hollywood, Spotlight, Stage, Television*

Mouth—The symbolism of the mouth is closely associated with its functions of eating and speaking. See: *Eat, Teeth.*

Details and actions involving the mouth help define the symbolism. For example, an alligator's mouth is big and can symbolize a "big mouth." A gummy substance in the mouth can symbolize difficulty with articulation.

Stuffing something like a sock or fist into a mouth can symbolize wanting to shut someone up, or saying something that embarrasses yourself. A mouth that's blocked like that can symbolize the feeling of being prevented from expressing yourself. It can mean you need to watch what you say.

Swallowing something sharp can symbolize holding back something sharp you want to say or express, as in "bite your tongue." It can symbolize self-criticism.

Bleeding from the mouth can symbolize saying something that embarrasses or harms you.

There are many variations of this theme, and the symbolism often boils down to what you say, want to say, or have said. See: *Teeth.*

See also: *Abscess, Bite, Body, Eat, Face, Food, Lips, Talk, Teeth, Vomit*

Murder—Murder in a dream is a particularly important theme to understand as symbolism. It's probably not a moral judgment or judgment about your character, but the tendency is to think that dreaming about murder indicates something wrong with you. But if you murder someone in a dream, it doesn't mean you are capable of murder or should be locked up. Like everything else in a dream, murder is symbolism.

The first possibility to consider is that murder is an expression of frustration or anger. For example, you dream about murdering your spouse and connect the act with the feeling that your frustration level is through the roof. If you say, "Oh my God, I could just murder my husband!" it doesn't mean you actually want to murder him. Or if you say, "I want to kill my wife!" it means she is doing something, or did something, that really annoys or angers you. Dreams create symbolism the same way through exaggeration. The exaggeration expresses how you feel.

Those strong feelings can be directed at yourself, too. Murdering a dream-character can mean you want to change something about yourself that's represented as a character. For example, you meet someone you are attracted to and stick your foot in your mouth, blowing your chances, as usual. You want to change that part of yourself that gets nervous when interacting with someone attractive, and you dream about sticking a gun in someone's mouth and pulling the trigger. The symbolism is acted out with the gun, and the mouth is the target because you are frustrated with what you say (or can't say) under certain circumstances. To kill someone with a gun is to "blow them away." In a way, your mouth "blows your chances."

Murdering a dream-character can be a raw expression of feeling sick and tired of a situation, circumstance, person, yourself, or your life.

The key to understanding these dreams is the strong feelings involved. Unless someone is truly sick in the head, he or she doesn't just go around murdering people. It's a crime of passion, usually. Murder is what you might call "next level." Dreams have several levels to choose from when expressing symbolism of this type—death, killing—and murder is used to express the strongest feelings, harshest thoughts, and direst situations.

Murder can be used as a way of saying something has come to an end. For example, when dismissed from a job, a person is "terminated." A relationship that ends is said to be "dead." Murder shows that the feelings involved are toxic, volatile, or crazy.

Dreams create symbolism by using comparisons, and murder in a dream can be used to compare with something that's wrong, shameful, insane, or unimaginable. For example, you feel ashamed because your life is in shambles, or you have inappropriate sexual feelings, and your dream symbolizes your feelings as murder because the shame and guilt you feel are comparable. The dream actually has nothing to do with murder. Murder is only used to trigger the feelings.

Along this line, murder in a dream can compare with something forbidden by society, something that deserves the severest punishment, something that could make a person an outcast. It can mean a line has been crossed that will forever separate a person from society. When you murder another human being, something inside yourself dies, too.

In some cases, the act of murder in a dream is less important than the method. Refer to the list below. Also, look up the entries for *Death* and *Kill*.

See also: *Body, Death, Execution, Gun, Hang, Jail, Kill, Knife, Serial Killer, Strangle*

Murky—See: *Water*

Museum—The symbolism of a museum connects with the idea of "relic from the past." Museums are terrific dream settings for looking at your past. They can show you what you really value about yourself, your history, and your heritage.

Museums are associated with the idea of "untouchable." For example, a young woman dreams about rescuing a child in a museum, symbolizing how she is trying to escape the restrictions of her childhood. As a high achiever with overprotective parents, she watched other children have fun and take risks, but wasn't allowed to participate. The "look but don't touch" association with a museum describes her childhood. Now that she's an adult, she has more freedom to decide for herself what she wants to participate in, but she needs to overcome the programming of her childhood that makes her feel she needs permission to do things merely for the fun of it.

See also: *Child, Time Travel*

Music—Music in a dream can connect closely with mood and emotion. It can express the thoughts you can't consciously express and the emotions you can't consciously feel. You have a DJ in your head who has access to every song you've ever heard, and who can pull out the right one at the right time to perfectly match the situation.

Music can express harmony or disharmony within yourself. To hear beautiful, harmonious music can mean you are experiencing positive emotions. Your life is harmonious, especially your inner life. Disharmonious music can indicate negative emotions, or express the state of your mind or life. It can tap into the deepest layers of your being.

Music can tie in with the subject of the dream. For example, the song "Material Girl" by Madonna is heard in a dream, a song the dreamer would never listen to voluntarily, and hearing it sums up his thoughts about living in a material world but seeing through it to recognize the beauty of it, too. The dreamer lives in a rundown urban neighborhood. It makes him feel pessimistic, but shifting how he views it helps him to see the beauty in the people and the ways that nature expresses itself in urban environments. The song is the catalyst for a flip in his perception.

If you wake up with a song in your head, pay attention to the lyrics—they could have a message for you—and also to the song's general mood and tone. For example, feeling energetic could be reflected in waking up with a techno beat in your head. Feeling angry could be symbolized by Death Metal.

See also: *Ears, Emotions, Hear, Kanye West, Snoop Dogg, Urban, Vibration*

Naked—Nakedness is a common dream theme. It tends to get your attention, and thus it stands out from everything else you dream about.

Nakedness has a variety of symbolism. The most common is "exposure." Nudity reveals the person beneath the clothes. It can mean you are seeing a person for who and what the person really is, or seeing beneath the surface of something such as a situation or idea. If you are naked, it can mean you are showing your true self. You have nothing to hide. Or maybe you do have something to hide, but it is exposed anyway. See: *Hide*.

When naked, you are exposed to the elements, and this use of the symbolism implies some sort of risk or personal exposure. It's a physical representation of a personal situation. For example, feeling exposed because something personal about you has been revealed. Feeling exposed to risk, such as in a financial dealing, or because of risky behavior. A similar idea is expressed when nakedness symbolizes vulnerability. Naked exposure can symbolize fear of being personally exposed, such as when a flaw or weakness is exposed. For an example, see: *Job*.

The word "exposure" has another sense, meaning learning something new or having new experiences, and this sense can be expressed by nakedness.

Nakedness in a dream can mean you feel unprepared. See: *Test*.

Nakedness in a dream can mean "stripped of pretense" or "naked truth." Everything is out in the open. This use of the symbolism suggests openness and honesty. The symbolism can combine with exposure or vulnerability in situations such as when you have opened up to reveal your true thoughts and feelings and feel vulnerable because of it.

Nakedness can mean "obvious," as in the truth should be obvious, or a person's intentions, motives, or feelings are obvious.

Getting undressed, then dressing again, can symbolize wanting to reveal your thoughts and feelings, then thinking it's not a good idea. Being without a shirt can symbolize being financially broke, or giving the shirt off your back to someone who needs it. See: *Dressed, Undress*.

Clothing is closely associated with a person's outer identity and social image. Conspicuous nakedness can mean something important to your identity is missing. For example, you quit your job to be a stay-at-home parent and dream about being naked at the place where you used to work, symbolizing that you gave up part of your identity by leaving the job.

Of course, nakedness can be associated with sexuality and sexual fantasy. This use of the symbolism will be accompanied by sexual situations and feelings. Just be careful to avoid jumping to conclusions. In a pretty common dream scenario, the object of your affection or infatuation strips naked in front of you, or is seen naked; sometimes such a dream is interpreted as a sign that the person wants you. However, it's more likely to be an expression of what you want, or even what the naked person wants.

For example, a man dreams that he sees his girlfriend naked in the bathroom. He reacts by thinking it's "sexy time" and approaches her seductively. She says, simply, "I want more," and he understands her statement to mean "I want more than just sex."

Context and feelings are the most important clues to determining the meaning of nakedness in a dream. For example, in many situations a person would feel embarrassed or ashamed to be seen naked in public. But if you feel proud or liberated being naked in public, the dream obviously has nothing to do with embarrassment or shame.

Feeling ashamed while naked can be a sign that something has been revealed about yourself that you'd rather keep hidden, or some part of your identity has been taken away. You have nothing to hide behind. It's a theme known to arise after a romantic relationship ends.

Nakedness in public can symbolize doing something embarrassing. On the other hand, it can connect with a situation where you were seen naked and it embarrassed you.

For example, a college student who is self-conscious about his body uses the group shower in his dorm while no one else is around. Then suddenly a group of schoolmates comes in. They don't say anything to him, but he feels like his naked body is scrutinized. That night he dreams he is taking an exam and finds himself naked. Someone makes a derogatory comment about his body. He runs out of the classroom and back to his dorm, feeling humiliated. It would be easy to conclude that the dream is about anxiety related to an upcoming exam, but instead it's about the situation in the shower. The clue that gives away the meaning is the fact that the dreamer runs back to his dorm—that's where the incident took place.

A young woman dreams that she is trapped in a bathroom stall by a group of men and they rip her clothes off. She feels violated and ashamed. The dream reflects her feelings about men judging her body. See: *Clothing*.

See also: *Body, Clothing, Dressed, Hide, Job, Sex, Shower, Test, Undress*

Nazi—To understand the symbolism of Nazis in dreams, begin with what is commonly associated with them: murder, cruelty, domination, conquest, delusion, grandiosity, torture, bigotry, genocide, discrimination. Basically, Nazis are as bad as it gets. Of course, dreams exaggerate, so whatever dreams symbolize as Nazis is probably not as bad as the real thing, but in some exaggerated way it is comparable or appropriate.

Dreams use comparisons the same way that people do in everyday conversation. If you say, "The boss at work is acting like a Nazi," you don't mean that the person sends employees to concentration camps. You mean that he or she is acting like a tyrant or being cruel.

Keep in mind that dreams can use Nazis to describe internal dynamics as well as external ones. Perhaps in the image of Nazis you see something about yourself. This is exactly the sort of situation dreams will focus on, because sometimes it's hard to admit when you act tyrannically or cruelly. Seeing yourself as a Nazi is the sort of wake-up call that dreams are known to deliver.

Psychologist Ann Faraday dreamed about seeing a weekend house guest dressed as a Nazi. The man was charming and well-spoken in the daylight world, and Ann puzzled over why her dream portrayed him as a Nazi. The answer soon became clear when she found out he was only there to make another woman jealous. Beneath the charming exterior was a selfish, manipulative person. Ann's deeper senses picked up on the situation and warned her in the dream.

See also: *Army, Evil, Hitler, War*

Neck—The neck is the connector between the head and body, making it a great symbol for communication between the mind and the body. If you "live in your head" at the expense of connection with your body, you could dream about your head detached from your neck. Or if you're driven by instinct and don't listen to your head, you could dream about that idea as a shrunken neck, or inability to pass air through your neck. See: *Strangle*.

Because the vocal cords are in the neck, it's associated with ability to articulate, and in general with articulation and self-expression.

Cutting or constricting the neck can symbolize that something isn't getting through to the head, or a conversation is "cut off." See: *Hang, Hear, Knife*.

The thyroid gland is in the neck, along with lymph nodes that help remove toxins from the body. Swollen lymph nodes in the neck are a common sign of illness, so if a dream presents the imagery of a swollen neck, consider the possibility of its warning about illness developing in the body, or an issue with your thyroid.

The throat is a vulnerable area of the body, so dreaming about protecting it can symbolize protecting yourself from being vulnerable. It can symbolize a "weak spot" in your character, or be similar to the symbolism of an Achilles heel. Perhaps you aren't as well protected as you think. Or you are "sticking your neck out."

If you dream about an elongated neck, see: *Giraffe*.

See also: *Body, Decapitate, Giraffe, Hang, Head, Knife, Strangle*

Needle—See: *Inject*

Neighbor—It's possible to dream about your neighbors, especially if you're involved in some sort of conflict or intrigue with them. Consider what you know about them and your recent interactions, if any. Dreams have a lot of possibilities to work with to create symbolism based on your neighbors.

For example, if your neighbors are loud and keep you up at night, they could be used to create symbolism related to a troublesome situation unrelated to them. For example, a big problem at work could be keeping you up at night, and it's symbol-

ized as a problem with your neighbors. If your neighbors appear to be well-off financially, in your dreams they could symbolize your desire to be well-off. If you hear them fight and argue, they could be used in your dreams to symbolize conflict.

Neighbors are close geographically, generally, so in dreams they can be used to symbolize something that is close in the figurative sense. Someone who is gravely ill might dream about death as a neighbor because he feels that death is nearby. See: *Barn, Garage*.

Neighbors can symbolize other people close to you, such as relatives, friends, or co-workers. For example, the co-worker in the office or cubicle next to yours is said to be your neighbor.

When you compare yourself with other people, whether or not those people are your neighbors, dreams can use neighbors to symbolize those thought processes and related feelings. Neighborhoods are generally homogeneous ethnically, racially, economically, and socially. The people in your neighborhood are in the same general grouping as you are and therefore can be used to symbolize the idea that "we're all in this together."

For example, a dream about looking out over the neighborhood and seeing the souls of children being sucked up into the night sky is related to the dreamer's thoughts about the sacrifices that have to be made in order to sustain a high standard of living. Parents in that neighborhood have to work long hours and that means less time with their children. In turn, the children lose something essential, symbolized as their souls.

A dream about a Chinese family moving into her neighborhood symbolizes that the dreamer feels out of place. She stands out in her peer group as a bit eccentric, the same way that a Chinese family stands out in a neighborhood composed of other ethnicities.

Neighbors can be used to symbolize divisions, particularly if fences or other obstructions are involved. For example, a dream about a fence being built between the dreamer's house and a neighbor's house is related to the dreamer's perception that his family is better off financially than his neighbors, and the disparity creates a divide between them.

Dreaming about your old neighborhood under attack or demolished can symbolize a break with your past. A way you used to think about life and the world is under attack or gone. You've been through big changes. Buildings such as houses and stores are structures, and metaphorically so are belief systems, values, and morals.

See also: *Building, City, Fence, Garage, Group, Home, Trespassing*

Nephew—When deciphering the reason that a nephew or niece is in a dream, follow the same process as with other dream-characters. Generally, a dream-character that is presented as someone you know symbolizes something about the person or something about the person that you see in yourself.

For example, if your nephew is good with computers and you've been struggling with a computer issue, you might dream about your nephew as a way of symbolizing your thoughts and feelings related to the issue.

If you have had recent interaction with, or thoughts about, a person and that person appears in a dream, then there is a good possibility the dream is related to the interaction or thoughts. For example, you see your nephew during a family gathering. Judging by the state of his life, you get the sense that he is making poor decisions that will have long-term consequences. You then dream about seeing him as a homeless person begging for handouts on a city street, symbolizing your hunch that his life is going nowhere.

Of course, it's possible the nephew in the above scenario is a projection of fear that *your* life is going nowhere, in which case he symbolizes something you see in him that you also see in yourself. It depends on the circumstances. Obviously, if you have no such fear about your life going nowhere, the likelihood is that the dream is making an observation about your nephew, not about yourself. If you have not seen or thought about your nephew in a while, his presence in your dream is more likely to be symbolism for something related to you.

Also consider that a nephew or niece in a dream can symbolize other people in the family tree. For example, if your nephew is your brother's child, he could symbolize your brother. For example, a man dreams his nephew is getting divorced from a woman named Ann, but in reality he's not married or even dating. However, he senses that his brother's marriage is going down the tubes—his brother is the father of his nephew. And, his sister-in-law's middle name is Ann. The nephew in the dream is a surrogate representing the dreamer's brother.

See also: *Family, Brother, Sister, Tree*

New York City—When a place such as NYC is a setting or reference in a dream, begin deciphering the symbolism by thinking of your associations with the place. New York is a city of glamor, wealth, and opportunity. You might dream about being in New York when you have been the center of attention, are thinking about money, or are looking for a job opportunity. New York is the center of many industries, such as fashion, media, publishing, and finance. People looking for opportunities or recognition in those fields can dream about NYC in relation to that desire.

For example, an author has a recurring dream about flying to NYC. She never actually makes it to the city. All the dreams involve getting to the airport, buying a ticket, and finding the correct terminal. In her waking life the author is trying to find a publisher, as symbolized in her dreams by trying to fly to NYC. She seeks a "ticket" to the next stage of her career.

Of course, NYC has its down side, too. It's crowded. It's dirty. It's ruthless. Those associations can be used to create dream symbolism. For example, lately you have taken some hard knocks from life, and they manifest in your dreams as walking through a tough Bronx neighborhood at night.

Because of the attacks of September 11 and the powerful impression made on the individual and collective psyche, NYC is associated with tragedy and terror and a symbol of being attacked, but also with resilience and defiance. The events of September 11 were viewed on television by billions of people, and dreams can use the city as a symbol of being attacked or witnessing it. For example, you see a schoolmate get ruthlessly bullied, or witness an incident of senseless road rage, and dream about such things as a plane flying into a building.

See also: *City, Famous, Skyscraper, Terrorist, Urban*

Niece—See: *Nephew*

Night—A nighttime setting in a dream can reference something you're trying to keep hidden. Nighttime is when people do things they don't want others to know about. See: *Hide.*

Nighttime is when you can have difficulty seeing, and if that's a theme in the dream, consider that the difficulty might be related to seeing ahead in your life or seeing your way through a situation. Or perhaps you don't "see the light at the end of the tunnel." A situation seems to have no end. See: *Dark.*

Night in a dream can refer to a change in atmosphere or behavior. People can act differently at night than the way they do during the day. See: *Moon.*

Night carries an air of mystery and hints at danger or strange encounters. See: *Black, UFO.*

Night implies that something is over or finished. For example, when one dreams about an ex, the scene is often depicted as occurring at night as a way of saying the relationship is over.

See also: *Black, Dark, Light, Midnight, Moon, Shadow, Space, UFO, Witch*

Nightmare—A nightmare can be a big flashing sign that warns, "Something's wrong!" A situation has gone on too long. Stress levels are too high. Something about you or your life needs to change, pronto.

Think of a nightmare as shock therapy, an attempt to break a pattern or get your attention after gentler methods fail. Dreams usually try to get through to you in what you might call a normal speaking voice, and they crank up the volume if you don't get the message. It's like shock therapy, a last resort.

Dreams tend to focus on unprocessed emotions. You haven't worked them through your system, so your dreams take up the slack. If you want to lessen the odds of having nightmares, process your emotions consciously. Don't give your nightmares fuel for the fire.

Fear is the number-one emotion behind nightmares, and some fears are more obvious than others. For example, if you fear spiders and dream about them crawling all over you, the dream could be a way of amplifying or confronting the fear. And if you successfully confront a fear in a dream, you're likely to reroute your brain's neural pathways away from that fear, creating a lasting change. Or if you fear heights, you might find yourself dreaming about being stuck on top of a skyscraper, and your choice is to overcome the fear or succumb to it.

Don't worry. If you fail the first time, you'll be put back into the scenario again, and again, and again—as many times as necessary till you get it right.

It's very important to understand that the imagery in your nightmares is not to be taken literally. It's symbolism. It's telling a story. For example, see: *Incest.* Incest, the ultimate taboo, is symbolism in a dream. If you take it literally, you'll end up judging yourself for it and completely miss the point.

Nightmares come in three general varieties.

1. *Trauma.* You can also call them "shock to the system" nightmares stemming from sudden, dramatic, and traumatic events. You find out your spouse is cheating. A layoff is coming at work. Someone close to you dies, and the death provokes a nightmare. Trauma nightmares tend to be meaningful, but often there isn't much that can be learned from them or changed as a result. These nightmares reflect the events that spark them—events that are probably beyond your control—and act as a release valve. Your best bet to avoid this sort of nightmare is to consciously process your thoughts and emotions after a shocking or traumatic event. If you have been through trauma, for example, because of fighting in combat or abusive parents, then you will dream about it, and it will hurt. It might seem cruel

to relive traumas in dreams, but if you believe what Carl Jung said, all dreams—nightmares included—are for your benefit. In a moment we'll discuss why.

2. *Abuse.* Chronic stress. Some sort of addiction or compulsion. Self-abuse. A prolonged situation that's harming you, or something untenable. Abuse nightmares are most likely to be potentially beneficial, because they're often brought on by something that can be changed or addressed. For example, you are aware that a work or home situation is stressful, but it takes a nightmare for you to realize how much of a toll it's taking. You can change the situation or take steps to alleviate stress. Or you know you have been ignoring the warning signs that your health is deteriorating, but it takes a nightmare about dying to spur you to action.

3. *Illness.* Fever dreams and "something I ate" nightmares are brought on by indigestion and certain medications. Spicy foods and heavy dairy products are known to produce nightmares, especially if eaten just before bed. Also, SSRI and other psychoactive drugs are known to cause them. Withdrawal from the drug Cymbalta® even has the term "Cymbalta nightmares" associated with it, noted for extreme gore and violence. Often, there isn't a deeply personal message or meaning. The body reacts to something inside it, and dreams translate it into scary imagery. Or in the case of withdrawal, the body reacts to something taken from it.

Nightmares help you by putting psychological distance between you and the event, trauma, or situation. Once the dream is finished, it is "in the past," behind you. It creates a mental cushion.

A nightmare provides emotional release. Think of it as a safety valve for pressure. If you don't dream about the trauma and let the emotions out, the pressure building inside you might erupt.

Nightmares give you ways of viewing situations in your life as stories and working with the imagery to find resolution. Dreams function at a neurological level to reroute neural pathways, called "neuroplasticity," a process of reorganizing and rerouting the brain. See: *Letter.*

For example, let's say you were a soldier and are haunted by the blood on your hands. No matter how you justify it, it's just wrong, and your conscience won't let up. You can't change what happened, but dreaming can give you some distance from it. It can give insights. It can help you reprocess the experiences in a way that heals the trauma.

You can work with the imagery consciously as a sort of therapy. It's amazing what apologizing to a dream-character and resolving to learn from your mistakes can do. And you don't have to be dreaming to do it. A heartfelt daydream can do the trick, or try *dream rescripting* and *active imagination technique.*

In some nightmares, what makes them so frightening is obvious—the serial killer pursuing you; the tidal wave enveloping you; the evil presence haunting you—but sometimes your reactions stand out. When you react powerfully to imagery in a dream, it's because you subconsciously know what it symbolizes.

For example, you dream about going into the basement of an abandoned home and seeing a young child. It floats in the air and its head spins around like in the movie *The Exorcist.* For some people, such imagery might be disconcerting or frightening but not terrifying. They wouldn't necessarily describe it as nightmarish because what it represents to them is not at that level. Hell, they might even think it's funny.

But for other people, such a scene is no laughing matter. It might induce panic and cause them to wake up screaming. Why? Because they recognize something about themselves in that child, such as repressed memories from childhood causing current emotional problems. To them the child symbolizes something they have been avoiding at all costs, while to someone who reacts more mildly the child might symbolize that he or she acted childishly the previous day—not exactly nightmare material.

Which brings up the point that everything in a nightmare is a projection of something about you and your life, except on occasion when it's a direct representation of a nightmarish experience.

Nightmares are easy to confuse with sleep paralysis. See: *Sleep Paralysis.*

Chronic nightmares can be caused by airflow obstruction while sleeping, such as from snoring or sleep apnea. It causes your body to send panic signals to the brain—*Help, I need to breathe!*—which the brain then translates to scary, even life-threatening imagery and scenarios. Oftentimes, the dreams have themes or imagery related to lack of air, or to ventilation. For example, a man dreams recurrently about being stuck upside down in a chimney. He has sleep apnea, and the chimney symbolizes his airway. To help determine if your nightmares have a physical cause, you can ask your sleeping partner to monitor your sleep, or use a voice-activated recorder to record the sounds you make while asleep. A popular phone app, *Sleep Talk Recorder*, turns your phone into a voice-activated recorder.

And finally, chronic nightmares can be caused by *REM deprivation*. It's a serious problem in this age of twenty-four-hour schedules, night work, and the constant distraction caused by electronics, especially phones. Search online and check whether the symptoms of REM deprivation, which include drastic mood swings and inability to focus, match what you are experiencing. A hallmark of REM deprivation is dreaming about being fatigued or sleepy.

See also: *Attack, Creature, Dream Within a Dream, Emotions, Enemy, Evil, Fear, Fight, Hell, Monster, Panic, Sleep, Sleep Paralysis*

Noose—See: *Hang*

North—If you live in the Northern hemisphere, north can symbolize the harder route, because the northern latitudes are colder and more rugged. In dreams, references to the north can symbolize a rough road in life or difficult challenges. "North" can mean you take the road less traveled and the more difficult path in life that leads to personal and spiritual fulfillment. See: *Left*.

If you live in the Southern hemisphere, south is the direction of the more difficult route.

North can mean you face a physical difficulty. For example, you break your leg and have to use crutches, and dream about taking the north road

through rugged terrain, reflecting the physical difficulty of getting around.

In some spiritual traditions, north is the direction of spirit and rebirth. Because winter lasts longest in northern latitudes, north can symbolize a time of dormancy or spiritual malaise.

See also: *Crutches, Left, Map*

Nose—To dream about your nose can indicate the need to "sniff out" a situation or trust your instincts. Perhaps you "smell a rat" or "something smells fishy." Or, like a bloodhound, you might be on the hunt, following a trail of clues or signs. In such a dream you will probably follow a trail of clues or have something you need to find. You might even detect a smell.

The nose in a dream can be a play on the word "nosy." Someone is snooping or sticking his nose where it doesn't belong.

Damage to the nose can indicate you aren't using your instincts. It can mean you fail to notice something.

Cutting off the nose can be a way of visualizing the expression "cut off your nose to spite your face," meaning overreact to a situation in a way that creates embarrassment.

To smell a scent while dreaming can mean you are actually smelling something as you sleep, such as smoke, or it's used as symbolism. For example, if you smell rot while dreaming, it can mean something is figuratively rotting or in decay, such as a relationship that should have ended long ago. Most people don't have the sense of smell as part of their dreams, except for people who use scent regularly as part of their occupation, such as perfume testers and chefs.

See also: *Body, Face*

Nuclear War—When a situation in life "goes nuclear" it means it is highly dangerous and explosive. We use the term to describe a huge and momentous event or battle. Dreams exaggerate, so it's not as if bombs are dropping, but in some way the imagery fits. A nuclear war implies that a situation is really bad, beyond just the normal squabbling and bickering that can be symbolized in dreams as fighting or warfare. The situation is in "meltdown."

Take the idea further and it can apply to situations in which all other options have been exhausted. Dialogue and negotiation have stopped. You're helpless to change the situation or prevent the inevitable. Extreme measures are needed.

In this sense, nuclear war is like the symbolism of war, only more of it. It's war on steroids.

Bombs in dreams can symbolize something explosive, such as a temper, and a nuclear bomb takes the symbolism to the next level to describe something *really* explosive—blow-your-top explosive. The wording is seen in the dream imagery.

It implies hostility, destructiveness, even rage.

Symbolism is based subjectively on your perceptions and feelings, not necessarily on objective analysis. For example, you wreck the car and tomorrow your spouse returns from a trip. You haven't said anything about the accident. You expect the situation could "go nuclear." The imagery of a nuclear bomb exploding is fitting.

Nuclear war ties in with "end of the world" and "apocalypse." When used figuratively it means a situation changes drastically for the worse, or threatens to. The symbolism applies to situations such as bad health problems, divorce, and death. Again, it's an exaggerated way of expressing the dynamics of a situation, especially the feelings and emotions involved. Facing a major decline in your health, wealth, or status can seem like the end of the world because it means the end of your world as you know it.

The idea can apply broadly. For example, "bombing" a college entrance exam can mean the end of your college plans. Royally screwing up at work can mean you might be fired. Saying something really inappropriate can mean the end of a relationship or ruin of your reputation. Getting into trouble with the law can cause devastation in your life. It's the possibility of it that gets translated into dream imagery of mushroom clouds and nuclear missiles.

A mushroom cloud is an apt metaphor for a feeling of dread or something that's inevitable or unstoppable. Most of the analogies used in this entry connect with extreme situations, but don't limit yourself. Usually the connection with the feelings is most important.

Nuclear war can describe extreme inner conflict. Something inside you resists change and will fight to the end, even take you down with it. See: *Shadow*.

It can mean you're facing big changes in yourself and your life, or so sick of being the way you are that you are ready to wipe it all out and start over again. That idea can apply to "nuking" a relationship or situation. It's over, finished.

A nuclear explosion can't be escaped. It destroys everything, and that destruction can be a metaphor for death. It will come for you eventually, and there's no escaping it. However, the same idea can apply to any sort of end that's inevitable.

Your dreams can visualize bodily processes happening as you sleep. If you eat some five-alarm chili and go to bed with it burning away in your bowels, you might dream about it as a nuclear blast.

See also: *Apocalypse, Armageddon, Bomb, Death, Rocket, War*

Nude—See: *Naked*

Numb—Dreaming that you are numb in a dream can indicate emotional numbness. Dreams will use a physical representation to describe a personal situation, and numbness means "unable to feel."

On the other hand, numbness can be your body communicating to you that blood circulation is constricted, as when you fall asleep on your arm.

See also: *Drugs, Drunkenness, Emotions*

Numbers—In meaningful dreams, every detail is related to the dream-story and the dreamer. Nothing is random, so there are reasons you dream about specific numbers. It's a subject that can reach great depth. Here is a brief overview.

When you dream about a number related to a grouping, such as three dogs or five babies, ask yourself whether it connects with something in your life. For example, three dogs might represent three friends. Five babies might represent five projects you call your "babies."

A ten-story building might represent your life at age ten. Each year of your life builds on the previous years, just as floors of a building build on the ones below.

Numbers are part of many aspects of our world that can be referred to by dreams: addresses, phone numbers, bank accounts. Dreams are often quite clever in the ways they make these references.

For example, let's say that you work in television production and have aspirations to move up in the profession. You have a dream about finding thirty rocks. The dream is oddly specific about the number thirty. You sense that it has significance. Then it hits you: Surprised that no mention made here of TV show *30 Rock* in New York! It's the mecca of network television production in the United States. Understanding that reference can be used to decipher the rest of the dream, because now you know it's related to your profession.

Numbers can be used to create an impression, as opposed to a specific meaning. For example, to most people the number 459,824 is simply a big number and can mean "abundance." Whereas the number "two" is small, especially if it's how many dollars you have in your pocket!

In numerology, numbers have spiritual and cosmic significance. It takes an expert to explain how numerology works, but it doesn't take an expert to recognize the significance of numbers in your dreams. It's something you intuit and feel. With some searching of the Internet, you can find many resources, and when you find something that explains the significance of a number in your dreams, you will feel a ping of recognition. Try *dreamhawk.com* and look up numbers.

See also: *Alimony, Bail, Elevator, Gamble, Group, Lottery, Money, Octopus, Time*

Obese—See: *Fat*

Ocean—Because water in the ocean is always moving and because emotion moves like fluid, the two have a strong connection. If you want to create a metaphor for emotions, the ocean in particular is a terrific symbol because of how it affects people emotionally, and because of the many analogies that can be made comparing emotions to the ocean.

For example, a calm ocean can symbolize calm emotions. A rough ocean can symbolize turbulent emotions. A murky ocean can symbolize clouded emotions. A frozen sea can symbolize frozen emotions. Emotions can be powerful. They can toss you about. They have depth.

Other characteristics and associations with the ocean can be used as symbolism. The ocean is a place where lives and treasure are lost. Its vastness is associated with seeing the big picture, with opportunity, wide-open possibilities, and freedom. It's associated with long voyages, isolation, and exploration. See: *Boat*.

Another strong association is between the ocean and the unconscious mind. Both are vast, deep, and mysterious. The conscious mind is like an island in the ocean of the unconscious, or a boat atop it, signifying how small it is in comparison. Islands and boats are frequent themes in dreams that illustrate the relationship between the conscious mind and the unconscious mind.

When you expand your consciousness, you can dream about discovering land that has been claimed from the ocean, or about the ocean receding, or an island forming, or walking along the beach and finding strange creatures washed up. The strangeness is a reflection of the newness, such as when a person seems strange to you till you get to know him or her better. It's a projection of your perceptions.

A submarine in the ocean can symbolize exploration of your inner depths. The depths of the unconscious mind can't be overstated because in theory the unconscious mind contains all of the memories and experiences of the human species going back to the beginning. Basically, it has no bottom. See: *Unconscious Mind*.

The analogy comparing the ocean with the unconscious has a deeper layer because you have a *personal unconscious* that connects with the *collective unconscious*. Your personal unconscious is like a warehouse for all of your experiences, potentialities, memories, and components of the deep psyche. The collective unconscious is the warehouse for the experiences of *every human being who has ever lived*, going back to the beginning of the species. You, the individual, are just a tiny speck floating atop all that.

THE 𝒟REAM INTERPRETATION 𝒟ICTIONARY

So now you see why the ocean is a great metaphor for the individual's relationship with the unconscious.

Creatures that live in the ocean, such as dolphins, whales, rays, and octopi, can symbolize aspects of the unconscious mind or your means of exploring it. For example, octopi live deep in the ocean and can symbolize the aspects of the unconscious that are strange or foreign to the conscious mind. Whales can symbolize the strength and power of the conscious mind to go deep down into the unconscious. Dolphins can symbolize the love of exploration and playful attitude that keep the conscious mind from getting overwhelmed by what it finds deep down inside.

See also: *Beach, Collective Unconscious, Creature, Dolphin, Emotions, Fish, Heat, Ice, Monster, Octopus, Treasure, Water, Wave, Whale, Unconscious Mind*

Octopus—The symbolism of an octopus is usually derived from its tentacles and the way it engulfs prey. It can symbolize a situation or problem that has many facets or layers, or something entangling or ensnaring: multitasking, possessive relationships, juggling several relationships, being ganged up on. You're involved in too many things at once, feel pulled in too many directions, overwhelmed, overpowered.

An octopus can symbolize ability to camouflage and to squeeze through tight spaces. Think in terms of a physical representation of a personal situation. Such as camouflaging to avoid notice or scrutiny, or just to blend into your social environment. Squeezing through a tight space can represent getting out of a tight situation. *Phew!*

An octopus attacking or ensnaring you can symbolize some way that your unconscious mind is pulling you into its realm. This imagery is common in the dreams of people who resist the call from deep within them to find out what's down in their depths. They feel that something lurks beneath the surface, and it terrifies them because they know if they "go there" they'll never come back. The experience will change them significantly.

Like other sea creatures, an octopus can symbolize something from the deep reaches of your mind, the foreign, wondrous, sometimes frightening things encountered in the unconscious. See: *Unconscious Mind.*

In psychoanalytic tradition, the octopus is seen as a symbol of an overwhelming mother figure, someone who will devour and possess you; an octopus sums up the idea in one image. People who lack security, solid identity, and healthy boundaries can be terrified of separation or loneliness. They attach to and feed off the light and energy of people around them. And if that person is the mother who raised you, an octopus is an apt metaphor for your relationship with her.

Remember, though, that dreams are subjective, and if someone you know is represented as an octopus, it's your subjective perception. Perhaps you feel that way because you have trouble setting boundaries or making attachments.

The clinging, devouring octopus might represent something about you with which you need to contend. Clingy, afraid of separation, needing close attachments, sucking people in. Does that describe you? This use of the symbolism is more likely if you battle an octopus, or the dream recurs. The symbolism shows in the actions.

An octopus has eight tentacles and is therefore associated with the number eight.

As with all dream symbolism, the meaning depends on your feelings. If you see an octopus and react with fear, it suggests that whatever it symbolizes bothers you, is difficult, or arouses your emotions. On the other hand, if you eat an octopus it might mean you are looking forward to taking on several tasks at once, or are happily involved simultaneously in several relationships. Or maybe you just want to try something different.

See also: *Animals, Fear, Numbers, Ocean, Unconscious Mind*

Old—See: *Elderly*

Old Friend—Dreaming about an old friend in a dream can mean you miss the person, or the person recently crossed your mind. Sometimes a seemingly random thought or dream about a friend you have not spoken to in a while can indicate it's a good time to get in touch.

However, the majority of dream-characters represent something about you, and in the case of an old friend, dreams have many references to draw on to create symbolism. Dreams can be packed full of references to people you used to know, and figuring out the symbolism is tricky because a dream can use anything you associate with that person to create symbolism, such as personal qualities and traits, what the person means to you, and the time of life you shared together. So as with any symbol in a dream, begin by making associations, then ask yourself whether any of them fit the dream-story.

For example, in a dream about an old college friend holding a map in the passenger seat of a car driven by the dreamer, the old friend represents the help the dreamer needs with organizing a big project. The friend taught the dreamer a trick long ago for how to organize big projects, and the dreamer had forgotten it. See: *Map*.

An old friend appears in a dream as a guy who is working hard and being disciplined in order to be more successful. The old friend is someone the dreamer associates with success through hard work and discipline, and is used in the dream to refer to those qualities in himself.

An old friend shows up in a female's dream when she is dealing with conflicted feelings about being too assertive and opinionated. She fears she will be perceived as acting too masculine. The old friend—an assertive, opinionated female—is someone she remembers as not caring what people think. Her presence is a way of reassuring the dreamer she is all right so long as she doesn't care what people think of her.

An old friend shows up in a dream when the dreamer is trying to be more compassionate and engaged with people in his life, two qualities of that old friend.

An old friend appears when the dreamer is having financial difficulties. The friend is someone she knew when they were both poor and scraping to get by.

Dreaming about old friends can reference the time of life when you were close. It can be a way of saying that something started then that continues now: a thought pattern, a tendency, a circumstance. It can refer to something you did together, such as attend school or work together, or to a feeling you shared.

It's common to dream about old friends when you miss the feeling of closeness and camaraderie—you don't have that sort of friend in your life anymore.

When you dream about an old friend, begin the decoding process by asking yourself what the person reminds you of—it's often portrayed in the dream or found in your feelings.

Of course, an old friend in a dream can be used symbolically, the same as other friend-characters. The person is used to tell a story about you and your life. See: *Friend*.

See also: *Childhood Home, Friend*

Opponent—An opponent in a dream can indicate conflict, either with yourself, with someone in your life, or with a situation. Sometimes the imagery is pretty straightforward. If you have been in conflict with someone in your waking life and dream about that person as an opponent, the likelihood is high that the dream relates to the conflict. Or if you're battling yourself over a decision and dream about wrestling a bear, then perhaps the decision is a "bear to deal with."

Dreams have all sorts of ways of telling a story and using opponents to do it. The key is to figure out what an opponent represents, and to understand the opponent as deliberately chosen by the dream to tell the story.

In simplest terms, an opponent is something you oppose or that opposes you. That word can apply to a wide variety of situations and circumstances.

Sometimes, a conflict with a person in your life is symbolized as a surrogate dream-character who opposes or works against you. For example, the coach you're at odds with reminds you of your father, so you dream about your father as a surrogate for your coach. Perhaps they're both inflexible and demanding. The supervisor you're in conflict with reminds you of a teacher you disliked, and you dream about the teacher instead of the supervisor. Both have the power to judge whether you succeed or fail. The arguments you have with your spouse are just like the arguments you had with your ex-spouse, and you dream about your ex.

Using a surrogate gives you distance to step back and observe and react from your gut. Remember, while dreaming, you already know who and what the characters represent, and you react according to that subconscious knowledge.

Conflicts with yourself symbolized by an opponent will usually feature a character or characters that don't look like you, but that's not always the case. For example, a young doctor dreams that he is in an arena, in a fight to the death with a character that's himself. The opponent is "clean and angelic," while the doctor sees himself as muddy and sweaty. The dream illustrates internal conflict about upholding the image of a doctor. He thinks doctors have to maintain a clean image, but he knows that's not who he really is.

An opponent might represent something positive about yourself that needs to be integrated into your personality. An adversary in a dream can be anything with which you have an adversarial relationship, and it's presented as an adversary because of your conflict with it.

The adversary in your dream can actually be a part of you that works against you or challenges you in ways that make you uncomfortable. Or it's a rejected or unwanted part of yourself. It might represent a fear or bad character trait, something about yourself with which you struggle.

Dreams about an opponent can arise from conflicts with your morals, values, ideals, principles, or best interests. Something inside you disagrees with what you're doing. Or you have competing desires. Your head and heart disagree. You are your own opponent.

The opponent(s) in a dream can symbolize a situation that's difficult, a struggle. For example, a school office worker dreams about an apocalyptic battle against strange alien creatures, illustrating the battles she faces every day at work to accomplish everything that needs to be done. The opponent in the dream is represented as strange aliens because the battle against the constant onslaught of work is impersonal. See: *Fight*.

That last point is very important. When something is close and personal to you, the related symbolism is likely to be close and personal. The opponent in your dream is in your face. And the degree of the conflict is symbolized through the characterization. An opponent isn't the same as an enemy. An enemy implies a greater degree of conflict or feeling.

An adversary can symbolize an obstacle, including your internal obstacles, and overcoming an adversary is a good sign of overcoming the obstacle. Dreaming about an adversary overcoming you implies that you are unsuccessful at overcoming something.

What do you see about yourself in your opponent? Do you recognize someone you know, on the basis of appearance, role, or demeanor? Are you battling yourself over something, or is your daily life like a battle?

See also: *Arena, Enemy, Fight, Games, Sports, Tackle, War*

Oral Sex—See: *Cunnilingus, Fellatio*

Orange—You can dream about an orange, the fruit, to indicate what your body needs and that an orange will do the trick. Your body gives nightly status reports through dreams and tells you what it needs. See: *Food*.

The color orange is expansive and can be a sign that your life or mind is expanding.

Orange is a friendly, exciting, and energizing color that can connect with related emotions. See: *Colors*.

Orange is associated with creativity and fertility. Fertility is associated with procreation, and a baby is a creation, so the two ideas can easily intermix. Women trying to get pregnant are known to have dreams with objects and scenery colored orange.

Examples:

Opening an orange door, from a dream about entering a new area of sex life.

Taking off in an orange plane, from a dream connected with starting a relationship with an enthusiastic lover.

Trying on an orange sweater, from a young woman's dream about starting a sex life.

Juggling oranges, a dream image illustrating the complexity of juggling several sexual relationships at the same time.

The pumpkin is a classic symbol of sexuality or sex-related themes. It's ripe and ready.

See also: *Carrot, Colors*

Orgasm—See: *Sex*

Orphan—To understand the symbolism of an orphan in a dream, begin with the definition of an orphan as a child without parents. Now ask what that can compare to: feeling abandoned; needing guidance, love, or care; the sense that parents or other adult figures are absent physically or emotionally; facing the challenges of life alone.

Stretch the idea of an orphan further and it can symbolize being away from your family or missing them. It's a way of expressing feeling alone or without family, even if temporarily. See: *Family*.

For example, a woman dreams about being in a home and finding an orphaned child in the basement. She asks the child why he's there, and he says he's waiting for the mail to arrive. It's a way of saying she misses her father, who takes long business trips. Waiting for the *mail* to arrive to the home symbolizes her waiting for this all-important *male* to come back. The child is in the basement because the basement is where things are put out of mind. She's trying not to miss him too much.

Dreams with the theme of orphans and orphanages arise commonly in people who feel estranged from, or abandoned by, their parents or family. Being an orphan in a dream is a comparison that sums up their feelings and perceptions, albeit in an exaggerated way. You are not necessarily an orphan but might as well be because you feel unloved, unwanted, or excluded.

Those feelings can be projected onto a surrogate-character; e.g., an orphan. It's likely to be a projection of something about you, though a dream can use that image to symbolize encountering something that's been abandoned, such as a project, idea, or pet.

For example, a woman dreams about driving through an unfamiliar neighborhood and finding an orphaned child on the side of the road. She pulls over and asks the child where her parents are, and she replies that they died. She tells the child that she will find her a home. The orphan symbolizes a house she visited while house hunting. The real estate agent told her that the elderly couple who used to live there died suddenly, and the house sat for months with no attention or care. It is, in a sense, orphaned, and the woman's motherly instincts are pulling her toward buying the home and giving it the attention and care it needs.

"Orphan" can capture the idea of taking care of people who need guidance and parenting. People can be described as orphans when they lack direction in life or behave like unruly children.

Even as adults we can have figures in our lives who are like parents. If you are cut off from that support, then your dreams can symbolize the situation as involving an orphan.

An orphan can symbolize something in your psyche that's left out, not integrated. It's a comparison used to describe something that's left out or unwanted, and it can be used far and wide. For example, a project is said to be orphaned when it's abandoned, and adults can be described as orphans when they lack direction or are isolated and friendless.

Any of these ideas can be symbolized by an orphanage. It's a dream setting that sets the scene and gives an overview of the subject.

See also: *Adopt, Child, Childhood Home, Family, Family Home, Museum, Pet, Psyche, Stranger, Widow*

Outer Space—See: *Space*

Outfit—See: *Clothing*

Outlaw—See: *Bandit*

Outsider—See: *Foreigner, Stranger*

Ovaries—A woman's dreaming about ovaries can be similar to a man's dreaming about testicles, in that the dream can refer to what makes her unique and to how strongly she identifies with being female. Is there a female equivalent of having "big balls?" Yes, having big ovaries.

Of course, for women the idea has a different twist. Her "big ovaries" refer to the feminine traits she has in abundance. When a fetus becomes male, the ovaries turn into testicles. Testicles begin their biological life as ovaries, so perhaps the idea of "big ovaries" isn't such a stretch.

Ovaries, as part of a female's reproductive system, can tie in with ideas discussed at length in the entry for *Vagina*.

Dreams can use the ovaries to refer to reproduction and creating a family. For example, a woman dreams about seeing her ovaries on an ultrasound, and inside of each one is a beetle. The ovary on the left contains a female beetle, and the one on the right contains a male beetle. The beetles symbolize the germ of the idea she has about having children—she's married and wants children, so the subject is prescient for her. The ovaries contain her eggs that will become her children, and the reference to the sex of the beetles connects with her thoughts about her husband's wanting a boy first.

In this sense, the male beetle on the right means "correct," or, even better, "preferred." Which doesn't mean she won't be happy with a girl; she just has the idea that she should have a boy first.

See also: *Egg, Menstruation, Uterus, Vagina, Woman*

Ovation—An ovation or applause in a dream can symbolize doing a job or task well, or deserving recognition. It can relate to an accomplishment in your external life for which you did or should be praised. But also consider the possibility that an ovation can be given for doing the right thing, being a good parent or spouse, or it can be recognition from deep inside that you are making good decisions and generally conducting yourself well.

An audience applauding you can be a way of saying you're living your life in a way that makes you proud or gains you recognition. It can be a way of praising yourself for your effort.

The good things that people do in everyday life can be largely overlooked, but the unconscious mind notices everything and has ways of rewarding you for being a good person or trying your best at whatever you do. If you dream about receiving an ovation, ask yourself how you deserve it, or whether someone in your life—spouse, child, coworker, friend—deserves it.

Applause can connect with something that deeply moves you. People applaud when something moves them, or is of exceptional skill or quality.

See also: *Actor, Arena, Famous, Music, Spotlight, Stage, Television*

Oven—To bake something in a dream can symbolize preparation for something new in your life, particularly something creative. You're "cooking up" a creative project, plan, or idea.

Baking involves combining ingredients, then applying heat to create something new. That idea applies to processes that occur both in your life and inside yourself. Ingredients combine, such as experiences, feelings, personality traits, personal qualities, desires, values, observations, principles, and knowledge. Then the pressures of life, or of your ambition or desire, create a sort of internal heat that sparks change.

Baking is a way of saying the heat is on! See: *Heat*.

Baking can symbolize the creation of a child, a "bun in the oven." Pregnant women are known to dream about baking because pregnancy involves combining ingredients (genetic material; the mother's bodily resources) and adding heat for a length of time. Moreover, the womb is roughly shaped like an oven, with the birth canal as the door.

Baking can symbolize a healing or growing process. Areas of the body can heat up when they are healing.

Another possibility to consider is that baking something can relate to the everyday activities of life. "Our daily bread," meaning "that which sustains and nourishes us." It can relate to physical or spiritual nourishment, or the nourishment of the body, mind, heart, and spirit.

Baking can mean "getting baked"; i.e., getting high. For example, after getting baked smoking cannabis all day, a young man dreams about crawling through an oven and coming out the other side. People "get baked" in the sun. It means "overdone."

Any of these uses of the symbolism can be created by the dream image of a baker or bakery.

See also: *Chef, Fire, Heat, Hell, Kitchen, Pregnant, Sun, Uterus*

Overdose—In simplest terms, an overdose means "too much," and while that's commonly associated with drugs, dreams can apply the symbolism broadly. For example, eating too much in one meal is an overdose. Binge-watching is an overdose. Spending too much time with someone is an overdose. It's too much of a good thing.

Overdose is associated with situations that get out of hand. It's something you can't stop yourself from doing, taking things too far.

It can symbolize danger.

It can reflect fear for yourself or someone in your life related to drug use. While dreams are often oblique with their messages, sometimes they are direct—especially when it comes to reflecting fears or drawing attention to something that is overlooked.

See also: *Alcohol, Drugs, Inject*

Overweight—See: *Fat*

Owl—The "wise owl" is a popular image, and in dreams it can represent you or an aspect of yourself connected with knowledge and learning.

The owl's presence can be a way of saying, "This dream is related to learning something or gaining knowledge." Or you are trying to think deeply about a situation. You're pondering, pensive.

It can symbolize the feeling of being watched from the shadows.

However, the symbolism can go much deeper. Unlike most birds, owls are nocturnal. That their night vision is unmatched creates a strong association with intuition and hunch. They connect with the parts of yourself that are in the dark of the unconscious mind. They act as intermediaries to help you tap into your instinctive wisdom, especially in regard to protecting and rearing children and trusting your intuition.

They help you see what is hidden—especially what's hidden about yourself.

In this sense, owls are like crows. They help bring your hidden potential to the awareness of the conscious mind. They initiate you into the mysteries of life and death. See: *Crow*.

The owl can symbolize something within you that helps you find your way when you're not sure where you're going, that is stealthy and aware, that can navigate dark environments without much information or guidance.

A white owl is known to be a good omen in dreams. It can mean that the time is right to move ahead with something you've been planning or thinking about. You have the internal resources you need.

See also: *All-Seeing Eye, Animals, Birds, Crow, Dark, Night*

Pain—If you experience pain in a dream, it can stem from feeling pain as you sleep. Dreams translate any input into symbolism, including input from physical stimuli. For example, you dream about getting hit in the head with a rock and wake up with a migraine, or dream about getting stabbed in the back and wake up with a stabbing pain in your back. Dreams translate physical stimuli into imagery.

Another possibility is your dream uses pain as a physical representation of a personal situation. You really are hurt emotionally or personally and the hurt manifests in your body. The body has nerve bundles in the heart and stomach, and related feelings are processed and felt there, such as love in the heart and fear in the gut.

What the mind believes to be real becomes real, to an extent, and your body can make real something from your dream to the point of pain and injury. Author Robert Moss shared a dream he had about seeing through the eyes of someone else as the person was shot in the chest. He woke up with welts on his chest where the bullets struck.

Pain and its causes are referenced in language, such as when a comment cuts like a knife, your pride is wounded, or you feel someone's pain. In dreams, the wording translates into imagery and you actually feel a lesser version of, for example,

the pain of a snake bite or acid thrown in your face. If the imagery doesn't cause some sort of corresponding pain, you can bet there's a reason. For example, the snake bite in your dream doesn't hurt because you subconsciously know that the snake symbolizes your lover and the bite is a "love bite."

People are amazed that they can dream about hurting a body part and wake up with a pain in that part of the body. Dreams are fully realistic simulated environments. In most cases, while dreaming you actually believe it is really happening, and your body can respond, even to the point of injury.

See also: *Abscess, Beat, Body, Fight, Wound*

Panic—If you are experiencing panic or anxiety in your waking life, you can bet you will dream about it. Dreams zero in on these feelings to try to help you with them. It might seem cruel for your dreams to induce panic or anxiety after you have been feeling it all day, but it's actually helping you to relieve the pressure, put some distance between you and it, and understand the source. Dreams can even suggest treatments and solutions.

A common source of panic in dreams is lack of preparation. You know something important is coming up, such as a test, meeting, or interview, and you aren't ready. Depending on the situation, your response in a dream can range from mild anxiety to full panic. *Oh, crap, the interview is tomorrow and I'm not ready!* See: *Test*.

Whatever causes panic in a dream is likely to connect with you and your life but be disguised as symbolism. You can tell what underlies a symbol in a dream by how you react to it. You subconsciously know what it means and react according to that.

Discrepancies will really stand out, too. For example, you react with panic because a drink spills, and it symbolizes fear of getting pregnant. The glass spilling symbolizes an accident with a contraceptive, and that's the sort of situation that can cause panic, but you normally wouldn't expect such a reaction.

Dreams exaggerate, so if you experience panic in a dream, the situation it reflects from your waking life might not be as bad as portrayed. For example, you dream about people panicking, jumping off buildings and stabbing themselves with big knives. However, in the dream you are relatively calm. Thinking back on what occurred the day before the dream, you remember that your co-workers were panicked about a situation that you viewed as just another day at the office. The actions of the people in the dream are an exaggeration of how your co-workers behaved and the contrast with how you perceived the situation.

Along these lines, a feeling of unease or trepidation can trigger panic and anxiety in your dreams. While dreaming, your defenses are down and filters off. The full impact is felt. Add in dreams' tendency to exaggerate, and something that is felt mildly while awake can return as panic in your dreams. It might mean you aren't taking something seriously enough, or you've allowed something important to slip your attention. You might have good reason to panic!

For example, your doctor says you are on the verge of becoming diabetic. You laugh it off at the time, but on a deeper level the news hits you hard. Seeing the situation as full-blown panic in a dream might express how you really feel.

Consider also that a source of panic is what *could* happen instead of what *did* happen. You fear

the worst, or see a tendency in yourself that is cause for alarm. Or your Mr. Hyde is showing. For example, you are normally cool-headed but lose your temper one day, and are reminded of your father's ferocious temper. You fear that ugliness coming out in yourself again.

Sometimes not panicking during a dream is a good sign, especially if that's how you would normally react. Dreams create scenarios to help you learn and grow, simulations that test you and drive home lessons. Think of it as pressure under fire. If you can handle panicky situations in your dreams, you are more likely to handle them in your waking life.

For more thoughts on this subject and how to use your dream imagery to lessen panic and anxiety, see: *Anxiety*.

See also: *Anxiety, Chicken, Emotions, Fear, Test*

Panther—See: *Leopard*

Panties—See: *Underwear*

Pants—See: *Clothing*

Paralysis—Paralysis in a dream can be a physical representation of a situation where you can't act or make a move. You are paralyzed by doubt or fear, for example.

Dream paralysis can be an exaggerated way of saying you have difficulty moving, such as when pregnant, obese, or infirm.

Paralysis can symbolize lack of power or control, or paralyzing fear or doubt.

Paralyzed means you can't move a part or parts of your body, and movement in dreams is associated with movement in life, getting to where you want to be, reaching your goals and ambitions. Being paralyzed can symbolize being unable to move forward in life. It can be because of a situation that's holding you back, or something about yourself holding you back. Depression, panic, stress, and character flaws are common causes. So are lack of options, heavy restrictions, or a controlling parent.

For some people, paralysis is their worst fear, so for them it can symbolize a worst-case scenario.

Keep in mind that the dream can express a fear that the worst case *could* come true, not that it has or will.

A final possibility is that paralysis in a dream can represent a physical condition called sleep paralysis, or REM atonia. See: *Sleep Paralysis*.

See also: *Coma, Crash, Handicap, Sleep Paralysis, Wheelchair*

Paramedic—Paramedics can symbolize help during a crisis in your life, or coming to the rescue. Like lifeguards, paramedics save people, and dreams can associate that idea with saving someone or something: coming to the rescue of a friend, saving a relationship. It's a physical representation of a personal situation.

The same symbolism is possible in the image of an ambulance. Most details in dreams are symbolic and tie together to tell the story, but some details are used because they go together. For example, a paramedic goes with an ambulance, and they combine to create symbolism related to coming to the rescue. See: *Rescue*.

Paramedics are associated with emergencies.

They're also associated with hospitals. See: *Hospital*.

Paramedics give special attention, especially related to health, and dreams can use the idea of health to apply to a variety of scenarios: physical health, mental health, emotional health, financial health. For example, you dream about paramedics being called because a man is found lifeless in a bank vault. It occurs after you check on your 401k and are shocked to find out it has plummeted in value.

See also: *Doctor, Hospital, Lifeguard, Rescue*

Parasite—A parasite can represent something going on inside your body—you might actually have contracted a parasite. Or it can be an analogy for an illness caused by a virus or bacteria, such as a flu bug. Dreams give warnings about threats to health, so always consider the obvious. If you dream about a parasite, pay extra close attention to your health and how your body feels.

Expand on the idea of parasite and it can mean "eaten at" in nonphysical ways, such as by stress or worry. In simplest terms, it means something is harming you from the inside, and it might be something that's too small to notice consciously. See: *Cancer*.

The most common use of parasite symbolism is in connection with parasite meaning "someone who relies on or exploits others and gives nothing in return." It's an analogy that can sum up your opinion of someone or even a situation.

For example, a woman dreams that her young child contracts a parasite and she immediately suspects the babysitter. It reflects her suspicion that the babysitter's first priority is to chat all day on her phone and run personal errands, all but ignoring the child. The babysitter is like a parasite living off the goodness of the dreamer's child.

See also: *Bug, Cancer, Disease, Infect, Infest, Insects, Invasion, Vulture*

Parents—The dynamics of your relationship with your parents and what they mean to you open up many possibilities for symbolism. People commonly assume that their parents in their dreams represent their actual parents, when they're actually characters in a story based on the dreamer's associations and common associations with parents.

The first clue is in the fact that they appear together in a dream, instead of separately. It's a clue that the symbolism might be tied to what parents represent: authority, protection, restriction, expectations, guidance. Parents together can symbolize anything they're in agreement or "of the same mind" about.

Of course, the symbolism depends on your experience and perceptions. If your parents are not protective or restrictive, for example, then they're unlikely to symbolize protection or restriction—unless they are used to symbolize lack of it, or need for it.

A lot depends on whether your parents are actively part of your life and whether they've been on your mind. If yes, you have to consider that their presence in your dream reflects your recent activity or thoughts. The dream is about a recent event in your life and your parents' involvement.

Otherwise, it's safe to assume that your parents are in the dream because of what they represent to you.

Things get interesting when your parents act out of character. Discrepancies with reality scream, "This is symbolism!" They're characters following a script in a story. For example, you dream that your hands-off parents tell you that you absolutely cannot marry your boyfriend. It's something they'd never actually do, so you look at it as symbolism. Perhaps you're trying to tell yourself something and the dream uses your parents to deliver the message because you're more likely to listen.

Your parents are your primary example of parenthood, probably. If you're a parent, you will draw on your examples to guide you in what to do and what not to do. In which case, your dreams can use parent-characters to tell a story about your own experience as a parent. Again, though, it depends on your experience and perceptions. Maybe your parents are a better example of how *not* to be a parent.

Stretch the idea further and your parents can be used in your dreams to tell stories about growing into adulthood and beyond. They are your example, and they shape your ideas about the adult you want to be, even long after you're an adult yourself.

Parents dictate behavior for their children. They set rules and expectations. As a child, how did you respond? Did you behave as expected? Did you follow the rules, or defy them? Did you try your hardest to meet expectations, or not give a care? Did you act like an angel when they were watching, and let the little devil in you come out when their backs were turned?

These patterns that start in childhood can carry into adulthood. For example, if you find yourself defying a supervisor or undermining authority figures, does it remind you of your relationship with your parents? Do you work hard while being watched, and slack off when you think no one is watching?

How do your parents view you at this point in your life—are they, or would they be, proud? Are

you living your life in a way that reflects them, the example they set, and what they taught you? Did something come up the day before the dream that reminded you of them? Are you being treated like a child?

These are the questions that can help you understand their role in a dream-story.

Grandparents in your dreams can be surrogate-characters for your parents. When grandparents are used as surrogate-characters, the dream could be related to your parents as role models. Grandparents act as role models for your parents, so it is an easy association for dreams to make.

Dreaming about parent-characters that are not your parents is a clue that the dream could be about the general symbolism of parents and parenting. Also consider the possibility that the unfamiliar parent-characters can symbolize people in your life who are in some way like parents to you.

See also: *Archetypes, Boss, Child, Childhood Home, Deceased Loved Ones, Family, Family Home, Father, Grandfather, Grandmother, Guide, Mother, Orphan*

Paris—A city that's specifically referred to in a dream can have symbolism based on your associations. Paris has a special place in the minds of people around the world as a mythic city of romantic love and deep history. It's known as a world center for intellectual thought and great literature.

Along this line, an author has recurring dreams about trying to fly to Paris but something always gets in the way. He arrives late for his flight. He doesn't have money to buy a ticket. He can't find the terminal. The theme of wanting to go to Paris connects with his desire to write and publish books that demonstrate his intellect and that gain him recognition. For him, arriving in Paris means he's arrived where he wants to be in his career.

Paris can symbolize being disappointed by the difference between expectation and reality. People with romantic notions about Paris are known to be sorely disappointed by the reality of it.

For example, a young man dreams he's in Paris and expects the food to be great and the women to be exotic and beautiful. Instead, the food is crappy, the women indifferent and not particularly attractive, and everything costs a fortune. It symbolizes a situation in which he finally persuades this really hot girl he knows to go out with him. He takes her to dinner and it's the most excruciating two hours of his life. The girl shows little interest in him, mumbles most of her responses, and when he gets the bill for the meal, it's shockingly expensive.

See also: *Famous, Hollywood, New York City*

Party—To dream about a party or festival can indicate you are in a happy mood or feeling good, energetic, and ready to have fun. You have something to celebrate. You feel festive. It can relate to anything to do with sociability and dealing with people.

Parties and festivals can be chaotic and unorganized, which can symbolize a chaotic or unorganized situation in your life. It can be an external situation, such as your merry but crazy home life with your young children, or it can show the chaos in your mind or heart.

The possibilities for symbolism get deeper when you consider that a party in a dream can be used to show the opposite of what the typical party scene implies. Maybe you don't want to socialize, aren't in a happy mood, or lack the energy to deal with a group of people. In which case a dream will show you avoiding a party, not enjoying yourself at one, or arriving in a hobbled state, such as in a wheelchair.

The intermingling of a party can depict the intermingling between parts of yourself. Your psyche has many aspects, all of which can be portrayed as dream-characters. Therefore, the intermingling of different types of people at a party is a great analogy for times when your internal barriers come down and various parts of you can get together. This symbolism is especially likely if the party in your dreams shows widely different types of characters: the punk rocker, the intellectual, the athlete, the misfit. Stereotypical characters in dreams are a sign that parts of the psyche are taking form. See: *Archetypes, Group.*

Parties are where people are more likely to say what they're really thinking or give their true opinion, and where personal items get mixed up. For example, coats and purses are known for getting lost or stolen at parties. In dreams, these associations can be used to tell a story about finding out what people really think of you, or losing something valuable or important to you. For example, losing a purse at a party can symbolize losing something about your identity when in groups of people. See: *Lost Item.*

Dreaming about a carnival suggests the need for variety. Perhaps your life has become routine. The symbolism of parties, festivals, and carnivals can all connect around the idea of fun, activity, and variety.

The symbolism can connect with something inside you that needs expression, perhaps by your being looser, less inhibited. Carnivals and parties are loose environments.

A carnival or party setting can connect with a recent event, such as attending a rock concert.

The theme of the party can identify the symbolism of it. For example, a going-away party can symbolize that a time of life is over. A baby shower can symbolize trying to have a baby.

See also: *Alcohol, Amusement Park, Archetypes, Baby, Boy, Candle, Clown, Drugs, Drunkenness, Fiancé, Fireworks, Girl, Group, Lost Item, Music, Roller Coaster, Zoo*

Passenger—In simplest terms, a passenger in a dream is along for the ride. Someone else leads or makes the decisions. When you're the passenger, it means you're not in control—in your life or a specific area of it.

For example, parents can lead the lives of their children, even into adulthood. They are "behind the wheel." A supervisor leads your work life. A spouse or significant other is in charge of the relationship. A friend is the one who decides what you do together.

When you are in the driver's seat and someone else is the passenger, it means you make the decisions and determine the direction. For example, as a parent, you lead the lives of your children, and your dreams show you in the driver's seat. Driving together in a car is a heck of an analogy for going places together in life. But if you dream that your child is in the driver's seat and you're the passenger, it might be saying that your child makes the decisions.

A passenger can symbolize a side of yourself that prefers to follow rather than lead. It can symbolize a feeling that you don't have the power to get to where you want to be in your life, you're unable to take charge.

Planes are closely associated in dreams with getting to the big goals in life. Being a passenger in a plane can mean you've created a vehicle to get you there, to be successful and reach the destinations in life where you want to be. For example, creating a business or career that "takes off." A car can be used to create similar symbolism, except that generally the pace is slower and the goals more related to everyday life.

See the entry for *Mother* for some good examples of dreams that illustrate the symbolism of being a passenger.

See also: *Airplane, Boat, Car, Mother, Train*

Pastor—As spiritual leaders, pastors and related characters such as priests, rabbis, imams, and ministers can be used in dreams in connection with spirituality, religion, faith, and belief. But don't stop there, because pastors are also associated with clean living and helping the less fortunate, for example, and dreams have many ways of telling stories using your personal associations and common ones.

For example, pastors are people to turn to when advice is needed, someone to talk to who can help see the good in people and ourselves. In that role, a pastor-character is a mask that a dream puts on an aspect of yourself, that delivers answers or gives advice.

Even if you dream about a pastor you know, it's still likely to connect with an internal issue—something about your thoughts, feelings and perceptions. The pastor is a mask for what that person means to you.

A dream can help you to digest an interaction with that person or lesson he or she taught you,

such as in a sermon. Anything new to integrate into yourself is likely to be dreamed about with some reference given to the source, because a primary function of dreams is to help integrate things into your personality. So the pastor represents something about the person's influence on you.

A bad pastor in a dream can symbolize something about yourself that resists a call to clean living or self-sacrifice, is hypocritical, or is basically the opposite of what you expect from a good pastor. It's not to say that you are like a bad pastor—although it's possible—just that the idea fits the dream-story.

A pastor can symbolize your ability to delve into spiritual life and see into the spiritual world, your ability to minister to others and bring into the world the goodness of spiritual teachings. You are the medium through which the message is delivered, in word and example.

Related subjects can be referred to obliquely, such as in a dream a man has about being told that the pope is coming to his friend Christian's house and he's responsible for making preparations, terrifying the man. The dream is about the man's fear of dying without being ready to go. The pope and the friend Christian are both references to Christianity, and preparing for the pope symbolizes being in the right place before the man dies. He's an atheist who, deep inside, fears the consequences of being wrong about the existence of God.

See also: *Afterlife, Altar, Church, God, Heaven, Hell, Jesus, Temple*

Pedophile—See: *Molest*

Pee—See: *Toilet*

Penis—The penis has many phallic symbols to represent it: towers, flagpoles, cigars, snakes. And if you go down that road, you'll start seeing phallic symbols everywhere. But more often, a penis is a penis, no phallic symbol needed. Rather than use a symbol for the penis, dreams represent it directly.

However, a penis in dreams is usually symbolism for associations with it—mainly traditional masculinity and related traits. The penis isn't just the male organ, it's a whole set of ideas summarized in one image.

The penis is the masculine—not just the masculine personality traits, such as strength, domination, assertiveness, firmness, and independence, but also the masculine principle, the yang. The penis gives the energy of life, and the vagina receives it, same as the sun gives energy and the earth receives it and turns it into an abundance of life. Where you have one, you have the other, working together to create life and everything about it. See: *Vagina.*

It's easy to lose the point of the imagery when you view it solely in sexual terms. What it really shows is the process of creation that brings the universe into being, according to some belief systems. Opposites unite in a state of bliss and create our world. Your body and mind are a microcosm of the universe, and sexual imagery can be used to show the creation process going on inside you. It can show your internal relationship with it and ability to master it.

A penis is obviously symbolism when a female dreams she has one, or a female dream-character has one. At its most basic, it means she's assuming a masculine role or masculine personality traits. She plays the role of father to her children, siblings, friend, or spouse. She's independent, strong, logical, dominant. She starts a business, manages a project, establishes a home, protects the nest.

For example, a woman dreams that an old friend she hasn't seen in a long time—a woman with whom she used to train for triathlons—talks her into having sex. They get naked, and her friend has a penis.

When a dream features someone you haven't seen in a long time as a character, it's a good bet that the person is symbolism for something about yourself, because you have no reason to dream directly about the person or a recent event with him or her. And you know it's symbolism when the character's depiction obviously differs from reality, such as when a woman has a penis.

In this case, the old friend represents someone who doesn't care what people think of her, a trait associated with men. You could say that she lets it all hang out, and the dreamer is the same way, opinionated and outspoken. But unlike her friend, she fears coming off as too masculine. Agreeing to have sex with the friend is agreement within herself that the best thing to do is adopt the friend's "I don't care what anyone thinks" attitude. Intercourse in dreams can mean, simply, "take in."

A popular and misguided interpretation of dreaming about being intimate with a woman with a penis is that it shows latent homosexuality, a secret wish, or penis envy. Usually, it couldn't be further from the truth. Take the example of a young man who dreams that his girlfriend has a penis and he sucks it. The dream occurs after she accuses him of being selfish in bed and just a terrible person, and he grovels all night begging for forgiveness. Her penis symbolizes her dominance, and sucking it symbolizes the dreamer's submissiveness and attempts to mollify her.

Biting and sucking a penis has many associations. See: *Fellatio.*

A girlfriend with a penis can symbolize sexual dominance or assertiveness, such as in the dream a woman has about having a penis and being in bed with her boyfriend, who tries to comfort her by playing with it. It's simply a way of depicting her assertiveness in the bedroom and his getting used to it.

A man depicted in a dream with a tiny or detachable penis, presuming it differs from reality, can symbolize having a tiny sex drive, or exhibiting little or no traditional masculinity.

On the other hand, a huge penis can symbolize an oversized male ego, or machismo, such as in the dream a woman has about seeing her brother get out of the shower with an elephant trunk dangling between his legs. Her brother, who has done time in prison, constantly makes a point of proving he's an alpha male, and her dream symbolizes it as a huge penis.

Seeing someone with his penis out also has possibilities for symbolism related to private life, or being embarrassed.

An erection generally symbolizes readiness and virility. For example, in the dream a young man has about using his raging erection to plow a field, his phallus means he's ready to have sex, to plow a field. His sex drive is revved up. Remember, though, that dreams create symbolism by making comparisons, and an erection can symbolize anything related to readiness or excitement, such as being excited about an upcoming trip—really excited—or feeling charged up with creative energy.

A flaccid penis can mean something isn't ready; there's no excitement or virility. It can characterize a person or situation as dull or boring. It can mean that a person can't muster the courage, moxie, or energy to meet a challenge.

In this sense, you could think of the strength of an erection as a sort of measuring stick. The idea begins with the penis or erection as a measure of a how big a man you are, or how much masculinity you can handle as a woman, and branches out to include potentially a variety of ideas about taking the measure of a person and gauging interest, excitement, desire, and so on.

How much do you think your man wants you? Well, in dreams, you could use his erection to gauge. Or how much does he love the kids you have together? Don't jump to conclusions, though. Always look at a symbol in the context of the dream-story and let your feelings guide you to the meaning. An erection might simply point to where you think someone's priorities are, and the strength of an erection is a measure of the strength of a person's sex drive or emphasis on sexuality.

Being aware of someone's erection beneath his clothes can mean that you know something about him that others don't. If you reach your hands inside the person's clothes to touch the penis, it can mean that you have access to his private life (the penis is also known as a private part). It can mean you know him better than most other people.

In the dreams of women who fear that their mate is sleeping with someone else, seeing him in bed with another woman, especially if he's erect, is a way of creating a scenario that reflects their fears.

Women who are coming to terms with male energy—especially sexual energy—can dream about it as a snake, and a woman's reaction to the snake reflects her feelings and attitudes. For example, a woman who is not receptive to male sexual advances can dream about letting a snake out of her home, or locking the doors and windows to keep it out. Now contrast that reaction with her hunting the snake down with an ax or beating it to death with a hammer. The different reactions reveal how she feels.

The penis can be used in dreams to tell a story about obsession, immaturity, and absurd attitudes toward sex. The symbolism often shows in dreams about inappropriate uses of the penis, such as to have intercourse with a relative or an animal. Or the penis is disfigured or disproportionate, showing the disproportionate hold it has on the person's psyche and the damage done by obsession. Dreams compensate, meaning they go just as far in the opposite direction to show what's out of balance in the psyche. See: *Compensation*.

Sometimes, dreams need to create personal distance to explore a subject without interference from the ego, so they represent the subject with symbols and allow the dreamer to react from the gut. In which case, phallic symbols come in handy. See: *Phallic Symbol*.

To explore this subject further, use the entries listed below.

See also: *Bite, Compensation, Fellatio, Genitals, Incest, Man, Masturbate, Men, Old Friend, Phallic Symbol, Sex, Snake, Sun, Testicles*

Period—See: *Menstruation*

Persona—Persona is defined in Jungian psychology as the aspects of yourself that show publicly, the image you project, your "public persona." In simplest terms, it's your identity, strongly connected with your ego. Actors are said to adopt a persona when they play a role—they become the characters they play. So for our purposes, think of persona as being like a mask. It might differ from who you truly are, or it might not.

Going deeper, you can think of persona as the human face on your eternal spirit. Becoming a person—everything that you are—is like creating an identity so you can play a role in this story we call life, and eventually (after death, or upon attaining enlightenment) that identity is assimilated into the larger structure of what's called the "higher self."

See also: *Clothing, Disguise, Dressed, Ego, Mask, Mirror, Psyche, Undress*

Pet—In this entry we will discuss "pet" in the senses of "family pet" and "petting."

Pets are associated with friendship and companionship, and qualities such as loyalty and trust. But the possibilities expand far and wide when you consider the characteristics and traits of your pet, what the animal means to you, and ways it can be used to tell a story.

Your pets can be used 10,000 ways to create symbolism, so covering all of them isn't possible. However, the interpretation process begins the same way as with any dream-character. What are your associations with the pet? What do you observe about its personality and character? Does the dream show any obvious discrepancies with reality, such as an animal presented as your pet when in reality you don't recognize it? How does the character fit the story?

For example, a woman dreams that she's told by her mother to poison her pet dog. It dramatizes a situation in which her mom is actually pressuring her to marry her best friend. It's going to poison the relationship with her friend, she fears. Her pet symbolizes her friend.

You can dream about your pets in relation to their care and well-being. In this way, it's a lot like a parent dreaming about his or her children.

A pet can symbolize something you tend, something close to you, something you invest yourself into, something important that's like a pet to you, such as a responsibility, long-term project, or endeavor. That's a good possibility for symbolism when the pet in the dream isn't one you own. Parents with young children, in particular, are known to dream about caring for young pets.

A pet can symbolize the feeling of being loved, wanted, and appreciated unconditionally. Pets don't judge or play head games—unless, of course, it's to get a treat! A pet can symbolize something

you look forward to, such as when the best part of your day is taking your dog for a walk after work.

It can symbolize something that you train, that obeys, that loves you unconditionally, that can be expensive.

To be attacked hard by a pet can symbolize a dispute with a friend or damage to the relationship. It can symbolize betrayal or misplaced trust, or vulnerability to people close to you. For example, criticism from a friend can bite a lot harder than criticism from someone outside your inner circle. Because of the closeness you can have with pets, they're great as symbols for close relationships such as those with friends. Dogs, in particular, are "man's best friend."

Pets can symbolize something you invest your energy into.

See the entries for *Cat* and *Dog* to get more ideas.

It's common to dream about pets after they die, a normal part of grieving and healing. Our pets can be as close to us as family, and the death of a pet can be a hard loss. Two themes predominate in this sort of dream. One, you get a chance to reunite and enjoy time with your pet, like the good old days. It shows that the healing process is progressing as it should, and the memory of your beloved pet is alive inside you. Or two, something's seriously wrong, like in a scene in the movie *Pet Sematary*. It shows that something is stuck in the healing process. You aren't handling the grief, or you feel guilty because you think you didn't do enough to save your pet. See: *Deceased Loved One*.

Petting a cat has associations with sexuality because cats are "felines," which dreams can use to mean "female." Further, they're known as "pussies." Cats are soft and generally responsive to being petted. It can symbolize giving pleasure. On the other hand, petting a cat is associated with indulging thoughts of revenge (as evidenced in such movies as *The Godfather* and even *Austin Powers: International Man of Mystery*).

Petting is another word for "foreplay," and dreams can depict it as petting an animal—especially when the animal responds by getting aroused, or the dream setting is sexually suggestive, such as a bedroom.

Other associations with petting involve calming someone down, making a personal connection, and showing care and concern. Petting a wolf, for example, can symbolize coming to terms with someone's wild side, including your own, especially in regard to sexuality. Petting a wild animal like a wolf or gorilla can symbolize playing nice with someone who is potentially dangerous. Petting a whale can symbolize coming to terms with something overwhelming or too big to handle.

To explore this subject further, begin with the entry for *Animals* and branch out to look up the specific type of pet animal in your dream.

See also: *Adopt, Animals, Cat, Deceased Loved One, Dog*

Phallic Symbol—When you start looking for phallic symbols, you can see them everywhere. Don't be fooled. Most phallic-shaped objects in dreams have nothing to do with the erect penis.

However, phallic symbols are useful when a dream needs to create distance from a subject that involves masculinity or sexuality, or when a phallic symbol can sum up an idea in one image. In this sense, it's the most efficient means of communicating an idea or set of ideas.

For example, holding on for dear life to a missile as it launches can symbolize a powerful orgasm or learning how to get a grip on male sexual energy. A boy in puberty could dream about this theme when he's getting a handle on the surge of testosterone in his body. But the same imagery could symbolize dealing with powerful emotions, or the desire to quickly leave a situation, so never jump to conclusions just because a symbol has a phallic shape.

As noted in the entry for *Penis*, dreams don't use phallic symbols unless they need to—usually the penis is shown directly. However, it can be instructive and amusing to consider the possibilities for phallic imagery. Bear in mind, the symbolism shows in the actions and other details involving a

symbol, and the meaning is often found in your reactions and feelings.

Some common phallic symbols are listed below, shown in the context of actions that are sexually suggestive. And by the way, the female equivalent of a phallus is the yoni, and it is often represented as a receptacle, hollowed-out place, or sacred passageway such as the entrance to a temple or cave.

Eating a hot dog, banana, or sausage.

Swinging a bat or hammer.

Milking a teat.

Handling a snake or eel.

Smoking a cigar.

Climbing a skyscraper.

Licking a popsicle.

Launching a rocket or torpedo.

Popping a cork, shooting a gun, or an erupting volcano (male orgasm).

Beating a child or snake or climbing a tree (male masturbation).

What can get lost in a discussion about phallic symbols is why dreams would use them. Back in Freud's day, in Vienna, sexuality was highly repressed and rarely if ever referred to directly. These days, we're saturated with sexual imagery and references, and every aspect of sexuality is out in the open, so phallic symbols aren't needed as much. Dreams use the most effective means to tell a story, and if a phallic symbol tells the story better than a straightforward reference to a penis or erection, or you need an oblique reference over a direct one, then that's what you get.

See also: *Penis, Rocket, Snake*

Phone—Phones serve many functions and have many uses, and in dreams they have a wide variety of possibilities for symbolism and meaning.

The first function to consider is that phones are used to communicate. Being on the phone with someone can symbolize expression of your feelings and thoughts. Dreaming about wanting to phone someone can mean you want to say or express something to that person. The idea can be used to express the desire to know what that person feels and thinks about you or some situation. See: *Talk*.

The symbolism often arises in connection with romantic relationships and possibilities for them. For example, wanting to phone a romantic interest in a dream occurs after the dreamer has dropped hints about being interested in dating a certain person but has not received a reply. The dream is simply a reflection of the dreamer's thoughts about calling the person and being more direct.

Wanting to phone an ex in a dream occurs as the dreamer has thoughts about getting back together. A call to an ex that goes to voice mail symbolizes the mixed signals the ex is giving about getting back together. See: *Ex*.

A phone dropping the call or malfunctioning is a classic sign of symbolism for communication problems. In this sense, connection means personal connection, and if the phone doesn't work the way it's supposed to, it can mean that a personal connection is lost or fails to establish. It can express the feeling that something is wrong with the relationship or the person.

A bad signal can symbolize that you're not getting your point across, or feel that someone isn't really listening. Someone ignoring you on the phone, either by avoiding the call or not responding during the conversation, can express the feeling that the person is ignoring you or not meeting your needs.

Modern phones have uses that go beyond basic communication. For one, they can contain a lot of personal information. Someone going through your phone can symbolize privacy invasion or fear of exposure. For example, people cheating in a relationship are sometimes exposed because their mates find incriminating evidence on their phones.

Losing your phone can symbolize the loss of something important to you. Branch out to consider any type of loss of something important: of a relationship, of opportunity, of personal identity, of face. Such as in a dream about losing a phone after

someone has lost a job. The phone is used to mean the job.

Modern phones are used for getting information through the Internet, keeping track of appointments, and playing games, and dreams can start there and potentially branch out in many directions. For more ideas along this line, see: *Computer*.

Phones can be a huge distraction, and can symbolize being ignored or inattentive. A person using a phone is distracted, and this idea is used in dreams to symbolize situations and feelings related to not getting the attention you want. Dreams can project aspects of yourself onto dream-characters, so keep in mind that what you see in a dream-character may actually be what you see in yourself.

For example, a mother dreams about being at a park with her child as other mothers and children play. She notices that one of the children is walking quickly toward a busy street, and its mother doesn't notice because her attention is consumed by her phone. The dreamer yells at the mother to get her child, and the mother, when she notices what's happening, jumps up and rescues her child. She apologizes, saying that she hates her phone sometimes because she constantly feels the need to engage with it.

It would be easy to assume that the dream-character represents someone the dreamer knows or a specific situation she observed, but the dream is actually pointing out the mother's own distractions with her phone. She's careful about using it while driving and is conscious of staying off it during family time. However, it's still a distraction, and the statement at the end of the dream about needing to be engaged with it is actually how the mother feels. Maintaining her social and business relationships requires her to be on the phone more than she wants to be.

A phone call can symbolize the process of communication between areas of the mind and between the mind and body while dreaming. Dreaming is well known in neurology for facilitating communication between areas of the brain. See: *Letter*.

See also: *Computer, Ears, Email, Hear, Lost Item*

Pie—See: *Circle*

Pig—Begin with common associations with pigs, such as selfishness and overindulgence, hogging the spotlight, and eating like a pig. Pigs are associated with chauvinism, obstinacy, and crude behavior, and with the expression "men are pigs."

Rolling around with pigs is a metaphor for excess and a dirty reputation or dirty behavior.

Then again, spend enough time around pigs and you'll see that they have sweet qualities, too. As with all dream symbolism, the meaning depends on your personal associations and the context of the dream.

For example, a woman dreams about a cute pig given to her as a gift, and the actions of the dream involve her doing the same activities as in her daily life, except with the pig along for company, which she greatly enjoys. The pig symbolizes her husband, and to the woman it's a very positive symbol. Of course, her husband might take it the wrong way if he knew that her dream depicts him as a pig!

See also: *Animals*

Pilot—A pilot-character can symbolize the part of yourself that leads you to your destinations in life and navigates your way through life. See: *Captain*.

Characters that pilot a vehicle—plane, boat, car, starship—can symbolize leadership and decision-making. Piloting a vehicle can symbolize personal direction, vision, and organization. A dream will use a pilot in connection with a plane when it wants to add the dimensions of quick movement in your life and/or a big or important destination.

A woman dreams that she and her boyfriend take a flight together and the pilot angrily refuses to fly the plane. It occurs during a time when she's frustrated by her boyfriend's not shouldering his share of the load around the house. Her "inner pilot" refuses to accept the situation any longer.

A woman's dream about a pilot jumping out of a plane in flight occurs after a project leader at work suddenly quits. He abandons ship.

See also: *Airplane, Captain, Embark, Guide, Journey*

Pink—The color pink is closely associated with affection and romance. It's a gentle, calm, soothing color, and since it's a shade of red it can symbolize soothing anger or hard feelings.

It can show the need for the aforementioned ideas: need for affection, romance, calm, or soothing.

It can mean that emotions are moving toward red in the sense that you have a new feeling of energy, vitality, passion, or aggressiveness. The emotions aren't fully charged yet, but are headed in that direction.

See also: *Colors*

Pitch—See: *Baseball*

Plague—See: *Infest*

Plane—See: *Airplane*

Planet—See: *Earth, Jupiter, Mars, Mercury, Moon, Saturn, Space, Sun, UFO, Venus*

Poison—See: *Venom*

Police Officer—Police officers in dreams are among the most common "generic characters," meaning they are not usually depicted as someone you know and instead are like actors playing a role or extras in a movie. The high frequency of reports of police characters in dreams probably stems from the wide variety of ways they can be used as symbolism.

To begin, police officers are associated with authority, rules, settling disputes, justice and determining right from wrong. Now consider how those associations connect with areas of life, and how a police officer can be used as symbolism. For example, defying a cop can symbolize defying authority or rules—either specific authorities or rules, or just in general. Running from a cop can symbolize fear of getting caught doing something wrong.

Police officers make arrests. See: *Arrest*.

Police officers restrain people. Lack of restraint can mean you "shoot first and ask questions later," meaning you react to tense situations by getting angry or defensive. Or you pursue sexual encounters even when they cause trouble or put you at risk.

Police are associated with conformity. Police in dreams can symbolize societal or cultural forces that promote or enforce conformity and norms of conduct and behavior.

Police out to get you can mean that you are knowingly doing something that's wrong, illegal, or reckless. For example, people with drinking or drug habits will dream about police searching or detaining them because police enforce alcohol-and-drug laws. If you make a decision to clean up your life, you might dream about police officers at your home removing unruly guests or intoxicants, as a way of symbolizing removing something causing trouble in your life.

Dreaming about running from the police can mean you don't want to control or restrain a habit or behavior—or even acknowledge there is a problem. It can show that you deny your inner authority, authority structures, blame, responsibility, or your conscience.

Police are used in dreams when you feel that an injustice has been committed against you, or that you have been unfairly treated.

Police can be used to symbolize taking the blame for something—rightly or not. For example, you know that a snafu at work was your doing, but you haven't been exposed as the source. That night you dream about police searching your computer because you know it's where the evidence can be found.

Looking for evidence is another common theme in dreams involving police, and it arises most often when you're trying to figure why and how something happened, or are protecting yourself from blame. See: *Detective*.

Police in dreams can connect with issues of privacy or intrusion. You might dream about the police because you wish someone would butt out of your life or stop making trouble. Or someone is behaving in a way that makes you uncomfortable, crosses a line, or just isn't right. It might not be illegal behavior, but you still dream about the police because you wish an outside authority would intervene or correct the person.

The possibilities for symbolism go on and on. For example, a recurring dream about making a right turn and crashing into the back of a police car symbolizes that the dreamer feels punished for doing the right thing. She had turned in her brother to the police for committing a serious crime, and their father resented her for it.

A dream about a police officer coming into a scene as the dreamer is rolling a joint symbolizes his self-knowledge that his marijuana usage is putting him in danger of getting caught.

A dream featuring the dreamer in a role of a cop ignoring a crime symbolizes a situation in which the dreamer witnessed blatant cheating on a test and didn't say anything about it.

See also: *Addict, Arrest, Chase, Cheat (Exam), Court, Crime, Detective, Drugs, Guilt, Intruder, Jail, Judge, Lawyer*

Pond—See: *Water*

Pool—Like other bodies of water, a pool has associations with emotions. It can describe your emotional state or the emotional dynamics of a situation or relationship: calm, turbulent, hot, cold, deep, shallow.

A pool can be a metaphor for a group, such as a "job pool."

When associated with bathing or nudity, it can express sexual feelings or desires. Remember, however, that dreams can use scenes that evoke feelings of desire and sexuality as symbolism for something else related to pleasure, attraction, or desire. For example, a beautiful sex partner beckoning you to a pool can symbolize your love of swimming. See: *Naked*.

A lifeless body in a pool can be an image of something about yourself that has receded into the depths of your mind. Some part of yourself is "dying" in the figurative sense. Sometimes it is necessary—a part of your personality or character needs to change or mature. Sometimes it is caused by circumstances or pressure. See: *Body*.

Pools can be used to tell a story. For example, if you have a young child, you know what can happen if you turn your back for a moment. Stories abound of young children drowning in pools, often when adults are distracted. Even if you do not have a pool near your home, you are aware of the association between pools and danger to young children. Thus, a pool can be used in a dream to tell a story about fears related to your young children inadvertently getting hurt.

See also: *Body, Empty, Fish, Fishing, Lifeguard, Naked, Ocean, Rescue, Water*

Possessed—To be possessed in a dream can symbolize that something has taken over a person. When people don't act like themselves, they are said to be possessed. People can be "possessed" by a mood, idea, or feeling. In dreams, these relatively innocuous meanings can be exaggerated into possession by a spirit or demon.

Possession can symbolize seeing something hidden about a person, something lurking in the background. And the worse the possession, the worse the thing that person hides. For example, being possessed by a ghost spirit is one thing, and being possessed by a demon is another. See: *Demon, Spirit.*

Possession can be a way of saying that something is beyond your control. For example, a woman dreams that her stepfather, possessed, kills her mother and siblings. The dream follows an incident in which her mother is caught cheating with another man, and it most likely means the end of her marriage. The dreamer likes her stepfather and considers him to be a father figure. The dream is a way of expressing her thoughts and feelings about her mother "killing" the family in the sense of causing it to break up. The action is projected onto her stepfather because he's the one the dreamer will miss more.

See also: *Demon, Devil, Ghost, Infest, Nazi, Spirit*

Precognitive Dream—Precognition happens when an event is foreseen ahead of time or information is gained through a nonphysical source. It happens most often in dreams, though it can happen during wakefulness, too, in which case it is commonly referred to as premonition. It happens more often in dreams because the senses are shut down and the mind is more open to receiving the signals.

Most people have experienced some sort of premonition or precognitive dream. It's not as if you need to be psychic or anything. In fact, in yogic tradition, precognition is the first special mental ability to appear, and it's treated simply as the first rung of the ladder, no big deal. Precognition runs the gamut, from previewing seemingly mundane events to showing the most dramatic ones. Incidents depicted in most precognitive dreams come to pass within a few weeks of when they occur. However, some are known to come true far in the future.

And some don't come true at all. The critical fact to keep in mind is that most instances of precognition are like a weather forecast. Precognition is based on probability, and probability is not the same as prophecy. You can take action if needed to avoid an unwanted outcome. For example, you know before driving through an intersection that a truck is about to barrel through it. Or you can use what you learn from a precognitive dream to prepare ahead of time. For example, you know before you walk into a meeting that you're going to be waylaid.

Thousands of cases of precognitive dreams have been documented, and serious researchers such as Dean Radin and Stanley Krippner, applying rigorous scientific methods, have studied the subject and affirmed the high likelihood that it's a real phenomenon. Some cases thought to be precognition certainly are explainable as faulty memory or wishful thinking, but others have so many overlapping details and show such prescience that only precognition can adequately explain them.

Precognitive dreams have some distinguishing characteristics:

Extra vividness. The dreams are unusually lifelike and strongly impact you.

Directness. Symbolism can be used, but often a precognitive dream shows a future event pretty much exactly as it could happen.

Strong feelings. People report feeling strongly that their precognitive dream is not ordinary.

Repetition. If you don't get the message of a really important precognitive dream the first time, it's likely to recur.

A related phenomenon is *déjà vu*. Sometimes, precognitive dreams aren't remembered until they come to pass. Then the person is struck with a feeling of strong familiarity. Precognitive dreams aren't the only source of *déjà vu*—it can result from faulty memory and the proclivity of the mind to make connections between close memories. However, be aware of the possibility of precognition so that the next time you are struck by *déjà vu,* you can search your memory to check if it's connected with a dream.

To explore this further, see *youaredreaming.org*.

See also: *Deceased Loved One, Magic, Psychic Power*

Pregnant—Pregnancy in a dream can mean that something new about you is brewing, developing, growing. A new part of your personality or character is getting ready to emerge, but for the moment it's still gestating in the unconscious mind. See: *Childbirth, Unconscious Mind.*

It can mean you have a new project or idea, something you might refer to as "my baby." You might be pregnant with an idea or a feeling, or a situation is "pregnant with possibilities." Children are creations, so being pregnant in a dream can mean you are creating something. See: *Child.*

For example, a woman dreams that she's pregnant with five babies, symbolizing five projects she was given for a work-study program. She refers to them as "my babies." See: *Baby.*

Being pregnant can mean there's something you need to get out of you. If the baby feels heavy, it can symbolize the feeling of being weighed down.

Pregnancy can mean you are anticipating something important. Pregnancy is referred to as "anticipating," and the dream uses anticipating a baby to symbolize the importance of something, or high level of anticipation.

Men dream about being pregnant. See: *Childbirth.*

Dreaming about being pregnant with your ex's baby can mean something from the relationship is still inside you. If you dream your ex is pregnant with your baby, it carries the same idea. You left a part of yourself behind with that person. See: *Ex.*

A pregnancy dream can mean you are working through personal issues before getting pregnant. The dream is preparing you by showing what needs to be done ahead of time, such as getting your finances in order, preparing your body, finding the right mate, judging whether a relationship is ready to handle a pregnancy, and addressing fears.

In this sense, a dream can be like a simulation. It runs through scenarios to help you think about pregnancy, and it can ask, "What if?" For example, what if you really were pregnant? How would you react? See: *Baby.*

A positive pregnancy test can indicate positive prospects or feelings about pregnancy. The time is right, conditions are good. It can mean "stay positive," especially if you've been trying for a while to get pregnant. In rare cases, a positive pregnancy test in a dream can foretell you will imminently be pregnant.

On the other hand, a negative pregnancy test can indicate negative feelings or prospects. The time is wrong, conditions are bad. But remember that dreams associate between ideas, and a pregnancy test in a dream might have nothing to do with pregnancy. Instead, it can be used to indicate positive or negative feelings or prospects.

Dreams are very creative with the ways they use associations to create symbolism. For example, a teenaged female dreams that she's pregnant and immediately worries about how she'll tell her family. She feels that she's done something terribly wrong, but doesn't remember doing anything to get pregnant. The situation connects with the feeling of being blamed for things she doesn't do. Her parents constantly guilt-trip her.

Along a similar line, being pregnant can symbolize a worst-case scenario come true.

Finally, consider the obvious. If you are female, sexually active, and able to conceive, a dream about being pregnant might mean you are or soon will be pregnant.

See also: *Abortion, Baby, Boy, Child, Childbirth, Ex, Family, Fetus, Girl, Miscarriage, Test, Unconscious Mind.*

President—As a leadership figure, a president in a dream can symbolize a leader in your life, such as a supervisor, coach, or parent.

Begin there and consider the scenarios that a dream can create around that symbolism. For example, a president dying, leaving office, or taking office can represent a change in leadership. New managers take over at work. A new teacher takes over a class. A new coach takes over the team. It's like getting a new president.

A president can symbolize your leadership qualities, including the ability to lead your psyche. Everyone has a "leader" archetype within him- or herself, in the deep psyche, which can be represented as a president-character. It's referred to as the King or Queen archetype, the part of you that sets a vision for life and marshals resources to advance the cause. See: *Archetypes, King, Queen.*

Consider the qualities of a president and how they can be used as symbolism. Presidents are strategic thinkers. They organize. They have vision. They inspire trust—and sometimes, derision.

Presidents are authority figures. A president-character or reference to the authority of a president can arise in dreams related to the exertion of authority. For example, in a dispute with a neighbor, you turn to the your homeowners association or property managers to mediate. In a dispute within yourself, you seek out your internal sense of authority to resolve it.

A president can symbolize your relationship with authority. See: *Police Officer.*

Presidents are admired. People put their faith in them. A president-character in a dream can symbolize someone who is admired or trusted. It can symbolize something about you that's admirable or trustworthy.

Presidents are famous. See: *Famous.*

Dreaming about a president, or about being a president, can mean you want to take charge. Action

is needed. Decisions need to be made. Dreams can use a president-character in the negative sense, too. Decisions are not being made. A person can't be trusted. Authority is abused. Leadership is absent.

Look at the character in the context of the story, and make associations to come up with your own ideas. Also, explore further by reading the entries below.

See also: *Archetypes, Castle, Famous, Father, Hero, King, Mother, Parents, Police Officer, Queen*

Priest—See: *Pastor*

Prince—As a king-in-waiting or descendant of royalty, a prince-character in a dream can symbolize someone who is next in line to get a position of prestige or authority. Or it can be a satirical way of describing someone who acts entitled or privileged, like "mom's little prince."

A prince can symbolize the budding king within you. It shows the leader in you learning and emerging, your leadership qualities developing.

A prince-character can be the face of the Hero archetype, or a young version of the King archetype. For males in their teens and twenties, the Hero is particularly important because it's a psychological foundation for becoming fully mature and masculine. It acts as a bridge for becoming a man who rules his kingdom. See: *Archetypes, Hero, King.*

A prince can symbolize confidence in your abilities or position, or just confidence in general. Princes are known for their confident bearing. They're smarter, stronger, and more charismatic than the average male. They have something special about them.

A prince can symbolize loyalty, especially loyalty to a family, spouse, leader, social circle, or organization.

A prince-character can depict your "Prince Charming," a love interest for whom you pine, or someone you put on a pedestal.

A prince can symbolize learning from a person above you such as a father, coach, teacher, or supervisor. You are the prince to that person's king.

A prince is the classic image of an animus figure, the male face of a female's unconscious mind or soul—especially in the dreams of young females. See: *Animus.*

See also: *Animus, Archetypes, Father, Hero, King, Princess*

Princess—Princess can mean "next in line."

A female who acts entitled is called a "princess." A prom queen or pageant contestant is a sort of princess. "Princess" can be a way of describing someone who lives or acts the role.

Portrayal as a princess can characterize an entitled female or effeminate male. It can mean she has something special about her.

A princess can sum up in one image a female's confidence, attractiveness, savvy, authority, or decisiveness.

Females learn from the queens in their lives and the strong women they observe from afar: the mothers and mother figures, heroes, idols, teachers, mentors, supervisors, and coaches who show them how it's done. In that sense, a princess is a female learning to be a queen, and a queen, in simplest terms, is a woman with authority and power.

A princess-character can be the face of the Hero archetype, or a young version of the Queen archetype. It's a psychological foundation for becoming fully mature and feminine, and it acts as a bridge for becoming a woman who rules her life and controls her environment.

A princess-character can be a characterization of a love interest, or someone put on a pedestal.

A princess is the classic image of an anima figure, the female face of the male soul—especially in the dreams of young males.

See also: *Anima, Archetypes, Hero, Mother, Prince, Prom, Queen*

Principal—In simplest terms, a principal is an authority figure and can symbolize authority structures. School is generally the first authority structure that a child encounters outside the home, and it makes a lasting impression.

A principal is generally someone you see when caught misbehaving or breaking the rules; the principal is the person who dishes out consequences. Therefore, a principal can symbolize consequences of misbehavior, and the dream-character represents a specific person you don't want to encounter, or sums up in one image fear of getting caught or punished. This use of the symbolism is often shown through actions of running from, hiding from, or defying a principal.

If the principal in your dream is a familiar person from your life, consider associations based on what you know about the person and the time of life when the person was an active part of your life.

A principal can symbolize a strong authority—he or she is the highest authority in a school. See: *President.*

A principal can symbolize someone admired for leadership or concern for children.

A principal can symbolize the part of yourself that governs anything in life related to learning and academics.

A principal can be a reference to childhood and school days. See: *School.*

Another definition of principal means "chief" or "central person," and dreams can branch out from there to mean "chief concern" or "central idea." It can refer to a principle, meaning "a fundamental truth." Dreams play with words and create symbolism through comparison and substitution.

See also: *Captain, Child, Coach, General, President, School, Student, Teacher*

Prison—See: *Jail*

Prisoner—To dream you are a prisoner can symbolize the feeling of being isolated or withdrawn. The situation might be due to circumstances beyond your control, but also consider that some people choose isolation in order to know themselves better and make personal progress.

In this sense, a prisoner is like a monk or nun in a cell, deprived of freedom and social contact to gain a closer relationship with God. A dream about a cell might be a suggestion from your unconscious mind that you need more time alone in order to find yourself. On the other hand, it can mean you have too much time alone.

You can be a prisoner of your beliefs or of your own mind. In this sense, a prisoner connects with the idea of restriction and limits. See: *Cage, Jail*.

A dream's depiction of a character as a prisoner instead of a captive or hostage adds the dimension of punishment and guilty conscience.

Prisoners can be used as characters to symbolize control by an outside influence or authority. For example, addicts are sometimes described as prisoners because they can't control their addiction. "Prisoner" has a more helpless or slave-like connotation to it. See: *Hostage*.

People who live in poverty can be described as prisoners of their situation.

People in cults are like prisoners if forcibly prevented from leaving. An abused domestic partner can be kept prisoner through coercion and threat. The question to ask is, what's keeping you where you are? Use the list below to fully explore this subject.

See also: *Accomplice, Addict, Attack, Cage, Court, Crime, Escape, Fugitive, Guilt, Hostage, Jail, Police Officer*

Professor—See: *Teacher*

Prom—Prom can be used in a dream-story to create symbolism based on associations with it—common associations and personal ones.

Some common associations with prom are that it's a big date, a formal occasion, a highly anticipated event.

Some less common associations are that it's costly, brings out insecurities and anxieties in people, and the person you take as your date says a lot about your social status and dating skills. Those are possible reasons that you dream about being at prom ten or twenty or thirty years after your last prom.

Also consider that prom for some people is when they lose their virginity, so it can be associated with sexuality and sex life.

For example, a teenaged female dreams that she and her peers walk single file across a plank over a dark pit. Some of her peers fall off, but she makes it across to a room with an overhead sign that says "PROM." Inside she finds bored teens and a picked-over food buffet.

The dream symbolizes her first sexual experience. The risky maneuver over the pit represents the inherent risks, such as pregnancy and disease. Making it to the other side represents that she didn't fall into those traps during her first sexual experience. The bored teens and picked-over food buffet show how she feels about the experience. It didn't live up to expectation.

Prom is connected with inclusion and exclusion. For example, a man who didn't attend prom because he was an outcast in high school dreams about it years later as a recurring theme. His dreams use prom anytime they want to address a subject related to exclusion and the bitter taste it leaves in his mouth.

Prom can connect with the symbolism of school. See: *School*.

It can connect with dating. See: *Boyfriend, Girlfriend*.

It can connect with marriage, both as a formal occasion and as a precursor, such as when you marry your high school sweetheart. See: *Marriage, Wedding*.

And of course, you can have personal associations that your dreams use as symbolism. Begin by thinking about prom and what you associate with it personally.

See also: *Boyfriend, Dress, Girlfriend, Limousine, Marriage, School, Student, Teenager, Wedding*

Prostitute—See: *Hooker*

Psyche—The psyche is the complete picture of the mind, made up of separate and interacting structures like pieces of a puzzle fit together. Structures of the psyche include ego, persona, the unconscious, archetypes, and anima/animus, each of which has an entry, listed below.

The core of the psyche—aka the "archetypal Self"—is modeled as an octahedron. Each face of the top pyramid of the octahedron represents a primary archetype and connects with its contrasexual counterpart, represented by a bottom face of the pyramid. (Contrasexual means "traits of the opposite gender.") Each archetype branches out to connect with other parts of the psyche, like chess in 3-D. Explaining how it all works is a book in itself.

For our purpose, the psyche is important because it is the internal environment of the mind illustrated by *subjective dreams*. (Much-less-common *objective dreams* focus on events of your life and the conditions of your external environment.) Dreams are produced in the unconscious by a structure known as "the Self," which is the complete picture of who you are, both conscious and unconscious. At the core of the Self are the primary archetypes. The Self is the painter, a dream is the painting, and the psyche is the thing painted.

The psyche is a self-regulating system that uses dreams to help create balance and advance its development. Understanding how the psyche works is foundational knowledge for understanding dreams and how they show developmental processes within it. Explore further by using the entries listed below, especially: *Circle, Spiral*.

See also: *Anima, Animus, Archetypes, Circle, Collective Unconscious, Compensation, Ego, Group, Individuation, Mental Functions, Persona, Psychologist, Pyramid, Shadow, Shapes, Spiral, Subconscious, Unconscious Mind*

Psychiatric Ward—See: *Insane*

Psychic Power—Psychic power in dreams can symbolize personal power or ability. For example, telekinesis can symbolize the power to "move" or influence people, or to influence events. Prophecy or precognition can connect with the ability to analyze trends and situations and foresee where they are headed. Levitation can symbolize the ability to "rise above" and see from a higher perspective. Telepathy is akin to the ability to communicate nonverbally.

Alternately, dreaming about having psychic ability can indicate you truly have those abilities, either in the figurative or literal sense. It might not be symbolism. Instead, your dreams are awakening you to new possibilities in your personal development. Decades of research at places like Princeton University, University of Virginia, and Stanford Research Institute have proven that psychic abilities are real, and most people, under the right circumstances, can tap into their own abilities.

However, the majority of people either do not believe psychic power is real or possible, or do not recognize their own ability. To explore this subject further, refer to the work of Dean Radin, especially his groundbreaking book, *The Conscious Universe*.

Dreams can create symbolism based on root words, and the root of psychic is psyche. At its simplest, psychic power is a power of the psyche, and the psyche can be immensely powerful without venturing into the territory of parapsychology. See: *Psyche*.

Read the entry for *Magic* for a discussion of how a psychic power can be symbolism for something that can't be explained conventionally.

Finally, consider personal associations. Such as, if you think that people who claim to be psychics are shams (and some of them certainly are), you could dream about a psychic or psychic power in relation to something or someone you don't believe. In which case, you will react in the dream with disbelief or derision.

See also: *Magic, Precognitive Dream, Psyche, Telepathy*

Psychologist—A primary use of the symbolism of a psychologist or psychiatrist in a dream relates to needing help working things out in your mind and heart. Something's out of whack and you know it, so you go searching inside yourself for how to fix it. You need help, need to talk with someone who knows.

In simplest terms, a psychologist is someone who understands the psyche, and whether you know it or not you already know everything going on in there. The psyche is a self-regulating and balancing system, and dreams are its chief spokesperson. What better way of providing information about the psyche than through a psychologist-character or variation like a psychology teacher or even a friend or relative with a well-balanced psyche? See: *Psyche.*

You could think of a dream-character psychologist as representing your own inner psychologist. The role of psychologist can be played by other parts of the psyche, such as your unconscious mind or the Magician archetype. In which case, the image of a psychologist or therapist is a mask, your dream's attempt to create a story that helps you help yourself.

The things that drive you to see a professional psychologist are usually long term; they don't just pop up overnight. Such as your relationship with your family, bad habits and patterns, experiences of early childhood, trauma, abuse, and perceptions of yourself created by experience.

But if you take a personal blow that knocks you out of balance, you can dream about a psychologist to help get back on track. For example, your spouse leaves you, or you lose your job, and suddenly you're in turmoil, and dream about seeing a psychologist and explaining the situation. It's a pretty straightforward representation. Basically, you're talking things through with yourself.

You don't have to have a problem to see a psychologist—especially your dream psychologist. That character can be used to address any aspect, function, or development of your psyche. Your inner psychologist is there to help you understand yourself better and develop yourself as a person, through what Carl Jung calls *individuation.*

A psychologist can symbolize someone in your life who helps you keep yourself together, listens to your problems, dreams, and desires, and provides advice and perspective. Or perhaps a psychologist in a dream expresses a wish for such a person to be part of your life.

If you're seeing a psychologist or therapist, you're likely to dream about it, and the possibilities for symbolism and meaning it raises are too numerous to address. Just keep in mind, the person is a character playing a role in your dream, not necessarily a reflection of the actual person.

As with all dream-characters, your personal associations are the basis of your dream symbolism. While psychologists are generally seen as skilled professionals of the mind, some people view them as quacks and would rather have a root canal than be analyzed.

For other people, dreaming about a psychologist can connect with thoughts about choosing a profession that pays well. As with all symbolism, use your personal associations as well as common ones to decode what a psychologist means to you and the role the character plays in a story.

See also: *Addict, Doctor, Emotions, Hospital, Individuation, Insane, Pain, Psyche, Rescue, Talk, Unconscious Mind*

Psychopomp—See: *Jesus*

Puke—See: *Vomit*

Punch—See: *Fist*

Pupil—See: *Eyes, Student*

Puppy—Dogs are companions and friends, and a puppy is something new. Put the two ideas together and a puppy can symbolize a new friendship or something that makes you feel good.

A puppy can symbolize a playful and carefree nature.

A puppy can symbolize a child, or the relationship between a parent and child. Do you follow your parent (or sibling, or best friend) around like a puppy? Is your child like a puppy—happy, enthusiastic, and always on the go and at your side?

It can symbolize someone who is a follower, who trusts to the point of gullibility, who's innocent. Think of someone described as "such a puppy." It's often a jaundiced way of characterizing someone who's too eager for attention and can be exploited or mistreated.

Rescuing a puppy can symbolize trying to preserve something "puppy-like" about yourself. It's a common theme to summarize the experience of losing childlike innocence. It can symbolize rescuing a friendship. See: *Rescue.*

Harming a puppy can symbolize taking advantage of innocence, or doing something reprehensible. The dream creates symbolism by making a comparison, and harming a puppy is generally considered reprehensible, something only a monster would do.

And that's just the beginning of the possibilities, because puppy symbolism can be an offshoot of dog symbolism. See: *Dog*.

Also, as an animal, a puppy can connect with animal symbolism. See: *Animals*.

A key fact about puppies that can be used as symbolism is that they're young. To explore that idea, see: *Kitten*. You can go a step further and read the entry for *Baby*. A puppy can symbolize anything that's new about you and your life.

Another key fact is that puppies are small, and in dream-speak that can mean easily overlooked or unimportant.

If you've been thinking about adopting a dog, you can dream about it as a sort of dress rehearsal or way of exploring whether it's what you really want.

See also: *Adopt, Animals, Baby, Child, Dog, Kitten, Pet, Rescue, Young*

Purse—Purses in dreams are associated with the items kept inside, such as money, financial documents, identification cards, and personal items such as makeup.

The symbolism of a purse can tie in with the idea of something important you don't want to lose. It can be symbolized by the purse itself, or what it contains.

Losing your purse is a common dream theme related to money and financial worries or loss of identity. It can reflect hard financial times. For a more thorough discussion, see: *Wallet*.

Because makeup is kept in a purse, and expensive purses are status symbols, the symbolism can connect with appearance and creating impressions.

Buying a new purse can connect with a time of life that ends and a new one that begins. For example, a woman who just got hired for a new, professional job dreams about shopping for a new purse. Her usual taste in purses leans toward quirky and fun, but this time she picks an upscale businesswoman's purse, reflecting the persona she's adopting to fit her new job.

To further explore the connection between wearable items and dream symbolism, see: *Clothing*.

See also: *Bag, Clothing, Dressed, Fashion, Money, Lost Item, Persona, Wallet*

Puzzle—Puzzling over something means figuring out how the pieces fit together. Putting the puzzle together means fitting pieces together, for example, when solving a math problem or figuring out what to do with your life. Something puzzling is inexplicable. Working on a puzzle with someone can symbolize trying to figure the person out.

See also: *Lost, Maze, Wilderness*

Pyramid—A pyramid is essentially a three-dimensional triangle, and a triangle can symbolize anything that comes in threes, such as a love triangle or the Trinity.

However, the possibilities for symbolism can get much deeper because a triangle is also how an archetype is modeled, with its positive polarity represented at one bottom corner, and the negative polarity across from it. These opposite polarities are said to be in conflict, basically what's meant by the term "bipolar." In Jungian psychology, it's referred to as the *conflict of opposites*, and the goal is to *transcend* it. Transcendence is symbolized in many esoteric traditions as the All-Seeing Eye, or Eye of Horus, which sits atop the pyramid. See: *All-Seeing Eye*.

In dreams, these ideas manifest as opposite characters or ideas and conflicts between them.

Archetypes are deep structures of the psyche. See: *Archetypes, Psyche*.

For our purpose, the point is that if you dream about a pyramid, you might be seeing the structure of your psyche. It's quite common to dream about the psyche because a central purpose of dreams is to show movement and development in it.

Dreams featuring monumental pyramids tend to connect in some way with power—personal or other power. They're symbols of power for the rulers and societies that build them.

Dreams can use a pyramid in relation to the belief that they're used for burials, and that association can connect with any subject related to mortality and death. See: *Bury, Death, Graveyard.*

The massive size of some pyramids can be used to create symbolism, such as for having a huge amount of respect, looking up to someone, idolizing, or placing on a pedestal. See: *Giant.*

Climbing a pyramid can symbolize "reaching for the top," meaning being the best or the top dog; it can have the same symbolism found in the phrase "climb the mountain." It can symbolize the steps to reach a "peak" position or to achieve a lofty goal.

A pyramid that crumbles can symbolize an authority or power structure that crumbles.

See also: *All-Seeing Eye, Archetypes, Bury, Death, Giant, Graveyard, Group, Numbers, Psyche, Shapes*

Python—See: *Snake, Strangle*

Quarantine—See: *Infect*

Quarrel—See: *Argument*

Queen—A queen-character in a dream can symbolize a role of leadership or prestige played in waking life. A wife can be like the queen to her husband's king. As owner or manager of a business, she can be like a queen. As a mother, she can be like a queen to her little princes and princesses.

Usually this use of the symbolism in a dream involves the dreamer actually playing the role of queen or being identified as one, but the queen can be projected onto a character separate from the dreamer, especially if a dreamer needs distance from this part of herself in order to see it.

A queen-character in a dream might show your connection with a queen's qualities of confidence, leadership, grace, authority, vision, inspiring respect, authority, wielding power, and so forth. Every woman has an inner queen who begins life in the psyche as a princess. The image of a queen sums up how those qualities and characteristics manifest in a person's life and personality.

Or not. A queen-character can just as easily be used to show what's missing, denied, or undeveloped.

This learning-and-development process shows in dreams about being at a queen's side, conversing with her, and getting advice, or learning from her example. It's a positive interaction, though it can be pointed if hard lessons must be learned or big obstacles overcome. Connection with this part of you is almost sure to feel good.

The queen can be thought of as the "All-Mother," the ultimate female authority figure. Dreaming about being a queen can indicate that a woman is identifying with the highest qualities and characteristics of being female. For men, it can mean finding and developing in themselves a masculine version of what are traditionally feminine traits, such as grace and consensus-building.

Men dream about queens most commonly in connection with a female authority figure in their lives, such as a wife or mother. Or she might represent someone the dreamer wants to please, or who must be obeyed.

A queen in a dream can symbolize a man's anima, the face of his unconscious mind. She appears as a queen after a man outgrows his fascination with the princess and wants more maturity. This development of the psyche can show in his life as his taste in women changes. See: *Anima*.

Anima is an archetype. See: *Archetypes*.

Look up "queen archetype" online to explore in more depth.

For either gender, a queen can symbolize wanting to do things perfectly, to put forth best effort, to impress. If the queen is coming for dinner at your house, you're going to make damned sure you do everything in your power to impress her.

Also consider the idea of a queen representing a situation in which everything is done for you—for example, on a luxury cruise, or at a resort. You feel like a queen.

Queens have their dark side. They can be bossy, demanding, imperious, arrogant, impossible to please. In the image of a queen can be seen a shadowy side of a woman's character or personality. People can have difficulty seeing this part of themselves, so dreams can project those qualities onto a character. Does it describe anyone you know?

Read the entries for *King, Prince,* and *Princess* to approach this subject from different angles.

See also: *Anima, Archetypes, King, Prince, Princess, Woman*

Quicksand—Quicksand in a dream can represent the potential for danger. It implies being careful about the next steps you take in your life.

Quicksand slowly sucks a person in—what a terrific analogy for something that slowly consumes or overwhelms you. For example, a bad relationship or work situation you can't escape, or an addiction, are things that slowly consume you. An extramarital affair can suck you in.

Also consider the possibility of quicksand as symbolism for being stuck in a situation or place in your life. For example, you graduate from college but don't find a job in the profession for which you trained. Or at work you know you can't advance until the person ahead of you quits or retires, and that's not likely to happen anytime soon. You feel stuck in your life.

Rabbi—See: *Pastor*

Rabbit—As with other animals and creatures in dreams, the symbolism of a rabbit depends on associations—common associations and your personal ones.

Begin with the association rabbits have with sex and love. They are frequent visitors in dreams of people who have been doing a lot of cuddling and petting. Rabbits have long been associated with sexual activity, expressed in such phrases as "mating like bunnies." Rabbits used to be sacrificed for pregnancy tests. And a "bunny" is a term used to describe a sexually attractive female.

White rabbits in particular are associated with purity and faithfulness, black rabbits with impurity and promiscuity or faithlessness.

Rabbits are associated with luck and good fortune. A rabbit's foot is a good-luck charm, and in dreams a good-luck charm can be a sign that you feel lucky or fortunate, or wish to be more lucky. See: *Lottery.*

Dreams can use rabbit symbolism in the negative sense. For example, a dead rabbit can symbolize feeling unlucky, or the end of a sexual relationship.

Rabbits hide at the first sign of danger and can symbolize being shy or reclusive, which could be characteristics of yourself or someone you know symbolized as a rabbit in your dream.

Rabbits are associated with being in a hurry, as in the story of the tortoise and the hare.

See also: *Animals, Hide, Lottery, Sex, Speed.*

Raccoon—Raccoons are commonly associated with scavenging and sneakiness, behaviors they exhibit. The black band of fur around their eyes makes them look like bandits. The associations extend to include ideas like struggle for survival, going it alone, getting back to nature, and living simply.

However, associations based on personal experience are fair game for dreams to use to create symbolism. Such as in the dream a man had about being in a tent and suddenly the ground gives way and he tumbles down hundreds of feet into a raging river. He washes up on a rock outcropping and sees a raccoon that's trapped and can't swim across the river. He tries to help it, and it attacks him and shreds his tent.

To understand the dream, you have to know about an experience he had as a child. While camping, he fed the raccoons at the campsite and his parents admonished him for it. It created an association in his mind between raccoons and being punished for trying to be helpful. A recent incident has made him feel that way. It feels like a personal attack, and it shreds the flimsy protection he has around his ego, symbolized by the tent. It puts his emotions in turmoil, symbolized as the raging river. Ultimately, the dream raises the point that he shouldn't be so sensitive.

This example points out why no dream dictionary can cover all possibilities for symbolism, and you should always think of personal associations for your dream symbols.

See also: *Animals, Bandit*

Race—See: *Run*

Rage—Dreams create scenarios that trigger emotions. If you dream about being in a rage, it's a strong indicator that you feel really strongly or are really angry about something. Whatever triggers the rage in the dream symbolizes something in your life. The entry for *Anger* goes into more depth about decoding the symbolism.

For example, a man dreams about being back in high school and being told he won't graduate, triggering his rage. He throws desks and stalks off to the counselor's office. In reality, he graduated four years before the dream. His reaction of flying into a rage is disproportionate to the situation and indicates a deeper layer of meaning. The dream is actually about having graduated and four years later finding he's going nowhere in his life. High school is supposed to be preparation for adult life, so failing to graduate really means he fears he'll get nowhere in his life. And that's what triggers his rage. See: *Teacher.*

A dream about flying into a rage after a lover spills a drink on the mattress while having sex connects with the dreamer's fears about getting pregnant. Expressing rage under the circumstances stands out as symbolism because it's an overreaction, a clue that the spilled drink (spilled semen) symbolizes something about which the dreamer feels really strongly (accidentally getting pregnant).

See also: *Anger, Emotions, Fire, Hate, Teacher*

Railroad—See: *Train*

Rampage—See: *Anger, Rage*

Rape—Some of the most powerful and traumatizing dreams involve rape. Females and males have rape dreams. The first possibilities for symbolism to consider revolve around nonsexual definitions of the word. Think of times it's used to mean something other than physical rape. It's heard in reference to losing badly in sports or video games, with one side dominated and humiliated by another. It's used in reference to exploiting the natural resources of the planet, and as an expression of helplessness and anger.

Dreams enact other definitions of rape, such as domination, exploitation, and violation, turning them into scenarios of sexual rape.

Another way that dreams use rape is to express the feeling that you're being forced to do something you don't want to do or be someone you don't want to be. It's a frequent theme in the dreams of males and females who resist living up to the cultural ideals and expectations of their gender.

Some females resent having to wear makeup and heels, and are discriminated against when they don't. Some males don't want to act tough and distant, or spend hours in the gym buffing up. Cultural pressure to live up to gender ideals can be intense, and the consequences of resisting it can be extreme. Even if a person tries to live up to gender ideals, it can still feel like being coerced or forced. It's not necessarily "consensual."

A man has recurring dreams about being raped and connects it with being forced to hide his homosexuality. Instead, he tries to force himself to feel and act straight and to be attracted to women. Rape sums up how he feels.

For another man who dreams about being raped by a woman, it's shows his powerlessness over his sexuality. Sex and sensuality have too much hold on his mind. See: *Sex.*

When rape is used to symbolize the force and coercion of gender ideals and cultural expectations, it's often shown in dreams as gang rape. See: *Men.*

Being gang-raped in a dream can be an exaggerated way of expressing the idea of being ganged up on. It can express the feeling that everything and everyone are out to get you or hurt you.

Rape is "next-level symbolism," meaning not just humiliated, violated, or hurt, but very humiliated, violated, or hurt. Not just coerced, but forced. It captures the dynamics of a situation and your feelings.

Rape in a dream can have roots in your inner life. In a graphic way, it shows how you treat yourself. Your ego uses threat, domination, and humiliation to get what it wants, or some aspect of your psyche overpowers the others. This is especially true of the Shadow aspects of the psyche and sadist/masochist dynamics of the Warrior archetype. If that's how life is in your head, it's likely to show outwardly. Some people are best described as rapists just on the basis of their personality and character, and some people live the role of victim.

Rape in a dream can have roots in personal experience. People who have been raped are likely to dream about what happened. It seems cruel to bring up a traumatizing event like that, but it actually helps by creating a psychological cushion between the present moment and what happened in the past. Once the dream is over, it is in the past, and when something can be thought of as in the past it creates personal distance. The same sort of process happens with other traumas, such as combat and abuse. Further, such dreaming gives you opportunities to run through threat simulations and devise strategies for protecting yourself.

On the other hand, rape dreams can show that you're still chained to the experience even though you have the potential to move on.

For example, a woman dreams about finding her rapist working beneath a car. She coldly pulls out a gun and pumps rounds into him. The dream is an expression of her thoughts of revenge. She didn't report the rape because her best friend's brother did it, and it's eating her up inside. Her thoughts of revenge rip open the scab and keep the wound fresh. In a bipolar way, she's bouncing back and forth between being a victim and wanting to be the oppressor. See: *Revenge*.

Dreaming about being raped can be a way of saying you feel *very* disrespected. For example, you decide to sleep with someone you've been dating, thinking it will be a special experience, and all your partner wants is sex.

Dreams exaggerate, and rape in dreams can be used to exaggerate a situation related to sexual tension or exploitation, such as when a person is used as a sexual plaything.

Rape may connect with a recent or ongoing situation that's dangerous, sexually or otherwise. It's the sort of comparison dreams are known to make because dangerous situations can lead to rape. For example, passing out at a wild party puts you in danger, especially if you're young and female.

A rape dream can come in response to feeling vulnerable or powerless. For example, after being hit on at a gas station by a creepy guy, a woman dreams that night about being raped at that gas station by a similar guy. It's an expression of feeling raped in the sense of having her dignity attacked, compounded by recognizing her vulnerability to men who are stronger than she is.

Dreams can act as simulations, and a dream about rape can be a way of acting out an issue related to it. For example, you hear a graphic story about a friend who is raped, then dream it happens to you. It's a way of really understanding what that friend went through and perhaps fearing it could happen to you—or taking steps to prevent it, which is a possibility if you dream about fending off a rapist.

Dreaming about rape can express a rape fantasy. Something about the idea of domination and humiliation turns you on.

For example, a young man with a rape fantasy has two dreams that when looked at together present a choice. In one, he has normal sex with a girl he is attracted to, an imaginary character, and in the other dream he rapes a random girl and enjoys seeing her fear. The dreams are showing him his choices. On the one hand, sex with someone he is attracted to (normal sex) appeals to him but lacks the stimulation he feels at the thought of raping someone. The rape dream shows that the stimulation of rape comes at the expense of any sort of intimacy. He can have one or the other, but not both.

A vivid rape dream is discussed in the entry for *Devil*.

If you were raped and want help, try *dream rescripting* for nightmares and post-traumatic stress disorder (PTSD). Look it up online.

See also: *Attack, Crime, Devil, Hate, Men, Nightmare, Penis, Revenge, Sex, Victim*

Rat—Rats are associated with pests and disease, so dreams of rats can relate to anything that pesters you or rubs off in a bad way. For example, anxieties and worries pester you. Bad influence rubs off on you. Negativity spreads like a disease. See: *Anxiety, Disease.*

A person described as a rat can't be trusted. He or she has a bad character.

An informant or tattletale is called a rat. It can symbolize feeling betrayed. For an example, see: *Bed*.

Rats are connected with anything that plagues you and won't go away. See: *Infest*.

Rats are associated with fear and disgust. See: *Fear.*

However, people who keep rats as pets might describe them as lovable or harmless, so rats in their dreams can have different positive symbolism related to protecting something that's small and harmless. For example, a young man who used to have a pet rat dreams about protecting it from a cat, symbolizing how small he feels when his mother lectures him and how he tries to protect his sensitive inner nature.

Pet rats can be associated with rat-like instincts that have been tamed, or with trying to find your way through "the maze of life." Dreaming about taming a rat could symbolize overcoming a habit of being a tattletale, or improving your living conditions.

Rats scrounge for food and shelter, and in dreams they can symbolize struggling for survival.

"Rat race" describes competition and crowding.

A dream about a house infested with rats can represent that your life or emotions are in disarray. See: *Infest*.

As with other symbolism, consider the context of the dream-story and your feelings. Obviously, if a rat in a dream is running on a wheel and you feel sorry for it, then the dream is most likely using the rat in the context of "rat race."

Rats running throughout your child's room could symbolize worries about him or her.

See also: *Animals, Anxiety, Disease, Fear, Infest, Maze, Mouse*

Raven—See: *Crow*

Read—See: *Book*

Rectangle—When a dream draws attention to a four-sided object or structure, the symbolism can be based on the shape. Many aspects of the psyche are configured in groups of four, and a dream can use anything four-sided to show the configuration and structure of the psyche.

The trick with a rectangle is to see it as an elongated square, which in dream-speak can mean emphasized, overemphasized, or out of balance. Balance is shown in the square, so if a dream picks a rectangle instead to give you a peek behind the curtain separating your conscious mind from the rest of the psyche, there's a reason for it.

The rectangle could symbolize the four primary mental functions of the psyche. If you see a rectangular configuration, the dream is showing something out of balance. For example, you can be overly rational at the expense of your feelings (meaning value-based judgment, not emotions). You can discount your intuition and overemphasize "just the facts." See: *Group, Mental Functions*.

If the rectangle is a door or window and it's the focus of the action or the dream-story, then the symbolism might not have anything to do with the shape. Doors and windows have their own symbolism. However, if none of the possibilities fits your dream, perhaps the door or window symbolism really is connected with its rectangular shape.

A rectangle connects with order and structure. Dreams use a physical representation for a personal situation connected with the order and structure of your life. Dreams use rectangles to create symbolism related to grounding yourself in the physical, material world, and a rectangle can show too little or too much grounding. Or, because rectangles make strong structures, a rectangle can show solidity and strength. You have created a secure life for yourself. You have a strong mind and internal integrity. Your house is built on a strong foundation.

The four sides of a rectangle can connect with the symbolism of number four and groups of four. Four is two 2s, two pairs, and it shows interrelated strength. In this way, the strength of the psyche is similar to the strength of anything else that's well-constructed. See: *Archetypes*.

See also: *Archetypes, Basement, Building, Group, Numbers, Psyche, Pyramid, Shapes, Square, Window*

Red—Colors in dreams are likely to connect in some way with emotions, and emotions associated with red include love, passion, anger, lust, shame, and embarrassment.

If you're really angry you "see red," and that association extends to aggression and war.

But at its most essential, red says "energy" and "intensity." It says "zest" and "vitality."

Wearing red in a dream can mean you feel sexy, full of vitality, assertive, and forceful. You want to draw attention to yourself.

And since red is the color of blood, it can be associated with illness or injury. Associations with blood branch out in many directions to create symbolism. See: *Blood*.

Use the entries listed below to explore further.

See also: *Blood, Colors, Clothing, Emotions, Fight, Heart, Love, Mars, War*

Reflection—See: *Mirror*

Rental Car—A rental car is a temporary vehicle. Translated into your life, it can symbolize a temporary situation, such as a temp job. See: *Car*.

Reptile—People described as reptilian are concerned about one thing: survival. They look at the world solely in terms of what they can get and how they can dominate. They are emotionless and remorseless, ruled by impulse and survival instinct, so if any of those subjects was part of the day, reptiles might appear in dreams that night.

The reptilian brain—the part of the human brain shared with all reptiles and mammals—governs instincts, and a reptile can symbolize any base instinct associated with the reptilian brain: survival, fight or flight, aggression, fear, revenge, territorial behavior, and reproduction.

The reptilian brain also controls basic functions of survival such as heartrate, breathing, and body temperature. When your dreams refer to these functions, it can symbolize them as reptiles.

When reptiles appear in dreams, search yourself for feelings related to struggle and dominance. They're easy to overlook, especially when the struggle is emotional, or the need to dominate is instinctual. We tend to discount how it feels to be exposed in large groups like school and work environments, with rules of the game that revolve around cold-blooded dominance and survival. It's not a stretch to see how dreams can describe these conditions with reptiles or even insects; the imagery only has to be comparable on some level.

From the viewpoint of the dreaming mind, emotional survival is as important as physical survival. Dreams use scenes of physical peril to describe what it feels like to defend yourself emotionally. The violence is a metaphor for how it feels to "take a beating" emotionally from cold or impersonal sources comparable to reptiles. People literally "fighting for survival" will dream of reptiles to describe how it feels to scrape for something to eat, or struggle for heat on a cold night.

These associations, while common, sell reptiles short. Yes, they're primitive and instinctual, but they can also come across as noble and strong. They're survivors, and ability to survive is an admirable quality.

See the entry for *Animals* and *Pet* to get an overview of how dreams use creatures to create symbolism.

See also: *Alligator, Animals, Birds, Devil, Pet, Snake*

Rescue—Being rescued in a dream can tie directly to a situation in your life where you need rescue or are doing the rescuing. It might be an external situation, such as drowning in work or debt, or an internal situation, such as depression or making a mistake. Rescue can reflect a role you play in life, with other people and with yourself.

Dreams create physical representations of personal situations. A dream about physically rescuing someone or something can represent the idea of rescue in the personal sense. Think about ways the words "rescue" and "save" are used figuratively.

For example, a woman about to get married dreams that it's her wedding day, and she's at the altar in front of family and friends when her ex-boyfriend barges in and says he's there to rescue her. It symbolizes her inner knowledge that she's about to marry the wrong man and needs to be rescued from making a terrible mistake.

Dreams can make direct references to situations in your life, though often those situations are couched in symbolism. A dream might present it as literally saving someone or being saved—from drowning, a fire, an attacker—when really it's meant in the figurative sense. For example, being saved from drowning in emotion or debt. See: *Drown*.

The theme of rescue can arise in a more general sense of giving and receiving assistance. It might not be tied to a particular situation but instead to a tendency or habit. For example, a man dreams repeatedly about being in situations in which he can rescue people, but instead either refuses to do it or waits till later. It symbolizes being sick of coming to the rescue of people in his life who make a habit of dumping their problems on him.

A dream about rescue can tie in with reluctance to receive assistance. Perhaps you don't want to be a burden, are too proud, or think it's a sign of weakness.

A dream about rescue can symbolize that something inside yourself needs help. You're mentally or emotionally out of whack. See: *Psychologist*.

Or you're in danger of losing something about yourself. For example, a man dreams about rescuing a kitten from drowning in a pool. The kitten symbolizes the happy, playful part of himself threatened with "submerging" down into his psyche and no longer being a conscious part of his personality. He's a teenager, and peer pressure is forcing him to toughen up.

In a dream about saving a baby from drowning in a pool, the dreamer is trying to save a side of himself from receding into his psyche. He's drowning in the drudgery of adult life and wants to enjoy himself again.

A woman dreams about saving a beached whale and connects it with her sense that some recent bad experiences are making her leery and bitter. She associates whales with kindness, so saving the whale is a way of saying she is trying to save her naturally kind nature.

If you are saved in a dream, or an attempt is made to save you, ask yourself whether you need help or support. Is your workload getting to be too much? Are you struggling? Does someone need to be cheered up or guided? Are you trying to save something, such as a relationship? Think along these lines for the figurative ways that something is saved and how the word is used in expressions and figures of speech, such as "save the day" and "save me from myself." Remember that your dreams can project these thoughts and feelings onto a dream-character that you observe.

For example, a man watches a horse drown and does nothing to save it. It symbolizes his inability to ask for help when he's drowning in work.

Dreams make wordplays, so "save" can be a play on the word "safe," as in playing it safe, and safe from danger. "Safe" can be used to say that a marriage or relationship is safe, or a job is safe, and it can be represented in a dream as physical safety. For example, a dream says your marriage is safe by showing a house safe from a storm.

See also: *Doctor, Guide, Lifeguard, Paramedic, Pet, Psychologist, Whale*

Restaurant—A restaurant setting in a dream presents a variety of possibilities for symbolism.

Consider what you do at a restaurant and a restaurant's function and purpose.

Restaurants are where you consume food, and consumption in a dream relates to the larger idea of what you choose to take into yourself. See: *Eat, Food.*

Restaurants are where you make choices. See: *Menu.*

Restaurants are popular settings for dates and special occasions. Some relationships begin and end at restaurants. Business deals are struck. Anniversaries are celebrated. These associations can be used by dreams to create symbolism and refer to events in your life.

For example, a woman wondering whether her boyfriend is going to "pop the question" dreams about being in the restaurant where they had their first date. A chef-character says that a special meal is being prepared for them, symbolizing her anticipation that her boyfriend will soon give her that "special moment."

Another woman dreams about being in a restaurant with her ex-husband. He tells her that things are being worked out, and a contract is drawn up. It symbolizes her decision to finally put the relationship completely behind her. Her ex is a lawyer, so the idea of a deal fits with how she would expect him to behave under the circumstances. The restaurant setting is used because it's where people can meet in neutral territory.

Restaurants can be busy and hectic, and if your life is busy and hectic, then your dreams can symbolize it as working in a restaurant. This association is even stronger in people who have worked in restaurants.

For example, a man dreams that he has two jobs, both in restaurants, and decides to call off one of them. Having two jobs symbolizes his feeling of being overextended. He has a career and home to take care of, and he's too busy with work related to his career, so his job at home has to wait. His career involves juggling many responsibilities at once, which is the nature of restaurant work. And cleaning up his home involves many of the same tasks involved in restaurant work, such as preparing meals and sweeping floors.

A lot of preparation goes into getting ready for "the rush," a restaurant term for the busy hours of service. It's a ready-made analogy for rushing to get ready for a big event, such as preparing for relatives to come over for the holidays, or working on a project that requires attention to detail and multitasking. Another characteristic of working in a restaurant is that it can alternate between periods of idleness and periods of busy-ness.

See also: *Chef, Dinner, Eat, Food, Kitchen, Knife, Menu, Waiter*

Restroom—See: *Bathroom*

Revenge—Revenge in a dream can tie in directly with a situation in your waking life. You feel wronged, and it's payback time. Or you want someone who has hurt you to know how it feels. Or you fear that something you've done invites retribution.

A woman who was raped dreams about getting revenge on her rapist by murdering him. The dream ties directly with her thoughts of revenge. See: *Rape.*

A young woman who had been mercilessly bullied by her classmates dreams about being forced to perform fellatio on one of the bullies. She decides to pretend that she wants to do it, then bites off the penis. The henchman laughs as if he was expecting her to do it. She vomits up long, stringy pieces of the penis.

The dream relates to her thoughts of revenge. Years after the fact, she is still very angry and fantasizes about getting revenge, symbolized as biting off the penis of her tormentor. But the situation backfires, showing that her thoughts of revenge only keep her chained to the situation. Vomiting up pieces of the penis shows that she wants to rid herself of the remnants of the experience of being bullied that are still inside her. She's still internally chained to the feelings of humiliation and powerlessness. See: *Bully.*

Also consider the connection between revenge and something that really makes you emotionally hot or keyed up. For example, a dream about getting revenge against someone connects with your determination to do better on the next test. It's your revenge. Or a dream about seeing your ex while out on a date connects with hoping he or she knows that you're dating someone else, and so will feel jealous.

See also: *Bully, Emotions, Ex, Fire, Kill, Rape*

Reverse—See: *Backward, Car*

Right—A common use of the symbolism of direction to the right is that it means correct. For example, a young woman dreams about making a right turn in her car and crashing into the back of a police car, and it symbolizes feeling punished for doing the right thing. See: *Turn.*

A man dreams that he's escaping from hell and makes a right turn while burrowing through a wall. The dream is about learning to take responsibility for his actions, and the right turn symbolizes that it's the right move for his life. See: *Hell.*

Right is the direction of the conscious mind, whereas left is the direction of the unconscious mind. Dreams about movement to the right can symbolize that something unconscious is becoming conscious.

Dreams featuring objects or structures to your right can connect with the tangible, physical, material aspects of your life.

Right is the direction of the masculine and the masculine principle. See: *Penis.*

In the Muslim world, the right hand is the "hand of honor," used for shaking hands and eating. Using the left hand is a major faux pas, tied with the old tradition of always wiping the butt with the left hand.

A reference to the right foot can mean "get off on the right foot."

The right-hand path or road is the conventional or orthodox one. To understand the symbolism in contrast, see: *Left.*

See also: *Eyes, Feet, Guide, Left, Map, Spiral, Turn*

Ring—See: *Circle, Finger*

Rise—See: *Ascend*

River—A river is, essentially, an obstacle, and trying to cross a river in a dream is a strong indicator of trying to get past an obstacle. The condition of the river, whether raging or calm or in between, and its size can indicate how much of a challenge the obstacle presents.

For instance, a student graduating from law school must pass his bar exam before starting work. He dreams about traveling through a city before coming to a bridge over a raging river. Crossing the bridge is perilous, but he makes it to the other side, symbolizing passing the bar exam so he can take a job that has already been offered on contingency. It's what's waiting for him on the other side of the river, and the bar is his bridge to getting there. The dream predicts his success with the exam—he knows he's well prepared—and indeed he passes it.

The conditions of the river have many other potential uses as symbolism through comparison. For example, a rushing brown river can symbolize diarrhea. Rapids can symbolize rapid progress or pace to life or some aspect of it. It can mean you're in rough water figuratively. Standing on the other side of a river from someone you know can show that something stands between you and that person, and/or there's a division in your mind related to him or her. It can mean a difference of opinion or outlook.

The same ideas apply to standing across from a group of people. You're far apart from them about something.

Rivers have currents, and "current" in dreamspeak can mean the flow of life, the direction you're headed, the natural progression of things. You can go with the flow or against it.

Going with the flow shows you are in harmony—in your life in general, or in a specific aspect of it. For example, a harmonious marriage can be like a calm river. On the other hand, a stormy marriage can be symbolized as a raging river.

Going against the current can be a way of saying you wish to go in another direction. You don't like where things are headed. You want your own way. Or, you resist the natural progression. You're going against your instincts. The symbolism shows in the actions involving the river and in your actions and reactions as a dream-character in the story.

A river can be an analogy for the course of your life, with stops representing its phases and stages—school days, getting married, starting a career, having your first child, retirement. The river connects these points of reference. Rivers are used for travel, too, adding another layer to use as symbolism, because travel and movement in dreams can symbolize the movement of your life, its progress or lack of it. The symbolism will show in your movement along the river, or a view of it.

A river that splits can mean facing a decision, especially one that means your life will split off in a new direction.

Family is like a river, with your immediate family as the main waterway. Rivers combine to form bigger ones, and families combine through marriage to form bigger families. Day-to-day life with family can be like floating together on a river.

Time progresses like a river. The pace of travel on a river makes it a good symbol for watching the days and nights flow by. See: *Time, Time Travel*.

A river can symbolize your emotions. They flow. They move. And the condition of the water can say a lot about the state of your emotions. See: *Water*.

Drowning in a river can mean that something about your life is too much—too much work, too much responsibility, too much turmoil, too much sadness or disappointment, too much emotion.

A meandering river is a great metaphor for a meandering life.

And of course, your personal experiences come into play. An experience such as almost drowning in a river can create a strong impression that's likely to be used at some point in your life by your dreams, perhaps years later, as a way of comparing to some other sort of jeopardy in which you find yourself. Or a river in a dream can be a way of referencing an incident from your life.

For example, a man dreams about a cold ghost, which just got out of a river, getting into his bed with him. It references the time as a child when he caught typhoid after swimming in a river. The illness made him deathly cold like the ghost, and he almost died and became a ghost himself! Ghosts are associated with the past, too, and he had the dream many years after the incident.

See also: *Boat, Bridge, Calendar, Captain, Drown, Flood, Journey, Road, Time, Time Travel, Water*

Roach—Roaches can symbolize disease, including "dis-ease" caused by anxiety, irritation, and stress. See: *Disease*.

Insects in dreams may refer to something or someone "bugging" or irritating you. See: *Bug*.

The symbolism of cockroaches has possibilities related to living in a low state physically, emotionally, or spiritually, or having the lowest possible opinion of someone or something. They are associated with filth and squalid living conditions, and are used as an analogy for people with low character or bad reputation.

Roaches are almost universally disliked, and people react to them with disgust, creating associations with something shunned, something that you want to keep out, something that disgusts you. Or something, perhaps, that you can't keep out, just as roaches will find ways into your home.

The symbolism of the roach can be similar to other insects. See: *Insects*.

Dreaming about roaches in your home can show that something disgusting has gotten into your head, such as after you view a snuff film or nasty porn, or indulge in dark or nasty thoughts.

An infestation of cockroaches in a dream can be a way of saying that your mind is infested—with negativity, bad memories, disgusting thoughts, or irritations—or your life is infested with problems or misunderstandings that won't go away. See: *Infest*.

See also: *Bug, Disease, Infest, Insects*

Road—A road in a dream can symbolize the road of life you are on or a path you are taking, not just with life, but maybe with a project or relationship.

It's common to dream about being on a road with someone important in your life, such as a family member or co-worker, reflecting the fact that your lives are parallel or move together.

A road can show the direction of your thoughts or feelings.

A road that splits can symbolize that your opinion is split. It can mean that you face a choice, and whichever one you make will lead you in a new direction. It can mean that you split with someone and your lives go in separate directions.

The entry for *Car* has many references to road conditions, and the entry for *River* can give you many ideas about symbolism related to the "road of life."

See also: *Alley, Backward, Bridge, Car, Construction, Dead End, Detour, Empty, Highway, Left, Right, River*

Robber—See: *Thief*

Robot—Dreaming about a robot can mean that your life has become predictable, routine, and repetitive. For example, every day at work or school is the same old routine. You are like a machine. You're expected to perform and conform.

For example, a woman dreams about directing a robot at work, symbolizing her work in a call center where she follows a script and her answers are programmed. She feels like a robot.

Robots can symbolize lack of humanity. They can express the feeling of being ground up by the machinery of society and treated like you don't have feelings, dignity, or intrinsic value.

Dreams about killer robots are known to express the perception of living in a world that lacks humanity, in a system that only wants conformity, which can kill off individuality, and that violates a primary reason that you're alive in the first place. You're here to fully live your life, not be a cog in the machine.

This idea extends to any automated process, good or bad. Automation is for robots.

A robot is a ready-made analogy for a person who doesn't show emotion, or for a feeling of being dead inside. However, as robots get more human-like, they can be used as symbols for someone who *pretends* to be normal and show emotion. That symbolic use can connect with a sense that something isn't quite right, or isn't an exact copy.

For example, you run across your ex, who's now dating a younger version of you, and dream that your ex built a robot in your image.

The idea can expand to capture the feeling and perception that people aren't acting human or in ways expected. For example, a spouse acts differently and you can't quite put your finger on why. A friend who is normally warm and responsive is suddenly distant. A co-worker gives answers that don't make sense.

Turn this idea on its ear and a dream can use it to show the spark of life within you, the resistance to conformity, the love of nature.

See also: *Computer, Doll*

Rocket—The symbolism of a rocket depends largely on what type it is. An ICBM in a dream paints a much different picture than a bottle rocket does. A dream will use an ICBM as a way of saying "the big guns come out," or the danger represented by the missile is particularly big or far-reaching, whereas a bottle rocket is comparatively minor. Instead of a big response, which is what's implied by launching an ICBM, it's a weak one. Instead of a big boom, it's a small one.

If a dream needs to tell a story about movement in your life, it uses a rocket to symbolize getting somewhere quickly, such as when someone rockets to fame or rockets to the top. If you ride a rocket, it's a wild ride! The image captures a feeling of exhilaration, or holding on for dear life. See: *Speed*.

A rocket takes off suddenly, perhaps symbolizing love at first sight or anything else that starts intensely and quickly.

The symbolism of a guided missile can connect with hitting a target. It can symbolize accuracy and precision, or closing in on a target.

A rocket is a classic phallic symbol, and a rocket taking off or exploding is a metaphor for good sex and orgasm, particularly male orgasm.

Rockets and missiles can symbolize fear of sudden change, especially when they come in bunches.

The same imagery of incoming rockets can symbolize personal attacks and hostile competitors' advances or moves. It can connect with a feeling of wariness or trepidation. It can mean you feel threatened.

As with all symbolism, it depends on what happens in connection with a symbol like a rocket and how it fits into the dream-story.

See also: *Attack, Bomb, Embark, Fireworks, Guide, Nuclear War, Phallic Symbol, Speed, War*

Rodent—See: *Mouse, Rat*

Roller Coaster—Roller coasters are associated with thrills, excitement, and unexpected twists and turns. The symbol can be used to trigger a particular feeling or emotion that's also experienced while one rides a roller coaster. It can connect with risk-taking and what you do to amuse yourself.

A roller coaster is a great metaphor for the ups and downs of life, and also for the highs and lows of being in love and taking certain drugs.

It's also a great analogy for the twists and turns of life. Figures of speech such as "my life has been a roller coaster ride lately" show how the analogy of a roller coaster ride can fit a variety of situations.

Bear in mind that dreams can use a roller coaster to point out what's *not* happening, or to create contrast. Such as when a crumbling, unused roller coaster symbolizes nostalgia for a more exciting time of life, or for the fact that you're bored.

A roller coaster can have symbolism similar to that of a train. See: *Train.*

See also: *Amusement Park, Party, Passenger, Rocket, Speed, Train*

Roof—See: *Home*

Rooster—A rooster rules the hen house, and that behavior is comparable to people who "rule the roost" by displaying their dominance or authority, or who act "cocky."

A cock can refer to a penis and related masculine traits and behaviors.

See also: *Animals, Bully, Chicken, Penis, Phallic Symbol*

Roots—Roots in dream can symbolize your roots as a person, indicating a deep layer of what makes you the person you are. For example, your personal roots are your values, principles, upbringing, and faith.

Roots are associated with family or heredity—"family roots." Many dreams about trees and roots connect in some way with your family or the idea of family. See: *Tree.*

Relationships can be said to have "deep roots." Something deeply rooted in your being is a permanent part of you.

Roots can refer to the roots of a situation or event, the roots of a problem.

Putting down roots means establishing yourself in the physical world, such as when you buy a home or become involved in a social circle. You decide that this is the ground where you're going to stay for an extended period. See: *Home.*

"Uprooted" is a way of saying "upended." Your life is upended. For example, a young man dreams about a massive tree in the front yard of his family home being uprooted in a powerful storm. The roots of the tree are exposed, and in the dream he notices that detail in particular. The imagery symbolizes the uprooting of his family, who have all gone their separate ways. The family has lost the cohesion it once had.

See also: *Family, Family Home, Tree*

Round—See: *Circle*

Rug—See: *Carpet*

Run—Running or racing in a dream can symbolize trying to escape something in your life. Think of situations in which you might ask, "What are you running from?" Of course, if this symbolism is used, the dream is likely to show you running from something.

For example, a woman dreams about running from an evil shadow. The shadow symbolizes her precarious financial situation, and running from it symbolizes that she doesn't want to think about it. She's not acknowledging the depth of her fear about the possibility of things getting really bad.

Another woman dreams recurrently about running from a monster. One night she finally has had enough, stops running, turns and confronts the monster. It morphs into a little girl, symbolizing the "inner child" she's been ignoring.

The action of running in a dream is often a physical representation of a personal situation. It can mean you're in a hurry to get somewhere in your life. A race against time. You want to get ahead of the competition. You're afraid. You run from the truth. The symbolism creates a comparison that can connect with your life.

Running in a dream can connect with the emotions triggered, such as exhilaration or enjoying a challenge. It can connect with why people run regularly, such as to stay healthy and young-looking.

A man dreams about running against a competitor, just a random man. The race is only for ten meters, and in the dream he uses a starting block to launch himself and get up to full speed as quickly as possible. He repeatedly starts and is timed, but the starting block is configured for him to launch with his left leg, not his right leg, his dominant leg, and his start is slower than expected. It symbolizes "starting off on the wrong foot" in the morning.

Feeling weak can reflect a physical condition while dreaming known as sleep paralysis. You think you're running, but your brain isn't registering motion. See: *Sleep Paralysis.*

See also: *Backward, Car, Chase, Crutches, Feet, Fly, Handicap, Leg, Monster, River, Rocket, Shoes, Sleep Paralysis, Weak, Wheelchair*

Sacred—See: *Temple*

Sad—See: *Cry, Depressed*

Safe—A locked safe can symbolize keeping a secret. It's safe with you.

Something locked away in a safe can symbolize that it's out of sight or hidden. That idea can include memories you don't want to think about, and aspects of yourself that are unknown. It can be something that's subconscious or unconscious.

A safe can be a wordplay for the feeling of being safe or wanting to be safe.

Unlocking a safe can symbolize getting past a person's defenses, or finding a way around safeguards.

See also: *Door, Key, Lock, Locker, Subconscious, Thief, Unconscious Mind*

Satan—See: *Devil*

Saturn—The planet Saturn has interesting possibilities for dream symbolism based on its astrological characteristics. You might not know anything about astrology, but you might have heard of the word "saturnine," which is commonly thought to mean "dour" or "pessimistic" when really it might be better defined as "gloomy."

Saturn shatters illusions. It punctures the bubble of hubris or delusion. It teaches the hard lessons.

On the other hand, the god Saturn from Roman mythology rules the harvest. Think along the lines of "reap what you sow." Saturn can be used in the negative sense of paying for your actions, or the positive sense of being rewarded for your actions and steps you take to prepare for the future. Saturn is linked with the idea of planting the seeds for tomorrow's harvest. When done with wisdom and insight, it leads to a golden age.

See also: *Earth, Jupiter, Mars, Mercury, Moon, Venus*

Save—See: *Rescue*

Scar—A scar on your body in a dream can symbolize an old emotional or psychological wound. Think along the lines of "that experience left scars." It means you were hurt. It is often used in reference to bad experiences in dating, but has a wide array of applications.

Remember that dreams can speak to wounds inflicted on you *and* wounds you inflict, intentionally or not. For example, you dream about seeing a co-worker covered in scars. You angrily declare that you will find and punish the person who did this, then look down to see a knife in your hand. It's a message that you have been walking over your co-workers and not caring about hurting their feelings.

See also: *Body, Fight, Pain, Tattoo, Wound*

Scent—See: *Nose*

School—A school setting in a dream has a wide variety of possibilities for symbolism. The most obvious are related to learning and knowledge, but school symbolism extends much further to include topics such as authority, success and failure, social life, and preparation for adult life and career.

Begin by noting whether the school is familiar or generic. A familiar school is more likely to represent something about that time of your life or what you experienced there. If you're in school, it's likely to be a frequent setting of your dreams. A generic school is more likely to relate to the general idea of school, authority, or learning. See: *Campus*.

Think expansively about what you learn. You can learn about yourself, another person, your limits, lessons in life, and new skills. Life is a continual process of taking in new information and experiences and learning.

School challenges you in a wide variety of ways. It's not just about learning. It establishes patterns and perceptions—good and bad—that can last a lifetime. For example, a woman who was mercilessly bullied in high school dreams about being trapped by her tormentors in a bathroom stall at school and forced to perform oral sex. See: *Revenge*.

If you are out of school, dreaming you are in a school you once attended can reference that time of your life. Some people think nostalgically about their school days—the "glory days." Dreams about school days can be a nostalgic wish for a return to that time, though usually a dream has a larger purpose than just reminiscence. These dreams are a frequent theme in the lives of adults who wish they could go back and do things over, or whose adult lives lack fun and freedom. For example, see: *Teacher*.

Some people peak at a young age and can search for the rest of their lives to get back that magic.

Think about what you experienced during that time of your life, the decisions you made, your living conditions, the major events, as well as daily life, and especially the kind of person you were and what you wanted to be when you grew up. Compare and contrast with your life now to help lead you to the meaning of a dream about school.

Dreaming about being in a classroom can mean you are learning, either directly, such as when studying a subject, or indirectly, such as when learning about life or learning a new skill. See: *Classroom, Student*.

Extend the idea further to consider your experiences in, and impressions of, classrooms. If you were a kid who had difficulty staying focused, and sitting still in a classroom was torturous, compare that time with your life now. Is it torture sitting at a work desk all day, or enduring another meeting? Do you text-message all day, like passing notes in class? What's the connection with your life now?

See also: *Book, Campus, Child, Classroom, College, Computer, Desk, Library, Locker, Principal, Prom, Student, Teacher, Teenager, Test, University*

Scratch—See: *Wound*

Scream—Dreams provide outlets for emotions, and screaming in a dream can be a sign that some strong emotions need to be expressed. It can mean you're in pain—physically, emotionally, personally. You're in shock. You are under extreme stress or worry.

Screaming can mean someone isn't listening—including you. When you feel that you aren't being heard or acknowledged, screaming gets attention. Screaming progressively louder can mean your frustration or anger level is rising. See: *Yell*.

Yelling is more closely associated with anger, while screaming is more associated with fear.

Screaming can be a way of drawing attention to something that needs it. For example, you have been ignoring your health, and then you dream about a doctor screaming at you.

See also: *Anger, Fear, Pain, Panic, Rage, Yell*

Sea—See: *Beach, Ocean*

Serial Killer—As with most dream-characters, a serial killer is symbolism based on common perceptions and personal situations.

A serial killer-character can be a dream's way of saying that someone or something methodically works against you. For example, people in business who play a "zero-sum game" are out to win at any cost, including by eliminating their competition. They are killers in the sense that they can kill your business.

Serial killers are often indistinguishable from ordinary people. They can disguise themselves behind a facade of friendliness and affability in order to avoid getting caught and to take their victims unawares.

A man who owns a business dreams that he knows a serial killer is in his warehouse, and he warns himself to be careful. He's working and gets a text message, which he ignores, then another, more insistent message that reads, *The serial killer is here, be careful.* It symbolizes his subconscious knowledge that he's being set up.

The serial killer is not depicted in this dream, but its presence in the dreamer's workplace is a clue that points to where the danger is coming from. He's making some big business decisions and feels exposed to subterfuge because he's dealing with new people. But no one sticks out as suspicious enough to be characterized as a serial killer, even in an exaggerated way. Then it dawns on him that one of his suppliers is also a competitor, and that rival is positioning himself to wipe out the dreamer's business. The rival has cleverly maneuvered for the kill, and the dream tells the man what he knows subconsciously but has been too busy to realize. His dream gives him the prompting he needed to connect the dots.

Dreams can use a serial killer-character to take you inside the mind of such a person. For example, a student of psychology studying serial killers dreams recurrently about a serial killer. Some of the scenes are very intense, as in the movie *Silence of the Lambs*. The dream acts as a simulation to take the dreamer inside the mind of a serial killer.

See also: *Fear, Kill, Murder, Pain*

Serpent—See: *Snake*

Servant—The symbolism of a servant in a dream can be based on the association with doing duties for others, such as cleaning up after messy kids or a spouse. This association is especially true if you feel subservient, used, or unappreciated.

The association extends to doing someone's dirty work. Remember that a servant-type-character in a dream can be a projection of something about yourself. You don't actually have to play that role in a dream for the symbolism to apply.

Servant-types have low social status, so dreaming about a servant can symbolize low social status or struggling to rise above circumstances.

The root word "serve" can mean to serve food and drink, or even serve a tennis ball. A dream can use either sense of the word separately or together. See: *Waiter*.

Servants make things more convenient and can be associated with a situation involving convenience. For example, a dream about in-laws hiring a nanny for a young couple who just had a baby symbolizes their help taking care of the baby. They didn't hire a nanny, but they're being helpful like one.

Also consider inner dynamics that might be in play. The psyche is composed of many parts, some of which are autonomous. The interplay among parts of the psyche can be described in terms of the interplay among people. For example, if you use your intellect properly, it can help you advance your ambitions.

See also: *Janitor, Slave, Waiter*

Sex—Sex is commonly used by dreams to create symbolism. Even virgins and celibate priests and nuns dream about sex—very intensely and realistically, too.

Interpreting a dream featuring sex or arousal doesn't have to go very deep, in some cases. The dream simply means that sex is on your mind, or you're aroused during sleep. People can experience periods of intense arousal while asleep. Dreams turn physical input into dream imagery, so arousal while dreaming is likely to be turned into sexual imagery or symbolism.

However, the "chicken or egg" question has not been answered: Does arousal cause sexually related dream imagery, or does sexual dream imagery cause arousal?

Most dreams connect in some way to the process of integrating new material into the psyche. Sex is a terrific analogy for this process because sex is essentially about integration. Two bodies integrate. Two hearts integrate. You give and take, physically and emotionally. You "make" love, a very telling verb to use, basically saying that sex is a creative process. It's something that grows and develops and takes on a life of its own.

Think about it. Dream sex is sex (metaphorically speaking) with yourself.

The same idea applies to celibate people, who can have intensely sexual dreams that provide outlet for their sexual energy, and at its heart it's healthy. It can be a way of pouring energy into an area of life, especially related to creativity and personal development, and encouraging bonding between parts of the psyche.

It's common to dream about someone you know who arouses you. If you have sexual thoughts or fantasies about the person and dream about having sex, the dream might simply reflect your thoughts. It might not be wise to pop awake and tell your bedmate about your "sex with someone else" dream, but it's not something to feel guilty about, which is a typical reaction. Sex in a dream is symbolism.

Whatever you repress or deny in your waking life will be given extra emphasis in your dream life, so it's better to allow it outlet in your dreams.

If you already know that a person turns you on and you dream about having sex with that person, you're not learning anything new. Instead, it could be a safe forum to think through the situation, or a safe outlet for your feelings and desires. At least you get a taste of that fruit, perhaps enough to satisfy. It's a simulation to help you work through related issues such as attraction, desire, performance, anxiety, comfort, and orgasm. Being comfortable with sex in a dream can make you more comfortable with sex in your life, or with sexuality in general.

For example, a woman who has never had an orgasm, and has been racking her brain trying to figure out why, dreams about having sex with a man who really turns her on. Rather than the usual "wham, bam" sex she's used to, he takes his time, unlike the men she's been with. She reaches orgasm in seconds—it's mind-blowing. And when she wakes up she thinks to herself that she has to find a man who can do it the way her dream lover does it. It's her dream's way of showing her—not just telling her—what she needs to orgasm.

Your physician would probably agree that sexual arousal in dreams is healthy for you, especially if you are not having any sex in your waking life. A wet dream helps the prostate and Skene's gland. It releases stress and anxiety. Enjoy it!

Unrequited sexual feelings can show in dreams, too. It's quite common to dream about your crush and *not* get what you want. It can be a way of expressing frustration, of thinking you won't get what you want, or of thinking through strategies for getting it.

For example, a young man dreams that his best friend—for real, not imaginary—has sex with every girl he likes. It's awful as time after time he watches his friend take a girl into a bedroom, while he can only weep. The dream is not tormenting him. It shows him he has a great example in his friend for learning how to get the girls he wants. His friend is good with the ladies and an example to follow.

Sex in a dream can symbolize intimacy of any kind. You can be intimate with a person without having sex with him or her. You can be intimate with a subject or idea. For example, a student dreams about having sex with a professor. The professor is not at all physically attractive to the student in waking life, but in the dream he is a real Casanova. The dream helps the student realize that the professor is intellectually stimulating. His lectures are dynamic. The subject of the class and the professor's teaching ability are what actually turns on the student.

Sex can be used to symbolize forced intimacy. A teenaged girl dreams recurrently about being told by her mother that she must have sex with her father. She reluctantly follows him into a bedroom, where he casually disrobes. The dreams end just before they do the deed. She's disgusted. In her waking life, her parents are divorced and her father is distant from the family. Her mother pushes her closer to her father, forcing her to have a relationship with him, but she doesn't want to be close with him. Her dreams turn the situation into a scenario of being forced to have sex with him. See: *Incest*.

Sex in a dream can express personal intimacy with what you create. A writer dreams about a sexually charged situation with a character he invented for a book he is writing. The dream reflects the closeness and intimacy he feels with the character. Our creations are often expressions of our inner lives. Story characters, in particular, reflect the writers that create them, so the leap from a story character to a dream-character is a short one.

A college-age female in a committed relationship with her boyfriend dreams about having sex with their mutual friends. She wonders whether she has a repressed desire to cheat, but instead the dreams reflect the intimate conversations she's been having with those mutual friends. It feels like cheating because she's sharing thoughts and feelings with them that she isn't sharing with her boyfriend.

Sex in a dream can be used to express thoughts and feelings that are intimate or private.

It can be used in association with jealousy. For example, a man dreams that his wife is having sex with her co-workers. He does not suspect she is cheating in waking life, but does feel a bit jealous of all the time she spends at work. The dream amplifies his feelings so he will consciously deal with them rather than ignore them. See: *Cheat, Jealous*.

It's easy to lose sight of the fact that the most basic purpose of sex is reproduction. Sex in a dream can be about pregnancy and related matters. See: *Pregnant*.

Sex in a dream can symbolize dominance and submission, giving and receiving. The symbolism derives from the roles played and positions assumed during sex. For example, dreaming about being on top during sex can symbolize being in a dominant position in a business deal or relation-

ship, or in some way taking the lead or getting on top. The dream can be about getting what you want and relate to sex only because it's used as a comparison to getting *something else* you want.

Sex that finishes soon after it starts can symbolize disappointment. Something doesn't live up to expectation. Something exciting or pleasurable ends too soon.

Sexual dream imagery that is absurd, inappropriate, or outrageous can be a sign of something out of kilter in a person's sexual attitudes and perceptions.

Interrupted sex in a dream can symbolize lacking privacy or opportunity for sex or masturbation. See: *Masturbate*.

If none of the other possibilities covered in this entry fits your dream, the possibility is strong that the dream is about integrating something new into yourself.

Dreams can draw on hundreds of euphemisms for sex to create symbolism: plowing a field, climbing a flagpole, hitting a home run. Just keep in mind that your dreams don't bring up sex just for the fun of it. Or do they? With dreams, anything is possible.

The possibilities for symbolism are endless, and this book goes to great lengths to explain the symbolism of sexually related dream imagery and themes. Use the entries listed below to continue your exploration of this subject.

See also: *Anal Sex, Bed, Bird Cage, Body, Breast, Castrate, Cheat, Cunnilingus, Egg, Fisting, Fellatio, Fireworks, Gay, Genitals, Incest, Lips, Love, Masturbate, Orange, Ovaries, Penis, Phallic Symbol, Pregnant, Rape, Testicles, Undress, Uterus, Vagina*

Sexual assault—See: *Rape*

Shadow—Shadow in a dream can represent something unknown. Shadow is an unseen area, and "to see" in a dream can symbolize awareness. At its simplest, a shadow is a dark area, and "dark" in a dream can mean bad or wrong. It can symbolize the dark side of people and situations, dark thoughts and feelings. But dark can simply mean unknown or mysterious. See: *Dark*.

Shadow can symbolize fear, especially when you react with fear to seeing a shadow. The shadow may represent an intangible fear, such as fear of the dark. It can symbolize danger, especially when you run from it. See: *Black, Fear*.

A shadow is cast by an object blocking light, so it can symbolize living in the shadow of another person, for example, a parent, sibling, or authority figure.

Shadow is a name given to the dark side of the ego, in which case it is capitalized. The ego is the CEO of the psyche, and the psyche is made of structures that interact together. But imagine that some or all of the employees (structures of the psyche) decide to follow a different leader, seduced over to the "dark side." That they rebel in secret against the ego, and are led by one particularly powerful character. The *Star Wars* mythology perfectly captures this idea because the Dark Lord, Emperor Palpatine, is in the midst of the good guys the whole time, secretly scheming and dividing people against each other, creating a void he fills to become supreme ruler.

Another classic shadow-character from the movie world is Scar from *The Lion King*, who kills Mufasa (the king) and takes over the pride. Scar is arrogant, devious, malicious, volatile, tyrannical. These are characteristics of the Shadow of the psyche. Shadow has "gone rogue" and takes over parts of the psyche or the whole thing. And the bigger the ego, the bigger its shadow. Shadow encompasses everything about you that's unwanted, unaccepted, unacknowledged, rejected, and repressed. See: *Ego*.

When you do something out of character, especially something that works against the agenda of your ego, you can bet that Shadow is at work. Shadow is known as the Trickster because it's slippery and misleading. It gets you to work against yourself.

For example, you forget about an important appointment but didn't really want to go, anyway. You inexplicably fall sick on the day of a test for which you're unprepared. You get into a car accident on a day when you really don't want to go to work. Notice in these cases that Shadow makes you act from your true feelings. Ha ha, joke's on you.

Shadow is why people sabotage their carefully constructed lives, go against their best intentions, or do the wrong thing despite knowing better. Shadow is a rebel, and it steps in when you don't have the guts to do something yourself. It brings to light everything you don't want to know about yourself.

Obviously, Shadow can be personally dangerous, especially when it's totally out of control and influences people and events against you. But the danger is compounded because your personal Shadow connects with the collective Shadow, what we call *evil*. It's all too easy to project your Shadow onto other people and hate them for it. And when that happens on a mass scale, it leads to horrible tragedies and abuses, such as the Holocaust and slavery. Know your own Shadow and own it, or it will own you. See: *Evil*.

However, Shadow is the gateway to the unconscious mind and a tremendous source of creativity. It prepares you for a deeper relationship with your unconscious—a relationship that potentially leads to an inner marriage with your anima or animus. You can think of Shadow as the person who stands up when the minister asks whether anyone objects to this marriage, and says, "Yeah, I do. That fool ain't ready." See: *Anima, Animus*.

Shadow usually manifests in dreams as a dark or shifty character, usually a human-character with dark skin and dressed in dark clothing, though it can take the form of an animal, monster, or invisible presence. Its face can be blurred or distinct— a blurred face is a hallmark of Shadow because it's a great way of depicting something that's missing in your self-awareness, and as you get to know your Shadow it'll take on more distinction. However, Shadow can take the form of any racial or ethnic group or subgroup: Hispanic, Asian, Italian, Gypsy, Latino, Polish, Russian—any group viewed as threatening or discriminated against.

Shadow's depiction as a particular race or ethnicity is based on stereotypes, fears, and perception, not on objective reality. Racial and ethnic stereotypes are deeply embedded in most cultures and closely connected with Shadow. It doesn't matter how enlightened you are, your dreaming mind can draw on these associations to create symbolism.

Shadow is the dream-character that helps you work against your interests. It convinces you that something's OK when it's really not. It seduces you into doing the wrong thing. It's the snake in the Garden of Eden that tells you to go ahead and eat the apple. It's the image in the mirror that points back at you when you wrongly try to blame someone else, and the part of yourself lurking behind the façade, just waiting to burst your bubble.

People who most strongly deny the existence of their Shadow side are often the most strongly in its grip. Think of the evangelist who rails against unmarried sex, then is caught with a prostitute. Or the politician who rails against gays and drugs, then is caught snorting coke off the naked body of a gay lover. They're victims of their own lack of self-awareness.

As Carl Jung said, "The shadow is a moral problem that challenges the whole ego-personality, for no one can become conscious of the shadow without considerable moral effort. To become conscious of it involves recognizing the dark aspects of the personality as present and real. This act is the essential condition for any kind of self-knowledge."

Shadow is an archetype. See: *Archetypes*.

See also: *Accomplice, Anima, Animus, Archetypes, Black, Dark, Emotions, Enemy, Evil, Fear, Gang, Psyche, Unconscious Mind*

Shallow—See: *Fishing*

Shapes—Shapes may show the internal configuration of your mind and how parts of the psyche fit together. In dreams, shapes often are shown through objects. So your dream doesn't just show you a circle, it shows you a basketball or a pizza. It doesn't just show you a rectangle, it shows you a rectangular house or pool. Then it weaves together a story around the symbolism of the shape.

Alternately, you can think of shapes as things that "shape" you, or what sort of "shape" you're in. The condition of an object or structure with a specific shape can speak volumes. For example, a deflated ball can symbolize feeling deflated, but if it's overinflated it can symbolize an inflated ego. A box can symbolize feeling "boxed in."

When shapes are important in a dream, you will sense it. They will stick out somehow to you.

The entries listed below go into depth about this subject.

See also: *Ball, Building. Circle, Group, Psyche, Pyramid, Rectangle, Spiral, Square*

Shark—Dreaming about sharks can be a sign to watch your back. People can be like sharks—predatory, stealthy, relentless—and swimming with sharks is inherently dangerous. Someone could be out to get you, or you have a general sense to be wary. For example, women who mistrust men and their intentions can dream about men in general as a pack of sharks, and about specific men as sharks.

A shark can symbolize something you fear. See: *Fear*.

A shark can symbolize a person or situation that can turn on you at any moment.

It can symbolize wild or predatory instincts, such as an instinct to attack or to take advantage of weakness. It can symbolize taking advantage of misfortune or trust.

It can symbolize dangerous emotions. Water is associated with emotion, and sharks are dangerous. See: *Water*.

A shark can symbolize something dangerous lurking below the threshold of your awareness. See: *Subconscious*.

"Shark" is used to describe a person who is almost unbeatable at card games or billiards, or at any game or competition. The word is used on Wall Street to describe its top players, and used to describe lawyers. The association is derived from sharks being merciless predators.

Sharks in a frenzy can symbolize something that drives people wild, or hysteria.

Sharks are unpredictable, and people can be unpredictable, too, especially when gathered in packs or groups. Sharks prey on weakness and smell blood in the water. Does that describe someone you know, or characterize a situation you're in or something you've observed?

See also: *Animals, Attack, Eaten, Fear, Panic, Subconscious*

Shed—See: *Barn*

Ship—See: *Boat*

Shirt—First, read: *Clothing*.

As a covering for the upper part of the body, a shirt can symbolize a way that you protect your feelings and emotions. The color of a shirt, in particular, is connected with emotions that arise in conjunction with memories as your mind sorts and collates your memories from the previous day. For example, wearing a red shirt can connect with emotions related to anger, love, vitality, or shame. Wearing a yellow shirt can connect with emotions related to optimism and hope. See: *Colors*.

Being shirtless in a dream can symbolize being broke.

Stealing a shirt can symbolize scrounging for the basic necessities of life. If you feel guilty about it, it can simply connect with something you feel guilty about. Stretch the idea and it can connect with ideas such as feeling like a fake or imposter, or taking credit for something you don't deserve. Stealing a shirt that belongs to someone you know can symbolize wanting to assume something about that person's identity or life. See: *Imposter*.

A stain on your shirt can symbolize a stain on your emotions or reputation. A shirt is particularly visible to people who view you, so it can connect closely with the impressions you make. Keep in mind that dream-characters can be projections of you, so you can see a stain on someone's shirt in a dream and it still connects back to you. Or, characters can represent people you know. For example, you dream about a neighbor with blood on his shirt after you hear that neighbor getting into a heated argument.

A torn-up shirt can symbolize tattered emotions, or just generally that things have been rough. You feel beat up, tattered. Or you need time to compose yourself. Think of some way that you have to present yourself or make an impression and how a torn-up shirt can say that you aren't ready. The same idea applies to the other variations of shirt symbolism listed here.

Washing a shirt can symbolize cleaning up your emotions or self-image.

Ironing a shirt can symbolize organizing yourself, or preparing to present yourself. It can mean you're straightening out a situation, straightening out yourself, or getting ready to make a good impression. In this sense, it's similar to talking to yourself in a mirror. It can symbolize preparing yourself mentally. For women, ironing a shirt can symbolize her body preparing for menstruation. See: *Menstruation*.

A wrinkled shirt can symbolize an emotional life in disarray, or something related to putting in the time and effort to make the best presentation. The wrinkled shirt is a physical representation of a personal situation.

See also: *Blood, Clothing, Closet, Colors, Imposter, Menstruation, Mirror*

Shit—See: *Excrement*

Shock—See: *Lightning*

Shoes—Shoes are put on when one is ready to travel, ready to move. Movement in dreams is associated with movement in your life. You're "going places," or at least are ready to make progress.

Work is a common area of life addressed through the use of shoe symbolism, because work is closely associated with movement in life. Some types of shoes are associated with work, such as boots or pumps.

Feeling confident about your shoes can symbolize feeling confident about your job or a role you play in life, such as friend or spouse. It can mean you have standing, meaning authority, power, or influence. See: *Leg*.

Missing or lacking shoes can mean you feel that you don't have standing. It can symbolize being financially broke, or lacking what you need to go to the places in life where you want to be.

Losing your shoes can mean you've lost your motivation, desire, or energy.

Shoes are associated with wear and tear, and a dream can use that association to speak to the wear and tear on your body. It shows the mileage you've accumulated. Dreaming about worn-out shoes can connect with having a busy life and feeling the effects of it.

Shoes are associated with preparation, especially preparation to be busy. For example, a woman dreams about cleaning her running shoes, reflecting her thoughts about getting ready for the Christmas holiday. She knows she'll be doing a lot of running around to get ready, and is preparing psychologically. Notice that running shoes and running around connect, and are a clue to the meaning that's hidden in plain sight.

Buying new shoes can symbolize taking on a new job or relationship, and related ideas. For example, a newly divorced woman dreams about buying stiletto heels, which are connected with her thoughts about getting back into the dating scene. This detail stands out because she never wears stilettos, but she associates them with attractive women. It means she's thinking about ways of attracting another man.

Shoes are associated with moving on—from a relationship, a time of life, a pattern or habit. For example, a woman dreams about going back to her ex-boyfriend's place to retrieve shoes she left behind. She's determined to get them back, but in reality she didn't leave any shoes behind, so the shoe-dream must be symbolism. It represents her readiness to move on from the relationship. Her thoughts had been lingering on it, and she decided that time had come to cut all ties.

Heavy shoes, or being unable to find your shoes, can symbolize difficulty moving on, such as after a breakup. It can symbolize being stuck in place, such as in a job or relationship. It can symbolize lack of progress in your career or inner life.

Heavy shoes can symbolize lethargy, lack of motivation, depression, or difficulty with physical movement, especially if movement is hindered by heavy body weight.

Shoes are put on before leaving, so if you dream about your shoes missing, it can mean you lack something you need to move forward in your life: opportunity, gumption, money, personal vision.

Because shoes come in pairs, they can be used to symbolize a pairing, such as a couple. And because shoes have soles, they can be used as a wordplay for "soul." Put soul together with the idea of a pairing, and shoes can symbolize the desire for a soulmate.

Shoes are closely associated with feet. See: *Feet*.

Tying shoelaces can symbolize final preparations.

See also: *Clothing, Embark, Feet, Journey, Leg, Locker, Run, Soul*

Shoot—See: *Gun*

Shop—Shopping in a dream can symbolize making choices or decisions. It's associated with options, such as when choosing from a menu. See: *Menu*.

Shopping for clothes can tie in with a person's importance and image. It can connect with making choices and decisions about your outer identity or persona. Clothes cover you and say a lot about a person in one glance. For example, a "man in uniform," an executive in a Brooks Brothers suit, a woman out on the town wearing an Armani gown, and a person wearing a T-shirt emblazoned with the words "I'm with stupid" across the front. Each creates a distinctly different impression. See: *Clothing*.

The type of shop and what you shop for can indicate the subject of the symbolism. For example, shopping for groceries can relate to your food choices and things you consume, including nonmaterial things, such as information, entertainment, and opinion. See: *Eat, Food, Grocery Store*.

Shopping in a toy store can connect with childhood and maturity. Choosing to return items to a toy store can mean you have decided to present a more adult image. See: *Toys*.

Shopping can mean "shop around." For example, you can shop around for a spouse or just a date, for a job, for a better deal—anything involving choices and decisions. To explore this idea further, see: *Mall*.

Obsessions and addictions involve choices, and shopping can be an obsession or addiction, creating two potential layers of association. See: *Addict*.

For some people, shopping is a major part of their social lives. See: *Friends*.

Having disposable income with which to shop is a sign of status and an indicator of having leisure time. See: *Money*.

Shopping is related to finances—stories abound of spouses and children costing a bundle and running up the credit cards. See: *Wallet*.

The price of something can connect with the personal price, such as the price of friendship or of failure.

Think further and consider associations such as bumping into someone unexpectedly while shopping. For example, dreaming about bumping into an old friend at a store can symbolize the choices you make about your friends. The dream is making a comparison or contrast between then and now. See: *Old Friend*.

The front of a store is the public face of a business, and in dreams that idea can connect with public aspects of your work life, such as your reputation, image, or publicity. It can connect with the idea of "open for business" or "accepting new clients." For an example of a storefront used as symbolism, see: *Fisting*.

See also: *Addict, Bankrupt, Chase, Clothing, Eat, Fisting, Food, Grocery Store, Job, Mall, Menu, Money, Old Friend, Toys, Wallet*

Shoreline—See: *Beach*

Short—When dreams refer to the size of something, it can be a physical representation. For example, you dream about looking in the mirror and appearing shorter than you think you should, symbolizing that you do not have the "high" social status you want. Or you've been "taken down a notch."

"Short" can be used in the sense of "the time is short" and "short-tempered."

"Short" can mean "low opinion" or "low status." See: *Below*.

When "short" is used in the sense of a shirt or coat that's too short, it can mean that something doesn't fit you. It's a physical representation, such as when you try to be a tough guy, but the image doesn't fit your personality.

See also: *Below, Clothing, Giant, Little*

Shot—See: *Ammunition, Bullet, Gun, Inject*

Shoulder—Shoulders are associated with the idea behind the phrase "shoulder the load." The symbolism connects with taking on the majority of work or carrying a heavy load of responsibilities.

The shoulder is a multidirectional joint and that association can be used to symbolize multiple approaches to the same situation, or personal flexibility.

See also: *Body, Elbow, Job, Knee*

Shout—See: *Yell*

Shower—Taking a shower in a dream can mean you want to cleanse yourself of something. When people feel dirty they need to take a metaphorical shower, to cleanse. The same idea applies to guilt and related feelings of shame and disgust. You want to rid yourself of the residue.

For example, a young woman dreams she is taking a shower and the shower head turns into the face of her boyfriend. She screams at him to leave, feeling violated. The dream is about her feeling that her boyfriend is invading her life, especially her personal space, and her reaction to his sudden presence speaks volumes.

Along these lines, a shower is a place where privacy is usually expected, so intrusions while showering can symbolize intrusions into your privacy, or embarrassment.

On the other hand, perhaps you want to be seen. You're not embarrassed when people see the real you, stripped of all pretense. A dream can express that idea as people watching you as you shower and you enjoy it or allow it. See: *Naked*.

A shower in a dream can connect with a physical need for cleansing, a message from your body to cleanse it, especially of impurities and toxins.

A dream could put a clever twist on a shower to mean "shower with attention" or "shower with gifts" and actually show it as a shower of water or objects. You'll be able to tell by your feelings and other details of the dream. For example, to shower with attention can be symbolized as taking a shower in public and enjoying it. To shower with gifts could be symbolized as taking a shower beneath a Christmas tree.

See also: *Bathroom, Clean, Intruder, Locker, Naked, Undress, Water*

Shrink—Shrinking in a dream can mean "diminish." Such as when your respect, hope, fear, prospects, enthusiasm, or bank account diminishes.

The symbolism shows in a dream a man had about having sex with a super-hot woman. Halfway through, she starts shrinking and gets tinier and tinier. The woman represents his wife, and her shrinking while having sex with him is a way of saying he's enjoying sex less with her. She's gained a lot of weight since they got married, and it means more work for him in the bedroom because their bodies don't fit together the way they used to. He still loves his wife and loves sex with her, but his enjoyment of it is shrinking.

A woman dreams about being pursued by a huge monster. The dreams recur and every time she sees the monster she runs for her life. Finally, one night she gets sick of running and turns to confront the monster. When she does, it shrinks, and what's left is a small child looking scared and alone. The story is about her running from the needs of the child within her. The big monster is a classic image of overblown fear. Once it's confronted, it shrinks back to a manageable size.

See also: *Fear, Giant, Little, Psychologist*

Sick—See: *Illness*

Sister—A sister can be used in a wide variety of ways as symbolism. Begin narrowing down the possibilities by answering two questions. Is the person used as a character in the dream your actual sister (not an imaginary character), and if yes, has she been part of your life recently, or on your mind?

If you don't have a sister, you can bet that the character in the dream symbolizes something about you, or is a surrogate for someone in your life who's like a sister. There's no chance that the character depicted as a sister could be in the story in relation to recent interaction with her, thoughts and feelings you have about her, or parts of yourself that you also see in her, symbolized by the character. Those possibilities are in play only if you actually have a sister, or if the character is a surrogate for someone in your life who's like a sister.

If you have a sister and she's been part of recent events in your life, you're likely to see her in your dreams. Your mind will touch on those memories at some point while doing its nightly review and brain tune-up, otherwise known as dreaming. Your dreams will touch on your thoughts, feelings, and emotions connected with your interaction with your sister(s) and everything associated with that event.

It's possible that your sister is only in the story in reference to the event. If so, she's unlikely to play a central role in the story because the dream isn't about her.

The character can symbolize your thoughts, feelings, and emotions about her—a projection of you, not necessarily her. In the dream, if your sister behaves out of character, it's almost certain to be a projection. The character is following a script you wrote subconsciously, to show what's happening in your inner world. Even when her actions and behavior in the dream are based on something you've observed about her, it's still based on your perceptions. With dream-characters, a dream can use exaggeration and comparison, the same as it does with other symbols.

For example, a young man dreams about his sister competing in a pageant, reflecting his observations about her love life. See: *Casino*.

Then again, in a dream your sister can act just like she is in your waking life—the good, bad, and everything in between. In which case, pay more attention to how you act and react in the dream, because while some dreams can replay events pretty much as they happen and show people as they are, ultimately the dream is about you, not them.

Your sister can appear in a dream in reference to a past event, situation, or time of life together, such as while you were growing up together. See: *Childhood Home, Family Home.*

She can symbolize something you associate with her, such as a trait, quality, or ability, and it's likely to be something that's either a way of telling the story, or something about yourself that you also see in her.

For example, your sister is good with words and you're writing a memoir or a wedding toast, or you're thinking through how to say something to someone in just the right way. She's in your dream because she's good with words and you're trying to be good with words, too.

Or your sister is emotionally open and you're not, but you need to be because you have emotions you need to express. You then dream about your sister as a symbol of being more emotionally open. The dream might even use her to show you what you need to know and convey advice from the unconscious.

Any sort of sister in your dream can symbolize general associations with sisters, such as someone to confide in, or a "sisterly talk."

A sister in a dream can represent a relationship with someone in your life who's like a sister to you, such as a best friend. It's a way of saying that a relationship with a female is special. People have been known to have sex dreams about their sister, and the character is used as a surrogate for someone in your life who's like a sister. It's often in connection with exploring the idea of taking the relationship beyond the friend zone, into being romantic or sexual.

Does the relationship have that potential, and do you risk ruining it if you try to take that next step? Your dream will try to answer those questions for you, or at least do its best to help you answer them for yourself. In many cases, you already know the answers and just need help making the connection.

dream-characters are shown together in the same scene or adjacent scenes as a way of making connections between them. For example, if your sister is a mother and she appears in the same scene with your mother, it can connect with something related to parenthood. Sister and mom are shown together because they're both moms. A sister and a friend can appear together because you think of your friend as a sister, or your sister as a friend.

Sexual interaction with a sister in a dream can symbolize something that's forbidden or taboo. See: *Incest.*

A sister-character can be used as a surrogate for another family member, such as a mom, and vice versa—especially if they are a lot alike.

A sister-character can be used in the sense of something related to you, not a family relation but a personal one. Such as, you're known publicly because of a particular talent of yours, and though it's something people know about you, it's not *you*. It's what you do, not who you are, closely related to you, like a sister. This use of the symbolism is particularly likely if the sister-character is imaginary.

A sister is someone you witness going through changes, such as from child to adult, an association your dreams can use to tell a story about changes you see in yourself or someone you know.

A female who was recently dumped by her boyfriend for someone else dreams about seeing him and his new girlfriend in bed together. No sex is involved; they are just happy and in love, the same as they are in the Facebook pictures of them together that the dreamer recently saw. Then the dreamer's sister—not her real sister, an imaginary character—comes in and hops into bed with them and it's all clean fun. It's a projection of the dreamer's desires. She wants to be the girl with whom her ex is happy and in love. It's a way of projecting herself into the scene, but without being obvious. If she saw herself in bed with her ex and his new girlfriend, she'd react differently.

Finally, a sister in a dream can mix and match with other meanings of sister, such as a nun or sorority sister.

Read the entry for *Brother*, too. The symbolism works much the same.

See also: *Brother, Childhood Home, Incest, Family, Family Home, Friend, Old Friend, Woman*

Skin—Skin is the most visible part of your body. As an outer covering it can be used to symbolize something about your outward identity, the part of you seen publicly. Wounding to the skin can symbolize a blemish on your reputation or damage to your persona. See: *Persona*.

For example, a young woman dreams that a skinless creature with a knife wants to skin her alive. They fight epically and end up in the street, where the creature is hit by a city bus. The dream symbolizes a situation with her former employer. She sued the company and her former supervisor retaliated by spreading rumors about her. In the skinless creature, she sees a projection of her raw and wounded feelings related to a public dispute.

Because skin is sensitive, it can symbolize emotional or physical sensitivity. For example, a painful burn on your skin can symbolize being "burned" emotionally, or burned by an argument. It's a physical representation of a personal situation. The same idea can be expressed by scratches, bruises, and stings. These ideas are fleshed out more in the entries listed below, especially: *Knife, Wound*.

Skin can be used to refer to pain in another part of the body. Skin is a part of the body more likely than others to experience pain, so it can be used by dreams as a general reference to pain, especially pain experienced while sleeping. For example, a dream about being too close to a fire and feeling a burn can symbolize the pain of a sunburn. See: *Pain*.

Figures of speech come into play as possibilities for the symbolism. Dreams can enact phrases like "skinned alive" and "get under my skin" as a way of expressing the dynamics of a situation and your feelings. Something under your skin in the figurative sense can be portrayed in a dream as an object such as a splinter or an insect. You can feel as if you want to crawl out of your skin. Something can make your skin crawl, which is a way of saying it disturbs, frightens, or disgusts you.

The bark of a tree can symbolize skin, as can the outside of a house or skin of a tent. In this sense, skin is what protects you.

See also: *Body, Creature, Knife, Makeup, Mask, Naked, Pain, Snake, Tree, Undress*

Skinny—See: *Emaciated*

Skyscraper—The size of something in a dream can be used as a comparison, and a skyscraper is ripe for comparison with high ambitions, huge ego, tremendous standing, or monumental effort. It can be used to indicate a big amount, such as how much you love or admire someone and look up to that person.

It can be used in the sense of "stand tall," meaning confidence in abilities and recognition for achievements, or "stand your ground," "top of the heap," "king of the hill," or "top-level."

A skyscraper can symbolize your body. It can symbolize an aspect of your mind, or your psyche. See: *Building*.

A skyscraper can symbolize a center of power, in your outer life or inner life. For example, a man dreams about going to a fortified skyscraper and finding his dark nemesis on the top floor, symbolizing the place in his mind where his Shadow side is entrenched.

A tall building can be used to give perspective, because the view from the top oversees everything.

A skyscraper can even symbolize a tall person. From the perspective of a child, adults appear to be giants.

The top of a skyscraper can be a lonely place and can symbolize a feeling of isolation.

See also: *Above, Building, City, Elevator, Shadow, Tree*

Slave—See: *Servant*

Sleep—Falling asleep in a dream can reflect thoughts about being able to go to and stay asleep, especially if you have concerns about getting to sleep or getting enough of it. People who toss and turn while trying to go to sleep are known to dream about frustration related to sleep.

Sleep can be used in the sense of being unaware. The symbolism is the same as coma. If a person is described as asleep, it means he or she is blissfully ignorant. Falling asleep in a dream can symbolize a period of time when you drifted away from reality. It means "zoned out" or "asleep on your feet." Reflect on the day before the dream and try to remember if that happened. See: *Coma*.

Falling asleep in a dream can indicate a need for rest and recuperation. It can mean it's better presently just to get deep sleep rather than to dream intensely. And it simply reflect the sleeping state of your body while dreaming.

See also: *Body, Coma, Dream Within a Dream, Nightmare, Sleep Paralysis, Wake Up, Zombie*

Sleep Paralysis—Sleep paralysis is a state of muscle paralysis while dreaming so that you don't act out your dreams or harm yourself. Also known as REM atonia, it's normal, and a source of much confusion and some of the most intense experiences a person can have.

The experience of waking up paralyzed is terrifying enough, especially if you don't understand what's happening. Add to it the fact that dream imagery overlays what your open eyes are seeing—and the feeling of terror, and that your dreaming mind responds to feelings and other stimuli by producing symbolic imagery—and you have a recipe for what's called a "waking nightmare."

Sleep paralysis is believed to be a source of reported experiences of alien abduction and demonic presence. That's not to say that it explains all experiences of abduction or demons, but it can explain why there are so many reports of people being in bed asleep, waking up paralyzed and seeing creatures in the room. The person experiences fear and terror because he or she is paralyzed, confused, and afraid. The dreams translate the feelings into imagery of something frightening. For some people, aliens are frightening, perhaps their worst fear. Other people see shadowy figures, demons, or something along that line.

It's simply your dreaming mind translating the feelings of fear into related imagery.

If you experience sleep paralysis, focus on your breathing. Breathe deeply. The extra oxygen will wake up your system, and knowing you can control at least one bodily process helps to lessen fear. Subjects have reported that a few deep breaths breaks their sleep paralysis and dispels the hallucinatory imagery.

See also: *Demon, Dream Within a Dream, Nightmare, UFO, Weak*

Slow—See: *Speed*

Snake—Interpreting dreams about snakes depends primarily on your associations with snakes and how snakes are used in the dream-story. The variations run the gamut. To some people, snakes are feared and loathed. Just the thought of a snake makes their skin crawl. To others, snakes are symbols of temptation and evil. To still others, snakes are associated with good health, virility, transformation, and the presence or blessing of God.

These associations form the basis of dream symbolism. The process of making associations can be as simple as whatever comes to mind first in relation to a snake. If I say "snake," you say "_____?"

The snake is an enigmatic dream symbol that can't be interpreted using pat definitions. Instead, dig into the story and analyze.

How a snake is presented in your dream and how you react to it gives you a good idea of what it symbolizes. Is the snake dangerous, or just chillin'? Do you run in terror at the sight of it, or play with it? What role does the snake have in the dream-story, and what actions, if any, does it take? Where is the snake encountered and who, if anyone, is with you?

Begin with a common use of snake symbolism. Snakes are known for being venomous, and as symbolism snakes can represent venomous people and situations. For example, venomous people poison your thoughts or feelings. They're a bad influence and say things that hurt; they're "mean as a snake." They strike and lash out. They're reptilian in their approach to life, only looking out for themselves. Everyday comparisons between people and venomous snakes are common, so for dreams it's an easy connection to make. See: *Venom*.

If that's how the symbolism is used in your dream, you'll see it in the dream-story. The snake will be a venomous variety. It will bite and inject venom, or you will fear that happening. If the snake is not venomous, does not strike out, does not bite or provoke fear, then it's probably not related to the symbolism of venom. See: *Inject*.

Dreams make comparisons based on your personal associations, and fear is a common association with snakes. They can symbolize anything that you fear: people, places, situations—or just the idea of something, such as speaking in public or health problems. If you fear it, a dangerous snake can symbolize it. The idea can be stretched from here to Mars. For example, fear of getting into trouble, of failing a test, or of losing something you love can be symbolized as fear of a snake. See: *Fear*.

But if you don't fear snakes, then they're not likely to be used in your dreams to symbolize fear. Or if the snake is not a killer, then you have nothing to fear. Of course, some people fear any snake, so again, it depends on you and how you react to snakes in general and specifically to the snakes in your dreams.

If you dream about overcoming fear of a snake, it's a strong indicator of overcoming a fear of snakes or some other fear symbolized by them.

Another word that sums up a situation with a snake is "danger." This use of the symbolism is especially likely in scenarios where a snake rattles, or the situation is dangerous.

A snake blocking your path can symbolize an obstacle to getting to where you want to be in life.

Constricting situations in life are comparable to the killing method of boa constrictors and pythons. You feel suffocated, such as by a relationship, expectation, or duty. Something has a hold on you and won't let go. The life is squeezed out of you. Situations in the work world can feel like a noose around the neck as the demands of the job sap the life out of you. People can become "ensnared" in all sorts of ways. See: *Strangle*.

However, dreams are clever and varied with how they use symbolism. A constrictor snake can symbolize the need to loosen up. You're wrapped too tightly.

A snake wrapped around the neck can describe a restricted airway while asleep, or poor blood circulation. A snake wrapped around a limb of the body can be a way of visualizing the sensation of a limb that's "dead" because you fell asleep on it.

Snakes are known for attacking out of the blue. They can lie still and hidden for hours waiting for lunch to wander past. This characteristic of snakes can describe people and situations, too. Some people lie in wait for an opportunity to attack. Situations can be fraught with potential for danger summed up in the image of a snake waiting to attack. See: *Ambush, Attack*.

Picture how a snake eats. It engulfs, opens its mouth and swallows whole. Imagine the possibilities for how that image can be used as symbolism. A relationship can engulf. A job can be all-consuming. An addiction or desire can encompass a person's life. See: *Devour*.

In the story of the Garden of Eden, a snake tempts Eve to eat of the fruit of the Tree of Knowledge of Good and Evil. It symbolizes humans' separation from nature and natural instincts, and has evolved as a general symbol of temptation and evil. That association can be used for a snake to symbolize Shadow. See: *Shadow*.

But wait, snakes aren't all bad!

The possibilities covered so far are all negative, but snakes are marvelous creatures that have many positive associations that can be used as symbolism.

Snakes live in the ground and that closeness to the Earth creates a strong association with nature. Nature is associated with wisdom, fertility, and instincts. Snakes are used in rituals to bless crops for a good harvest and bless people with fertility and health. Cultural associations play a strong role in dream symbolism, especially with snakes because of the broad spectrum of perceptions and associations from culture to culture. See: *Earth*.

Snakes are connected with nature, which goes through cycles, and with renewal and health. When you're ill, sometimes the best medicine is to listen closely to your body and give it what it needs. Snakes are highly sensitive to their environment and sense the slightest vibrations. That sensitivity can be used to create associations with sensitivity to the subtle signs and signals from your body.

Women thinking about starting a family are known to dream about snakes; in particular, green snakes. The color green is associated with nature and fertility. A green snake in a tree is a particularly strong indicator because trees are also associated with families. See: *Tree*.

The color of a snake can be a modifier that defines the symbolism. See: *Colors*.

A snakebite, especially a bite on the wrist or hand, is known to be associated with a call from inside a person to "shed your skin" and transform. The idea extends further to include the need to take action. The hand is used to take action, so a bite to the hand can be a reminder or warning to act while you can. This use of the symbolism extends to any situation in which a snake strikes. For more ideas, see: *Bite*.

Snakes are used on the Rod of Asclepius, which is the basis of the caduceus, a symbol associated with medicine. The good-health associations stem from a snake's ability to renew itself by shedding its skin. This idea has strong connections also with personal development and the psyche, because "shedding your skin" means letting go of the old to allow something new to emerge.

Another very positive association exists between snakes and kundalini. Kundalini is an energy that rises out of the hips, travels up the spine, and emerges out of the forehead or crown of the head to connect with the "upper realm." It's visualized as two snakes intertwined and traveling up the spine. A snake emerging from the head is a symbol of deep insight and enlightenment.

The long, cylindrical shape of snakes creates an association with the penis. The association is easily stretched to include males in general. "All men are snakes," a frustrated woman says. Taken further, snakes are associated with everything about men and masculinity, positive and negative. See: *Penis, Phallic Symbol*.

As with all symbolism, look at the action to determine the meaning. If the snake crawls up your leg under your pants, it might be a phallic symbol. But if the snake is on a rock sunning itself, it might symbolize something "warming up," as in "warming up to the idea."

See also: *Bite, Cage, Colors, Devour, Evil, Inject, Penis, Phallic Symbol, Reptile, Shadow, Skin, Strangle, Venom*

Snoop Dogg—Famous people and celebrities appear often in dreams, but few of them are in the Hall of Fame. Snoop is a huge figure in the cultural landscape, so it's not surprising that he appears in dreams. The surprise is the frequency, at least from a macro perspective.

As with other famous people, the key is to connect your associations with Snoop Dogg with the dream-story and ask what it says about you.

Snoop Dogg is used in dreams in connection with the association with him as a party animal. He's almost always high, and his persona is shaped around it.

He's used in dreams in connection with his success as a musician, which dreams can use to launch into a story about musical ability or desire for fame and success.

He's used to symbolize someone who's admired, someone who grew up in a tough environment and made good. That association could be used in a dream-story about overcoming adversity.

He can represent someone respected for his style and social prominence.

Check out the entry for *Kanye West*, too.

See also: *Addict, Drugs, Famous, Kanye West, Music*

Snow—See: *Winter*

Sodomy—See: *Anal Sex*

Soldier—See: *Army*

Son—See: *Daughter*. The entry covers many possibilities for symbolism and all you have to do is substitute "son" for "daughter" and masculine traits for feminine traits.

Soul—Soul is commonly perceived as the inner essence of a person, also thought of as your internal self. But think more broadly, and remember that dreams create physical representations of personal situations.

For example, a dream about the souls of neighborhood children rising into the sky connects with the dreamer's perception that people must sacrifice something essential about themselves to afford to live in his neighborhood, and for parents who work all the time, it means sacrificing time with their children.

Soul can also be used in the sense of "that guy has soul." It means a person has depth and special personal qualities. He or she is authentic. If you dream that someone does not have a soul, it can mean you perceive him or her as shallow. He has no heart. She's fake. See: *Fake, Imposter.*

Soul can refer to something that affects you deeply, "heart and soul."

A dream about losing your soul can symbolize the sense that you're losing something essential about yourself. Something is draining the life out of you. Or you are losing a special connection, either with another person or with something related to spirituality or your inner being. See: *Blood.*

Soul in a dream can refer to a man's anima or a woman's animus. See: *Anima, Animus.*

Soul can refer to your connection with God and spirituality. See: *God.*

It can be used in a story about your inner development and spiritual life, or your connection with your fellow human beings. See: *Collective Unconscious.*

It can show your positive connections with other people and with nature. See: *Earth.*

Be sure to also read: *Spirit.*

See also: *Ancestor, Anima, Animus, Ascend, Blood, Collective Unconscious, Earth, Fake, God, Imposter, Possession, Spirit*

Space—Outer space is commonly associated with mystery, wonder, and unfathomable vastness.

Dreams can use these associations to create stories about the mysteries of human existence and the wonder of life. They can paint pictures about something that, while obviously not as vast as outer space, is comparable in some way, such as the vastness of the mind and the ability to imagine anything.

Space is associated with the unknown. It can be a theme in dreams about venturing into new territory in your life. For example, you go to college and a whole new world opens up for you for exploration. Or you desire to travel and have new experiences.

Outer space can be used to symbolize something that's far, far away. Extremely remote or distant, or seems that way—having children, retirement, the love you used to feel for your ex, the help you need.

Space captures the imagination, especially in young minds, and it certainly can be used to symbolize your imagination, or even the potential of it for those of you who don't think you're very imaginative. But we don't really know what's out there, and what we do know only scratches the surface. That desire to know is the same burning passion that's compelled people to scale the highest mountains and explore the deepest oceans. In this sense, space can symbolize something strongly alluring. The idea is tied up with destiny and finding your calling.

Inner space is also mysterious and endlessly vast, making outer space a great metaphor to describe your inner world and the exploration of it. If you look at your body from the standpoint of the nucleus of an atom, it's mostly empty space, and if you take out all atomic-level gaps from a body, you can fit what's left—what's actually there—in the bottom of a teaspoon. In other words, you are mostly empty space.

Long-time meditators and other people who train their minds to be still report experiences of sensing the incredible vastness within themselves. Like a fish suddenly aware of the immensity of the ocean, or astronaut Edgar Mitchell flying in a metal can between the moon and Earth. You are a microcosm of the macrocosm. To say it another way, the universe is within you, and your mind *and* body are made in its image.

When space in a dream is accompanied by a sense of loneliness or isolation, it can symbolize the feeling of being lonely or isolated. Perhaps you have difficulty relating to, or connecting with, people.

A similar situation is when a person feels misunderstood. People don't "get you." You can feel as if you are from another planet. The dream makes the connection through the feeling. See: *Stranger*.

Being on another planet in a dream can symbolize the sense that you and another person or group of people are on a different wavelength, or see the world from completely different viewpoints. "Men are from Mars, and women are from Venus."

Being on another planet can mean "outside of reality."

Space is thought of as a void—thought it's really not—and that association can be used to say that something is missing. You have a void in yourself or your life.

Space is airless, and that association can create symbolism connected with difficulty breathing. You dream you suddenly find yourself in space and unable to breathe. See: *Strangle*.

Out in space is a great metaphor for being lost. See: *Lost*.

See also: *Earth, Empty, Jupiter, Lost, Mars, Mercury, Meteor, Saturn, Stranger, Strangle, UFO, Venus*

Speed—Speed in a dream can symbolize the pace of your life. A snail's pace means things don't happen quickly enough. Driving too fast can mean things happen too quickly. It's a physical representation of a personal situation, and it applies widely to situations and events in life and to what's happening in your head and heart.

Think about the speed of a romantic relationship. Some people cautiously feel their way forward, and others jump right in, full speed ahead, like riding a rocket. One's a tortoise and the other's a hare. See: *Rocket*.

Speed is associated with vehicles. See: *Car*.

Speed can be used to symbolize fast or slow talking. Health can decline or recover quickly. Life can go by slowly or quickly. A situation can change rapidly, not fast enough, or too fast for comfort. A heart can beat rapidly, which will translate into dream imagery if it happens while you're asleep.

Speed can be used in the sense of the pace toward getting to a goal, or pace of a project. It can refer to how long it takes to learn something, to do something, or to get a point.

High speed is associated with excitement. For example, riding a racing roller coaster in a dream can symbolize something that excites you, especially related to accomplishment, drug use, and good sex. Or it can be used by a dream to trigger similar feelings, and that's how you connect the imagery with your life. You ask, What's going on in my life now, or what am I looking forward to, that's thrilling or exciting or terrifying or a rush like a roller coaster?

Use the entries listed below to explore the many ways dreams can use speed as symbolism or to modify symbolism.

See also: *Airplane, Boat, Bullet, Car, Highway, Hummingbird, Jet, Meteor, Motorcycle, River, Rocket, Roller Coaster, Tornado, Turtle*

Sphere—See: *Circle*

Spider—Creatures that cause anxiety, such as spiders, snakes, and roaches, can symbolize it. The imagery is used to trigger feelings and emotions relevant to your waking life; so if you have been feeling anxiety, then your dreams are likely to produce imagery that triggers it. Doing so helps process the feelings and expose their source, even provide ways of dealing with them. And if you can overcome an anxiety symbolized as a spider, the benefit can carry over directly into your waking life.

Spiders are known for their webs, associated in dreams with webs that people weave and situations that entangle. Extramarital affairs and business schemes are situations known to spark dreams about webs or spiders.

Fear of spiders can be fodder for dreams. In a dream, a guy at work sees a big spider. A co-worker traps it in a jar and the refraction of the glass makes it look massive. The magnifying effect symbolizes the dreamer's "blown up" fear of spiders, and the co-worker symbolizes the fearless quality the dreamer needs to gain perspective.

Some spiders are venomous and therefore dangerous, so something like a black widow bite in a dream can describe poisons such as excessive drinking, a poisonous voice in your mind, or a person who is a terrible influence. See: *Black Widow*.

However, most dream symbols have an alternate definition, something that makes sense when you step back. Spiders are most closely associated with fear and treachery. But judge from your feelings and reactions, not the overt image. For example, a mother dreams that spiders are all over her house and they completely wrap it in silky webs. Someone enters the house and the spiders wrap the person in silky strands. She's no fan of spiders, but these spiders make her feel loved and protected.

The dream occurs at a time when she's thinking through ways of bringing in extra income. She's the breadwinner in the family and for the past decade has supported her family well. She's a little worried about how she's going to bring in extra income, and the dream is showing her that the love and protection she gives her family will carry her through. The spiders represent her protective, motherly instincts, like the mother spider in *Charlotte's Web*.

See also: *Black Widow, Cocoon, Fear, Venom*

Spiral—Spiral shapes are common in dreams about the development of the psyche in the quest toward wholeness. The spiral is basically a circle leading toward a center, and that image sums up the process of becoming whole as a person, of actualizing your potential, what Carl Jung calls *individuation*. See: *Individuation*.

In the image of a spiral you see progress, coming to points in life where you were previously, but this time are further along, and next time around you'll be further along still. Whether or not it represents progress in your outer life or inner life depends on the direction of movement. Center-out movement shows progress in your outer life. Out-side-in shows progress in your inner life. Clockwise movement is toward your outer life, and counter-clockwise movement is toward your inner life.

Circular movement around a central point, especially if it's a tornado, symbolizes the energy of the psyche. See: *Circle, Tornado*.

A dream could use a spiral to show lack of progress, too. You can tell the difference from your feelings. When you make progress in your life or your consciousness, it feels good.

To further explore the symbolism of spirals and relation to consciousness, look up Dan Winter's explanation of infinite nondestructive compression.

See also: *Chakras, Circle, Ego, Individuation, Psyche, Pyramid, Tornado*

Spirit—A spirit in a dream can be a pun for enthusiasm, fight, zest, and determination—full of spirit, or "uplifted spirits." A person with spirit has strong character and makes the best out of things. The person "rises above."

Spirit is the root of the word "spirituality," which can be boiled down to your relationship with yourself and life. It's your goodness. It's your search for meaning and truth. It's your better nature. See: *God*.

Spirit can symbolize something that "gets into a person" and makes him or her act strangely or out of character. See: *Possessed*.

It can symbolize an unseen influence or feeling that something isn't quite right. Spirit can be used interchangeably with ghost. Spirit can refer to something affecting you from outside your conscious awareness. It's something unseen. Moods can seem to "come from nowhere." Events and circumstances can turn for you or against you, seemingly without cause. See: *Ghost, Psychic Power*.

A spirit that talks to you in a dream might be a messenger from the unconscious mind. Spirits are commonly believed to be messengers who come either to aid or harm humans. In dreams this association can be used when a person needs to "get the message." It's probably important so pay attention! See: *Unconscious Mind*.

An evil spirit can symbolize something that's negative and intangible, such as influence and coercion. See: *Evil*.

Be sure to read: *Soul*.

See also: *Ascend, Demon, Devil, Evil, Fire, Ghost, God, Possessed, Psychic Power, Sleep Paralysis, Soul, Unconscious Mind*

Sports—Generally, sports symbolize competition and striving to do your best. They capture feelings of being energetic and healthy, or contrast with feelings of being rundown and unhealthy. They're associated with discipline, practice, competition, preparation, and recognition.

But as always, dreams can expand far and wide to create symbolism. Sports can be a public spectacle or event, especially sports that attract many fans or are played in big venues. For example, a young man about to become a father dreams about being in a football stadium packed with fans—a way of saying that having a child is a public event. See: *Football*.

The terminology and phrases associated with sports are ripe for use as comparisons, and comparison is the heart of dream symbolism. For example, if you score in a game, it can relate to scoring in life. Sports have goals, and so do people. Sports can require getting around obstacles. They involve assistance. They're associated with fame and glory.

See also: *Animal, Arena, Athlete, Baseball, Basketball, Boxing, Coach, Famous, Football, Locker, Monster, Opponent, Tennis, Tiger, Wrestle*

Spotlight—A spotlight can symbolize focus—focus on you, or on something, such as when you focus your attention. It can mean something is the object of attention. It's important or central. It's connected with recognition and fame.

See also: *Actor, Camera, Director, Famous, Stage*

Spouse—See: *Husband, Wife*

Spy—A spy can characterize a situation in which you feel spied on or lack privacy, or it can represent the use of underhanded or furtive means.

For example, a man dreams that he sees a drone flying right outside his windows with the camera on it pointed at him. He goes outside and sees a work crew doing a geographical survey. He then lectures one of the workers about spying on him. The dream sums up a situation in which social workers were called to check on the welfare of a family member in his home. It feels like an intrusion, like he's being spied on in his home.

A spy can symbolize secrets—keeping them, or finding them out.

See also: *Computer, Detective, Lock, Phone, Safe*

Square—As a shape with balanced sides, the square is a symbol of strength and solidity. Square shapes are closely associated with our material world, and in dreams they can connect with being grounded or materially secure. A square missing a side, such as when a room is missing a wall, implies insecurity. Your life is shaky in some way.

Squares are often shown in the shape of an object such as a room or other structure, or a door or window. A rectangle is an elongated square.

A square can show strength of character or personality.

It can show balance in the psyche.

It can show squareness of thinking, from within the box, not outside it (a box is a 3-D square). The person is "square."

See also: *Building, Psyche, Rectangle, Shapes, Window*

Stab—See: *Knife*

Stadium—See: *Arena*

Stag—A stag in a dream can be a symbol of strength, sexual potency and male virility. It can symbolize a bachelor or a male who lives and acts like a bachelor.

See also: *Animals, Antlers, Deer*

Stage—Being on stage in a dream can symbolize feelings and perceptions related to public scrutiny or performance. People on stage are the center of attention, where they're seen in public and are under the public eye—a good symbol for when you want to be noticed, to make a spectacle, or to openly declare support for something.

Being on stage speaking to an audience can mean you have something to say. It can mean you consider what you've learned from life or about a specific subject to be valuable and you're looking for a venue to express it.

On stage in front of an audience, in simplest terms, means you're being watched, and that association can branch out to include *The Truman Show* delusion or the feeling that people are keeping an eye on you.

For example, a man dreams that he's on stage as an actor in a play when he gets a text from a co-worker that says he should come to work now if he wants to catch the boss in the office. He remembers that it's his only time to do it, and he has something important he wants to say, but he can't get away while on stage. Especially not while all eyes are on him, and some of his co-workers are in the audience.

The dream reflects his thoughts related to a situation at work in which he wants to do an end-run around his work group and appeal to the boss directly to have his way—but they can't find out. His strategy is to try to catch the boss after hours, but lately too many prying eyes have been around.

To dream about being in front of an audience can indicate that you seek public recognition. It can connect with embarrassment in public.

To dream there should be an audience—but no one is there—can symbolize feeling that no one is listening to you or recognizing your talents, abilities, or accomplishments.

To dream about being in an audience can symbolize being part of the crowd. Or it might express the idea of "outside looking in." You are a spectator instead of a participant.

An audience can be associated with the general idea of "in public." Perhaps you don't want your feelings to be known in public, or there is something you don't want to be public knowledge.

The possibilities for symbolism expand when you consider what happens on stage. For example,

many stage performances center around stories of romance and tragedy, and your life can resemble these stories. Stages are where fantasies and dramas play out. It's an ideal set piece for acting out the major events, fantasies, and dramas of your life.

Dreaming about being on stage and forgetting your lines can symbolize the feeling of forgetting something important, especially something important you wanted to say. It can mean you're having difficulty playing a role in your life, or you missed an opportunity to say what you want to say.

Something "staged" is made to appear a certain way. Behavior and circumstances can strike you as staged when they are deliberate or manipulative, or are meant for appearances. To stage-manage means to carefully arrange and control to create a desired effect. See: *Imposter*.

A dream about an audition can indicate preparation for a big event or challenge.

An audition can be a way of saying "test the water." You're not sure whether you're ready to commit to something and want feel your way through it before deciding. Or you're not sure you're good enough for something and want to find out.

See also: *Actor, Arena, Costume, Director, Imposter, Makeup, Movie, Spotlight*

Stairs—Stairs have steps, and steps in the figurative sense mean the steps you take to reach a point in your life. Phrases like "taking steps to reach my goal" and "steps in my career" mean tasks, actions, achievements, and accomplishments that build on each other. The entry for *Dungeon* provides an example.

Stairs are associated with personal development, each step being like a stage of development.

Stairs are associated with movement up or down, and movement in life can go up or down. See: *Ascend, Descend*.

The idea also applies to when dreams move into areas of yourself such as your intellect (moving up) or emotions (moving down). The association is created through the intellect's being centered in the head, and emotions' being felt in the heart and gut. See: *Elevator*.

Steps can trip you, and "tripped up" means you hit a snag on your way toward a goal or personal destination. Tripping up stairs can symbolize "falling forward," meaning failing but still advancing.

Also consider the idea in the phrase, "Take steps to protect yourself." In a dream about finding a crocodile in a pool of dark water, the dreamer walks away from the area and finds steps leading up into the air, seemingly to nowhere. When the crocodile is understood as representing someone the dreamer can't trust, the steps make sense as a message to take steps to protect herself from that person.

Spiral stairs can symbolize progress in your inner or outer life. See: *Spiral*.

See also: *Ascend, Climb, Dark, Descend, Elevator, Home, Spiral*

Steal—See: *Thief*

Steer—See: *Car*

Steps—See: *Stairs*

Sting—See: *Bee*

Stomach—The stomach is, of course, associated with food, and that association can branch out in many directions to include nutrition and diet. See: *Food*.

But more often, dreams refer to the stomach in the sense of "gut feeling." The stomach has more nerve endings than the spinal cord, and emotions such as fear, nervousness, and anxiety are felt in the gut because it has nerve bundles that act as processing centers for these emotions. Some instincts and hunches are also felt in the gut. They're "gut instincts."

Vomiting in a dream or an ill feeling in the gut can mean you can't "stomach" something.

See also: *Body, Eat, Food, Vomit*

Store—See: *Mall, Shop*

Storefront—See: *Shop*

Storm—When people say they sense a storm coming, they usually mean it in the figurative sense of "trouble brewing." Something bad is about to go down. A situation or person is stormy or explosive. Emotions can be described as powerful or electric. Feelings can be turbulent.

Perhaps the trouble brewing is inside you. Or you see it on someone's face—a "storm on the brow."

You can think of a storm as something disruptive. A storm can disrupt travel plans and outdoor events, for example, making it a candidate for dreams to use as symbolism for something else disruptive, such as a relative who storms back into your life.

A storm can symbolize an illness or dark mood.

Also consider physical causes. You might have heard a storm outside as you slept.

See also: *Hear, Hurricane, Illness, Lightning, Tornado*

Stranger—To decode the symbolism of a stranger in a dream, begin with what's strange and foreign to you, such as people, behaviors, subjects, and situations. "Stranger" can symbolize feeling strange or out of sorts, or dealing with something different or new. "New" and "strange" are used interchangeably.

You start working at a new job, or attending a new school, and feel like an outsider. Or you tackle a new subject or learn a new skill. You are in a new place in your life. Being outside your comfort zone really stirs the deep reaches of the mind and is likely to spark dreams in response.

You're like a stranger when you're unwelcome or feel like a foreigner. It can mean you feel uncomfortable, unwelcome, or tense. For example, you find yourself in a circle of people you don't feel comfortable with, or outside a social clique. Or a business situation turns tense or goes into uncharted territory. Strangers are associated with tense and unpredictable situations.

A stranger can symbolize someone you haven't seen in a long time. See: *Lock*.

When you say that someone you know is a stranger, it means you don't really know the person, so a stranger or foreigner in a dream can symbolize not knowing who the person really is, or the person doesn't really know you. See: *Mask*.

Dreaming about being in bed with a stranger can express the feeling that you don't really know someone close to you, or that that person is acting out of character.

A stranger can symbolize an unknown or estranged aspect of yourself. This use of the symbolism is quite common because a stranger is a human-character and a sort of blank canvas on which a dream can paint your self-portrait.

dream-characters are usually projections of something about yourself, so if you dream about a foreigner, ask yourself whether you're seeing something about yourself depicted as a dream-character. Many aspects of a person are unconscious, meaning outside the scope of conscious awareness and control. They can be depicted as foreign because they are foreign to you, but they're still you.

The meaning of a foreigner in a dream is often found in his or her culture and your associations with it. For example, you dream about a Frenchman and associate French people with high society. Doesn't matter if your association is accurate, it's something your dreams can use to tell a story. You think back on the day before your dream and remember that you dined in a super-formal foreign restaurant, a situation that could be described as "foreign," and thus be summed up in the image of a Frenchman in your dream.

Another possibility to consider is that a foreigner in your dream could be sparked by something you watched on television, read about, or heard on the news. Also, consider whether you recently interacted with someone from the same foreign culture as the character in your dream. The character could be a surrogate for that person.

See also: *Border, Dark, Foreign, Orphan, Trespassing, UFO*

Strangle—Strangling, hanging, or asphyxiating in a dream can symbolize that something isn't getting through to your head. You don't want to acknowledge or know it.

For example, a young man dreams about finding his mom hanging from a rope in the basement of their home. In his waking life he's doing something that his mom has told him not to do. The message isn't getting through to his head. And on another level, the symbolism connects with his fear of committing relationship suicide if his mom finds out.

Strangling in a dream can symbolize "choking on your words." You have difficulty articulating, or can't express your emotions. Or you are repressing something, holding it down. See: *Neck*.

Strangling is a very personal method of killing, so strangling can symbolize feeling angry—so angry you could strangle someone. It's personal.

Strangling can mean a situation or relationship in your life is choking you. You feel suffocated. You need room to breathe. See: *Snake*.

Many dreams about trouble breathing or suffocation are related to a constricted airway or something related. For example, a young man dreams about suddenly finding himself in outer space without a spacesuit and experiences a vivid sense of suffocation. It occurs after a night this nonsmoker smoked half a pack of cigarettes and his lungs felt abused. See: *Chimney*.

To choke can mean freezing when the spotlight falls on you, or blowing an opportunity, such as when an athlete gives a bad performance in a big game.

See also: *Chimney, Hang, Neck, Snake, Suicide, Talk*

Student—Students are associated with learning and can be used as symbolism whenever you are learning. Learning extends far beyond academic learning to include learning about people, about life, about the ways of the The Force or whatever. See: *School, Teacher*.

Expand the definition of student. It applies to many situations in life, including your inner life as you learn what makes you tick and how to navigate your inner world, and your outer life as you learn to navigate in your outer world.

Students are associated with a free lifestyle—at least, freer than what life can be like with a career, family, and many responsibilities. See: *Campus*.

Students are associated with lack of money. For example, a woman living on unemployment benefits dreams about being a student and living in a bare apartment. The benefits don't equal her former salary, and she's had to find creative ways of saving money.

Dreaming about students as an adult can symbolize that in some way you're unprepared for adult life. You have more to learn.

Of course, for someone who is actually a student, a dream featuring students can be a reflection of daily life.

The symbolism of students in a dream can connect with their age. See: *Child, Teenager*.

See also: *Campus, Child, Childhood Home, College, Desk, Guide, School, Teacher, Teenager, University*

Subconscious—Subconscious and unconscious are often misunderstood or used interchangeably, but technically they're different. Subconscious means "below the threshold of conscious awareness." The word on the tip of your tongue is subconscious. The thought or memory that's just out of your reach is subconscious.

Unconscious means the unconscious mind, or just *the unconscious*. The unconscious mind is everything about the psyche that's not conscious. The unconscious is a structure of the psyche. See: *Unconscious Mind*.

The subconscious is the gray zone between conscious and unconscious. It's more readily accessible to the conscious mind, whereas the unconscious is a deeper layer that's largely inaccessible.

See also: *Psyche, Unconscious Mind*

Suffocate—See: *Strangle*

Suicide—While suicide is usually symbolism, it can reflect actual thoughts of suicide and be a warning, either for yourself or someone you know. In rare cases, people dream about loved ones committing suicide just before it really happens, or just

in time to prevent it. However, dreams usually mean suicide in a figurative or symbolic sense. For example, see: *Hang, Mother*.

In one sense, suicide means to give up. That association can be used to create symbolism related to giving up—an idea, relationship, endeavor, hope, desire, dream. Think broadly about what you can give up. For example, you can give up trying to be nice, or give up a bad habit (or good habit!). See: *Abortion*.

Suicide is "the end," and in dream-speak "the end" can mean the end of something important in your life. It's probably something about which you feel strongly.

People who commit suicide are perceived to be deeply unhappy, so suicide can reference being unhappy. It doesn't mean you're suicidal, but in an exaggerated way it might describe your feelings.

Suicide can mean the death of something about yourself. Something's got to change. See: *Death*.

Sometimes suicide is not intentional, it's the result of carelessness or recklessness. When someone gets blasted drunk or high and barrels down the highway at 120 mph, he or she is asking to die. When a diabetic guzzles soda, it's virtual suicide.

Suicide can be a way of saying that a person messed up badly. For example, flunking out of school can kill your future. "Career suicide" is something that discredits you or hinders your chances for advancement, or spells the end of your career.

Be careful of confusing suicide in a dream with the method of doing it. The method is often where the symbolism and meaning are found.

See also: *Abortion, Death, Drown, Gun, Hang, Knife, Kill, Mother, Strangle, Terrorist*

Suitcase—See: *Baggage*

Sun—The sun in a dream can reference qualities of the sun. It is bright and makes people feel happy. It brightens mood. A sunny outlook means optimism. See: *Yellow*.

The sun is associated with good health, whereas a setting sun is associated with declining health and advanced age.

A rising sun is associated with ascendance. See: *Ascend*.

A setting sun is associated with descent. See: *Descend*.

For thousands of years, the sun has been associated with masculine qualities and the moon with feminine qualities. The sun is the masculine face of God, the yang, the Father. It is strong, dominant, assertive, aggressive. It sends the life-giving energy received by Mother Earth, the yin, the endless fertility of nature. See: *Penis*.

The sun can symbolize a strong masculine person, such as a father or other male authority figure.

A sun in a dream can be a wordplay for "son." For example, a young man dreams about the world ending and a hole in the sun, symbolizing the hole in his life after his father died. The son is the sun. His world ended with the death of his father.

See also: *Ascend, Descend, Desert, Earth, Father, Heat, Moon, Penis, Space, Yellow*

Surf—See: *Coast (Action)*, *Wave*

Supervisor—See: *Boss*

Surgery—Having surgery performed on you in a dream can be a way of saying you want to change something about yourself or remove something from your personality or memory. It can be something you are ashamed of, that's unwanted, or that's troublesome for you.

Brain surgery, in particular, is known as an analogy for removing something from your thoughts or thought processes.

For example, a young man dreams that his female friend performs surgery on his brain. He's calm and relaxed as some parts are removed and some disconnected. The dream symbolizes rewiring his brain to accept that his friend will not be his girlfriend or lover. He has strong feelings for her, and in order to save the friendship he has to disconnect from them or turn them off. He's relaxed during the surgery because he knows subconsciously what the surgery symbolizes.

Surgery can symbolize something tedious or very serious. It can reflect health fears.

"Surgical" means precise, sometimes ruthless or cold.

Be sure to read: *Amputate*.

See also: *Amputate, Dissect, Doctor, Hospital, Knife*

Swim—See: *Dolphin, Fish, Float, Pool, Shark*

Sword—See: *Knife*

Tackle—Tackling someone or something in a dream can symbolize trying to gain control of some aspect of yourself or your life. You might need to get a grip on yourself, or control a habit.

For example, being tackled by police officers in a dream can symbolize inner conflict over a drug habit or something that could get you into trouble.

Figures of speech like "tackle the problem" use the word "tackle" to mean grasp an issue and take action to address it.

Be sure to read: *Football*.

See also: *Arrest, Football, Police Officer, Wrestle*

Talisman—A talisman or amulet in a dream can be a protective symbol, and if that's the meaning behind the symbolism, then it will make you feel safe. It can show that you have the inner strength and integrity to withstand the pressures of life and achieve your potential as a person.

It can symbolize a potential source of strength or insight. It's a good sign, usually, and can indicate that you are at a particularly important moment in your life, such as at a crossroads or facing big decisions.

For example, while struggling in a blizzard in a dream, the dreamer finds and picks up a talisman in the snow. The snow symbolizes depression, and the talisman is a sign that the dreamer has the strength to get out of it.

The talisman is also a symbol loaded with energy in the psyche. By picking up the talisman the dreamer is accessing it, or claiming it, making it conscious—she is going to need it to battle the depression. Until that happens, the energy is only potential, locked away behind the symbol, and willingness to claim it is the key. In the next scene, the dreamer finds a white horse, and in time she learns to ride it and escape her depression.

Carl Jung said that these symbols can appear as the psyche individuates, and within them is everything needed to help the process along. Sketch the talisman. Research it. Wear it as a necklace or ring, or get it tattooed. Make it part of you.

Amulets are known to ward off bad energy, and that can connect with warding off negative people and situations, or dealing with negativity and darkness in yourself. Your dreams will translate these ideas into scenarios such as using an amulet to ward off a pack of wolves, or to teleport away.

Amulets protect from invisible forces, and that association can symbolize recognition of pernicious influences or unconscious aspects of oneself, two examples of things that are intangible (invisible) but real and influential. This use of the symbolism in dreams is often accompanied by themes of magic and sorcery.

The shape and composition of an amulet can be significant. For example, an amulet shaped like a triangle can symbolize willpower, energy, or transcendence. An amulet shaped like a circle can symbolize wholeness or completeness of the psyche. An amulet made of precious metals and gems can symbolize something precious to the dreamer. See: *Circle, Gem, Jewelry, Pyramid.*

The unconscious mind can, in one image, say a thousand words. An entire idea or set of ideas is summed up in the amulet symbol.

See also: *Circle, Gem, Gold, Individuation, Jewelry, Magic, Psyche, Pyramid, Shapes, Spiral, Unconscious Mind*

Talk—Talking is a common action in dreams. Some dreams are basically just conversation, the brain spitting out memories from the day or communication among various parts of yourself. Your body can talk with your mind. Your head can talk with your heart. The components of your psyche talk among themselves, taking form as dream-characters and other symbols such as talking animals, or just as voices.

Yup, the voices in your head can be completely normal.

Talking to people you know in a dream can reflect your conversation from the day—it's basically just memories—but it can be a way of articulating something you are not articulating consciously, or continuing the conversation, specifically the train of thoughts. It can be a way of connecting with the emotions felt in response to what you said and heard.

For example, a woman dreams about talking to friends about her deepest personal thoughts, reflecting the discussions she has been having with them. But then she has sex with them and wakes up feeling as if she's cheated on her boyfriend. It feels like cheating, in a sense, because she has not been talking about those same deep thoughts with him.

Conversations in dreams can be used to admit something to yourself, too. Don't be surprised if what you hear is shocking or discomfiting.

Conversations with important figures such as leaders and celebrities can be a way of getting your attention and communicating something important. Dreams of talking with holy figures and higher powers can serve the same purpose. See: *Famous.*

Symbolism can be built around associations with talking, such as openness and guardedness, glibness and sincerity, social acceptance and isolation, candor and deception, and gossip and rumor. In a conversation with dream-characters, or conversations between them, you can see your own tendencies. It's all you talking something over with yourself. See: *Psychologist.*

Trouble with hearing someone talk can mean you aren't listening, or have trouble understanding something being communicated to you. For example, a man's dream that his girlfriend is deaf means he thinks his girlfriend doesn't listen to him. Having trouble hearing what a supervisor says in a dream reflects the dreamer's confusion over understanding an assignment. See: *Ears.*

See also: *Accent, Angel, Ears, Famous, Guide, Hear, Lips, Mirror, Mouth, Neck, Phone, Psychologist, Strangle, Whisper*

Tall—See: *Giant, Skyscraper*

Tattoo—People sometimes get tattoos as permanent reminders of another person, so getting a tattoo in a dream can mean that you want to remember someone—or conversely, don't want to forget the person. Especially a loved one who passed away.

Tattoos are reminders of events and times of life.

Tattoos are part of you, and as symbolism they can mean that whatever is tattooed on your body is part of you. For example, a man's dream about getting a tattoo of a wolf ties in with recognizing wolf-like qualities in himself: good instincts, protective, sociable. The tattoo symbolizes his connections with those qualities of himself.

A tattoo is a record of who you are and where you've been.

Getting a tattoo with another person can be a bonding ritual. It shows the personal bond between you. On the other hand, if the tattoo is forced on you, it might symbolize a feeling that you're forced to commit to something or bond with someone or something.

A temporary tattoo can symbolize a temporary situation or relationship.

See also: *Artist, Body, Deceased Loved One, Scar*

Teacher—For students, dreams featuring their teachers and professors are common and usually connect with their classes and education, or relationship dynamics with the educators.

Dreams love to create comparisons and trace problems to their source. For example, a student has difficulty with a demanding teacher. Everything the teacher says, he does the opposite, and he's openly hostile to her. He's fine with the class and its subject matter, but doesn't understand his reaction to the teacher till he dreams that his mother teaches the class ... his demanding mother whom he's too scared of to openly defy. Instead, he acts out his feelings with his teacher.

When you dream about a teacher or professor from your past, the dream can connect with something you learned from that person. For example, you dream about your former English professor when you're struggling with the wording of a report you're writing for work. Or you had a teacher who told you that your innate talent and intelligence would carry you only so far in life, and that eventually you would need to prepare better and be consistent. Years later you realize you have hit a wall and need to prepare better and be more consistent. Voila! The teacher appears in your dreams. Oftentimes, the meaning of the symbolism pops to mind when thinking of your initial associations with the person and the subject they teach.

Teachers help you live up to your potential. They advise. They guide. They give answers, and you can dream about teachers whenever you need them. See: *Guide*.

A teacher in a dream can symbolize a mentor, counselor, friend, parent—anyone who teaches in any sense.

You can dream about a teacher in connection with a specific incident and the impression it makes on you. For example, say that one time you were late to class and the teacher wouldn't let you into the classroom. It's a harsh lesson about being on time. Then the other day you were late to an appointment, triggering a dream featuring the teacher represented as a character, and you wonder why you'd dream about someone you haven't seen in years. It's because the past connects with the present.

Dreaming about a group of teachers can symbolize your perceptions of them as a group. See: *Group*.

A teacher in a dream can be a representation of your attitudes toward learning. For example, a dream about being chosen for a special program to develop psychic powers, then sneaking out of the classroom, leaving the teacher to be beaten to death while the dreamer is doing his own thing, summarizes the dreamer's overall attitude toward being taught. He has plenty of innate ability, but his stubborn insistence of doing things his own way holds him back. The death of the teacher dramatizes his inability to live up to his potential.

You can dream about teachers as completely imaginary characters that play teacher-related roles. The symbolism is based on common associations with teachers, and with teaching and learning. Teachers and professors are known for being well-educated, sometimes pompous, sometimes challenging, and sometimes lecturing. For example, you dream about enduring a teacher's seemingly endless lecture the night after sitting through a seemingly endless meeting.

Dreams use associations with teaching, such as inspiration, authority figure, and someone you can or can't count on. It depends on how the teacher is presented in the dream and your feelings and associations. The possibilities deepen when the teacher is someone you know, your teacher or former teacher. The symbolism can connect with the person, the subject he or she teaches, the school he or she teaches at, your experience with the teacher, the time of life you knew the person, and the person's role as a teacher. For ideas about how to decode the symbolism of someone you know, see: *Sister*.

Along this line, a big part of a teacher's job is to prepare students for the challenges they will face. You dream about a teacher from your past (a real-life person) when you face a challenge that the teacher warned you about or prepared you (or didn't prepare you adequately) for.

A young man four years out of high school dreams he's back there, in a classroom led by a teacher he doesn't recognize as one he used to have. The class is given an assignment to work on. It confuses him and he asks for help and still doesn't understand. His peers tell him he isn't going to graduate, enraging him. He hurls desks across the room, then storms out and hunts down the school counselor, who is out of the office.

The dream symbolizes the young man's struggle to figure out where he fits in the adult world; specifically, what he should be doing as an occupation. That's his assignment, and his confusion about the assignment reflects his overall confusion about what to do with his life. His rage in the dream is an amplification of his feelings—he's really upset with himself and the teachers and counselors who haven't given him the answers he needs. It's why he reacts with rage—he subconsciously knows that failing to graduate means he won't have the adult life he wants. By understanding the dream he is able to grasp the situation and make a decision. He joins the Navy. Six months later he's happier than he's ever been.

And it all begins with the teacher, because ultimately the dream is about understanding his situation. That's his assignment. The question is about his life, and the answer is to find a way to "graduate."

A teacher can symbolize teaching what you know. For example, as a parent you want to teach your children what they need to know to grow up to be healthy adults.

Teaching in dreams can apply to situations in which you want to get across your ideas and knowledge, as teachers do. For example, a man dreams about being a professor teaching a classroom of students about a subject in which he's an expert. The dream reflects his efforts to assume the role of teacher by giving public presentations.

The symbolism of a teacher can connect with the settings in which teachers are found. See below.

See also: *Campus, Classroom, Friend, Guide, Library, Parents, Principal, School, Sister, Stage, Student, Talk, Test*

Tears—See: *Cry*

Teenager—The first consideration for the symbolic use of a teenager-character in a dream is that it is related to qualities and perceptions of teenagers, such as that they're rebellious, impulsive, rowdy, mischievous, moody, and immature. Teenagers can also be daring, optimistic, and free-thinking.

Those associations have myriad ways to be used in dream stories. For example, you dream about a teenager disobeying her mother, symbolizing a situation at work in which you rebel against the direction of a supervisor. Or you dream about fighting with a teenager after an incident the day before when a bad attitude took you over and made you surly. The teenager represents your attitude.

A teenager in a dream can symbolize someone pushy and disruptive, no matter how old the person is. The symbolism is based on how he or she acts.

A teenager can symbolize the courage to go in a new direction or start afresh. See: *Hero*.

As an adult it's easy to forget what you were like as a teenager, especially the idealism you felt. As a teenager you have ideas about the person you want to be as an adult and the ways you are going to live your life and even change the world. Then you turn around years later and realize the world changed you, and the idealism you espoused ran up against the wall of reality.

Dreams can remind you of what you used to believe by putting you into a story among groups of teenagers. It can be hard to admit to yourself that you are disappointed in your inability to achieve what you once thought you could. Your dreams won't let you forget—maybe it's not too late. Groups of teenagers can symbolize the roots of your sociability, how you act in groups, the persona you adopt, the roots of anxieties and fears, and how you think people react to you. See: *Anxiety, Group, Persona.*

Take the idea further and a teenager in a dream can symbolize idealism versus reality. Teenagers, generally, think they can do anything. It's a great mindset, and as adults we need that can-do attitude, but you learn what your limits and constraints are.

The new life that begins at puberty—no longer a child, not yet an adult—continues as long as you deal with the same issues and questions, no matter how old you are. For example, for the rest of your life, fitting in with people is likely to be a theme, and when it is, your dreams can show you among teenagers as a way of pointing toward the source of your present thoughts, feelings, perceptions, and patterns.

The same idea applies to many areas and aspects of life: dating, sex, work and study habits, attitudes, addictions. No matter what age you are, your dreams will take you back to when things began and even show you as that age.

Of course, if you are an adult and deal with teenagers, you are likely to dream about them. And if you are a teenager, then teenagers are your peer group and you will dream about them.

A common perception is that teenagers think they know it all and don't want some doesn't-get-it adult telling them what's up. This perception of teenagers can be used by dreams to symbolize situations in which someone doesn't listen, or thinks he knows it all. And it cuts both ways. Sometimes teens are right to tune out adults who try to tell them the facts of life.

To better understand the dreams of teenagers, see: *Archetypes, Hero.*

See also: *Addict, Anxiety, Archetypes, Boyfriend, Ego, Girlfriend, Group, Hero, Job, Parents, Persona, Prom, Sex, School, Student*

Teeth—Teeth in dreams have a wide variety of uses as symbolism, giving you a lot to consider. But as with other symbols, the meaning is usually found in how teeth connect with other details, especially actions, and the context.

Teeth can be a source of anxiety, especially for their care and appearance, and many dreams about problems with teeth connect with anxiety. Stress too, "the daily grind." Broken, crumbled, or ground-down teeth are metaphors for feeling worn down, nervous, or anxious. See: *Anxiety.*

Crumbling teeth can connect with something in your life or yourself that's falling apart, such as physical health—your body is falling apart, or you fear it is—or your mind or emotions are falling apart, or threatening to.

Then again, the first rule of dream interpretation is to consider the obvious. A small anxiety about your teeth can be turned into a major one in your dreams. It might be time to see a dentist.

Another popular dream theme involves loss of teeth. That can connect with any sort of loss, but it's especially good as symbolism for losing something close to you. For example, it's common to dream about losing a molar after having a miscarriage or losing a child or other loved one. Molars are deeply embedded in the mouth, and children and other loved ones are deeply embedded in your life.

Losing a front tooth can symbolize loss of prestige, status, or reputation. Front teeth are part of the face, so losing front teeth means losing part of your face—a dream's way of saying "lost face." See: *Face.*

For expectant parents, dreaming about losing a baby tooth can symbolize fear of miscarriage. However, the symbolism has other meanings, such as loss of innocence or a reference to childhood. On the other hand, losing baby teeth is a rite of passage and can mean you are growing, maturing. Your feelings and reactions tell you the difference in the meaning. See: *Miscarriage.*

Loss of teeth in a dream can mean you lose hope, lose touch with reality, lose out on an opportunity, lose a relationship, lose part of yourself, and so forth—anything involving loss.

It can symbolize feeling lost in your life. See: *Lost.*

Losing a tooth creates a gap, and a gap can symbolize something missing from your life. For example, you lose custody of your child, or a child goes off to college, creating a gap in your life.

Anything involving the mouth in a dream can relate to articulation and speech. For example, dreaming about teeth falling out while you're trying to speak to a group of people can symbolize fear of speaking in public or in front of groups. It can connect with lacking confidence in what you say, or lacking honesty. See: *Mouth*.

A young man dreams about having dinner with his dad, and every time he opens his mouth to speak, teeth fall out. It symbolizes anxiety about talking with his father. The young man recently came out as transgender, and his father isn't taking it well.

Chewing on something too big like a big wad of gum that makes speech difficult can symbolize inability to find the right words or to communicate a thought or idea.

Chewing on glass or sharp objects can symbolize saying things that hurt people, or being careful to avoid saying something that could hurt someone.

Chewing can mean chewing on a thought or idea.

False teeth can symbolize lying and other false words that come out of your mouth, or giving off a false impression.

For example, a young woman dreams that she has false teeth that smell putrid. The night before the dream her mom asked her whether she was using drugs and she said no, knowing that she smokes cannabis. False teeth in this dream represent her lie, and the putrid smell represents her guilt about lying to her mom.

On the other hand, confidence in your teeth can symbolize confidence in what you say or how you say it.

Teeth are closely tied with personal presentation and the impression a person gives off. You can tell a lot about a person from his or her teeth, and dreams can use those associations to tell stories about reputation, appearance, self-consciousness, and personal presentation.

The idea of presentation extends to your place in the world and your standing within it—how you present yourself to the world. For example, a young man dreams about having a hollow tooth and being told by a dentist that the problem will fix itself in time. It connects with his worries about paying for college. Getting a degree is tied closely in his mind with the sort of social image he wants, and hollowness in this case connects with the hole in his finances to pay for college.

Food stuck in teeth can symbolize appearing foolish, or bad presentation.

Brushing teeth is connected with preparation—especially preparation to present yourself, such as in dating and mating. Perfect teeth, hair, body, clothes. Perfect résumé. Brush teeth before going out or meeting a date. Brushing and preparation go hand in hand.

Here's a good example. A woman dreams she's brushing her teeth in her female friend's bathroom when her friend's boyfriend steps out of the shower and she gets a peek at his penis, and is embarrassed. In the next scene, she's trying to get to a wedding when she spills tea on an old chair, embarrassing her again, and she has to clean it up, so she misses the wedding.

The dream is about finding a husband, and brushing teeth symbolizes the woman's thoughts about how she presents herself as a potential mate. The dream uses the boyfriend as a character because he's the sort of man she'd like to attract. Her embarrassment when she sees him, and later when she stains the old chair, connects with her embarrassment about her age. She's no longer a maiden, and in her mind it's the stain on her presentation.

Teeth are connected with attractiveness. Attractive teeth can indicate attraction to someone, or to something such as a subject or prospect, and unattractive teeth carry the opposite idea. For example, you dream about meeting Mr. (or Ms.) Right, and everything is great until he opens his mouth and he's missing teeth, or half-chewed food drops out. It helps you realize that the guy you've been dating lacks something you want in a relationship. See: *Beauty*.

Removing teeth, or agreeing to have them removed, can symbolize a loss that you initiate or acquiesce to, such as breaking off a relationship, dropping a class, or leaving a job. See: *Amputate*.

See also: *Anxiety, Baby, Beauty, Body, Face, Guilt, Lips, Lost, Mirror, Mouth, Talk, White*

Telekinesis—See: *Psychic Power*

Telepathy—Telepathy can symbolize being on the same wavelength with someone. Your thoughts are in sync. It can mean you have a deep connection with someone.

Telepathy can symbolize something that invades your mind, especially if it seems to come out of nowhere.

It can symbolize putting thoughts into someone's head, or thoughts put into your head.

See also: *Magic, Psychic Power*

Telephone—See: *Phone*

Television—Television and video are so pervasive and varied that the possibilities for symbolism are wide open. Basically, anything that's part of your life can be represented on screen, including projections of your inner world. This entry will cover some of the obvious possibilities.

The most obvious possibility is that watching something on television or in a movie in a dream is a reflection of something you actually watched or saw in person. The memories play back like video. However, usually dreams will translate memories into symbolism, so although obvious, this possibility is not probable.

Television is associated with fantasy and illusion, and can connect with your fantasies and illusions, but you should go deeper. Imagination is the basis of your waking life—you first imagine what you want to do or be, and in this sense a television is like your simulator to run through possibilities and scenarios and test them out. For example, you think that you might want to marry someone

you've been dating, then dream about playing a married character on television. Afterward, do you still want to marry the person?

Television and movies can tell the story of your life. They show what's happening, if it's live television, or what has happened, if recorded. See: *Movie*.

Television and movies can symbolize something you know isn't real even though it's presented that way.

They can symbolize something that influences your thoughts, feelings, perceptions. And expand to include your values, beliefs, behavior, and desires.

Television can connect with a desire to be recognized or famous. See: *Famous*.

It can connect with thoughts related to a career in television or the movies.

See also: *Actor, Camera, Director, Documentary, Hollywood, Movie, Stage*

Temple—A temple in a dream can be a setting symbolizing your innate spirituality, uncomplicated by teachings, beliefs, dogmas, or ideologies. It's simply your natural expression of connection with something greater than yourself, whether it be nature, society, or a higher power. See: *Church, Earth, God, Goddess*.

A temple can be a place of refuge, a place for quiet contemplation. This use of the symbolism arises often, ironically, with people who are stressed out or really busy. A temple in their dreams can point to the need to slow down and find inner peace, or help provide at least a semblance of it in their dreams. In that sense, dreaming of a temple is compensation for something missing in their lives. See: *Garden*.

There is also the saying that your body is your temple. Perhaps a temple in a dream symbolizes your body, and the overall message is, "Take care of it." See: *Body*.

A temple can be a stage on which the dramas of your deep inner life play out. These dreams often involve mythological and archetypal themes. See: *Archetypes, Castle*.

Dreaming about trying to find a temple can mean you're looking for your inner center. See: *Circle*.

See also: *Altar, Body, Candle, Castle, Church, Circle, Earth, Garden, God, Goddess, Pastor, Psyche, Pyramid, Stage, Talisman*

Temptation—See: *Addict, Affair, Drugs, Sex*

Tennis—The symbolism of tennis can connect with the action of hitting a ball back and forth, meaning going back and forth about something, or tossing around an idea. Taken further, it can symbolize the idea in the phrase, "pass the buck" or "serve a purpose."

Any action that involves a ball can represent your process of personal development. The ball symbolizes personal wholeness, and hitting it with a racquet symbolizes your success or lack of it in your progress toward becoming a more complete person. See: *Ball, Baseball, Circle*.

Elements of playing tennis, such as accuracy, easily connect with accuracy related to thought processes and verbal statements. It can show how close you are to a target, especially a personal target such as becoming the sort of person you want to be, or getting to where you want to be in life. Branch out from there and you can connect with many aspects of life.

In tennis, the point is to hit the ball within the lines, and lines of a tennis court can symbolize boundaries in your life or an area of it, staying on task or within a defined structure. For example, a graduate student working on her dissertation has recurring dreams about playing tennis and wanting to hit the ball outside the lines, symbolizing her desire to venture "outside the box" of accepted thinking in her field. However, anyone who ventures outside the accepted boundaries risks ruining her career, so she stays within the lines.

Gender roles are like boundaries. Rules and limits are boundaries. Beliefs and dogmas are boundaries.

Playing tennis without a racquet can symbolize feeling ill-equipped.

For more ideas, see: *Games, Sports*.

See also: *Ball, Baseball, Circle, Coach, Games, Referee, Sports*

Tent—A tent can symbolize flimsy protection, and the idea of protection extends to sensitivity and how you protect yourself personally and emotionally. For an example, see: *Raccoon*.

In this sense, the covering of a tent is like one's skin. See: *Skin*.

See also: *Animals, Forest, Raccoon, Wilderness*

Tentacle—See: *Octopus*

Terrorist—"Terror" is the root of the word "terrorism," so as symbolism the first thing to consider is that a terrorist or terrorism in your dream symbolizes something terrifying. For example, death or declining health can terrify you. The thought of losing someone close to you can be terrifying. The feeling can be exaggerated, too, so perhaps you're just worried or frightened.

Terror and chaos go hand in hand, so a dream about terrorism can symbolize chaos or confusion in your life or your mind. Things are in real disarray. For example, a situation at work is really mucked up, and you dream about it as a terrorist strike—a way of capturing the dynamics and your feelings. See: *Zoo*.

Terrorism is synonymous with fear. Terrorists have become a universal bogeyman, a general symbol for fear, especially of things you can't control. In dreams, that association can connect terrorists with anything that you fear or can't control. See: *Fear, Panic*.

Along this line, terrorists are associated with paranoia and delusion and synonymous with "crazy." See: *Insane*.

A terrorist can symbolize the part of yourself that rebels or fights the system.

It can symbolize something that's gone haywire in your body or mind. See: *Cancer*.

Terrorism is, by definition, the use of violence, threat, and fear to achieve an objective. These ideas could be used to compare with someone who uses similar tactics to get his way.

Terrorism is closely associated with the news because that's the primary way it's heard about.

Terrorism is associated with battles, bombs, and guns. See: *Fight, Bomb, Gun*.

Battles, bombs, and guns are associated with apocalypse. See: *Apocalypse, Armageddon*.

Some places are associated with being prime targets for terrorist attacks. See: *Airport, New York City, Skyscraper*.

Terrorists, while heard about widely, are a mystery to the general public. We can speculate about what in their background or experience makes them turn to such an extreme, but ultimately we can only guess, and that association can be used in connection with something unexplainable, especially in connection with the actions and behaviors of certain people.

See also: *Apocalypse, Armageddon, Asylum, Bomb, Fear, Fight, Gun, Insane, Panic, Suicide, War, Zoo*

Test—Taking a test is one of the most commonly reported dream themes, especially among populations such as students, who regularly take tests. If you're in school and take tests, a dream about taking a test can connect directly to aspects such as preparation, fear of failure, progress toward a degree, where you want to end up after college (are you a high-achiever or not?), class ranking, and recognition or lack of it.

The symbolism is found in phrases and situations in which people refer to a test or being tested. You can "test the water," "pass the test," and "test patience." The phrases can apply to situations such as testing a person's intentions or commitment, or being admitted into a social circle after passing the "sniff test." Situations in life can test you, and so can people.

You are tested when you stick to your guns and uphold your values, principles, beliefs, and ideals. Your resolve is tested. Anytime you break a habit or start a good routine you are tested.

Being unprepared for a test is a common dream theme often connected with feeling unprepared to meet a challenge in life. Most often the situation is related to what's happening in your life, such as when you encounter something in your job that you don't know how to do; but other situations come into play, such as a challenging relationship or living situation. See: *School, Test*.

Your thoughts and feelings about taking a test in a dream reflect the meaning. For example, if you arrive late or unprepared to take a test, the dream might be about preparation or feeling behind in life. Being naked in an exam is a classic symbol of coming unprepared or neglecting something important. See: *Naked*.

Test is synonymous with "challenge," and the challenges of life extend far beyond the classroom. Long after you are out of school you can dream about taking a test. In which case, consider the idea of feeling tested or challenged. For example, at work you get an assignment that really challenges you. At home, a rough patch tests your relationship with your spouse or children.

A common dream theme for people out of school is the dreaded "show up for a test and have no idea what's going on." For example, a man dreams that he is back in college and shows up for class on the day of a test. He feels totally unprepared and worries he will fail. The dream comes after an incident the day before when he was asked questions to which he didn't know the answers. Tests involve giving answers, and you fail if you can't give the correct answers.

Failing a test in a dream can connect with general fear of failure. The dream creates a scenario to bring out the fear.

Tests are associated with "making the grade." Dreaming of a test can be a sign that you drive yourself hard and hold yourself to high standards.

Dreaming about being tested in order to get a reward or pass on to a new level can connect with thoughts and feelings about your future and what you need to do or accomplish to get to where you want to be. It can connect with meeting a challenge. For example, think of the tests that a relationship passes before moving to the next level.

Other associations with tests can be used as symbolism, such as feeling crunched for time, or pressured to perform.

Wordplays are possible. "Exam" can mean "to be examined," in which case, see: *Doctor*.

Cheating on an exam can mean cheating in the sense of being unfaithful or breaking the rules. In which case, see: *Cheat (Exam)*.

See also: *Anxiety, Armageddon, Cheat (Exam), Doctor, Fear, Job, Naked, School, Student, Teacher*

Testicles—This symbol opens up some interesting possibilities, especially considering the many figures of speech and euphemisms for testicles. Dreams have a penchant for acting them out.

For example, in a dream you're asked how big your cannon balls are. What you're really being asked is how bold you are, and that connects with working up the courage to ask someone out. You're hoping it ends with a bang.

Testicles are associated with fortitude and courage, with masculinity and alpha characteristics. See: *Man, Penis*.

Testicles are where a man's children are stored, and from there a dream can really branch out. See: *Child, Pregnant*.

For example, a woman dreams about looking at her husband's testicles with an ultrasound, which connects with her wondering how many more children he wants to have. It's not just a question of sperm count, but of longevity, health, and desire.

Testicles are associated with the penis and sex. See: *Penis, Sex*.

They're otherwise known as balls. See: *Ball*. And the scrotum is a bag. See: *Bag*.

The possibilities go on and on. A key point to remember is that dreams can be funny when the humor serves a purpose, and references to testicles and balls not only tell you something about yourself, but also do it in a way that gets the point across.

See also: *Bag, Ball, Bull, Bully, Castrate, Child, Penis, Pregnant, Sex*

Thief—A thief in a dream can symbolize that something valuable is being taken from you, but it's probably not material. Instead, it's a physical representation of a personal situation, and whatever item is stolen in the dream symbolizes the thing of value.

For example, a woman dreams about a man stealing her phone while she's looking at a map. The phone symbolizes her personal direction in life. See: *Ex*.

Heavy drinking affects your performance at work or school, robbing you of a sense of accomplishment or opportunity for advancement. Anxiety robs you of peace of mind. Depression robs you of motivation. A friend moves away, robbing you of his or her company. Illness robs you of energy. Working a menial job robs you of dignity.

You can dream about a thief when something material has been taken from you, but otherwise you know it's symbolism, and clues to the origin are right there in the story.

For example, a young woman dreams that a man steals a box of items associated with her childhood from her, and she steals it back. She tells her father, and he tells her she's going to get into trouble if she doesn't give it back. The dream symbolizes that her father has controlled her life since childhood, taking her ability to make her own decisions. Now, as a young woman, she's trying to take it back, depicted as stealing back something that's hers because she still feels that she doesn't have permission to make her own decisions.

You can feel like a thief when you do something wrong, or are sneaky. Doesn't matter if your intentions are good or bad—the thief in your dreams symbolizes your feelings. You feel like a thief.

An adult woman dreams about stealing makeup, symbolizing her restriction from wearing makeup as a teenager. When she uses makeup as an adult, years after the fact, she still hears her mother's voice in her head and feels as if she's doing something wrong.

You can "steal the limelight" or "steal someone's heart."

You can feel robbed when you lose something valuable for yourself, such as when you rob yourself of an opportunity by dropping the ball. That part of you that trips you up and makes you do stupid and careless things is called Shadow, and it's notorious for getting people to sabotage themselves and slip up. It tends to pop up unexpectedly, like a robber, and pull the rug out from underneath you. See: *Shadow*.

You can dream about yourself as a thief when you know you have been lying or portraying yourself in a false light. A thief-character in a dream can portray someone you know, or a situation. See: *Fake, Imposter*.

Thieves are associated with deception, low character, and poverty. They take advantage of vulnerability in people.

Stealing can mean "something for nothing." What's taken isn't deserved, such as when a co-worker "steals" a promotion by manipulating perceptions, rather than through dedication and superior work.

Stealing is linked with taking the easy way out.

Stealing is called a crime of opportunity because something is a lot less likely to be stolen if it is protected or watched. So dreaming about a thief can mean you are vulnerable. You need to take steps to protect yourself or take better care of something. See: *Bicycle*.

Robbery and anxiety go hand in hand. Anxiety can rob you of your peace of mind, just as fear of being robbed takes away your peace of mind. Along these lines, robbery can be used to symbolize something that makes you anxious, wary, or defensive.

Dreams use the best symbolism to describe a situation and your feelings. Instead of a thief, your dreams could use a bandit or burglar. See: *Bandit, Burglary*.

See also: *Anxiety, Backyard, Bandit, Bicycle, Burglary, Baseball, Car, Crime, Depression, Detective, Door, Ex, Fingerprints, Gun, Illness, Intruder, Lock, Police Officer, Safe, Shadow, Shirt, Shop, Walmart, Window*

Thin—See: *Emaciated*

Throat—See: *Neck*

Throne—A throne in a dream can symbolize self-importance, respect, or admiration. For example,

admiring someone is sometimes expressed as putting the person on a pedestal, meaning elevating him or her in your mind to a high position. A throne takes the symbolism to the next level by saying you *really* admire that person. See: *Famous*.

A throne can symbolize authority. From your throne you make decisions that carry inner authority. Your life is like a kingdom, and you either rule it or abdicate your throne to someone or something else. See: *Shadow*.

Use the entries listed below to explore further.

See also: *Boss, Castle, Famous, King, Queen, Shadow*

Throw—See: *Ball, Baseball*

Throw Up—See: *Vomit*

Thunder—See: *Lightning*

Tidal Wave—A tidal wave is overwhelming, and life too can be overwhelming, at least at times. The image of a tidal wave or tsunami captures that idea. It's something unstoppable.

Water in dreams can symbolize emotions, so in this sense a tidal wave can symbolize overwhelming emotions. They won't be held back. An emotional situation threatens to sweep you away. You experience a huge emotional swing. See: *Flood*.

A tsunami sweeps away everything in its path, as does a tidal wave but with a further reach and longer duration. For example, you don't just lose control of your emotions, you have an emotional breakdown. The tsunami is bigger and more overwhelming, destructive, dangerous, fearsome, inescapable, and emotionally powerful. The symbolism often plays out in connection with the biggest sorts of changes and transitions in life. See: *Emotions, Teenager, Water*.

A tidal wave can symbolize a huge impact, such as a huge argument or change in your life. Such an impact could come from a sudden downturn in health, unplanned pregnancy, or end of a relationship.

It can symbolize a disaster or breaking point, something that sweeps away everything in its path, comparable to situations and events that change your life. See: *Disaster*.

A tidal wave creates a crisis, so in dreams a tidal wave can symbolize a crisis—one that happened, is ongoing, or is anticipated. Extend the idea to include situations that spiral out of control or are turbulent.

As something feared, a tidal wave can be a general symbol for fear, such as fear of sudden change. Because of a tidal wave's massive size, the symbolism is reserved for big fears. Anything you are really afraid of can be symbolized as a tidal wave. The idea applies to certain types of people who are unstoppable, and extends to something that is inevitable or that seems to be that way.

Water can symbolize the unconscious mind, and tsunamis are noted for pouring ginormous amounts of water onto land. That can symbolize unconscious content pouring into your conscious mind. This experience is sometimes called a nervous breakdown or psychotic break. Something has to change, and the unconscious mind forces the issue by creating a crisis. See: *Unconscious Mind*.

The answer to a question that can get right to the heart of the symbolism is, What won't be held back any longer?

What can't be denied or avoided?

At heart, such an experience is an attempt to create balance in the psyche. As Carl Jung said, the psyche is a self-regulating system. If it gets out of balance, it will correct itself. A breakdown can be exactly what's needed to confront what's wrong and force needed changes. See: *Compensation*.

A tidal wave or tsunami can symbolize a massive surge of creativity. Highly creative people are known for outpourings of intense productivity. A tsunami is an apt metaphor. See: *Artist*.

See also: *Anxiety, Artist, Compensation, Disaster, Emotions, Fear, Flood, Ocean, Rescue, Storm, Unconscious Mind, Water, Wave*

Tiger—Tigers are closely associated with temper, because they're known for being ferocious. Tiger dreams can follow after situations in which you lose your temper or get into a ferocious argument.

Perhaps you need to be ferocious in order to get your point across or to motivate, including motivating yourself. Or perhaps someone is ferocious toward you.

Along this line, a tiger can symbolize someone harsh or severe. You might be too harsh and severe with yourself.

Tigers are fierce and powerful. As a dream symbol they can represent an aspect of yourself—your inner strength and potency, especially. "Tiger" is used to describe people who are highly competitive and dominate opponents. They have the "eye of the tiger." Tigers pounce when the time is right and opportunity presents itself. They stalk and camouflage and have keen instincts. See: *Games, Sports*.

Tigers are territorial. They take no guff. They are proud and noble, virile and seductive. Do these qualities and characteristics apply to yourself or to someone you know? Is it a characterization of your ego? See: *Ego*.

A caged tiger in a dream might indicate you're being held back. You can't show your true strength, or don't have freedom to roam. You need to be free of your constraints, whether physical or personal. You need challenge and adventure. See: *Cage*.

Containing your temper is another possibility for the symbolism of a caged tiger. It's a part of yourself you deliberately hold back. A tamed tiger has similar associations with taming part of yourself.

A tiger can symbolize a dangerous or potentially life-threatening situation, because if you encounter a tiger in the wild you are probably in deep trouble.

Tigers are known for tearing prey to shreds. In the figurative sense, you can be torn to shreds when you make a mistake, get caught doing something wrong, or take on something you can't handle, for example. See: *Attack*.

A white tiger is a powerful symbol, often for the protective side of yourself.

A tiger cub can symbolize a young child—your "little tiger." See: *Child*.

Be sure to read: *Leopard, Lion*.

See also: *Ambush, Animals, Attack, Cage, Cat, Child, Eaten, Ego, Leopard, Lion, Zoo*

Time—Dreams can alter your perception of time to help tell the story, the same way that a movie or novel can compress or expand the sense of time passing. For example, a movie can jump forward or flash back in time and the audience plays along. You can live a lifetime in a half-hour dream and it is completely believable.

Time in a dream can be used to refer to a variety of situations in life. For example, finding the right time to do something, time to work on a task or project, wasting time, and giving enough time to do something right. You can want to turn back time, or you can run out of time.

Time is associated with patience and lack of it.

Running out of time in a dream can express the feeling that you have something to do and the clock is ticking. For example, a dream about having only a short amount of time to be with a friend, and constantly getting distracted, occurred while the dreamer's friend was close to dying after a prolonged illness. The dreamer wanted no distractions so he could spend as much time as possible with his friend. Time runs out for having children or changing careers or telling someone you love him.

See also: *Calendar, Clock, Elevator, Love, Midnight, Numbers, River, Time Travel*

Time Travel—Time travel can connect with thoughts about the past or future, such as the desire to go back in time and change something, or a desire to get a better idea of what the future holds for you.

It can symbolize reminiscing, taking a trip down memory lane.

The television show *Doctor Who* helped popularize the idea of time travel and is a frequent theme in dreams about going back or forward in time to correct a mistake or achieve a desired outcome. What if you took the other fork in the road?

Time travel in a dream can mean this point in your life is momentous. The decisions you make now are going to have a big impact on your future.

Time travel can mean the time you live in now reminds you of a previous time of life.

A similar idea is that time travel can symbolize when things stay the same despite significant time passing. You "step back in time." For example, you return to your hometown after a long absence and everything looks pretty much the same. The people haven't changed much.

See also: *Calendar, Clock, River, Time*

Toe—See: *Feet*

Toilet—Using a toilet in a dream can connect with the need to eliminate something from yourself or your life, especially if you vomit, defecate, or urinate into the toilet.

For example, you relieve yourself of pressure, burdens, guilt, negativity, high expectations, tension, or stress. Your dreams go through a nightly process of washing that stuff away, at least enough to reset and get you through another day. It's a physical representation of a personal situation.

Toilets are associated with privacy. Using the toilet is supposed to be a private moment. Along that line, being intruded upon while on the toilet can symbolize embarrassment, or feeling vulnerable or exposed. See: *Bathroom, Intruder.*

Dreaming about a toilet can symbolize feeling that something has been dumped on you, such as when a friend dumps all his troubles on you, or a supervisor dumps a load of work on you.

A dirty toilet can symbolize a messy situation or dirty feelings. It can symbolize dirty emotions, especially when the water is dirty.

A toilet dream can be a way of saying that your mind is in the toilet.

Flushing a toilet can be associated with letting go of something, especially pressure or negativity.

Toilet symbolism can be created by side associations, such as when a toilet is needed and can't be found, creating anxiety. Dreams make comparisons that trigger related feelings and emotions, so a dream about being unable to find a toilet can connect with a situation in your life making you worried or nervous. Dreaming about a disgusting toilet can connect with your disgust about something. See: *Anxiety*.

Toilets are associated with the one place where you can find peace and privacy. It brings to mind the image of the father in a house full of kids who reads a magazine while sitting on the toilet. It might be the only moments of peace and privacy he gets.

If you pee or defecate in a dream, first consider the obvious. The dream might reflect the fact that you feel as if you need to use the toilet.

Peeing or defecating in public can symbolize vulnerability, embarrassment, or exposure. You did something or showed something about yourself in public that you'd rather not have. See: *Naked*.

Peeing in a way that disrespects a place or person can be an expression of hard feelings. For example, you dream about peeing on someone who insulted you, as a way of expressing your feelings about wanting to return the insult. You pee on a church as a way of saying you don't respect its teachings. Someone pees on your bed, symbolizing a disrespect or insult that's personal.

A bowel movement can symbolize a period of introspection after breaking off a relationship. You work it out of your system like a bowel movement.

Constipation can symbolize holding onto something you should let go.

Along this line, a bowel movement is related to digestion, and digestion is used as an analogy for processing experiences, memories, feelings, and emotions. The bowel movement is the tail end of the process, a perfect analogy for the nightly process of discarding unneeded memories.

A bowel movement can be a graphic commentary about how you feel about something. To be "shit on" means that someone dumped his problems on you, or treated you disrespectfully. It can be a raw and honest expression of your feelings about yourself, your life, or someone in it as "shit." See: *Excrement*.

A bowel movement in public suggests regret over something said or done that's publicly known. You showed a shitty side of yourself.

A rushing river of brown water or similar imagery can symbolize diarrhea.

Exaggerated bowel movements can symbolize moral depravity or extremely dirty thoughts. Shit all over the walls. Piles of it everywhere. These dreams are extremely graphic and reflect the condition of the dreamer's mind or life. It's not to say that the imagery automatically has this meaning, but it's common.

A dream about a toilet can come in response to the feeling of needing to urinate or have a bowel movement while asleep. Dreams can create imagery and scenarios based on physical stimuli. Along this line, bowel problems can trigger dreams about toilets. They're sending strong signals as you sleep and these are translated into your dreams as imagery.

See also: *Anxiety, Bathroom, Bathroom Stall, Excrement, Naked, Shower, Vomit, Water, Yellow*

Tornado—Tornadoes are terrific symbols for frantic activity. When your life is like a whirlwind, it can't slow down. It's frenetic, busy. Things happen quickly, suddenly.

For example, in a dream about two tornadoes, the dreamer, an author, is thinking about two writing projects he has going. He realizes it's too much to take on at once and has to drop one of them to give his best to the other one.

Tornadoes are destructive, flinging objects and debris in all directions. That association can be used to compare with someone you know, such as a child leaving a trail of destruction. It can symbolize personal destruction, or something in your life that leaves a trail of destruction in its wake. See: *Destruction*.

In simplest terms, a tornado is a disaster. See: *Disaster*.

Tornadoes can show the powerful force inside you that's going to shake up your life. It's the force of change, unstoppable. For a great example of such a dream, see: *Family Home*.

In this way, tornadoes are commonly misunderstood as nothing but bad. Sometimes you need to mix things up. You need change—dramatic change. You have something big inside you trying to come out, and it takes a big change to make it happen.

Before making a big change, especially a change in their psyche, people are known to dream about tornadoes hunting them. And ultimately it's a sign to let go and allow the powerful forces of the unconscious to work within you. See: *Unconscious Mind.*

Those forces will unleash tremendous energy. A tornado is, after all, powerfully energetic. And as a funnel whirling around a core, it's a great symbol for the energy of the psyche. See: *Spiral.*

Or the spinning motion could symbolize arguments that go round and round, or thoughts that do—your head is spinning. It can mean your life is turned around by a powerful event. You suddenly find yourself going in a different direction, just as tornadoes are known for suddenly switching directions.

Tornadoes can have a devastating impact, and that association can be used by dreams to symbolize something that devastates you: separation, failure, loss, addiction, illness, mental breakdown. A feeling of devastation can stem from a specific situation, or from stress.

A tornado is a particularly good metaphor for heavy stress—it's destructive, turbulent, electric, stormy—and captures the related emotions in one image.

The damage to a city, town, or neighborhood caused by a tornado in a dream can symbolize forces bringing down structures in your life such as values, beliefs, and assumptions. You're rethinking something—or everything. See: *Building, Construction.*

Damage to a home, on the other hand, tends to symbolize damage to your life or body. See: *Home.*

A tornado can symbolize something avoided or run from because it brings up strong emotions or bad memories. See: *Storm.*

As something feared, tornadoes can symbolize any fear, but particularly fears associated with sudden changes and uncontrollable circumstances. Tornadoes drop down from the sky—death from above—and that association connects them with fear of sudden death, war, or something that comes out of nowhere to upend your life or your psyche. See: *UFO.*

The buildup to a tornado coming (sirens, weather alerts) can symbolize a sense of doom or gloom. Something you dread is coming. It can be specific—for example, a big test or confrontation—or general, such as fears and phobias. It can mean that you sense a crisis coming, or something big.

Dreams can use associations with tornadoes such as how people tend to reveal their true thoughts and feelings during disasters.

Flouting the danger of a tornado can symbolize ignoring a danger or warning, such as the danger of provoking someone or defying an authority figure, or of stirring up emotions you can't control.

Seeking shelter from a tornado can be a way of saying you need a break. Tornadoes cause huge changes, a metaphor for how certain times of life can be.

Tornadoes cause insecurity and can pop up in dreams when you feel insecure. They're unstoppable forces of nature.

See also: *Clouds, Destruction, Disaster, Family Home, Psyche, Spiral, Storm, UFO, Unconscious Mind*

Torture—Dreams create physical representations of personal situations, and torture can be a way of describing something that figuratively tortures you. People talk about torture to mean something that ranks as less than actual torture, but in an exaggerated way it fits:

"Sitting through that lecture was torture."

"Listening to that music is torture."

"I'm tortured by guilt."

Imagine how a dream could take those statements and turn them into a scene. The torture of sitting through a lecture could be turned into a scene of being strapped into an electric chair. Listening to torturous music translates symbolically into nasty insects crawling into your ears. Being tortured by guilt could be depicted as being forced to watch an innocent person executed for something you did.

A key point is that torture in dreams is often a way of describing what's going on in your emotions, according to how an event feels, rather than how it really is.

Torture is an exaggerated way of saying something is awkwardly painful. For example, "The meeting tomorrow is going to be torture."

Extend the idea further and it can apply to situations you dread, such as having dental work done or a proctology exam.

Torture is used to expose secrets, and might be used in a dream in relation to keeping a secret.

Torture in a dream can mean you torture yourself or are tortured by guilt or shame.

You hate yourself, or your life is hell. Something really needs to change. See: *Guilt, Hell*.

It can mean you can't forgive yourself for something, or you focus on the pain and suffering in the world and these give you a bleak view of life.

Of course, in some cases the traditional meaning of the word "torture" might be closer to the truth. For example, a painful illness or physical condition can be portrayed as torture, because torture is used to create physical pain. Or torture is an apt way of describing how you receive some shocking news. For example, you hear that a neighbor's child was in a horrific accident, and it affects you deeply. You then dream about a child being tortured.

See also: *Dungeon, Guilt, Hell, Prisoner, Terrorist, Torture, Wound*

Toy—Toys in a dream can refer to childhood, either to that time of life specifically, or to the sorts of activities, behaviors, and feelings typical of children.

Toys are for fun. They're used spontaneously and creatively and spark feelings of happiness and contentment. You can dream about playing with toys as a way of capturing those feelings or symbolizing something else you do for fun. Adults can

have toys, too: your boat, your tools, your guns, your high-tech drone, your computer, your liquor cabinet. Anything associated with fun. Include activities under that umbrella: going to the beach, playing in the snow or rain, playing a game.

You can toy around with a person or idea, meaning you are giving it less than serious consideration. If you toy with a person's feelings it means you manipulate him or lead her on. In a dream, that use of the symbolism could be expressed in a scene in which you dress the person up like a doll or action figure. See: *Doll*.

Toys tend to pop up in the dreams of teens and adults whose lives have become too serious or mechanical. It can be a sign of missing the spontaneity and freedom associated with childhood and playing. You need to lighten up, and you need time to play.

It's only a rule of thumb, but if you recognize the toys in your dream as ones you played with as a child, they're more likely to refer specifically to your childhood, instead of to what childhood can symbolize. The meaning is found in what a toy means to you.

It's always important to consider what a symbol means to you. For example, if you dream about a toy that you and a sibling used to fight over, consider that it could represent issues related to arguing and sharing. If the toy is one a beloved grandparent gave you, it might connect with family, security, and guidance. Or it acts as a reminder of that person and what he or she gave you: love, attention, security, confidence, advice.

If you dream about a toy you are highly protective of, ask yourself whether protecting the things dear to you has been a theme in your life lately. It might refer to protecting your inner, sensitive nature. See: *Frog, Turtle*.

The symbolism can connect with maturity. For example, you start dating someone and dream about the person playing with toys, a way of saying you perceive the person to be young at heart. Or you dream about a co-worker playing with toys at her desk, a way of saying she plays around instead of working.

Childhood toys taken from you can symbolize something about your childhood taken from you: innocence, fun, freedom. In a dream detailed elsewhere, a box of childhood items connects with the dreamer's ability to make her own decisions. See: *Thief*.

See also: *Child, Childhood Home, Doll, Family, Frog, Guide, Parents, Shop, Teenager, Thief, Turtle*

Train—The symbolism of trains can be created by the fact that they're interlinked rail cars pulled by an engine. That can symbolize a job or duty with interlinked responsibilities or people, and the leader is the engine that makes it move and gets things done. It can be a metaphor for leading an endeavor and pulling other people along.

Trains take you places, especially toward distant destinations, a metaphor for distant places you want to reach in your life. For someone just starting college, graduation is far off. For someone just starting a family, raising the kids to adulthood is a distant objective. A train is a great metaphor for a family because both are interlinked, with a head of the family who pulls everyone along and determines the direction they go together.

For example, a young man who's about to graduate from college dreams about being at a big, festive gathering of people at a train yard. A marching band plays as people walk one at a time through an open, empty train car. Each person gets a moment in the spotlight before moving on. It symbolizes graduation and moving to the next phase of life.

Physical movement in a dream can symbolize personal movement in your life, and a train is going in only one direction. For example, you want to avoid someone, but have no choice but to run into the person. It's inevitable, just as there's no stopping a speeding train.

Symbolism can be created by the limited options for a train's movement because it runs on tracks. For the same reason, trains can symbolize a "one-track mind" and similar ideas related to being forced to go in a certain direction or having only one option in mind. Trains and tracks can

symbolize "staying on track," meaning staying focused and heading toward a goal.

Boarding a train can symbolize embarking on a journey. See: *Embark, Journey*.

Trains run on schedules, and another word for schedule is routine. Breaking a routine can be symbolized as a train going off its track.

For ideas about what a train station can symbolize, see: *Airport*.

A train can connect with the symbolism of a bus or car. See: *Bus, Car*.

A train can be a wordplay for "in training."

See also: *Airport, Bus, Car, Embark, Journey, Passenger, Roller Coaster, Spotlight*

Treasure—See: *Diamond, Gem, Gold, Money*

Tree—Trees are used in analogies to compare with the organizational structure of business, family, and military, so that's the place to begin interpreting the symbolism.

A tree in a dream can symbolize a family tree. It's a terrific analogy because trees have roots, trunks, and branches. See: *Family*.

The analogy works also for the body: Roots represented as feet and toes. The trunk represented as legs and torso. Arms represented as branches. Skin symbolized as bark. The image of a healthy tree can symbolize a healthy body, and problems with parts of a tree can symbolize problems with the body. See: *Body*.

A tooth has enamel, comparable to the bark of a tree, and it has roots, so a rotted tree could symbolize a rotted tooth. See: *Teeth*.

Because a tree is associated with family lineage, it can symbolize ancestry and lineage. See: *Ancestor*.

Roots of a tree can symbolize your personal roots, not just family, but your background and upbringing, the roots of who and what you are as a person. See: *Roots*.

A leaf falling from a tree can symbolize a child leaving home—leaving the "family tree." Leaves falling can symbolize a period of personal decline, the autumn of life. Leaves can be a wordplay for "leave," meaning depart or exit.

Trees provide shelter, and this idea can be used to symbolize something that shelters you. Think figuratively, such as about the shelter a strong friendship can provide, or beliefs or doctrines that shelter you from the outside world. But also think literally. Most houses are made primarily of wood, so a tree can symbolize your home—your "tree house."

A fallen tree can represent losing your home, or some major issue with it. See: *Building, Home*.

A tree's collapse can symbolize the collapse of a big hope, or the fall of a prominent family member. For example, soon after the death of her grandfather a young woman dreams about a tree falling over in her family's front yard.

Planting a tree can symbolize starting a family or something else that you hope will grow. This use of the symbolism is especially likely if you plant a tree in your front yard, symbolizing your public life, and if family members are present.

A tree blocking your way can symbolize something blocking you from getting what you want or where you want to be, especially wanting to be close personally or geographically with family members.

Trees are associated with nature, opening more possibilities for symbolism. For example, relaxing under a tree in a dream captures the image of peace and contentment. Being among trees can symbolize harmony and relaxation. It can show your connection with nature through your body and your being. See: *Garden*.

Trees have long been associated with spirituality, and the "One Tree" or "Sacred Tree" is a mythological image that represents the Self as defined by Carl Jung, the innermost "you." It appears in dreams as you take steps toward finding out what you're really made of inside and developing your full potential. A sacred tree can symbolize "the Self" archetype, described in the entry for *Psyche*. See: *Circle, Psyche*.

In a general sense, a tree can be a symbol of spirituality because its roots go into the Earth, and from that soil springs all life. It is the ultimate connection with Mother Nature. Keep in mind that the symbolism is largely determined by your feelings and the context of a dream. See: *Earth*.

People going through personal changes are known to dream about a strong connection with trees in general, or with a particular tree. The symbolism is derived from the ways that deciduous trees change with the seasons, shedding their leaves in autumn and growing them again in spring. A tree losing its leaves can symbolize a person entering the twilight of life. A barren tree can symbolize the ravages of old age or bad health. Or it can symbolize the idea of a tree that doesn't bear fruit, meaning a lack of personal or spiritual growth, or being unable to conceive children. A tree sprouting new leaves can symbolize the feeling of being physically or mentally renewed.

Branches of a tree in a dream can symbolize the branches of a family. A branch can symbolize a child or dependent.

Branches can refer to less formal relations, too. For example, organizational structures such as religions and businesses have branches. Bank locations are referred to as branches.

A broken branch can symbolize something you can no longer support. For instance, you can no longer support someone financially or emotionally, or support a cause or political organization. A broken branch can symbolize the loss of a family member or someone close to you, or breaking a limb (arm or leg). It can symbolize stress that threatens to cause a mental break.

Branches are associated with growth and can connect with thoughts about which direction to grow in, which areas of life to devote your time and energy to. People are said to "branch out" in new directions.

A dead branch can indicate that something has run its course, or that a direction you are headed in will not lead to growth. Another possibility to consider is that you are feeling weak; your health is frail. A dead branch can symbolize the loss of a family member or someone close to you.

See also: *Ancestor, Arm, Body, Break, Building, Circle, Earth, Family, Forest, Garden, Legs, Lightning,*

Psyche, Roots, Skin, Snake, Spiral, Storm, Tornado, Wilderness, Winter

Trespassing—Knowing that dreams create physical representations of personal situations, imagine the possibilities for what it means to trespass.

It can mean venturing into someone else's territory.

It can symbolize the feeling of being unwelcome. See: *Stranger*.

It can be a sign that you've gone too far.

It can mean you're in foreign territory, especially the territory of your psyche.

See also: *Border, Fence, Foreign, Home, Neighbor, Stranger*

Triangle—See: *Pyramid*

Trip—See: *Journey*

Truck—A truck in a dream can symbolize feeling heavy or fatigued. The feeling might stem from a physical condition, but consider personal feelings, too. For example, a heavy responsibility or workload can be symbolized as a big, lumbering truck. A workload is especially likely as truck symbolism because trucks are associated with work. Then again, trucks come in light-duty models, too, perhaps a way of saying that you aren't living up to your capabilities or taking on as much of a workload as you can.

Be sure to read: *Car*.

See also: *Bus, Car, Highway*

Trump, Donald—See: *Donald Trump*

Tsunami—See: *Tidal Wave*

Turn—Turning in a dream can be used in the sense of "turn for the worse or better," or "turn within." When dreams refer to movement, it usually means movement of your life, your psyche, or the direction that something is headed, such as a project or relationship.

To turn can mean you change your mind—or if you can't turn, that you can't or won't change your mind.

Read the entries for *Left* and *Right*.

See also: *Car, Left, Map, Psyche, Right, Spiral*

Turtle—Turtles are associated with long lives and protective shells. Dreaming about a turtle can connect with protecting yourself, especially your emotions and inner sensitive nature. Or your need to "come out of your shell." The entry for *Lion* discusses a dream that uses this symbolism. See: *Armor, Lion*.

Turtles can snap, and people are known to snap, too. In this sense, a turtle could symbolize a tendency for you or someone you know to lash out with sarcasm or grumpiness.

Turtles are slow movers and can be associated with taking your time. That association can be used to symbolize obstinacy, serious consideration, deep thought, dawdling or lagging behind.

See also: *Animals, Armor, Speed, Time*

UFO—UFOs and their occupants are an enigmatic dream symbol, with meanings ranging from fear of something inexplicable to an unknown part of yourself. Dreams about UFOs and aliens have physiological causes, too.

A UFO in a dream is commonly a symbol of fear. The association is tied with portrayals of aliens as hostile, and the threat of death from above: missiles, bombs, nukes. Fears associated with UFOs range from fear of spiders, which can drop down from above, to fear of death, to fear of change. After all, encounters with UFOs and aliens would be life-changing experiences. See: *Fear*.

UFOs are "unexplained," so the symbolism can tie in with anything you can't explain, especially in connection with someone's behavior or your inner life. For example, you can't explain why you feel distant from your spouse, symbolized in a dream about sleeping next to an alien.

The occupants of UFOs are known as "aliens," and alien can mean "foreign." The symbolism can refer to a foreigner or illegal alien, or it can mean foreign in the sense of strange, different, or outside the scope of your experience. See: *Foreign, Stranger*. For an example dream, see: *Fisting*.

Perhaps what is foreign or alien to you, or what you fear, is something about yourself. An alien can symbolize something you don't recognize about yourself. It might be something about yourself that's outside your conscious awareness, or that you don't recognize. Anything about yourself that's highly repressed can take form as an alien, because it's "alienated." For example, imagine the homophobe who's actually homosexual but deeply represses the tendency, then he (or she) dreams about his sexuality. It's like encountering an alien.

Aliens and alien planets in a dream can relate to feeling alienated or disconnected from everyday reality, or being in a situation you've never encountered previously. It can symbolize feeling isolated, alone, or misunderstood.

The sexuality of aliens is ambiguous in our popular conceptions of them, and that association can be used in relation to androgyny and asexuality.

Aliens are often shown with slender bodies and great big heads, and that picture can be used by a dream to tell a story about having a big mental life, a heavy emphasis on intellect.

UFOs and aliens might symbolize a calling from within you to higher consciousness or deeper spirituality. The symbolism is created by the association between aliens and knowledge, wisdom, and intelligence. In addition, they come from above, usually, and above is associated with heaven.

Dreaming about aliens, alien abduction, or UFOs can be caused by called sleep paralysis. Ba-

THE *D*REAM INTERPRETATION *D*ICTIONARY

sically, you wake up but are still dreaming. See: *Sleep Paralysis*.

To be abducted by aliens can symbolize being taken away from your usual life and its everyday reality. Some "alien" part of yourself wants expression in your life and won't wait any longer for you to acknowledge it. You are forcibly "taken away" by the unconscious mind because of an attitude or stance of the ego that won't allow the process of self-discovery to unfold naturally. Such dreams can be part of experiencing a psychosis or badly needing to completely change your life and way of looking at it.

People who repress their spirituality or have no outlet for it are known to dream about alien abduction. Aliens and UFOs are associated with beliefs, and beliefs are at the heart of notions about spirituality and religion. For some people, belief in aliens is like a religious belief, so it's easy for dreams to connect aliens with other beliefs to create symbolism.

See also: *Ego, Fisting, Fly, Foreign, Head, Sleep Paralysis, Space, Stranger, Unconscious Mind*

Ugly—Knowing that dreams create physical representations of personal situations, you can begin deciphering the symbolism of something ugly by asking whether it is a characterization, such as:

An ugly situation, experience, or habit. See: *Addict*.

Ugly feelings and emotions, such as jealousy and revenge, or ugly thoughts. See: *Jealous, Revenge*.

Ugly qualities and characteristics of a person, such as arrogance, greed, and indifference, and ugly behavior such as bullying and arguing. See: *Bully*.

Ugliness in a dream can be compensation for an inflated sense of self-worth. See: *Compensation*.

You can think of ugly as something unattractive to you in the personal sense. For example, the opposite of an attractive job offer is an ugly one. See: *Beauty*.

A young adult male dreams that his girlfriend suddenly turns very ugly and nasty. In waking life they live in different countries and are considering moving to be together. Nothing about their relationship or her appearance, behavior, or character can be described as "ugly," so he considers the possibility that the dream symbolizes something that should be attractive to him but isn't. That perfectly describes a recent situation in which he took a job, an attractive offer, that turned out to be an ugly situation. He quit soon after.

See also: *Beauty, Bully, Compensation, Deformed, Ego, Emotions, Jealous, Revenge*

Uncle—See: *Family*

Unconscious Mind—If you're new to dream psychology, you may not know that "unconscious" is not the same as knocked out and unresponsive. In dreams, the definition of unconscious is more akin to being comatose or asleep. See: *Coma, Sleep*.

Everything about your mind that isn't conscious is, by definition, either subconscious or unconscious. The subconscious is the gray zone between the conscious mind and the unconscious. See: *Subconscious*.

The unconscious mind is simply called *the unconscious,* and it's basically everything that's behind the curtain, below the waterline, beyond conscious awareness. The conscious mind—basically, the ego—is an island in the vast ocean of the unconscious. See: *Ocean*.

You can think of the unconscious as the soil from which the conscious mind grows. Or think of it as the Basic Input/Output System (BIOS) of a computer motherboard, the root programming that connects all the parts and attempts to make them work together optimally. That's why the unconscious is not associated with any one area of the brain. Instead, it's found everywhere in the brain.

The unconscious mind sees the big picture of you and your life, and is aware of everything happening inside you and in your life. It's independent and autonomous of your ego. And it has its own agenda. This is a really important point to grasp. Most people don't even know that they have an unconscious mind, let alone that it's as vast as an ocean, connected with all other human minds at a root level, and that it greatly influences thoughts, behaviors, and cognitive processes from behind the scenes.

Knowledge of the unconscious is crucial for understanding your dream life, because its agenda is to help you grow and it uses dreams as the primary means for communicating with its counterpart, the conscious mind. Think of it as a life coach who knows you better than anyone—knows how you tick and what motivates you, even your innermost thoughts and desires—and it creates dreams to give you coaching from within. See: *Individuation.*

The long-term goal of dreaming is to prepare the conscious mind to unite with the unconscious in a sort of inner marriage. You begin life in this world as undifferentiated from everything in it. You are unconscious. Then you separate from it. You create a unique identity, an ego. Then, if you complete the journey, you reunite with the unconscious in a higher state of being. See: *Circle, Ego, Love, Wedding.*

The unconscious takes form in dreams as anima figures for males, and animus figures for females. Be sure to read: *Anima, Animus.*

The personal unconscious of the individual is part of the collective unconscious connecting all individuals. See: *Collective Unconscious.*

Archetypes are the core of the unconscious. See: *Archetypes, Psyche.*

A major archetype of the unconscious is called the *anima* in males and the *animus* in females. See: *Anima, Animus.*

See also: *Amulet, Anima, Animus, Archetypes, Basement, Beach, Bear, Black, Boat, Cave, Circle, Collective Unconscious, Crow, Descend, Dragon, Dungeon, Ego, Elephant, Erupt, Flood, God, Individuation, Left, Love, Marriage, Ocean, Psyche, Right, Shadow, Spiral, Subconscious, Tidal Wave, UFO, Water, Whale*

Underwear—Since underwear covers the genitals and is associated with sexual desire, seeing someone in underwear can connect with sexual desire, either for a specific person or just in general. You might be well aware of your feelings of sexual desire, or the dream might boost your awareness of them.

For example, a middle-aged man dreams about seeing his attractive neighbor strip down to her underwear to sunbathe in her yard. He hides behind the curtains to watch her. Then he hears his wife call for him and he tries to pretend that he was just watching the neighborhood for trouble. In reality, he has only seen his neighbor fully clothed, which is a big clue that seeing her in her underwear is symbolism. In waking life he undresses her with his eyes, doing so furtively because he doesn't want his wife to get wind of what he's thinking. He's the neighborhood watch in the sense of being the guy who watches out for sightings of any attractive woman in the neighborhood!

Although underwear is commonly associated with sexuality, more often it's actually about seeing the person beneath the clothing, seeing beneath the surface, or feeling vulnerable or exposed. See: *Clothing, Naked.*

When people are dressed only in underwear, they generally want privacy. If you dream about barging in on someone wearing only underwear, or vice versa, it might connect with invasion of privacy or finding out something that's hidden. See: *Bathroom.*

Wearing only underwear can symbolize revealing too much, or embarrassment.

On the other hand, being dressed only in underwear can be a way of saying, "See the real me." Clothes are associated with the persona, a person's public image. This can differ from the inner person. Dreaming about yourself wearing only underwear in front of people can be a way of saying that you feel comfortable showing the person you are inside. On the other hand, if you are uncomfortable in the scene, it can mean you don't want people to see the person you really are.

A young man dreams about seeing his mom in her underwear at the library. There is nothing sexual about the scene—she simply reads a book—but he wonders whether he might have some sort of Oedipal desire for her. However, the dream is simply saying that he's starting to see his mother for the person she really is, rather than seeing her only as a mother—*his* mother. Her undergarments in the dream symbolize her role as a mother, so lack of clothes is a way of saying he sees the person behind the role. The library setting is used as a way of saying he is learning something new about her.

Panties or other types of underwear can symbolize a barrier to getting what you want. They can be used to tell a story about obsession or fetish.

See also: *Bathroom, Bikini, Clothing, Genitals, Naked, Persona, Shower, Undress*

Undress—To see a character undress in a dream—or yourself undressing—might symbolize something revealed to you. Truth is "bared." Secrets are "exposed." It can be revealing, or a way of saying you have nothing to hide. See: *Hide.*

Now expand your thinking to include other definitions of those words. "Exposed" can mean vulnerable. It can mean something is made known or obvious, such as your support for a person or proposal.

The symbolism of undressing ties in with other symbolism like clothing and nakedness. See: *Clothing, Naked.*

Undressing in a dream can be used to provoke your reaction. For example, you dream about a romantic rival undressing in front of your spouse—a way of saying you worry about competition, or are jealous of the attention given to your spouse.

Undressing can have sexual meaning, too. It can mean you find someone (or something) attractive, or have sexual feelings for someone you know.

See also: *Bathroom, Beauty, Clothing, Dressed, Hide, Naked, Sex, Shower, Skin, Underwear*

Unemployed—Being unemployed in a dream can be a way of saying "doesn't want to work," or misfortune, a big change, a delay in your career, or a stoppage of work.

It can mean your circumstances are poor. You are adrift. You seek opportunity. You aren't doing for work what you really want to be doing. You are bored. You are worried about your job status.

See also: *Employee, Job*

Uniform—See: *Clothing*

University—As a place of learning, a university has many possibilities for symbolism in a dream, related to learning, teaching, and intelligence. It is an academic setting, but dreams expand the idea beyond book learning and academics to include learning about yourself, life, people, and other subjects. These possibilities are covered in entries for *Classroom, College, School, Student, Teacher.*

A university dream setting can be used to create symbolism based on related associations. Universities are associated with getting ahead in life. People with a university degree are supposed to rise higher, have more opportunity, and earn more income. However, that's not always the case. You might dream about being in a university setting because you have or haven't been as successful as you like—in your career, life, relationships, social standing.

Universities are associated with recognition for intelligence and achievement, as well as for praise and criticism. The university is an environment that exposes what people are made of, how smart they are, and what they're willing to do to get ahead.

You can be reminded of a university when working on something such as an analysis at work or research for a home to buy. The process and work are similar to how you would research a paper for school.

A university can symbolize thinking long and hard, with depth, analysis, and strategy. Universities are where the toughest questions are answered, and subjects are tackled.

Symbolism can be created based on experiences outside the classroom and the overall university atmosphere. For example, a big part of university life for some people revolves around friends and socializing. It's a time of freedom. Even if you never set foot on a university campus or your experience was different, the associations can be used to create symbolism. See: *Campus.*

The word "university" can be read as two words fused into one, "universe" and "city." That symbolism has appeared in dreams about a "cosmic university," as big as a major city, where all subjects are studied, including math and philosophy at higher levels than are presently known on Earth, and the brightest minds in the universe gather.

See also: *Campus, Classroom, College, School, Student, Tackle, Teacher*

Unlock—See: *Lock*

Urinate—See: *Toilet*

Uterus—The entry for *Vagina* has a thorough discussion about the female reproductive system's symbolism and connection with the foundations of the psyche and personal identity. The uterus can be thought of as an extension of those ideas, and incorporating ones covered under *Ovaries*.

The uterus is very closely tied with a female's gender identification and role. It's involved in reproduction, yes, but it goes much deeper to speak to the heart of her instincts, personality, and innermost desires. For thousands of generations, females have built their lives around motherhood. It's something a female starts thinking about from a young age, from the moment she fully realizes that her body is the vessel for making and delivering a baby, and it fundamentally affects everything about her.

The uterus can have symbolism specific to the idea of the place where something gestates and grows before coming into the world, and that describes the unconscious mind's role in creating the personality. The personality is like a flower growing out of the soil of the unconscious. Everything you are consciously begins there, and everything you will be is stored there, like the blueprint for a person found in the DNA. See: *Psyche, Unconscious Mind.*

The uterus is also one heck of a metaphor for the imagination. Creative ideas often begin life as just a seed deep in the mind. If the idea catches on, it's like a fertilized egg embedded in the uterine wall. Artists and other imaginative people can feel the ideas move inside them before becoming consciously aware of them. For some of them, the gestation period can be long. They have to work an idea through their entire being before it emerges into the mind as the idea for their next creation.

Of course, the uterus in a dream can refer to the organ itself and its health. And it can refer to your choice in a father for your children. Even if that decision is far off, the ideas can form now. It can refer to fertility, and your hopes and dreams for the future.

See also: *Child, Egg, Lotus, Menstruation, Ovaries, Oven, Mother, Psyche, Unconscious Mind, Woman*

Vacant House—See: *Home*

Vacation—Dreaming about a vacation might mean simply that you have been thinking about it or need it. Perhaps you have thoughts about where you would like to go and what you'd like to do. Or you might be thinking about side issues such as your budget or babysitting needs.

As symbolism, a vacation in a dream might mean you feel as if you have a reprieve from the usual hustle and bustle of your life, or you are avoiding work. You might be in a time of life when you relax and let things come to you. You have time to do things you enjoy.

See also: *Airport, Beach, Boat, Embark, Hotel, Island, Job, Journey*

Vagina—Sigmund Freud had interesting things to say about dreams that refer to female genitalia, most of which turned out to be overblown or just not true. For instance, most of time when a male dreams about a vagina, it doesn't mean he has a mother-complex or infantile desire to return to the womb, but it can indicate some sort of obsession—especially considering the plethora of pornographic imagery that's in your face these days. In which case, the dreams will be accompanied by absurdity and obsessiveness.

Otherwise, think in broader terms of what a vagina is used for—not just for sex, but for receiving the penis as symbolism for taking in masculinity and the masculine principle, the yang. See: *Penis*.

The masculine gives, it asserts, it moves the outer world. And the vagina—the yin—receives, it shapes, it moves the inner world. More than just feminine personality traits such as empathy, sensitivity, sensuality, intuition, affection, and patience can be symbolized as the vagina. It's the entire idea of taking into oneself, molding and outputting something new. That analogy for procreation also applies to creating life at its most essential, and women are the experts.

Psychological life is basically about taking in and absorbing everything on a personal level and responding in some way. For the feminine, the change is internal. She's the child-bearer, the vessel of creation, the one who builds from within, then brings her creation into the world. She receives the sperm, the assertive energy of the masculine, absorbs it, and uses it to create life.

For the masculine, the change is external. He's the nest builder, the protector of the vessel and the nest, the one whose energy is directed outward to build the outer world for mother and child. He generates. He gives the life force symbolized as the sperm. And remember, by "he" we mean the masculine principle, and by "she" we mean the feminine principle. Individual men and women can choose to play their respective gender roles, or not. Masculine and feminine roles exist throughout nature, and indeed throughout all of creation.

This concept strikes at the very heart of the forces that create not only people, but also the world and everything in it. The analogy of the masculine penetrating the feminine and the feminine receiving it and using it for creation applies across the sciences, philosophies, and religions of the world. It's summarized in the yin-yang duality. It's seen in Father Sun giving his energy, his light, to Mother Earth, who turns it into abundance of life. Everything, it seems, works in pairs. Masculine and feminine can exist without each other, but are only complete with each other. See: *Archetypes.*

Sound familiar?

This libidinal, creative energy begins its movement into the psyche at the foundational level, the archetypes, and works its way upward. The archetypes begin the work of forging shape from the raw material of life, and the ego finishes it. And what starts as something as basic as the instincts for sex and reproduction ends with owning a home and having a spouse, kids, and a life shaped around them. That's pretty much how things have been since the beginning—with exceptions, of course, which are part of the design, too.

For men and women, the vagina sums up these ideas in one image. You don't have to be consciously aware of them, either. They're part of your hard-wiring.

Dreams can express these ideas and show how the energy works in you through imagery and references to the vagina, or through images of females and female animals, or even references to traditionally feminine activities such as nursing babies and raising children. Sex involving the vagina, especially, ties in with the dance of feminine and masculine energy and its magic power to create the universe and all life in it.

When dreams refer to sex, the symbolism is more likely to refer to some sort of giving and receiving, entering or leaving, than just to the mechanical motions of penis and vagina.

When a male dreams that he has a vagina, it can mean that he's adopting a traditionally feminine role, personality traits, or the feminine principle's role in creation. He plays the role of mother to his children or siblings. He's intuitive, tender, receptive, sensual, surrendering. He takes into himself and creates new life.

This imagery is commonly misunderstood to mean he's a girly man—just imagine being a guy telling your rugby buddies about your vagina dream. While it's possible that a man with a vagina in a dream reflects a perception of lacking cojones, it's much more likely to mean he identifies in some deep and fundamental way with the feminine principle. It shows that he can be both masculine and feminine while fully living up to the role of a man in his society. In fact, only the strongest and most secure men are likely to dream about a vagina in this sense. Most men are too insecure and caught up in traditional gender roles to venture outside whatever narrow definition they have of what it means to be a man.

A vagina can connect with sex and sexual desire, but dreams are very creative with stretching associations to make symbolism. For example, a vagina can symbolize a goal, because for some people the goal of dating is to "get to the good part."

It can symbolize something that grabs your attention.

It can symbolize something that you don't have to see to know it is there.

It can symbolize a wish fulfilled or a dream come true.

It can symbolize openness and receptivity. The vagina opens to receive the penis, and if you get past the sexual connotations, you can see all sorts of ways that imagery can be used as symbolism, such as for being open to new ideas or interpersonal connections.

A bald vagina that's been waxed or shaved can symbolize the extent to which a woman can go to be attractive. It can symbolize early puberty or childhood. It can symbolize frank talk about sex or reproduction, or exposure of something private.

For a man, it can symbolize something he doesn't have, or something he wants. That association applies to gay females and transgender males, too.

For a woman, it can symbolize the most special thing she has to give about herself in a romantic relationship. The vagina is not just a sex organ, it's intimately connected with her heart and her very being. It might explain why giving her virginity is—or at least used to be—such a special event for a female—and for males, meh, not so much. It's tied in with the idea that males are able to produce billions of sperm per month, but a female gets only one egg, so she'd better treat it with delicacy and reverence.

With dreams, always think outside the box. Make connections between ideas. Any association with the vagina can be used to creative symbolism.

Dreams like to connect the past with the present. They not only speak to what's happening now, but they also trace the roots and sources, and those roots extend into early childhood. All of a woman's notions and ideas about all of the subjects connected with the symbolism of the vagina can be addressed in her dreams.

Dreams can refer to the vagina through symbols such as a cave, a tunnel, a lotus, an orchid, a vase, a soccer goal, a valley, or any sort of recessed space. A woman dreams about her vagina as a tunnel leading underground and her womb as an underground parking garage. These are known as yoni symbols. For a complete description of this dream, see: *Car*.

See also: *Archetypes, Bald, Body, Egg, Genitals, Masturbate, Menstruation, Ovaries, Penis, Phallic Symbol, Pregnant, Sex, Underwear, Uterus, Woman*

Vampire—The symbolism of a vampire in a dream is often tied to common associations. The most popular is the association with vampires drinking blood. Blood is life and energy. Vampires drain the life out of you. A vampire can symbolize a person or a situation draining you. The analogy covers everything from a person who feeds off your energy to a job that sucks you dry. You give and something else receives. See: *Blood*.

Expand that idea and a vampire can represent a person who is constantly borrowing from you, or is emotionally needy—an "emotional vampire." Expand further to include people who are overly emotional or demonstrative, aka "emo," an impression gained from heavily dramatized vampire movies and television shows.

A vampire can symbolize an illness that drains you. A condition such as anemia can be symbolized as a vampire because it involves blood and is noted for producing weariness. See: *Illness*.

Vampires are perceived as evil. As a dream symbol they can characterize someone who is cold, predatory, or remorseless. See: *Evil*.

Becoming a vampire in a dream can symbolize changing for the worse, or feeling threatened with it. For example, certain professionals, such as homicide detectives and bartenders, regularly see the worst in people and society, and it can rub off. Vampires are portrayed as able to corrupt people, to influence and hypnotize. Vampires are people transformed into evil. They generally don't start out that way.

Another association is that vampires are creatures of the night. A vampire in a dream can mean you had a bad night—tossing and turning, sick, in turmoil—or stayed up all night.

Vampires are seductive, a description that applies broadly to people and situations. Seduction is usually referred to in the sense of sexual seduction and conquest, but it applies broadly. You can be seduced by a person, idea, temptation, or mood, for example. Seduction is a powerful internal dynamic, too, because in many cases of seduction you actually talk yourself into doing something or going along with it.

Also, the dark side of the ego—the Shadow—uses seduction as a means of persuasion and manipulation. See: *Shadow*.

Vampires can symbolize something out to get you, or the feeling of it, because they stalk their prey and are relentless in pursuing it.

The traditional image of vampires has expanded because of portrayals in movies and media as emotional, moody, passionate, and lovesick—a perfect description of some teenagers. See: *Teenager*.

The final and most important consideration for the symbolism is that maybe you see something about yourself in the image of a vampire. You identify with it personally. See: *Persona*.

See also: *Blood, Creature, Dark, Disease, Evil, Illness, Monster, Persona, Shadow, Teenager, Teeth*

Vengeance—See: *Revenge*

Venom—Venom is the root of the word "venomous," and venomous is a way of describing mean, nasty people. They lash out. They're full of venomous words and thoughts. They cause division and strife. They're a bad influence.

"Venomous" can describe situations and circumstances in life that figuratively suck the life out of you. For example, prolonged abuse and stress are like venom in your system, killing you from the inside. Working or living in a bad environment slowly eats at you. See: *Cancer*.

Situations and thoughts can be venomous, too. Thoughts like "I'm good for nothing" and "I can't do anything right" are venomous to the ego. They kill you from within, as do feelings such as shame and self-loathing.

Venom can symbolize something that works into you, such as an ideology or belief system, or a harmful group dynamic, such as when your attitudes and beliefs are shaped in a bad way because of group influence.

Venom can be used to describe anything that attacks the body and mind from within, such as certain substances: sodas, alcohol, drugs, heavily processed foods, bacteria, fungus, viruses. Remember that the symbolism is based on your perceptions and how your body and mind react to the intake of something. Some people can eat Twinkies morning, noon, and night and are fine. For other people, that would be slow death. Some people can drink alcohol and it doesn't bother them. For others, it's poison.

The obvious message to take away from a dream about venom getting into your body is that you're in danger, so protect yourself. The antidote is found in your positive thoughts and feelings. It is found in your resolve to block the negative influence. It's found in your healthy lifestyle and diet.

And it is found in your sympathy. A snake can't help but be a snake.

See also: *Black Widow, Cancer, Ego, Infect, Inject, Parasite, Snake, Spider*

Video—See: *Camera, Computer, Games, Television, YouTube*

Village—A village in a dream is a surprisingly versatile symbol with a variety of associations. The first possible meaning to consider is that a village represents simplicity. A village is an image of the simple life, where the residents all know each other and take life slowly. The association with simplicity can be applied to situations such as simplifying your life or cutting down a busy schedule.

A village can represent a desire to get away from public notice or crowds, or to be alone. It might relate to a social phobia, or to feeling out of place. Most people in the busy modern world would feel out of place in a simple rural village.

A village can be used as a dream setting to symbolize eccentric or unexplainable behavior. It ties together with the perception that people in villages are unconcerned about social image and have different standards, values, and mores.

Another possibility for symbolism is based on the association that villagers are people who will talk your ear off. They have nothing better to do.

See also: *City, Native, Talk, Wilderness*

Violence—See: *Attack, Beat, Fight, Fist*

Violet—Violet is a magical color. A commonly associated word with it is "mystical." It makes people feel connected with something greater than themselves, perhaps related to violet's being in the highest frequency range of the visible color spectrum.

Violet is closely associated with intuition and deep insight, especially when the shade leans toward indigo.

Violet makes people feel close, intimate, connected, even erotic. It's the color of fantasy and imagination—perhaps at the expensive of living fully in reality.

Because colors are closely associated with emotions, judge first by how you respond emotionally to violet. Picture it in your mind—how do you feel?

See also: *All-Seeing Eye, Colors, Emotions*

Virus—See: *Body, Bug, Disease, Parasite*

Voice—See: *Talk*

Volcano—A volcano erupting sums up anger, fury, and fiery temper in one image. People are said to blow their top when they lose their temper. Anger is hot and fiery.

A rumbling volcano can symbolize grumpiness, complaints or threats. It can warn of imminent danger, such as anger building up or a meltdown coming. On the other hand, a dormant volcano can symbolize anger cooled or a situation defused. However, the potential for eruption can reemerge. See: *Erupt.*

The symbolism of a volcano can be built around other associations with an eruption, such as disaster, major change, and chaos.

See also: *Anger, Disaster, Erupt, Heat, Fire, Rage*

Vomit—The simplest way of describing vomiting is that you need to relieve yourself of something. You can't hold something down anymore.

Begin there. What do you need to get out of you? It could be guilt, pain, burden, expectations, or negativity.

Vomiting means eliminating something from yourself that's harming you from within, something you can't hold down anymore, such as toxic feelings and emotions. For example, a woman dreams about vomiting heavily into a toilet. The vomit is black and fills the toilet bowl. A thought crosses her mind that she really needed to get it out of her because it was making her sick. What she sees in the black mess in the toilet is the childhood abuse she endured. She's an adult and has moved on, but has held down all the pain and bitterness. She can finally let it go.

Vomit comes out of the mouth and the mouth is used to speak, so needing to express something, to say something, is an especially strong possibility.

Or it can characterize something that's spoken as vile, nasty, disgusting, worthless, premature.

Vomiting is used to symbolize a sudden outpouring of talk or feelings. Perhaps you had to listen to someone ramble on and on, or a friend poured out her troubles.

Vomiting can indicate revulsion. The thought of something makes you sick.

Vomiting food is a theme in the dreams of people with eating disorders. It reflects the belief that vomiting food will lead to weight loss, and is a graphic illustration of their relationship with eating.

It's also possible that vomiting in a dream is caused by an upset stomach or the feeling of wanting to throw up.

Vomiting champagne in the dream of a high school girl is an expression of her feelings about people not being very good friends. She's sick of her peers being fake and inconsistent, one day acting like friends and the next day acting distant. Champagne is used by the dream to symbolize friendship because of its association with celebration and friendship.

A dream about vomiting pieces of penis expresses graphically the dreamer's feelings about giving oral sex. Even the thought of it makes her sick.

See also: *Eat, Food, Mouth, Stomach, Toilet*

Vulture—Vultures feed on decay and rot, so the dream symbolism is often based on this association to tell stories about taking advantage of weakness and misfortune. For example, vulture capitalists look for weak companies they can swoop in and feed on.

Vultures can symbolize people who prey on the weak. They help to set a scene involving struggle or desperation. It can mean the end is near. You've almost given up, or you feel vulnerable.

People described as vultures are shameless. They will do anything to get what they want.

To be watched by a vulture means you feel as if someone is just waiting for you to slip up.

A vulture can symbolize a mindset—a readiness to take advantage of weakness or swoop in when rivals fall.

A vulture can be a sign of illness or death. Remember that illness and death are highly symbolic. See: *Death, Illness.*

And keep in mind, the vulture you see in a dream might be there to characterize something about yourself and help you understand it. Vultures perform a necessary role and are maligned for it. Something has to eat the waste.

In this sense, a vulture can be a symbol of strength and fortitude to resist disease and parasites, including symbolic varieties. For example, a vulture could symbolize a person resistant to negative influence, or with the fortitude to stomach situations that make other people sick.

See also: *Animals, Birds, Death, Disease, Elderly, Infest, Illness, Parasite*

Waiter—Waiters take and deliver food orders. That association can be used to create symbolism related to delivering something needed, such as information, knowledge, or other things that are consumed. For an example dream, see: *Eat*.

Waiters take orders. In this sense the symbolism can be similar to that of a servant or even a soldier. Another word for waiter is server. Do you feel like someone's servant, or treat people that way? See: *Servant*.

A waiter can symbolize someone who waits. It could be in the figurative sense of delivering the things you want or making sure your needs are met—good mom plays a similar role—or it can mean you're always waiting for someone, or you're waiting to hear back from someone after leaving a message, or waiting to get the results of a test.

Doing a waiter's job can symbolize times when you hustle and juggle multiple responsibilities, symbolized as tables full of people, orders to take, food to serve, etc. A waiter can be used as symbolism for any subject related to food and drink service; for example, after hosting a dinner party. See: *Restaurant*.

See also: *Eat, Food, Job, Restaurant, Servant*

Wake Up—See: *Coma, Dream within a Dream, Sleep*

Walk—See: *Feet*

Wall—Dreams create physical representations of personal situations, and a wall can represent an obstacle, barrier, or divide. See: *River*.

A wall might symbolize a "wall between us," meaning you are distant emotionally or personally from someone. See: *Bridge, Fence*.

A wall blocks your view, and ability to see in a dream can connect with awareness—especially self-awareness—and comprehension.

Walls can be used in the sense of lines you won't cross, or barriers to your freedom, including freedom in your mind. See: *Cage, Jail*.

For example, in a dream about trying to escape by burrowing through a wall, the dreamer is trying to escape from self-restraints. See: *Hell*.

Consider the symbolism of a wall in the larger context of the dream, and pay attention to any action that takes place with it. Such as a collapsed wall, which can symbolize that an obstacle or barrier is removed. You are now able to get to somewhere in your life that you want to be. Or something is unblocked from view. For example, after getting to know a new neighbor, you dream about climbing over a wall that divides your homes.

A big clue is given when dreams create discrepancies with reality. In the last example, the wall between you and a neighbor exists only in the dream. That's a clue that it must be symbolism.

Walls are used in figures of speech such as "climb the wall" to mean get past an obstacle or feel frustrated or cooped up. You need freedom, elbow room. See: *Climb*.

Walls are used as support for a larger structure. See: *Square*.

See also: *Border, Building, Cage, Climb, Door, Fence, Home, Jail, Square, Window*

Wallet—Wallets are associated with what they're used to carry: money, bank cards, identity documents, and so on. Now branch out from there and your dreams have all sorts of subjects they can address and ways to tell the story.

Finding a wallet belonging to someone else can symbolize borrowing money or accepting someone's financial support. It can symbolize an unexpected windfall. It can mean finding within yourself a new capacity to make or manage money.

Losing a wallet can be used to tell a story about a crisis in your life, especially a financial crisis. It can be associated with feelings of panic and making poor decisions. After losing a wallet, a person might ask, "How could I be so stupid?" A dream could use that association to create symbolism for a situation in which you used poor judgment or mucked up your finances.

Losing a wallet is a theme that pops up in dreams when a person is in a personal crisis. You lost something important related to your self-worth, finances, identity, or personality, such as a job or relationship. A lost wallet can symbolize a crisis of confidence. The connection between the dream and yourself is found in the thoughts, feelings, and emotions triggered by thinking that you lost your wallet. Now your task is to identify how it connects with something you recently thought or felt.

Losing a wallet can symbolize losing something else that's important to you, such as your emotional or personal security. A common fear when a wallet is lost is that someone will find it and exploit the situation by using your credit cards, stealing your identity, or even showing up at your home. Your sense of security is lost.

Rummaging through someone's wallet can symbolize invasion of privacy or getting a view into his or her personal life. For example, you find out your spouse has been secretly reading your personal email, and dream about catching the person with your wallet. Or you see a friend's bank statement.

But don't stop there. Dreams are creative storytellers and can test your reactions. For example, you find a wallet that's not yours. What do you do? Search for the person who owns the wallet and return it, or "finders keepers?" Your reaction says a lot about the sort of person you are.

Then again, perhaps subconsciously you know the wallet symbolizes something that belongs to you anyway and you have every right to keep it. You can tell the difference by your feelings about finding it and what you decide to do with it.

See also: *Bank, Gamble, Lost Item, Money, Panic, Purse, Shop, Subconscious*

Walmart—Associations with Walmart can be satirical and funny: low value, nothing better to do, mindless consumerism. The dream storyteller in our heads can be a funny one, using observations and perceptions of a retail chain to tell stories about our lives using common associations such as:

Walmart is jokingly referred to as the land of the walking dead. See: *Zombie*.

It's referred to as hell on Earth. See: *Hell*.

It's associated with boredom and depression. See: *Depression*.

It's associated with employment sought only because there's no other choice. See: *Dead End, Job*.

And it gets even better (or worse) when you work there.

A man who works in the back at Walmart dreams he's running around doing his job when a siren goes off in the receiving area. A truck with three guys in the back pulls in and they all get out and go to an empty folding chair on the loading dock. One of the guys sits down and allows his throat to be cut, as in a sacrifice, and it's treated like no big deal, business as usual, by his co-workers and a manager who's present. It's a poignant metaphor for the personal sacrifices the dreamer makes to work there. He does it only for the money. Otherwise, he'd never work in such a dreary and inhumane environment.

Note that the dream isn't telling him what he doesn't already know, but it is amplifying the depth of his feelings. Until having the dream and understanding it, he didn't realize just how much of a personal toll working at Walmart was taking on him. The man in the chair is a projection of himself as a Walmart employee, and voluntarily allowing his throat to be cut acts out the symbolism of voluntarily taking the job. "Business as usual" means that high personal sacrifice is just part of the deal— it's that way for everyone who works there.

As with all dream symbols, the best route to the meaning is to make personal associations and see how they fit the dream-story. What are the first words that come to mind when you think of Walmart? Walmart isn't all bad. For some people, it's associated with finding the best deal, and convenience, which could connect with personal qualities of thriftiness and finding the best route to a goal.

See also: *Boss, Co-Worker, Dead End, Employee, Hell, Job, Money, Shop, Zombie*

War—War is a heck of a metaphor that can apply widely to situations in life, such as a confrontation—especially a protracted confrontation—or battling a workload, or a hostile environment. Keep stretching the metaphor and it can apply to situations such a stressful exam week, or being treated like an enemy—and the enemy could be, for example, the hateful ex of someone you're dating, or the side of yourself you treat with hostility.

A war isn't a skirmish or squabble or even a fight. It's a protracted situation. That's how the symbolism is differentiated. It's stronger.

Decoding the meaning of a dream symbol like war begins in your feelings and emotions, because you react to symbols according to subconscious knowledge of what they mean. You'd expect scenes of war to trigger strong feelings and emotions, but

if they don't, that's a clue that the symbolism connects with milder associations.

For example, if battling a workload is just a fact of daily life for you, the war in your dream isn't likely to make you feel horrified or desperate. The war metaphor is based on the idea of battle.

If you react strongly, that's a clue that the dream connects with a meaning of war that's more charged.

Look at details, too. Such as a blasted battlefield representing a protracted confrontation. You've been dropping bombs on each other for a while, and it shows in the dream landscape. On the other hand, if the battle hasn't begun yet, it's likely to mean the war represents something you're expecting, instead of what's happening or has already happened. It's the week before exam week, and you're still gearing up, not yet taking exams. That's when the battle begins.

Look at your enemies—are they general or specific? If they are targets seen at a distance, or non-human, or just average Joes, then they're more likely to represent something that's non-personal. The war might symbolize the way you go about advancing your career, and the enemies are simply targets you're trying to reach.

On the other hand, if the enemy pounces on your chest and looks at you hatefully before ramming a combat knife into your head, then the meaning is more likely to tie in with something very personal, such as the ex who hates you or the war of the roses you're in with your spouse. See: *Enemy, Opponent.*

Look at the actions—it's all part of the story. Such as in the last example when the knife is rammed into the head—that's specific to the situation. It could mean that your enemy is getting into your head, or the enemy *is* in your head.

Consider facts about war that fit the dream-story. War is when two or more sides face off. War is organized. War is chosen, whereas battles erupt. War has a bigger buildup and bigger consequences or rewards. It's inevitable. That differentiates war symbolism from ordinary fighting symbolism. A fight can be a temporary or one-time thing, something that's comparatively less serious than a war. War is next-level. Nuclear war is "next next-level." See: *Nuclear War*.

War can be used to symbolize a situation in your life or inside yourself, but also consider the state of mind a war situation creates. It can mean you're constantly on guard or wary. It can symbolize paranoia and fear. It can symbolize a "war mentality," such as a person being at war with the world. It can represent one side imposing its will on another. It can be used to create scenarios related to brutality and compassion. The possibilities go on and on.

As with other dream symbols, the symbolism of war is captured in figures of speech. "At war with yourself" means self-conflict to the extreme. Sides of yourself are battling for supremacy in your mind or heart, or you are making decisions contrary to your values, ideals, or true feelings.

A "war footing" is similar to a "war mentality," meaning you are alert, ready to attack and defend. Sometimes you have to be because you don't know from where the next psychological or emotional attack is coming.

Dreams are known to create scenarios to make a subject more personal and understandable inside-out. For example, you hear stories about a relative's experiences in war and dream about being in the heat of battle. Or you read about a heroic World War II battle, then dream about it.

Dreams are also known to show what it is like on the other side. Portrayals of war tend to focus on the victors and the glory of conquest, but there is nothing glorious about war for the people in the thick of it. A dream might show the dark side of war—children mangled, cities destroyed, grief and sorrow—to shatter the illusion that war is something to be envied or desired.

Then again, maybe in an exaggerated way, that imagery sums up your childhood.

A civil war can symbolize a war within a family or organization. It can be an apt way of describing your relationships, job, or neighborhood.

See also: *Armor, Army, Destruction, Documentary, Enemy, Erupt, Family, Fight, General, Gun, In-*vasion, Movie, Nuclear War, Opponent, Subconscious, Warrior*

Warrior—In the image of a warrior in your dream, you might see the side of yourself that fights your battles and defends yourself and your turf, whether the dream shows you as the warrior or that side of yourself that is projected onto a dream character.

When it's projected onto a character, the warrior symbol can be a way of showing potential to be warrior-like in how you go about your life or defend yourself personally, psychologically, and emotionally, or give you a chance to step back and recognize something about yourself.

The warrior is a set of traits and characteristics that you may or may not have: duty, honor, discipline, restraint, structure, aggression, persistence, sacrifice. It can symbolize living by a code.

Warriors can have specific symbolism related to situations and circumstances in your life and the roles you play. You're a warrior when you protect your children and build a home for them, not just a roof over their heads but the home in their minds and hearts. Or if you go to battle daily at work, you might dream about yourself as a warrior. See: *War*.

You're a warrior as you plow ahead in your life, trying to reach your goals and personal destinations.

Many daily activities are warrior-like, such as when you plan and prepare. You might not see yourself as a warrior, but you still are one every time you act disciplined, enforce a boundary, draw a line in the sand, or make a sacrifice.

You're a warrior whenever you draw on your courage. A warrior can symbolize the hero within you, or one in your life. See: *Hero*.

A warrior can symbolize high skill and keen ability or instincts.

Dreams speak to the sources of these traits and characteristics in you, to the people, teachings, and experiences that instill them in you and to the roots of your ideas, notions, and feelings. From parents and family members to teachers, coaches, masters, and personal heroes, and from your experiences in games, sports, and conflicts to everything you've taken in from media and advertising, your dreams have a tremendously broad and deep pool of possibilities from which to draw.

A warrior in your dream might represent something about yourself tied to self-image as a warrior, or an archetype in your psyche. The Warrior archetype governs your energy related to discipline, effort, and sacrifice. It shapes your thoughts, feelings, and perceptions. It sends imagery into your mind related to your capacity for bringing that energy into every area of your life: home and family, work and career, relationships and social life, intellect and leadership. See: *Archetypes*.

When you dream about a famous warrior such as Bruce Lee or Dwayne "The Rock" Johnson, or someone else, famous or not, who embodies the qualities of a warrior, you might see something about that person that you also see in yourself. In these dreams you're likely to feel kinship or friendship for the warrior-character. See: *Famous*.

See also: *Ambush, Anger, Archetypes, Armor, Army, Attack, Bully, General, Famous, Fight, Gun, Hero, Home, King, Knife, War*

Wash—See: *Bathroom, Clean, Shower, Water*

Water—Water in a dream has close associations with emotions. The symbolism is created by the fact that things can be immersed in water. It moves, and moves you. Water can be ineffable, the same as emotions. Bodies of water can spark strong emotions, such as when you look out over an ocean. Emotions are sometimes described as "wet," whereas the opposite idea is expressed if someone is said to be dry and emotionless.

The state and condition of water presents a wide variety of uses as symbolism related to emotions: calm, turbulent, hot, cold, frozen, deep, shallow. See: *Emotions, Ice*.

Plus, being in water is very much an experience of feeling sensation within the body, and emotions are felt in the body. It's a great metaphor to describe the mind's experience of emotions. It's like floating, swimming, or immersion. See: *Float*.

Water can be used figuratively to characterize a situation, such as "in hot water," or "fish out of water."

A flawed argument "doesn't hold water."

An inexperienced person is "wet."

The symbolism of water can be expressed by figures of speech such as "going under" and "stay afloat." See: *Drown*.

Water is associated with the unconscious mind because the content of the unconscious is largely outside conscious awareness, just as underwater objects and creatures can be difficult or impossible to see from the surface. Plus, the unconscious mind is like a womb, and the aware ego "floats" within it—that's how it feels.

When water is used to symbolize the unconscious mind, it is usually vast like the ocean, because the unconscious is vast, especially in comparison with the conscious mind. The ocean is mysterious, and the unconscious mind is mysterious, too. See: *Ocean, Unconscious Mind*.

Water is used in baptism and other spiritual rites because of its associations with cleansing of sins and impurity. Spirit is compared with water because it flows, overcomes resistance, and shapes itself to any container. People are said to "thirst" for truth, and Jesus Christ said he gave "living water," another way of saying his teachings moved the spirit within people. See: *Clean, Jesus, Spirit*.

In psychoanalytic tradition, water is associated with birth and infantile desires, because a fetus is surrounded by fluid while in the womb, and a pregnant woman's water breaks when she is ready to give birth. Water connects people back to their mothers, and if Sigmund Freud is to be believed, everyone has a basic desire to return to the warmth and safety of the womb. See: *Baby, Childbirth, Mother*.

This idea extends to water as a medium for creation, and that describes yin in a nutshell. Water is ultimately where all biological life originates. The human body is made up mostly of water, and water is essential for life. See: *Uterus, Vagina*.

Murky water in a dream can symbolize clouded emotions. It can symbolize a situation that is murky, dark, gloomy, immoral, or not fully understood. See: *Blind, Dark.*

These possibilities are only the tip of the iceberg, but use the entries listed below to uncover more of it.

See also: *Bathroom, Beach, Blind, Childbirth, Clean, Dark, Desert, Drown, Earth, Emotions, Fish, Float, Flood, Heat, Ice, Jesus, Mother, Ocean, Pool, River, Shower, Spirit, Swim, Tidal Wave, Unconscious Mind, Uterus, Vagina, Wave*

Wave—Waves can symbolize something that makes an impact. The larger the wave, the larger the impact. See: *Tidal Wave.*

Making waves means causing trouble or provoking reaction. A co-worker makes waves at work, and it's visualized in a dream as making waves in pool, or a baby making waves in a bathtub.

Waves can symbolize problems or tension. The size of the waves is roughly equal to the size of the problems or tension.

A wave can symbolize the size of a reaction or conflict. For example, a tidal wave can symbolize an overreaction or big conflict.

Waves are the product of interplay between forces such as wind and momentum. In a dream featuring waves you might be seeing the result of your actions and how they affect other people's actions, like ripples in a pond. You might see the momentum built up from your effort. Surfing on a wave can symbolize moving forward in life on the basis of your previous effort, summed up in the phrase "carried forward by momentum." It means things are getting easier. The heavy lifting has already been done.

Waves and currents can symbolize your emotions. See: *Emotions, Water.*

Big waves that create rough conditions can symbolize having a rough time in life. Something is rocking the boat. Seas are rough. See: *Boat.*

See also: *Boat, Flood, Ocean, Pool, River, Tidal Wave, Water*

Weak—To be weak in a dream can symbolize a personal weakness, such as for sweets, or weakness of character. It's a physical representation of a personal situation.

It can mean you feel as if you can't handle your responsibilities or carry your burdens. See: *Back.*

Weakness in a dream can be compensation for an overinflated sense of strength. Dreams are known for using opposite imagery as a way of compensating for something that's out of balance in the psyche. See: *Compensation.*

Weakness in a dream can reflect a physical condition; for example, feeling ill or frail. See: *Illness.*

The Weakling is an immature expression of the King or Queen archetype and shows lack of empowerment to live your life the way you want to. See: *King, Queen.*

REM atonia is a physical cause for feeling weak in a dream. While you're dreaming, nerve signals to the muscles are mostly or completely muted. Otherwise you might physically act out your dreams. The discrepancy between dream reality and physical reality can cause a feeling of weakness—it's your mind's way of explaining what is happening. You sense that you can't move, and that feeling is translated into a dream as feeling weak. See: *Sleep Paralysis.*

For example, you dream about running, but hardly move, resulting from the fact that you can tell while dreaming that you're not actually running. The dreaming mind tries to explain the situation and expresses it as a feeling of weakness. Weak punches and kicks in dreams are also a common manifestation of this condition.

See also: *Archetypes, Beat, Compensation, Coward, Elderly, Fight, Fist, Handicap, Illness, King, Run, Sleep Paralysis.*

Weasel—The symbolism of a weasel in a dream is often connected with weasel-like qualities in people, such as shiftiness, sneakiness, and unreliability. It can mean a person acts uncaring and selfish. Think of situations in which a person might be labeled a weasel, and ask yourself how that description fits what's happening in your life.

See also: *Animals, Raccoon*

Weather—Weather in a dream can be compared in many ways to mood and emotion. Gloomy weather can symbolize gloomy moods and emotions. Sunny weather can symbolize optimism and good cheer. Stormy weather can symbolize a rough time, conflicts, or a stormy relationship.

Weather is forecast and can be used to symbolize outlook and prospects. Is the coast clear, or are dark clouds forming on the horizon?

Weather is associated with measurements such as temperature and barometric pressure. Measurement of weather can be used to symbolize other measurements, such as of value, opinions, or success.

See also: *Air, Blizzard, Clouds, Heat, Hurricane, Ice, Lightning, Storm, Tornado, Winter*

Web—See: *Spider*

Wedding—Dreams about weddings can have waking-world roots if you have recently been to a wedding or are planning one or even just thinking about the subject.

Dreaming about planning a wedding can symbolize getting ready for another big commitment. For example, an author planning her next book might dream about it as planning a wedding. Writing a book can be a big commitment of time and energy. It weds the person to the creative project. Any similar sort of situation is covered under the same umbrella. A wedding is, first and foremost, an event at which a big commitment is made.

A wedding can symbolize other sorts of commitments, such as to a cause, routine, or your kids. When you decide to do something you make a commitment to it. When you agree to do something you make a commitment. The saying "married to your job" captures the idea. See: *Marriage.*

Commitments you make to yourself can be symbolized as a wedding. It's a way of saying you link parts of yourself in common cause. For example, sticking to a routine marries together personal qualities such as discipline, self-worth, and commitment.

Dreaming about running away from a wedding can symbolize avoiding commitment.

Weddings are associated with urgency. You have something you need to do—now. A wedding also requires extensive preparation and handling of family dynamics. Those associations can be used to symbolize a similar situation, such as hosting family members for a holiday celebration.

Another situation known to spark wedding dreams is when you hear about an ex either getting engaged or making a commitment to a relationship. Dreaming about that person getting married can be a way of telling yourself you have no chance of getting back together.

If you are in a relationship with a potential for marriage, you might dream about marrying the person as a sort of dress rehearsal. You want to know whether the match is right. It might be time to put up or shut up. Your reaction in the dream to the prospect of marrying the person says it all.

Turn the tables and married people can dream about a wedding as a way of asking themselves whether they want to remain married. Dreaming about being at the altar with your spouse can be a test, and again, your reaction says it all. Along this line, dreaming about a wedding with your spouse can relate to some aspect of your relationship. A wedding reception under the circumstances might symbolize the difference between your wishes for married life and the reality of it.

A wedding can symbolize the union of the ego and unconscious mind, body and mind, or spirit and flesh. See: *Anima, Animus, Bride, Groom.*

See also: *Alimony, Altar, Anima, Animus, Bride, Divorce, Dress, Ego, Ex, Family, Fiancé, Groom, Marriage, Music, Pastor, Psyche, Unconscious Mind*

Werewolf—A werewolf is a heck of a metaphor for the dark side of someone, something that lurks beneath the surface. It can mean that a person has an inner Mr. Hyde.

The idea extends to situations, too, such as when you know that people are being friendly with you only because of the circumstances. The key association is the change from human to monster. See: *Monster.*

Werewolves are ordinary people who transform under certain circumstances, then wake up and don't remember what happened. That association can be used to create symbolism of being "out of it." You aren't your normal self. A period of time is missing from your memory. See: *Sleep*.

Werewolves are also used by dreams in association with sexuality. They can symbolize animal passion and lust or a person's wild side. A werewolf dream can be a way of saying you have something powerful inside yourself that needs to find expression. It can mean that passions and instincts take over.

With werewolves, a situation can quickly spiral out of control. Emotions can explode. Dark forces threaten. You could dream about a werewolf in connection with the potential for trouble.

Also consider that werewolves can symbolize general fear or paranoia. Any creature that sparks fear can symbolize these.

See also: *Dark, Midnight, Monster, Moon, Sleep, Vampire, Wolf*

West, Kanye—See: *Kanye West*

Whale—The symbolism of a whale in a dream can derive from its immense size, expressed in sayings like "whale of a good time" and "whale of an argument." Size in a dream is like an adjective that modifies the symbol connected with it. For example, you have huge expectations before meeting a person, but end up disappointed afterward. You then dream about looking forward to going to Sea World and seeing the whales, only to get there and find out the exhibit is closed.

Trying to figure out how to transport a whale can symbolize a huge problem. A whale that lands on your head can symbolize a big idea. See: *Giant*.

A whale can symbolize feeling overweight or bloated. It can symbolize feeling weighed down. See: *Fat*.

Whales are associated with spirituality and wisdom. They can dive deep under water, and water is associated with emotion, spirit, and the unconscious mind. In dreams a whale's journey

through the water can symbolize your personal or spiritual journey through life, or your exploration of the unconscious mind. It's a very positive image and bodes well for your personal development. See: *Ocean, Water, Unconscious Mind*

A baby whale can symbolize a child, especially given that babies emerge from the mother's womb all wet. See: *Childbirth*.

The languid movements of whales are associated with feelings of tranquility and calm. They're inspiring and uplifting.

Whales make strong bonds among each other and can symbolize strong bonds between people. For example, a closely knit family can be symbolized as a pod of whales.

Whales can communicate over vast distances using ultrasonic frequencies that are beyond human hearing. That ability to communicate can symbolize a connection you have with a person who is physically distant but personally close. You have a sixth sense.

Being near such a big creature as a whale is inherently dangerous. Therefore, a whale in a dream might symbolize something from which you want to keep your distance.

Rescuing a whale can symbolize saving something about yourself symbolized as the whale. For example, a woman dreams about finding a beached whale and trying to save it. She associates whales with kindness, and what she's trying to save is her own kindness after a series of incidents made her start feeling jaundiced. Always consider your personal associations when you dream about a whale. See: *Rescue*.

See also: *Animals, Beach, Childbirth, Family, Fat, Giant, Ocean, Rescue, Unconscious Mind, Water*

Wheelchair—A wheelchair in a dream can symbolize restriction. Movement is restricted for someone in a wheelchair, and movement in a dream can symbolize movement in your life.

For example, a teenager might dream about being in a wheelchair when pushed into a certain course of study or occupation by an authority figure. Coercion restricts one's choices. Or think of movement in the literal sense. Mom and dad take the car keys, restricting the mobility of their child, or your car breaks down.

A physical disability that requires the use of a wheelchair can be a physical representation of a personal situation. You feel disabled in some way, perhaps emotionally, personally, or financially, or you have a personal weakness. Disability and weakness can limit you. Then again, the dream might be about overcoming adversity, limits, or weakness.

Along this line, think of the symbolism as possibly related to obstacles, feeling hampered, or at a disadvantage. For example, you dream about racing in a wheelchair against someone on a motorcycle, symbolizing being at a disadvantage.

A wheelchair might symbolize being treated as if you have a disability or personal weakness, not necessarily that you have one. This idea of how you are treated may be the case when you dream about being forced into a wheelchair. For example, people with autism can feel that they're treated differently and dream about it as being strapped into a wheelchair, when they actually function just fine. See: *Handicap*.

A wheelchair can symbolize special consideration. For example, a young man dreams about being in a wheelchair at a martial-arts tournament. He really is taking martial arts and expects special consideration, such as a person in a wheelchair might receive. The dream is showing him that he is overdoing it. He doesn't actually need special consideration; he's just trying to avoid having to do everything the other students do.

See also: *Crutches, Elderly, Handicap, Paralysis, Weak*

White—White says "new." Something is just beginning or is new to you—new feelings, new beginnings, new lease on life, new outlook.

White says "purity," particularly white clothing and dress. See: *Angel*.

White says "innocence," even gullibility. See: *Innocent*.

White can be used to symbolize your thoughts and feelings about spirituality. Expand on the idea and white becomes a sort of umbrella under which any thought or feeling related to spirituality can be found. See: *Spirit*.

Spiritual and holy figures in dreams can be identified by their white clothing, but more important to making that determination is how you feel about the figures and how they act. Holy figures sometimes have a white glow around their bodies or are bathed in white light. Then again, white is worn by novices, too.

Something bathed in white light can also be a sign of respect or admiration. It is common to dream about deceased loved ones surrounded by white light. In these cases, white is associated with the afterlife. See: *Afterlife, Deceased Loved One*.

White can mean that something is undefined. The picture hasn't taken shape.

White is associated with depression, implying a lack of vitality in the person. It's associated with sterility, coldness, and loneliness. See: *Blizzard, Depression*.

White animals and creatures are associated with harmony between the conscious mind and the unconscious, and with your instincts.

See also: *Afterlife, Angel, Animals, Blizzard, Colors, Deceased Loved One, Depression, Emotions, God, Heaven, Ice, Innocent, Light, Spirit, Unconscious Mind, Winter*

Whore—See: *Hooker*

Widow—A widow can symbolize loneliness, grief, or sadness. It can symbolize feeling abandoned, or the fear losing someone close to you.

On the other hand, a widow can mean "free of someone or something." For example, you retire from work and suddenly find yourself able to do whatever you want.

Being a widow in a dream can symbolize a feeling that you have lost something essential about yourself.

The entry for *Deceased Loved One* has a great example of a widow's dream.

See also: *Black Widow, Death, Deceased Loved One, Husband, Marriage, Orphan, Wife, Window*

Wife—For people who are married, dreaming about their spouse is likely to connect with something about the spouse or the relationship. However, be careful of assuming that your wife in a dream must represent the person. Instead, she can symbolize something about yourself or a situation or circumstance. A big clue is given when your wife in a dream acts out of character. Discrepancies with reality are a sign of symbolism. They indicate that either she really is acting of character, or you are projecting something onto her.

For example, you dream that your wife is cheating on you. It's completely out of character for her. If you look only at the surface story of the dream, then you might suspect she is really cheating. However, cheating actually symbolizes your feelings about her lack of attention lately. She hasn't had as much time or energy for your relationship. This situation is portrayed in the dream as cheating because it feels unfair. See: *Cheat.*

If you do not have a wife, or the person in the dream is not your wife, the possibilities for symbolism expand like a big balloon. Consider what a wife means in general, and to you specifically. For example, a wife is someone you might perceive as being supportive and encouraging. Someone such as a co-worker, mother, or classmate can play that role in your life.

Turn the tables and consider those same ideas if you are not married and find yourself playing the role of wife in a dream. Perhaps you are a source of support and encouragement for someone else, or you "play house." For example, if you always seem to be cleaning up after a roommate or sibling, you might feel like a housewife whose work is never done. See: *Servant.*

Dreaming about your girlfriend as a wife can be a dress rehearsal. You wonder about the potential for the relationship. The same idea applies to dreaming about a close female friend as a wife. Perhaps you wonder whether the two of you should be together as a couple. Or maybe the friend is already like a wife. See: *Girlfriend.*

If you are friends with a woman who is married, you can dream about the dynamics of the relationship between you, her, and her spouse. All sorts of issues can arise, especially if her spouse doesn't like you or is suspicious.

Dynamics can arise between you, your wife, and her friends—especially friends who are potentially romantic rivals. Jealousy is a powerful emotion and is almost certain to be a subject of dreams. These dreams tend to be loaded with conflict and even violence, symbolizing your inner conflict and the violence you do to yourself. See: *Jealous.*

A wife can symbolize feminine aspects of yourself. For a woman, it can show the more mature female emerging in her, or a man "wedding" his feminine traits with his masculine personality. See: *Woman.*

For a man, a "dream wife" can symbolize his anima. See: *Anima, Bride.*

A wife-character in a dream opens the door for symbolism based on the feminine principle, or yin. A detailed discussion is included in the entry for *Vagina.*

See also: *Anima, Bride, Cheat, Girlfriend, Husband, Jealousy, Marriage, Parents, Servant, Vagina, Wedding, Woman*

Wilderness—A wilderness in a dream can symbolize being in an unfamiliar place or situation in your life. It can mean you're unsure about what to do and in which direction to go. You feel lost or are searching for something. You are experiencing hardship.

A wilderness or jungle is a place where it's easy to get lost. There are few roads or paths to follow. As symbolism, wilderness can express the feeling that you don't know where you are going in your life, or don't know how to reach a goal. See: *Lost.*

Some people are at home in the wilderness. They want the freedom to do things their own way. In this sense, a wilderness can symbolize getting back to nature, or experiencing new freedom. See: *Earth.*

A wilderness can symbolize your wild side or a wild situation. It can mean "uncontrollable."

The jungle is commonly perceived as a place that is wild and uncivilized. You can dream about a jungle setting when in a situation in which the normal rules of society don't apply. The "law of the jungle" means that the strongest survive, and it can be used as symbolism for situations in which you are in a sort of "winner-take-all" competition and the participants use any tactic to get ahead. For example, a jungle could be used as a setting in a dream about the brutal competition to get ahead at work, or to make a business deal, or win someone's affection or attention.

See also: *Animals, Dark, Earth, Forest, Lost, Maze, Native, Tree, Village*

Wind—See: *Air, Balloon*

Window—See: *Eyes*

Winter—A wintry setting in a dream can symbolize something in decline, such as health or fortune.

It can symbolize a feeling of dreariness or a time of hibernation. You might be conserving your resources. See: *Bear*.

It can mean you are experiencing hardship, especially if you dream about trudging through snow or getting blasted by wintry weather. Anything that hinders travel in a dream can symbolize something that hinders you in life. Snowstorms are a common metaphor for having difficulty in life—personal difficulty or depression, or hassles and delays. See: *Blizzard*.

Then again, snow has good connotations, too. Some people associate it with the Christmas holidays. It's fresh and new, even pure and innocent— pure as driven snow. Waking up in the morning to see a landscape covered in virgin snow can awaken your sense of wonder and bring out the kid in you (build a snowman, anyone?). It can mean you are excited by new possibilities. You're starting over. You have a fresh outlook.

Winter can characterize feelings, emotions, and personal situations that are cold or frosty, or the cold feeling of depression or unhappiness. See: *Blizzard, Depression, Ice*.

A frozen winter setting can mean you feel "frozen out" or distant. Relationships are described in terms of hot and cold. If you are "out in the cold" or "left in the cold," it means excluded or forsaken.

Think along the lines of something that can make you cold inside: the thought of your mate leaving you, fear of death or declining health, rejection, or finding out you failed a test. Those situations can be symbolized by snow and cold.

A cold house in a dream can symbolize emotional distance. Life lacks emotion, personal warmth, or vitality. It can characterize a relationship with someone shown in the home with you in the dream.

A cold feeling accompanies feelings of fear. When an illness strikes, you can get the cold feeling that your life is changing in a bad way. It can relate to the feeling of something that is inevitable, such as the cold realization that an important relationship is irreparably damaged, or a course of events is leading to an unwanted conclusion, or a goal or ambition will not be reached.

Take the idea further and feeling cold can be associated with fear of exposure, because you can be cold when exposed to cold weather. You might fear that a hidden part of yourself will be revealed, or that actions or behaviors you have tried to conceal will be revealed.

Winter cold can symbolize lack of activity or inspiration. No progress is made.

Another possibility for the feeling of being cold relates to physical condition. You really are cold! Perhaps a blanket fell off the bed while you were sleeping, or a window was left open, allowing cold air in. Dreams translate physical sensations into imagery, so in such a situation you might dream about a wintry landscape or walk-in cooler.

See also: *Blizzard, Car, Ice, North, Storm, Weather, White*

Witch—A witch is associated with the dark side of the feminine. See: *Shadow*.

Witches scheme. They act selfishly. They're wicked.

In an exaggerated way, a witch describes someone who is cranky, nosy, manipulative, or divisive.

A witch can characterize a situation where a person feels cursed, or evil lurks beneath the surface. See: *Evil*.

See also: *Evil, Magic, Midnight, Monster, Shadow, Vagina, Vampire, Werewolf, Woman*

Wolf—A wolf in a dream can symbolize something wild or dangerous, a person or situation. And like most dream symbols, the possibilities expand far beyond the typical.

The symbolism of wolves can be associated with their ferocity and defensiveness. Wolves appear threatening and will fight to the death. They growl over their food and snarl. They are predators.

In people, those associations can be tied to traits and qualities such as aggressiveness, territoriality, relentlessness, and ruthlessness. In situations, those associations can describe fear, danger, competition, or ganging up. For example, a group of family members gang up on you like a wolf pack. See: *Gang.*

A wolf—especially the action of following a wolf or a pack—can symbolize following instincts to protect the young, defend turf, display aggression, or mate.

A wolf pack can symbolize "pack mentality."

A situation in which you argue heatedly or get into an altercation can be symbolized by wolves snarling and fighting.

Wolf packs are said to be led by an alpha, creating an association for dreams to describe a "leader of the pack." Alphas are the strongest and most assertive. A pack of wolves in a dream can symbolize a group of bullies led by a chief or alpha. See: *Bully.*

For example, a family man dreams about three wolves breaking down his front door, led by a fearsome alpha. Outmatched, he decides to befriend the alpha, so he pets it and says nice things. The alpha says to the other wolves, "Let's meet and decide how to handle these humans." The dream sums up a legal situation in which the dreamer was threatened with being sued by a team of three lawyers for violation of intellectual property rights. Instead of fighting back, he called the lead attorney—the alpha—and framed the dispute in terms of providing for his family. He offered to freely share his innovations. His reasoning persuaded the lead attorney, a mother and family provider, to settle the situation amicably. The dream occurred a few months before any inkling of trouble. See: *Precognitive Dream.*

As wild and instinctual creatures, wolves can symbolize raw sexuality and passion.

The relentless way that wolves pursue prey can be used to create symbolism for exhaustion and being worn down.

A wolf attack in a dream can mean you are doing something to provoke a person or otherwise court danger. Wolves don't generally attack humans unless provoked or threatened. The symbolism of a wolf attack can connect with the general symbolism of being attacked or ambushed. See: *Ambush, Attack.*

It can symbolize an adversarial relationship with your instincts.

Provocation and threat are not just physical situations. Emotional and personal situations can be described that way, too, such as when you're facing a threat from someone getting too friendly with your spouse, or you are a threat to yourself.

A wolf in sheep's clothing is someone or something who's threatening despite outer appearances.

While many associations with wolves are negative, some are positive. They're closely associated with nature, especially its wild and unpredictable side, and native cultures. "Run with the wolves" means in one sense to be uninhibited and free to roam. Wolves are loyal to each other. They mate for life and form strong family bonds.

A white wolf can symbolize a feeling that you're protected, or a strong, positive connection between the ego and the unconscious mind. See: *White.*

See also: *Ambush, Animals, Attack, Bite, Bully, Earth, Guide, Precognitive Dream, Werewolf, White, Wilderness*

Woman—A woman-character in a dream is a blank canvas, especially when the character doesn't resemble anyone you know. For a breakdown of how to decode the symbolism of such a character, see: *Sister.*

When a woman-character doesn't appear to be based on someone you know, begin narrowing down the possibilities by asking yourself whether she symbolizes a role women traditionally play, feminine personality traits, or the feminine principle, the yin. Yin is discussed at length in the entry for *Vagina*.

Recent interactions with a woman can influence the dream. Did you bump into someone on the street, or speak with a stranger? If so, the woman in the dream might represent the person. Most likely you won't make the connection solely on appearance. Instead, something else will be familiar: the setting, your interaction, the feeling you get. You can assume that the person or situation made an impression on you in order to get into your dreams and be memorable.

The dream-story might be more important than the person or character. For example, say you were shopping at a busy store and your credit card was declined. Thoughts race through your head. The salesgirl looks impatient, and waiting customers grumble. That night the salesgirl—or a character that reminds you of her—appears in a dream as the teller at your bank. You raise hell with the bank manager. In which case, the character is a symbol for your feelings about the incident that day. Maybe you are angry at your bank, or at yourself for not better managing your money. The salesgirl is in the dream only because she ties in with the incident reviewed by the dream.

An indistinguishable woman-character in a dream can be a surrogate for someone you know. Dreams use surrogates to create personal distance, so people you know are not obviously recognizable.

For example, say that you argue with your mom and that night dream about an argument with a random woman. She's probably a surrogate for your mom. The dream uses a surrogate-character because you still feel hot about the argument, and if you see your mom in a dream you will be too disturbed to work through the situation. You need distance from the subject in order to observe it.

A woman in a dream can symbolize your thoughts, feelings, and perceptions about women in general. For example, a man who thinks that all women belong in the home raising children might dream about a woman who acts as his maid. She symbolizes his thoughts about all women. See: *Women*.

A woman in a dream can symbolize feminine characteristics of the dreamer, male or female. First, ask yourself what you associate generally with women: nurturing, receptiveness, intuitiveness, bitchiness, and motherhood are some examples. Now ask yourself whether those associations fit the character's role in the dream-story.

For example, a man dreams about observing a woman happily tending to her home, and the lifestyle appeals to him. He feels envious. It connects with his feelings about wishing he could stay home and tend to his home and family rather than spend so much time at work.

As a woman, you might struggle with some aspect of the expectations of being a woman in your culture. For example, say that you are a woman who lives in a culture in which women have to cover themselves in public. You dream about getting into a fight with a woman on the street who is covered, and in the process you tear away her clothing. The dream symbolizes your struggle with the dictates of your culture, and your desire to be free of the restrictions.

A common dream theme for women is to see aspects of their own femininity and womanhood projected onto female dream-characters. Sometimes those characters will be familiar people from their lives, such as mothers, sisters, and friends. Other times the characters will be unfamiliar. These characters are a way of comparing yourself with, and a way to learn from the examples of, other women. Dreams can address every aspect of feminine identity and trace the roots and sources back to early childhood. See: *Girl*.

These dreams can arise after a woman sees or interacts with another woman who raises her admiration, respect, or jealousy. For example, a woman who prefers ponytails and sweatshirts runs across her husband's co-worker who always looks as if she just stepped out of a salon, raising questions in the wife's mind about how she compares and about what women are valued for in society.

The most important clue for identifying the character's purpose in a dream is found in the context of the dream and the role the character plays. A dream is formed around a central idea, and everything in it points in that direction. Characters play roles and are used to advance the story, so a woman in your dream is used as part of the story. Understanding roles that way, you can identify the symbolism of any dream-character. A woman-character doesn't even necessarily represent a person.

For example, let's say that you are a man who recently quit smoking cigarettes. You are tempted to start again. You have a dream that a "smokin' hot" woman tries to seduce you into bed. The character represents temptation to smoke. A woman is used by the dream because of the associations with temptation and the visual pun on "smokin' hot."

Of course, a woman in a dream can symbolize straightforward sexual thoughts and temptations. The constant bombardment of sexualized imagery in daily life can be reproduced in dreams. Female characters that play sexual roles in dreams might be there to help you work through related thoughts, feelings, questions, and issues. They're actors in a story, and sexuality is the subject. See: *Sex.*

This subject is ripe for further exploration. Use the entries listed below, especially: *Girl, Man.*

See also: *Anima, Childbirth, Daughter, Girl, Home, Lady, Man, Mother, Ovaries, Sister, Stranger, Uterus, Vagina, Wife, Witch, Women*

Women—A group of women in a dream can symbolize something related to your perception of women in general, or some women in particular.

For example, a group of women in a dream can symbolize cultural expectations and ideals. See: *Doll, Rape.*

They can symbolize common perceptions of women such as that they're not as physically strong as men, and are more in tune with their feelings.

They can symbolize traits commonly associated with femininity, the feminine principle, and

the yin, in particular its connection with creation. See: *Vagina.*

Women in dreams—especially groups—can symbolize how you interact with women in general. For example, as a woman you might view all other women as rivals or untrustworthy. As a man, you might view them as sex objects or mother figures. See: *Group.*

Finish this sentence: "All women are ..." Whatever thoughts come first to mind might be the associations your dreams use to create symbolism.

Be sure to read: *Men, Woman.*

Also read the entry for *Men.* It explores the same ideas from the opposite perspective.

See also: *Doll, Group, Men, Numbers, Rape, Vagina, Woman*

Woods—See: *Forest, Wilderness*

Work—See: *Job*

Worm—A common use of the symbolism of a worm is to represent something worming into you. It's usually something you don't want, or even something that disgusts you.

Worms around the head and face can symbolize something that worms into your thoughts. Worms in your eyes can symbolize something that you see and can't forget. Worms around your heart can symbolize feelings eating at you, or something trying to worm into your heart, such as a suitor or a negative attitude. Worms in your ears can symbolize something you've heard that bothers you, or a song or sound stuck in your head, aka an "ear worm."

On the other hand, worms are associated with Mother Nature and ability to survive. Cut a worm in half and it becomes two worms. They're really amazing creatures when you think about it. See: *Earth.*

Finally, worms are associated with bait. They can symbolize something used to lure and entice. See: *Fishing.*

See also: *Bug, Earth, Fishing, Insects, Maggots, Music*

Wound—As a physical representation of a personal situation, a physical wound in a dream can symbolize a personal or emotional situation: hurt feelings, a hard blow, a personal attack. A wound can mean, simply, "wounded."

Wounds in a dream can symbolize harm that's been done to you, or that you have done to someone else. For example, a careless comment to a friend hurts his or her feelings, but you are not consciously aware of it. You then dream about that friend having a big wound in the chest, over the heart, and you think to yourself, *If only I could get my hands on the jerk who did this to my friend ...* And actually, it was you. Wounding amplifies the situation so you recognize it for what it is.

Injuries in dreams can be a graphic way of symbolizing damage that's not physical, such as damage to emotions, reputation, and self-image. We say that a person who makes a bad decision "hurts" herself. It's a "self-inflicted wound."

For example, a young man dreams that he drives sports cars with two of his buddies. They do daredevil maneuvers and one of his buddies wrecks badly, mangling his leg. In the next scene, the dreamer and his buddies are with a large group of their friends. The guy with the mangled leg tears off pieces of it and passes it around like popcorn.

The dreamer and his two buddies really are daredevils who push the limits, and the opening scene in the sports cars reflects the fact. The wreck and injury are an observation that the one friend takes things too far and does real damage to his life. The last detail, about passing around pieces of his mangled leg like popcorn, shows the meaning of the symbolism. It's a way of saying that the friend brags about doing things that harm him. You pass around popcorn while listening to a story. *Hey, remember that time I downed that bottle of vodka and had to get my stomach pumped? That was sooo cool!* The character is not a projection of the dreamer, but instead is a depiction of the dreamer's friend, and the symbolism of the mangled leg is based on the dreamer's subjective perception.

Keep in mind, surrogate-characters can be used to represent people you know, or yourself, and a dream will provide clues to the character's real identity. For example, you dream about a delivery driver getting badly injured in a crash, symbolizing a friend's bad decision to break up with his pregnant girlfriend. Babies are delivered during birth, so the delivery driver is identified as the friend through that association.

"Wounded" in another sense can describe a state of being. A wounded person carries the pain of the past with him. Some wounds can be healed only with love and time, or by finding purpose and meaning in life.

Areas of the body affected by wounds point toward areas of life affected by pain or damage. A wound on your body can indicate an emotional or psychological wound, something bothering you from beneath the surface of your mind, just as a bruise sits under the skin. The symbolism becomes more specific depending on the part of the body. For example, since the face is associated with social image, a wound to it can symbolize damage to reputation. See: *Amputate, Body, Face*.

A wound in a dream can symbolize wounded pride or bruised ego—again, a physical representation of a personal situation. See: *Ego*.

It can represent damage you do to your life from poor decisions or reckless behavior, such as in the mangled-leg example.

Wounds are vulnerable to infection, and that association can be used to create symbolism associated with personal vulnerability. For example, you ended an abusive relationship long ago, but the wound it left on you still affects your ability to trust people. See: *Infect*.

Wounds inflicted by an animal can symbolize wounds inflicted by a person in your life represented as the animal. For example, a dream about being bitten and scratched up by a cat follows an argument with a female friend or relative. The possibilities for animal symbolism vary widely. See: *Animals*.

Dreaming about injury or wounding can be a warning to be more careful—you might be taking risks that can lead to harm, and in the back of your mind you know it. It's a common theme in the dreams of motorcycle riders, people who deal a lot with crazy traffic, and people in dangerous professions. So if you dream about being injured, then consider the obvious and look at your life for ways in which you're taking risks—especially physical risks. Drinking and driving is an example of an obvious risk that can be consciously ignored and amplified by your dreams. See: *Grim Reaper*.

If you experienced an injury the day or two before the dream, you can dream about it. Remember that dreams exaggerate, so the dream about slicing your throat with a razor blade and gushing blood might be an exaggeration of a nick while shaving. Perhaps the thought crossed your mind that the nick could have been worse, or maybe it bled a lot. The experience made an impression on you and is amplified in your dream.

See also: *Abuse, Amputate, Animals, Attack, Beat, Blood, Body, Callus, Cry, Divorce, Ego, Face, Fist,* *Grim Reaper, Gun, Illness, Infect, Knife, Pain, Precognitive Dream, Skin, X-ray*

Wreck—See: *Car*.

Wrestle—Wrestling in a dream can symbolize struggle. Figuratively, you can wrestle with someone over a business deal. You can wrestle with yourself to control a habit or make a decision. You can wrestle with a problem or idea. See also: *Tackle*.

Wrestling can symbolize thinking about ways to come out ahead or win.

Consider the dynamics of wrestling. It is about domination, submission, and competition. Think of times the word is used other than in reference to a wrestling match. For example, a sibling rivalry is sometimes described in terms of wrestling.

Wrestling has erotic overtones. See: *Gay, Sex*.

See also: *Body, Fight, Gay, Sex, Sports, Tackle*

X-ray—An X-ray is a view inside something, to see through the surface, see what's hidden. It can symbolize seeing beneath the surface or through a facade, or showing that you have insight into the inner nature of a subject or situation.

Fear of getting an X-ray can symbolize fear of scrutiny or of people seeing the "inner you."

See also: *Body, Doctor, Hospital, Spy*

Yell—To understand the symbolism of yelling in a dream, think about why you might yell while awake: to get attention, express anger, make sure you are heard. Now consider situations where yelling is used and how dreams can expand on the idea.

You might want attention because you are being ignored, your needs aren't being met, or you enjoy the spotlight. Yelling in a dream can be a way of acting out symbolism related to doing something that gets you noticed in a good way or a bad way. For example, your promotion at work causes a big stir among your co-workers, and you dream about being in the lobby at work when a commotion breaks out, and people yell your name.

Yelling as an expression of anger is a common use of the symbolism, as opposed to screaming, which is connected with fear and losing your cool. It often arises in dreams when anger isn't being ex-

pressed or isn't effective in changing the situation causing anger. Yelling that increases in volume and urgency can relate to attention, either trying to get it—you feel that someone isn't really hearing you—or needing to give attention to something. For example, you know that a big test is coming up and you haven't started studying for it, and the urgency is increasing. In your dream a yell becomes louder and more urgent. You need to study for that test!

Yelling is a raw expression of frustration and desire to get your point across. There is a difference between hearing and listening. Just because someone hears you doesn't mean the person is really listening.

See also: *Anger, Ears, Hear, Panic, Rage, Scream, Talk, Test*

Yellow—The color yellow is associated with emotions such as joy and happiness and feelings such as optimism, hope and alertness. It's connected with the sun and sunny days. Read the entry for *Colors* to learn more about the connection between color in dreams and emotions.

Yellow is bright. It says, "Hey, look at me!"

Yellow has a flip side to it connected with finding your way out of a difficult situation and acting impulsively. And it's associated with cowardice, usually when it's depicted as a pale shade, implying a lack of willpower. A strong shade of yellow implies strong willpower.

See also: *Colors, Coward, Emotions, Joy, Sun*

Young—To dream about being younger than you are can symbolize nostalgia for the way things were, such as for simplicity and adventure.

It can point to a time of life when something began or took root. For example, the age when you first decided what you wanted to be when you grew up, or a habit began. See: *Teenager.*

Another possibility is that you are trying to reconnect with a young part of yourself. You might need more fun and play in your life. See: *Child.*

Young can mean "premature," "immature," "undeveloped," or "early."

Look at the subject from another direction by reading the entry for *Elderly.*

See also: *Animals, Baby, Boy, Child, Elderly, Girl, Kitten, Puppy, Teenager*

YouTube—Watching YouTube has similar possibilities for symbolism as watching television. See: *Television.*

A YouTube video can identify the subject of the dream or help tell its story. For example, a dream about watching a YouTube video of someone driving recklessly through traffic actually shows the dreamer's own recklessness. A YouTube video is a better choice to convey the symbolism than, say, a movie, because popular YouTube videos involving driving tend to be about everyday moments just before something extraordinary happens, such as a car wreck.

Also consider situations and circumstances involved in watching YouTube videos in waking life. For example, for some people it's a way of relaxing or killing time. Watching YouTube with friends is a social activity, and dreaming about it can be a way of pointing toward your social life. See: *Friend.*

YouTube is, for some people, a way of being seen and noticed. It can connect with that desire and motivation.

So many personal associations can come into play—impossible to cover them all. To decode the symbolism, start by considering the content of a video in your dreams, then make general associations about YouTube.

See also: *Computer, Documentary, Facebook, Friend, Movie, Phone, Television*

Zebra—A zebra in a dream can be a visual pun for something that is "black and white," no shades of gray.

See also: *Animals, Black, Colors, Horse, White*

Zombie—One of the primary ways zombies are used in dreams is to symbolize mindlessness. Being surrounded by zombies in a dream can symbolize the feeling of being surrounded by stupidity. Your world is full of the walking dead. People are driven by the most primitive of instincts. Your opinion of people and society are very low. It's an easy connection to make, bearing in mind that the comparison with zombies is an exaggeration.

Extend the idea to situations in which you are bored out of your mind. Conversations are tedious. Silence is deafening.

Extend the idea further to situations in which a person can't think of what to say or freezes with panic. A blank expression on someone's face is comparable in an exaggerated way to a zombie's blank expression.

A zombie can symbolize something that won't die, such as a bad habit or negative attachment. It can symbolize a change that isn't completed.

Zombies are awesome symbols for feeling sluggish and lifeless. Energy level is low. You have no inspiration. "The walking dead."

Zombie often goes hand in hand with "apocalypse." See: *Apocalypse.*

A zombie is dead but still alive, and that association can be used to describe a situation such as hoping to get back together with an ex. The relationship is dead, but your hope for it is alive.

See also: *Apocalypse, Coma, Creature, Death, Ex, Fire, Grim Reaper, Infest, Monster, Sleep*

Zoo—A zoo in a dream can symbolize a crazy or uncontrollable situation. A classroom full of rowdy children, chaotic work environment, or houseful of guests coming and going is a "zoo."

A messy, hectic, or unorganized environment or situation can be symbolized as a zoo.

Symbolism can be created from the cages and "animal prison" aspects of zoos. Dreaming about a zoo might mean you feel restricted or caged in. See: *Cage*.

A zoo is a perfect dream setting to speak to things you observe. Creatures at zoos are there to be observed.

An animal escaping from a zoo can symbolize escaping restriction, including restriction of your movement and decision-making.

A zoo can be simply a setting to tell a story about an animal. See: *Animals*.

See also: *Amusement Park, Animals, Cage, Family*

FIGURING OUT YOUR DREAMS

First, Three Simple Facts

Even simple dreams present so many possibilities for symbolism, it's a wonder they can be understood at all. But you have a big factor working in your favor. Not just big. Huuuge.

Simple Fact #1: You know (subconsciously) what your dreams mean.

Deep inside yourself, you know what your dreams mean because they are created in your *unconscious mind. You* create your dreams. If you don't know what the unconscious mind is, stop now and look up the entry in the dictionary part of this book. Go ahead. You'll find a thorough description that's easy to understand, even if you don't know the first thing about psychology.

The fact that you know what your dreams mean gives you an approach to understanding them. *Remember what you already know.* When you already know something, you don't have to learn anything new. Your approach is different than if you don't know something.

If it sounds easy, that's because it is—well, it may not be fair to say *easy*, but neither is it as *hard* it can seem. It really depends on the person. Be confident that anyone—you, too—can understand dreams. And by the time you take in everything offered by this book, you'll have the confidence of an expert. Seriously. Just keep reading.

Simple Fact #2: Dreams are stories.

They can be crazy stories that don't follow normal logic, but nonetheless, they're stories, and figuring them out is similar to analyzing a novel or movie. Literature 101. If you can analyze a story, you can analyze a dream.

Dreams that aren't structured as stories are better understood as *dreaming*, a succession of images and sensations you experience while asleep. Dreaming can start soon after you close your eyes and it doesn't really mean anything important.

A dream, on the other hand, is a story and it's always meaningful. It *engages* your thoughts, emotions, feelings. It *moves* you. It's *memorable*. You can start experiencing meaningful dreams soon after falling asleep, but usually, your mind needs time to warm up.

Dreaming is the rehearsal. *Dreams* are the performance.

Dreams are stories you tell yourself. Stories are interesting and they sure beat a lecture!

For tens of thousands of years, humans have used stories to learn, grow, adapt, pass down history, teach the truth and find meaning. Think of when a student approaches a teacher with a complex question and the teacher tells a story, and contained in that story is the answer. It paints a picture and engages the imagination. When the student "gets it," they really get it. The lesson sinks in.

That's what dreams do. They allow you to figure it out for yourself. They respect your intelligence. And they are very clever about tailoring stories just for you. It's like having the world's best life coach living in your head. Your own personal Jesus.

Simple Fact #3: Everything in dreams is symbolism.

Dreams use symbolism to tell stories about you and your life. Your unconscious mind takes all input from other areas of the mind and body—memories, emotions, thoughts, feelings, perceptions, physical conditions, and stimuli—and spits out the symbolism. It's all put through the grinder and out pops your dreams.

Symbolism is the native tongue of your dreams, the language of the unconscious mind. If you want to understand dreams and your unconscious mind, begin with symbolism. We'll talk more about symbolism later.

This simple fact has an exception—dreams can sometimes create direct representations that are not symbolism—but it's a solid rule of thumb.

These three facts—you know what your dreams mean, they're stories, and everything in them is symbolism—prepare you for launch to explore the mysterious and exciting world within you. Dreams truly are experiences unto themselves, like living another life or many lives simultaneously. Deep in your mind, dreams are no less real than "real" life. Treat them that way. They're never "just a dream."

The Dream Interpretation Dictionary entry for *Ego* goes into more detail about the right approach to your dream life.

Oh yeah, one more simple yet important fact: *Dream imagery is figurative, not literal,* even the most shocking and absurd dreams about subjects such as incest, murder, Armageddon, and even anal fisting can be figurative. Yes, the dictionary has an entry for *Fisting*, and just wait till you find out what it can symbolize. The dreams used to illustrate the subject are real, really shocking, really revealing, and might just crack you up.

Go check it out and come back. The best is yet to come. And remember, it's all symbolism.

What the Heck Is Happening in There?

In simplest terms, while dreaming, your brain processes and consolidates memories, and those memories are encoded into symbolism for easy reference. Dreaming makes room for tomorrow, taking what you experience today and figuring out how it fits into the existing structure that is you: your mind, psyche, personality, and character. Anything unneeded or not useful is set aside. Dreaming—especially REM-stage dreaming—is critical for brain development.

Infants sleep 16 hours per day and spend half that time in REM stage—brain development in overdrive!

Dreaming heats up your neural pathways, making them malleable—also known as *neuro-plasticity*. Some of the neural pathways are pruned and some are strengthened. Read the dictionary entry for *Letter* for more detail about the neurological process of dreaming.

Emotions are processed and sorted in parallel with your memories while dreaming, and they're combined with imagery charged with meaning and significance. You can think of your dreams as your viewing station for internal processes as you sleep, especially emotional ones. To explore this idea in more depth, read the entry for *Emotions*.

Your brain runs through stages of intensity while performing the activities described above, interspersed with stages of deep rest with little or no dreaming. It's called the *sleep cycle* and you should look it up online. The highest intensity stage is the REM stage, which is short for *rapid eye movement*. During this stage, *the brain is just as active as while awake and concentrating on a task.*

Dreams perform two stages of memory processing: the immediate processing of daily memories, and a second stage about a week later that processes memories more deeply into your being. Those dreams tend to be particularly potent, memorable, and metaphorical. Think of it as a whittling process, and left at the end are the experiences most important to your growth as a person and to your life.

The opening to the entry for *Childhood Home* continues this discussion.

Your body runs processes, too, as cells clean house and various systems and organs report in and give status updates. When something is off in your body, your mind will try to fix it, and your dreams give you a view into this process—and even make you part of it.

You can choose in your dreams to be sick or well, to heal or not, all based on what you believe to be true while dreaming—based on how you react to the imagery and story. I'm not saying it's that way for everyone—dreaming is a widely varied phenomenon—but for most folks, their dreams trigger all sorts of reactions in the body, and that fact adds to the many reasons to know as much as possible about your dream life.

For example, a man dreams that a fish with big teeth is going to enter his body and eat the coffee *grounds* in his knee. He thinks about it and says sure, go ahead. The fish does its thing, and the next day the strange *grinding* sound he'd been hearing in his knee is diminished. The fish in the dream represents antibodies, and his consent sets them loose in his bloodstream. Usually, a bodily process like this is subconscious, but he actively decides to allow it in this case.

Why? A clue is found in the next scene of the dream. When the fish is done, it's tossed into a pool with other fish and eats them, too. Antibodies are not picky. They eat their target and everything like their target. The dreamer's consent is needed because of the risk involved to address the issue with his knee by attacking it with antibodies. If he had reacted by saying he didn't want the fish anywhere near him, his body would not have loosed the antibodies. Simple fact #1: he subconsciously knows what he's agreeing to.

That bird's-eye view into your health is invaluable. It's saved many lives by giving timely warnings. Read the entries for *Cancer* and *Disease* to continue exploring this subject.

Then Something Magical Happens

You are dreaming. You experience emotions. Imagery and thoughts run through your mind. You follow them down the mystery hole. Then something magical happens.

It's magical by the standards of science because it happens even though it's apparently unnecessary for the adaptation of the human species to its environment, and all physiological processes such as dreaming are viewed in this evolutionary light. How does dreaming help the species and the individual survive and thrive?

We've discussed some examples, but none of them explain why we have deeply meaningful dreams. Some researchers say it's simply because of a human proclivity to look for meaning in everything, even where there is none. It's hardwired. But that explanation, while true in some cases, stretches too thin when used to assert that no dreams have meaning.

Dreams don't have meaning because we mistakenly ascribe it to what's merely a succession of meaningless imagery. *Dreams have meaning because something at the core of the mind steps into the dreaming process and uses it for a deeper purpose.*

That "something" is known as *the Self* and it's an archetype of the complete person, a blueprint for personal development. The Self's mission is to unify the psyche, the conscious mind with the unconscious mind, and in dreams, it appears as shapes such as circles, squares, and mandalas, and as imagery such as the Great Tree, as holy figures such as Christ and Krishna, and as talking animals. To learn more about archetypes, see: *Archetypes.*

Read the entries for *Circle, Psyche,* and *Unconscious Mind.* Explore the entries listed under "see also" to better understand why you dream in the deepest sense and what's involved. You will learn to view every meaningful dream through the lens of what it's ultimately trying to accomplish: unification of the psyche, beginning with the processing of day to day events in your life, and ending with *self-actualization.*

This book is designed to give you trails to follow as you explore your dreams. To help you understand the dreaming mind. And to make the magic of personal growth and transformation a bigger part of your life.

Dreams help you process, help you learn, help you grow, and somehow it all ties in with why consciousness exists in the first place and its role in an infinite universe.

The map for higher consciousness is embedded in the mind from birth.

The directions for following it are given to you nightly.

THE DREAMS 1-2-3 SYSTEM OF DREAMWORK

DREAMS 1-2-3 is a system for decoding and interpreting dreams to make the process as easy as possible. It has three steps:

1. Break down the dream into story elements and narrative components.

2. Use interpretation techniques to analyze the symbolism and the story.

3. Build up the interpretation by considering context and making connections.

Looks simple, doesn't it?

We still have a lot of ground to cover, but soon you will see that dream interpretation is not the big mystery it can appear to be. Anyone can do it. But remember, it requires dedication to truth and authenticity because you can just as readily believe illusion and dance with shadows as see the truth in your dreams. *It's easy to be wrong about your interpretations, and just as easy to convince yourself you are correct.*

Leave your ego at the door.

Story Analysis Step 1: Story Elements and Narrative Components

Your dreams are stories told through symbolism.

By breaking down a dream into elements and components, you look at the story and the symbolism of each detail separately. Then, in steps two and three, connect it all together and figure out how it applies to you.

A dream in its entirety can be too much to swallow at once. It's better to take it in bites and savor it for a while. Plus, it helps you to recognize the thematic threads and tie together details.

If you can figure out one part of a dream, you can use the answer to decode other parts. For example, if you know that the symbolism of a school setting in a dream connects with something you're presently learning, it might explain the presence of certain characters and the reasons for certain actions.

Think like a storyteller.

Every detail of a motion picture or novel is chosen deliberately. Your dreams take the same care and pay the same attention to detail. By analyzing how a dream-story is put together, you gain insights into its meaning and message. Reverse-engineer the dream.

Three Story Elements: Settings, Characters, Symbols

Story Analysis—Settings

Far, far away, there is a beautiful Country which no human eye has ever seen in waking hours. Under the Sunset it lies, where the distant horizon bounds the day, and where the clouds, splendid with light and colour, give a promise of the glory and beauty which encompass it. Sometimes it is given to us to see it in dreams.

—Bram Stoker

A dream's setting sets the scene. It's the stage on which the story unfolds. Without a setting, the story is not anchored to place and time.

The setting usually is symbolism, such as when a home improvement store setting symbolizes improving yourself, or your home life or a train setting symbolizes steady progress toward a goal.

Some settings don't have specific or separate symbolism. For example, if you dream about a tiger in a cage, you might expect to see it at a zoo, and the zoo is not as important to the story as the tiger and the cage. But sometimes the setting really *is* the story. It's the thread that ties together all the other details.

Settings that are incongruous with the rest of the story must be deliberate, and it must be symbolism. It could be the key for decoding the rest of the dream. The tiger and cage in the above example are in your bedroom, not a zoo. The dream deliberately places them in that setting. It could mean you are fiercely protective of your private life—bedrooms are private places for some people, and tigers are fierce—so much so that it hampers you, symbolized as the cage. Or you heavily restrain your sensuality. Tigers are sensual beasts, and bedrooms are sensual places.

A setting can represent your inner landscape, especially your emotional landscape. Or it can be a snapshot of your life—past, present, or future. For example, a scarred battlefield can represent the devastation to your life caused by fighting or stress. A meadow full of butterflies can symbolize feeling hopeful or peaceful.

Sometimes in dreams, you know where you are without being told. For example, you fly over a landscape and know it's France without seeing any identifiable landmarks. When the dream identifies the setting as France instead of just a random landscape, the detail helps tell the story.

Settings can show the big picture and subject of a dream. Figure out why a dream chooses the setting. It's deliberate and part of the story. Nothing is random in dreams, so whether your dream is set in your childhood home, France, or on the moon it means something.

Think Like a Storyteller

—What does a bank setting say about the subject of a dream? It could relate to money. See: *Bank*.

—What does a campus setting say? It could relate to school and learning. See: *Campus*.

—A library says "information" and "knowledge." See: *Library*.

—An airport or hotel says "transition." See: *Airport, Hotel*.

—A hospital says "emergency" or "health." See: *Hospital*.

Interconnected

Dreams can shift settings on the fly and they appear separate but actually continue the story. For example, you dream about flying over France and noticing a spectacular tree, and next thing you know you are in your family home talking with your grandfather about wine-making. The two scenes appear unrelated, but if the dream is telling a story about your heritage, and your family has roots in France, you see how your family home connects with France. In which case, the tree is your family tree, and your grandfather connects with your heritage. His family hails from France, and France is famous for its wine. You take pride in your French heritage.

The symbolism is understood when the setting interconnects with other details to paint a picture.

Even if a dream setting is only referred to and not actually shown, it's still part of the story. For example, you dream about trying to find your way back to your family home and never make it there. Although the setting is not shown, you should look up the entry for *Family Home*. Go ahead and do it now; it's a popular dream setting.

Read the entries for *Bedroom, Classroom, Home, Jail, Stage,* and *Zoo*. They show how these settings are used as symbolism.

Story Analysis—Characters

> The Universe is a dream dreamed by a single dreamer where all the dream characters dream too.
>
> —Arthur Schopenhauer

Dream characters are usually central to the dream-story. They move the action forward and enact the symbolism. They provide the drama. Characters generally symbolize the dynamics of your life, especially your inner life, though they can depict or represent people you know or even subjects or ideas.

Think of dream characters as actors chosen for the roles they play. Some are main actors, some are supporting actors, some are like movie extras. They generally follow a script.

The appearance of a dream character is like a costume and its behavior is programmed. Remember that.

Some characters have no choice, no real intelligence. They never veer off script. But some are distinctly intelligent and able to think and react on the fly. Noting these differences between characters is essential to understanding their symbolism. Characters with distinct intelligence are more likely to represent an aspect of yourself personified, a part of the psyche, or even the complete you, *the Self* archetype. Characters that act programmed are more likely to represent someone who is part of your life, or a subject or idea.

They're All You

Think of your dream as a movie projector, the screen as your mind's eye, and the film as a picture of your inner world. Everything you see on the screen is a projection from within you, especially the characters. In your dreams, parts of yourself personify, and while they can take form as objects and settings, they usually take form as dream characters. They're all you.

Even when dream characters look like people you know, they're still actors. They're *characterizations*. If your parent or best friend is characterized in a dream as an ax-wielding maniac, it's based on your thoughts, feelings, and perceptions—assuming that it's not a representation of the person's actual behavior! Which is highly unlikely, yes, but not impossible.

Or the character represents something about you. See: *Brother*.

Think of it as separating the actor from a role they play. It's tempting to think of the actor as the character, but instead, the character is role-played, and the person might be far different from the character they portray.

Most people think that dream characters based on people they know must represent those people when the opposite is usually the case. Dreams can directly depict people you know, but more often the characters are projections of your inner world.

For example, you dream about your mom. In the dream, she looks and acts as she does in your daily life, but she's still a character in a story. It's not her; it's an actor playing her role in a story. The script she follows can be based on reality, or it can be completely imaginary.

Or, say that you wake up from a dream with a feeling that your mom is in danger, and at that moment she's being rushed to the hospital after taking a bad fall. What you see in your dream is a direct representation of her. People can and do subconsciously communicate in dreams and pick up on what's happening with each other. We're all connected via our unconscious mind. To explore this idea further, see: *Collective Unconscious*.

See the entry for *Wound* for an example of a dream that dramatizes the behavior of the dreamer's friend. The character in the dream is based on the dreamer's perceptions of that friend, which provide the programming for the character's appearance and behavior. In this case, the dream is observing something about the friend. The character is not purely a projection of the dreamer's inner world, nor is it a direct representation of the person. Instead, as in most cases, there's overlap between the dreamer's outer and inner worlds.

And remember, the stronger you react to a dream character, the more it might be showing you something about yourself you don't like or want to know. Ridiculous and exaggerated dream characters tend to compensate for one-sided attitudes of the ego. See: *Compensation*.

It's safe to assume that dream characters tie in with the subject or theme of the dream. So, for example, you dream about being naked in front of people you know from work or school. You can bet that the dream's subject or theme involves work or school. Next, figure out what nakedness symbolizes in this case and you're well on the way to figuring out the meaning.

However, a rule of thumb like the one above always has exceptions. Dreams are known to use some details purely to create a believable atmosphere for a story to unfold.

Groups of Characters

Some characters are used as a group. For example, if a dream wants to address the subject of your place in society, it can show you among thousands of people in a stadium and they all play one role: to represent society. Or, one character can represent a group, such as when one family member is used to represent the entire clan, or one co-worker is used to represent them all. Read the entries for *Family, Group,* and *Men* for more discussion about this subject.

Surrogates

Dream characters can be surrogates for people you know. Surrogates don't necessarily look like those people, but something will connect them symbolically. Such as when a dog ("man's best friend") is used to represent your friend, or a nun (a "sister") represents your sister or a sister-like relationship.

Dreams have a variety of reasons for using surrogates. Oftentimes, it's done to give you the distance to observe. For examples, see: *Co-Worker, Daughter, Ex, Girl*.

Characters can symbolize something intangible such as authority or ambition. For example, principals and police officers are authority figures and can be used to represent authority. A celebrity can symbolize ambition. Stephen Hawking, the famous physicist, can symbolize intelligence. These sorts of characters symbolize subjects or ideas. For further example, see: *Donald Trump*.

Even if a dream only refers to a character or type of character, analyze it as part of the story. *"Everyone hide, the police are coming!"* If that's part of a dream, look up *Police Officer* to get ideas about what it means.

To get a better idea of how to approach interpreting familiar people in your dreams depicted as characters, see: *Employee, Fiancé, Friend, Sister.* For unfamiliar characters, see: *Doctor, Fugitive, Stranger*. For non-human characters, see: *Animals, Doll, Monster, Snake*. For characters that represent aspects of the psyche, see: *Animus*, *Shadow*. For famous people, see: *Famous*. To better understand your relationship with your dream characters, check out: *Archetypes, Ego, Jesus*.

And remember, you are a character in the story, too, an actor playing a role. Everything, including your actions and behaviors, is scripted. You act out the symbolism. More about that later when we discuss action as a narrative component.

A dream can present a scenario and allow you to react on the fly. You can determine where the story goes. It's not entirely scripted. We'll dig more into that subject later when we discuss reaction as a narrative component.

Story Analysis—Symbols

What we call a symbol is a term, a name, or even a picture that may be familiar in daily life, yet that possesses specific connotations in addition to its conventional and obvious meaning.

—Carl Jung

Everything in dreams is symbolism, except on occasion when they're literal. It might seem pointless to differentiate a symbol from symbolism, but there is a difference, and it's important:

- A symbol is a thing that represents an idea or set of ideas.
- Symbolism is the use of that thing in a story.

Compare it to the difference between a snapshot and a video recording. A symbol is like a snapshot, a moment captured in time. No action and limited context. It might be obvious what's really happening in a snapshot, but you must make some assumptions. Symbolism is like a video recording of the same scene. It shows the action and context and leaves less room for guessing. The meaning is right before your eyes—if you know how to see it in the actions and other details.

Symbolism gives definition to your dream *symbols*.

You have heard the famous saying, "A picture says a thousand words"? Well, the person who coined that phrase might as well have been describing dream symbols. They are loaded with information that can be communicated all in a glance: thoughts, emotions, feelings, ideas, opinions, perceptions, and interconnections.

And here's the rub: a symbol or dream can have multiple meanings. For example, the flood that overtakes you could symbolize a situation that overwhelms you, plus the emotions that pour out of you, plus, well, a pipe burst in your kitchen and flooded it, creating the situation that overwhelms you and hits your emotions hard.

Dreams choose symbols carefully and deliberately to capture dynamics. Dreams are not likely to symbolize an argument as a war, for example, unless the argument is part of a protracted struggle or heated battle, which are associations with war. A nuclear war is stronger symbolism. It's not just any argument, it's the mother of all arguments. It's Armageddon!

Or maybe it just feels like Armageddon. Your dreams use symbols subjectively, not objectively. The person you argue with, who doesn't feel as strongly as you, might dream about the same situation as firecrackers or balloons popping.

Dreams use symbolism that fits best. It gets the point across and captures your feelings, emotions, thoughts and perceptions. Plus, it's good storytelling.

Your dreaming mind starts with a conflict you're in, for example, then picks the best symbolism for telling the story. And the strength of the symbolism depends on the strength of the conflict, the dynamics of the situation, and how you feel about it. A small conflict can be symbolized as a wind howling outside your home, but a big conflict is a hurricane that rips the roof off!

Ripping the roof off can be appropriate symbolism for losing your head—your head representing the roof, and the hurricane representing the turbulent conflict. Or it's a conflict that threatens your security, the "roof over your head." Specific details in the dream-story match the situation.

Specific or General

When a conflict is with a specific person or thing, a good rule of thumb is the dream is more likely to feature a specific opponent. A battle that's not personal is more likely to use the battle theme without showing specific or individual opponents. The battle is with a pile of work and is shown as enemy troops overrunning a defensive position. The enemy troops are not emphasized and few details are given about them. They are all lumped together. On the other hand, another battle is with a dark side of your personality, and the enemy presented by the dream is a dark knight determined to lop off your head with a huge sword. The dark knight is a specific opponent. The battle is personal. To explore further, see: *Enemy, Opponent*.

The entry for *Earthquake* shows the same process at work when analyzing a story about a disaster. The entry for *Storm* is another good resource.

Think Like a Storyteller

Dreams carefully choose every detail, so question those details. See the reasoning behind them. Reverse engineer.

Take modes of transportation, for example. Oftentimes, they are used to symbolize the movement of your life, the progress or lack of it and ways you go about your business. Your life "moves." You "go places." You have destinations.

For example, marriage is a destination. Retirement is a destination. Learning a new skill is a destination. Now think like a storyteller and consider the options you have: car, train, boat, plane, bus, bicycle, hot air balloon, rocket, spaceship. Choose the mode of transportation that best fits the situation.

Cars tend to symbolize daily life and present circumstances. Trains tend to be associated with ideas such as "on the right track" and "interrelated." Boats tend to symbolize long-term goals and destinations and movement in the psyche. Planes, on the other hand, get you to destinations quickly. To dig deeper into this subject, see: *Airplane, Balloon, Bicycle, Boat, Bus, Car, Rocket, Train*.

Prominence

A symbol's prominence in the dream-story is a clue. For example, it's one thing to dream about seeing a knife on a counter, and another thing to dream about using your father's favorite knife to cut free someone trapped in a sinking car. In that case, you use the knife instead of just seeing it, and it's not any ol' knife, it's your father's. It has greater importance and prominence, and so does the symbolism. Using your father's knife can symbolize using something he taught you, or following his example. It's a stronger situation requiring stronger symbolism.

A nondescript knife on a counter can symbolize a counter-argument. The knife is neither prominent nor specific.

See the difference?

Symbols by themselves generally don't say much. Or they potentially say too much—the possibilities are so broad—and the meaning is hard to pin down. But they have rich meaning and significance when put together with other details and shown in the context of the dream-story.

Modifiers

Symbols are modified by details such as color, movement, conditions, position, shape, speed, and size. These modifiers are the adjectives and adverbs of dream language. Learn more by reading the entries for *Backward, Colors, Ear, Ice, Shapes, Tidal Wave* and *Whale*.

Step 1: Three Narrative Components: Action, Reaction, Resolution

After noting the dream's settings, characters, and symbols, it's time to analyze the narrative. Dreams are narratives, and when fully formed they have three narrative components:

1. Action

2. Reaction

3. Resolution

In these components, the story of the dream—especially its meaning and message—really stands out.

Story Analysis: Action

Actions speak louder than words.

—Famous Idiom

The action component of a dream is a primary place to focus for decoding the symbolism. Action *shows* symbolism. Action adds definition to your dream symbols by *showing* the meaning.

Stop for a moment and fully absorb that last paragraph. Most people don't know that the actions in their dreams are symbolism. A symbol in motion is symbolism.

Action tells the dream-story. It moves the plot forward and is found in the verbs you use to describe the dream: run, swim, hide, fall, swim, float, talk, eat. Flying can symbolize quickly getting to a destination in your life. Hiding can mean to conceal or avoid. Eating can mean to take something into yourself such as opinions, beliefs, or knowledge. These actions have entries in *The Dream Interpretation Dictionary* and have more possible meanings than described here. Point is, learn to identify the actions of your dreams and think of them as symbolism.

Another important point: you, as a character in the dream-story, act out the script. You act out the symbolism. You are an *actor*. Anytime you do something in a dream and don't have a choice, assume it's symbolism. It's the bulls-eye for interpreting the dream. Focus there.

When people commit a horrible act in a dream, they assume it must be a moral defect or judgment when it's just symbolism acted out. For examples, see: *Beat, Murder, Suicide.*

You act out your feelings, emotions, thoughts, perceptions, and so on. For example, you act out feelings of frustration by kicking someone in a dream or act out feelings of elation by flying in a dream. You act out thoughts of regret by cutting off a limb. You act out perceptions of a person as untrustworthy by locking doors.

Now expand that idea and consider actions that happen to you. For example, you dream about a friend lighting you on fire and it expresses fear that the person could "burn" you by exposing intimate secrets. You dream about a co-worker crashing her car into yours, symbolizing a conflict in your schedules and her refusal to budge.

The action can be a modifier of other symbolism and point right to where meaning is found such as how you drive a car—fast, slow, forward, in reverse. The car symbolizes your life or something about it, and the movement—speed, direction, control—tells the story.

Read the entry for *Climb*. It's a great example of symbolism in motion. And while you're at it, look up the entries for *Amputate, Bury, Construction, Fall, Fight* and *Run* to fill out the picture.

Story Analysis: Reaction

For every action, there is an equal and opposite reaction.

—Sir Isaac Newton

The virtuous man contents himself with dreaming that which the wicked man does in actual life.

—Sigmund Freud

The reaction component of a dream shows how you feel and provides clues for what the symbolism means. It's raw, honest, from-the-gut. Subconsciously, you know what the symbolism means and, while dreaming, react to that, *not to the overt imagery or actions.*

Your reaction can be the most important clue to the meaning of a dream or a scene within it if you answer the question, "Why did I react that way?"

Your reaction can really stick out, especially when it's disproportionate to the situation. Why run from the baby in your dream if it's just a baby, right? Because it symbolizes a small problem you fear will grow big and want no part of it. Or it answers the question of whether you want to have children. In this case, the answer is *hell no!*

You know what the baby symbolizes, and your reaction says everything. Remember, though, a baby in a dream has a wide variety of possibilities for meaning. See: *Baby*.

Choose Your Own Adventure

Reactions can determine what happens next in the story, affecting the direction of the plot, like a *Choose Your Own Adventure* book. For example, instead of running from the baby in the dream, you take it in and love it, showing a willingness to address the problem, or to have children, or to nurture yourself, or to take on a new challenge. That reaction changes how the story unfolds.

Your reaction says everything when someone you've been dating says, "I love you," or when you hear that your ex is dating someone, or you get a Christmas present other than what you really want, or a friend asks for help moving. When you dream about scenarios such as these, your reaction shows your true feelings.

Or your reaction might act out the script, just part of the story. You can tell the difference based on how much control you have. Is your reaction the result of your free will, or is it beyond your control?

For example, a man dreams that he watches another man get stomped to death and does nothing to intervene, then dreams about a fire at a nightclub and he gets out before warning anyone else. In both scenarios, he's put into situations that test his reactions, and what they show is that by not coming to the aid of people during emergencies, he's acting out his feelings about always coming to the rescue of people in his life. It's an old pattern and he's ready to break it. His reactions are based on the symbolism presented by the dream scenarios, and his feelings show in his reactions. While dreaming, he acts out the symbolism, and what it shows is he wants to break the pattern.

Now look at those dreams without knowing that the dreamer's reactions are symbolism. You might think he's a heartless bastard and has a secret wish to commit violence or watch the world burn. You might think he's been watching snuff films or gets off by torturing puppies. The man himself wondered if his dreams show a serious moral defect or latent wickedness.

A common misconception is that dreams allow Mr. Hyde to emerge from Dr. Jekyll, that dreams remove the mask of civility and allow the wild animal in us all to emerge, and that's just not the case. The opposite is true. Yes, dreams can act as wish fulfillment. They strip away the filters. They allow the real inner you to show. And, except in cases of strong repression or psychosis, what they usually reveal is the virtuous person within you.

Reactions in dreams are largely based on feelings and emotions, and strong reactions tell you that the related feelings and emotions are strong.

Alternatively, if you don't react strongly to dream imagery that should provoke potent feelings—such as witnessing a murder or watching the world about to end—you can bet that the underlying symbolism isn't connected with strong feelings. For example, reacting mildly to the world ending could mean that your favorite television show is ending, but reacting strongly can mean that something about your world is ending, such as when a loved one dies.

Testing, Testing

Dreams can create scenarios to test your reactions as a way of showing you your true thoughts and feelings, preparing you for future scenarios, or simulating situations. For example, if you normally freeze up when the spotlight of group attention shines on you, you might dream about being on stage with all eyes in the audience on you. How do you react? If it's with new-found confidence, it could be a turning point for you.

Or, you are deathly afraid of spiders and dream about a big, nasty spider. If you quell your fear of the spider while dreaming, it will carry over to your waking life.

The entry for *Emotions* has good examples. You can also check out: *Amputate, Anger, Bed, Beggar, Blood, Brother, Cry, Descend, Drugs, Friend, Hate, Machine Gun, Nightmare, Shower, Wallet.*

Story Analysis: Resolution

Dreams are the presentations of the experiences necessary for the development [of the person], if the [person] would apply them in the physical life. These may be taken as warnings, as advice, as conditions to be met, conditions to be viewed in a way and manner as lessons, as truths.

—Edgar Cayce

The resolution component of a dream is often the most difficult part to identify and interpret. It's either hidden somewhere in the dream-story or left to you to figure out. To find the resolution, you might need to wait until the end of the interpretation process or longer. Some dreams take years to resolve, and that's all right. You have time.

A resolution is a main way you can make your dreams part of your waking life. It's how you really benefit from a dream. A resolution gives you the opportunity to live your dreams in the truest sense, to apply what you learn, to make them an active part of daily life by taking to heart their messages and acting on them.

Oftentimes, a resolution is what's left over after all other parts of a dream have been deciphered. It's the part that doesn't fall under any other category.

Dreams give you another way of looking at yourself and your life. They offer perspective by breaking down complex personal situations into stories to help you find your own resolution. Sometimes it's right there in the dream if you have the eyes to see it, but oftentimes the dream meets you halfway and leaves the rest up to you.

If a dream suggests something, run with it.

If it asks a question, answer it.

If it points out a problem, solve it.

If it shows you a sore spot, heal it. If you're not sure how, ask for help. Ask your dreams, they're listening.

If a dream shows you wearing a color or symbol, wear it. Dreams speak in pictures, and color can speak volumes.

If a dream shows an activity, consider what it's really saying. For example, you dream about taking a yoga class. You don't necessarily need to do yoga. It could be simply a way of saying, "Hey, you feel stiff. Stretch!"

Or perhaps the activity in the dream is a straightforward suggestion. Yes, do yoga or whatever activity is performed in the dream.

If a dream brings up a subject, research it. People are known to dream about a subject out of the clear blue about which they know little—astrology, Taoism, sacred geometry, gardening, marine biology, a period of history—and find a personal gold mine by digging into it.

Work with the Story

You can find resolution at a story level without understanding everything about a dream. The dream presents its suggestions, questions, and problems in story form, and *when you are awake you can continue the story*.

For example, I had a dream about three rough-looking young men searching my home, presumably to rob me. One of the young men took the string from a hoodie I was wearing. It was a tense moment as I wondered if he was about to strangle me with it.

The puzzling image stuck in my mind, and I told a wise friend about it. She asked me, "Is the young man there to rob you, or does he need something?" My body twitched with recognition. The young man needed something from me, and when understood that way I was only happy to offer it, along with my heartfelt wish for his well-being. I pictured in my mind offering him the string and feeling at peace as he reaches toward my neck to take it. When I was his age I lived through many hardships, and I know well what it means to need something and search for it. Part of me is still searching, and since the dream's setting is my present home, it means the part of myself symbolized as the young man is still looking. I don't know exactly what "it" is, and don't need to. Using my imagination to address the situation at a story level is the catalyst for a needed change.

Resolution can take time to figure out, to know what you're supposed to do, or it can be obvious from the moment you wake up. Some dreams are indecipherable until more insight and self-knowledge are gained or a situation plays out.

Even the best dream interpreters can be puzzled by their own dreams. Dreams show you what you don't already know, and most people are naturally drawn to finding out what they don't know—especially when it's something they don't know about themselves.

As one of the most famous dream interpreters of all time, Edgar Cayce, says, "Dreams are today's answers to tomorrow's questions." You don't know for sure what tomorrow will bring, but you can get a good idea by closely following your dreams.

What you see in a dream is still partly or completely unconscious, so of course it's foreign and puzzling to the ego. Turn it over in your mind. Give it your attention. Reach out with your feelings. The resolution will come to you.

Your dreams want you to understand their messages and act on them.

Examples

A woman dreams about meeting actor Steve Buscemi in an art store, and a romance is sparked. She's aware while dreaming that she has a boyfriend and feels conflicted. Steve wants her to *run off* with him, but she says she can't leave her boyfriend. She decides that Steve should meet her boyfriend, and that's the resolution.

See, Steve Buscemi represents her love of art. She's about to *run off* to graduate school to study art and fears that her relationship with her boyfriend won't survive. But if he understands that only something she loves so much as art would take her away, it might show him how much he means to her and create the sort of bond that can survive long-distance. Her boyfriend needs to really *meet* this side of herself symbolized as Buscemi.

A different woman dreams that she's working at the family business when a commotion breaks out in the lobby. She dreads getting involved, but no one else is around to help. She's the only worker. Bruce Lee is in the lobby, and he's legless. Near the front door, the exit, she sees a young boy who appears to want to leave. Dream ends.

Working for the family business in this dream symbolizes planning holidays, cleaning house, and running errands. She does it out of love for her family, but she feels alone and resentful. The lion's share of the work falls on her. She wishes she could muster the courage to tell off family members, who cause commotions and don't contribute, to kick some ass Bruce Lee-style, or to just walk away and let them deal with everything. But Bruce is legless, meaning she can't walk away; she loves her family despite how they can make her crazy. Plus, her sense of duty overrides her personal desires.

The boy's position near the front door is the dream's suggestion to at least know she can exit the situation when she needs to. If she's going to continue working for the family business, she must find a way of dealing with the commotion it causes in her life. And she must feel like *she has a choice*.

The young boy represents the resolution, which is implied by his positioning near the exit.

Sometimes, the dream itself is the resolution. A young man dreams that he sees his ex-girl-friend and invites her to get into his car. Instead, she stands at the window and tells him he needs to let go of her—the relationship is over and holding onto it is tearing him up inside. She tells him that he's been through other breakups and knows how to let go. He wakes up in the morning knowing he can move on.

Life Is But a Dream

People think of being asleep and being awake as two distinctly separate states of being with no overlap, but the truth is you can continue to dream while awake, especially if you are sleep-deprived or have big, personal blind spots. Stop for a moment and really consider the implications. How do you know that you aren't dreaming *right now*? Dreams create completely believable, simulated realities. They can make you think you are awake when you're not. You can live an entire life while dreaming. Are you truly awake? How do you know?

Deep in your mind, in your unconscious, there's no difference between what you experience while dreaming or while awake, no difference between fantasy and reality. In dreamland, they're one in the same.

Some of the smartest and wisest people say that imagining something is the first and most essential step to making it "real." In the words of Albert Einstein: "Imagination is more important than knowledge. For knowledge is limited, whereas imagination embraces the entire world, stimulating progress, giving birth to evolution."

Look up *Childhood Home, Emotions, Ex, Family Home, Lottery* for more examples of resolution and ways that unresolved issues, situations, and questions can manifest in your dreams.

Step 2: Dream Interpretation

The interpretation of dreams is the royal road to a knowledge of the unconscious activities of the mind.

—Sigmund Freud

A dream which is not interpreted is like a letter which is not read.

—The Talmud

"Dream interpretation" is a loaded term. It brings pictures to mind of psychiatrists' offices with leather couches, gurus in white robes, and mysterious psychics with penetrating gazes and crystal balls. Dream interpretation can be intimidating because it's a rarified area of knowledge and expertise, but it shouldn't be such a big mystery. Yes, a gifted dream interpreter can see things in your dreams that you can't. At heart, though, dreams are stories, and anyone can understand a story. Sharing your dreams with a dream interpreter or dream group can be very helpful, but don't let anyone force their views on you. The power is in your hands.

Remember simple fact #1: *You already know (subconsciously) what your dreams mean.*

Let's add another fact: dreams have multiple meanings and layers of significance. The renowned dreamworker Jeremy Taylor says there is no such thing as a dream with only one meaning.

Now get ready to put on your guru hat and step into the heart of the mystery.

After breaking down the dream into story elements and narrative components, the next step is to understand the symbolism and the story. To do so, *use interpretation techniques* and *analyze the storytelling devices.*

Dream Interpretation—Interpretation Techniques

You have three primary interpretation techniques to choose from for analyzing your dreams, and you can use one or all them to decode the meaning:

1. Associate

2. Simplify

3. Amplify

Interpretation Techniques—Associate

Association is the most popular interpretation technique. It's simple. Boil down a detail from a dream to a word, phrase, or image, and what comes to mind associated with it?

Associations are your thoughts, feelings, emotions, and perceptions related to a symbol, subject, or idea raised by a dream.

Dreams use associations to create symbolism. They begin with a basic idea and associate it with something else. For example, dogs are commonly associated with friendship. A dream can use a dog to symbolize a specific friend, a friendship, or the subject of friendship.

Assume that the following four words are details from a dream and see what associations come to mind with each of them, the first words that pop into your head. It's an exercise and no context is given, as would be the case if they were symbols in a dream.

Sports car

School

Sex

Sun

Associate freely. Just get in the flow and let it tumble out. Avoid judging or second-guessing. And remember, associations should always lead back to the dream. Don't stray too far!

Association allows your intuition and feelings to speak, to end run around your filters. It bridges the gap between what you know consciously and what you know subconsciously.

Associations: Personal and General

Begin with personal associations. Pretend the sports car in your dream is a Mustang and it reminds you of one your cousin owns—your cousin who's a real go-getter. That's a personal association. The Mustang is cherry red, brand new, and sits idly in a garage, and to you that seems like a waste of a great machine. Now we have detail and context. Note the type of car, its color and condition, who it's connected with, the setting in which it appears, what it does (actions), and how you feel about it. In Step 3, you will figure out how details like these fit together to tell a story about you and your life.

After making personal associations, think of general associations with sports cars. They're fast, expensive, showy. Your dreams can use any or all of those associations to create symbolism.

The entry for *Mountain* has a discussion of a dream that shows how a personal association with a sports car is used as symbolism.

Association is brainstorming. Some of your ideas won't feel right or lead you anywhere, but hitting the mark gives you a snap of recognition. You subconsciously know what the symbolism means, so making the right association is like remembering something on the tip of your tongue. *Snap!*

You acquire a personal library of associations throughout your lifetime from personal experience, exposure, culture, DNA, society, and media. You are born with some associations, such as knowing that mom is life, and acquire the rest. As you learn and grow, your dreams have more to work with, eventually accumulating many thousands of potential references for use as symbolism. See the entry for *Collective Unconscious* to better understand the associations you are born with.

The Dream Interpretation Dictionary is loaded with entries showing how associations are used to create symbolism. For examples of specific associations, see: *Banana, Butterfly, Kitten, Raccoon.* For general associations, see: *Army, Crack House, Gun.*

Interpretation Techniques: Simplify

Explain your dream in simplest terms. Summarize it as a sentence, phrase, or word. Identify the central theme. Otherwise, the powerful drama and imagery of a dream can prevent you from seeing the simple, obvious meaning.

So, you dream that a dragon hunts you with the intent of eating you, and you run for your life. In simplest terms, you are running from something symbolized as the dragon, perhaps something that scares you, or that you can't face.

Look at the story from the perspective of the dragon. Perhaps it simply represents a problem you ignore and it only gets worse the longer you wait. From the point of view of a dragon, a person is a small problem, right? In fact, when you use your imagination to ask what's its beef with you, Mr. Dragon replies that it eats anyone that ignores it. Now you know whatever the dragon represents is probably something you ignore. Plus, it pegs the top of your anxiety meter, and that tells you it must represent something serious. It's strong symbolism. A dragon isn't a fly buzzing around your head, a minor annoyance or problem that can be ignored. It's a dragon!

You dream about losing control while driving and the car skids all over the road then straight off a cliff, and you wake up just before impact, your heart pounding. In simplest terms, what does that say about you? How are you out of control? What sort of danger are you in?

Notice the Obvious

Because you are in the thick of the action, it's hard to see the obvious, even hours or days later when you reflect on the dream, but the meaning is right there if you explain it in simplest terms. The theme of the car example is about *control*. One word says it all. The car represents the movement of your life, and skidding off a cliff shows a lack of control. Or you dream about flying like an eagle, and the word that comes to mind is "soar." It sums up how your life is going and how you feel.

Keep it simple, or at least start simple.

Here's a dream with a meaning that's obvious to everyone except the dreamer. He's 16 years old and has been in a relationship with his girlfriend for six weeks. Things are fantastic, couldn't be better, except for one thing, and it shows in a dream he has about his girlfriend locking him out of his bedroom. When he asks her to let him in, she refuses, saying from the other side of the door, "It's not safe."

Put together the clues: girlfriend, bedroom, locked door, something isn't safe.

The only piece of information you lack is the fact that she won't have sex with him. Now it's obvious. Locked out of a bedroom (a room associated with sex) by a girlfriend who is putting off sex, and her reason is it's not safe, as in it's not safe because she fears she will get pregnant, or catch a disease, or her parents will find out, or whatever. It's obvious, but first the dream must be simplified as a one-sentence question the dreamer can ask himself: What am I being denied by my girlfriend?

To him, though, the meaning of the dream isn't obvious, and it's not a defect or anything, it's just a blind spot. Plus, he's young. As we experience life and accumulate associations, the dreaming mind has more to work with, and dream themes progress from general to highly personal. At 16 years old, his dreams tell the story as his girlfriend locking him out of his bedroom. At 60 years old, his dreams might tell the story of his girlfriend hiding his Viagra!

There's Obvious, Then There's Obvious

Noticing the obvious extends to dreams with obvious messages. The meaning and message are right in front of your eyes. For example:

- You dream that your car brakes fail while driving on a familiar road. It could mean you can't slow down your life, or you felt some softness in your brakes and subconsciously can sense they're about to fail. Maybe you are ignoring the obvious.

- You dream your tooth is infected. Could mean that you have allowed a situation to fester, or that you have an infection developing in a tooth. It's an early warning.

- You dream that you lose your wallet, and the next day you find yourself in the exact situation as when you lost it, except now you're awake. Do you secure your wallet?

Always consider the obvious. You can often tell the difference by how a dream with an obvious message mirrors reality. The car with bad brakes in your dream is your car, and the road you drive on when they fail is one you drive on regularly. It's not an imaginary car on an imaginary road. Dreams that closely mirror reality are more likely to have direct messages. See: *Precognitive Dream.*

Explain in Simplest Terms

In simplest terms, what is a baby? It's new life. See: *Baby.*

What does it mean to endlessly pack luggage? You get ready but never go anywhere. See: *Baggage.*

THE ⟨DREAM INTERPRETATION ⟨DICTIONARY

What is a pack of hyenas? Trouble.

What is a bridge? A route over an obstacle. See: *Bridge.*

Using this technique can also help you understand at least one part of a dream, then use what you know to interpret the rest. You know that the bridge in your dream represents a route over an obstacle, for example, and it explains why the river beneath it is filled with credit card bills and you are shirtless: because the obstacle is too much debt, the route over it is your plan to pay off the debt, and your fear is you will end up financially ruined (shirtless) if you don't get a handle on the situation.

For more examples, see: *Abortion, Addict, Climb, Dressed, Evil, Journey, Overdose, Vomit.*

Interpretation Techniques—Amplify

To amplify means to magnify, to increase, to crank it up, and for our purpose it means:

1. Bring forward parts of a dream that otherwise might be overlooked or unrecognized for their importance

2. A storytelling device, used especially to counterbalance minimization

Counterbalancing in the psyche is known as *compensation*. Look it up in the dictionary section. It's related to amplification.

Amplification in dreams is your inner storyteller's way of foreshadowing future growth and healing, and of showing potential and what stands in the way or needs to be done to realize it. It helps you see what stands in your way—especially parts of yourself that work against you.

The storyteller can only do so much, though, so pay close attention when you recognize the use of amplification. Dreams amplify when necessary. You aren't listening, noticing, or getting the message. Or you are in new personal territory. A page of the book of your life is turning and new information is only starting to come forward that will shape the next chapter of your life.

Or, as is often the case, it's just good storytelling. The master craftsman in your unconscious mind uses amplification because it works. It gets your attention.

When dreams amplify, they show you the truth, especially when you minimize and it causes issues, such as when stress eats at you and you say it's just the price to be paid, or you fail to recognize how your behaviors and attitudes affect people in your life. You then dream about a tornado tearing through your home, an amplification of the effects of stress, or about seeing a loved one bleeding head to toe, an amplification of an emotional or psychological wound, *perhaps one inflicted by you.*

Nothing Overlooked

Amplification draws attention to where it is needed, a big sign that says, "LOOK HERE, THIS IS IMPORTANT!!!" Read the entry for *Grim Reaper* and see how a dream amplifies the dangers of drinking and driving. The dreamer minimizes the risk and his dream responds powerfully.

Amplification helps you notice the small voices in your head and little-but-important things in your life. The entry for *Walmart* has a great example of one man's dramatic, amplified dream that acts as a response to minimizing his feelings about how crappy his job is. Look it up.

The man who had that dream can see himself in the character who is sacrificed. The character is, after all, a projection of himself. He can recognize that he truly feels like his job is taking something essential from him and he feels more strongly about it than he lets on. He can sympathize with himself for having to take whatever job is available because he needs the money. And if he wants to, he can decide that in the future he'll no longer have to work for Walmart. But until he recognizes what the job is taking from him, he minimizes his feelings, which keeps him right where he is—*he won't change the situation.*

Personal Narratives

Amplification helps you recognize the narratives that define your possibilities, limits, and boundaries. The person you are is largely constructed around narratives in your head. You are this, you are that, you are from whatever place and are a product of what's happened so far in your life and what you believe to be true. Dreams are, simply, narratives, and in them you see both the narratives you construct for yourself, and those constructed for you through external scripting and programming—especially through your beliefs. Dreams help you see yourself from different perspectives by amplifying your personal narratives.

Dreams amplify your narratives so you can more clearly see the scripts you follow. You then have a conscious choice to continue following them, reshape them, or completely rewrite them. Change the script. That's the first step to changing your life.

Your dreams provide everything needed to change the script. The symbols in your dreams are potential energy—set it in motion! You don't even have to know exactly what the symbols mean, just follow your feelings and work with them in your imagination. Working with your dreams activates and energizes subconscious processes and the energy feeds back into itself like a loop or vortex.

Your dreams are dramatizations. You aren't just alive, you are having an *experience of life.* In your dreams, you're no longer just a person, you're an important character in an important story. You are a living myth, and the story is written a day and a night at a time. The entry for *Archetypes* expands on this discussion.

Power of Imagination

Daydreaming is a potent way of working with your dream symbols and amplifying them. Carl Jung calls it "Active Imagination", and it's known by other names such as "Creative Visualization". Look it up online, or refer to chapter three of my book *Dreams 1-2-3.*

You can amplify a dream by stepping into the roles of the other characters and seeing the story through their eyes, such as in the dragon and Walmart examples discussed previously. You can question how they're used in the story, and even talk with them directly. Dream characters are products of your imagination, so it's not like you must be dreaming to use your imagination.

When, for example, the wolf leads you into a wilderness in a dream, you can at any time while dreaming or awake ask where it's leading you. Ask what its role is in the story, its feelings and thoughts. Ask what it thinks of you. Ask what it can do for you, and what you can do for it. It's there to help you, and your willingness to accept that help and offer it in return sends a very positive message to your unconscious mind. You can even question and encourage inanimate objects to speak from their perspective.

Psychologist Robert A. Johnson says that the unconscious mind has two ways of communicating with its counterpart, the conscious mind: dreams and imagination. With your imagination, you can continue where a dream leaves off and reap what it sows.

The Story of Your Life

Traditionally, amplification technique is used to connect your dreams with literature and myth to understand how your life mirrors them, especially when dreams have fantastic settings such as castles and magic towers, characters such as kings and wizards, and creatures such as dragons and centaurs. Anytime a dream reminds you of a story—novel, motion picture, biography, comic book, legend—refer to it for clues to the meaning. There's no rule in dreamland against building atop the work of other stories. To expand on this idea, see: *Archetypes*.

Search online for "Jung dream amplification" to further explore this topic. See the entries for *Cry, Documentary, Hear, Joy, Movie,* and *Wound* for more examples and ideas.

Dream Interpretation—Storytelling Devices

The dream is the theater where the dreamer is at once scene, actor, prompter, stage manager, author, audience, and critic.

—Carl Jung

Your dream source, *the Self* archetype in the unconscious mind, is a storyteller. In fact, it's a *great* storyteller and it draws from an endless well of history, knowledge, experience, and imagination. You don't have to read piles of books or watch tons of movies to understand instinctually how stories are put together and what makes them effective. Every day of your life is a story and you continually turn it into a narrative.

History is a story. Life in society is a story. Everyone has a story to tell.

Your dream source builds stories around what's most important in your life and inside you—especially in your emotions. It focuses first on areas ripe for the potential for personal growth, and on everything *overlooked, unnoticed, unwanted* or *underappreciated*. Then it sorts through its options for symbolism and chooses whatever best tells the story.

Question why a story element or narrative component in a dream is chosen over others. Question why particular details are used to set the scene and move forward the action. If you want to know how something works, think from the perspective of what it does and what it accomplishes. Story analysis is how you reverse engineer your dreams.

The details of a dream all fit together to form a picture. In that picture an entire story is told.

The dream-story unfolds the same basic way as stories told in books and motion pictures:

- Opening: Introduces the central theme, idea, question or issue. It's often found in the first sentence or two of the dream's description.
- Body: Expands on the opening scene, providing details to fill out the picture.
- Climax: Brings the story to a resolution or shows what's preventing resolution. Perhaps the dream-story is "to be continued."

And keep in mind, the dream-story must draw you in. It must be believable—believable enough to suspend your disbelief. The primary objective of a storyteller is to pull people out of their everyday reality and create one in their imaginations. Your dreams know how to do that, using just enough detail so you don't stop and say, "Hey, that's not right." And it jars you out of your belief that the actions and events of the dream are really happening.

To read more about how your dreaming mind constructs stories to keep you engaged till the end, see: *Dream Within a Dream*.

The entries for *Drugs* and *Drunkenness* show the process of breaking down the story, analyzing it, and thinking like a storyteller to make connections with your life.

Storytelling Devices

Dreams have at their disposal every storytelling device imaginable: backstory, perspective (first, second, and third-person), parody, parable, nested stories, allegory, satire and so on. See *www.literaryterms.net* for a full list. Some devices are used more than others, and they are discussed below.

Dreams can even use storytelling devices that deceive, such as equivocation and red herrings, but only if it helps tell the story and show you something important. It's not done to deceive you. It's to enlighten, to inform, to show you when you're lying, being lied to, or lying to yourself. Dreams are reliably truthful, otherwise.

Dreams use three primary storytelling devices:

1. Metaphor

2. Exaggeration

3. Comparison and Contrast

One, two, or all three devices (and others used less often) can be used.

Storytelling Devices: Metaphor

A metaphor is a figure of speech that creates symbolism. It's like an analogy in that it uses comparison, but metaphor is more humorous and poignant and grabs your attention. Analogy is used more to explain and clarify.

Metaphors show the meaning, and a dream would much rather *show you* what it means than *tell you*.

A metaphor creates symbolism and meaning through exaggerated comparison, such as *boiling mad*. Someone is so mad (hot), if they were water it would boil. The metaphor paints a picture in the mind that captures the dynamics. The person isn't just mad, they are *really* mad. *Steaming* mad. Ready to *blow their top*.

The image of angry, boiling water is a *physical representation of a personal situation*. That phrase is repeated throughout *The Dream Interpretation Dictionary*, and it's an important concept for understanding symbolism, and by extension, understanding dreams.

When a dream environment is dark, it's a physical representation, perhaps for being *in the dark*. See: *Dark*.

Think of floating high in the sky as a physical representation for a *head in the clouds*. See: *Float*.

Think of *skinny as a pole* a physical representation for something lacking energy, attention or input. See: *Emaciated*.

This insight will make a lot of dream imagery understandable that otherwise appears nonsensical. The symbolism is enacted. Dreams create metaphors drawn from the hundreds or even thousands of them you are familiar with, plus they can create on the fly.

This book is packed with examples of metaphor and physical representation. To read a few of the best, look up *Anger, Boat, Car, Fishing, Hide,* and *Hug.* The entry for *Car* is the granddaddy. A car is a versatile symbol used in tons of metaphors and figures of speech.

Storytelling Devices: Exaggeration

Dreams exaggerate. Exaggerated comparison is used in many metaphors and other devices of story, language, and literature, and when you learn to notice it in dreams you are likely to see it used a lot.

A fear of social situations, for example, can be exaggerated into a scene of running from a horde of zombies. When viewed that way, the fear is not only more obvious, it's humorous. Run for your life!

A need for perfection can be exaggerated into a scene of picking at a small flaw in your face until it grows into a bloody crater. It's a fitting comparison and adds a touch of drama.

An earthquake rattling your home could symbolize news that rocks your world. The bigger the news, the bigger the earthquake. An earthquake is a disaster that kills and could potentially impact millions of people, so it's exaggerated in comparison to a personal situation.

Exaggeration is often found in how dreams portray something, such as when your parent is depicted as 30 feet tall, symbolizing the respect you have for the person. Or your head is shown as big as a beach ball, a way of saying you put too much emphasis on intellect.

Dreams zero in on your personal illusions and blind spots. When the ego is out of balance, dreams compensate by putting more weight on the other end of the scale and it can show in exaggerated dream imagery. Exaggeration blows things out of proportion to be more noticeable.

Your dreaming mind knows how to push your buttons. And it knows that exaggeration gets across the point and grabs your attention. Exaggeration can be a dream's way of countering when you minimize or avoid something, especially emotions and uncomfortable facts. Dreams exaggerate to reveal underlying dynamics and show how you really *feel.*

When confronted by ridiculous and impossible dream imagery and *discrepancies with reality,* look for exaggeration. Think like a storyteller. Work backward and ask yourself why the dream uses that storytelling device. What is it really saying?

Continue learning about exaggeration by reading the entries for *Adultery, Dungeon, Giant,* and *Torture.*

Storytelling Devices: Comparison and Contrast

Comparison is at the heart of most symbolism. What is a metaphor? It's a comparison, often one that is exaggerated. What is a symbol? At heart, it's a comparison of one thing to another. When dreams compare things, they say that one thing is like another, and the dreaming mind is masterful at making comparisons.

For example, a man drowning in work dreams about a horse drowning in a pond. See: *Horse.*

Heat is comparable to intensity or scrutiny. See: *Heat.*

Marriage is comparable to a commitment or bond. See: *Marriage.*

Kidnapping is comparable to being forced to do something against your will. It's exaggerated, but it fits. See: *Kidnap*.

No stretching of a comparison goes too far. It's fair game if it creates symbolism and is effective for telling the story.

Dreams use contrast, too. Contrast can be a satirical way of seeing into your personal blind spots. Such as when a dream character appears to be completely opposite of you, and it represents something about yourself you have trouble seeing or don't want to know. The entry for *Eat* details a dream in which the dreamer contrasts sharply with an imaginary dream character, showing him something about himself that's in a personal blind spot.

Contrast is often created through comparison with dream characters—imaginary ones or ones based on people you know—that are opposite of how you behave and perceive yourself. The entry for *Co-Worker* details a dream that centers on a contrast between the dreamer and a co-worker. The entry for *Fear* has another great example.

Sharply contrasting characters that come in pairs of opposite such as young and old could be archetypal. See: *Archetypes*.

Opposites and dissimilar things appear together in dream scenes to create comparisons and contrasts. Your job is to figure out why.

Dreams can compare and contrast a time in the past with the present to show how the past connects with the present; between fantasy, reality, and expectation to show you what's possible and what's not; between how you think you are perceived socially and how you're actually perceived; between your traits and qualities and someone else's. See the entries for *Ex* and *Friend* for more examples.

Comparison and contrast can create obvious discrepancies with reality, and those discrepancies are indications to look for symbolism. For example, you dream about a mouse holding up an elephant, something only possible in the dream world. It's obviously symbolism, and it could mean that a person with a huge reputation, symbolized by the elephant, is supported by the comparatively little people around her or him.

An old rule of thumb in dream psychology is people react most strongly to what they see or don't see about themselves in other people. It can spark an overreaction if they compare themselves, subconsciously or not, to someone or something else and don't like what they see. For example, a parent harshly punishes a child for a minor infraction, not realizing what they react to so strongly is what they see and don't like about themselves in the child. They then dream about a child killer on the loose, an exaggerated comparison with their behavior and guilt. For example, see: *Beggar*, *Shadow*.

The entries for *Archetypes*, *Death*, *Demon*, and *Roller-Coaster* discuss ways comparison and contrast are used to create symbolism.

Other Storytelling Devices

Dreams use word plays and alternate definitions of words as storytelling devices. For example:

- A character named Christian in a dream refers to the beliefs of Christianity. See: *Pastor*.

- A safe can symbolize feeling safe. See: *Safe*.

- A bear can mean "bare." See: *Bear*.

- A bug, the insect, can mean "to bug," meaning "to bother." See: *Bug*.

- A hospital can mean "hospitality." See: *Hospital*.

- The sun can mean "son." See: *Sun*.

- Fire can mean "anger." See: *Fire*.

- A pupil is the light receptor of the eye, or it's a student, and one can represent the other.

Alternate definitions of words are used as symbolism and shown in the actions of a dream. Such as when "adopt" means "take on" and acted out as adopting a pet or child. "Ditch" can mean "abandon" and shown as leaving something in a ditch.

For a clever variation on how dreams stretch ideas, see: *Family Business*. What is a family business? It's any business conducted for the family.

Other than understanding symbolism, understanding how dreams tell stories is your best path to grasping their meaning. *The more you learn about storytelling, the more you learn about your dreams.*

Step 3: Make Connections

You break down the dream into story elements—settings, characters, symbols—and narrative components—action, reaction, resolution.

You use dream interpretation techniques—associate, simplify, amplify—and search for storytelling devices—metaphor, exaggeration, comparison.

Now you are ready to connect the dream with your life. You have three primary means:

1. Context

2. Connect the dots

3. Reflect on your life

Make Connections—Context

Dreams use story context to define symbolism. Otherwise, with so many possibilities for meaning that symbols present, it's hard to pin one down. But when viewed within the context of the dream-story, the possibilities narrow quickly.

Picture a limousine cruising down Wall Street. In that context, it suggests "wealth" and "power." Wealthy and powerful people ride in limos on Wall Street. The setting provides the context that defines the symbolism. But a limo in a ghetto is the image of excess. It's a sharp contrast to its surroundings. A limo at a wedding has a different context and might symbolize something like the happy married life you hope to have or do have.

As another example, consider what is a wall. At its simplest, it is a divider or barrier. But if used in the context of holding up a structure, a wall is a support.

Biting usually carries unpleasant associations, but in an erotic context, biting can be quite welcome.

A symbol with no context doesn't tell you as much. *The context is the bridge between the dream symbolism and your life.*

When a symbol appears somewhere it normally shouldn't be (out of context), or does something it shouldn't be able to do, it's deliberate. Ask why and reverse engineer the dream. If the limo in your dream has a dance floor and movie theater in it, you know it makes sense somehow. Perhaps it symbolizes the material means to have the adventures in life you want to have and fly first class.

Context is also provided by circumstances.

Some symbolism only makes sense when viewed within the context of the dreamer's life. For example, a woman dreams about folding laundry in her home when a scary, skinless creature comes at her with a knife. They battle and end up outside in the street. A city bus runs over the creature, and she's detained for it. It's a story about her life. She's embroiled in a lawsuit with a former employer and recently found out that her former manager is spreading rumors about her, saying she's a bad person and bad employee, and it's preventing her from getting another job. With that in mind, look at the story again. It's all understood within the context.

It starts off with the dreamer folding laundry. Clothing is associated with outward identity and persona, and the action of folding clothing—especially freshly laundered clothing—can mean putting your life and personal presentation in order. The phrase "straighten up my life" comes to mind.

The creature is skinless, and skin is associated with outward identity, so being skinless is a key detail that connects with folding laundry.

Skin is protection, and it's sensitive, so being skinless is a picture of feeling "exposed" and "rubbed raw."

The dreamer battles the creature, and it comes at her with a knife, a weapon for close combat, implying a close and personal conflict.

Then the creature is hit by a city bus and the dreamer is detained for it, symbolizing the beating she's taken in the battle with her former employer. Her battle is a public matter, symbolized by the city bus, and it continues to *impact* her life. She's detained at the end because she feels like she's paying a heavy price for something that's not her fault. Her life is detained as the lawsuit presses forward. She can't get a new job.

Make Connections: Connect the Dots

Notice how every detail in the last example fits together to tell the story. Notice how the symbolism is defined through the interconnections. Folding laundry, the skinless creature, the knife, the battle, the city bus, being detained. Understood in the context of the dreamer's life, these details paint a picture. Alone, they're harder to pin down.

We call this process "connect the dots." Or think of it as putting together the puzzle. When the dots connect and the pieces fit, the meaning of the dream becomes clear. The dots form a picture, and within that picture they cross-reference and interrelate—small pictures within the big one. The puzzle isn't put together all at once, but instead a piece at a time.

For instance, a man dreams about battling a hugely overweight character in a home improvement store. The home improvement store setting is understood as symbolizing his efforts to improve his body. The overweight character is understood as representing the dreamer. And the action is the battle with himself over dieting. The three details connect nicely, forming a smaller picture within the big picture of the dream. For more about it, see: *Fight*.

Carl Jung said that a dream in its entirety tells a story, and if a dot doesn't connect, maybe the interpretation is off track, or something important is missed, such as the dream's resolution. Dreams don't leave loose change.

Now let's dig into a dream with multiple details and see how they all connect.

A young adult man dreams that his grandfather drives him to his new home. He climbs a ladder to get to the house. Inside, he sees family and friends but avoids them, preferring to look around on his own. They all leave and he sits down by the front door, relieved to finally be alone in his new home. The doorbell rings, and no one is there when he opens the door. He sits down and the doorbell rings again. He sees an indistinct white figure outside that disappears when he answers the door. The action repeats till he's so frustrated he could punch someone.

This dream is packed with symbols, and they all connect to tell a story. Begin with the new home. The guy who had the dream is not actually moving anywhere, nor does he plan to, so the new home *must be symbolism*. It's a discrepancy with reality explained below.

A ladder is popularly used in the metaphor for "climb the ladder," but a ladder fits only one person at a time, and that possibility for symbolism seems like a better fit, especially once you know what moving into a house means in this dream. Are you getting ideas?

Family and friends are in the dream, and the key detail is he avoids them. Connect that dot with the observation about the ladder. One person at a time.

Then there's the disappearing white figure at the front door. The front door is the boundary between public and private life. Outside is your public life; inside is your private life. Notice the dreamer's reaction at being pestered. Also, notice that the figure is indistinct, not a specific person or type of person. They're clues.

Now, how does it all fit together? Connect the dots:

1. A new home
2. A ladder
3. Avoid people
4. Front door
5. Pestered by an indistinct figure

If you said the dream is about privacy and the dreamer is a reclusive person moving into a new phase of life symbolized as moving into a new home, where he can keep people out if he wants to, you'd be correct. Notice how the front door connects with the white figure and his reaction to being pestered by it. The dots connect. Otherwise, the figure could represent anything. But when understood as related to privacy, the meaning is clear. He's annoyed by intrusions into his life. Or, more specifically, by being unable to control or prevent those intrusions, even when they involve loved ones and friends.

The clincher is the last dot:

6. His grandfather. The dreamer associates his grandfather with "reclusive" and "private." His grandfather taking him to his new home makes sense once you understand what it symbol-

izes. The dreamer is becoming more like his grandfather. They prefer to be alone and able to protect their privacy.

The dots all fit together. They tell a story. At this stage, if all goes well, the meaning and message of a dream really start to stand out.

This is the basic process you will follow when analyzing a dream. The elements and components fit together. First, look at them individually (Step 1). Then analyze the symbolism and story (Step 2). Look at the context and connect the dots (Step 3). Finally, reflect on your recent life to see what the dream says about it (that's next).

Read the entries for *Shop* and *War* to continue connecting the dots.

Make Connections: Reflect on Your Recent Life

Dreams make things easier by limiting the possibilities for what they cover about you and your life. Most dreams connect with events and circumstances of the previous day or two, or anticipate what's coming up in the next day or two, a "preview of coming attractions." You don't need to look back to a month or year ago, or ahead to a month or year from now, because it's outside the scope of time that dreams usually cover. That is, unless they connect the distant past (or future) with the present. Even then, the connection is made because of the relevance to the present.

Dreams can start with something you experienced in your outer life and show how it affects you internally, or they show how your outer life is shaped by your inner one. It's a two-way street. Most dreams connect with events within you—what you think, feel, and perceive—and how you integrate new information and experience into the existing structure of who and what you are. Begin there.

Sometimes, dreams connect exclusively with outer events, turning them into stories told through symbolism, but this is the exception, not the rule. Identifying the source of a dream provides a huge boost toward understanding it, and the trailhead is found in your recent life. In this sense, your dreams are like a diary.

Studies have shown that most dreams are accurate representations of your everyday life and reflect everyday concerns. They connect closely with your emotions. Once you know what to look for, it's not hard to find what they speak to about yourself and your life.

Rarely do dreams just replay memories verbatim. Instead, they turn everything into symbolism, and it's up to you to hunt through your memories and think creatively to trace the symbolism back to its source.

That's half the fun. The dream is a mystery and you are the detective, which means your life is the crime scene. Ha ha.

Particularly potent and metaphorical dreams can connect with something that happened about a week ago that was the subject of a dream at the time. An outsider is not likely to see the connection between the two dreams—the stories often appear unrelated—but you will know intuitively that the recent dream connects with an earlier one.

See the entries for *Army, Cage,* and *Wallet* for more ideas about using events in your life to help interpret your dreams.

"What If?"

Dreams can act as simulations. They help you answer questions, resolve issues, and solve problems. They ask, "What if?"

- What if you marry your high school sweetheart, or pursue a different career?

- What if your crush takes interest in you?

- What if you win the lottery or become famous?

- What if an estranged friend or relative suddenly reappears in your life?

- What if you are walking down the street and are suddenly confronted by a person with a weapon?

- What if it's the final moment of a big competition and the ball is in your hands, literally or figuratively?

When no other explanation appears to fit the meaning of a dream, consider the possibility that it's a simulation. Dreams can preview coming events, acting as a sort of dress rehearsal. They can simulate threats and future situations. These dreams can act as launching pads for you to use your imagination to decide and prepare for future events or possibilities. See yourself making the big play, or adeptly handling a situation, or reacting adroitly to the unexpected. It's the first step to making it happen.

Then there are precognitive dreams, previews of the future. For more about that subject, see: *Precognitive Dreams*.

One Last Thought

Those are the steps of the DREAMS 1-2-3 system. It's a lot to digest, but once you start applying it, you will catch on quickly. It's fun and challenging. You are now ready to dive head-first into *The Dream Interpretation Dictionary* and use this Dream Guide as your answer key.

And you are ready for the ultimate Jedi dream trick: reexperience the feelings and allow them to guide you.

Sit quietly and just bring your dream to mind. Step into the memories. Relive them. Say to yourself that you'd like insight into the dream, then pay attention to your feelings and intuition. Pay attention to your body. Allow your brain to take a backseat. Just observe. Keep your journal handy so you can write down anything important that comes to mind. Associate freely, but remember that the meaning and message of the dream are the center of gravity, and everything that runs through your mind orbits around that point. The meaning of a dream has a gravity that will attract the right memories, thoughts, and feelings. It happens naturally.

Your feelings can tell you more about the meaning of a dream than anything else.

The answers are in your heart more so than your head.

YOUR ANSWER KEY

Now let's summarize the DREAMS 1-2-3 system so you have an easy reference. We'll take it from the top.

DREAMS 1-2-3

1. Break down the dream into story elements and narrative components.

2. Use interpretation techniques to analyze the symbolism and the story.

3. Build up the interpretation by considering context and making connections.

Three simple facts:

1. You know subconsciously what the dream means.

2. Dreams are stories.

3. Dreams use symbolism.

Dream interpretation reminds you of what you already know and bridges the gap between what you know consciously and what you know subconsciously or unconsciously.

Step 1: Story Analysis—Elements and Components

Settings:

• Set the stage

• Identify the subject

• Are symbolism

• Depict your personal and emotional landscape

Characters:

• Move the action

• Provide the drama

• Connect with the subject

• Are actors playing roles

• Are symbolism

• Are subjective characterizations

• Are Projections of your inner world, especially the psyche

• Can represent people you know, or subjects or ideas

Symbols:

• Are Understood in context

• Tie together with other dream details

• Capture the dynamics of you and your life

• Are Pictures that say a thousand words

• Are used subjectively

• Can have layers of meaning

• Are Modified by details such as size, speed, shape, and color

Actions:

• Act out the symbolism; symbolism in motion

• Act out thoughts, feelings, emotions, and perceptions

- Use symbolism, even heinous actions
- Are found in the verbs you use to describe the dream
- Are scripted
- Move forward the dream-story
- Modify other symbols

Reactions:

- Are based on subconscious knowledge of the underlying meaning
- Show your raw, honest thoughts and feelings
- Are clues—question your reactions
- Stick out when disproportionate to the situation
- Can determine the course of the dream-story
- Show patterns and how to break them
- Are tested in dreams

Resolutions:

- Can be found in the dream-story, but often it's left up to you
- Are the answers, solutions, suggestions, ideas
- Are your opportunity to apply what you learn
- Are the main way you "live your dreams"
- Can be found in your imagination and feelings

Step 2: Dream Interpretation—Interpretation Techniques and Storytelling Devices

Associate:

- First thoughts that come to mind related to a dream detail
- Brainstorm ideas
- Helps you sidestep mental filters
- Bridges the gap between what you know consciously and subconsciously
- Associations can be personal or general

Simplify:

- Explain the dream in a sentence, phrase, or word; keep it simple
- Explain a detail in simplest terms
- See the obvious meaning behind the drama and action
- When the message of a dream seems obvious, it might just be so
- Shortcut to the central theme and meaning of the dream

Amplify:

- Magnify small details; nothing overlooked
- Counterbalance minimization and ego inflation
- Recognize your life for the epic drama it truly is
- Dramatize your personal narratives
- Help the message get through

• Tap the power of imagination

Metaphor:

• Creates symbolism through comparison
• Symbolism is enacted
• Found in figures of speech
• Uses exaggeration to make something more noticeable
• Physical representation of a personal situation

Exaggeration:

• Is at the heart of various ways to create symbolism
• Creates dramatic portrayals, depictions, and characterizations
• Shows you the symbolism at the heart of the dream-story
• Reveals underlying dynamics of a situation, especially feelings and emotions
• Makes something more obvious by blowing it out of proportion
• Counterbalances the ego and punctures personal illusions

Comparison / Contrast:

• Comparison is the main way dreams create symbolism
• Metaphors and exaggerations are comparisons
• Contrast helps you see blind spots and uncomfortable truths
• Opposites and dissimilar things appear together to show what they have in common

Step 3: Make Connections

Context:

• Dream details are understood within the context of the story
• Defines symbolism; without context, possibilities are wide open
• Is the bridge between the symbolism and you
• Your life provides context, too
• Look for out-of-context details; it's deliberate

Connect the Dots

• All dream details connect to paint a picture
• If a dot doesn't connect, reconsider the interpretation
• Dots connect to create small pictures within the big ones
• Dots bring together the dream-story and reveal the meaning

Your Recent Life

• Most dreams tie in with your recent life
• The recent past, and the near future
• Look to events in your life, and inside you
• Particularly powerful dreams reach back further
• Dreams integrate new experiences and information

RECOMMENDED ONLINE RESOURCES

Academic Study and Research

AsDreams.org
DreamBank.net
DreamResearch.ca
DreamsScience.org
DreamStudies.org
LiteraryTerms.net

Creativity and Intuition

AwakeToYourDreams.com
CreativeDreaming.org
DreamResearch.ca

Dream Dictionary

DreamBible.com
DreamMoods.com
UncleSirBobby.uk.org
UrbanDreamDictionary.com

Dreamwork

DreamBible.com
DreamMoods.com
UncleSirBobby.uk.org

UrbanDreamDictionary.com
Dreams123.net
DreamHawk.com
Dreams.ca
DreamSymbolism.info
DrMarciaEmery.com
JeremyTaylor.com
MindFunda.com
Mossdreams.blogspot.com
TheNaturalDream.com

Health and Wellness

LetMagicHappen.com
WandaBurch.com

Lucid Dreaming

DreamViews.com
LucidAdvice.com
World-of-Lucid-Dreaming.com

Precognition and Deja Vu

Deja-Experience-Research.org
NationalDreamCenter.com
YouAreDreaming.org

INDEX

Note: italicized page numbers indicates main entry.